EXPLORING CORRECTIONS
in America

John T. Whitehead
Department of Criminal Justice and Criminology
East Tennessee State University

Mark Jones
Department of Criminal Justice
East Carolina University

Michael C. Braswell
Department of Criminal Justice and Criminology
East Tennessee State University

 LexisNexis®

 anderson publishing
A member of the LexisNexis Group

Exploring Corrections in America, Second Edition

Copyright © 2003, 2008
Matthew Bender & Company, Inc. a member of the LexisNexis Group
Newark, NJ

ISBN-13: 978-1-59345-512-5

Phone   877-374-2919
Web Site www.lexisnexis.com/anderson/criminaljustice

Library of Congress Cataloging-in-Publication Data

Whitehead, John T.
    Exploring corrections in America / John T. Whitehead, Michael C. Braswell, Mark Jones.
        p. cm.
    Includes index.
    ISBN 978-1-59345-512-5 (softbound)
    1. Corrections--United States. 2. Prisons--United States. 3. Criminal justice, Administration of--
    United States. I. Braswell, Michael. II. Jones, Mark. III. Title.
    HV9304.W464 2008
    364.60973--dc22   2008034588

Cover design by Tin Box Studio, Inc.

EDITOR   Ellen S. Boyne
ACQUISITIONS EDITOR   Michael C. Braswell

Foreword

We are trying to accomplish several goals with this book. First, we hope to provide a thorough introduction to the topic of corrections in America. We hope to cover as many aspects of corrections as possible and to cover them in as much depth as possible within the constraints of a typical semester of coursework. Second, we have attempted to provide a balanced account of the issues facing American corrections. We have tried to offer students a thorough and stimulating discussion of relevant correctional issues so that they can make their own judgments and arrive at an informed opinion regarding the process of corrections in America.

We are also trying to make this new edition as helpful as possible to students. At the beginning of each chapter we have included a section entitled "What You Need to Know" that highlights key points in the chapter to look for as you read the chapter. The feature "On the Web" provides web sites that you can go to for further information on a particular subject such as the latest prison population statistics or information about the death penalty. Web exercises give you some direction on what to pursue on the Internet for specific topics. At the end of each chapter, we list both books and movies that you can consult for another perspective or a vivid portrayal of a topic such as life in prison.

Years ago, one of the authors took a corrections course at the university he was attending. The instructor, Bob Vasoli, took him and the other students on a tour of the Indiana State Penitentiary. That course and prison tour got him interested in corrections to the extent that he became a probation officer. From that experience, he continued his education and now teaches and does research addressing correctional issues. Hopefully, this book, along with your instructor, will get you interested in corrections. It is not likely that all of you will choose to become corrections professionals, but perhaps some of you will choose that vocation. It can be a challenging and exciting career. It is our hope that this text and your teacher will get you more interested in corrections and more knowledgeable about this important area of criminal justice.

We are indebted to the authors who contributed to the first edition: Gordon Bazemore, Kimberly Dodson, Steven Engel, Florence Ferguson, John R. Fuller, Dennis Giever, Christine Ludowise, Kevin Minor, Joycelyn M. Pollock, Mara Schiff, Irina R. Soderstrom, Margaret Vandiver, Eugene Waters, James B. Wells, and Angela West.

We want to thank Jennifer Mongold for her work on the Instructor's Guide and PowerPoint presentation. We also thank Kristin Wells and Amanda Evans for assistance with the manuscript. We also want to thank the staff at LexisNexis Matthew Bender (Anderson Publishing) for their encouragement and support. The Anderson staff are a joy to work with. We are especially indebted to Ellen Boyne, our project editor, who has made this a better book.

John T. Whitehead
Mark Jones
Michael C. Braswell

Table of Contents

Chapter 5
Community Corrections   153

Understanding Corrections: Where Are We?

CHAPTER 1

What You Need to Know

▶ Corrections is a growth industry.

▶ There is popular support for punishing criminals.

▶ There is increasing concern for the costs of operating prisons and other correctional programs.

▶ The "war on drugs" has had a major impact on corrections.

▶ The rehabilitative ideal continues to exist through such programs as restorative and community justice.

▶ Important correctional themes include the impact of public opinion, evaluating correctional policy and program effectiveness, and trying to more accurately understand what is true.

INTRODUCTION

When most people hear the term "corrections," they probably think of prisons, striped uniforms, cellblocks, armed guards, and surly prisoners. Part of American corrections is prisons, but corrections is much more than that. Corrections includes prisons, jails, halfway houses, group homes, probation, parole, intensive supervision, electronic monitoring, restitution programs, victim-offender mediation, and even the death penalty. Corrections can be defined as all that society does to and with offenders after they have been found guilty of a crime. Corrections even includes some things done to offenders prior to conviction, such as detention in jails pending adjudication of guilt and programs for offenders who are diverted out of the criminal justice system.

This book will examine and explore American corrections. We will look at all that corrections encompasses. We will try to help you understand what is happening in American corrections and why corrections is taking some of the directions it is taking. For example, American corrections appears to be continuing to emphasize punishment over treatment. We will attempt to examine trends such as the emphasis on punishment, explain where such trends originated, and discuss their consequences. To begin this process, we will take a brief look at some recent trends in corrections. Then we will discuss correctional goals and the themes of the book.

THE CURRENT STATE OF AMERICAN CORRECTIONS: PRESENT TRENDS

• Growth •

One of the clearest trends in corrections is growth. Corrections is currently a major growth industry in our country. All aspects of corrections are growing. At yearend 2006, more than 7 million adults (about 3.2% of all adults) were under some type of correctional supervision in the United States. More than 4.2 million adults were on probation, more than 798,000 were on parole, more than 760,000 were in jail, and more than 1.4 million were in prison. These figures indicate a 3.6 percent average annual change from 1995 to 2001. However, the corrections population growth seems to be slowing down; the average annual change from 2001 to 2006 was 2.1 percent.[1]

The growth in corrections populations is causing concern. The Pew Center recently reported that more than one in every 100 adults is now incarcerated in a U.S. jail or prison.[2] Of even more concern is that this figure is even higher for men ages 20 to 34 (one in 30 is in confinement) and even higher still for black men ages 20 to 34 (one in nine is in prison or jail). Some states are taking action. Both Texas and California, for example, had decreases in their prison populations as of early 2008.[3] (See Chapter 13 on adminis-tration and management for further discussion of how such states are addressing prison growth.)

To find numerous reports and information on corrections, go to the National Institute of Corrections (NIC) web site at www.nicic.org, or the Bureau of Justice Statistics (BJS) web site at www.ojp.usdoj.gov/bjs.

• The Punitive Ideal •

A second major trend in corrections is a demand for greater pun-ishment of criminals. There is demand for capital punishment, lengthy prison sentences, truth in sentencing (making offenders actually serve most of the time announced in their sentences), "three strikes and you're out" laws (no parole after three convictions), "no frills" prisons, and little support for probation and parole.[4]

We will examine this trend by discussing the call for "no frills" prisons. "Frills" in prison can refer to a number of educational, recreational, psy-chological treatment, or physical fitness programs and equipment. The frills label has been applied to college courses, access to cable televi-sion channels, exercise equip-ment (such as weightlifting equipment, tennis courts, soft-ball diamonds, etc.), and more. One argument against frills is philosophical: the "least eligi-bility" principle. This argument contends that prisoners should fare no better than the least advantaged individuals in soci-ety. Therefore, if disadvantaged or low-income individuals do not have cable television, exer-cise equipment, and so forth, it is unjustifiable for prisoners to have such amenities. Another argument contends that prisons are meant to be both punitive and deterrent (harsh enough to frighten persons considering committing crime out of actu-

An inmate lifts weights at the Hendry Correctional Institution in Immokalee, Florida. Physical fitness programs and equipment in prisons have been labeled as "frills" by some who argue that inmates should fare no better than the least advantaged individuals in society.

ally committing the crime they are considering). Frills detract from both the punitive and deterrent dimensions of prison. Other arguments are that amenities are costly and that some, such as weightlifting equipment, can actually be harmful. Prisoners can use weights to become stronger and then assault other prisoners or guards (or both). The federal prison system has outlawed weightlifting equipment in new federal prisons.

BOX 1.1

"No Frills" Prisons

Angola State Prison in Louisiana is a prime example of a "no frills" prison. The prisoners receive long sentences and spend much of their time farming the agricultural fields that are an integral part of the prison complex (it is sort of a twentieth-century plantation but with prisoners instead of slaves). The prisoners do have a chance to watch television at night. If they work hard enough, they can move from hand labor (hoes, rakes, shovels) to the luxury of operating a tractor.

Eglin Federal Prison Camp, a federal minimum-security prison camp in Florida, is an example of a prison many would say is loaded with frills. Many of the offenders are white-collar criminals. There is no imposing concrete wall or fence around the perimeter of the institution. Instead, there is a painted white line. If an offender crosses it, he is considered an absconder and is subject to transfer to a traditional federal maximum-security prison. Cells are actually dormitory cubicles.

The prisoners work seven hours a day for a token wage (a paltry per-hour rate). What makes the prison seem soft, however, is the presence of tennis courts, baseball diamonds, and a jogging track. If an observer were to visit Eglin, he or she might confuse it with a college setting. At a minimum, a visitor might confuse the physical fitness facilities at Eglin with similar facilities at a college campus or a physical fitness club.

The comments of Gresham Sykes (1958) put these two prisons in perspective (see Chapter 8 for a complete discussion of Sykes's comments). Although one has traditional cells with iron bars and the other has dormitory cubicles, and although one forces the men out into the fields and the other may require federal prisoners to groom the adjacent Air Force golf course for seven hours a day, both facilities share more similarities than differences. Both deprive the inmates of freedom, autonomy, goods and services, heterosexual sex, and security. (Eglin is less secure because of its white-collar crime clientele, but every offender is still a criminal, and riots and disturbances have occurred at minimum-security facilities like it.) In both places, the offender is constantly reminded that he is a number rather than a whole person and that the staff does not really care what he thinks or prefers. He is there to follow orders or else. It is true that a sentence to a prison camp like Eglin is easier to endure than a sentence to Angola, but both places take away freedom and dignity. As allegedly "frilly" as Eglin might appear, travel agents have yet to put it on their list of vacation attractions.

Proponents of "frills" argue that educational, treatment, and recreational programs keep prisoners busy and help them develop life skills. Keeping inmates busy can reduce tension and aggression and thereby prevent problems such as riots or other forms of prison violence. Staff tend to like such "frills" because they help to keep prisons safe for prisoners and staff. One response to the "least eligibility" argument is to make societal conditions better for the disadvantaged. In other words, rather than argue that the disadvantaged have no access to college courses or exercise programs, perhaps society has an obligation to provide more for the disadvantaged rather than keeping them in their current underpriviliged state. (For more on frills in prisons, see Box 1.1.)

One author calls the emphasis on punishment the "penal harm movement."[5] Part of the reason for this emphasis on punishment is the conservative doctrine of individual responsibility and free choice. Because many persons assume that individuals are free to choose and are responsible for their choices, punishment seems to make sense. Those who commit crimes are seen as deserving of harsh punishments. Harsh punishments are also considered to be a deterrent; they are supposed to scare or intimidate would-be offenders from committing crimes. Punishment advocates also view harsh sentences as incapacitative. Putting offenders in prison removes their capacity or ability to commit crime. If offenders are in prison, they cannot commit new crimes on the street.

• The Search for Efficiency, Effectiveness, and Accountability •

Still another trend in contemporary corrections is a concern for efficiency, effectiveness, and accountability. Seventy-five years ago there was little or no emphasis on the financial bottom line in corrections. Prisons were considered necessary, and state legislators passed budgets that provided for their funding. Today there is increasing concern about the costs of operating prisons and other correctional enterprises. One reason for this is the mushrooming growth of prisons. As noted in the opening section of this chapter, prison populations have been growing at an alarming rate. That growth means that they consume an ever-larger portion of state budgets. When prisons were only a small part of state budgets, legislators did not have to give much concern to their costs. When prisons became more expensive than state spending on education, prison costs became an issue of intense concern and debate. To give one example of costs, California spent almost $9 billion on corrections in 2007.[6] (See Chapter 13 for further details on costs.)

One indicator of the emphasis on costs is the privatization movement in corrections. At yearend 2006, 113,791 state and federal prisoners were in privately run facilities. This was an increase of 5.4 percent (5,851 prisoners) over the previous year. The federal system had more than 27,000 prisoners in private facilities. Texas had more than 18,600 prisoners in private facilities. In 2006, 24 jurisdictions had increases in the number of prisoners in private facilities.[7] This number indicates that privatization continues to be an important issue in the field of corrections.

Another part of the focus on efficiency and accountability is simply a greater concern for results. Decades ago, both police officials and correctional officials did not have to justify their existence and their budgets. It was assumed that criminals had to be caught and locked up. Now, however, both law enforcement and correctional officials must state their goals and objectives and then demonstrate that they have been successful in achieving the desired results and achieving those results at the lowest possible cost. It is much like professional sports. If the team does not win, then the coach is in danger of losing his or her job. Part of the reason for this is greater systematization and analysis in all areas of life. In football, for example, coaches do not just rely on their instincts to devise winning strategies. They hire assistants who keep detailed statistics on which plays work in which situations. They watch films of opponents for hours on end in an effort to determine what plays the opposing team will use in certain critical situations. Furthermore, if the coach or owner wants to acquire new players, they may be operating under a salary cap that limits how much money they can spend each year for personnel. All this means that matters are growing more complex.

This emphasis on efficiency and effectiveness has been labeled the "new penology."[8] Whereas corrections used to be concerned with reforming or rehabilitating the offender, the new penology is concerned with managing prison and community corrections populations as efficiently as possible. In an interesting turn of events, what used to be considered failure is now considered success. In the new penology, it does not matter so much that an offender commits a new crime while on community supervision (probation, parole, or some other type of supervision). This used to be considered failure. What matters now is that the correctional workers note the offense and have the offender moved out of community supervision into a prison. If this is done and done quickly, the new penology claims to be efficient at properly classifying and monitoring offenders. Sometimes, however, what is efficient in the short run may not be effective in the long run. For example, if some rehabilitation programs prove effective with certain types of offenders, it may save the state money in the short run to eliminate the programs (efficiency) but cost more in the long run if offenders continue to reoffend because they did not receive appropriate treatment intervention (effectiveness).

• The Impact of the War on Drugs on Corrections •

In the 1980s, there was considerable attention—even hysteria—about drugs and drug offenders. One report alleged that 375,000 babies were born of mothers addicted to crack.[9] The Monitoring the Future Survey indicated that high percentages of high school seniors were using drugs. For example, in 1982, one-third of the seniors reported having used an illegal drug in the previous month. Almost 30 percent stated they had used marijuana, and 5 percent reported use of cocaine in the prior 30 days.[10]

These and other reports suggested that drug use and availability were out of control in the United States and that drastic action needed to be taken. In response, politicians started a "war on drugs." Former Presidents Ronald Reagan and George H.W. Bush implemented a strategy of vigorous law enforcement and harsh penalties for drug sale and possession. In 1986, Congress passed the Anti-Drug Abuse Act, which specified mandatory minimum sentences for drug crimes. For example, someone convicted of selling only five grams of crack cocaine (perhaps about 25 doses worth a few hundred dollars) could receive five years in a federal prison without the possibility of parole.[11] Former President Clinton continued this "war" by asking for an additional 100,000 police officers in 1994 and for still more officers in his 1999 State of the Union address. The George W. Bush administration has also pursued the "war on drugs."

One impact of the war on drugs has been an increase in the number and proportion of offenders convicted and incarcerated for drug offenses. In 2006, 53 percent of federal prisoners were in prison for a drug offense versus only 25 percent in 1980. In 2004 (the most recent year for which statistics for state prisoners are available), almost 20 percent of state prisoners were in prison for a drug offense.[12]

A second impact of the drug war has been a disproportionate increase in the incarceration of African Americans. Between 1985 and 1995, the number of black males in prison or jail more than doubled. By yearend 2006, one in every 33 black men was a sentenced prisoner, and the black male incarceration rate was 3,042 per 100, 000 black males, compared to a white male rate of 487 per 100,000 (approximately one in every 205 white men).[13] As noted above, as of 2008, the number was even higher for black men between the ages of 20 and 34: one in nine was in prison or jail.[14]

As a result of the war on drugs, there are more prisoners, more drug offense prisoners, and more African-American prisoners. One immediate need of American corrections is to change or adapt to these trends. Prisons and community correctional agencies need to adjust their programming for the high percentages of drug offenders and minorities who are being sentenced. Some argue that another important course of action is to point out problems in corrections stemming from the war on drugs and to urge politicians to retreat or curtail the war so that there will be fewer prisoners, fewer drug offenders in prison, and a reduction in the proportion of black individuals in prison.[15] The idea is that money and resources could be used more efficiently and effectively on other correctional problems. This response would require correctional officials to take the risk of angering some legislators by pointing out shortcomings in the legislation.

To find out more about America's war on drugs, visit www.usdoj.gov/ndic/index.htm.

• The Rehabilitative Ideal •

Still another trend is the rehabilitative ideal. This trend began decades ago, underwent harsh criticism in the 1980s, but has since regained momentum. In the 1950s and 1960s, states began calling prisons "correctional institutions" instead of "prisons" or "penal institutions." Colleges began using the term "corrections" instead of the term "penology" (the study of punishment) to refer to the study of prisons, probation, and parole. "Guards" were renamed "correctional officers." In some prisons, concrete changes accompanied these name changes. For example, in California, some prisoners were placed in rooms that bore greater resemblance to college dorms than to traditional cells. Inmates were given extra privileges such as permission to sit and chat over coffee in the dining hall at the end of a meal or even a key to their room (cell). Group counseling sessions were provided for inmates.[16]

The philosophy behind these changes was rehabilitation. It was thought that individual personality and behavioral defects explained why many offenders turned to crime. Offenders suffered from such defects in their upbringing, their emotions, or their education and job training. Offenders had psychiatric, educational, or vocational problems that influenced them to commit crime. It was further assumed that if these individual defects could be "corrected," then the offender would not need to turn to criminal behavior. He or she could achieve his or her goals by means of law-abiding behavior such as legitimate employment. Therefore, offenders were considered persons who would more likely pursue legitimate goals such as job training, education, or work in American society if enough assistance was offered them.[17]

At least in name if not in reality, the rehabilitation philosophy persisted for some time. Most prisons eventually became "correctional institutions" and every guard a "correctional officer." The rehabilitation philosophy came to a halt some time in the 1980s. Names such as "correctional institution" and "correctional officer" persisted, but the rehabilitation philosophy was no longer operating behind those names.

Several factors worked to diminish the rehabilitative ideal. One factor was empirical research, which was critical of the impact of rehabilitative correctional programs on recidivism (the commission of any new crimes by offenders). Several studies came out that appeared to show that correctional programs were not reducing or eliminating recidivism. Offenders who went through the programs that were intended to rehabilitate them and eliminate any need to commit crimes were still committing new crimes after their participation in the programs. So if the results were negative, many thought that the philosophy must be wrong.[18]

Another factor working against rehabilitation was a change in the political climate. Liberal citizens and politicians were more inclined to support rehabilitation. It was congruent with their general belief that government programs can have beneficial effects on the lives of individuals. Gradually, though, political conservatism began to compete with liberalism. Conservatives had a general distrust of government programs and specific questions about the usefulness of correctional programs. Conservatives also tend to emphasize the importance of individual responsibility and accountability over other explanations for criminal behavior. While sociologists, psychologists, and political liberals might argue that something in a child's upbringing accounts for his or her involvement in crime or delinquency, political conservatives often prefer to explain behavior as primarily a matter of free choice. And if free choice accounts for behavior, there is no need to offer psychological therapy to prevent crime. The solution is simple; the individual must choose to do right, to follow the law. A current way of phrasing this is that values are critical. If children are taught proper values, then they will choose to do the right thing. Of course, what sounds good in theory often falls short in practice.

Liberals also have been partially responsible for the downfall of the rehabilitative ideal. One part of rehabilitation has been the use of indeterminate sentences. Indeterminate sentences usually meant that the parole board decided the actual release date of a prisoner.[19] For example, the judge would sentence the offender to a term ranging from five to 15 years. Somewhere within the five to 15 years, the parole board would decide if and when the prisoner was rehabilitated or ready to be released on parole to society. Some liberals criticized this process as being arbitrary and unfair. Two prisoners could have committed approximately the same crime, but the parole board would release one early (e.g., after five years) and keep the other until he or she was more completely rehabilitated (e.g., after 10 years). Critics argued that offenders committing essentially the same crimes should serve the same length of time in prison. Like conservatives, liberals began to question the rehabilitative ideal, but for different reasons.[20]

It is important to note that rehabilitation is not dead. Although the rehabilitative ideal has received serious criticism and has been replaced as the dominant theme in corrections, it is far from vanquished. For example, when asked about what to do with offenders, many average citizens still report considerable support for rehabilitative measures (see Box 1.2). Likewise, there is a significant number of researchers who have continued to conduct empirical studies of rehabilitation that show considerable success. As we will discuss in later chapters, these researchers have found that certain principles and approaches appear to be effective with certain types of offenders.[21] Although rehabilitation is no longer the primary emphasis in corrections, any announcement of its demise is premature.

BOX 1.2

Attitudes about Rehabilitation

Research on public opinion about crime shows that the public is not as punitive as some contend. In a 1995 survey about criminals who commit violent crimes, 26 percent of the sample said that the government needs to make greater efforts to rehabilitate such offenders and 12 percent said that there needs to be emphasis on both rehabilitation and punishment. When respondents were asked what should be the most important goal of prison once offenders are incarcerated, almost one-half (48%) of the respondents stated that rehabilitation should be the most important goal, 15 percent said punishment, and 33 percent said crime prevention/deterrence (Maguire & Pastore, 1998; see also Cullen, Fisher & Applegate, 2000). Similarly in 2003, 72 percent of a national random sample of more than 1,200 adults agreed that the criminal justice system should try to rehabilitate criminals, not just punish them. These results remain when discussing punishment for the most heinous crimes also (http://www.albany.edu/sourcebook). Although 75 percent of respondents favor the death penalty when asked a simple question about it, considerable percentages of respondents switch to the option of life without parole when offered that option (Whitehead, Blankenship & Wright, 1999). Thus, it is important to take a balanced look at the research on attitudes toward rehabilitation versus more severe options and also to examine the wording of items used to measure such matters.

• Restorative and Community Justice •

Still another important trend in corrections is the call to reform corrections along restorative and community justice themes. Just as many are calling for police agencies to redefine their role from crime fighting to community problem-solving, so also restorative and community justice thinkers argue for a fundamental shift in how we think about corrections. Whereas the focus in corrections has often been on the offender and the state: "Community justice redefines the roles and goals of criminal justice agencies to include a broader mission—to prevent crime, address local social problems and conflicts, and involve neighborhood residents in planning and decisionmaking."[22]

Community justice began with a focus on restorative justice—mediation between individual offenders and individual victims—but has grown into concern for solving community problems and fostering community empowerment. Thus, it can include restitution, community service, community involvement in sentencing, fostering community crime prevention, encouraging accountability, and promoting volunteer participation.[23]

The objectives of community justice advocates are ambitious and require a restructuring of past practices. With community justice, citizens cannot just let the police officer or the probation officer do it. They must also get involved.

It is interesting that first community policing and now community justice have become popular in criminal justice. In one sense, both movements represent a return to our roots. Justice used to be more of a community task and responsibility. Professional police and prison personnel are relatively recent developments in the history of corrections. What may be problematic in this return to our roots of citizen and community involvement, however, is the form that community is taking in the twenty-first century. If people work at home rather than at an office, shop, or factory, and if people interact via e-mail and shop on the Internet rather than go to a mall (let alone a neighborhood store), then how do these twenty-first–century realities coincide with nineteenth-century definitions of "community"? If we live in a virtual world that transcends local boundaries and local governmental entities, does it make any sense to try to use the local, geographical community to practice "justice"? In other words, "community" does not mean what it meant even 50 years ago. It may be difficult to get citizens involved in community justice if "community" does not mean that people interact with and care about the people that live in the same geographic area. On the other hand, the Internet offers new ways for people to interact and form communities. So both community policing and community justice seem to be arising when community, in the traditional sense, seems to be declining—but other possibilities are multiplying. (Chapter 6 will examine community and restorative justice in greater detail.)

In summary, the trends characterizing American corrections include growth, an emphasis on punishment, the search for efficiency and accountability, the war on drugs, a reduced but continuing

To learn more about the current trends in restorative justice, go to www.restorejustice.com or www. restorativejustice.org.

emphasis on rehabilitation, and concern for community and restorative justice. Later chapters will add further details about these trends.

▶ Ethics Focus: Should We "Hurt" or "Help" Offenders?

Offenders are tried and convicted of all types of crimes, ranging from passing bad checks and theft of property to planning and carrying out the murder of another person. As human beings we often feel that those criminals who physically harm an innocent victim should themselves experience similar pain. While our laws, except in capital cases, don't support an "eye for an eye" justice, human desire to punish those who commit acts of violence against us runs deep throughout human history. There are other persons who believe we should attempt to understand why criminals, even violent ones, act the way they do and try to correct their behavior. These persons would be more supportive of encouraging and helping offenders to change into law-abiding, productive citizens. They would be more supportive of rehabilitation than punishment.

1. Which of these approaches do you feel is most appropriate?

2. Why do you feel your choice is more effective in correcting offenders?

3. What might be a just balance between punishing and helping offenders to change?

FOUR CORRECTIONAL GOALS

To better understand corrections it is important to understand the goals of corrections. The traditional goals of corrections are retribution, rehabilitation, deterrence, and incapacitation. In the previous section on trends, we discussed retribution (punitiveness) and rehabilitation in considerable detail. We will add a few comments on these two goals and give more attention to deterrence and incapacitation.

• Retribution •

Retribution advocates just punishment for the offense. Historically, retribution can be traced back to the ancient law of *lex talionis* (law of talion) or an eye for an eye. Many people understand the law of talion as justifying harsh vengeance, but it was actually intended to put limits on punishment. The original intent was that those punishing offenders could punish no more severely than the offender had harmed his or her victim. This was contrary to practice at the time, which often entailed punishment for the offender that was harsher than what he or she had done.[24]

Commentators argue that retribution is rooted in a search for justice. A crime is a violation of justice. Punishment or retribution restores the balance. Punishments also proclaim and enforce social values.[25] In other words, when judges pronounce sentence and guards take prisoners to prison, society is indicating its opposition to murder, rape, robbery, or whatever crime is involved.

Mackie,[26] however, sees the matter in a different light. He contends that there really is no justification for retribution other than an emotional desire for vengeance. There is no logical argument involved; society essentially wants to "get even" with the offender. Society is just striking back out of collective emotional outrage, much like a child strikes back when he or she is hurt.

• Rehabilitation •

Rehabilitation has already been discussed as one of the trends in corrections. Here it is simply necessary to note that rehabilitation is always included as one of the traditional goals or objectives of the criminal justice system in general and of corrections in particular. The intention of rehabilitation is to facilitate change in offenders so that they can become productive, law-abiding citizens.

• Deterrence •

At least since the writing of Beccaria in the eighteenth century, deterrence has been considered an essential goal of criminal justice and corrections. General deterrence refers to the use of severe penalties (such as prison) to frighten or intimidate persons who are not yet offenders but considering committing a crime out of doing so. Specific deterrence refers to applying severe penalties to convicted offenders in the hope of frightening them out of committing any additional offenses (e.g., after they are released from prison).

Deterrence is clearly part of the current climate in corrections. Many people believe that harsh penalties can and do scare individuals from committing crime. Deterrence is thus part of the rationale for the current expansion in prison populations. It is also part of the current emphasis on capital punishment. Later sections of the book will examine whether deterrence is effective—whether it actually has any substantial impact on crime rates. As will be shown, there is considerable research available on this issue.

• Incapacitation •

Incapacitation is defined as removing the capacity or ability of the offender to commit crime. The clearest example of incapacitation is imprisonment. Locking someone up eliminates that person's ability to commit a crime in the free world. Persons may commit crimes (e.g., an assault on a guard or fellow prisoner) in prison, but their placement in prison means they cannot commit any crimes on the street until they are released.

Much of the current enthusiasm for prison and capital punishment stems from fascination with incapacitation. Vitiello even claims that the current correctional climate is not so much a punitive climate as it is a quest for increasing incapacitation.[27] The simple logic that a locked up or executed offender cannot commit additional crimes is compelling to many people.

Although we will assess incapacitation in more depth later in this text, it is important to note several factors here. First, one problem with incapacitation is that new offenders can fill in the gaps created by incarcerating convicted offenders. If a drug dealer goes to prison, for example, former customers will be looking for someone to take his or her place to supply their drugs. Another problem is that incapacitation is based on predicting the future. A judge is predicting that Offender X will commit a certain number of crimes in the future. Such predictions are not error-free. A judge may incarcerate an offender who actually would cease his or her criminal career if placed on probation or otherwise be allowed to remain in the community. Related to this, it is difficult to separate out high-rate offenders from low-rate offenders. If judges incarcerate high-rate offenders, they achieve greater incapacitation. The more they incarcerate low-rate offenders, however, the less incapacitation they achieve. Still another problem is that if an offender commits his or her offense in a group (with others), that person's incarceration may do nothing to stop his or her accomplices who were not apprehended from continuing their criminal activity. In light of this, it is not surprising that a respected evaluation of incapacitation found that the strategy has only minimal effects on crime rates.[28]

A variation on the theme of incapacitation is a call to manage corrections around the theme of public safety. Smith and Dickey define public safety as "a condition, specific to places, in which people and property are not at risk of attack or theft and are not perceived to be at risk."[29] Corrections agencies should be built on the theme of creating, maintaining, and enhancing public safety. For example, a task force in Wisconsin believed that concern for public safety was strong enough to recommend the dismantling of felony probation and substituting Community Confinement and Control (CCC). Community Confinement and Control would be sort of a halfway-house system; it would combine features of prison (confinement) with some of the freedom and obligations of the community, such as employment and treatment. CCC would also be shorter in duration than felony probation and be used as a parole device for prisoners leaving prisons.[30]

THEMES OF THE TEXT

We will attempt to develop several themes throughout the text. Certain themes pervade corrections, and we think they need to be kept in mind no matter what specific area of corrections is under consideration. Although these themes may not be highlighted as such, they were always in mind as we wrote the book.

• What Does the Research Show? •

One theme of this text will be an emphasis on evaluation. Wherever possible, we will address the question "Does it work?" Whenever we discuss a program or policy, one key issue will be whether that program or policy achieves its objectives. We will summarize the latest research on programs and policies to see if they are effective. A key question in this area concerns the impact on recidivism: Is the program or policy reducing the new crimes committed by the offenders who have gone through the program?

This emphasis on evaluation is part of the trend toward emphasizing efficiency and accountability. In both business and government, it is imperative that programs be effective and efficient. They must achieve their goals and do so in cost-effective ways.

The emphasis on evaluation is important because at the initiation of many programs everyone "knows" or believes that they will work. A good example is the "Scared Straight" program that began in the 1970s. Prisoners in New Jersey and elsewhere began to lecture delinquents or youths considered pre-delinquent about the horrors of prison life. The juveniles were told that they would be attacked, sexually assaulted, or even killed in prison. Deterrence theory was the conceptual framework behind this program. Proponents thought that they literally could scare kids "straight"—out of crime and into a law-abiding life. Some judges were so convinced about the value of these programs that they ordered probationers to watch the documentary titled *Scared Straight* about the New Jersey program at Rahway State Prison. Judges thought that watching a movie about the Scared Straight program would so frighten the viewers that they would never commit another crime.

Unfortunately, research on the actual results of a number of different confrontational programs (Scared Straight–type programs) has shown that the effects are not positive. Although there have been a few isolated positive results, the clear conclusion is that such programs are not effective in reducing delinquency[31] (see Box 1.3). As with some other deterrence efforts, people often think that they will either not be caught or not be convicted, so they do not take the consequences as seriously as the program intends. It is interesting that even though the research on confrontational programs has been discouraging, many continue to believe in their worth. For example, a brand new *Scared Straight* documentary has been produced and aired on cable television.

BOX 1.3

Scared Straight Programs

One of the most famous confrontation programs in the United States is the Rahway, New Jersey, program that used "lifers" to tell delinquents and pre-delinquents about the horrors of prison life. San Quentin Prison in California, however, actually had a more detailed program. Rahway was a two-hour program in one day in which lifers used whatever they could think of to scare delinquents away from crime and prison. San Quentin required kids to come three Saturdays in a row. In addition, San Quentin involved both deterrence (trying to scare kids away from prison) and a sort of "big brother" approach. Prisoners acted as "squires" who would sit down with a youth and try to discuss important issues with him or her. An evaluation of the program found little or no difference between youths who went through the squires program and youths who did not go through the program. Specifically, 81 percent of the youths who went through the squires program were rearrested in one year compared to only 67 percent of the control group. One-third of the youths in the program and one-third of the controls had three or more arrests. The average number of arrests for both groups was about 2.1 (Lewis, 1983). This and other similar studies (Lundman, 1993) suggest that Scared Straight programs are not very effective in reducing or preventing delinquency. (See also MacKenzie, 2006.)

• Where Does the Truth Lie •

A second theme of this text is a balanced approach—where does the truth lie? By this we mean that we will try to avoid either liberal or conservative bias and discuss American corrections fairly and evenhandedly.

Many correctional issues stir up emotional debates. This is probably most apparent in the debate over capital punishment. Many conservatives argue that extreme punishment is necessary for those offenders who have taken a human life. They note the brutal nature of many homicides and argue that anyone who commits a brutal killing does not deserve to live. As capital punishment proponent Ernest van den Haag puts it, "Murder differs in quality from other crimes and deserves, therefore, a punishment that differs from other punishments."[32] A recent case in Texas in which an African American was killed by being dragged by a truck is a prime example of an especially brutal killing about which many people were so horrified that they demanded the death penalty in commenting on the case. Supporters of capital punishment also argue that executing such offenders will "teach a lesson" to anyone contemplating a murder. Moreover, conservatives argue that executions will save money because the murderers will not be locked up for 20 years at a cost to taxpayers.

On the other hand, many liberals argue that the death penalty is barbaric—that it is a throwback to more primitive times. One commentator notes that most other industrialized democracies have abandoned the death penalty and by keeping it "we place ourselves in the company of some of the cruelest and most repressive governments in the world."[33] They also argue that many murderers can change and even become productive citizens in society. Instances in which death-row inmates had their sentences reduced to life sentences and were paroled without committing new crimes demonstrate that even persons sentenced to capital punishment can succeed on parole. (For more on the death penalty, see Chapter 15.)

Many times, sincere thinkers on both sides of an issue such as capital punishment get carried away with their position on the issue and the arguments justifying their position. They think that they are completely right and that the other side has little or no merit.

We would like to avoid partisanship and bias and try to look at correctional issues with a fresh perspective. We want to assess the arguments on issues such as capital punishment as completely and fairly as possible. We state an opinion only after thorough discussion and debate. We think that such a balanced approach is necessary as corrections starts the new century. At times, both liberals and conservatives may have gone too far in some of their positions and arguments. It seems appropriate to go beyond the extremes and search for common ground. If solutions are to be found for many of the key correctional problems, we need to put an end to ideological bias and be willing to come up with solutions that can be supported by both sides of the political spectrum.

A balanced approach does not mean that the answer to every problem lies exactly in the middle of the political spectrum. If it appears that either liberals are correct or conservatives are correct, we will state our opinion about the optimum solution. We just want to assess the evidence as fairly and completely as possible before expressing an opinion.

Going beyond liberal or conservative bias, the authors also admit to a humane perspective or bias. Although we will attempt to be balanced and to look at both sides of issues such as the proper degree of punishment in prisons and the appropriateness of the death penalty, we think it is necessary to admit a humane bias up front. We will not advocate anything that is degrading or demeaning to prisoners, other correctional clients, or corrections professionals. Part of the reason for this position is the peacemaking perspective, which stems from ancient wisdom traditions. Based on such principles as human dignity as well as personal responsibilities and the equality of all men and women, we will always argue for prisons, probation programs, and other correctional strategies that recognize human dignity and aim to enhance rather than detract from it.

BOX 1.4

Prisons and Films in American History

The 1930s and 1940s have been referred to as the "Big House" era in American corrections. During this period, large prisons, some holding more than 1,000 inmates, sprang up around the country. It was during this era that Hollywood filmmakers began to romanticize prison life. Films featuring James Cagney and other macho actors presented the prison inmate, often wrongly convicted, as a tragic hero battling against unjust prison conditions and corrupt staff. The image of the oppressed inmate as martyr persists today. It is ironic that a society that relies so much on imprisonment and demonizes criminal behavior enjoys popular media images that depict prison inmates as heroes and correctional personnel as villains. Listed below are a few examples:

The Big House. This 1930 movie put the prison picture genre on the map and was greatly influential to future prison dramas. Screenwriter Frances Marion claimed to glean the dialogue and situations from a visit to San Quentin Prison.

Jailhouse Rock. In this movie, filmed in 1957 at the height of Elvis Presley's popularity, Presley portrays a rebellious but sympathetic character abused by prison staff.

Birdman of Alcatraz. Robert Stroud, a brilliant but maniacal killer in real life, is portrayed sympathetically by Burt Lancaster in this 1962 film. Stroud's contribution to the study of birds is chronicled, although the title is misleading. Stroud's experiments with birds took place at Fort Leavenworth, Kansas, not Alcatraz. Karl Malden plays a well intentioned but feckless warden and nemesis of Stroud.

Cool Hand Luke. Paul Newman portrays an inmate in a Southern (all-white) chain gang in this famous prison film of 1967. Luke, a witty, wisecracking, war hero imprisoned for tearing the heads from parking meters, is driven by brutal prison officials to make several escape attempts. Strother Martin, who portrays the warden, delivers the movie's most memorable quote. After striking Luke for a disrespectful comment, Martin tells the other inmates: "What we've got here is failure to communicate."

Papillon. This 1973 film is based on the recollections of the film's protagonist, Papillon, and his experiences in a French Guyanan penal colony. Papillon is portrayed by Steve McQueen. The film depicts the brutal life inside the penal colony and Papillon's many escape attempts. The brutalities of homosexual rape, solitary confinement, and physical brutality are highlighted. Dustin Hoffman portrays Dega, Papillon's loyal friend and fellow inmate.

The Longest Yard. This 1974 film stars Burt Reynolds as Paul Crewe, a disgraced former pro-football quarterback serving time in a southern prison. Crewe is coerced by

BOX 1.4 *(continued)*

a sadistic warden (played by Eddie Albert) into forming an inmate football team to play against a semi-pro team composed of prison guards. Once the game commences, the warden threatens to trump up murder charges against Crewe if he does not throw the game, the very activity that got him banned from professional football.

Gideon's Trumpet. Based on a true story about the landmark Supreme Court decision, *Gideon v. Wainwright*, this 1979 movie stars Henry Fonda as Samuel Gideon, who was tried and wrongfully convicted in a Florida court without benefit of counsel.

Brubaker. In this 1980 film, loosely based on the true story of Tom Merton, an Arkansas prison reformer, Robert Redford portrays a prison warden who, unbeknownst to inmates and prison staff, enters a prison posing as an inmate so he can discover the horrible conditions visited upon prison inmates.

Chained Heat. One of numerous "B" films set in a women's prison, this 1983 movie features tough, attractive female inmates who battle each other and brutal guards for power in the prison. Lesbian sex, not the penal system, is the primary theme underlying many such films.

The Silence of the Lambs. This 1991 film starring Jodie Foster as a young FBI agent, much of which is set outside prison walls, also features some scenes inside some correctional facilities. The star inmate is a serial killer named Hannibal Lecter (played by Anthony Hopkins), a former physician who is a brilliant but indescribably brutal and sadistic murderer. Lecter is such a danger to other inmates and staff that he must be kept in total isolation. He is so dangerous that his handlers must keep him totally strapped, including his mouth, one of his most dangerous weapons.

The Shawshank Redemption. Perhaps the premier prison film of the 1990s, in this 1994 film, Tim Robbins portrays Andy Dufresne, a mild-mannered Maine banker wrongfully imprisoned for killing his wife. Morgan Freeman turns in a memorable performance as Redding, a veteran inmate and Andy's best friend. The staff is portrayed as murderously brutal and corrupt, and Andy effects a sophisticated yet highly improbable escape.

CONCLUSION

We have defined corrections, discussed current trends in the field, noted the traditional goals of corrections, and highlighted the themes of the text. The following chapters will give further details about many of the points we have noted in this chapter. For example, Chapter 6 is entirely devoted to restorative and community justice, and Chapters 7 and 8 offer considerable detail on the state of prisons and prisoners in the United States.

Chapter 2 discusses the history of corrections. Individuals have broken laws for thousands of years, and their societies have devised numerous responses to such offending behavior. We will trace the history of such responses in an effort to understand the choices we have made and to explore whether some past choices were perhaps better choices than those made recently.

DISCUSSION QUESTIONS

1. Discuss the current state of corrections in the United States. What trends are taking place? How do you assess the current trends? Are we going where we should be going, or do you think that the direction of American corrections has taken the wrong turn? What needs to be done in American corrections?

2. What are the traditional goals of corrections? Which is the most important? Which is the least important? Is there another goal that should be mentioned?

3. This chapter (see especially Box 1.3) indicates that "Scared Straight" programs have not been very effective in reducing delinquency. Why do you think that "Scared Straight"–type programs have not been particularly effective in deterring youngsters from crime and delinquency?

4. Eliminating frills from prison has been one recent trend in corrections. What constitutes a frill? List what you consider to be necessities versus frills in prison life. How do you distinguish between the two categories? What would your prison look like? (Note: We will return to this issue in Chapter 7 on prison life.)

5. What do you think prisons will look like in 15 years? How might they be different from today's prisons?

6. Cost concerns constitute an important issue in corrections. How much should society spend on its prisons?

FURTHER READING

Austin, J., and J. Irwin (2001). *It's About Time: America's Imprisonment Binge*, 3rd ed. Belmont, CA: Wadsworth.

Miethe, T.D., and L. Hong (2005). *Punishment. A Comparative Historical Perspective.* New York: Cambridge University Press.

Toth, R.C., G.A. Crews, and C.E. Burton (2008). *In the Margins: Special Populations and American Justice*. Upper Saddle River, NJ: Prentice Hall.

Weisheit, R.A., and F.T. Morn (2003). *Pursuing Justice*. Belmont, CA: Wadsworth.

NOTES

1. Glaze and Bonczar, 2007.
2. Glaze and Bonczar, 2007.
3. Pew Center on the States, 2008.
4. Austin and Irwin, 2001.
5. Clear, 1994.
6. Pew Center on the States, 2008.
7. Sabol, Couture, and Harrison, 2007.
8. Feeley and Simon, 1992.
9. Walker, 2006.
10. Johnston, O'Malley, and Bachman, 1997.
11. http://www.pbs.org.pages/frontline/shows/snitch/primer
12. Sabol, Couture, and Harrison, 2007.
13. Sabol, Couture, and Harrison, 2007.
14. Pew Center on the States, 2008.
15. See, e.g., Walker, 2006.
16. Irwin, 1980.
17. Irwin, 1980.
18. Irwin, 1980.
19. See, e.g., Bennett and Cribb, 2008, and Bennett, 1993.
20. See, e.g., von Hirsch, 1976.
21. MacKenzie, 2006.
22. Kurki, 1999, 1.
23. Kurki, 1999.
24. Prejean, 1993, 194.
25. van den Haag, 1978.
26. Mackie, 1982.
27. Vitiello, 1997.
28. Zimring and Hawkins, 1995.
29. Smith and Dickey, 1999.
30. Smith and Dickey, 1999.
31. MacKenzie, 2006.
32. van den Haag, 1978, 67.
33. Costanzo, 1997, 153.

REFERENCES

Austin, J., and J. Irwin (2001). *It's About Time: America's Imprisonment Binge*, 3rd ed. Belmont, CA: Wadsworth.

Beck, A.J. (2000a). "Correctional Populations in the United States, 1997."*Bureau of Justice Statistics Bulletin*. Washington, DC: U.S. Government Printing Office.

Beck, A.J. (2000b). "Prisoners in 1999." *Bureau of Justice Statistics Bulletin*. Washington, DC: U.S. Department of Justice.

Bennett, W.J. (1993). *The Book of Virtues: A Compendium of Great Moral Stories*. New York: Simon & Schuster.

Bennett, W.J., and J.T.E. Cribb (2008). *The American Patriot's Almanac*. Nashville, TN: Thomas Nelson.

Bonczar, T.P., and L.E. Glaze (1999). "Probation and Parole in the United States, 1998." *Bureau of Justice Statistics Bulletin*. Washington, DC: U.S. Department of Justice.

Breed, A.F. (1998). "Corrections: A Victim of Situational Ethics." *Crime & Delinquency* 44:9-18.

Bureau of Justice Statistics. Available at http://www.ojp.usdoj.gov/bjs

Clear, T.R. (1994). *Harm in American Penology: Offenders, Victims, and Their Communities*. Albany, NY: SUNY Press.

Costanzo, M. (1997). *Just Revenge: Costs and Consequences of the Death Penalty*. New York: St. Martin's Press.

Cullen, F.T., B.S. Fisher, and B.K. Applegate (2000). "Public Opinion about Punishment and Corrections." In *Crime and Justice: A Review of Research* (Vol. 27). Chicago: University of Chicago Press.

Feeley, M.M., and J. Simon (1992). "The New Penology: Notes on the Emerging Strategy of Corrections and Its Implications." *Criminology* 30:449-474.

Frontline. Available at http://www.pbs.org/wgbh/pages/frontline/shows/snitch/primer

Glaze, L.E. (2002). "Probation and Parole in the United States, 2001." *Bureau of Justice Statistics Bulletin*. Washington, DC: U.S. Government Printing Office.

Glaze, L.E., and T.P. Bonczar (2007). "Probation and Parole in the United States, 2006." *Bureau of Justice Statistics Bulletin*. Washington, DC: U.S. Government Printing Office.

Harding, R.W. (1997). *Private Prisons and Public Accountability*. New Brunswick, NJ: Transaction.

Harland, A.T. (ed.) (1996). *Choosing Correctional Options That Work: Defining the Demand and Evaluating the Supply*. Thousand Oaks, CA: Sage.

Irwin, J. (1980). *Prisons in Turmoil*. Boston: Little, Brown.

Johnson City Press, January 12, 1999.

Johnston, L.D., P.M. O'Malley, and J.G. Bachman (1997). *National Survey Results on Drug Use from the Monitoring the Future Study, 1975-1996* (Vol. 1). Washington, DC: U.S. Government Printing Office.

Kurki, L. (1999). "Incorporating Restorative and Community Justice into American Sentencing and Corrections." *Bureau of Justice Statistics Bulletin*. Washington, DC: U.S. Government Printing Office.

Lewis, R.V. (1983). "Scared Straight—California Style: Evaluation of the San Quentin Squires Program." *Criminal Justice and Behavior* 10:209-226.

Lundman, R.J. (1993). *Prevention and Control of Juvenile Delinquency*, 2nd ed. New York: Oxford.

MacKenzie, D.L. (2006). *What Works in Corrections: Reducing the Criminal Activities of Offenders and Delinquents*. New York: Cambridge University Press.

Mackie, J. (1982). "Morality and the Retributive Emotions." *Criminal Justice Ethics* 1(1):3-10.

Maguire, K., and A.L. Pastore (1999). "Sourcebook of Criminal Justice Statistics 1999." *Bureau of Justice Statistics Bulletin*. Washington, DC: U.S. Department of Justice.

Maguire, K., and A.L. Pastore (1998). "Sourcebook of Criminal Justice Statistics 1997." *Bureau of Justice Statistics Bulletin*. Washington, DC: U.S. Department of Justice.

Mauer, M. (1999). "'Lock 'Em Up and Throw Away the Key': African-American Males and the Criminal Justice System." In K.C. Haas and G.P. Alpert (eds.) *The Dilemmas of Corrections: Contemporary Readings*, 4th ed., 30-43.

Office of National Drug Control Policy (1998). *The National Drug Control Policy*. Washington, DC: Office of National Drug Control Policy.

Pew Center on the States (2008). *One in 100: Behind Bars in America 2008*. Washington, DC: Pew Center on the States.

Prejean, H. (1993). *Dead Man Walking: An Eyewitness Account of the Death Penalty in the United States*. New York: Vintage Books.

Sabol, W.J., H. Couture, and P.M. Harrison (2007). "Prisoners in 2006." *Bureau of Justice Statistics Bulletin*. Washington, DC: U.S. Government Printing Office.

Smith, M.E., and W.J. Dickey (1999). "Reforming Sentencing and Corrections for Just Punishment and Public Safety." *Bureau of Justice Statistics Bulletin*. Washington, DC: U.S. Government Printing Office.

Snell, T.L. (2000). "Capital Punishment 1999." *Bureau of Justice Statistics Bulletin*. Washington, DC: U.S. Department of Justice.

Sykes, G. (1958). *The Society of Captives*. Princeton, NJ: Princeton University Press.

van den Haag, E. (1978). "In Defense of the Death Penalty: A Legal-Practical-Moral Analysis." *Criminal Law Bulletin* 14:51-68.

Vitiello, M. (1997). "Three Strikes: Can We Return to Rationality?" *Journal of Criminal Law and Criminology* 87:395-481.

von Hirsch, A. (1976). *Doing Justice: The Choice of Punishments*. New York: Hill and Wang.

Walker, S. (2006). *Sense and Nonsense about Crime and Drugs: A Policy Guide*, 6th ed. Belmont, CA: West/Wadsworth.

"Weighing the Options: Questions Remain about the Pros and Cons of Weight Training in Prisons" (1999). Available at http://www.rec-net.com

Whitehead, J.T., M.B. Blankenship, and J.P. Wright (1999). "Elite Versus Citizen Attitudes on Capital Punishment: Incongruity Between the Public and Policymakers." *Journal of Criminal Justice* 27:249-258.

Zimring, F.E., and G. Hawkins (1995). *Incapacitation: Penal Confinement and the Restraint of Crime*. New York: Oxford.

The History of American Corrections: Where Did We Come From?

What You Need to Know

▶ Ancient societies used some of the correctional practices found in modern America. For example, the Mesopotamians had a type of jail, and ancient Greece and Israel used capital punishment.

▶ Colonial Americans used shaming punishments such as branding, the ducking stool, and the stocks.

▶ The Quakers were very influential in the development of American corrections, especially the penitentiary.

▶ The Quakers used the separate system while New York State used the Auburn or congregate system, but both systems emphasized many similar features.

▶ The indeterminate sentence and parole have their roots in Australian and Irish corrections.

▶ The Progressive Era influenced the development of probation and at least the idea of treatment. It was at this point that science began to influence how we view criminals and how they should be punished or treated.

▶ After World War II, rehabilitation, at least in theory, guided the operation of prisons, especially in California.

▶ In the 1960s and 1970s, attacks on rehabilitation emanated from both political conservatives and liberals. Even the Quakers participated in criticisms of rehabilitation.

▶ Concerns over rehabilitation led to a punitive or "get tough" era in correctional policy and practice.

INTRODUCTION

The dilemma of how to treat those who violate the prescribed rules of a society or community is as old as settled life itself. The question of whether a community should assist or punish an offender is just as old. This chapter briefly examines the history of humankind's efforts at dealing with those who break rules and laws. Specifically, the development of American corrections is traced to its roots in previous time periods in America, as well as antecedents in Western Europe, and to several ancient civilizations that influenced Western thought, political philosophy, and penal practices. The focus is on the evolution and history of Western penal systems. Although penal practices in nonWestern societies are worthwhile topics of study, they did not influence American penal practices to the degree that European penal systems did.

CORRECTIONS IN THE PREHISTORIC ERA

Most information about life in the prehistoric era—the period before written history—comes from archeological discoveries. This information provides little insight into how people organized and administered life in communities. In fact, it was only relatively recently in history that human beings stopped living as nomadic hunters and settled into agricultural life. With so little known about prehistoric life, there is likewise very little known about how prehistoric communities dealt with those who would be labeled today as "lawbreakers." Actually, because there was no written law to govern people's activities, the matter of dealing with those who violated community norms or unwritten rules was most likely an informal, haphazard affair.

If prehistoric humans left no written documents, how can we study their social organizations, including correctional practices? One way is through art, which often reveals much about societal values, structures, philosophy, and social organizations. A Paleolithic (5000-4000 BCE) cave at Addaura, Sicily, contains an engraved scene of many human figures moving around one who is bound in such a way that any movement would cause choking, a common method of torture and execution in ancient times.[1]

This little snippet suggests that prehistoric punishment, at least at that time and location, was organized and ritualistic—that it involved community participation, that it was directed at the body as opposed to the mind, that capital punishment was sanctioned, and that punishment was deliberately cruel and torturous. As will be seen in the following pages, in some respects, correctional practices in Western society have changed little from that time until recently.

CORRECTIONAL PRACTICES IN ANCIENT SOCIETIES

• The Mesopotamians •

When and where settled life began on earth is a matter of debate. Some historians and archaeologists suggest it began in China; others contend that it began in Africa. Important for criminal justice purposes are the first written documents related to law and punishment. The oldest known legal documents come from around 2400 BCE. The Mesopotamian Code of Urikagina contained provisions for execution by stoning for convicted thieves and for women who committed adultery.

There were other Mesopotamian legal codes, such as the Code of Lipti-Ishtar, the Laws of Eschunnah, and the Code of Hammurabi (which is on display at the Louvre in Paris). Under these codes, there was scant mention of anything resembling modern-day incarceration. The jail in ancient Mesopotamia was a deep hole or cistern. Its primary purpose was as a holding facility for offenders awaiting trial or execution.

Based on prescribed punishments, these communities valued property more than life. Assaultive behaviors, and sometimes even certain forms of homicide, were often punished by mandatory compensation to the victim or the victim's family. Theft from a garden, if it occurred at night, was punishable by death. In some cases that would normally demand the death penalty, the offender was allowed to live but lost the offending body part—for example, a finger for theft, or emasculation for certain sexual offenses. This was referred to as a "sympathetic punishment." The Mesopotamian codes are among the earliest to expressly endorse the concept of *lex talionis*, commonly referred to as the "eye for an eye" doctrine.

• The Israelites •

Several hundred years after the appearance of the early Mesopotamian codes, the Israelite legal codes, commonly referred to as Mosaic Law, were written. The Mesopotamian influence on the Israelites is evident, particularly in the "eye for an eye" doctrine. The best source for examining Israelite laws and punishment is the Torah, also referred to as the Pentateuch, or the Biblical books of Exodus, Leviticus, and Deuteronomy. All Mosaic Law revolved around principles contained in the Ten Commandments, which are first listed in the book of Exodus. The commandments contained general rules for obedience to God and for treatment of other human beings. Moses, an Israelite who was reared and educated in Egypt and then led the Israelites out of slavery from Egypt, is believed to have written Israelite law and, presumably under divine guidance, prescribed the punishments for lawbreaking.

Because Mosaic Law was written while the Israelites were wandering in the wilderness, there is no mention of long-term incarceration as a punishment. The rationale for the absence of incarceration is fairly simple. People who were constantly moving could not erect permanent facilities. However, the Israelites must have been familiar with imprisonment as a sanction. One of their Israelite forefathers, Joseph, spent many years in Egyptian prisons before emerging as a leader of the Egyptian government.

Most Israelite punishments were administered in public as a deterrent to others. Additionally, public participation and involvement in punishing lawbreakers served as a form of religious ritual, a time of cleansing from unrighteousness and community-wide repentance. This is a recurring theme in other religious societies as well, including some modern Islamic countries.

While most Israelite sanctions were harsh by modern standards—more than 30 offenses called for the death penalty—there appears in the Mosaic law an element that was foreign to many societies of that day but is common to many of today: rehabilitation. Although the idea of slavery is abhorrent to Americans today, it was practically universal during the time the Mosaic law was written. Many slaves were war captives, and many were forced into slavery or indentured servitude because of failure to pay debts or for being unable to compensate the victim of a theft. In those cases, Israelite masters were required to treat slaves humanely, just as many today say that Americans should treat captive prison inmates in the same way. In addition, Israelite masters were required to assist in the development of a slave's moral, religious, and vocational welfare, the ancient Near Eastern equivalent to rehabilitation. Further, no debt could be held over a slave or debtor for more than six years. This prevented the rich from holding the poor in virtual lifetime bondage through usury.

The use of imprisonment is referenced numerous other times in the Biblical account of Israel and Judah's history. For instance, the poetic books of Job and Psalms contain several references to incarceration. At least two Jewish prophets, Zechariah and Jeremiah, had some first-hand knowledge of imprisonment.

• The Ancient Greeks •

Israelite culture and military prowess prospered in the Middle East from about the time the Mosaic law was written—between 1400 and 1000 BCE—for several hundred years. Around the seventh century BCE, Greek culture, thought, and military might took hold in southern Europe and the Middle East. Though ancient Greece is most often associated with the writings of its great philosophers, such as Socrates, Plato, and Aristotle, a number of Greek lawmakers contributed to Western ideas on punishment.

In most ancient societies, and until relatively recent years, most criminal offenses were regarded as private matters to be settled between the disagree-

BOX 2.1

The Ten Commandments

Not all religious faiths agree on the ordering of the Commandments. Many Christian denominations regard Statement #2 listed below as two separate Commandments, and do not recognize the first statement listed below as a separate Commandment. Many Jewish authorities recognize Statement #1 as a Commandment by itself, and view Statement #2 as one Commandment. This listing is taken from the Jewish Publication Society's translation of the Jewish Tanakh.

1. I am the LORD thy God, who brought thee out of the land of Egypt, out of the house of bondage.

2. Thou shalt have no other gods before Me. Thou shalt not make unto thee a graven image, nor any manner of likeness, of any thing that is in heaven above, or that is in the earth beneath, or that is in the water under the earth; thou shalt not bow down unto them, nor serve them…

3. Thou shalt not take the name of the LORD thy God in vain; for the LORD will not hold him guiltless that taketh His name in vain.

4. Remember the sabbath day, to keep it holy. Six days shalt thou labour, and do all thy work; but the seventh day is a sabbath unto the LORD thy God, in it thou shalt not do any manner of work….

5. Honour thy father and thy mother, that thy days may be long upon the land which the LORD thy God giveth thee.

6. Thou shalt not murder.

7. Thou shalt not commit adultery.

8. Thou shalt not steal.

9. Thou shalt not bear false witness against thy neighbour.

10. Thou shalt not covet thy neighbour's house; thou shalt not covet thy neighbour's wife, nor his manservant, nor his maid-servant, nor his ox, nor his ass, nor any thing that is thy neighbour's.

ing parties. Whatever government was in existence merely tried to mediate the differences—and very often did not even do that. While the Israelites viewed crime as an offense against God rather than against just an individual, the more secular-minded Greeks viewed crime as a disruption of the social order. One of the most notable Greek lawgivers, Draco, saw the need for a structured governmental role in controlling criminal procedures and punishment. One reason was that government refusal to intervene in criminal matters resulted in blood feuds between different families and clans, with bloody and economically damaging results. Draco's punishments were harsh by modern standards, so much so that the word "draconian" is still defined as a an excessively harsh punishment for a misdeed.

The main contributions from the Greeks were in the area of judicial reform and legal thought. Most punishments differed little from those of other cultures of the time. Physical punishments such as torture were common. Capital punishment was frequently used.

The most famous view of Greek justice comes from the trial of Socrates. Socrates was placed on trial in 399 BCE on the charge of being "an evil-doer and a curious person, searching into things under the earth and above the heavens, making the worse appear the better cause, and teaching all this to others."[2] Socrates was convicted and sentenced to death.

AP Photo

"The Death of Socrates," by French classical style painter Jacques Louis David. Socrates was detained the night before his execution in a holding cell. He chose to drink the poison hemlock rather than accept banishment.

The common method of execution for a person of Socrates' high social standing was being forced to drink hemlock. As in most past time periods, a jail was used merely as a holding cell for pretrial detainees and those awaiting execution. Socrates was detained the night before his execution. It was a common practice in the case of political prisoners for the prisoner to be banished with the explicit understanding that he or she leave the area, and never return, under penalty of death. Socrates refused the banishment and drank the poison.

The stories of Socrates and other Greek law violators demonstrate that modern methods of correction, long-term imprisonment, and supervision in the community were foreign to the Greeks. However, imprisonment of some variety did exist. It is mentioned in Plato's *Apology*, which was written around 399 BCE. Greek influence in thought and governmental philosophy was very evident in the next great European and Middle Eastern Empire: Rome.

• The Romans •

It was during the time of the Roman Republic that many innovations in the empire's justice system occurred. Juries were used to determine the innocence or guilt of accused criminals; checks against judicial power were instituted; and Roman citizens were granted the right to appeal criminal convictions. The most famous example of the right to appeal is found in the New Testament story of Paul, the early Christian apostle. Theologians speculate that Paul harmed his case, though perhaps not his cause—the spread of the Christian message to Rome—by insisting on his right to appeal.

Many of the reforms and rights granted during the time of the Republic withered away under the Caesars, but not the right of appeal. In the name of improving the efficiency of justice administration and as an emergency measure to combat a perceived lawlessness in the Roman Empire, many procedural rights were eventually curtailed or abolished.

The Roman government appeared to care little for the idea of assisting criminal offenders. Deterrence, ensuring the continuance of absolute rule over its subjects, and pure retribution were the primary aims of Roman punishment methods. The death penalty could be administered for crimes of numerous varieties—violent, property, or political. As with most other societies, jails were used primarily as short-term holding facilities for those awaiting execution or scourging with the whip.

The Tullianum underground prison was constructed under the Roman forum in the third century BCE. Conditions in the Tullianum were abysmal. Sallust, a second-century historian, described it as hideous, dark, and neglected by its keepers. Indications are that the Tullianum was used as a short-term holding facility and sometimes as an execution chamber.[3]

The Romans appeared to make use of house arrest, a noninstitutional sanction that has reappeared in the United States over the past three decades. The case of Paul, the early Christian apostle, provides a view of this punishment. Unlike modern-day house arrest programs, which often involve electronic monitoring devices and allow the offender to attend several types of pre-approved activities, house arrest under the Romans was much more uncomfortable. The offender would usually be kept chained and under guard while on house arrest.

House arrest took another form in Rome other than the one just mentioned. Many households, particularly those of the upper class, contained a jail cell in the house. Roman law gave the male head of the household the power to incarcerate and punish any member of the household—wife, child, or servant—by placing him or her in this "domestic prison cell."[4]

THE MIDDLE AGES

As the Roman Empire's influence began to crumble, the administration of criminal justice increasingly came under the influence of the Christian church and small Germanic kingdoms. Although imprisonment as a long-term punishment was seldom used, the seeds of the penitentiary were born during the Middle Ages. In most of Europe, criminals were still subjected to physical punishments, and some were given economic sanctions. In some cases, trial by ordeal, in which an accused would be required to undergo a procedure that supposedly would determine guilt or innocence through divine intervention, would act as both a trial and a form of punishment. If one did not survive the ordeal, the issue of further punishment was moot.

The seeds of the penitentiary planted during the Middle Ages focused on punishments administered by church authorities. Most of these medieval church-based punishments were administered against members of the clergy —priests, nuns, and monks. A holding area in the church or the monastery would be set aside to isolate—and, in some cases, physically punish—the offending clergy member. The physical punishment might involve being placed in stocks for several hours or being whipped with a rod.[5]

The idea behind these punishments was to coerce the offending member of the clergy to make penitence through the punishment and isolation of the prison experience. Toward the beginning of the Middle Ages, this ecclesiastical or church-based punishment was used only against the clergy. The idea of long-term punishment through isolation and coerced penitence survived, though, and carried over to the secular realm. By the end of the medieval period, around 1550, long-term imprisonment as a means of punishment was becoming more common throughout Europe.

The medieval European idea of long-term punishment was short by today's standards, with several months to a year considered long-term. Medieval prisons, including English "gaols," from which the word "jail" is derived, were not equipped to handle prisoners for longer periods. There were few, if any, mechanisms for long-term punishment of criminals. So many offenses were punishable by death that long-term imprisonment was not even considered, and many offenders were banished from their community for life as a long-term punishment. Jail conditions were usually so horrific that many prisoners died if incarcerated for a lengthy period. Many personal amenities, including blankets, clothing, and sometimes even decent food, were given only to those who paid the jailer, or for those who had friends or relatives to provide for them. As a result, jail conditions were particularly brutal for the poor.

ENGLISH CORRECTIONS DURING THE ENLIGHTENMENT

During the latter part of the Middle Ages and the early Industrial Era, England and other European powers began expanding their world presence by exploring or invading "new worlds." England also experienced substantial social unrest and increasing crime because of rapid population increases in its cities, particularly in London. English government officials sought ways to rid the streets of petty criminals—serious criminals were usually executed—and make money in the process.

One of the more original correctional measures taken in the late eighteenth century to relieve crowding was the use of hulks, or dilapidated ships anchored off English ports, to detain offenders. The hulks, sometimes referred to as "hell holds" or "floating hells," were notoriously inhospitable, filthy, and disease-ridden. They offered nothing in the way of rehabilitation. The hulks were merely temporary warehouses, an alternative to nothing. The conditions in the hulks prompted John Howard, the sheriff of Bedfordshire, to write *The State of the Prisons* in 1777. Howard's criticisms of hulk conditions encouraged the British Parliament to pass legislation providing for the building of more safe, secure, and sanitary prisons on land.[6]

The use of hulks continued for a number of years, but the promise of material riches in North America generated another innovative idea for disposing of England's criminal element. Private business interests stepped forward to offer transportation to the American colonies. Those who transported debtors and criminals often received a fee from government officials in England and a fee from commercial interests in the colonies. By no means were the majority of American immigrants in the seventeenth and eighteenth centuries released from English prisons, but thousands of petty criminals and debtors were sent to the American colonies during that time. The American Revolution brought a halt to importation of English prisoners to the United States.[7]

CORRECTIONS IN THE UNITED STATES

The village-style, communal life of colonial America did not lend itself to extensive use of institutional incarceration. Resources and expertise for erecting jails or prison facilities were for the most part nonexistent. A few jails were used as short-term housing facilities for those awaiting trial or imposition of sentence. Some offenders served short jail terms, but one reason jails were not used as frequently as in later times was due to economics. Even today, jails and prisons are a financial drain on society. It is expensive to feed and house prisoners. Another economic motive has been connected to the scarce use of prisons and jails. Incarcerated inmates could not contribute to the community's economy because they were not able to work. If a small town in colonial America had incarcerated its citizens on a frequent basis, very few of these inmates (most of whom would have been men) would have been able to work and feed their families.

The most common Colonial Era–sanction for crimes was the same as that of today: the fine. Though the fine was the most commonly administered sanction in colonial America, that era's hallmark was the public punishment.[8] Such punishments are the stuff of legend—in folklore, history, film, and literature. Thus, most punishments were precursors not to institutional corrections but to community-based corrections.

The primary purpose of Colonial Era–punishments was to shame and embarrass the offender. It was hoped that shaming would have both a punitive and rehabilitative effect. The offender would be so embarrassed by being publicly punished that he or she would be repentant, in the religious sense, and sin no more. The use of the terms "repentant" and "sin" is not an attempt at cryptic sarcasm. Among most colonials of European ancestry, the most common explanation for committing crime was religious in nature. According to them, all people were born sinners and, unless aided by a strong faith in God, were bound to fall astray and break the laws and community mores of the town.

Colonial Americans did not lack creativity when it came to administering public punishments. Nathaniel Hawthorne's *The Scarlet Letter* was a fictionalized account of one such punishment. In the novel, the protagonist, Hester Prynne, bore a child out of wedlock. While such behavior is not criminal in today's society, it was treated very seriously in many colonial communities. The woman would be required to have the letter "A" (for adultery) sewn on her garment and would be required to wear the garment in public for a specified length of time.

Other behaviors brought punishments similar to the "scarlet letter." Sometimes offenders were branded with a hot iron rather than being required to wear a sewn letter on their garments. Offenders might be branded with the letter "V" for vagrant or vagabond, "D" for drunkard, or other letters that denoted their crime.

The ducking stool was another punishment designed to shame the offender. It was usually used against women who were slanderers, chronic gossips, or general busybodies. The offender would be strapped into a chair, taken down to the river, and dropped into the water several times in public view. Such a punishment was designed to embarrass the offender's husband, in hopes that the husband would do more to control his wife's behavior.[9]

The stocks were used for a variety of offenses. Offenders were required to spend varying periods of time—anywhere from several hours to several days, depending upon the infraction—usually in full public view with their hands and head in the stocks. Very often the offender was allowed nothing but bread and water, and townspeople were not discouraged from verbally and even physically abusing the offender as they walked the streets of the town.

The brank, or "scold's bridle," was a painful punishment that was primarily used against women who committed verbal offenses such as excessive gossiping, slander, or being disrespectful to men (be it a husband or local leader). William Andrews described the brank as:

> . . . an iron framework, which was placed on the head, enclosing it in a kind of cage; it had in front a plate of iron, which, either sharpened or covered with spikes, was so situated as to be placed in the mouth of the victim, and if she attempted to

move her tongue in any way whatever, it was certain to be shockingly injured. With the brank on her head she was conducted through the streets, led by a chain, held by one of the town's officials, an object of contempt, and subjected to the jeers of the crowd and often left to their mercy.[10]

Did shaming punishments work? It is difficult to say. First, it is difficult to define or measure, let alone evaluate, whether a punishment "works." For shaming punishments to accomplish their intended effect, several factors must be present. First, an offender must be capable of feeling shamed. Some children in elementary school are ashamed to have their name put on the chalkboard for misbehaving, while other children snicker at this "punishment." In the same vein, being publicly branded as a criminal did not then, and does not now, embarrass all offenders.

Second, in order for shaming to have its desired effect, a community must mutually agree that certain behaviors are indeed shameful, as many colonial villages did. As the populations in American towns and cities grew larger and more diverse in culture, mores, lifestyles, and religious beliefs, there was less agreement on which behaviors were right and which were wrong. In recent decades, some jurisdictions have enacted "scarlet letter" punishments, such as requiring child sex offenders to have their picture posted on an Internet web page and requiring convicted drunk drivers to post a bumper sticker on their car indicating they have been convicted of drunk driving. Some offenders would be embarrassed by these requirements, but some would not. This might depend in part on the values possessed by that offender's peer group and family. If an offender comes from a family in which a criminal conviction is not a badge of shame or from a peer group where a criminal conviction is a badge of courage, that type of shame is absent.

Third, the offender who was supposed to be shamed and shunned sometimes became a martyr. The scorn would be heaped on those who decreed or administered the punishment. For example, Hawthorne took a sympathetic view of Hester Prynne in *The Scarlet Letter*. Many other punishments also engendered sympathy rather than hostility toward the offender.

Similar sympathetic attitudes existed toward some offenders in America's early years. Eventually, many Americans became disenchanted with public punishments and sought alternatives to the frequent use of capital punishment. The increased urbanization of American society, the growing belief that criminal behavior was associated with an evil urban environment as well as a sinful nature, and the revulsion against public punishment all generated efforts designed at reforming rather than simply humiliating the criminal.

The final question about the efficacy of public punishments does not pertain to whether it "works" in terms of recidivism or public outrage.

The U.S. Supreme Court has used the phrase "evolving standard of decency" in deciding whether certain punishments are Constitutional. The physically torturous punishments described here do not seem compatible with contemporary standards of decency.

If fines and public punishments were not effective in stopping the undesired behavior, or if the offense was severe, the individual may have been banished. This was often a death sentence in itself because the likelihood of surviving in the wilderness or reaching another settlement before dying of starvation, exposure, or other dangers was slim. The offender was often branded or otherwise given a physical marking to warn other settlements of his or her criminality. If the offender returned or refused to leave, then hanging was used as a last resort for the community to protect itself. Thus, imprisonment, as such, was used only until some other form of punishment was carried out, or until the individual (or his or her relatives) paid the fine imposed.[11]

THE BIRTH OF THE PENITENTIARY

In the 1700s, the cities along the eastern seaboard experienced a host of problems associated with urban growth. "Red light" districts emerged, and droves of immigrants and citizens descended upon the cities, burdening charity services and creating a population of vagrants and minor thieves. Because the older forms of punishment, which depended on public humiliation, did not work on this transient, heterogeneous city population, new forms of social control were necessary. The congregate care facility was born of the need to control and provide services to larger numbers of people.[12] Orphanages were used to house orphaned or abandoned youngsters; hospitals were created to house the sick and infirm; mental institutions were opened to take care of those who had previously been cared for by families or tolerated by communities; and workhouses or poorhouses were used to control and house those who had no work or means of making a living.

Soon the population of poorhouses or workhouses overlapped with those in jails, and eventually the jail was utilized not merely as a holding facility but also as a type of punishment. Because poor people would never be able to pay a fine (certainly not as long as they were being held), keeping them incarcerated became the punishment itself. There was little difference between the fate of the street person who ended up in a workhouse and that of the one who ended up in a jail. Houses of correction, an institutional model found in England, recognized this overlap and operated under the assumption that poor people must be taught a trade and "corrected" from their life of idleness.[13] In effect, this practice made it a crime to be poor, with the punishment being incarceration and forced labor. If the individual proved pliable and learned quickly, he or she could earn release and utilize the learned trade to become a productive citizen.

To a great degree, the origin of the penitentiary has religious roots. Correctional reformers wanted to make less use of publicly degrading punishments that did little to alter offenders' behavior. They sought to provide an environment in which offenders could, in solitude, make penitence with God. This would be done by coerced Bible study and religious instruction. It is ironic that penitentiaries are viewed today as centers of human degradation and violence. The original intention behind the penitentiary's creation held much higher promise.

If one state deserves credit (or blame) for the birth of the American penitentiary, it would be Pennsylvania. In 1682, thanks in large measure to the efforts of William Penn, a new penal code, commonly called "Penn's Code," was established in Pennsylvania. It provided for bail eligibility for all prisoners, free food and lodging for prisoners (historically, prisoners had been expected to pay a fee for their food and accommodations), and the provision of jails to replace pillories and stocks.[14]

Quakers (such as William Penn), whose numbers in early American history were greater in Pennsylvania than in other states, had a strong hand in creating the penitentiary, though they did not actually create American prisons on their own. In fact, New-Gate Prison, an underground prison was opened in an abandoned copper mine in Simsbury (now East Granby), Connecticut, in 1773. The prison was used to detain conventional criminals as well as to detain Loyalists (those who opposed American independence from Great Britain) during the Revolutionary War.

In Pennsylvania, Quaker ideals contributed to the move to make penal institutions a humane alternative to public, corporal punishments, and in some cases, to capital punishment. Sentiment against public and corporal punishments had been building since the late 1600s. It culminated in the conversion of Philadelphia's Walnut Street Jail in 1790 to America's "first true correctional institution."[15] Benjamin Rush—a signer of the Declaration of Independence—and others instituted innovations that were designed to change the jail from a place of incapacitation to one where reformation might occur.[16] At least a rudimentary system of classification was imposed; women and men were separated, as were children from adults and the sick from the well. In addition, those who were believed to be capable of reformation were separated from those who were perceived to be hardened criminals.

Some attempt was made to have those incarcerated inside the Walnut Street Jail work at some craft. With these changes, jails took a giant step toward the institution we now call a prison or a penitentiary. The Walnut Street Jail was designed to keep inmates busy through manual labor. Walnut Street was also supposed to require that prisoners work and live in solitude, away from the unhealthy influence of other prisoners. It was also designed to classify inmates, segregating inmates by gender, age, and type of offense. Walnut Street officials hoped to keep women away from men, children away from adults, and minor offenders away from serious offenders. Contact with the outside was nonexistent or kept to a minimum. The only influence on the offender was the Bible and a religious guide as an aid in finding salvation. After a due period of "penitence," the individual was to emerge a new person.[17] The transformation of a holding facility to one where correction was encouraged and expected was accompanied by an unbounded optimism about what such facilities might be able to do. Clergy members, politicians, and educators all believed that the institution was the perfect place to instill the characteristics of sobriety, regularity, and piety in the wayward inmates found within.

As with many penal experiments, the staff at Walnut Street found that reality got in the way of high expectations. Cells quickly became overcrowded, so the ideal of solitude was dashed, as was the ideal of segregating offenders. There was not enough work that could be done under secure environments, a problem that plagues corrections even today. After several years, the idealism of those who transformed the Walnut Street Jail deteriorated as a result of management problems such as overcrowding and corruption.

Despite its shortcomings, the Walnut Street Jail was viewed as a humane alternative to corporal and public punishments, which had fallen out of favor with a large sector of the public. The Walnut Street experiment gave rise to other correctional innovations, most notably the founding of the modern penitentiary.

• The 1820s: Eastern vs. Auburn •

The next significant developments in American prison history were the opening of Eastern State Penitentiary at Cherry Hill, Pennsylvania, in 1821, and the opening of Auburn Prison in Auburn, New York, in 1829. Alexis de Tocqueville made the prisons at Cherry Hill, Auburn, and Walnut Street one of the "subjects of inquiry" of his famous treatise on American democracy.[18] The method of discipline and administration used at Eastern came to be known as the "Pennsylvania system," and Auburn became associated with the term "congregate system." Under the Pennsylvania model, each inmate lived in a separate cell with a separate exercise yard. Clergy members visited inmates and attempted to help them attain a spiritual awakening or rebirth. Handcrafts were performed inside the cell. Complete and absolute separation from all other influences was enforced (or at least that was the intent). In actuality, though, inmates developed an ingenious method of communicating with each other through a code of tapping noises over the plumbing pipes.

The primary hallmarks of both the Pennsylvania and Auburn systems were total solitary confinement and religious instruction. Prisoners were confined to their cells for 23 hours a day, with one hour allowed for exercise. Inmates were allowed no contact with each other. The congregate system at Auburn was also characterized by confinement to individual cells. Unlike the Pennsylvania system, however, inmates were allowed to work and eat together, but were not allowed to speak to each other. Smaller cells could be built because the inmate did nothing but sleep in them. Instead of individual handcrafts, industrial manufacturing could be brought into the prison, and inmates could work on assembly-line projects. This was touted as a way for prisons to become profitable institutions for the state, rather than ones that drained public resources.

The two models of this new form of punishment were presented for public scrutiny and adoption. The Pennsylvania (or Philadelphia or Eastern or separate system) model and the New York (or Auburn or congregate care) model were compared and contrasted, becoming the topic of editorials, debates, and public speeches. Some Europeans even came to see the two prisons, seeing them as much a part of the American experience for tourists as the buffalo, "wild" Indians, and the transcontinental railroad.[19]

Both systems incorporated religious instruction into their programming. The only reading material most inmates had access to was a Bible. The thinking was that inmates, left alone with themselves and a Bible, and an occasional visit from a member of the clergy, would see the error of their ways, make penitence (hence the word "penitentiary"), and sin no more after leaving the institution.

Samuel Walker points out that although the systems differed somewhat in their operation, both reflected a new belief about the causes of criminal behavior.[20] Crime, which in the past was believed to be the result of inborn sin, was now believed to be the result of bad external influences. With that in mind, prisons were placed in remote areas in the hope that a pristine rural environment would help cleanse inmates of the evil influence of the big cities. This same thinking pervaded English corrections. In *The Fatal Shore*, the classic account of the Australian penal colonies, Robert Hughes wrote that nature is the unaltered fingerprint of its Creator, and that its monotony and solitude serve as a moral text for human betterment.[21]

Religious thinking was still pervasive in the institution, but religion came to be seen as linked with the cure for crime, not the cause of it. With both models, influences from the outside and other criminals were felt to be detrimental to the inmate's progress toward correction and therefore no visitation or outside reading material could be brought in. In addition, the silent system was enforced in both models, meaning that inmates were harshly punished for speaking to each other.[22]

The penitentiary was only part of a larger movement toward institutionalizing Americans that lived on the margins of society. Mental hospitals and orphanages sprang up around the country as well. The ascendancy of President Andrew Jackson and his egalitarian ideas signaled

American attempts to help (and isolate) those who could not fit into mainstream society. The institution was seen as the method for dealing with these people. David Rothman writes that the idea of the institution, or the "asylum," was almost utopian in its outlook because hopes were so high for what these institutions could accomplish.[23]

Although the penitentiary was created with noble intentions of assisting convicted criminals, it did not live up to its promise. Religious beliefs, no matter how lofty, could not be force-fed on nineteenth-century penitentiary inmates any more successfully than with anyone else, even in a humane peaceful environment. The penitentiary did not provide an atmosphere conducive to fostering religious ideals of love, repentance, and forgiveness. Most inmates left the penitentiary embittered rather than rehabilitated. Isolation, which was designed to be a healthy mental influence, instead resulted in increased mental illness among the inmates. Despite its shortcomings, the penitentiary was copied by other nations. It is still the preferred method of punishment for serious crimes in the United States and most other countries around the world.

PRISONS IN THE INDUSTRIAL ERA

The end of the Civil War created a huge labor vacuum in the American South. Because slavery had officially become outlawed, southern business interests (especially agricultural interests) turned to an alternative labor supply. Inmate labor had been a staple in northeastern penitentiaries. The factory models of inmate labor at prisons in Pennsylvania, New York, and Massachusetts mirrored the economic base of the region. An important source of revenue in the northeast was the factory. The main industry in the antebellum south was farming, which relied heavily on slave labor. The South, which had relied on slave labor to support farming before the Civil War, now turned to prison inmates to replace slaves.

Enterprising law enforcement and court officials were quick to supply convict labor. Under the "convict lease" system, a business interest or farmer would lease an inmate's labor from the state for a fee, or sometimes for free, in order to save the cost of feeding and housing the prisoner. Under the "state account" system, prisoners built or manufactured goods that would be sold by the state.[24]

These systems often led to outrageous abuses. States that leased the inmates took an "out of sight, out of mind" attitude. As long as the inmates were not costing the state any money or, better yet, if they generated revenue for the state, their care and welfare was of no concern. Likewise, private business interests were largely unconcerned with assisting prisoners or preparing them for life after prison. Making money, rather than looking forward to an inmate's behavior after release, assumed primary importance. Some landowners worked the prisoners 12 to 14 hours a day, gave them barely enough to eat, and provided

BOX 2.2

The Eastern and Auburn Systems: Comparison and Contrast

SIMILARITIES	DIFFERENCES	
	Eastern System	**Auburn System**
Strong belief in rehabilitation	Called the "separate" system	Called the "congregate" system
Belief in establishing strict routine, regimen, and military model as important to rehabilitation	Prisoners worked, ate, and slept in total confinement, and only saw selected visitors	Prisoners slept alone in their own cell. Prisoners worked and ate together, but were prohibited from speaking or exchanging glances
Believed that prison should fill the void left by inadequate or improper influence from family, church, school, or community	Saw itself as "purist" in terms of rehabilitation, and viewed Auburn as incomplete and inconsistent with rehabilitative ideals.	Stated that the "pure" isolation of Pennsylvania was impractical and believed it drove prisoners insane

Auburn

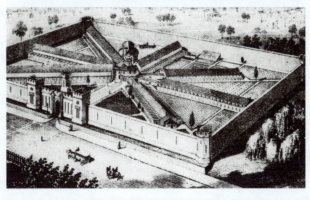

Eastern

them with inadequate clothing. Many prisoners died or became sick and injured. Periodic media coverage of the terrible conditions under which these prisoners lived spurred some oversight and change, but the system continued on into the 1940s.[25]

THE INDETERMINATE SENTENCE AND PAROLE

American parole was essentially imported from the British. After the American Revolution, England was no longer able to send debtors and those in trouble with the law to America. Instead, the British established penal colonies in and near Australia. One of the penal colonies was located at Norfolk Island, several hundred miles from the Australian coast.

As with the entire Australian penal experiment, the prison at Norfolk was beset with numerous problems, including inmate disruptions. In 1840, the British sent Alexander Maconochie to Norfolk to supervise the prisoners. Maconochie brought with him the idea that prisons should help to reform the criminal, punishing him or her (most were men but there were some females) for the past, but also training him or her for the future. Toward that end, he established an indeterminate sentence, in which the amount of time an inmate served depended partly upon his or her behavior while in prison.[26]

Maconochie established a gradual release system, by which inmates worked to earn "marks" for good behavior, which, if obtained, would grant them increasing amounts of freedom within the prison, and culminate in their release. This release method was referred to as the "ticket-of-leave" system, and it was usually 12 to 18 months in duration. If at any time during the ticket-of-leave period the prison received bad reports about the inmate, the offender could be returned to serve the remainder of his or her sentence in prison. The ticket-of-leave system had been established in 1834, six years before Maconochie's arrival at Norfolk. Maconochie refined the system, establishing a five-step release process: (1) strict custody, (2) labor in work gangs, (3) freedom in certain places on Norfolk, (4) conditional release (ticket of leave), and (5) complete freedom.[27]

Like many would-be penal reformers throughout both English and American history, Maconochie was criticized and eventually relieved of his position in 1844 for "coddling" inmates. Upon his return to Great Britain, Maconochie did not relent in advocating penal reform. His ideas were popular with other penologists, including a fellow Englishman named Walter Crofton. Crofton received an appointment as superintendent of prisons in Ireland, which at the time was under the dominion of the British.

Crofton established a system similar to the one used by Maconochie at Norfolk. Inmates who gained conditional freedom, or ticket of leave, were supervised by a police official if they lived in a rural area.

A civilian employee, a close approximation to the modern parole officer, supervised those who lived in urban areas.

Crofton's "Irish system" gained widespread attention in the Western world, including the United States. Zebulon Brockway, at the 1870 Cincinnati Congress of Penitentiary and Reformatory Discipline, advocated the Irish system in a speech titled "The Ideal of a True Prison System for a State." The necessary ingredient for Brockway's system was the indeterminate sentence. The thinking was that a prisoner's fate should be left in part up to the prisoner. The debate over the value of indeterminate sentencing persists to the present day, though it has fallen from favor in recent years.[28] Brockway espoused ideals of classification, earning levels of liberty, education, and training for amenable offenders. The idea that an offender should be the "master of his own fate" was an important principle of the meeting. Release should be earned, not given as a matter of course. Brockway had the chance to implement his ideas in the building and opening of Elmira Reformatory in Elmira, New York, in 1876.[29]

This institution was built for young offenders who could benefit from a strict regime of disciplined living and education. Staffed largely by ex-military personnel, the institutional program had a decidedly militaristic emphasis. Staff were given military ranks, uniforms were used, and inmates were led in marching formations. Inmates also had the opportunity to learn to read and write and study for some vocations. Discipline was harsh. Although Brockway believed in prisoners earning liberties, he was known for inflicting severe punishments as well.[30]

The reformatory model was often used as the pattern for newly built institutions for women. The first completely separate women's prison was built in 1873 near Indianapolis, Indiana, and followed a more custodial model, but several other states that built prisons for women in the late 1800s and early 1900s utilized a reformatory model instead. These institutions were usually staffed by women and built in rural areas where female inmates could work outdoors, a much needed reform from the cramped and unsanitary conditions that were present when they were housed in facilities for men. Together in a single room, women in prisons for men were usually ignored—and without programs, recreation, or attention, except for sexual exploitation.[31]

CORRECTIONS IN THE PROGRESSIVE ERA

The period from 1890 to 1920 is often referred to as the Progressive Era. It was a time of great social change in the United States. Linked with increasing socialism in Europe and the United States, many attempts at social reform were begun during the Progressive Era. Conservation and environmentalist advocates made great strides during this period. Antitrust legislation, designed to control the abuses of big business, also emerged at this time.

Organized labor gained strength during the progressive era. Many professional organizations were established during this time period. The National Prison Association, which was founded in the 1870s, became increasingly active during the Progressive Era. The National Probation Association was founded in 1907. The Mutual Welfare League, an early attempt at inmate self-governance, was created during the Progressive Era. The League was established at Sing Sing prison in New York with the approval of Warden Thomas Mott Osborne. The League succeeded initially, but problems at Sing Sing continued, and negative publicity about the attempt at inmate self-governance led to Osborne's resignation.[32] According to Samuel Walker, despite its failure, the League's significance is that it recognized the existence and legitimacy of a distinct inmate subculture, which had been ignored or suppressed for most of America's penological history. Most previous correctional administrators refused to acknowledge that inmates had their own communities within institutions. Inmate leaders, whether they were formally selected or merely informally acknowledged by other inmates, did exist in prisons. Many corrections professionals thought then (and many still do) that to acknowledge a power structure and leadership hierarchy among inmates is "giving in." In order to maintain absolute power over inmates, corrections practitioners should treat all inmates alike and not give deference to inmate wishes to deal with staff on an official basis. Osborne disagreed, and so did George Beto, who directed the Texas prison system from 1961 to 1972. Beto appointed seasoned inmates as "building tenders" to help maintain order in Texas prisons. His philosophy was that if prison officials did not choose inmate leaders, the inmates would instead.[33]

It was during the Progressive Era that the term "criminal justice system" began to emerge. The criminal justice system came under more intense scrutiny from the academic profession than it had in years past. Those who worked in criminal justice professions, including correctional wardens, came to view themselves as professionals, rather than just employees.

During the Progressive Era, the scientific method emerged as the answer to human problems. Phrenology and biological approaches to explaining crime reached their peak during this era, especially in Europe, though their influence was felt in the United States. Cesare Lombroso, an Italian prison physician, published his beliefs that criminals could be identified by physical traits.[34]

Although Lombroso's work did not have a major impact on prison officials, his work was part and parcel of the idea that medical science held the answers to dealing with criminals. It was during the period from the turn of the twentieth century to the early 1940s that the eugenics movement made headway into American mental hospitals and prisons. Eugenics is the study of methods of protecting and improving the quality of the human race by selective breeding. The thinking was that many criminals were morally or mentally defective from birth or as a result of their genetic makeup. The key to stop the breeding of such criminal types was sterilization, sometimes referred to at the time as asexualization. Indiana passed the first sterilization law in 1907. All institutions that housed "confirmed criminals, idiots, rapists and imbeciles" were required to have two surgeons on staff.[35] If in the opinion of a board of medical managers and prison personnel an inmate's mental or moral condition placed him or her beyond any affordable help, the prisoner would undergo sterilization.

Several states, including Virginia, followed suit with similar laws. Virginia's sterilization laws were upheld by the U.S. Supreme Court in the 1927 case of *Buck v. Bell*. Carrie Buck was a patient at Virginia's Colony for Epileptics and Feeble Minded at Lynchburg. She had been diagnosed as having a mental age of nine. The institutional physician, Albert Priddy, recommended that Buck be sterilized in accordance with Virginia's law, which allowed for the sterilization of certain convicted criminals and mental patients. During the judicial proceedings that would decide Buck's fate, she and the rest of her family were referred to as a group of "shiftless, ignorant and worthless class of anti-social whites."[36] Supreme Court Justice Oliver Wendell Holmes Jr. wrote the majority opinion upholding Virginia's sterilization law. Writing that "three generations of imbeciles are enough," Holmes went on to state that "cutting the Fallopian tubes" was the equivalent to vaccination. Buck was sterilized in 1927.[37]

Sterilization proliferated through the 1920s and 1930s. Ethnic minorities and the poor were frequent targets of eugenics. News of atrocities performed in the name of creating a master race in Nazi Germany eventually made its way to the United States. America was fighting to eliminate Nazism, and the eugenics movement had a Nazi flavor to it.

Amidst the American war effort against Germany, the U.S. Supreme Court dealt a blow to sterilization efforts in the 1942 case of *Skinner v. Oklahoma*. Justice William Douglas declared that marriage and procreation were basic civil rights, and that placing the power to sterilize in evil or reckless hands could cause races or types that are inimical to the dominant group to wither and disappear.[38] This signaled the end of most sterilization for a time. However, even today, some courts and correctional practitioners have called for chemical castration as the only viable solution for dealing with repeat sexual offenders.

Although the ideal of individualized treatment was popular, the reality was somewhat different in most states. California was the exception. This state led the way in individualized treatment for prison inmates and parole supervision and produced the first parole supervision manual. Still, parole supervision was minimal. Jonathan Simon states that few California jurisdictions had resources adequate to the task of individualized parole case management until the 1950s, a time by which all states had adopted parole and probation systems.[39]

BOX 2.3

A Correctional History Timeline

900–1400 BCE	The Mosaic Law is written.
451 BCE	The Twelve Tables, Rome's earliest laws, are written.
400 BCE	Athenian law prescribes stoning, compulsory suicide, and exclusion from social communication as punishment for crimes.
1066	William the Conqueror builds the Tower of London to house enemies of the Crown.
1166	The Assize of Clarendon authorizes the construction of English jails.
1180	Henry II orders jails for every English county.
1200	One of France's early prisons is built, the Chatelet.
1470	The use of French prisons increases under Louis XI. The Bastille begins housing prisoners.
1500	Galley servitude increases in France, Italy, and Spain.
1556	The first English prison is constructed at Bridewell.
1615	James I introduces forced transportation as punishment.
1679	The first American prison opens in Nantucket, Massachusetts.
1773	Chaplains and surgeons begin visiting English jails.
1775	Transportation of English prisoners to America ends.
1779	The Penitentiary Act calls for solitary confinement, religious instruction, work, and uniforms in English prisons.
1787	Transportation of English convicts to Australia begins.
1787	The Society for Alleviating the Misery of Public Prisons is founded in Philadelphia.
1790	The Walnut Street Jail is opened in Philadelphia.
1796	New York's first prison opens in Greenwich Village.
1811	Maryland State Penitentiary opens, one of the first "big house" prisons.
1815	Striped clothing is used by prisoners.
1816	Auburn Prison in New York opens.
1825	Ossining (Sing Sing) Prison in New York opens.
1829	Eastern Penitentiary opens in Philadelphia.
1840	Alexander Maconochie begins parole experiments on Norfolk Island near Australia.
1841	John Augustus begins his probation work.

BOX 2.3 *(continued)*

1847	The first American boys reformatory opens in Westborough, Massachusetts.
1850	Parole becomes part of French law.
1853	The English Penal Servitude Act provides for remission of sentences.
1854	The prison marks system begins in Ireland.
1869	English shipment of prisoners to Australia ends.
1870	The Cincinnati Congress convenes, includes first members of the National Prison Association.
1871	*Ruffin v. Commonwealth* — Supreme Court ruling perpetuates "slave of the state" doctrine.
1876	Elmira Reformatory opens in New York.
1878	Edward Savage of Boston becomes America's first paid probation officer.
1895	The first federal penitentiary opens at Fort Leavenworth, Kansas.
1899	The first American prison toilets are installed, in Maryland.
1910	First federal parole law signed.
1929	Federal Bureau of Prisons is set up.
1934	Alcatraz opens in California.
1944	In *Coffin v Reichard*, the "slave of the state" doctrine is overturned.
1964	*Cooper v. Pate* holds that prisoners may sue correctional officials for violation of constitutional rights.
1971	Attica prison riot results in 43 deaths.
1980	New Mexico prison riot results in 33 inmate deaths.
1982	Georgia establishes intensive probation.
1983	Inspired by a "Spiderman" comic strip and the New Mexico prison riot, New Mexico uses electronic monitoring.
1983	The Special Alternative Incarceration Unit opens in Georgia, triggering similar "boot camp" prison implementation in other states.
1985	Marion County, Kentucky, opens a private prison.
1992	The Wolds Prison becomes England's first private prison.
1995	Corrections commissioner Ron Jones brings back chain gangs in Alabama.
2006	The adult correctional population grew to nearly 7.2 million offenders under supervision.

Sources: Sam Houston State University. "Chronology of Criminal Justice History"; Newbold, G. (1999). "A Chronology of Correctional History." *Journal of Criminal Justice Education* 10(1):87-100; Walker, S. (1998). *Popular Justice.* New York: Oxford University Press; Friedman, L.M. (1993). *Crime and Punishment in American History.* New York: Basic Books.

THE "BIG HOUSE" ERA

Robert Johnson calls the early 1900s through the 1950s the era of the "big house."[40] One of the most famous prison movies of this era was *The Big House*, which was released in 1930. Prisons during this era enjoyed some improvements in conditions, but virtually no public interest was directed at them throughout both World Wars (1917-1918 and 1941-1945). Not until a rash of prison riots in the 1950s did public interest awaken. In the meantime, prisons proceeded to function largely outside of public scrutiny; some were run humanely, some were places of shocking cruelty. According to Johnson, "big houses" were "a world populated by people seemingly more dead than alive, shuffling where they once marched, heading nowhere slowly. . . ."[41]

Examples of "big house" prisons included Leavenworth (Kansas), which primarily functioned as a military prison; Alcatraz, San Quentin, and Folsom, all located in California; Sing Sing and Attica in New York; Eastern (Pennsylvania); the Georgia State Prison in Reidsville; Stateville (Illinois); and Jackson (Michigan). All of these facilities, and those like them, were either built, renovated, or expanded during the "big house" era. The "big house" prison still conjures up the image of the stereotypical prison in the eyes of the public.

REHABILITATION: THE "ANYTHING WORKS" ERA

The end of World War II brought a renewed sense of optimism in America. Americans believed that because they had conquered the Axis war machines, their ability to solve any problem was practically unlimited. There was a particularly strong belief that American wealth, industrial might, and scientific advancements in technology held the solutions to social problems, including crime. The positivist ideal that criminal behavior could be "cured" through scientific means greatly influenced American corrections throughout the 1950s and 1960s.

It was a time of great experimentation and innovation in the treatment of all forms of deviant or variant behavior. Radical interventions such as electroshock therapy and frontal lobotomies were fairly common methods of dealing with the mentally ill—or with criminals who were thought to be mentally ill. Recall that although sterilization had been used on habitual criminals and mental patients for several decades, Nazi abuses of the practice during World War II turned American opinion against it.

Eventually, more benign forms of intervention became common methods of assisting criminals in institutions and in the community. Religious programs, the bulwark of nineteenth-century penitentiaries, lost significance. Prisons began hiring more counseling staff. Educational, vocational, and substance abuse programs proliferated. Though security had always been the primary focus of the prison, prisons (particularly those in the northeastern United States) gradually began to place more emphasis on secular forms of rehabilitation.

In the 1950s, the disciplines of sociology, psychology, and psychiatry began to influence prison programming. Counselors (sometimes called prison sociologists) were employed to diagnose and classify the inmates according to their problems and security risk. In many states, inmates started their prison term in "classification centers" where they took a multitude of educational, aptitude, and interest tests and medical examinations to determine their needs, aptitudes, and interests.[42] The test results were then used to send the inmate to the appropriate prison, tag him or her with the appropriate custody level (based on violence and escape risk), and assign him or her to the appropriate mix of educational, vocational, and treatment programs.

By the 1960s, some prisons, most notably in California, were fully engaged in offering a wide array of programs. In addition to basic and advanced education, a prisoner might partake in group therapy, transactional analysis, or behavior modification; even transcendental meditation and yoga were offered in some prisons. The "big house" was replaced by the "correctional institution." Psychology replaced religion as the reform agent.[43]

It should be noted that even at the apex of the rehabilitative era, not all prisons displayed the same commitment to reform. For every Vienna, Illinois, there was a Tucker prison farm. Vienna was a federal institution known as the "prison without walls" because the enriched program offerings, including college classes, were available to townspeople as well as inmates. On the other hand, Tucker prison farm was the notorious Arkansas prison farm where inmates were brutalized with the "Tucker telephone," an electrical apparatus that transmitted electric shocks to the inmates' genitals and body parts. The litany of horrors that occurred at this prison farm (and the Cummins farm close by) was the impetus for the federal district court overturning the hands-off doctrine that had insulated prison authorities from court scrutiny for years. The federal court, shocked at the conditions under which prisoners lived, held that if the state chose to run a prison system, then it must run it in a way that met basic Constitutional protections.[44]

DEINSTITUTIONALIZATION AND "NOTHING WORKS"

During the 1960s, public opinion once again began to shift. The 1960s witnessed a tremendous proliferation in the amount of crime reported.[45] The 1960s was also a time of tremendous social upheaval in the United States. Civil rights concerns, opposition to American military involvement in Vietnam, the increase in illegal drug use by young people, and a general unease about the safety of walking the streets of American cities were among the problems that contributed to an anti-rehabilitation mindset within the public. Attitudes toward rehabilitation began to sour for other reasons as well. Rehabilitation programs, the indeterminate sentence, and correctional institutions in general came under attack from a number of sources.

BOX 2.4

Inmate Lawsuits in American History

The question of what legal rights prison inmates are entitled to is hotly debated by inmates, groups devoted to inmate rights, and civil libertarians on one side, with correctional administrators and state governments frequently on the other side. Most of the legal battles have been fought in the federal courts, and the Supreme Court of the United States has intervened on several occasions in the area of prisoner rights. Until relatively recently, inmates did not fare well in court actions against their keepers. In *Ruffin v. Commonwealth* (1871), the Court ruled that inmates are virtual slaves of the state and have few if any civil rights. Bear in mind that in 1871 the word "slavery" did not have the negative stigma that it does today. Slavery had only been abolished a few years prior. A state that had no objection to enslaving its citizenry would have little objection to treating inmates as slaves.

The situation changed little until the 1960s and 1970s. The civil rights movement, a more liberal public attitude toward treatment of inmates, and the interventionist philosophy held by some federal judges and members of the U.S. Supreme Court during Earl Warren's and Warren Burger's tenures as Chief Justice, led to many changes in prisons. In 1971, a federal court ruled in *Holt v. Sarver* that the entire Arkansas prison system violated the Eighth Amendment ban on cruel and unusual punishment. Similar rulings followed in Texas, Georgia, and other states. Federally appointed monitors controlled many prisons, especially in the South.

No area seemed off-limits to the courts when it came to inmate lawsuits. Lawsuits filed by inmates proliferated during the 1970s. The Supreme Court ruled in the areas of confinement conditions, access to legal information and counsel, damages against staff members who hurt inmates, due process during disciplinary hearings, racial segregation, use of force by staff, mail privileges, medical care, communication with the press, and freedom of religion. Although inmates lost many more lawsuits than they won, the perception that courts were allowing inmates to run the prisons became widespread.

BOX 2.4 *(continued)*

An anti-prisoner-rights backlash has ensued since the 1980s. Some of the trends that generated inmate litigation in the 1960s, 1970s, and early 1980s reversed themselves in the mid-1980s and 1990s. The U.S. Supreme Court, under the leadership of William Rehnquist, favored a more hands-off doctrine than the Warren and Burger Courts. Federal judges appointed by Presidents Reagan and Bush took a similar hands-off approach to inmate litigation. Public opinion shifted away from sympathy toward inmates.

Nevertheless, the impact of judicial intervention in prisons is still evident today. Prisons are much more humane institutions than they were prior to the 1970s. Staffs are more properly trained, inmates receive better medical care, and institutions and work conditions are more secure and safe than before. Though judicial intervention did not alleviate many of the problems in prisons, and some have argued that courts did more harm than good, it did make a lasting impact.

Sources: *Holt v. Sarver,* 309 F. Supp. 362 (ED Ark. 1970); *Ruffin v. Commonwealth*, 62 Va. (21 Gratt.) 790 (1871).

One source of discontentment with prisons lay in a growing antagonism toward institutions in general as an avenue for solving social problems. During the 1960s and 1970s, the feeling grew that institutional life was counterproductive in trying to deal with individual problems. Orphanages became increasingly unpopular with the public, thus greater efforts were devoted toward placing children in foster care. The mental hospital also became an increasingly unpopular institution; many mental patients were released and mainstreamed into the communities where they lived.

Likewise, prisons came to be viewed as counterproductive toward reforming criminal behavior. Prisons were viewed as breeding grounds or schools for criminals. The view was that prisons increase one's propensity to be bitter at society and therefore increase one's propensity to commit crime. The answer, as with the mental patients and orphaned or abandoned children, was to try to address the criminal's problems in the community rather than behind prison walls.

A second attack of sorts came from the White House. In 1964, President Lyndon Johnson, fulfilling an election promise to deal with crime, established a Commission to conduct a comprehensive study of crime and the administration of criminal justice in the United States. The result of the Commission's efforts was *The Challenge of Crime in a Free Society*, which was released in 1967. One suggestion made by the Commission was that more use be made of community-based sanctions such as probation and parole, with less reliance on the prison institution. The Commission's feelings mirrored the popular sentiment that prisons were not succeeding at rehabilitating criminals and therefore were not reducing crime.[46]

A third attack on rehabilitation efforts of the time came from a seemingly unlikely source: the Quakers. The Quakers had been advocating penal reform and rehabilitation efforts since the eighteenth century. In fact, the Quakers were very instrumental in the establishment of early American penitentiaries. However, in a 1971 report titled *Struggle for Justice*, the Quakers stated that prisons were failing to rehabilitate inmates. They further charged that the indeterminate sentence, one of the hallmarks of rehabilitation efforts and a necessary ingredient to a parole system, was being abused and manipulated by many prison and parole officials. The indeterminate sentence was merely being used as a tactic to coerce institutional conformity, not as an effective rehabilitation tool.[47]

A fourth element or event in the battle against prison rehabilitation occurred in 1971 at Attica prison in New York. On September 9, 1971, more than 1,300 inmates at Attica rioted and took 40 hostages. The inmates, including both whites and African Americans, issued a list of demands contained in a manifesto titled "To the People of America." They demanded better treatment and listed 15 specific demands, including more religious freedom, sensitivity to religious dietary demands, and better educational programs. The inmates were making many of the same demands that were being made in successful inmate litigation actions across the country.

Over the next four days, the siege continued. Attempts by Tom Wicker of the *New York Times*, Black Panther leader Bobby Seale, and defense attorney William Kunstler to mediate the situation proved fruitless. On September 13, Governor Nelson Rockefeller ordered that the prison be retaken. Prison guards and state police, who appeared to be inadequately trained in riot control, stormed the prison. In the ensuing nine minutes of mayhem, 29 inmates were killed, as were 10 of the hostages; four more people died later.[48]

The carnage was captured on film, and the clear message sent forth was that penal rehabilitation efforts in New York were a monumental failure. Though such a conclusion may have been shortsighted and further study would reveal that some assistance efforts did help some inmates, the visual image of the Attica riot carried much greater weight than anecdotal success stories or dry research studies. The tragedy at Attica was ironic because New York had been a pioneer in prison rehabilitation for well over a century. Since the establishment of the Auburn prison, and since Zebulon Brockway's rehabilitation efforts at Elmira in the nineteenth century, New York had prided itself on its penal rehabilitation efforts.

To make matters worse, a fifth attack on prison rehabilitation came from a research report commissioned by the New York Department of Corrections in the early 1970s. Robert Martinson and a team of researchers were hired to review several rehabilitation programs around the country. They reviewed programs in prison-based and community-based programs. Martinson's report gave a gloomy picture of rehabilitative efforts, especially those that were prison-based.[49] To avoid embarrassment, New York blocked release of the report. When court action on the part of inmates forced the release of Martinson's report in 1974, the phrase "nothing works" became the rallying cry of those who had long opposed prison rehabilitation, and of others who had recently become disenchanted with rehabilitation efforts.

Martinson's stinging indictment of rehabilitation efforts, however, was partly due to his bitterness toward New York officials who had quashed the release of his findings. Moreover, Martinson did not actually state that nothing worked. He was more optimistic about community-based rehabilitation efforts than about those based in prisons. After the initial release of the report and the anti-rehabilitation backlash it generated, Martinson backtracked, stating that the initial report was overly pessimistic about rehabilitation.[50] But the damage had already been done. Martinson's findings were the justification for dismantling many prison rehabilitation programs. The impact of the Martinson report is still evident today. Correctional officials often become nervous when evaluators and researchers use the phrase "what works" in research reports or journal articles.

Though gradual, perhaps the most significant development was a fear among many Americans that the social order had broken down and that an increase in crime was the result of that breakdown. One supposed remedy was a restoration of "law and order" to the streets and a sentiment that criminals should stop being "coddled" in prison and on probation and should start being punished. This sentiment, along with concern about the war in Vietnam, helped Richard Nixon in his successful 1968 presidential campaign. Nixon ran for office on a tough law-and-order campaign pledge. Ironically, Nixon would be forced to resign from office in 1974 because of crimes committed under his leadership.

In the 1970s, a number of events conspired to drive the rehabilitative ethic out of the rhetoric and mission of prisons. The Attica riot in 1971 brought the inside of the prison to the American public. The drama of prisoners holding knives to the throats of hostages played out in living rooms across the nation and did exactly the opposite of what the organizers of the riot intended. Instead of leading to better programs and treatment, and the right to be "treated like men," the public, which had been reasonably supportive of prison programming, turned away. It was hard to reconcile the prisoner wielding a machete and other crudely lethal weapons, with one who needed understanding and educational programs.

Another blow to the rehabilitative mission was the Martinson Report of 1974.[51] This report, paid for and then suppressed by the New

York Department of Correction, was a meta-analysis and evaluation of more than 200 prison and correctional programs across the country. Its "sound-byte" result? Nothing worked. Actually, the findings were a little more complicated. Martinson attempted in later years to modify his original harsh stance, but the damage had been done. Politicians interested in reducing the budget bottom line and/or wanting to appear "tough on crime" promoted the ethic of punishment first, and treatment not at all. Some academics also offered their support, promoting a philosophical justification for retribution and even managing to transform the attempt to correct into a moral wrong. Politicians and others continued to argue against rehabilitation, calling it "coddling" inmates, well into the late 1980s and 1990s, but the rehabilitative era was already gasping for air in the late 1970s and comatose by the mid-1980s.

CORRECTIONS IN THE "GET TOUGH" ERA

The movement away from rehabilitation impacted sentencing and penal practices. Among the academicians who recognized and discussed this shift were Andrew von Hirsch, Malcolm Feeley, and Jonathan Simon. Andrew von Hirsch advocated a "just deserts" model of sentencing and penal practice rather than one based on rehabilitation. Like many corrections professionals, von Hirsch has not advocated a total abandonment of offender assistance, nor has he advocated undignified treatment of offenders.[51] Feeley and Simon, in "The New Penology," recognize a shift toward an "insurance-based" model of penology. Under this conceptual model, the emphasis is on neither rehabilitation nor punishment but on accurate prediction, identification, and profiling of criminals. Under the new penology, corrections merely serves as a warehousing, or "waste management" apparatus, for criminals—especially those from the lower economic class.[52]

Todd Clear has stated that America is in the midst of a "penal harm" movement. Believers in "penal harm" advocate tough prison conditions designed to make inmates as miserable as possible. The rationale is partly based on specific deterrence and partly on retribution. If prison conditions are poor enough, inmates will not want to commit the crimes that bring them to prison. At the same time, the public exacts a matter of revenge on criminals. The penal harm idea places little if any emphasis on rehabilitation services, recreation programs, or anything designed to make the inmates' lives more pleasant.[53]

The 1980s witnessed numerous innovations in corrections, but one thing that did not disappear was the reliance on prison as the primary method of dealing with serious lawbreakers. Despite the continued reliance on prisons, corrections agencies across the country (especially in states that incarcerated large numbers of its populations) did at least attempt to devise some alternatives to incarceration. Georgia, which led the nation in the percentage of citizens in prison, pioneered many of these efforts. Other states, including Oklahoma, California, and New Jersey, devised programs designed to divert people from prison. Intensive probation, which had been tried and abandoned in some states two decades prior, was reborn in several states. Electronic monitoring, which had been developed on an experimental basis in the 1960s, soon followed. The boot camp prison was used in Georgia and Oklahoma. Halfway houses, under a variety of names, expanded.

Although these programs received much attention from the media as well as corrections professionals, they served very few offenders. The vast majority of criminal offenders continued to be punished by fines (for minor offenses such as traffic crimes), regular probation (for serious misdemeanors and minor felonies), and prison (for serious felonies). Although the penitentiary had been unheard of as a means of punishment early in America's history, by the 1980s Americans could conceive of no way to deal with serious crimes other than prisons, which have become increasingly expensive to build, staff, operate, and maintain.

In the 1980s, prison administrators struggled with a massive influx of offenders. Incarceration rates soared, prisons met and exceeded their maximum capacity levels, state-sentenced prisoners were held back in jails awaiting space, and then jails filled to capacity and beyond. Prisoners were housed in cafeterias, gyms, tents, and even in ships (harking back to the old barges used in the harbor of London during the 1700s). State legislatures increased prison budgets—doubling, tripling, and then quadrupling the amounts allocated for departments of correction.

Some web sites are devoted in whole or in part to the historical aspects of corrections. One is maintained by the New York Correction History Society, www.correctionhistory.org. Some state corrections departments' web sites include brief histories of corrections in that state. The Library of Congress web site, www.loc.gov, includes digital images of prisons and prisoners at various points in American history.

States went on building binges to meet the ever-expanding numbers. In the frantic attempt to find beds, programs were purely a luxury item. Classification efforts continued, but the decision where to send an inmate depended on space available, not program needs. Thus, the cycle was repeated. Ideals of reform and optimistic beliefs that institutions could change lives were strangled by overcrowding and other problems that drained resources. Once again, punishment became the only promise.

CONCLUSION

One lesson to be learned from history is that the rhetoric of correctional policy and reform often does not mesh with reality. Politicians and

AP Photo/Charlie Riedel

As punishment for breaking a smoking regulation, an inmate rakes rocks in the courtyard in Maricopa County Sheriff Joe Arpaio's jail in Phoenix. The Tent City Jail is one of Arpaio's most acclaimed and notorious creations.

correctional reformers frequently make either well-intentioned or self-serving promises about improving society by changing prisons. Most correctional reforms throughout American history have been aimed at either rehabilitating the criminal or ensuring that crime will be reduced through correctional practices. Although American corrections can claim some successes, the truth is that many correctional practices have done neither. A contemporary example is found in the case of Sheriff Joseph M. Arpaio of Maricopa County, Arizona. Sheriff Arpaio's tough, "no frills" administration of the Maricopa County Jail has earned him the nickname "America's toughest sheriff." Although many people around the country applaud his approach to jail administration, demonstrating a connection between the methods Sheriff Arpaio uses to run the jail and a reduction in crime is difficult. Historically, ruthless jail and prison administration has led to little more than riotous institutions and high recidivism. While get-tough rhetoric associated with corrections can claim little success, liberal-minded rehabilitation attempts cannot claim a large degree of success either. High-minded ideals of improving society through institutional rehabilitation often fail to meet expectations.

Many attempts at prison reform have unintended consequences. The penitentiary, which was originally designed with high religious ideals of repentance, forgiveness, and brotherly love, is now associated with human depravity and cruelty. Rehabilitation, which was designed to assist offenders, has been attacked as either hopeless naiveté put into practice, or as merely another guise for exercising social control over inmate populations.

Another lesson learned from history is that the level of civilization in a society is reflected by the conditions of its prisons. Societies both past and present that are viewed by many Americans as barbarous typically maintain inhumane prisons in which inmates have few civil rights. How will history judge the United States? Despite its shortcomings, American penal efforts, when compared to those of many other countries, may be viewed favorably. Prisoners have more civil rights in American prisons than in many other countries, and prison conditions are much more humane in America than in many other countries. The challenge for the twenty-first century is maintaining a proper balance between the well-being of inmates (i.e., rehabilitation) and ensuring that imprisonment is unpleasant enough to act as a deterrent to crime.

One mistake common to correctional administration is the attempt to shut out outside involvement in the administration of jails and prisons. Many people both inside and outside institutional walls wrongly assume that what goes on inside the prison has no relation to the community and that what goes on in the community has no effect on prisons. The civil rights protests in the streets during the 1960s and similar calls for civil rights in prisons during that time period are evidence that the "out of sight, out of mind" way of thinking about prisons is short-sighted. Just as advocates of community policing emphasize that law enforcement can best succeed with the support of the public, so should correctional administrators and policymakers realize that correctional programming, both institutional and community-based, must have public support to succeed.

As several later chapters show, the most recent history of corrections is marked by conflicting trends. On the one hand, practices such as mandatory sentencing, three-strikes laws, and life-without-parole sentences are part of the punitive or get-tough trend that has been part of correctional policymaking for the past three decades. However, some penologists argue that effectively administered correctional interventions can make a positive impact on recidivism.[54] Later chapters give additional information about these current trends in corrections.

▶ Ethics Focus: What is Barbaric?

History offers examples of practices that were considered acceptable and even praiseworthy at one time but are now considered either barbaric or simply antiquated. One example is the use of punishments like the stocks, where offenders were put on public display to both punish them and deter others from such offenses.

Are we doing anything in the twenty-first century that you think will eventually be considered barbaric or, at best, antiquated? For example, do you think that one day people might consider lethal injection barbaric? Will the idea of locking people up in prisons ever turn into a practice that will appear cruel and unusual or just terribly old-fashioned, or, conversely, will the future provide a primary means of punishment that is so harsh that imprisonment will seem quaint by comparison? What do you think? Discuss.

▶ At the Movies . . . .

Frankie and Johnny, 1991.

An ex-con works as a cook in a diner as he tries to readjust to live on the out-side after spending years in prison. The support he receives from the diner's owner and staff helps him through the transition.

Brubaker, 1980.

Based upon true events, a new Corrections Commissioner goes undercover as an inmate to see for himself what is really going on in the state prison.

DISCUSSION QUESTIONS

1. In what ways has corrections changed since the days of ancient civilizations? Compared to other civilizations, are Americans doing a better or worse job at sanctioning lawbreakers?

2. Compare the corrections systems of the Israelites, the ancient Greeks, and the ancient Romans. List some strengths and weaknesses of those systems.

3. Did America move in the right direction during the deinstitutionalizaton movement? Why or why not?

4. In view of the history of corrections, is the get-tough approach to dealing with offenders proper or misguided? Explain.

5. Describe the differences between the Pennsylvania (separate) system and the New York (congregate) system of prisons.

6. When viewing the history of correctional rehabilitation efforts, do you think those who said "nothing works" were correct? Explain.

7. Some say to ignore history is to be condemned to repeat its mistakes. Do you notice any current practices that seem to ignore the lessons of history?

FURTHER READING

Morris, N., and D.J. Rothman (1997). *The Oxford History of the Prison: The Practice of Punishment in Western Society*. New York: Oxford University Press.

Walker, S. (1997). *Popular Justice: A History of American Criminal Justice*, 2nd ed. New York: Oxford University Press.

NOTES

1. Drapkin, 1989.

2. Albert, Denise, and Peterfreund, 1988, 9.

3. Peters, 1995.

4. Peters, 1995.

5. Peters, 1995.

6. Senna and Siegel, 1998.

7. The English government began an even more adventurous project with unwanted petty criminals after the American Revolution. England began shipping convicts to Australia, effectively using the continent and some of its outlying areas as giant penal colonies. This gargantuan penal experiment is chronicled in Robert Hughes's *The Fatal Shore*.

8. Friedman, 1993.

9. Andrews, 1991.

10. Andrews, 1991, 39.

11. Barnes and Teeters, 1951.

12. Rothman, 1971/1990.

13. Durham, 1994.

14. Walker, 1998.

15. Walker, 1998.

16. Durham, 1994; Garland, 1990.

17. Johnson, 1997; Durham, 1994.

18. Beaumont and deTocqueville, 1994, 381.

19. Barnes and Teeters, 1951.

20. Walker, 1998.

21. Hughes, 1986.

22. Conley, 1992.

23. Rothman, 1990.

24. Walker, 1998.

25. Barnes and Teeters, 1951.

26. Walker, 1998.

27. Hughes, 1986.

28. Friedman, 1993.

29. Reichel, 1997, 80-81; Walker, 1980.

30. Sullivan, 1990.

31. Sullivan, 1990.

32. Rotman, 1995.

33. Crouch and Marquart, 1989.

34. Lombroso-Ferrero, 1994.

35. Friedman, 1993, 335.

36. Friedman, 1993, 337.

37. Friedman, 1993, 337.

38. Friedman, 1993, 338.

39. Simon, 1993.

40. Johnson, 1997.

41. Johnson, 1997.

42. Johnson, 1997, 37.

43. Johnson, 1997, 41.

44. Spencer, 1997.

45. It is still unclear whether crime dramatically increased in the 1960s or whether meth-ods of measuring crime improved. The Uniform Crime Reports, started in the 1930s, were largely ignored by most local law enforcement agencies. Many did not bother to keep track of the amount of crime in their jurisdiction. The FBI received increasing participation during the 1960s, which may have accounted for the increase in crime.

46. President's Commission on Law Enforcement and the Administration of Justice, 1967.

47. American Friends Service Committee, 1971.

48. Walker, 1998.

49. Martinson, 1974.

50. Martinson, 1979.

51. von Hirsch, 1976.

52. Feeley and Simon, 1992.

53. Clear, 1994.

53. See Lipsey and Cullen, 2007.

REFERENCES

Albert, E.M., T.C. Denise and S.P. Peterfreund (1988). *Great Traditions in Ethics,* 6th ed. Belmont, CA: Wadsworth.

American Friends Service Committee (1971). *Struggle for Justice: A Report on Crime and Punishment in America.* New York: Hill and Wang.

Andrews, W. (1991). *Old Time Punishments.* New York: Dorset.

Barnes, H.E., and N.K. Teeters (1951). *New Horizons in Criminology,* 2nd ed. New York: Prentice Hall.

Beaumont, G., and A. Tocqueville (1994). "On the Penitentiary System in the United States and Its Application in France." In J.E. Jacoby (ed.), *Classics of Criminology,* 2nd ed., 372-386. Prospect Heights, IL: Waveland.

Clear, T.R. (1994). *Harm in American Penology*. Albany, NY: SUNY.

Conley, J. (1992). "The Historical Relationship among Punishment, Incarceration and Corrections." In S. Stojkovic and R. Lovell (eds.), *Corrections: An Introduction*, 33-65. Cincinnati: Anderson.

Crouch, B.M., and J.W. Marquart (1989). *An Appeal to Justice*. Austin, TX: University of Texas.

Drapkin, I. (1989). *Crime and Punishment in the Ancient World*. Lexington, MA: Lexington.

Durham, A. (1994). *Crisis and Reform: Current Issues in American Punishment*. Boston: Little, Brown.

Feeley, M.M., and J. Simon (1992). "The New Penology: Notes on the Emerging Strategy of Corrections and Its Implications." *Criminology* 30:449-474.

Freidman, L.M. (1993). *Crime and Punishment in American History*. New York: Basic.

Garland, D. (1990). *Punishment and Modern Society: A Study in Social Theory*. Chicago: University of Chicago Press.

Hughes, R. (1986). *The Fatal Shore: The Epic of Australia's Founding*. New York: Vintage.

Johnson, R. (1997). "Race, Gender, and the American Prison: Historical Observations." In J. Pollock (ed.), *Prisons: Today and Tomorrow*, 26-51. Gaithersburg, MD: Aspen.

Lipsey, M.W., and F.T. Cullen (2007). "The Effectiveness of Correctional Rehabilitation" A Review of Systematic Reviews." *Annual Review of Law and Social Sciences* 3: 297-320.

Lombroso-Ferrero, G. (1994). "Criminal Man." In J.J. Jacoby (ed.), *Classics of Criminology*, 2nd ed., 116-131. Prospect Heights, IL: Waveland.

Martinson, R. (1979). "Symposium on Sentencing: Part II." *Hofstra Law Review* 7:243-258.

Martinson, R. (1974). "What Works? Questions and Answers about Prison Reform." *The Public Interest* 35:22-54.

Peters, E.M. (1995). "Prison Before the Prison: The Ancient and Medieval Worlds." In N. Morris and D.J. Rothman (eds.), *The Oxford History of the Prison*, 3-47. New York: Oxford University.

Pollock, J. (1997). "Rehabilitation Revisited." In J. Pollock (ed.), *Prison: Today and Tomorrow*, pp. 158-208. Gaithersburg, MD: Aspen.

President's Commission on Law Enforcement and the Administration of Justice (1967). *The Challenge of Crime in a Free Society*. Washington, DC: U.S. Government Printing Office.

Reichel, P. (1997). *Corrections*. Minneapolis: West.

Rothman, D.J. (1990). *The Discovery of the Asylum: Social Order and Disorder in the New Republic*. Boston: Little, Brown.

Rotman, E. (1995). "The Failure of Reform: United States, 1865-1965." In N. Morris and D.J. Rothman (eds.), *The Oxford History of the Prison*, 169-198. New York: Oxford University.

Senna, J.J., and L.J. Siegel (1998). *Essentials of Criminal Justice*. Belmont, CA: West/Wadsworth.

Simon, J. (1993). *Poor Discipline: Parole and the Social Control of the Underclass, 1890-1990*. Chicago: University of Chicago.

Souryal, S.S. (1998). *Ethics in Criminal Justice: In Search of the Truth*, 4th ed. Newark, NJ: LexisNexis Matthew Bender.

Spencer, D. (1997). "The Classification of Inmates." In J. Pollock (ed.), *Prison: Today and Tomorrow*, 84-115. Gaithersburg, MD: Aspen.

Stone, W. (1997). "Industry, Agriculture and Education." In J. Pollock (ed.), *Prison: Today and Tomorrow*, 116-157. Gaithersburg, MD: Aspen.

Sullivan, L. (1990). *The Prison Reform Movement: Forlorn Hope*. Boston: Twayne.

von Hirsch, A. (1976). *Doing Justice: The Choice of Punishments*. New York: Hill and Wang.

Walker, S. (1998). *Popular Justice: A History of American Criminal Justice*, 2nd ed. New York: Oxford University.

Walker, S. (1980). *Popular Justice: A History of American Criminal Justice*. New York: Oxford University Press.

COURT CASES

Buck v. Bell, 274 U.S. 200 (1927).

Coffin v. Reichard, 143 F.2d 443 (1944).

Cooper v. Pate, 378 U.S. 546 (1964).

Holt v. Sarver, 309 F. Supp. 362 (E.D. Ark. 1970).

Ruffin v. Commonwealth, 62 Va. (21 Gratt) 790 (1871).

Skinner v. Oklahoma, 316 U.S. 535(1942).

Corrections and the Courts

What You Need to Know

▶ The history of the relationship between corrections and the federal courts can be summarized as evolving from the hands-off phase to the hands-on phase, and then to a due deference phase. As the names imply, each particular phase involved more or less court involvement in correctional decisionmaking.

▶ Part of the reason for the recent due deference phase, which leaves most decisions with corrections officials, was growth in prisoner litigation.

▶ Prisoners have pursued both habeas corpus petitions and civil rights cases.

▶ Prisoner litigation has been concerned with such issues as freedom of religion and freedom of speech. The courts are concerned about the rights of inmates, but they are also concerned about the legitimate penological interests of prison officials in order and security.

▶ The courts have allowed prison officials great leeway in searching inmates, based on concern for prison security and order. The Fourth Amendment has little scope in prisons.

▶ Another major issue has been the Eighth Amendment issue of cruel and unusual punishment. The courts have ruled that solitary confinement and double-celling do not violate the Eighth Amendment.

▶ The courts have ruled that prisons cannot deny medical care, but the Constitution is only violated when failure to provide care is deliberate and intentional and the medical problem is a serious one. One of the standards used to decide whether an Eighth Amendment violation has occurred is the deliberate indifference standard.

▶ Recent court cases have dealt with the issues of boot camps, AIDS, and HIV.

▶ Resolving problems in the courts is both costly and time-consuming. Prison officials are wise to resolve as many problems as possible in the prisons so that inmates will not feel a need to take matters to court.

INTRODUCTION

• The Courts–Corrections Relationship •

In the strictest sense, the commonly used term "criminal justice system" is misleading because the components of criminal justice do not always work together smoothly and in unison toward agreed-upon goals. Instead, there can be a lack of coordination, even conflict, between and within components. Different and competing goals may be pursued. For example, in lawsuits filed by prison inmates against prison officials, courts are typically more concerned with pursuing fairness and due process for inmates than are prison authorities; the top priority of prison officials is usually the security of their institution. Even in the courts, however, there may be disagreements over prison issues between the state and federal courts, as well as disagreements between courts at different levels within both the state and federal structures (e.g., the U.S. Supreme Court overruling a lower federal appeals court).

What takes place in the courts has a great deal of influence on corrections, and vice versa. Consider the prosecuting attorney whose discretion helps dictate the volume and types of cases that enter corrections. In turn, correctional agencies impact prosecutors by providing diversion and sentencing options. Further, the effectiveness (or lack thereof) of correctional programs has much to say about the magnitude of the crime problem that a prosecutor's office must confront.

Another aspect of the relationship is that between judges and corrections. Judicial discretion is partly shaped by the availability and perceived quality of correctional programs. It can also be affected by the direct input of correctional staff, as when judges consider the pre-sentence recommendations of probation agents. In like fashion, judges influence corrections through their sentencing decisions and through their oversight of offenders who are serving sentences (e.g., probationers). Appellate court judges are responsible for overseeing the legality of correctional processes. Correctional personnel establish policies and engage in practices that correctional clients sometimes challenge on legal grounds. When this happens, the courts must rule on the acceptability of the policies and practices in question. The complex relationship between corrections and the courts—and the legal aspect of this relationship in particular—is the focus of this chapter.

• The Courts–Corrections Relationship in Historical Perspective •

It is common for discussions of the history of court intervention in correctional matters to begin with the 1871 case of *Ruffin v. Commonwealth*.[1] In this case, a Virginia court noted that "the prisoner has, as a consequence of his crime, not only forfeited his liberty, but all his personal rights except those which the law in its humanity accords to him. He is for the time being the slave of the state." By comparing inmates to slaves, the language of this case made it sound as though prisoners had no rights; indeed, a number of states had laws known as "civil death statutes" that denied inmates certain civil rights. On the other hand, as Donald Wallace demonstrates, state courts have shown at least some interest in reviewing and challenging correctional practices for more than a century, frequently on grounds of the Eighth Amendment protection against cruel and unusual punishment.[2]

As a general rule, prisoners want to have their cases heard in the federal courts because they see these courts as potentially more receptive to their claims than state courts. Additionally, the rulings of federal courts are more or less applicable across the nation. However, the federal system did not display much interest in correctional issues until the 1960s.

The role played by the federal courts in overseeing correctional policies and practices has been cyclical over time. These courts moved from a hands-off phase of the pre-1960s to a relatively active rights-granting or hands-on phase from the 1960s through the latter 1970s. Since then, they have returned to a minimalist phase that can be called the due deference phase, in which the courts generally (but not always) defer to the discretion of corrections officials.[3] These three phases did not unfold in smooth progression with one giving way completely to the next. As will be apparent below, principles from any given phase tend to be embedded as tensions and competing forces in the other phases.

During the hands-off phase, court officials were extremely reluctant to get involved in correctional issues unless extreme practices could be demonstrated (e.g., infliction of death or serious injury on inmates). Judges did not want to encroach upon or undermine the work of correctional authorities, and they claimed to lack the authority and expertise needed to address such issues.

Still, the federal courts were occasionally making decisions that were at odds with a true hands-off doctrine during the 1940s and 1950s. For example, in *Ex parte Hull* (1941), the U.S. Supreme Court established that prison officials could not impair an inmate's efforts to apply for federal habeas corpus, which is a mechanism for challenging the legal basis for confinement.[4] Then, in 1958, the Court gave the concept of cruel and unusual punishment a flexible definition in reference to "evolving standards of decency that mark the progress of a maturing society."[5] Thus, the hands-off tendency of this era was accompanied by countertendencies that, when combined with other developments, would lead to the prisoner rights movement of the 1960s and 1970s.

As others have pointed out, the prisoner rights movement did not take place in a vacuum; it can only be appreciated in the context of the wider society in which it transpired.[6] The movement arose with, complemented, and was complemented by other movements on the part of traditionally repressed groups (such as ethnic minorities and women) to establish and assert their rights in a democratic society. It also unfolded against the backdrop of considerable opposition to government authority that surrounded the war in Southeast Asia during the 1960s. In short, the prisoner rights movement was part of a cultural framework of protest.

While the prisoner rights movement consisted of more than a collection of court decisions, such decisions were essential to structuring the future treatment of inmates. One of the most important cases in ending the hands-off era was *Cooper v. Pate*.[7] Decided by the Supreme Court in 1964, this case dealt specifically with religious freedoms under the First Amendment to the constitution. However, *Cooper* is of added importance because it set a precedent for prisoners to use Section 1983 of the Civil Rights Act of 1871 to have their constitutional claims heard in federal court without first going through the time-consuming process of exhausting state court remedies.[8] Civil rights suits by state inmates gradually increased after 1964 and eventually surpassed the number of habeas corpus writs.[9] According to James Jacobs, the *Cooper* decision signified that "prison officials were not free to do with prisoners as they pleased. And the federal courts were permitted, indeed obligated, to provide a forum where prisoners could challenge and confront prison officials. Whatever the outcome of such confrontations, they spelled the end of the authoritarian regime in American penology."[10]

Once *Cooper v. Pate* was decided and the stage was set for inmates to bring Section 1983 actions against prison officials, a number of significant decisions followed. These cases addressed prisoners' access to the courts as well as their procedural and constitutional rights while incarcerated. A few of these decisions involved high-profile class action suits in which federal courts challenged the constitutionality of conditions and practices of entire prison systems in such states as Alabama, Arkansas, and Texas on Eighth Amendment grounds.[11] The Arkansas case, *Holt v. Sarver* (1970), even served as the basis for a film *Brubaker*, which featured Robert Redford as a warden.[12] Despite isolated landmark and media-popularized cases, however, the vast majority of inmate suits were unsuccessful even during the hands-on period.

The Southern Center for Human Rights is devoted to prisoner rights (www.schr.org), as is Human Rights Watch (www.hrw.org/prisons). The American Civil Liberties Union often takes up legal cases for prisoners (www.aclu.org/prison).

Remnants of the hands-off philosophy meant that courts had to struggle with a fundamental tension between the desire to align prison operations with minimal constitutional standards and the desire to give prison officials the leeway needed to administer their facilities effectively.

• The Courts–Corrections Relationship in Recent Times •

During the late 1970s and 1980s, the courts showed signs of retreating from their relatively active stance to a philosophy of due deference, and the deference trend continued into the 1990s. Under this philosophy, the courts are generally willing to defer to the expertise of prison officials while still maintaining an interest in major constitutional matters.[13] The former position is indicative of the hands-off era, whereas the latter is indicative of the hands-on period.

If the Supreme Court's decision in *Cooper v. Pate* was symbolic of the end of the hands-off philosophy, its ruling in *Bell v. Wolfish* (1979) symbolized the start of the deference period.[14] This was a decision with wide scope and significance. The case dealt with pretrial detainees who, it was argued, should enjoy a higher level of legal protections than convicted prisoners because of their unconvicted status. However, the Court rejected the notion that these cases need to be conceptualized differently from prison cases. Importantly, too, the Court refused to ban the practice of double-celling (i.e., putting two inmates in a cell designed for one) as a response to overcrowded conditions. The case is of even more significance because, as Justice Rehnquist's quotations in Box 3.1 show, the Court essentially drew a line on how far the judicial branch should go in the regulation of prison matters.

In recent decades, concern has grown about the sheer amount of prisoner litigation coming before the courts. For instance, a 1996 state and federal adult prison population of nearly 1.2 million inmates filed 57,644 habeas corpus and civil rights actions in the federal courts.[15] A belief that many prisoner lawsuits are frivolous or lacking in foundation has sparked a movement to limit inmates' access to the courts. As a result, state inmates generally must exhaust habeas corpus claims at the state level before making them at the federal level. With respect to these claims, a 1999 U.S. Supreme Court ruling required that "state prisoners must give the state courts one full opportunity to resolve any constitutional issues by invoking one complete round of the State's established appellate review process."[16] Furthermore, under the Prison Litigation Reform Act passed during the mid-1990s, any inmate must exhaust available administrative channels (e.g., prison-based inmate grievance procedures) prior to filing federal civil rights suits about prison conditions. The Act also requires court officials to make careful consideration of the impact of their rulings on prison operations.[17] In addition, it is becoming more difficult for inmates to avoid paying the court fees associated with filing suits, and prisoners can be penalized (e.g., with loss of good time credits) if suits are judged to be frivolous.[18]

As was true during the hands-on period, most litigation brought by inmates in recent years has not been successful. In fact, it is incorrect to think that: (a) most prisoners file suits against the government, (b) many of them are successful at getting courts to rule in their favor at trials, or (c) successful inmates often receive handsome rewards from the courts in the form of money or improved prison conditions and services. The reality is that few incarcerated persons file suits. Some inmates tolerate things they find objectionable until release, others informally manipulate the system to their advantage as best they can, and others rely on internal prison grievance procedures. Of those inmates who attempt to get cases into court, only a few succeed. Of those cases not initially dismissed by the courts, very few go to trial. Most are dismissed before trial, and some result in out-of-court settlements. Of those going to trial, few are "won" by inmates. Moreover, of those won by inmates, few result in much money or tangible improvements to prison conditions and services.[19]

The United States Supreme Court maintains a web site containing recent opinions: www.supremecourtus.gov.

INSTITUTIONAL CORRECTIONS AND THE COURTS

The legal bases for inmate litigation are found in constitutional law as well as statutes at the state and federal levels. The collection of court decisions interpreting constitutions and statutes creates another important component of inmate litigation: case law.

As mentioned earlier, two legal mechanisms that inmates have commonly used to get their cases to court include habeas corpus petitions and actions based on Section 1983 from the federal Civil Rights Act of 1871. Since the Supreme Court's 1973 ruling on this matter in *Preiser v. Rodriguez*, inmates have generally had to use habeas corpus petitions to challenge the legality and duration of their confinement and Section 1983 suits to challenge the constitutionality of conditions under which they are held.[20] In addition, inmates usually prefer to have their cases heard in federal court rather than the court system of the state where they are imprisoned. Therefore, they tend to prefer Section 1983 actions because, unlike with habeas corpus claims, 1983 actions do not require that state-level remedies be exhausted before moving to the federal system.

Much prison litigation is based on the First, Fourth, Eighth, and Fourteenth Amendments to the U.S. Constitution. In this section, each amendment will be presented and then followed with consideration of the primary issues and case decisions associated with it concerning prisons and prisoners. First, however, it is important to understand the provisions for giving inmates access to the courts. By virtue of their status as prisoners, inmates' activities in general, and their efforts to enter the courts in particular, have been much more restricted than those of free citizens.

• Access to the Courts •

The availability of constitutional guarantees and the legal mechanisms for protecting those guarantees are of little value to prisoners if prisoners are not permitted access to the court system. Although prisoner access to the courts is not specifically mentioned in the U.S. Constitution, the Supreme Court and other courts have affirmed that it is a fundamental right implied in the due process clause of the Fourteenth Amendment.

After the Supreme Court barred prison officials from impairing inmates' efforts to apply for federal habeas corpus in *Ex parte Hull* (1941), other noteworthy cases followed in this area. In the *Hull* case, an inmate challenged a Michigan prison regulation that required inmates to submit all legal documents to prison officials for review before these documents could be mailed to the courts. The Supreme Court found this regulation invalid. Three years later, a federal court ruled that inmates could seek federal action to challenge not only the legality of their confinement (which they had traditionally been able to do through habeas corpus petitions) but also to challenge the conditions of confinement.[21]

More recently, the Court has rendered important decisions concerning the access of inmates to counsel and legal materials. The Sixth Amendment provides a right to counsel for persons facing criminal prosecution that ends at the point of sentencing. However, the Fourteenth Amendment's due process clause protects everyone against government error in the deprivation of life, liberty, or property. The landmark 1969 case of *Johnson v. Avery*[22] addressed the constitutionality of a Tennessee prison regulation that prohibited inmates who had knowledge of law (sometimes called "jailhouse lawyers") from assisting or advising other inmates in legal matters. Reasoning that many inmates are unable to obtain legal assistance any other way, the Supreme Court ruled that unless the state provides some alternative form of legal assistance to inmates seeking postconviction relief, the regulation prohibiting jailhouse lawyers is not valid. In this way, the *Johnson* decision reinforced the momentum the prisoner rights movement had gained through the *Cooper v. Pate* decision.

Eight years later, the Court again addressed the issue of legal assistance in *Bounds v. Smith* (1977).[23] In this case, the Court held that inmates must be provided either adequate law library facilities or adequate assistance from persons trained in law (e.g., inmates working under the supervision of lawyers, law students, licensed attorneys). Today, most prisons have law libraries, although they vary considerably in size and quality.[24]

Almost two decades after the *Bounds* decision, the Supreme Court issued a ruling in *Lewis v. Casey* (1996) that is much more in line with the due deference philosophy of the present era.[25] In this case, the Court held that a prisoner must demonstrate that the alleged shortcomings of the prison's library (or other type of legal assistance program) caused actual injury and hindered the prisoner's efforts to build a case. This gives institutional officials considerably more latitude in providing acceptable access to the courts. Since *Lewis*, courts have dismissed many access-to-the-courts claims on grounds of failure to demonstrate injury.[26] With the *Lewis* decision and with the Prison Litigation Reform Act of 1996 (mentioned earlier), efforts to expand the access of inmates to the courts have subsided.

• The First Amendment •

The First Amendment states that "Congress shall make no law respecting an establishment of religion, or prohibiting the free exercise thereof; or abridging the freedom of speech, or of the press; or the right of the people peaceably to assemble, and to petition the government for a redress of grievances." Thus, the main issues affecting prisoners include (a) freedom of religion, (b) freedom of speech and press, and (c) the right to assemble.

• *Freedom of Religion* •

The First Amendment keeps the government from establishing a religion and from prohibiting free exercise of religion.[27] A balancing act is required when the state must provide the opportunity for all prisoners to practice their religions without creating the image of promoting one religion over others. This potential conflict, combined with prison officials' concerns about how religious rights may interfere with prison order, security, and budgets, have produced complex and sometimes ambiguous interpretations of this amendment. Nevertheless, the Supreme Court has made it clear that inmates are entitled to practice their religions, and historically, it was in the area of religious freedoms (in the *Cooper v. Pate* case) that the Court initiated its efforts to end the hands-off philosophy.

Early decisions in this area tended to involve Black Muslim inmates' claims that they were being denied religious freedoms because of their specific religious preference. The early decisions that were decided in favor of inmates laid the foundation for the position that it is unacceptable under the First Amendment and the equal protection clause of the Fourteenth Amendment to grant freedoms to prisoners of certain religions while disallowing freedoms for inmates of other religions.[28] The Supreme Court solidified this position in *Cruz v. Beto* (1972), a Texas case in which the Court held that inmates cannot be denied the opportunity to practice an unconventional American religion (Buddhism, in this case) when other inmates are given the chance to pursue conventional faiths.[29]

Although the courts have recognized the rights of inmates belonging to many different faiths to hold religious services, the courts have also declared that the First Amendment does not extend to religions that mock established institutions, are "obvious shams," or whose members lack religious sincerity. For instance, in *Theriault v. Silber* (1977), it was concluded that the religion devised by inmate Theriault (called the Church of the New Song or CONS) was a "masquerade designed to obtain protection for acts which otherwise would have been unlawful and/or reasonably disallowed by various prison authorities."[30]

One of the most important Supreme Court cases on prison religious freedoms is *O'Lone v. Estate of Shabazz*, which was decided in 1987. Unlike *Cruz v. Beto*, this decision is reflective of the deference era.[31] Ahmad Uthman Shabazz, a Muslim inmate, challenged the refusal of prison officials to relax work regulations so he could participate in religious activities. The Court ruled that religious rights are not violated by such regulations when the regulations are related to the legitimate interests prison officials have in order and security; the Court had previously articulated this concept of legitimate penological interests in *Turner v. Safley*.[32]

Congress challenged the *O'Lone* ruling (and related ones) by passing the Religious Freedom Restoration Act of 1993 (RFRA). This law stipulates that religious freedoms can be constrained only if the constraint imposed is the least restrictive way available to advance some compelling interest of the government. As passed, the law did not exempt correctional institutions.[33] Thus, prison officials wishing to limit religious freedoms must demonstrate, first, that they have a compelling interest (i.e., order, security, and/or rehabilitation) in doing so and, second, that the limitations involved are as nonrestrictive as possible. Amidst court decisions surrounding RFRA, some correctional institutions have decided not to fund any religious programs if they are unable to support all religions equally.[34] This is likely to create fertile ground for future First Amendment claims.

Inmates have also filed freedom-of-religion suits on more specific points, such as their dietary and literature needs. In general, prisoners are allowed diets that are consistent with their religious beliefs unless prison officials can demonstrate an acceptable rationale for doing otherwise. Examples of rationales that have been found acceptable include budgetary constraints, a desire to avoid the image of giving select inmates preferential treatment, a desire to control security and contraband risks, and the availability of substitute foods that ensure adequate nutrition.[35]

Courts have often required prison officials to demonstrate justification for not allowing inmates to have religious literature. Some justifications that courts have found acceptable include claims by officials that certain publications are not necessary to practice a religion and claims

Federal inmates gather to smoke tobacco before participating in a sweat lodge ceremony at the Torrance County Detention Center, in Estancia, New Mexico. The goal of the sweat lodge is the same as the other religious services provided to inmates of various faiths.

that certain material may encourage activities that jeopardize institutional order and security.[36] A good deal of the litigation in this area has involved Black Muslim publications that correctional officials perceive as inflammatory and detrimental to security. One court said that the prison library must make the Koran available to Muslim prisoners and that prisoners should be allowed to receive *Muhammad Speaks* unless it could be demonstrated that a specific issue of this publication would undermine prison discipline.[37]

• Freedom of Speech •

Along with freedom of religion, freedom of speech is among the most cherished components of the U.S. Constitution. Courts have extended the right to free speech to prisoners by requiring prison officials to show why restrictions on speech should be imposed.[38] The term "speech" is used rather broadly in this context to mean not only what one says but also what one writes, reads, and hears. The concept of censorship refers to efforts to impose constraints on such communications. Prison officials have historically maintained that censorship is necessary to preserve security and contain contraband.

Rather than seeking to eliminate prison censorship, the courts have chosen to regulate it. The first major Supreme Court ruling on the issue came in 1974 in the case of *Procunier v. Martinez*.[39] In this case, the Court held that censorship is allowable only if it can be shown to be necessary to maintain the interests of prison authorities in order, security, and rehabilitation. Furthermore, where censorship is imposed, it should go no further than what is required to protect the interest involved.

In the 1987 case of *Turner v. Safley* (mentioned earlier), the Supreme Court again took up the issue of prison censorship when it ruled that mail between inmates could be banned if justified by "legitimate penological interests." Missouri prison officials justified a policy regulating inmate-to-inmate mail on grounds that such mail might be used for such things as communicating about escapes, fostering gang activity, and arranging to assault other inmates. The Court found this justification to represent a legitimate security consideration and indicated that there was no reasonable alternative available to prison authorities. The *Turner* decision was used as precedent in another case, *Thornburgh v. Abbott* (1989).[40] In this case, the Court held that the prison administration can reject inmates' incoming publications (e.g., magazines) if these publications are detrimental to such legitimate penological interests as order, discipline, and security, or if these publications might facilitate criminal behavior. Courts have also ruled that prison authorities can restrict sexually explicit materials if there is concern that these materials may lead to violence or sexual behavior that violates prison rules.[41]

In 2001, the Supreme Court decided *Shaw v. Murphy*.[42] Kevin Murphy, a Montana prisoner, was disciplined by institutional officials for writing a letter in which he tried to assist a fellow inmate with that inmate's defense against charges of assaulting a correctional officer. Murphy brought legal action claiming that the First Amendment free speech protection entitled him to give other inmates legal advice. The Court rejected Murphy's claim. The justices unanimously held that inmates do not have a First Amendment right to give fellow inmates legal assistance in a manner that would enhance the legal protections already afforded under the *Turner v. Safley* ruling.

Clearly, then, freedom of speech is rather far from being absolute in prison settings. The courts have shown considerable willingness to uphold censorship practices that prison officials are able to justify. At the same time, however, it is important to realize what censorship generally entails. Clair Cripe's remarks are instructive in this regard:

> Some people have in mind prison officials opening mail and poring over every word, to make sure there is nothing objectionable. In practice, that is pretty far from the truth. There is so much mail coming into and going out of the typical prison or jail that the thorough review of all mail is impractical. . . . What is done most often is to (1) search the contents of incoming mail for contraband, and (2) identify those inmates (or groups of inmates) who are of most concern, as security threats, and look closely at their mail.[43]

• Freedom of Press •

Among the most important rulings on freedom-of-press issues affecting prisons are from *Pell v. Procunier* and *Saxbe v. Washington Post Co.*, both decided in 1974.[44] In the first case, the Supreme Court upheld a California prison regulation that denied inmates personal interviews with members of the media; in the second case, the Court ruled that members of the media enjoy no special constitutional right of access to a specific inmate beyond that available to members of the public. The gist of this case law is that inmates can be denied interviews with the media (and vice versa) on grounds of the need to preserve institutional order and security. Some states have passed legislation that restricts an inmate's access to the media.[45] These initiatives essentially transform the Supreme Court's decisions in cases such as *Pell v. Procunier* and *Saxbe v. Washington Post Co.* into statutes.

• Freedom of Assembly •

Citizens of this country have the right to assemble peacefully for purposes of engaging in lawful activities, including those protected by the First Amendment (e.g., religious services, speeches, discussions, debates, etc.). Yet it has been said that there is power in numbers. Prison officials sometimes grow concerned that sizeable assemblies of inmates exercising First Amendment freedoms pose more of a threat to order and security than individual inmates doing so alone or in small groups. This concern was addressed by the Supreme Court in *Jones v. North Carolina Prisoners' Union* (1977).[46] Fearing that a prisoner union (which was really a prison reform organization) had grown too large, North Carolina prison officials began to restrict activities of the union that were intended to attract more members. In a ruling that began to signal the entry of the due deference era in penology, the Court upheld the restrictions of prison administrators on grounds that the restrictions were needed to prevent disruption in the prison environment. Combined with the other decisions covered in this section, the Jones ruling demonstrates that the courts tend to be more receptive to the First Amendment challenges of individual inmates than to collective challenges.[47]

A final aspect of assembly pertains to inmate visitation. Although visitation privileges can be strong incentives for inmates to maintain acceptable conduct and can even have therapeutic value, most facilities (especially the more secure ones) regulate the frequency, duration, and nature of visits. This is done to promote order and security and to control entry of contraband into the prison. The courts have generally been supportive of the efforts of prison authorities to regulate visitation processes. For example, the Court has held that pretrial detainees can be denied contact visits due to security concerns.[48] Furthermore, courts have upheld the authority of correctional officials to ban certain categories of visitors (e.g., former inmates) and to ban conjugal visitation (i.e., visits in which spouses are permitted privacy).[49]

• The Fourth Amendment •

The Fourth Amendment says that "the right of the people to be secure in their persons, houses, papers, and effects, against unreasonable searches and seizures, shall not be violated, and no warrants shall issue but upon probable cause, supported by oath or affirmation, and particularly describing the place to be searched, and the persons or things to be seized." The aspect of this amendment that affects prisons and prisoners is the search and seizure clause. Persons, houses, papers, and effects are protected against unreasonable searches and seizures, and inmates have used this terminology to argue that they are entitled to some degree of privacy in the prison environment. By contrast, prison officials have maintained that any attempt to grant this right might compromise institutional security and contraband regulations.

The Supreme Court examined this issue in *Hudson v. Palmer* in 1984, a Virginia case in which an inmate sued a correctional officer for violating his Fourth Amendment rights by conducting what the inmate saw as an unreasonable search of his cell.[50] Disagreeing with a lower court's assertion that an inmate has a limited right to privacy in his or her cell, the Supreme Court declared that because prison officials must look for contraband and maintain sanitary conditions, the Fourth Amendment has no applicability to a prison cell. The Court called the Fourth Amendment "fundamentally incompatible" with prison security and order. In an earlier ruling in 1979 (*Bell v. Wolfish*), the Court had reached basically the same conclusion, but it had gone further to rule that inmates have no right to be present to oversee the "reasonableness" of searches of their cells.

The *Bell v. Wolfish* decision also addressed the issue of strip searches wherein inmates are required to remove their clothing and submit to bodily searches (including inspection of body cavities). As part of contraband control efforts, institutions routinely conduct strip searches after events like contact visits, work release, and furloughs; pat-down searches of outer garments are conducted even more frequently. *Wolfish* dealt specifically with searches of body cavities following contact visits. A majority of the Court ruled that such searches are reasonable for purposes of contraband control and do not require probable cause to believe

BOX 3.1

Excerpts From the U.S. Supreme Court's Ruling in Bell v. Wolfish

Justice Rehnquist's Majority Position: "We have held that convicted prisoners do not forfeit all constitutional protections by reason of their conviction and confinement in prison. . . . But our cases also have insisted on a second proposition: simply because prison inmates retain certain constitutional rights does not mean that these rights are not subject to restrictions and limitations. . . . The inquiry of federal courts into prison management must be limited to the issue of whether a particular system violates any prohibition of the Constitution. . . ."

an inmate is concealing contraband. However, a federal court has held that prison staff may not conduct strip searches of inmates who are of the opposite gender (or supervise bathing or toilet use); similar restrictions have been imposed in other cases.[51] The courts seem most likely to impose regulations on bodily searches, including pat-down searches, when inmates are able to demonstrate that the searches are carried out in a way that is abusive, unduly intrusive, humiliating, or degrading.[52]

• The Eighth Amendment •

The Eighth Amendment states that "excessive bail shall not be required, nor excessive fines imposed, nor cruel and unusual punishments inflicted." Because this chapter deals with corrections and the courts, the focus here is on the clause prohibiting the infliction of cruel and unusual punishments.

As mentioned earlier in this chapter, the Supreme Court defined cruel and unusual punishment in the 1950s as deriving meaning in relation to evolving standards of decency indicative of social progress and maturation. This rather subjective definition implies that what is defined as cruel and unusual punishment will change over time with a society's cultural conceptions of acceptable punishments. Consistent with this logic, in 1981, the Court stated that "no static 'test' can exist by which courts determine whether conditions of confinement are cruel and unusual. . . ."[53] However, the Court has also defined cruel and unusual punishment in more static and objective terms as that which is grossly disproportionate to the seriousness of the crime and which far exceeds what is needed to achieve a legitimate penological goal.[54]

Just as cruel and unusual punishment has been defined in various ways, the prohibition against it has been applied to different aspects of prison life. These include the overall or total conditions of confinement, solitary confinement, double-celling and crowding, excessive use of force, and medical treatment and services.

• *Overall Conditions of Confinement* •

Some of the most well known applications of the Eighth Amendment have come in so-called "totality of conditions" cases. In these cases, inmates allege that a combination of problems (such as crowded living quarters, excess noise, lack of exercise opportunities, unsanitary conditions, etc.) makes the conditions of their confinement cruel and unusual. Basically, the claim in these cases is that the entire prison (and sometimes even the jurisdiction's entire prison system) is unconstitutional. Two of the best known cases of this type are *Holt v. Sarver* (1970), the Arkansas cases mentioned previously, and *Ruiz v. Estelle* (1980), a case in which the totality of conditions in the Texas prison system was declared unconstitutional. Examples of Eighth Amendment concerns cited in one or both of these cases include crowding, unsanitary conditions, inadequate diet, inadequate programs and services, use of inmates to control other inmates, and prison violence.

Unless conditions of confinement are extreme, however, courts generally defer to the judgment of correctional officials and the interest these officials have in maintaining orderly and secure institutions. Because of the increase in filings of conditions of confinement suits, the Supreme Court has created barriers to such filings.[55] For example, in *Wilson v. Seiter* (1991), when an inmate claimed his Eighth Amendment rights were violated by a combination of conditions, the Court ruled that a consideration of broad "overall conditions" is not sufficient to ascertain if cruel and unusual punishment exists; greater specificity about particular conditions is required.[56] This means that the Supreme Court did not follow the totality of conditions approach taken by lower courts in decisions such as *Holt* and *Ruiz*.[57] Moreover, the Wilson decision requires inmates to show that the conditions being challenged, regardless of what they may be, exist because of "deliberate indifference" on the part of correctional officials. This can be a difficult state of mind to demonstrate to the satisfaction of an appeals court.

An interesting Eighth Amendment issue in the area of confinement conditions stems from the movement toward having private companies operate entire correctional facilities under contract arrangements with the government. Illustrative of this issue is a recent class action settlement against a private prison company in the amount of $1.65 million. This settlement, the first of its kind, took place in April 1999. It required various reforms at a private prison and established a prison monitor and medical monitor position so that compliance with requirements could be reviewed.[58] Privately operated facilities are frequently accused of minimizing inmate services and programs more so than government operated facilities in order to minimize expenses. To the extent that this is true, privatization may require courts to spell out more clearly the minimally acceptable conditions of confinement and to re-examine the applicability of the deliberate indifference standard.

Another intriguing development in corrections that has Eighth Amendment implications is the effort of some states to reinstitute chain gangs, an arrangement whereby inmates are placed on work details outside the prison and restrained by chains or similar devices to prevent escapes. Earlier in the twentieth century and in previous centuries, the main force behind the use of chain gangs (particularly in the South) was the desire for profit from exploiting inmate labor. Today, by contrast, the main force is a desire to symbolize toughness on crime.[59] The former motive is economic, whereas the latter derives from emotions—fear, anger, and vengeance. In determining whether the chain gang is a con-

AP Photo/stf

Inmates working on Alabama's chain gang near Prattville, Alabama, in 1995. A 1996 settlement between state officials and attorneys of the Southern Poverty Law Center now prevents the state from shackling inmates together.

stitutional condition of confinement, courts will need to inquire whether this practice: (a) is offensive to contemporary standards of decency, (b) is excessive of what is required to achieve legitimate penological objectives, or (c) inflicts pain that is unnecessary and out of proportion with the crime. The retributive mood of the public and government officials, combined with the argument that restraints are needed to prevent escapes (a legitimate penological objective), make it seem unlikely that inmate litigation against chain gang policies will ultimately have much success. Like the economic motives of previous times, the emotional motives of the present age are strong barriers to successful Eighth Amendment challenges.

• *Solitary Confinement* •

Most prisons regularly place inmates in solitary confinement or isolation (known among inmates as "the hole") to discipline them for rule violations, to protect the general prison population and staff from dangerous inmates, and to control against escapes. The federal courts have rejected the position that solitary confinement, in and of itself, constitutes cruel and unusual punishment. Solitary confinement is seen as a legitimate tool to further important institutional goals.[60] When considering the legality of solitary confinement, courts generally examine the overall conditions under which the person is being confined (e.g., sanitation, allowance for exercise and diet, and duration of the isolation) in reference to the rule the inmate has violated or the threat he or she poses. Although one particular condition may not violate the Eighth Amendment, this same condition, when combined with others, may be considered a violation. For instance, in *Hutto v. Finney* (1978), the Supreme Court ruled that punitive isolation exceeding a 30-day limitation policy was cruel and unusual punishment but stressed that the length of confinement was only one factor in the decision.[61]

Many institutions have guidelines or policies regulating the conditions and duration of solitary confinement. These policies often require that inmates have contact with prison staff and periodic reviews of whether continuation of solitary confinement is necessary. Courts tend to look upon the mere existence of such regulations with favor when reaching decisions.

• Double-Celling and Crowding •

The Supreme Court has addressed prison crowding as an Eighth Amendment consideration in two landmark cases. In the first of these, *Bell v. Wolfish* (1979), jail inmates in New York challenged the constitutionality of placing two inmates in living quarters designed for one. The Court ruled this practice to be constitutional because the practice had been implemented as a necessity for dealing with the problem of jail crowding, which the Court found to be a legitimate purpose of government. The second case, *Rhodes v. Chapman* (1981), was a class action lawsuit filed on behalf of a group or class of inmates. Inmates challenged double-celling at the Southern Ohio Correctional Facility (SOCF) in Lucasville, a high-security facility housing some of the state's most serious and violent offenders. This case addressed the same basic issue as the *Wolfish* case, only this time on behalf of sentenced prisoners in addition to pretrial detainees.[62]

The lower courts had found double-celling at Lucasville to be cruel and unusual punishment because, among other things, it had become a routine rather than temporary practice, and the prison far exceeded the capacity for which it had been designed. The Supreme Court reversed the lower courts' rulings, failing to find evidence that double-celling at the prison inflicted unnecessary pain or was disproportionate to the magnitude of the crimes for which the inmates were in prison.

As prisons grow more crowded, it seems likely that there will be an increase in inmate suits relating to the various problems that tend to go hand-in-hand with crowding (e.g., fewer services and programs to go around and sanitation issues). In particular, as the potential for violence and disruption increases, there is likely to be an increase in lawsuits challenging the inability of the prison system to protect inmates from harm. There is precedent for the position that cruel and unusual punishment exists when staffing shortages compromise inmate safety.[63]

• Excessive Use of Force •

As in police work, there are situations in which correctional officers are permitted to employ necessary force against inmates. Some examples of these situations are self-defense, defense of third persons, and enforcement of prison rules and regulations.[64] The courts tend to analyze the factual elements of each case that comes to their attention to determine whether the force employed was excessive for the situation. However, as Hawkins and Alpert point out, the Eighth Amendment has done little to protect inmate populations from staff brutality because such brutality is often conceptualized as a tort or private action rather than a constitutional violation.[65]

In brutality cases, the standard established by the Supreme Court is also very demanding. In *Whitley v. Albers* (1986), a decision clearly reflective of the deference era, the Court held that an Oregon inmate who had been shot in the leg during a riot needed to demonstrate an "unnecessary and wanton infliction of pain" to win an Eighth Amendment case.[66] The Court concluded that the shooting took place in a good faith effort to restore prison order rather than for malicious or sadistic purposes. However, remains of the hands-on philosophy and a counterbalancing of the *Whitley* ruling are evident from the Court's 1992 ruling in *Hudson v. McMillian*.[67] In this case, the Court held that use of force against an inmate need not cause a significant degree of injury to constitute cruel and unusual punishment. Even a relatively mild injury (e.g., minor bruising from a slap to the face) might offend standards of decency if imposed in a manner that is unnecessary and wanton.

One development in corrections that has interesting implications for Eighth Amendment use-of-force claims is the expansion of what are typically called "special operations response teams" (SORTs). Prior to being professionalized and formalized, these units were simply referred to as "goon squads." Just as many police agencies have special weapons and tactics (SWAT) units to respond to intense, high-risk emergency situations (e.g., hostage taking), prison systems increasingly maintain specially trained tactical units to accomplish such tasks as cell extractions, disturbance control, and escapee captures.[68] Some observers suggest that prison tactical units could decrease the likelihood of successful suits by helping to ensure that: (a) the staff most likely to employ force are well trained and (b) the application of force follows approved procedures that have been established with an eye toward the posture of the courts. On the other hand, a lack of or nonadherence to training will almost certainly increase the probability of suits resulting from the employment of SORTs.

• Medical Care •

The first landmark Eighth Amendment case to come from a prison setting, *Estelle v. Gamble* (1976), dealt with the issue of health care.[69] Inmate Gamble claimed that the Texas Department of Corrections (TDC) had inflicted cruel and unusual punishment on him by not adequately treating a back injury sustained during a work detail. The Supreme Court acknowledged that prisoners are entitled to adequate medical care but ruled in favor of the TDC. Based on evidence that Gamble had been treated for the injury several times by prison medical staff, the Court concluded that Gamble had not shown evidence of "deliberate indifference" to his medical needs.

The Supreme Court noted that "deliberate indifference to serious medical needs of prisoners constitutes . . . unnecessary and wanton infliction of pain" and argued that denial of medical treatment runs counter to "contemporary standards of decency." However, the Court made it clear that such concepts as negligence, inadvertent failure, or even medical malpractice do not equate with deliberate indifference. It must be demonstrated that the failure to provide medical care (or the provision of improper care) was deliberate and intentional and that the medical problem was serious.

Estelle v. Gamble set the standards by which subsequent cases of prison medical care have been judged. In addition, lower courts quickly applied the deliberate indifference standard to cases involving mental health treatment. As noted earlier in the chapter, the Supreme Court has since ruled that successful Eighth Amendment challenges of prison conditions (medical or otherwise) require demonstration of deliberate indifference on the part of correctional authorities.

Although inmates enjoy a constitutional right to medical treatment, the courts have been much more reluctant to find that inmates have a right to receive rehabilitative treatment (e.g., counseling, education, vocational training, etc.) during incarceration.[70] On occasion, however, a lack of rehabilitative programs has been cited in totality-of-condition cases. While a lack of opportunity for rehabilitation may be declared an Eighth Amendment violation in combination with other factors, it is not likely to be considered unconstitutional in its own right.

Debates over the right of inmates to refuse medical or rehabilitative treatment stem mainly from the privacy and due process clauses of the Fourth and Fourteenth Amendments, respectively. However, when the treatment in question involves unpleasant side effects or other undesirable consequences, the Eighth Amendment can become relevant. Courts have been rather inconsistent in this area. For instance, the Supreme Court has ruled that psychiatric medication can be administered to an inmate against his or her wishes, provided that the drug is used for medical (as opposed to purely behavioral) purposes and is needed to help keep the inmate from hurting himself or herself or others.[71] On the other hand, aversion therapy programs, in which inmates are given a noxious stimulus (e.g., an injection to produce nausea) for undesirable behavior (e.g., rule breaking), have frequently been struck down on Eighth Amendment grounds for inflicting unnecessary and wanton pain.[72] At the same time, the courts have generally supported institutional requirements that inmates participate in vocational and educational programs. Courts tend to consider the purpose of the refusal of medical or rehabilitative treatment when determining whether the refusal is justified.[73]

The above considerations have assumed added significance as many areas have undertaken efforts to remove patients from mental hospitals. The result of such "deinstitutionalization" has sometimes been an influx of mentally unstable persons to prisons and jails.[74] As the need grows for mental health treatment in jails and prisons, courts will be forced to keep considering the right-to-treatment issue. Some courts have already laid out what they see as the minimally acceptable elements of mental health care for incarcerated offenders. These include mental health screening procedures for incoming inmates, suicide prevention programming, treatment provisions for inmates in solitary confinement, and so forth.[75]

Women prisoners present most all of the same healthcare concerns as male inmates, in addition to posing unique concerns. As an example of the scope of their healthcare needs, women prisoners, like their female counterparts in free society, regularly need competent examinations for breast cancer and gynecological disorders. Depending on a woman's condition, these exams can become quite specialized and complicated. Additionally, pregnant inmates require a variety of prenatal care services including not only medical monitoring of the mother's and baby's conditions, but also special nutrition, precautions to maintain an environment that is as low in stress as possible, and, in some cases, education and counseling services. Women's prisons must also provide (or make arrangements for) labor and delivery services and care of newborns. Some female inmates, even those who are still young, have relatively serious health problems complicated by their limited income and lack of medical insurance and preventive health care. Among other things, this means that many female facilities are likely to be confronted with a disproportionately large volume of high-risk pregnancies.

Many institutions are ill-equipped to address the above considerations in any consistent and adequate way. With isolated exceptions,[76] this state of affairs has resulted in minimal Eighth Amendment litigation favoring women inmates. As discussed later in the chapter, when the courts have addressed gender issues, it has usually been done under the Fourteenth Amendment's Equal Protection Clause. In this regard, courts have taken the basic position that unless government officials can demonstrate a valid rationale, there should be no differences between the programs and services offered to male inmates and those offered to female inmates. This position can be questioned, though, in view of the fact that women have medical needs that are clearly different from those of males, and these needs require specialized attention.

Recent years have witnessed an increase in the population of elderly prisoners. This population contains a number of geriatric inmates who, compared to the general prison population, are more likely to have special dietary needs and serious medical problems, which often have escalated due to years of neglected health care. Furthermore, these inmates sometimes require special housing assignments, either to accommodate their disabilities or to keep them from being victimized by younger inmates. These considerations can be expected to drain further institutional budgets that are already overburdened. The potential for successful Eighth Amendment litigation will lessen as prison systems take steps to avoid deliberate indifference to the serious needs of these inmates.

Another contemporary health issue in prison parallels the controversy about smoking in general society—specifically, there are debates regarding exposure to secondhand smoke. As anyone who has ever worked in (or even toured) a prison can attest, relatively high numbers of inmates and staff smoke. Historically, they have done so inside buildings where proper ventilation and filter systems are lacking. Increasingly, however, prison administrators are taking steps to regulate smoking in correctional facilities, in part because of court decisions such as the Supreme Court ruling in *Helling v. McKinney* (1993).[77] In this case, inmate McKinney claimed that he developed health problems because of being required to share a cell with an inmate who was a heavy smoker. McKinney said this state of affairs amounted to cruel and unusual punishment. The Court accepted the position that the failure of prison officials to address such a known health risk could represent deliberate indifference. This ruling suggests that instances of deliberate indifference to conditions promoting either current or future health problems are unacceptable from a constitutional standpoint.

• The Fourteenth Amendment •

The Fourteenth Amendment holds that "all persons born or naturalized in the United States, and subject to the jurisdiction thereof, are citizens of the United States and of the state wherein they reside. No state shall make or enforce any law which shall abridge the privileges or immunities of citizens of the United States; nor shall any state deprive any person of life, liberty, or property without due process of law, nor deny to any person within its jurisdiction the equal protection of the laws." While federal courts have routinely used this amendment since the 1960s to make various protections in the U.S. Constitution binding on the states, prisoners have used the due process and equal protection clauses in and of themselves to secure important rights.

• Due Process •

The due process clause is most commonly thought of as giving criminal defendants the right to be treated fairly and according to legally prescribed procedures. However, prisoners have employed the clause to file actions challenging prison disciplinary decisions as well as classification and transfer decisions.

Disciplinary Actions. When inmates violate institutional rules, they may be subjected to various disciplinary actions, and efforts are commonly made to match the seriousness of the action to the seriousness of the violation. Some of the more serious disciplinary actions can affect inmates' sentences (e.g., a reduction of good time credits) and/or temporarily alter their living conditions (e.g., movement from the general population to segregation). As such, disciplinary actions are perhaps the most frequently contested and litigated area in prison.[78]

The landmark U.S. Supreme Court case dealing with due process in prison disciplinary actions is the Nebraska case of *Wolff v. McDonnell* (1974).[79] Some of the stronger language that the Court has ever directed at prison officials was contained in Justice White's remarks, which illustrate well the philosophy of the hands-on era:

> But though his rights may be diminished by the needs and exigencies of the institutional environment, a prisoner is not wholly stripped of constitutional protections when he is imprisoned for crime. There is no iron curtain drawn between the Constitution and the prisons of this country. . . . Prisoners may also claim the protections of the Due Process Clause. They may not be deprived of his life, liberty, or property without due process of law.

Inmate McDonnell lost good-time credits for what prison officials defined as serious misconduct, and officials claimed their decision required no due process. The inmate, on the other hand, said that the absence of due process surrounding the decision was unconstitutional because his liberty was taken away in the form of lost good time. Because liberty rather than a privilege (e.g., commissary visits, furlough, etc.) was at stake, the Court agreed with the inmate. The Court ruled that when disciplinary actions threaten liberty interests, the following due process elements are required:

- a disciplinary proceeding by an impartial body

- 24 hours advance written notice of the claimed violation

- a written statement from the fact finders as to the evidence relied on and the reasons for the disciplinary action

- an opportunity for the inmate to call witnesses and to present documentary evidence (provided this is not hazardous to institutional safety or correctional goals).

At the same time, the Court reasoned that prison settings pose special hazards and that prison disciplinary hearings should not be overly adversarial. Thus, the *Wolff* ruling did not guarantee inmates a right to: (a) retained or appointed counsel, (b) confront and cross-examine witnesses, or (c) appeal the decision to higher levels.[80] It is also worth emphasizing that the decision did not apply to all disciplinary actions. As Christopher Smith says of the ruling, "the right to due process exists because of state regulations that give something valuable to prisoners, and therefore the prisoners are entitled to fair procedures when the state decides to take that valuable thing away for disciplinary reasons."[81]

Wolff v. McDonnell was one of the major cases (some might argue *the* major case) of the hands-on era. As the courts gravitated toward the deference era, some of the momentum created by *Wolff* gradually weakened. To illustrate this point, consider a Supreme Court decision rendered nine years later in *Hewitt v. Helms*.[82] This case is sometimes seen as expanding on the *Wolff* decision because the Court held that when states require (through laws or regulations) that inmates be placed in administrative segregation for certain violations, a liberty interest is created and due process is required. However, the *Hewitt* decision may be better seen as reflecting the deference era because the Court concluded that the discretionary (as opposed to mandatory) use of administrative segregation with inmates does not create a liberty interest, even though such segregation may entail many more restrictions on inmate freedoms. Again drawing on Smith's analysis, one can see that "the Court's reasoning effectively discouraged prisons from writing careful regulations. Corrections officials suddenly had an incentive to leave many matters under the discretionary control of wardens and others so that no mandatory language would appear that could be used by prisoners to trigger due process protections."[83]

In a 1995 case, *Sandin v. Conner*, the Court overruled the position it had taken in *Hewitt*.[84] The majority of the Court held that inmate Conner's placement in administrative segregation without the benefit of each of the due process components granted under *Wolff* was constitutional because the disciplinary action did not fundamentally alter the length or nature of the original prison sentence. The majority reasoned that due process no longer depends on whether there is language mandating a particular disciplinary action for a particular violation; the nature of the discipline is what counts. Moreover, only if discipline constitutes an "atypical, significant deprivation" and is not "within the range of con-

BOX 3.2

Excerpts From the U.S. Supreme Court's Ruling in Sandin v. Conner

Chief Justice Rehnquist's Majority Position: "We believe that the search for a negative implication from mandatory language in prisoner regulations has strayed from the real concerns undergirding the liberty protected by the Due Process Clause. . . . Following *Wolff*, we recognize that States may under certain circumstances create liberty interests which are protected by the Due Process Clause. But these interests will be generally limited to freedom from restraint which, while not exceeding the sentence in such an unexpected manner as to give rise to protection by the Due Process Clause of its own force, . . . nonetheless imposes atypical and significant hardships on the inmate in relation to the ordinary incidents of prison life."

finement to be normally expected" is a liberty interest created and the due process of *Wolff* required. As Barbara Belbot explains the ruling in *Sandin v. Conner*, "if the punishment imposed for misconduct does not entail a significant departure from the basic conditions of a prisoner's sentence, a prisoner has no liberty interest in avoiding that punishment."[85] Justice Breyer's minority opinion relied upon the constitution and upon the precedent established by the Court.

Classification and Transfers. Classification is based on assessments of the risks and problems posed by an inmate as well as the inmate's rehabilitative needs. It involves making decisions about what an inmate's custody level should be, at which particular facility the inmate should be placed, where the person will live within the facility, what programs he or she needs to participate in, and so forth. Inmates undergo classification shortly after being sentenced to prison and then are reclassified periodically throughout their sentences. Because decisions to transfer inmates between institutions are incidental to classification decisions, court rulings in transfer cases have been applied to classification cases.[86]

In *Meachum v. Fano* (1976), the Supreme Court ruled that the Fourteenth Amendment does not entitle an inmate to a due process hearing when the inmate is transferred from one prison to another, even if the conditions at the receiving prison are substantially less favorable to the prisoner.[87] The Court reasoned that the Constitution does not require prisoners to be placed in a particular prison. Therefore, inmates are not entitled to due process protections in matters regarding inter-prison transfers. (Notice the consistency of this logic with the logic applied by the Court in *Sandin v. Conner* almost 20 years later.) In *Vitek v. Jones* (1980), however, the Court ruled that involuntary transfer from a prison to a mental hospital setting involves a liberty interest and therefore necessitates a due process hearing. As the Court stated, "A criminal conviction and sentence of imprisonment . . . do not authorize the State to classify [the inmate] as mentally ill and to subject [the inmate] to involuntary psychiatric treatment without . . . additional due process protections."[88] *Vitek* gave inmates facing transfer to a mental hospital essentially the same due process protections spelled out in *Wolff v. McDonnell*, plus an opportunity to cross-examine witnesses provided there is no compelling rationale for disallowing cross-examination. Taken together, then, *Meachum v. Fano* and *Vitek v. Jones* provide further evidence of the tension between the due deference and hands-on philosophies.

• Equal Protection •

The equal protection clause of the Fourteenth Amendment has been used by inmates to file claims regarding both racial and gender discrimination. Reflective of the wider society, racial segregation policies were commonplace in American prisons until about the 1970s. Prison officials

III. SCALE SUMMARY AND RECOMMENDATIONS

CUSTODY LEVEL INDICATED BY SCALE ....
1 = Minimum 2 = Medium 3 = Maximum   Code

Custody Classification Scale

7 or more points on items 1 - 3 .... Maximum
5 or fewer points on items 1 - 7 .... Minimum
5 or fewer points on items 1 - 7, with detainer/warrant ..... Medium
6 to 10 points on items 1 - 7 .... Medium
11 or more points on items 1 - 7 .... Maximum

B. SPECIAL MANAGEMENT ISSUES (Check all that apply to this inmate.)

_____ Protective custody   _____ Known management problem
_____ Psychological impairment   _____ Suspected drug trafficker
_____ Mental deficiency   _____ Suicide risk
_____ Escape threat   _____ Medical problem
_____ Serious violence threat   _____ Physical impairment
_____ Known gang affiliation   _____ Other (specify): _____
_____ Substance abuse problem

C. OVERRIDE OF SCALE CUSTODY LEVEL IS RECOMMENDED ....
1 = Yes   2 = No   Code

If yes, give rationale (required): _____
_____
_____
_____

D. RECOMMENDED CUSTODY LEVEL ....
1 = Minimum   2 = Medium   3 = Maximum   Code

Specialist Signature _____ Date _____

IV. SUPERVISOR APPROVAL OF OVERRIDE

A. RECOMMENDED CUSTODY LEVEL
1 = Approved   2 = Disapproved

B. FINAL CUSTODY LEVEL (if override di
1 = Minimum   2 = Medium

Rationale (required if different from recommenda

Supervisor Signature_____

V. RECOMMENDED HOUSING ASS

INITIAL CUSTODY ASSESSMENT SCALE

IDENTIFICATION   Inmate ID # _____

Inmate Name (Last, First, MI) _____

Assessment Date _____   Classification Specialist _____

II. CUSTODY EVALUATION   Score (1)

1. SEVERITY OF CURRENT CHARGES/CONVICTIONS (Use the Severity of Offense Scale: Rate the
   most serious charge/conviction, including any detainers/warrants.)   0
   Low _____   2
   Moderate _____   5
   High _____   7
   Highest _____

2. SERIOUS OFFENSE HISTORY (Use the Severity of Offense Scale: Rate the most serious prior   Score (2)
   conviction.)   0
   None or Low _____   1
   Moderate _____   4
   High _____   7
   Highest _____

3. ESCAPE HISTORY (Excluding current charges.)   Score (3)
   No escape or attempts _____   0
   Walkaway or attempted escape from minimum security facility or failure to return   3
   from authorized absence _____   7
   Escape or attempted escape from medium or maximum security setting _____

MAXIMUM CUSTODY SCORE (Add items 1, 2, and 3.)   Score (1-3)
With a score of 7 or higher, assign to maximum custody. (Always complete the remaining items, but do not
total score if the inmate has already been assigned to maximum custody.)

4. INSTITUTIONAL DISCIPLINARY HISTORY   Score (4)
   None or minor with no segregation time _____   0
   One or more major disciplinary reports and/or time in segregation _____   3

5. PRIOR FELONY CONVICTIONS (Excluding current charges.)   Score (5)
   None _____   0
   One _____   2
   Two or more _____   4

6. ALCOHOL/DRUG ABUSE   Score (6)
   No social, economic, or legal problems related to abuse _____   0
   Abuse resulting in social, economic, or legal problems _____   1
   Abuse resulting in assaultive behavior _____   3

7. STABILITY FACTORS (Deduct indicated points.)   Score (7)
   Age 26 or over _____   -1
   Employed or attending school for 6 months prior to arrest _____   -1
   Lived at same address for 12 or more months prior to arrest _____   -1

COMPREHENSIVE CUSTODY SCORE (Items 1-7)   Total Score (1-7)

Figure 3.1
Intial Custody Assessment Scale

justified segregation as necessary to maintain order and security. It was not until an Alabama case in 1968 (*Lee v. Washington*) that the U.S. Supreme Court declared racial segregation in prison unconstitutional.[89] However, the Court conceded that in extreme situations, in which there is a clear and immediate threat to institutional security, it might be necessary to separate races for a temporary period. Even in cases involving temporary segregation, prison administrators may be required to show that segregation was the only viable alternative available.[90] In the daily routines of prison life, however, inmates often self-segregate along racial lines. This can be seen in dining area seating preferences, club memberships, sporting/exercise activities, and the like.

Some correctional department and local detention web sites include information about how inmates are assessed and classified. You can visit your state's web site and try to locate this information. For an example of prison classifications, see the North Carolina Department of Correction web site at www.doc.state.nc.us. For an example of a large county jail inmate classification system, see the Harris County (Houston), Texas, web site at www.hcso.hctx.net.

The U.S. Supreme Court has yet to make any firm ruling on the equal protection rights of female inmates. However, the lower courts have established a parity standard as precedent, in which there must be a basic equivalence of treatment for male and female inmates. To illustrate, in *Glover v. Johnson* (1979), a federal court ordered Michigan officials to establish educational and vocational programs for female prisoners that were substantially equivalent to those offered for male inmates.[91] However, because there are fewer women inmates and women's prisons, identical treatment is not necessarily required. The main issue is whether prison officials can demonstrate a valid justification for differential treatment by gender.[92] For example, in *Pargo v. Elliott* (1995), a court found that if prison authorities can justify gender differences in programs on grounds of such considerations as security and rehabilitation, there is no violation of the equal protection clause.[93] A program's financial cost, however, is not viewed as a legitimate justification.

There are a number of other issues that are either unique to female inmates or much more applicable to them than to their male counterparts, thus calling into question the logic of the parity standard. As one example, consider provisions for arranging child custody and child visitation. Most institutions have regulations that prohibit incarcerated mothers from retaining newborns in the prison environment, although some programs permit infants to remain with their mothers temporarily (e.g., six months or a year). Courts have tended to uphold regulations prohibiting retention of newborns by prison mothers.[94] Because many women inmates are mothers (or expectant mothers) at the time of incarceration, and because many of these persons lack a husband or male partner who can or will provide child care, children must usually be placed either with relatives or under state control (e.g., in foster care). There is considerable variation in regulations across jurisdictions, and there is even much variation across cases, but it is not uncommon for incarcerated women to be faced with the threat of permanently losing legal custody of their children.

Compared to male inmates, there are few women prisoners, so there are few women's prisons in most areas of the nation. This means that most female prisoners are incarcerated at long distances from their home communities where their children generally reside. Given limited resources to cover travel expenses, mother-child visits are often infrequent and may be practically nonexistent. Considering what is known about the importance of positive mother-child interaction to child maturation and development, it may be prudent to rethink the general rule established in *Meachum v. Fano* (a case involving male inmates) that the decision to place an inmate at a particular facility requires no special due process.

• *Recent Fourteenth Amendment Issues* •

As part of the so-called "truth in sentencing" movement, a number of jurisdictions have enacted legislation and policies that either prohibit or curtail the possibility for inmates to reduce their prison terms by earning good time. Fourteenth Amendment issues become relevant because these laws involve a liberty interest. Ohio recently went a step further and passed a "bad time" law that permits the parole board to extend inmates' sentences by 30, 60, or 90 days for each crime committed while in prison.[95] Extensions could result in a sentence that is as much as 50 percent longer than the judicially imposed term. Critics of this law have challenged it on due process and equal protection grounds, but Ohio's intermediate appellate court upheld the constitutionality of the law in 1998.[96]

Over the past two decades, increasingly more jurisdictions have opened boot camp or shock incarceration facilities with the intent of teaching offenders discipline and respect for authority, thereby appearing tough on crime. Offenders who lack serious instant offenses and extensive criminal backgrounds are sent to these programs as an alternative to regular prison with the understanding that, while the boot camp stay will be more intense and demanding, it will also be shorter.

The boot camp movement raises equal protection issues. In general, boot camps are used with younger males who are in good enough physical condition to complete a rigorous program of exercise and work. Because boot camps feature the benefit of a shorter sentence (and tout other benefits as well), an obvious legal question is whether there is discrimination against females, older offenders, and persons with physical disabilities or problems (e.g., asthma) that might preclude participation. Some jurisdictions avoid potential for gender discrimination by establishing boot camp programs for women offenders, but discrimination on the basis of age and physical condition is more difficult to avoid. Future litigation will address such Fourteenth Amendment issues.

Faith Lutze and David Brody point out that some boot camps inflict what amounts to mental abuse through intense verbal confrontations and various activities meant to degrade and humiliate inmates. Using precedents established by the courts, these authors show that programs that rely on mentally abusive tactics risk being held in violation of the Eighth Amendment.[97]

The presence of acquired immune deficiency syndrome (AIDS) and the human immunodeficiency virus (HIV) in the prison population has raised Fourth, Eighth, and Fourteenth Amendment issues in recent years. With respect to the Fourteenth Amendment, one issue is the extent to which HIV-positive inmates should be segregated from the rest of the prison population. There is potential for a "Catch 22" situation here. HIV-positive inmates can argue that they should not be subjected to unequal treatment in housing, work assignments, and programs. The remaining inmate population can argue that they have a right to be protected from those who are HIV-positive. The former position is supported by the fact that the virus can be transmitted in a very limited number of ways, while the latter position draws strength from the realities of prison assault (especially sexual assault) and drug use. Given these realities, prison staff argue that they could be held liable if they are unable to protect inmates from infection.

With respect to the Fourth Amendment, arguments have been made that inmates who are HIV-infected are entitled to have this medical information remain confidential. As such, there is debate about screening policies that permit officials to test all inmates (mass screening) or selected inmates entering prison for HIV. There is additional debate about exactly who should be informed of positive test results (e.g., medical staff, security personnel, program personnel).

A major Eighth Amendment concern relates to the circumstances under which correctional systems may be judged deliberately indifferent toward the medical needs associated with HIV/AIDS, which is obviously a serious medical condition but, at the same time, is expensive to treat. Specifically, there is debate about whether deliberate indifference exists when prison officials do not provide needed dosages of AZT, a costly drug that is designed to prevent or postpone HIV infection from transforming into AIDS.

A number of cases have addressed these issues; all in all, the inmates bringing claims have not been successful at convincing the courts to intervene. In *Harris v. Thigpin* (1991), for example, Alabama inmates challenged the state's policy of compulsory mass screening followed by segregation of prisoners who tested positive; challenges were made on Fourth, Eighth, and Fourteenth Amendment grounds.[98] The court sided with the state and granted prison officials deference on the issues of testing, segregation, and medical treatment. By the same token, a court has held that a refusal by prison officials to segregate HIV-positive inmates does not constitute cruel and unusual punishment toward other inmates.[99] However, requiring a prisoner to share a cell with an HIV-infected inmate known to have committed sexual assaults, and then not protecting the prisoner from assault, was held to be cruel and unusual.[100]

• Other Legal Issues Affecting Prisons and Prisoners •

Until now, this section has focused on the rights courts have granted to prisoners on the basis of constitutional law. However, as noted at the outset of this section, statutory law is another basis for inmate suits. One example of such a law is the Religious Freedom Restoration Act covered earlier when considering First Amendment issues.

As a second example, all states have tort laws that permit one party (e.g., an inmate) to bring civil action against a second party (e.g., a prison and/or an individual prison official) for some harm inflicted by the second party. The kind of tort suit that is probably most frequent in prison settings involves claims by inmates about lost or damaged property resulting from staff negligence.[101] Inmates have also brought tort claims against institutional staff for such things as assault (both staff-on-inmate assault and inmate-on-inmate assault arising from staff negligence) and medical malpractice. From the standpoint of prison staff, the greatest liability threat arises when staff members can be shown to have not followed a law or policy that they were required to follow and a harm was produced as a consequence. (This is true in the case of both torts and constitutional violations.)

A final example of statutory law affecting prisons is the Americans with Disabilities Act (ADA) of 1990. This legislation is meant to provide disabled persons physical access to government activities, services, and programs and to ensure that whatever special needs are involved get reasonably accommodated. (In prison, an example would be provision of an adequate aid for a hearing-impaired inmate who is participating in group counseling or a parole hearing). In *Pennsylvania Department of Corrections v. Yeskey* (1998), the U.S. Supreme Court made it clear that prisoners are protected under the ADA.[102] Segregation of disabled inmates cannot be a solution to ADA requirements because the law calls for mainstreaming such inmates into extant programs and services to the extent possible.[103] The ADA takes on added significance with increases in the population of elderly inmates because a greater proportion of these inmates display some type of disability covered by the law and have special living amenity needs.

LIMITATIONS OF CORRECTIONAL LITIGATION

Any treatment of corrections and the courts would be incomplete if it did not address some of the limitations of relying on court intervention to change problematic correctional practices and conditions. A number of limitations exist.[104] Probably the most basic and widely shared concern is that litigation is costly, often far more so than alternative strategies such as fair grievance and mediation procedures that, in the end, may produce more satisfactory outcomes for all parties. Some prison systems get caught in a cycle that is difficult to escape. They spend money defending themselves from inmate lawsuits, and on occasions when inmates win, more money is spent to comply with court rulings. In many instances, it would have been less costly to alter from the outset the practices or conditions that caused inmates to file suits. When considerable money is being spent on litigation, there is less available to spend on changes that might preempt future suits. These future suits ensure that a steady stream of expenditures will have to be directed toward legal defense and compliance fees. It is easy to get so caught up in the complexities and details of litigation that less formal yet potentially more effective ways to address problems are overlooked.

Another limitation is that lawsuits are time-consuming, particularly when judges, attorneys, and other court personnel are overburdened with cases. Even if inmates manage to win their cases and if courts order changes in correctional conditions or practices (the former in no way guarantees the latter), it often takes much time for corrections authorities to comply; and getting them to comply can require significant monitoring and assistance from court-appointed officials. Years may pass before timelines and the specifics of change are negotiated and implemented. In some situations, there is instability and disorder in the prison as a result of this process.

Finally, litigation tends to be piecemeal in its effects. Most court decisions have narrow rather than wide and far-reaching applicability; only the plaintiff(s) and a select few prison officials are affected. There are instances in which court decisions like those mentioned in this chapter lead to a false sense of knowledge and predictability. Few decisions provide clear, steadfast rules that can be followed like recipes in present and future situations. Each case poses a unique combination of circumstances that often defy any attempt to apply general rules or principles from prior court decisions. Past decisions merely provide guidance for considering those circumstances. When these considerations are combined with the fact that the vast majority of suits filed by correctional clients are not successful, the piecemeal nature of litigation is readily apparent.

It is instructive to bear in mind Justice Powell's remarks about the limitations of correctional litigation in 1974. In the *Procunier v. Martinez* decision, he wrote:

> The problems of prisons in America are complex and intractable, and, more to the point, they are not readily susceptible of resolution by decree. Most require expertise, comprehensive planning, and the commitment of resources, all of which are peculiarly within the province of the legislative and executive branches of government. For all those reasons, courts are ill equipped to deal with the increasingly urgent problems of prison administration and reform.[105]

BOX 3.3

Landmark Supreme Court Prison Cases

CASE	HOLDING
Cooper v. Pate, 378 U.S. 546 (1964)	Inmates who are denied the right to practice their religion may sue for civil rights violation.
Cruz v. Beto, 405 U.S. 319 (1972)	Prison officials violated the First and Fourteenth Amendments by discriminating against the Buddhist religion through denying the inmate plaintiff a reasonable opportunity to practice his faith comparable to the opportunity afforded fellow prisoners who adhered to conventional religious precepts.
Procunier v. Martinez, 416 U.S. 396 (1974)	A prison regulation that banned the use of law students and legal paraprofessionals to conduct attorney-client interviews in prison constituted an unjustifiable restriction on the prisoners' due process right of access to the courts and served no justifiable governmental interest.
Estelle v. Gamble, 429 U.S. 97 (1976)	Deliberate indifference to an inmate's medical condition violates the Eighth Amendment ban on cruel and unusual punishment.
Bounds v. Smith, 430 U.S. 817 (1977)	A court order requiring prison officials to provide prison law libraries and other forms of legal assistance was affirmed. States were required to assure the prisoners an adequate opportunity to present their claims fairly in order to guarantee their constitutional right of access to the courts.
Bell v. Wolfish, 441 U.S. 520 (1979)	In a case involving conditions in a pretrial detention facility, the Supreme Court ruled that courts should defer to the expertise of correction officials in the absence of evidence indicating that officials exaggerated their response to the issues involved in providing detainment.
Rhodes v. Chapman, 452 U.S. 337 (1981)	Minor deprivation of privileges due to double-celling constitutes cruel and unusual punishment in and of itself.
Daniels v. Williams, 474 U.S. 327 (1986)	A prison official's mere lack of care—leaving a pillow case out so an inmate slipped and injured himself—did not constitute a deprivation of liberty.
Whitley v. Albers, 475 U.S. 312 (1986)	Prison officials who shot and injured an inmate as part of a good faith effort to restore order during a prison riot did not violate the inmate's Eighth Amendment rights.
Turner v. Safley, 482 U.S. 78 (1987)	There was no legitimate penological interest in a ban on inmate marriages.
Wilson v. Seiter, 501 U.S. 294 (1991)	A prisoner claiming that conditions of confinement constitute cruel and unusual punishment must show a culpable state of mind on the part of prison officials, and the applicable legal standard in this context is the "deliberate indifference" standard.
Farmer v. Brennan, 511 U.S. 825 (1994)	Prison officials are liable if, having foreknowledge that an inmate faces significant risk of being harmed, they fail to act to protect the inmate.
Shaw v. Murphy, 532 U.S. 223 (2001)	Written inmate-to-inmate legal advice is not protected under the First Amendment.
Booth v. Churner, 532 U.S. 731 (2001)	The Prison Litigation Reform Act of 1995 requires prisoners to exhaust all administrative remedies before filing suit.
Hope v. Pelzer, 536 U.S. 730 (2002)	Punishing an inmate by handcuffing him to a pole for seven hours, while shirtless, deprived of all but a minimum amount of food and water, constituted cruel and unusual punishment.

CONCLUSION

As pointed out at the start of this chapter and as should now be clear, there is a great deal of interaction between corrections and the courts. The functions of these two system components even overlap, but they do not always share the same goals and priorities. While the courts have more often than not deferred to the judgment of correctional authorities, there have been several major occasions when courts have set down parameters within which correctional officials must remain.

There are three identifiable phases in the history of courts' efforts (or the lack thereof) to regulate corrections. By and large, before the 1960s, the courts adhered to a policy of staying out of correctional matters; this was especially true of the federal courts. For a relatively brief period during the 1960s and 1970s, the courts, under the leadership of the U.S. Supreme Court, stepped in to establish basic constitutional protections for prisoners, probationers, and parolees. Since the late 1970s, the courts have clearly retreated from their more active stance of the hands-on era. They have shown a willingness to grant deference to correctional officials, but this deference is tempered by keeping an eye on the constitutional boundaries set forth earlier in this text. Contemporary correctional law, then, is the product of tensions between all three stages. It is a compromise formation that contains ambiguous, contradictory, and ambivalent elements.

To illustrate this point, prisoners were granted access to the courts (after access had traditionally been denied) because of concern about hidden prison conditions and practices. Recently, however, efforts have been made to curtail access due to concern over excessive and groundless suits. Likewise, case law has granted inmates various First Amendment rights, but their rights are not nearly as free of restrictions as the rights of unincarcerated citizens. Case law also permits prison authorities to limit First Amendment freedoms in ways that are not unnecessarily restrictive, given that the restrictions can be justified by broad correctional objectives.

The ebb-and-flow pattern between expansion and restriction of rights that is apparent with access to the courts and First Amendment issues is far less apparent with respect to the Fourth and Fifth Amendments. Prisoners and clients in community correctional programs can expect little if any privacy and confidentiality from criminal justice officials. This is true unless the courts determine that the practices of officials are abusive, unnecessarily intrusive, or overly degrading.

The U.S. Supreme Court has been unreceptive to the position that a combination or totality of prison conditions can constitute cruel and unusual punishment under the Eighth Amendment, choosing instead to require a focus on a specific condition(s). The Court clearly insists that correctional clients enjoy Eighth Amendment protections. Yet, before reaching judgments of unconstitutionality, the Court has required that the specific conditions or practices in question be (a) the result of deliberate indifference on the part of correctional staff, (b) unnecessary to further legitimate correctional goals, or (c) inflicting of unnecessary and wanton pain.

The Court has insisted that prisoners, probationers, and parolees are entitled to due process in the face of threats to life, liberty, and property. The Court, however, has recently determined that for prisoners to be given due process, the actions taken by correctional officials must depart significantly from the basic conditions or length expected from a sentence of imprisonment. This position gives prison officials great latitude because it is they who, over time, construct what the "typical" prison sentence entails and what is to be expected during its course.

In addition to due process, the Fourteenth Amendment promises equal protection. Courts have shown a willingness to examine differential treatment by ethnicity and gender and have sometimes ordered such differences to be addressed where these could not be justified on legitimate grounds. At the same time, the courts have been somewhat more tolerant of differential treatment by gender than by ethnicity, frequently citing the relatively low number of women prisoners and prisons as a valid justification for gender differentials.

A central theme of this chapter has been the manner in which tension and competition between the hands-on and hands-off philosophies of the courts have always shaped developments in correctional litigation. Given the heavy reliance of courts on precedence law, decisions in future cases are sure to reproduce this tension and the contradictions and ambi-

---

▶ Ethics Focus: "It's a Matter of Paperwork"

An inmate named Billy was sexually assaulted over a month ago. He is having difficulty filling out the grievance paperwork claiming that the guard on duty that night ignored his calls for help. The prisoner only has a tenth-grade education. He has asked you for some help in filling out the forms.

Your supervisor has told you in the past not to help inmates with their paperwork. According to Department of Corrections rules, if inmates do not meet the filing deadlines, then the matter will be dropped. The courts are very technical about such deadlines and will not hear any appeals after a deadline has been missed.

You feel sorry for the inmate. He is not that strong and has a difficult time defending himself. You know the guard in question, and he does not always do everything he should. The guard claims that he did what he could and followed institutional guidelines. You were not present that night, though, so you do not know exactly what happened.

What would you do?

guities that go with it. This is true regardless of what names (hands-off, hands-on, due deference, etc.) are assigned to future eras. Moreover, while noteworthy benefits have been and will no doubt continue to be achieved through correctional litigation, litigation will remain a limited means of transforming corrections.

▶ At the Movies . . . .

Brubaker, 1980.

This film, starring Robert Redford and Yaphet Kotto, is loosely based on the story of Arkansas prison official Tom Murton, who goes undercover as an inmate to discover firsthand the brutalities suffered by prison inmates.

Gideon's Trumpet, 1980.

This made-for-television movie starring Henry Fonda and José Ferrer, tells the story of Clarence Gideon, who mounted a successful legal challenge to his original criminal conviction by conducting his own legal research while imprisoned.

DISCUSSION QUESTIONS

1. Describe the hands-off, hands-on, and due deference approaches to corrections. Which do you think is the most appropriate philosophy?

2. Which court cases have addressed inmates' freedom of religion? What rationales for denying religious requests do you think should be acceptable?

3. How have the courts chosen to regulate prison censorship? Describe the court decisions that have affected this issue and tell whether you agree or disagree with the courts.

4. What have the courts deemed to constitute cruel and unusual punishment? What sanctions do you believe to be cruel and unusual?

5. Do you think inmates involved in prison disciplinary actions deserve the same due process considerations that defendants receive before sentence? Why or why not?

6. What procedures have the courts required for the revocation of probation and parole? Do you think these procedures are fair?

7. A frequent criticism of prisoner lawsuits is that they are frivolous. Cite examples from this chapter that either support or dispute this claim.

FURTHER READING

Chilton, B.S. (1991). *Prisons Under the Gavel: The Federal Court Takeover of Georgia Prisons*. Columbus, OH: Ohio State University Press.

Crouch, B.M., and J.W. Marquart (1989). *An Appeal to Justice: Litigated Reform of Texas Prisons*. Austin, TX: University of Texas Press.

DiIulo, J.J. (1992). *Courts, Corrections and the Constitution: The Impact of Judicial Intervention on Prisons and Jails*. New York: Oxford University.

NOTES

1. *Ruffin v. Commonwealth*, 62 Va. 790, 796 (1871).
2. Wallace, 1997.
3. Jones, 1992.
4. *Ex parte Hull*, 312 U.S. 546 (1941).
5. *Trop v. Dulles*, 356 U.S. 86, 101 (1958).
6. Irwin, 1980; Jacobs, 1983.
7. *Cooper v. Pate*, 378 U.S. 546 (1964). The *Cooper* decision was predated by another important decision, *Monroe v. Pape*, 365 U.S. 167 (1961). In *Cooper*, the Supreme Court held that persons could have cases involving alleged violations of the Civil Rights Act of 1871 (Section 1983) heard in federal court before having their cases heard in state courts.
8. Hawkins and Alpert, 1989.
9. Thomas, Keeler, and Harris, 1986.
10. Jacobs, 1983, 37.
11. *Pugh v. Locke*, 406 F. Supp. 318 (1976), *Holt v. Sarver*, 309 F. Supp. 362 (1970), and *Ruiz v. Estelle* 503 F. Supp. 1265 (1980).
12. Redford's real-life character was Warden Tom Murton, and Murton's books make very interesting reading. See Murton and Hyams, 1969, and Murton, 1976.
13. Jones, 1992.
14. *Bell v. Wolfish*, 441 U.S. 520 (1979).
15. Simon, 1999.
16. *O'Sullivan v. Boerckel*, 526 U.S. 838 (1999). See also Hawkins and Alpert, 1989.
17. Hass and Alpert, 1999, 227-228. See also Shook and Sigler, 2000.
18. Simon, 1999. See also Steinmann, 1999, and Smith, 2000.
19. This state of affairs is analogous to the familiar criminal justice funnel effect, which begins at the top with a high number of crimes and gradually ends at the bottom with exceedingly few of these crimes resulting in prison terms.
20. *Preiser v. Rodriguez*, 411 U.S. (1973). See Hawkins and Alpert, 1989.
21. *Coffin v. Reichard*, 143 F.2d 443 (6th Cir. 1944).
22. *Johnson v. Avery*, 393 U.S. 483 (1969).

23. *Bounds v. Smith*, 430 U.S. 817 (1977).

24. Cripe, 2004.

25. *Lewis v. Casey*, 116 S.Ct. 2174 (No. 94-1511, 1996).

26. Hass and Alpert, 1999.

27. Palmer, 2006. See also Cripe, 2004.

28. *Fulwood v. Clemmer*, 206 F. Supp. 370 (D.C. Cir. 1962).

29. *Cruz v. Beto*, 405 U.S. 319 (1972).

30. *Theriault v. Silber*, 547 F.2d 1279 (5th Cir. 1977).

31. *O'Lone v. Estate of Shabazz*, 482 U.S. 342 (1987).

32. *Turner v. Safley*, 482 U.S. 78 (1987).

33. Cripe, 2004.

34. Wilson, 1996.

35. See for instance *Kahane v. Carlson*, 527 F.2d 592 (2nd Cir. 1975) and *U.S. v. Huss*, 394 F. Supp. 752 (S.D.N.Y. 1975).

36. Palmer, 1997.

37. *Northern v. Nelson*, 315 F.2d 687 (N.D. Cal. 1970).

38 Cripe, 2004.

39. *Procunier v. Martinez*, 416 U.S. 396 (1974).

40. *Thornburgh v. Abbott*, 490 U.S. 401 (1989).

41. *Giano v. Senkowski*, 54 F.3d 1050 (2nd Cir. 1995) and *Aikens v. Jenkins*, 523 F.2d 751 (7th Cir. 1976).

42. *Shaw v. Murphy*, 532 U.S. 223 (2001).

43. Cripe, 2004, 131.

44. *Pell v. Procunier*, 417 U.S. 817 (1974) and *Saxbe v. Washington Post Co.*, 417 U.S. 843 (1974).

45. Kirtley, 1996.

46. *Jones v. North Carolina Prisoners' Union*, 433 U.S. 119 (1977).

47. See Hawkins and Alpert, 1989.

48. *Block v. Rutherford*, 468 U.S. 576 (1984).

49. *Polakoff v. Henderson*, 488 F.2d 977 (5th Cir. 1974). *Lyons v. Gilligan*, 382 F. Supp. 198 (N.D. Ohio, 1974).

50. *Hudson v. Palmer*, 468 U.S. 517 (1984).

51. *Lee v. Downs*, 641 F.2d 1117 (4th Cir. 1981). *Forts v. Ward*, 621 F.2d 1210 (2nd Cir. 1980).

52. Cripe, 2004.

53. *Rhodes v. Chapman*, 452 U.S. 337 (1981).

54. Hawkins and Alpert, 1989.

55. Palmer, 1997.

56. *Wilson v. Seiter*, 501 U.S. 294 (1991).

57. Cripe, 2004.

58. American Lawyer Media, 1999.

59. Allen and Abril, 1997.

60. Palmer, 1997.

61. *Hutto v. Finney*, 437 U.S. 678 (1978).

62. The second author of this chapter began working at SOCF as a correctional officer within a month of the Supreme Court's decision in *Rhodes v. Chapman*.

63. Hawkins and Alpert, 1989.

64. Palmer, 1997.

65. Hawkins and Alpert, 1989.

66. *Whitley v. Albers*, 475 U.S. 312 (1986).

67. *Hudson v. McMillian*, 503 U.S. 1 (1992).

68. Bryan, 1995.

69. *Estelle v. Gamble*, 429 U.S. 97 (1976).

70. Palmer, 1997.

71. *Washington v. Harper*, 494 U.S. 210 (1990).

72. *Knecht v. Gillman*, 448 F.2d 1136 (8th Cir. 1973).

73. Palmer, 1997.

74. Spence, 1997.

75. Johnson, 1999.

76. *Todaro v. Ward*, 431 F. Supp. 1129 (S.D. New York, 1977).

77. *Helling v. McKinney*, 509 U.S. 25 (1993).

78. Cripe, 2004.

79. *Wolff v. McDonnell*, 418 U.S. 539 (1974).

80. A prison system may opt to allow any or all of these three things.

81. Smith, 2000, 140.

82. *Hewitt v. Helms*, 459 U.S. 460 (1983).

83. Smith, 2000, 148.

84. *Sandin v. Conner*, 515 U.S. 472 (1995).

85. Belbot, 1997, 276.

86. Palmer, 1997.

87. *Meachum v. Fano*, 427 U.S. 215 (1976). See also *Montanye v. Haymes*, 427 U.S. 236 (1976).

88. *Viteck v. Jones*, 445 U.S. 480 (1980).

89. *Lee v. Washington*, 390 U.S. 333 (1968).

90. See *Blevins v. Brew*, 593 F. Supp. 245 (W.D. Wis. 1984).

91. *Glover v. Johnson*, 478 F. Supp. 1075 (E.D. Mich. 1979).

92. See Cripe, 2004, for an excellent and thorough discussion of this topic.

93. *Pargo v. Elliott*, 49 F.3d 1355, 69 F.3d 280 (8th Cir. 1995).

94. Pollock-Byrne, 1990.

95. Civic Research Institute, Inc. (1999), 17, 31.

96. *State ex rel. Bray v. Russell*, CA 98-06-068 (12th App.Dist. Ohio, 1998).

97. Lutze and Brody, 1999.

98. *Harris v. Thigpin*, 941 F.2d 1495 (11th Cir. 1991).

99. *Robbins v. Clarke*, 946 F.2d 1331 (8th Cir. 1991).

100. *Billman v. Indiana Department of Corrections*, 56 F.3d 785 (7th Cir. 1995).

101. Cripe, 2004.

102. *Pennsylvania Department of Corrections v. Yeskey*, 118 U.S. 1952 (1988).

103. Cripe, 2004.

104. Jacobs, 1983.

105. *Procunier v. Martinez*, 416 U.S. 396 (1974).

REFERENCES

Allen, H.E., and J.C. Abril (1997). "The New Chain Gang: Corrections in the Next Century." *American Journal of Criminal Justice* 22:1-12.

American Lawyer Media, Inc. (1999). "First Ever Class Settlement Against Private Prison Company Approved." *Criminal Justice Weekly* 1:19-20.

Belbot, B. (1997). "Prisoner Classification Litigation." In J.W. Marquart and J.R. Sorensen (eds.) *Correctional Contexts*, 272-280. Los Angeles: Roxbury.

Bryan, D. (1995). "Emergency Response Teams: A Prison's First Line of Defense." *Corrections Compendium* 20:1-3.

Civic Research Institute, Inc. (1999). "Ohio's New 'Bad Time' Law Upheld." *Community Corrections Report on Law and Corrections Practice* 6:17,31.

Cripe, C.A. (2004). *Legal Aspects of Corrections Management*, 2nd ed. Sudbury, MA: Jones and Bartlett.

Hass, K.C., and G.P. Alpert (eds.) (1999). *The Dilemmas of Corrections: Contemporary Readings*, 4th ed. Prospect Heights, IL: Waveland.

Hawkins, R., and G.P. Alpert (1989). *American Prison Systems: Punishment and Justice*. Englewood Cliffs, NJ: Prentice Hall.

Irwin, J. (1980). *Prisons in Turmoil*. Boston: Little, Brown.

Jacobs, J.B. (1983). *New Perspectives on Prisons and Imprisonment*. Ithaca, NY: Cornell University Press.

Jones, C.H. (1992). "Recent Trends in Corrections and Prisoners' Rights Law." In C.A. Hartjen and E.E. Rhine (eds.), *Correctional Theory and Practice*, 119-138. Chicago: Nelson-Hall.

Kirtley, J. (1996). "Limiting Media Access to Prisoners." *American Journalism Review* 18:50.

Murton, T.O. (1976). *The Dilemma of Prison Reform*. New York: Holt, Rinehart and Winston.

Murton, T.O., and J. Hyams (1969). *Accomplices to the Crime: The Arkansas Prison Scandal*. New York: Grove Press.

Palmer, J.W. (2006). *Constitutional Rights of Prisoners*, 8th ed. Newark, NJ: LexisNexis Matthew Bender.

Pollock-Byrne, J.M. (1990). *Women, Prison and Crime*. Pacific Grove, CA: Brooks/Cole.

Shook, C.L., and R.T. Sigler (2000). *Constitutional Issues in Correctional Administration*. Durham, NC: Carolina Academic Press.

Simon, K. (1999). "Are Inmate Lawsuits Out of Control? No." In C.B. Fields (ed.), *Controversial Issues in Corrections*, 249-255. Boston: Allyn & Bacon.

Smith C.E. (2000). *Law and Contemporary Corrections*. Belmont, CA: West/Wadsworth.

Spence, C.N. (1997). "The Impact of the Deinstitutionalization Movement upon the Criminal Justice System: A Georgia Case Study." In J.W. Marquart and J.R. Sornesen (eds.), *Correctional Contexts*, 281-287. Los Angeles: Roxbury.

Steinmann, R.M. (1999). "Are Inmate Lawsuits Out of Control? Yes." In C.B. Fields (ed.), *Controversial Issues in Corrections*, 239-247. Boston: Allyn & Bacon.

Thomas, J., D. Keeler, and K. Harris (1986). "Issues and Misconceptions in Prisoner Litigation: A Critical Review." *Criminology* 24:775-797.

Wallace, D.H. (1997). "Prisoners' Rights: Historical Views." In J.W. Marquart and J.R. Sorensen (eds.), *Correctional Contexts*, 248-257. Los Angeles: Roxbury.

Wilson, J.C. (1996). "RFRA: More Harm than Good." *Corrections Today* 58:21.

COURT CASES

Aikens v. Jenkins, 523 F.2d 751 (7th Cir. 1976).

Bell v. Wolfish, 441 U.S. 520 (1979).

Billman v. Indiana Department of Corrections, 56 F.3d 785 (7th Cir. 1995).

Blevins v. Brew, 593 F.Supp. 245 (W.D. Wis. 1984).

Block v. Rutherford, 468 U.S. 576 (1984).

Booth v. Churner, 532 U.S. 731 (2001).

Bounds v. Smith, 430 U.S. 817 (1977).

Coffin v. Reichard, 143 F.2d 443 (6th Cir. 1944).

Cooper v. Pate, 378 U.S. 546 (1964).

Cruz v. Beto, 405 U.S. 319 (1972).

Daniels v. Williams, 474 U.S. 327 (1986).

Estelle v. Gamble, 429 U.S. 97 (1976).

Ex parte Hull, 312 U.S. 546 (1941).

Farmer v. Brennan, 511 U.S. 825 (1994).

Forts v. Ward, 621 F.2d 1210 (2nd Cir. 1980).

Fulwood v. Clemmer, 206 F.Supp. 370 (D.C. Cir. 1962).

Giano v. Senkowski, 54 F.3d 1050 (2nd Cir. 1995).

Glover v. Johnson, 478 F.Supp. 1075 (E.D. Mich. 1979).

Harris v. Thigpin, 941 F.2d 1495 (11th Cir. 1991).

Helling v. McKinney, 509 U.S. 25 (1993).

Hewitt v. Helms, 459 U.S. 460 (1983).

Holt v. Sarver, 309 F.Supp. 362 (1970).

Hope v. Pelzer, 536 U.S. 730 (2002).

Hudson v. McMillian, 503 U.S. 1 (1992).

Hudson v. Palmer, 468 U.S. 517 (1984).

Hutto v. Finney, 437 U.S. 678 (1978).

Johnson v. Avery, 393 U.S. 483 (1969).

Jones v. North Carolina Prisoners' Union, 433 U.S. 119 (1977).

Kahane v. Carlson, 527 F.2d 592 (2nd Cir. 1975).

Knecht v. Gillman, 448 F.2d 1136 (8th Cir. 1973).

Lee v. Downs, 641 F.2d 1117 (4th Cir. 1981).

Lee v. Washington, 390 U.S. 333 (1968).

Lewis v. Casey, 518 U.S. 343 (1996).

Lyons v. Gilligan, 382 F.Supp. 198 (N.D. Ohio 1974).

Meachum v. Fano, 427 U.S. 215 (1976).

Monroe v. Pape, 365 U.S. 167 (1961).

Montanye v. Haymes, 427 U.S. 236 (1976).

Northern v. Nelson, 315 F.2d 687 (N.D. Cal. 1970).

O'Lone v. Estate of Shabazz, 482 U.S. 342 (1987).

O'Sullivan v. Boerckel, 526 U.S. 838 (1999).

Pargo v. Elliott, 49 F.3d 1355, 69 F.3d 280 (8th Cir. 1995).

Pell v. Procunier, 417 U.S. 817 (1974).

Pennsylvania Department of Corrections v. Yeskey, 118 U.S. 1952 (1988).

Polakoff v. Henderson, 488 F.2d 977 (5th Cir. 1974).

Preiser v. Rodriguez, 411 U.S. (1973).

Procunier v. Martinez, 416 U.S. 396 (1974).

Pugh v. Locke, 406 F.Supp. 318 (1976).

Rhodes v. Chapman, 452 U.S. 337 (1981).

Robbins v. Clarke, 946 F.2d 1331 (8th Cir. 1991).

Ruffin v. Commonwealth, 62 Va. 790, 796 (1871).

Ruiz v. Estelle, 503 F.Supp. 1265 (1980).

Sandin v. Conner, 515 U.S. 472 (1995).

Saxbe v. Washington Post Co., 417 U.S. 843 (1974).

Shaw v. Murphy, 532 U.S. 223 (2001).

Theriault v. Silber, 547 F.2d 1279 (5th Cir., 1977).

Thornburgh v. Abbott, 490 U.S. 401 (1989).

Todaro v. Ward, 431 F.Supp. 1129 (S.D. New York 1977)

Trop v. Dulles, 356 U.S. 86, 101 (1958).

Turner v. Safley, 482 U.S. 78 (1987).

U.S. v. Huss, 394 F.Supp. 752 (S.D.N.Y. 1975).

Viteck v. Jones, 445 U.S. 480 (1980).

Washington v. Harper, 494 U.S. 210 (1990).

Whitley v. Albers, 475 U.S. 312 (1986).

Wilson v. Seiter, 501 U.S. 294 (1991).

Wolff v. McDonnell, 418 U.S. 539 (1974).

Jails

CHAPTER 4

What You Need to Know

▶ Jails can be traced to England to the time of King Henry II.

▶ In 2006, jails housed almost three-quarters of a million inmates.

▶ Jails house a disproportionate percentage of minorities. In 2006, African Americans comprised almost 40 percent of the jail population. Hispanics comprised about 16 percent.

▶ More than half of the people housed in jails are pretrial detainees. More than 40 percent are inmates serving a sentence for a misdemeanor conviction. Less than 10 percent of jail inmates are awaiting transfer to a state or federal prison for a felony sentence.

▶ Jail design can be either traditional, second-generation, or new-generation.

▶ A major problem in jail operation is inmate lawsuits.

▶ Jail administrators must deal with problems of crowding and addressing inmate needs such as alcohol and other drug abuse.

▶ Also problematic are mentally ill inmates and the prevention of suicide.

INTRODUCTION

Jails play a unique role in our criminal justice system. For many, the jail is the point of entry into the criminal justice system.[1] While the importance of jails is unquestioned, the jail is often the most misunderstood of the agencies that make up the criminal justice system. In this chapter, we will take a look at this unique institution within the criminal justice system, first exploring the history, both in England and the United States, then addressing concerns with modern jail facilities and their management and operation. To begin this journey, let us first define what a jail is and, for that matter, what it is not.

The Bureau of Justice Statistics defines jails as "locally-operated correctional facilities that confine persons before or after adjudication. Inmates sentenced to jail usually have a sentence of a year or less."[2] These facilities, with some exceptions, are administered locally, by an elected county sheriff. In this fact lies the first of many unique problems endured by the modern jail. For the most part, sheriffs tend to focus on the law enforcement aspects of the job and have little interest in or knowledge about their role in the jail operation.[3] Adding to this problem is the fact that jails are almost totally dependent on other agencies within the criminal justice system and, as such, have little control over their own destiny.[4]

Jails house a rather diverse population made up of both pretrial detainees (those who have not been convicted of any crime) and those convicted of a misdemeanor. While the majority of the jail population could be classified in one of these two categories, it does not tell the whole story. In fact, the Bureau of Justice Statistics lists 10 other categories of inmates often housed in jails, ranging from the mentally ill awaiting movement to appropriate health facilities to transfer inmates from federal and state authorities.[5] Jails are often the institutions of last resort, and many times are called on to house those with whom no other agency is willing to deal. For this reason, jails have been classified as the "dumping ground" for society's problems.[6] John Irwin referred to these inmates as society's rabble or those who are "irksome, offensive, threatening, capable of arousal, even proto-revolutionary."[7]

Often the terms "jail" and "prison" are used interchangeably by the media and public alike. However, jails are not prisons. To add to this identity problem, one must also make a distinction between jails and police lockups. Police lockups are facilities authorized to hold persons awaiting court appearance for periods that usually do not exceed 48 hours.[8] These facilities are usually housed in and administrated by the local police agencies. Examples of police lockups are drunk tanks and holding tanks. Often these facilities are little more than a steel cage set up inside a police station.

A number of important distinctions can be made between jails and prison facilities. The major ones are: sentencing, location, administration, population, and programs (remember these with the mnemonic device "SLAPP"). The first factor that distinguishes jails from prisons is the length of the sentence. Jails are institutions for short-term confinement, usually less than one year (in some states, jails house inmates for less than two years). Prisons, on the other hand, are places of long-term confinement, ranging from one year to life; in states with the death penalty, they also house those awaiting execution. While jails, by definition, are facilities designed for short-term confinement, they often find themselves holding inmates for longer periods due to crowding in both federal and state facilities. To a novice, short-term confinement may seem like less of a problem than long-term confinement, but one has to realize that there are about 17 million persons that pass through our nation's jails in a given year, many of them more than once. Prisons have, by contrast, a relatively stable population. This constant changeover in population causes numerous problems for jail personnel.

A second important distinction between jails and prisons is location. Jails are most often located in or near the central business districts of most cities. In many cases, jails are located in or very near the county courthouse. This facilitates the quick transfer of pretrial detainees to various court hearings. Prisons, on the other hand, are often located in remote locations.

The third distinction is how these facilities are administered. Jails, for the most part, are administered locally by an elected county sheriff. In only a small number of jurisdictions are jails administered by a local department devoted specifically to corrections. As mentioned above, this in itself can cause problems. Most sheriffs have law enforcement backgrounds with little or no training in corrections or jail administration. While the vast majority of jails are locally operated, a number of states (Alaska, Connecticut, Delaware, Hawaii, Rhode Island, and Vermont) operate their jails at the state level. Prisons, in contrast, are operated exclusively at the state or federal level.

The fourth major distinction between jails and prisons is the population they house. In the United States, the vast majority of prisons are single-gender institutions that house those convicted of a crime. In the past, a distinction was made that only adults were held in prisons, but due to the increased number of juveniles that are waived into the adult system, this distinction can no longer be made. Nevertheless, prisons still house a rather homogeneous population. Jails, on the other hand, have a heterogeneous population made up of both males and females, juveniles and adults. As of 2007, females made up 12.9 percent of the jail population in the United States,[9] up from about 7.1 percent in 1983.[10]

Despite a mandate by the federal government to remove juveniles from adult jail facilities, about 1.1 percent of the jail population in this country are juveniles age 18 or younger. On June 30, 2006, there were

6,104 juveniles housed in jails in the United States, about 21 percent of whom were held as juveniles; the other 79 percent were being held as adults (including juveniles who were tried or awaiting trial as adults).[11] These figures may be misleading because a one-day count does not give a full picture. It has been estimated that approximately 100,000 juveniles are incarcerated in adult jails each year.[12]

The final factor that distinguishes jails from prisons are the programs offered in each facility. While it is common to hear complaints about the lack of programs in prisons, such programs are far more prevalent than in most jails. This is due to the nature of the population they serve. As mentioned above, more than 17 million people flow through jails in this country every year, some staying for as little as a few hours. It is difficult to offer any meaningful programs or technical training with such an inmate turnover. As jails are utilized to house increasingly more inmates awaiting transfer to prison facilities, the need to occupy these inmates becomes a major concern. With too few programs and too much idle time, inmates become restless and bored; problems are bound to follow.

In the section that follows, we will take a brief look at the history of jails. As with so much of our criminal justice system in the United States, the roots of the modern jail can be found in our heritage in England. So let us begin our look at the history of jails with a look at the history of jails in England.

THE HISTORY OF JAILS

• Jails in England •

The term "jail" is derived from the English term "gaol" (pronounced "jail"), which can be traced back to the time of King Henry II. In 1166, King Henry II ordered the reeve (the official law enforcement officer for the crown) of each shire (county) to establish a place to secure offenders until the next session of the king's court. These shire reeve's (sheriff's) had a wide variety of law enforcement responsibilities for the crown, only one of which was to maintain the gaol. These early jails served the single function of holding accused persons until such time as a trial could be held. There is some evidence that even at this early stage in their history, jails were sometimes used to house those convicted of crimes as well.[13]

The conditions in these early jails were horrendous at best. No real attempt was made to separate prisoners by age, gender, or seriousness of offense. They were often all thrown into a single dungeon or cellar and had to fend for themselves. If they were small or weak, "other prisoners would literally strip the clothes" from these new prisoners' backs.[14] The sheriff did not receive additional resources to construct or operate these facilities. As such, they often relied on existing structures such as dungeons, cellars, or towers to serve their needs.[15] Because the sheriff received no compensation for housing inmates, these jails were operated on a fee system. Under the fee system, prisoners were charged a fee upon entering the jail. Any food or medical attention needed by the inmate had to be paid by the prisoners or his or her family or friends. Prisoners often had to wait long periods of time before the crown convened a court. If they had no money and family and friends were not available to pay, prisoners would often die long before they had their day in court.

No real change in these horrendous conditions occurred until the beginning of the sixteenth century. During that period in England, a large number of people were migrating to the cities looking for work. This influx of vagrants and beggars caused a huge economic strain on these large cities. Large numbers of crimes were committed, and attempts were made to deal with such crimes by branding and mutilation. When these measures failed, houses of corrections or bridewells were established. The first was established in London in 1553 at St. Brigit's Well (Bridewell), which had previously been a mansion built to house royal visitors. These houses of corrections, or workhouses, were used to house sentenced offenders and provide a place for inmate labor.

It was not until the eighteenth century that the first attempt at jail reform began. Much of the reform in that century can be attributed to the publication of John Howard's *The State of the Prisons in England and Wales with Preliminary Observations and an Account of Some Foreign Prisons in 1777*. Howard, who at that time was a sheriff in Bedford County in England, wrote of the deplorable conditions of jails in Europe. Soon after that publication, Howard, along with Sir William Blackstone and William Eden, authored the Penitentiary Act of 1779, which was passed by Parliament. This act had four basic principles of reform: secure and sanitary structures, systematic inspections, abolition of fees, and a reformatory regime. After stepping down as sheriff, Howard continued to work to improve the sanitary conditions of jails. In a somewhat ironic twist, Howard died of a disease ("jail fever," or typhus) that was common in the unsanitary jails of that time.[16] Many of the reforms that Howard worked so tirelessly to achieve did not occur until long after his death, but his impact was felt throughout Europe as well as in the American colonies.

• Jails in America •

As was the case in England, jails in the Americas remained the responsibility of the local government, most often the sheriff. The fee system found in early English jails was retained in the colonies along with many of the deplorable conditions. It is believed that the first jail in the Americas was established in Jamestown, Virginia, in the early part of the seventeenth century. As was the case in England, jails in America were used largely to hold persons awaiting trial. Punishment was, in many cases, a form of corporal punishment such as whipping posts, stocks, or pillories.

It is important to remember a number of factors about punishment in colonial America. First, in the colonies, the most direct and least expensive form of punishment was most often used. Second, the punishment imposed in the colonies was more humane than that found in Europe.[17] The latter fact was due largely to economic conditions. In the colonies, labor was needed and the citizens were reluctant to execute anyone who had not committed a very serious crime. Europe, in contrast, had high unemployment and a surplus of labor. At one time in England, there were more than 200 crimes that were capital offenses.

Reform in America, as in Europe, was slow in coming. The first serious attempt at reform occurred in Pennsylvania under the direction of William Penn, a leader of the Quakers. Penal reform was at the cornerstone of the Quaker movement, and Penn believed that hard labor in a house of corrections was the most effective way of handling crime. Penn and his followers did not believe in corporal or capital punishment. In 1682, the Quaker code or "great law" was enacted in Pennsylvania. This code emphasized fines and hard labor in a house of corrections for most crimes. During that same time period, the first jail designed to house convicted offenders, the High Street Jail, was opened in Philadelphia. Soon after it opened, it too became overcrowded and it deteriorated. The reform movement that Penn had started died with him in 1718. Pennsylvania, like other colonies, reverted back to corporal punishment for most criminal offenses. Change was not to occur again until the Revolutionary War.

Soon after the end of the Revolutionary War, a number of reformers, including Benjamin Franklin, led a movement to reform the English criminal code of 1718, which had been in effect since the death of William Penn. On September 15, 1786, the new law was enacted that allowed prisoners to be put to work repairing roads and sweeping streets. Prisoners would have their heads shaved or were put in iron collars and chains to distinguish them from others.[18] Soon after this code was enacted, the Quakers formed the Philadelphia Society for Alleviating the Miseries of Public Prisoners. The main goal of the Society was to bring religious services into the Walnut Street Jail, which had been built in 1776 to relieve the poor conditions at Philadelphia's Old Stone Jail.

In 1790, the Society for Alleviating the Miseries of Public Prisons was able to pass legislation that was almost identical to the Penitentiary Act of 1779 in England. The Quakers focused their efforts on reforms at the Walnut Street Jail in Philadelphia. For example, they were able to get females segregated from the male population, separate the most serious prisoners from others in 16 large solitary cells, and abolish the fee system. The society provided food and clothing for all inmates, and medical care was offered weekly.[19] As had occurred before, the conditions soon began to deteriorate. By 1816, the conditions at the Walnut Street Jail had deteriorated back to the condition before the reform. The only exception was that inmates were still segregated by sex and offense.[20]

As state prisons began opening in the late 1700s, those convicted of more serious crimes were housed in these facilities. States that did not have prisons either executed those convicted of serious crimes or confined them in the local jail. Corporal punishment soon began to disappear from America, although the process was gradual. During the mid-nineteenth century, the jailing of persons for debt was generally abolished.[21] At about the same time period, a number of private juvenile facilities began opening in America, the first opening in Boston in 1826, followed closely by Philadelphia in 1828. In 1847, the first state reformatory was opened in Massachusetts.

A bust of William Penn in the Hall of Fame for Great Americans in New York. Penn, a Quaker leader, was instrumental in reforming corrections. The Quaker "great law" emphasized fines and hard labor in a house of corrections for most crimes.

en.wiikipedia.org

JAILS TODAY

The growth of jails in America can best be explained by a careful look at the inmate population growth. Table 4.1 shows the jail population from 1880 until 2006. The data for this table were compiled from U.S. Census, Law Enforcement Assistance Administration, and Bureau of Justice Statistics sources.

It is important to note the explosive growth that has occurred in the jail population especially since 1980. From 1980 until 1990, the population grew by 147 percent, while the growth in the 1970s was only 27 percent. Relative to the U.S. resident population, the jail population more than doubled in 16 years, from 96 inmates per 100,000 residents in 1983 to 222 per 100,000 residents in 1999. At midyear 1999, nearly one in every 450 U.S. residents was in a local jail. From 1995-2005, the number of jail inmates per 100,000 U.S. residents rose from 193 to 256.[22] An interesting number to study when looking at the jail population is the percent of capacity occupied. This number gives

TABLE 4.1
Jail Population

Year	Number of jail inmates
1880	18,686
1890	33,093
1940	99,249
1950	86,492
1960	119,671
1970	129,189
1980	163,994
1983	223,551
1986	274,444
1987	295,873
1988	343,569
1989	395,553
1990	405,320
1991	426,479
1992	444,584
1993	459,804
1994	486,474
1995	507,044
1996	518,492
1997	567,079
1998	592,462
1999	605,943
2000	621,149
2001	631,240
2002	665,475
2003	691,301
2004	713,990
2005	747,529
2006	766,010

Sources: Cahalan, M.W. (1986). "Historical Corrections Statistics in the United States 1850-1984." *Bureau of Justice Statistics Bulletin*. Washington, DC: U.S. Department of Justice; Bureau of Justice Statistics (1995). *Jails and Jail Inmates 1993-1994*. Washington, DC: U.S. Government Printing Office; as quoted in Champion, D.J. (1998) *Corrections in the United States: A Contemporary Perspective*, 183. Upper Saddle River, NJ: Prentice Hall; Gilliard, D.K. (1999). "Prison and Jail Inmates at Midyear 1998." *Bureau of Justice Statistics Bulletin*. Washington, DC: U.S. Government Printing Office; Beck, A.J. (2000). *Prison and Jail Inmates at Midyear 1999*. Washington, DC: U.S. Government Printing Office; Beck, A.J., and J.C. Karberg (2001). "Prison and Jail Inmates at Midyear 2000." *Bureau of Justice Statistics Bulletin*. Washington, DC: U.S. Government Printing Office; and Beck, A.J., J.C. Karberg, and P.M. Harrison (2002). "Prison and Jail Inmates at Midyear 2001." *Bureau of Justice Statistics Bulletin*. Washington, DC: U.S. Government Printing Office; Beck, A.J, J.C Karberg, and P.M. Harrison. "Prison and Jail Inmates at Midyear 2005." *Bureau of Justice Statistics Bulletin*. Washington, DC: U.S. Government Printing Office; Harrison, P.M., and A.J. Beck. "Prison and Jail Inmates at Midyear 2006." *Bureau of Justice Statistics Bulletin*. Washington, DC: U.S. Government Printing Office; Sabol, W.J., T.D. Minton, and P.M. Harrison (2007). "Jail Inmates at Midyear 2006." *Bureau of Justice Statistics Bulletin*. Washington, DC: U.S. Government Printing Office.

us an indication of how crowded our jails are. In 1990, our jails were operating at 104 percent of their rated capacity, meaning that they had 4 percent more inmates than they were rated to hold. Since then, prison crowding has fluctuated. By 1995, the percentage of capacity occupied had dropped to 93 percent; by 1998, it had risen to 97 percent; and by 2001, it was down to 90 percent.[23] The growth in jail capacity during the 12-month period ending on June 29, 2001, was less than the average growth of 25,591 beds every 12 months since midyear 1995, and was less than the growth in beds during 2000 (25,466).[24]

The discussion above leads to an interesting note. How much of the jail construction is driven by population needs versus how much of the population increases are due to increased jail space? A term often heard is "if you build it, they will come" from the popular *Field of Dreams* movie starring Kevin Costner. Often new jails are built that, in fact, double the jail capacity for a given jurisdiction, and within six months that facility is full. Did the crime rate suddenly increase drastically, or did the courts change their practices to utilize newly acquired jail space? We know that crime has been declining gradually since about 1990, but prison and jail populations continue to rise. Much of this increase is due to the more punitive nature of the criminal justice system. Much is also due to the fact that judges, who had few options just a few short years ago, will take advantage of jail space if it is available.

While the jail population is climbing, the number of jails is remaining fairly constant and, in some cases, actually declining. In 1983, there were 3,338 local jail facilities. By 1988, that number had dropped to 3,316, and by 1993 it had dropped even further to 3,304. The midyear 2000 figures showed 3,365 local jails,[25] which indicates an increase. Two factors may explain why the number of jails does not necessarily increase as populations increase; they are regionalization and replacement. Regionalization occurs when two or more governments join forces to build one regional jail serving multiple jurisdictions.[26] When jurisdictions are faced with the rather expensive prospect of replacing an old crowded facility, they often find it cost-effective to pool resources with a neighboring county and build a regional facility. In some areas, as a way to encourage regionalization, the state will reimburse a large portion of the construction cost of the new jail when three or more jurisdictions are involved in such a joint venture.[27] Such arrangements are not without problems. For example, the transportation of inmates to court hearings becomes a problem because they now have to travel to another jurisdiction. Some facilities are dealing with such problems by having video arraignments, by which the inmate and the judge stay in their respective locations and the arraignment takes place before a two-way video link.

The second factor, replacement, occurs when an existing facility is either expanded or replaced with a larger facility. While the number of jails has not changed much in the past 15 years, the size of these jails has increased drastically. The rated capacity of jails in 1990 was 389,171 prisoners, and by 2007, that capacity had risen to 813,502.[28] The number of jails during the same period has risen only slightly. This indicates that existing jails are adding beds or are being replaced by newer, larger facilities.

BOX 4.1

The Andy Griffith Show

"The Andy Griffith Show," which aired on CBS television from 1960-1968, is one of the most popular programs in television history. Even though it ended 40 years ago, the show still has millions of fans; an annual festival in Andy Griffith's hometown of Mount Airy, NC, attracts thousands of visitors. The show depicted two of its principal characters, Sheriff Andy Taylor and his inept deputy, Barney Fife (played by Don Knotts), and their lives and jobs as law enforcers in a fictional southern town called Mayberry.

Crime in Mayberry was as quaint as life there itself, reflective of how television depicted life in the United States throughout most of the 1960s. Crimes like murder, rape, and child molestation did not exist. The social problems that were plaguing America in the 1960s did not find their way into Mayberry. African Americans were either invisible or nonexistent in Mayberry, a highly unrealistic scenario in most Southern towns at the time. The most common offense committed by Mayberry residents was moonshining, and the brew produced by Mayberry moonshiners (unlike actual moonshine) was not the deadly sort that killed or poisoned its consumers.

One could hardly claim that "The Andy Griffith Show" was supposed to serve as a realistic portrait of crime and law enforcement, but some interesting observations can be made about the jail in the show. The jail and courthouse were in the same room. The jail only had two cells, neither of which included a toilet or a sink. The cells were seldom occupied (and often by troublemakers from out of town and criminals), let alone full. The facility was hardly secure, and in addition to housing criminals, was also used as a babysitting facility or as a holding cell for barking dogs. The most frequent occupant was Otis Campbell, a recurring character portrayed by Hal Smith. Otis was the affable and immature town drunk, an alcoholic who was afraid to go home to face his wife when he was inebriated. Although he was a frequent prisoner, Otis was also a good friend of Andy and Barney's. He was allowed to effect his own incarceration and release. Otis even had his own set of keys to the courthouse.

Small-town jails sometimes bore slight resemblances to the Mayberry Jail. Although it was not the case on "The Andy Griffith Show," it was not unusual for the sheriff and his spouse (usually the sheriff was a man) to live at the jail, and it was not unusual for a sheriff's wife to cook for prisoners. Many small-town jails were (and some still are) about as secure as the Mayberry jail. Inmates had little protection from each other, and the jails were hardly escape-proof. Many small-town jails, both then and now, were frequent destinations for alcoholics with sad home lives, like Otis Campbell. Unlike the comical Otis, many such frequent visitors to local jails were and still are examples of one of the uglier sides of American life. Alcoholics and those addicted to other drugs, that like Otis Campbell often find themselves constantly in and out of local jails present a problem to jail administrators, the courts, and mental health systems; to their own health; and to the lives of their families. It is a problem that still has not been solved and shows little sign of being solved.

JAIL INMATE CHARACTERISTICS

There were a reported 780,581 inmates housed in American jails on June 30, 2006, an increase of more than 14,000 from the previous year and more than 270,000 from 1995.[29] Table 4.2 shows that in 2007, 100,572 of the jail inmates were females. Women in jail face a number of unique problems. Not only do they face the shock of incarceration, but they must often face the shock of losing contact with their children. More than 65 percent of women in jails have children under the age of 18.[30] Two-thirds of these women were living with their children before entering jail. While a vast majority of these children will be placed with either their father or a close relative, almost 10 percent are placed in foster care or some other institutional setting.[31] Males also suffer the shock of losing contact with their children. While not as prevalent as studies on the impact on women, studies are being undertaken to look at the impact on fathers separated from their children while in jail or prison.[32] Not only must the parent deal with the loss of the child, the child is faced with dealing with the loss of a mother or father. Thus, the sanctions imposed on the parents are imposed on the children as well.

TABLE 4.2
Average Daily Population and Number of Men, Women, and Juveniles in Local Jails, Midyear 1990, 1995, 2000, and 2007

	1990	1995	2000	2007
Average daily population[a]	408,075	509,828	618,319	773,800
Number of inmates, June 30[b]	405,320	507,044	621,149	780,581
Adults	403,019	499,300	613,534	773,744
Male	365,821	448,000	543,120	680,009
Female	37,198	51,300	70,414	100,572
Juveniles[c]	2,301	7,800	7,615	6,837
Held as adults[d]	—	5,900	6,126	3,652
Held as juveniles	2,301	1,800	1,489	1,185

Note: Data are for June 30 in 1995 and 2000 and for June 29 in 1990 and 2001. Detailed data for 1995 were estimated and rounded to the nearest 100.

— Not available.

[a] The average daily population is the sum of the number of inmates in a jail each day for a year, divided by the total number of days in the year.

[b] Inmate counts for 1990 include an unknown number of persons who were under jail supervision but not confined.

[c] Juveniles are persons defined by State statute as being under a certain age, usually 18, and subject initially to juvenile court authority even if tried as adults in criminal court. In 1994 the definition was changed to include all persons under age 18.

[d] Includes juveniles who were tried or awaiting trial as adults.

Sources: Beck, A.J., J.C. Karberg, and P.M. Harrison (2002). "Prison and Jail Inmates at Midyear 2001." *Bureau of Justice Statistics Bulletin*. Washington DC: U.S. Government Printing Office, 9; Sabol, W.J., and T.D. Minton (2008). "Jail Inmates at Midyear 2007." *Bureau of Justice Statistics Bulletin*. Washington, DC: U.S. Government Printing Office, 5.

Women are more likely than men to have been the victim of physical or sexual abuse. Almost half of all women in jail reported being physically or sexually abused prior to admission. Table 4.3 shows the percentage of jail inmates in 1996 who had been physically or sexually abused before admission.

TABLE 4.3
Physical or Sexual Abuse Before Current Admission

Abuse before admission	Percentage of Jail Inmates		
	Total	Male	Female
Ever	18.2%	13.4%	55.3%
Before age 18	10.9%	9.7%	20.3%
After age 18	4.9%	2.3%	25.2%
Physically abused	15.1%	11.2%	44.9%
Sexually abused	7.7%	4.0%	35.9%

Source: James, D.J. (2004). "Profile of Jail Inmates 2002." *Bureau of Justice Statistics Special Report*. Washington, DC: U.S. Government Printing Office, 10.

Accounting for a little more than 12 percent of the total jail population, women face a number of other problems as well. In general, programs are rather scarce in jails, but the problem is intensified for women. With so few female inmates, jails are faced with offering programs that meet the needs of the majority of their inmates. Once again, women find themselves at the short end of the stick. On average, women spend about 17 hours per day in their cells, and are less likely than their male counterparts to have work assignments.[33] In addition, their medical needs are often not addressed. The American Correctional Association points out, "There is a lack of gynecological care for jailed women and seldom any special health care for pregnant women; use of contraceptive pills is often interrupted because they are not available in jail."[34]

The vast majority of women serving sentences in jails are in facilities that also house male inmates. There is a small but growing number of jail facilities that are exclusively for women. Gray and her colleagues identified 18 such jails in the United States in the mid-1990s.[35] While one might think that such facilities designed to house females would offer specific programs and treatments that meet the particular needs of women, their study found that the programming in these women's jails was "woefully inadequate."[36]

The racial composition of American jails is another important population characteristic. Jails, like prisons, house a disproportionate number of minority inmates in comparison to their distribution in the general population. In 2007, black, non-Hispanic inmates made up 39 percent of the jail population, while white, non-Hispanic inmates made up 43 percent of the jail population. The Hispanic population was 16 percent of the total jail population.[37] According to a *Bureau of Justice Statistics Bulletin*, at midyear 2007, relative to their number of U.S. residents, black non-Hispanics were five times more likely than white non-Hispanics, more than two and a half times more likely than Hispanics, and 11 times more likely than persons of other races to have been in jail.[38]

In order to get a clear picture of the jail population in America, one can look at the jail incarceration rates. These rates are based on the number of jailed inmates per 100,000 U.S. residents. Since 1990, the nation's jail population on a per capita basis has increased by more than one-third.[39] At yearend 2006, the nation's prisons and jails held one in every 131 U.S. residents.[40] These numbers do not reflect the many individuals who pass in and out of jail each year, some staying for only a few hours. Much of this turnover is concentrated during peak periods, such as Friday and Saturday evenings.

THE ROLE OF THE JAIL IN THE AMERICAN CRIMINAL JUSTICE SYSTEM

As mentioned earlier, jails were originally conceived as places to hold pretrial detainees until their appearance in court. While much of the inmate population in jails fits that classification, many others fit into some other category. According to the Bureau of Justice Statistics, jails perform the following functions:

1. Receive individuals pending arraignment and hold them awaiting trial, conviction, or sentencing.

2. Readmit probation, parole, and bail-bond violators and absconders.

3. Temporarily detain juveniles pending transfer to juvenile authorities.

4. Hold mentally ill persons pending their movement to appropriate health facilities.

5. Hold individuals for the military, for protective custody, for contempt, and for the courts as witnesses.

6. Release convicted inmates to the community upon completion of sentence.

7. Transfer inmates to federal, state, or other authorities.

8. House inmates for federal, state, or other authorities because of crowding of their facilities.

9. Sometimes operate community-based programs as alternative to incarceration.

10. Hold inmates sentenced to short terms (generally under one year).[41]

As mentioned in the list above, jails supervise offenders outside jail facilities in a number of programs, such as community service, electronic monitoring, work release, and other alternative programs. At midyear 2006, local jail authorities supervised 60,222 offenders outside jail facilities. This number, like so many others, has grown drastically. In 1995, that number was 34,869, so in 10 years, supervision outside a jail facility grew dramatically.[42] Table 4.4 shows the types of programs and the number of offenders in each.

TABLE 4.4
Persons Under Jail Supervision But Not Confined, by Type of Program

Type of Program	2001	2006
Electronic monitoring	10,017	10,999
Home detention (without electronic monitoring)	539	807
Day reporting	3,522	4,841
Community service	17,561	14,667
Weekender programs	14,381	11,421
Other pretrial supervision	6,632	6,409
Other work programs	5,204	8,319
Treatment programs	5,219	1,486
Other/unspecified	7,729	1,273

Source: Beck, A.J., J.C. Karberg, and P.M. Harrison (2002). "Prison and Jail Inmates at Midyear 2001." *Bureau of Justice Statistics Bulletin*. Washington, DC: U.S. Government Printing Office, 8. Sabol, W.J., T.D. Minton, and P.M. Harrison (2007). "Prison and Jail Inmates at Midyear 2006." *Bureau of Justice Statistics Bulletin*, 8. Washington, DC: U.S. Government Printing Office.

• Pretrial Detainees •

More than half of all people housed in jails are pretrial detainees. Such individuals have been arrested for a wide assortment of offenses and, for one reason or another, are either unable to afford or are denied bail. As such, they are housed in the local jail until trial. Pretrial detainees present some unique circumstances with which jail administrators must contend. Our justice system is based on the principle of "innocent until proven guilty." Pretrial detainees have not been convicted (proven guilty), but are often housed in the same cells as those serving sentences. Jail administrators have little control over the number of convicted misdemeanants sent to their facilities, but efforts have been undertaken to limit both the number of pretrial detainees and to shorten their stay. In 1974, Congress passed the Speedy Trial Act, which mandated that federal charges must be filed against a defendant within 30 days of the arrest. A preliminary hearing must be held within 10 days of that date, and the trial must begin within 60 days of the arraignment. While states are not bound by the Speedy Trial Act, the Sixth Amendment of the Constitution claims that "the accused shall enjoy the right to a speedy and public trial." Many states have adopted legislation similar to the federal Speedy Trial Act.

State laws vary on how quickly a newly arrested suspect has to wait before making an appearance before a judge or magistrate. In *County of Riverside v. McLaughlin*, the United States Supreme Court heard a challenge to a county policy that required defendants to face a magistrate within 48 hours of their arrest, excluding weekends. The Supreme Court affirmed this policy, indicating that any jurisdiction that followed a similar policy would be adhering to Constitutional standards.[43]

Another method of reducing the number of pretrial detainees is to release inmates on bail. The Eighth Amendment to the Constitution states that "excessive bail shall not be required . . ." The original purpose of bail was to ensure that the defendant would appear for trial. A problem is that those who can afford it will pay the bail and be released, while only those who are unable to pay will stay in jail. These are not necessarily the more dangerous offenders and are often the individuals who possess the least risk of flight. A number of reforms have added to the problem as well. In 1984, the Bail Reform Act was passed. One of the provisions of the Bail Reform Act, which was affirmed by the U.S. Supreme Court in *United States v. Salerno et al.* permitted judges to deny bail to those charged with a violent crime, those charged with crimes that carried a possible life sentence, those charged with crimes that carried a possible death sentence, those charged with some major drug offenses, and those defendants charged with a felony who have a serious past criminal record.[44]

• Misdemeanants •

A second function of jails is to house offenders serving short-term sentences. Offenders convicted of misdemeanors and sentenced by the local courts to incarceration for a period of less than one year (in most jurisdictions) typically serve their sentence in a local jail. A number of states house misdemeanants for up to two years. In 1998, about 43 percent of all inmates in jail were serving sentences. This percentage has fluctuated in the past decade. In 1994, the percentage of all inmates in jail serving sentences was 49 percent.[45] Since that time, the percentage has been declining; in 2002, the figure stood at 43 percent.[46]

The average time served by inmates in local jails tells an interesting story. For example, the average sentence length for persons serving time in local jails in 2002 was 24 months,[47] even though most states purport to limit the time served in jail to one year. To understand this information, one must understand two facts. First, remember that the data for such reports is collected on a single day of each year: June 30. Those persons who serve shorter sentences leave jail more quickly, resulting in a longer reported average sentence (those with short sentences are less likely to be interviewed). A second factor is that while the rule is to house only those inmates who are serving sentences of less than a year, in practice, with prison crowding, many inmates are serving longer sentences in the local jails. Another interesting factor is the median sentence. Fifty percent of the inmates serve sentences less than the median and 50 percent serve sentences greater than that amount. In 2002 , the median maximum sentence length was eight months.[48] When you take into account the time already served and the expected date of release, about one-half of those sentenced to jail are expected to serve six months or less.[49]

• Felons •

Jails also house inmates convicted of felonies who are awaiting transfer to a state or federal prison. In some cases, these inmates have been found guilty of a felony and are waiting for the court to sentence them, often after a presentence investigation (PSI) is undertaken. In most such cases, the local jail is reimbursed by either the state or federal government for housing the individual.

Today, jails find themselves holding convicted felons for longer periods of time, due to crowding at state and federal prisons. If sufficient bed space is not available to accommodate an inmate, the state or federal government may enter into a leasing agreement with the local jail to house the inmate. In 1994, an estimated 61,200 jail inmates were being held for other authorities.[50] About 6 percent of jail inmates were being held for state correctional authorities and 2 percent for federal agencies.

Jails are also finding themselves being used by the courts as a sentencing option for convicted felons. Between 1986 and 1992 alone, the number of convicted felons who were sentenced to confinement in local jails almost doubled and the number continues to increase.[51] These convicted felons sentenced to jail amounted to 30 percent in 2002, up from 26 percent in 1992, and up from 21 percent in 1986.[52]

Research has been undertaken to look at the effect of determinate sentencing laws on jail use.[53] One study found that the implementation of determinate sentencing guidelines increased the judicial use of jail sanctions. Due in part to overcrowding in state prisons, judges often circumvent these new laws as a mechanism to shift the burden of incarcerating offenders from the state to the local level.[54]

• Juveniles •

Jails often find themselves housing juvenile offenders when no juvenile detention facility is available in a jurisdiction. Many juveniles find themselves in adult facilities despite a mandate in the federal Juvenile Justice and Delinquency Prevention Act that banned the jailing of juveniles.[55]

Juveniles present a number of problems for jail administrators. First, the Juvenile Justice and Delinquency Prevention Act of 1974 requires that any juvenile housed in a jail receive sight and sound separation from the adult population. The act states that juveniles "shall not be detained or confined in any institution in which they have regular contact with adult persons incarcerated because they have been convicted of a crime or are awaiting trial on criminal charges."[56] This provision of the Act was interpreted to mean that juveniles could be held in adult jails as long as there was sight and sound separation. Often this means that juveniles will find themselves in solitary confinement because this is the only place in many small jails in which sight and sound separation can be ensured. Such arrangements can have an impact on the number of suicides in jail, as we will see below.

On June 30, 2006, there were 6,104 people under age 18 held in local jails, down from 9,615 in 2000. The majority, of these juveniles were being held as adults. These juveniles are either awaiting trial as an adult or have already been tried as an adult, and are either serving their sentence in jail or awaiting transfer to another facility. A minority were being held in local jails as juveniles. These numbers represent one-day totals and tell nothing of the thousands of juveniles who pass through adult jails each year.[57]

While the issue of jailing juveniles in adult jails is not as hot a topic today as it was a few years ago, the following recommendations by Schwartz are still timely:

1. The most effective way to eliminate the jailing of juveniles is to enact legislation prohibiting the practice under any circumstances. Such legislation, as was the case in Pennsylvania, should include a grace period so that the deed could be accomplished within a reasonable time period.

2. Experience has shown that there are a variety of policies and community-based alternatives to jailing that can be implemented without significantly increasing the risk to the community. Also, many of these options can be implemented at relatively low cost. For example, one of the most effective strategies for limiting juvenile jailing would be to develop and utilize objective detention intake criteria, particularly those recommended by the National Juvenile Justice Advisory Committee. In addition, such programs as home detention, family-operated shelter care, report centers, and staff-operated shelter care have proved to be effective options.

3. There are some juveniles who need to be detained pending their court appearance. Experience has demonstrated that the number of youths who fall into this category is relatively small. Because of this, and because secure detention facilities are costly to build and operate, a careful and comprehensive needs assessment should be completed to determine how many secure beds may be needed in a particular jurisdiction or jurisdictions, and how those needs can be met best.[58]

Schwartz and his colleagues[59] go even further to make the recommendation that legislation should be passed to make the jailing of juveniles a crime. Of even greater concern is the jailing of female juveniles. In some areas, females account for as many as one-quarter of the juveniles admitted to adult facilities, and a vast majority of these female juveniles are of no risk to the community.[60]

• Others •

There is a large percentage of persons held in local jails that do not fit into any of the categories enumerated above. Examples are the mentally ill or homeless, who are often housed in jails for their own protection and welfare. Such inmates have been referred to as the "rabble" of society, the "disorganized" and "disorderly," or the "lowest class of people."[61] It has been estimated that about 670,000 mentally ill people are admitted to U.S. jails each year.[62] These mentally ill are often jailed because there are no community-based treatment programs to accommodate them. Jails are not equipped to handle the needs of such inmates. Studies have shown that jail administrators cite mental health services as one of the most serious institutional needs.[63]

Jails also hold probation and parole violators. Such persons are entitled to a hearing to determine whether their probation or parole should be revoked, but if they are suspected of committing a serious crime, they are often held in jail. These violators share many of the characteristics of the pretrial detainee. Another group of persons held in jail are wanted for crimes in other states. Often they are stopped for traffic violations and it is discovered that a warrant has been issued from another jurisdiction. They are often taken to jail until extradition proceedings can take place.

As can be seen, jails often act as "catch-all asylums for poor people."[64] If no other outlet exists, jails must pick up the slack. They have to provide for the wide variety of persons who move in and out of their facility.

JAIL DESIGN

Jails in America have gone through a number of distinct design stages in the past quarter century. While there are many variations, it is useful to divide jail design into three different classifications: traditional jails, second-generation jails, and new-generation jails. Each of these designs is based on a number of underlying philosophies, presenting a number of important distinctions. While we can classify most jails into one of the three design categories, it is important to remember that most jails in the United States are relatively small and, as such, are limited in design options. In 1995, more than 55 percent of American jails housed fewer than 50 inmates.[65] Many of these jails house 10 or fewer inmates.[66] At the other end of the spectrum are the nation's largest jails. In 2004, the nation's 50 largest jail jurisdictions accounted for one-third of all jail inmates.[67] Jails in Los Angeles, New York, Phoenix, Chicago, and Houston together housed approximately 60,000 inmates on any given day, more than 25 percent of the national total. While we can clas-

Ellen S. Boyne

Located a little south of Seattle in Kent, Washington, King County Regional Justice Center comprises a direct supervision jail with a rated capacity of around 900. In contrast to traditional jails, new-generation jails such as this house groups of inmates together in a unit or pod arranged around a common multipurpose area.

sify most jails into one of the three designs, many jails are hybrids that do not fit perfectly into any of the three listed categories.

• Traditional Jails •

Most jails in America are traditional in design. These jails, also referred to as having the linear design, have a long history dating back to the time of the Walnut Street Jail in Philadelphia. Traditional jails house inmates in cells situated along corridors. The staff must monitor inmates by walking the corridors in front of each cell block. This design type is often referred to as intermittent surveillance design. When staff are not present in the corridors, the inmates enjoy a free rein in their cells. Thus, the staff cannot monitor all of the inmates in a housing unit at one time; they can provide only what is referred to as intermittent surveillance.[68] Fighting and other behavioral problems can occur between these intermittent patrols.

Inmates will often watch out for the jailer and warn others when he or she is coming. The familiar image of inmates holding mirrors from their cells to observe the corridor is a striking example of this reality. As one might imagine, these linear designs present a number of security issues. In 1996, 14 percent of all inmates had been involved in a fight or hit or punched since entering jail.[69] This number represented one in five inmates 24 years of age or younger, and about one in 10 inmates age 35 or older. So how safe are jails? When asked, 57 percent of jail inmates felt as safe or safer in jail than the streets where they had lived.[70]

The linear design is clearly the most dangerous for inmates. This was exemplified by a 1960s account by a female inmate in the Cook County Jail in Illinois. The inmate, Dorothy West, was labeled a snitch by other inmates, and fearing for her safety, had requested protective custody. The jail personnel had only laughed at her. Later that night, West was attacked by eight other inmates.

> Rudy's first blow caught me on the side of my head. As soon as she hit me, a scream went up from the others. "Kill the stool-pigeon bitch." All eight of them fell on me at once. Somebody set fire to my skirt, and my nylon petticoat went up in flames. I tried to beat at my burning legs, but they were banging my head against the bars. I felt my nose crumple, and start to gush blood. I fell and they kicked me repeatedly in the left eye. They kicked my breasts and jumped up and down on me. Then somebody pulled off my panties, thrust them into my mouth as a gag, and I was raped. My hair was burning and I could feel the skin on my forehead crack and begin to peel. I'm told the beating went on for an hour.[71]

The materials used to build these traditional jails are designed to hold up to the most intense punishment. The toilet facilities and beds are not designed for aesthetics but for durability and function. Light fixtures are either encased in metal or are outside the actual cell to prevent inmates from having access to them. These hardened fixtures are often very expensive. As a consequence of hardened fixtures and concrete floors and walls, the traditional jail is very noisy because the floors and walls do not absorb sound. When metal doors clang shut, their sound reverberates throughout the facility.

The noise level and lack of supervision add to the stress that inmates face when confined to a traditional jail. Inmates, who are already experiencing stress, frequently exhibit signs of psychopathy soon after their arrival in jail when they find themselves locked up in a noisy and often hostile environment.[72]

• Second-Generation Jails •

"Second-generation" is the term given to jails that have remote or indirect surveillance of inmates. This design has been put into use in many areas and is, in many cases, the design used for new facilities. Under the remote design, cells are situated around a central dayroom, and jail personnel occupy a secure control room that overlooks the dayroom and the individual cells. While they have a number of design improvements over traditional jails, these second-generation jails often limit the verbal interactions between inmates and jail personnel. Communication between inmates and jail personnel is frequently undertaken through an intercom. While the inmates are more closely monitored in second-generation jails than in traditional jails, most such jails still employ high-security fixtures, furnishings, and finishes.[73]

• New-Generation Jails •

The design of new-generation jails began with an effort by the U.S. Bureau of Prisons in the mid-1960s. The government commissioned three architectural firms to design three new federal jail facilities in Chicago, New York City, and San Diego. These architectural firms were given three criteria: single cells for inmates, direct supervision by staff, and functional living units.[74] The concept of direct supervision, by which staff and inmates share a common area, had practical significance. No longer were inmates locked in cells with other inmates out of sight from jail personnel. In these new-generation jails, inmates and staff share the facility, with jail personnel in constant contact with the inmates. Jail personnel actually occupy a space within the dayroom or housing pod.[75] Each living unit is made up of manageable groups of between 16 and 46 inmates. The ultimate goal of the new-generation jail is to provide a safe, violence-free environment for both inmates and staff that treats inmates in a humane fashion.[76]

The concept of functional living units was significant. In such units, all sleeping, food, hygiene, and recreational facilities are located in a self-contained unit. A number of benefits have been identified with these functional units. For example, program flexibility is increased. Because they are self-contained units, programming needs for the specific group of inmates can be met without affecting the total institution.[77] These units also increase the frequency of contacts and intensity of the relationship between staff and inmates.[78]

New-generation jails also have the advantage of lower building costs. As mentioned above, traditional and second-generation jails use a more costly high-security design for their furnishings, fixtures, and finishes. As jail personnel are sharing the living space with inmates, less expensive, commercial-grade fixtures can be utilized. Nelson determined that savings in building costs for a single unit housing 48 inmates would be very substantial when compared to a traditional jail. While there is a substantial savings in the original building cost, there is a savings in the operating cost as well. With inmates and staff in constant contact with one another, the incidences of vandalism and graffiti are greatly decreased. An example is the Contra Costa County Detention Center in California, the first local jail facility to incorporate the new-generation design. Administrators there claim that in the older traditional design facility in that county they had to paint the facility every year, but with the new facility a fresh coat of paint was not needed until after five years of operation.[79] New-generation jails also incorporate carpeting and acoustical tile to reduce the noise level and add to the aesthetics of the environment. Instead of steel gates and bars, solid walls and doors with impenetrable glass are used.

Staffing is another important issue with new-generation jails. Two questions must be addressed when looking at staffing. Do jail personnel prefer the new-generation jail over the more traditional designs? Is there a savings in the number of personnel needed to staff these new facilities? The answer to the first question seems to be yes. Although it is difficult to measure at an absolute level, studies have found that jail personnel seem to prefer working at these new facilities. For example, in a study reported by Nelson,[80] the National Institute of Corrections found that sick leave taken in the new-generation jails was significantly less than the average leave taken in the four other houses of detention. In fact, the savings amounted to about 1,810 staff days, or the equivalent of eight full-time positions.

As to whether staffing is reduced, there seems to be no definitive answer. Often the level of staffing is tied to state jail standards and, as such, will not change with a new-generation jail. In other cases, a substantial savings could be found. In Dade County, Florida, it was found that only half the staff was required to operate the new direct-supervision facility compared to the older linear jail.[81] Much of the answer to this question is dependant on the efficiency and size of the traditional jail. Often direct comparisons cannot be made because jurisdictions replacing an existing traditional jail with a new generation jail will build a much larger facility.

New-generation jails are not just about architecture and cost savings. It is important to remember that the new-generation philosophy includes the process of direct inmate supervision. Six objectives have been identified for direct inmate supervision:

1. Staff, rather than inmates, will control the facility and inmates' behavior;

2. Inmates will be directly and continuously supervised, and custodial staff, rather than inmates, will direct and control the behavior of all inmates;

3. Rewards and punishments will be structured to ensure compliant inmate behavior;

4. Open communication will be maintained between the custodial staff and inmates, and between staff members;

5. Inmates will be advised of the expectations and rules of the facility; and

6. Inmates will be treated in a manner consistent with "constitutional standards and other applicable codes and court decisions," and will be treated equitably and fairly regardless of their personal characteristics or the reasons for which they are in jail.[82]

Correctional staff in new-generation jails must be trained to use a number of sophisticated human relations skills such as conflict management and problem solving.[83] This is in stark contrast to the traditional custodial skills now taught, such as physical control techniques and fire-

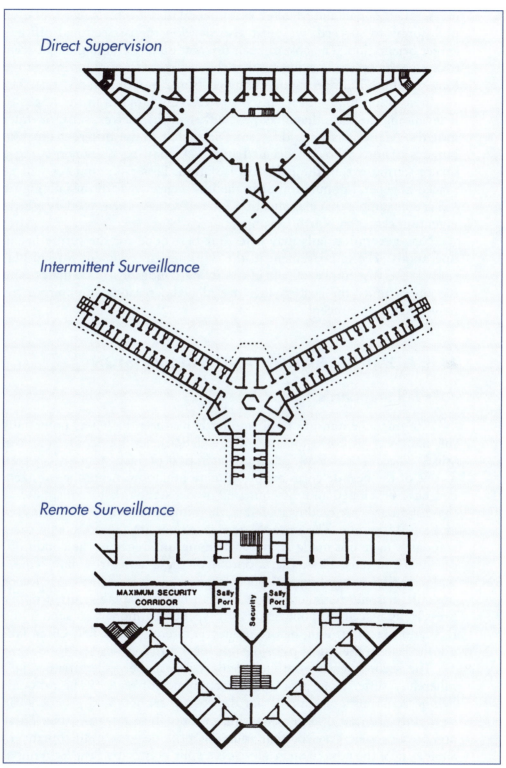

Direct Supervision

Intermittent Surveillance

Remote Surveillance

MAXIMUM SECURITY CORRIDOR   Sally Port   Security   Sally Port

Figure 4.1
Typical Jail Designs

arms usage. Zupan and Menke[84] recommend that, for the new-generation philosophy to succeed, we must also develop the correctional officer's career orientation. The cost of such orientation and training might seem excessive, but there is evidence that there is a substantial savings in the long run, both in lowering operating costs and in reducing lawsuits.

In addition many local jails interview new inmates in the hopes of determining the risks they may pose either to themselves, staff, or other inmates. Many jails have different wings that house different types of inmates. Those who are deemed high-risk may be placed in a more secure setting within the jail or in isolation. Less risky inmates will be placed in general population or in the less secure areas of the jail. Figure 4.2 is an example of a classification interview instrument used by a local detention center in North Carolina.

New-generation jails may offer our best hope for the future in jail operations. The improvement in the working environment for jail personnel, the vast improvement in the living conditions for inmates, and the opportunity for cost savings are all valid reasons to embrace the new-generation concept.

JAIL ADMINISTRATION AND SUPERVISION

• Jail Standards •

The implementation of jail standards has been hailed as potentially the best way to correct many of the deficiencies found in American jails.[85] The development and implementation of such standards is seen as one of the best defenses against inmate litigation. A number of agencies have developed and disseminated model standards for jails.[86] While these standards are readily available, their implementation has been slow at best. Mays and Thompson[87] give three possible reasons why these standards have not made an overwhelming difference in the conditions of American jails. First, the adoption of these standards may require major capital expenditures.[88] Such large expenditures just may not be possible in some jurisdictions. Where money is available, often public pressure is placed on policymakers to spend tax money on school and recreation facilities long before money is filtered into a jail. Often jails are the last on the list of priorities for local jurisdictions.

The second reason outlined deals with smaller jails. Smaller jails inherently suffer from problems of economics of scale.[89] The rationale behind economics of scale is that the cost of services and products can be greatly reduced if larger quantities are purchased at one time. There are certain basic services that must be provided for each inmate. In smaller jails the cost of such services is split between a smaller number of inmates, and in larger jails, by a larger number of inmates. The same rationale holds for many treatment programs. It is not feasible for many small jails to offer such programs with too few inmates. For example, for a small jail to provide medical care, it must divide the initial cost among only a small number of inmates. In a large metropolitan jail (such as Cook County, which houses more than 9,000 inmates), however, the

How did you end up at the Pitt County Detention Center? _____

_____

Have you ever been convicted of a felony? _____
How many? _____

What was your most violent conviction? _____

Have you served time with the Department of Correction?_____ If so, what was the charge/crime? _____

Do you drink alcoholic beverages? _____

Has drinking ever caused you any legal problems or to be arrested? _____

Has drinking ever caused you to hurt anyone? _____

Have you ever used drugs of any type? _____

Have you ever committed a crime under the influence of drugs or alcohol? _____

Have you ever hurt anyone while using drugs? _____

Have you ever been confined to a mental institution? _____

If so, what institution(s) and why? _____

_____

Have you ever been und_____

Have you ever received dr_____

Assessment date: _____

Classification Officer: _____

Interviewer's comments: _____

CLASSIFICATION INTERVIEW QUESTIONS

DATE: _____

Inmate Name: _____
           Last   First   Middle
Social Security Number: ___/___/___   Race/Sex: _____ AGE: _____

Current Address: _____ How Long: _____

_____

Education Achieved: _____
                    Elementary/High School/GED/College

Did you have a job/were you a student when entering the Pitt County Detention Center? _____ How Long: _____
Where: _____

Do you have any health problems that would limit housing or work assignments? Are you subject to any type of seizures? _____

Do you have any trouble walking up or down stairs? _____
Do you know anyone at the Pitt County Detention Center with whom you might have problems? : _____
If   so,   what   are   the   names?

Is there anyone here at the PCDC that you "hang around with" on the outside? _____

_____

Have you had any recent stressful experiences (such as loss of a loved one, divorce, loss of a job, major health problems, serious financial problems, etc)?: _____

_____

Have you ever attempted or contemplated suicide? _____
Are you now feeling or think you may attempt suicide? _____

Figure 4.2
Classification Interview Questions

cost is divided among a large number of inmates so that the relative cost per inmate is small. The rationale holds true for many services, such as food and supplies and, to a certain extent, labor costs. The jail standards place a huge burden on the resources of these small jails.

The third reason that the implementation of these jail standards has been slow is that even if they are put in place, rarely do mechanisms exist to enforce them.[90] Without the legislative authority to conduct inspections and enforce compliance of these standards, true change is unlikely to take place.

A number of organizations are devoted to the continued improvement and operation of local jails. These organizations are also dedicated to improving training and professionalism among jail staff. They act as information resources for jail administrators. These organizations include the American Jail Association, www.aja.org, and the American Correctional Association, www.aca.org. In addition, the National Sheriff's Association, www.sheriffs.org, collects and disseminates information on jails.

The ideal approach would be for states to develop jail standards. Short of that, it is necessary for local jail administrators to move toward the implementation of jail standards at the local level or face the possibility that the court will, at some point, force compliance.

• Legal Issues •

One of the most pressing problems facing jail administrators today and in the future is the issue of inmate lawsuits. Inmate lawsuits have the potential of costing local governments millions of dollars. Inmates have sued for such rights as mail censorship, cell searches, and inmate discipline. While most would claim that the courts have been moving back in the direction of the hands-off era, there is still substantial risk of liability. As discussed in Chapter 3, prisoner litigation has gone through three major periods in our history. The first, referred to as the hands-off period, was in existence until about 1964. Before 1964, inmates enjoyed few rights and were often referred to as being civilly dead, having few, if any, rights in the eyes of the court. Recall that in 1964, the U.S. Supreme Court held in *Cooper v. Pate* that state prisoners could bring lawsuits against correctional officials under Title 42 U.S.C. Section 1983, the Civil Rights Act. This case came on the heels of *Monroe v. Pape* (1961), which held that abuse of state-delegated authority constituted action under color of law for purposes of Section 1983 jurisdiction. Such lawsuits provided a remedy for deprivation of civil rights. This period of activity by the courts in issues of inmate rights has been referred to as the hands-on period.

After *Cooper v. Pate*, the flood gates were opened for inmate litigation. The federal court reviewed numerous cases and ruled in favor of inmates on a number of important issues. Cases were decided that affirmed that prisoners still retain certain fundamental rights relative to speech, religious freedom, the right to access the courts, the right to equal protection under the law, the right to due process, and to be free from cruel and unusual punishment. Most such cases were filed under the Title 42 U.S.C. Section 1983 lawsuits, but there are two other major avenues that jail inmates can follow for filing lawsuits: habeas corpus petitions and mandamus actions.[91]

The rationale for such suits is that administrators at all levels are responsible for the actions of subordinates. If it can be shown, either through neglect in hiring, training, or retention, that the administration or county officials should have been aware of inappropriate actions by their subordinates, then they can be held liable. When something happens, both the jail employee and the supervisor are responsible. Section 1983 suits are the most prevalent jail inmate litigation mechanisms.[92]

Habeas corpus lawsuits are the second most prevalent form of inmate suit filed. Under habeas corpus lawsuits, inmates challenge either the legality of their confinement or the conditions of confinement.[93] A person who is confined can use this writ to obtain a hearing regarding the legality of his or her detention. In 1944 the courts ruled in *Coffin v. Reichard* that inmates are entitled to habeas corpus relief, even though they are lawfully held, if it is shown that they have been deprived of some right to which they are entitled.[94]

The final major avenue of inmate lawsuits, mandamus actions, are often filed to compel jail personnel to perform their administrative duties. If a jail is under a court order to provide a service or reduce crowding and the jail fails to carry out that order, a mandamus action can be sought. Due to the nature of the jail population, mandamus actions are problematic. Often the inmate who is filing the mandamus action is no longer in the facility when the case finally reaches the court. Lawyers often file class action suits rather than individual suits in order to avert such problems.

The hands-on period lasted until the mid-1980s. Since the mid-1980s, the courts have moved toward a more restrained judicial approach to correctional litigation, what is referred to in Chapter 3 as the due deference phase. While not retreating back to the hands-off period prior to the 1960s, the court has shown an unwillingness to jump as deeply into inmate issues as they had. It is important to remember that the active role that the courts played in the 1960s, 1970s, and early 1980s provided a number of benefits to both inmates and jail personnel. Many of the improvements that have been made in jail administration and design can be attributed to the active role of the courts. Such lawsuits and intervention by the courts have forced local jurisdictions to take a serious look at the facilities and training afforded their staff. While large settlements are not the norm, such threats have forced local jurisdictions to look seriously at both their physical plants and their training procedures.

The best approach to litigation is to avoid the conditions for which lawsuits are brought. Jail administrators should design and run their facility in a preventive fashion.[95] Sechrest and Collins[96] offer jail administrators and jail personnel an alternative to simply dealing with lawsuits as they occur: they recommend that steps should be taken to avoid the possibility of lawsuits.

• Jail Personnel •

Many lawsuits that have been filed can be attributed to the deliberate indifference of jail personnel to the inmates they supervise.[97] Such a fact underscores the importance of training and supervision of jail personnel. In fact, when asked, jail administrators rank personnel concerns as second only to crowding as the major obstacle facing them.[98] Added to the problem are staff shortages in local jails that occur as a result of the "poor image of jail work and inadequate career incentives."[99]

What has led to the personnel problems in local jails? More importantly, what can be done? As pointed out earlier, in many jurisdictions, the local jail is operated by the county. The person most often responsible for the jail's operation is the county sheriff. The local sheriff has a large number of responsibilities, only one of which is the administration of the local jail. In most jurisdictions, the sheriff is an elected official who may or may not have law enforcement experience. For the most part, the public has one of two attitudes toward jails: at best, indifference; at worst, a strongly negative view.[100] As such, jails are often found at the bottom of the sheriff's list of priorities as well as at the bottom of funding lists. The local sheriff, like most elected officials, wants to appease the residents of his or her jurisdiction. The most visible way to accomplish this is to put more deputies out on the street, patrolling the neighborhoods, making arrests, and answering citizens' calls for service. As long as there are no major problems in the jail, such as a riot or escape, the public is often unwilling to put forth any efforts for jail improvements.

Jail work is often seen as less desirable than work as a deputy sheriff. Those working in jails may hope to move into the more lucrative and much higher-status deputy positions. Jail duty is often seen as only a temporary position. There are some cases in which the jail is staffed with deputies who are being punished for violating a departmental rule.[101] Such punishment does little to improve the image of jail work as a career move.

In an effort to change this image, a number of jurisdictions have added a second career track exclusively for correctional officers. While this first step is important, as early as 1982, the National Sheriffs' Association acknowledged that "jail officer careers will never achieve the status they deserve so long as counties continue to pay jail officers less money than the officers assigned to police duties."[102] Within the sheriff's office, jail personnel are often seen as second-class citizens. Adding to this image is the fact that jail personnel receive less training than their law enforcement counterparts, plus the environment in which they work is often less than desirable. Jail personnel suffer from a lack of potential advancement as well. Correctional officers account for more than 76 percent of all jail personnel, with promotions to supervisory positions highly competitive and sometimes nonexistent.[103]

It is interesting to look at the trends in expenditures for local police protection and corrections over time. From 1980 to 2003, annual corrections expenditures increased from $4.2 million to $36.9 million.[104] While expenditures in corrections increased substantially in that period, there is still a large gap in starting salaries between correctional officers and sheriff deputies. In Harris County (Houston), Texas, the starting salary for a detention officer is around $31,000; while the starting salary for a deputy is more than $37,000.[105] In Fulton County (Atlanta), Georgia, the starting salary for a deputy is more than $33,000, while the starting salary for a detention officer is $26,000.[106]

Poor working conditions affect employee morale and, consequently, affect the treatment of those under their care. Efforts must be made to bring about a number of changes for jail personnel. As Poole and Pogrebin have pointed out, we must "examine ways of maximizing the use of employee talents, skills, and abilities, thus enhancing both staff and program development."[107] If changes are made in the training and enrichment of the correctional officer's job, it will also enhance the environment in which we house inmates.

The philosophies underlying new-generation jails offer hope in improving the working conditions of jail personnel. As has been pointed

▶Exercise: Checking Out the Local Jail

Many local jails and detention centers have their own web sites. These web sites may include information about the jail, including information for families of jail inmates. This information may include rules and policies for visitation or rules and policies on what inmates can receive in the mail. Many jail web sites contain a roster of the jail's inmates, which may include information about the inmate's alleged offense and bond. Collect some information from the local jail or detention facility web site. You may search the web for the web site of the jail in your area, or visit www.cookcountysheriff.org/doc to view the web site for the Cook County (Chicago), Illinois, jail.

out, some of the end results of the direct supervision model include improved staff morale, decreased staff tension, reduced sick leave, improved treatment of inmates by staff, decreased staff–inmate conflicts, and reduced employee misconduct.[108] New-generation jails offer jail personnel greater control of inmate behavior and, as such, more interaction and control over what happens. Correctional officers in these facilities must more actively supervise the inmates, resulting in more responsibility and usually increased job satisfaction.

• Crowding •

Despite our attempt to build our way out of the jail crowding crisis, out nation's jails are still struggling with more inmates than they can handle. As has been pointed out, in 1990, our nation's jails were operating at 104 percent of their rated capacity. In 1998, this percentage stood at 90. While it seems at first glance that we have adequately dealt with the issue, one must look at the issue more closely. While jails are operating at 90 percent of their capacity generally, not all jails are at that level. Many jails are still housing more inmates than their rated capacity. In 2001, 19 of the 50 largest jail jurisdictions operated at more than 100 percent of their rated capacity.[109] If we look at a number of individual jails, we find, for example, in Clark County, Nevada, the percent of capacity occupied at midyear in 2001 was 171 percent, followed by Maricopa County, Arizona, at 134 percent, and both Philadelphia City, Pennsylvania, and Travis County, Texas, at 126 percent.[110] So, while we find an overall percentage under 100, many individual jails are still housing more inmates than they are rated to house.

It is important for readers to understand that rated capacity is just one measure of crowding. Many jails at or below their rated capacity might be very crowded due to the housing of females and juveniles in the same facility. As mentioned above, federal law mandates that there be sight and sound separation of the sexes and between juveniles and adults. In many smaller jails, if space is needed to house a female or juvenile, a whole wing of the jail must be emptied to accommodate this person. In a sense, you have one or two individuals staying in an area designed to hold 50 inmates, while the other displaced inmates occupy a much smaller area.

Prison crowding adds to the problem of jail crowding as well. In many areas when state correctional systems are at or above capacity, they rely on the local jails to house the overflow of inmates until space opens up. For example, in Louisiana in 2001, 16,050 state prisoners were being held in local jails.[111] This number accounted for almost 45 percent of all state inmates. While this figure is the worst-case scenario, there were 67,760 state prisoners housed in local jails because of crowded state facilities in 2001, representing about 5.4 percent of all state inmates nationwide.[112]

In an attempt to deal with the crowding problem, policymakers have decided to house many jail inmates in what have been called "makeshift jails."[113] These makeshift jails may range from converted gas stations or motels to barges or ferry boats converted to floating detention facilities. New York City took the lead in the use of decommissioned ferry boats and military troop transports as makeshift jails. The first two such floating detention centers were moored at Rikers Island to add much needed jail capacity.[114] Others have been added to the fleet as well, with the largest holding more than 800 inmates.

Offering promise in reducing crowding are alternatives to incarceration. Alternatives to incarceration include a number of programs in which jail inmates are supervised outside of the jail facility. In 2007, more than 68,000 inmates were under such supervision.[115] An inherent problem with these programs is the issue of "net-widening." Net-widening occurs when the courts use these alternatives to incarceration as alternatives to probation or some other penalty that does not involve jail time. If the court approaches programs such as electronic monitoring as a way to be more punitive to offenders who would have normally received only probation or a fine, then the "net" is widened because more people are "caught" by the criminal justice system. For alternatives to be effective, the courts must sentence those who would have normally received a jail sentence to one of these programs. Only then will we have reduced the number of inmates serving their sentence in jail.

Another solution to reducing jail crowding is to lessen the number of pretrial detainees in jail. Reducing their number would substantially reduce crowding. Much of this could be accomplished if we eliminated or completely overhauled the antiquated and biased bail system.[116] It is important to remember the intended purpose of bail: to ensure that the charged individual will show up for his or her court hearing. The poor or disadvantaged often end up serving their pretrial period in jail because they cannot afford bail. Even with the new provisions of the Bail Reform Act, about 14 percent of those on pretrial release are rearrested, 71 percent of whom were rearrested for a felony.[117]

• Inmates with Special Needs •

As has been mentioned, jails are often seen as institutions of last resort, housing a wide array of persons that no other agency is willing or able to handle. Many inmates entering our jails have special medical needs or are suffering from mental illness. Many jails are not equipped to meet the special needs of these inmates. Such conditions create additional problems on an already overtaxed system. In the section that follows, we will look at a number of these special-needs inmates.

• Alcoholics •

One of the most pressing problems facing jail administrators is dealing with individuals taken into custody who are under the influence of alcohol. The number of persons arrested who are under the influence of alcohol has grown rapidly in the past two decades, due largely to the efforts of public interest groups such as Mothers Against Drunk Driving (MADD). Such groups have applied pressure on the police and the courts to punish drivers who are under the influence of alcohol. In many cases, mandatory jail time has been legislated for those convicted of driving under the influence. The impact of alcohol-related arrests is immense, especially in terms of cost and jail space.[118] There are two major concerns that are important to note. First, this increased emphasis on arresting drunk drivers has added greatly to the crowding problems in many jails, especially during peak periods on Friday and Saturday evenings.[119] The Bureau of Justice Statistics[120] reports that more than 33 percent of jail inmates were under the influence of alcohol at the time of the offense (based on convicted jail inmates only).

AP Photo/California Highway Patrol

This police booking photo released in 2002 shows actor Nick Nolte after his arrest on suspicion of driving under the influence in Malibu, California. While media reports tend to ridicule celebrities arrested under the influence of alcohol and other drugs, it is important to remember that a significant percentage of inmates booked into jails are intoxicated when taken into custody, and jail administrators are expected to contend with the ramifications.

A second concern is the problems that can occur during the first few hours of confinement. Sickness, vomiting, and the possibility of slipping and falling are all very real concerns. Inmates may have compounding health problems that simply go unrecognized when they enter the jail. They may become despondent and try to commit suicide. It is not uncommon for individuals who seem drunk or under the influence of other drugs to be placed in a cell and later fall into a coma and, in some cases, die. As the number of these types of inmates increases, especially during the peak periods, such problems only compound.

• Drug Addicts •

Persons who use and abuse drugs other than alcohol also present a special problem to jail personnel. People who have a long history of drug abuse may often appear unaffected when they arrive at jail. The actual physical and medical problems associated with drug abuse do not materialize until the person begins to come off the drugs. Withdrawal symptoms may become severe and require the assistance of medical personnel. Often the drug user must be restrained to ensure that he or she does not hurt their captor or themselves. In 1996, the Bureau of Justice Statistics[121] found that 29 percent of convicted jail inmates were under the influence of drugs other than alcohol at the time of offense. Altogether, six in 10 convicted jail inmates were using alcohol or other drugs at the time of the offense.[122] More than 68 percent of jailed inmates reported being regular drug users.[123]

Jail administrators must be sympathetic to the special needs of persons who abuse drugs. They must train jail personnel to look for signs of drug use and be prepared to assist the inmates during withdrawals. In many cases, the drug problem is not outwardly apparent at the time of arrest, and symptoms of withdrawals do not materialize for hours (often in the late hours of the night). Jail personnel should be familiar with the side effects of a large number of different types of drugs so that appropriate action can be taken.

Jailers must also look out for illicit drug use within their institution. Inmates will often go to extraordinary lengths to obtain drugs within a jail. Jail and support personnel may be bribed or coerced into supplying drugs. If contact visits are allowed or outside contractors provide services to the jail, the potential for obtaining drugs becomes even greater. This potential smuggling problem often becomes a management nightmare. In some cases, illicit drugs are as readily available in jail as they are on the streets.

• Sex Offenders •

Another type of offender that can present a number of unique problems in jail is the sex offender. Many such offenders are seen as the "lowest of the low," hated by correctional officers and inmates alike. For example, if a person is accused of molesting a child, other inmates will often go to great lengths to injure or even murder the offender. Frequently, such inmates need to be separated from the general population for their own protection. Adding to the problem is the fact that jail personnel often have little or no sympathy for such inmates. Many such offenders become depressed and suicidal, and segregation affords the opportunity to carry out these suicides.

• Mentally Ill Inmates •

In 1971, in the case of *Wyatt v. Stickney*, the courts ruled that mental hospitals must either treat their mental patients or release them. The proverbial flood gates were opened as previously institutionalized patients were released onto the street. Many such individuals became public nuisances, and the police often had few alternatives to deal with them. As has been pointed out, jails are often the social agency of last resort. With the lack of other public facilities to house them, the mentally ill soon found themselves in jail. The treatment of mental illness has become one of the more pressing problems for jails in this country.[124]

Even in jurisdictions that have public or private facilities to deal with mental illness, the mentally ill will often be housed in jail for short periods of time until they can be committed to such institutions. In fact, it has been reported that nearly eight times the number of mentally ill persons are admitted to jail than are admitted to state mental hospitals.[125] As many as 13 percent of individuals arrested each year suffer from severe mental disabilities.[126]

A disturbing statistic from 2002 is that 64 percent of local jail inmates had a mental health problem, including 23 percent suffering from a major depressive disorder.[127] The jailing of the mentally ill is a problem both for the jail and for the inmates themselves. The actual environment in which individuals are locked up can have a profound effect on the symptoms of psychopathology. While mental illness may have been present at the time of arrest, once housed for a few days, these same inmates were found to have increased symptoms of psychopathology.[128]

What can be done about this problem? Without question, mentally ill persons who have committed very serious crimes must be housed in jails. The problem lies with those who suffer from mental illness who have committed less serious, nonviolent offenses. It is recommended that in such cases the mentally ill be diverted from jail into community-based mental health programs. Three reasons are outlined:

1. Community treatment programs provide a public safety benefit by reducing the likelihood that the mentally ill offender will be rearrested.

2. Community treatment programs provide a management benefit by enabling jails to operate more efficiently, to focus on keeping dangerous offenders off the streets, and to more effectively ensure the safety of jail staff and other detainees.

3. Community treatment programs provide more effective mental health treatment through an array of integrated services that most jails do not offer.[129]

Jail administrators must also make major operational changes in the delivery of mental health services.[130] Screening mechanisms must be put into place, with highly trained personnel conducting the intake process. When a need is identified, appropriate mental health care must be provided. Whenever possible, support must be sought from the community, but if community treatment is not available, the jail must take the lead in providing the service within the facility. The jail and its personnel must make every effort to reduce the environmental effects that can add to or cause the problems.

The direct supervision design offers a partial solution. In new-generation jails, the inmates and jail personnel are in constant contact with each other. These environments have been found to be less stressful for the inmates because they feel less threatened from predatory attacks. In addition, the noise levels in these jails are often greatly reduced, which in itself lessens the stress. A study by Zupan compared the stress levels between a traditional jail and a direct-supervision facility. It was found that inmates in the direct-supervision facility reported fewer symptoms of psychological and physical stress than those inmates housed in the traditionally designed jail.[131]

• Suicides •

Studies have found that the rate of suicide among jail inmates is five to six times higher than that of comparable individuals in the free world;[132] in fact, suicide is the leading cause of death in jails.[133] In 2002, 32 percent of jail inmate deaths were attributed to suicides,[134] while only 6 percent of prison inmate deaths were attributed to suicides.[135] Much of this difference can be attributed to two factors. First, jails serve an at-risk group of individuals. This can include young men abusing alcohol or other drugs as well as those suffering a mental illness. DuRand et al.[136] found that about 75 percent of those who committed suicide in correctional facilities communicated their intent in advance. Jail administrators must provide the necessary training to identify those at risk and to provide treatment and monitoring to ensure the inmate's safety.

A second factor is related to the fact that about 50 percent of all suicides in jail occur in the first 24 hours of incarceration. Inmates who find themselves in prison have spent time in jail already and have, to the extent possible, become accustomed to confinement. Jail inmates often have found themselves at one hour partying away at a local pub and the next locked in a jail cell. This shock of incarceration can lead a person to commit desperate acts. Jail personnel must be aware of this problem and provide the necessary surveillance, especially during the critical first few days.

A number of studies have offered profiles that jailers can use to identify potential inmates who might consider suicide. Such instruments must be approached with caution. First, a reliance on such a profile might cause jail personnel to overlook other inmates who may take their lives.[137] Second, the use of profiles may allow lawyers to attach tort liability to jail personnel when a death occurs if the individual who committed suicide fits the profile. Kennedy and Homant have suggested alternatives to profiles.[138] First, they suggest that we should develop jails that are suicide-resistant. By developing new designs that allow more careful monitoring of inmates, and using hardware that does not facilitate hanging, the opportunity for suicide can be reduced. The direct-supervision approach, which affords continuous monitoring of inmates, will also help. In such facilities, inmates are not afforded the opportunity to commit suicide, and jail personnel are more likely to notice warning signs and offer assistance.

A second alternative is to extend increased awareness to inmates' needs during the first critical 24 hours that they are in custody.[139] Whether the inmate fits the profile or not, realizing that the first few hours are the most critical and providing additional care during that crucial time period can reduce a substantial number of suicides.

• Jail Time •

A common adage mentioned by scholars is that "jail time is dead time." Many jails just do not have the resources to provide inmates with meaningful activities. Much of the problem lies in the high turnover in jail inmate population. More than one-quarter of the jail population is released after spending as little as one day or less in jail, and three-fifths spend only four days or less.[140] Jails then have little opportunity to help those housed in their facility, and they become, in a sense, "revolving doors." As Lightfoot, Zupan, and Stohr point out, "without appropriate programs that focus on changing the criminal behavior of inmates, the jail becomes a 'revolving door,' releasing individuals into the community simply to readmit them in a few months, weeks, days, or even hours, when they are arrested for another crime."[141]

One of the major challenges facing jail administrators is to develop initiatives to reduce inmate idleness. The Jail Industries Initiative in 1991 proposed a number of objectives to put inmates to work, both to generate revenues for jail facilities and to reduce inmate idle time. The Jail Industries Initiative included four objectives to deal with this dilemma:

1. The development of inmate work habits and skills;
2. The generation of revenues or reduction of costs for the county;
3. The reduction of inmate idleness, and
4. The satisfaction of community needs.[142]

While such programs might seem prohibitive to many smaller facilities, the report mentions a continuum of tasks that might fit within any jail. For the very small jails, the inmates might simply cut the grass in front of the jail, earning little more than the privilege to watch television for an extra hour. For the largest of jails, inmates might work for private-sector industry to earn real dollars that could be used to offset the cost of confinement.[143] In both cases, "the elements of labor, service provision, value, and compensation are all present."[144] The ultimate goal is to reduce inmate idleness; beyond this, such programs can improve work habits as well as defray the cost of housing and feeding jail inmates.

THE TWENTY-FIRST CENTURY

The important role that the jail plays in the criminal justice system is not likely to diminish in the twenty-first century. Persons entering the criminal justice system are still going to pass through the gates of the local jail to be processed. As society becomes more punitive, increasingly more persons will serve sentences in jail for crimes that, in the past, might have only warranted a fine or community treatment. Overflow from state and federal prisons will continue to add convicted felons to the mix of jail inmates, at least in the short term. What does the twenty-first century hold? Much is dependent on how we react today to many of the problems facing local jails.

A number of specific recommendations have been made to address the needs of jails today as well as to enable jails to operate efficiently in the future. The first four recommendations are addressed at the state level. The first recommendation deals with states providing the necessary resources for new jail construction or renovation.[145] We have seen some progress in this area, with an explosive growth in new jail construction in the 1990s. Much of this growth was fueled by the courts intervening in the operations of local jails.

The second recommendation deals with jail standards. According to Thompson and Mays,[146] states should develop mandatory jail standards. These standards should address critical issues dealing with construction and the training of jail personnel. These standards need to be developed with the assistance of local officials so they will be viewed as a "management resource" and not another burden imposed on officials by the state.[147]

The third recommendation is that states should develop an inspection and enforcement program for the standards.[148] Jail standards are of little value if there is not a mechanism in place to force local government into compliance.

The fourth recommendation is for states to adopt legislation that enables local jurisdictions to engage in cooperative agreements to build regional jails.[149] As mentioned above, in many jurisdictions, such arrangements are cost-effective because duplication of services is not a problem.

The next four recommendations offered by Thompson and Mays are at the local level. The first deals with community awareness programs, with the goal of informing the community both of the jail's functions and the conditions within its walls.[150] The public must be informed that "jails are not prisons" and they have unique legal and financial problems.[151] The local community must also develop long-term financial plans for jail construction or renovation, staffing, and operation.[152] This recommendation goes hand-in-hand with community awareness programs. Adequate funding must not be confused with the notion of "coddling criminals."[153]

The third recommendation at the local level deals with requiring local officials to have written policies and procedures.[154] Such written policies and procedures will serve as a valuable tool for the operation of the jail and the training of personnel. These policies and procedures, if implemented and followed, can also be used to prevent lawsuits.

The final recommendation is for communities to explore alternatives to incarceration.[155] As early as 1974, Hans Mattick was recommending alternatives to jail incarceration: "the simplest sentencing alternative for reducing jail populations are suspended sentences, summary probation, and probation without verdict."[156] Mattick further recommended that local communities look at other alternatives to jail, such as the use of fines, community service, electronic monitoring, day reporting centers, specialized treatment facilities, and the use of work-release and weekender sentences.[157] Much has changed since 1974, but many of the problems facing local jails remain the same. Local jails still house large numbers of persons, many of whom are of little danger to society.

CONCLUSION

The problems faced by local jails are not new, nor did they occur overnight. This means that their problems will not be solved quickly or inexpensively. The future of local jails depends on their ability to adapt to the changing needs of our criminal justice system. The explosive growth in jail populations that we have seen in the past two decades cannot continue at its current pace. We must take a careful look at the recommendations mentioned in this chapter and seriously consider alternatives to jail incarceration. We must also strive to improve the existing conditions in our local jails. These efforts require money. The public, courted through public awareness campaigns, must play a key role in any effort we undertake. Without public support, change cannot occur. As the courts begin to back away from intervening in the operation of jails, it is up to local officials and the public to step up and continue to improve the conditions, both for jail personnel and the inmates they house.

DISCUSSION QUESTIONS

1. Discuss the differences between jails and prisons. Give an example of the terms being used inappropriately in the news media or by a policymaker.

2. Discuss some possible explanations as to why we continue to see an enormous increase in the number of jailed inmates at a time when crime has continued to decline.

3. Discuss what it might be like to serve time in each of the three jail designs mentioned. If you were an inmate, which would you prefer? How about as a correctional officer?

4. Discuss some of the problems related to housing females in jail today. What policies might we implement to eliminate some of these problems?

5. Discuss whether you think it is fair to house both pretrial detainees and convicted persons in the same facility.

6. Discuss what planners and policymakers should be doing to prepare our jails for the twenty-first century.

FURTHER READING

Hall, J.U. (2007). *Just Visitin': Old Texas Jails*. Abilene, TX: State House Press.

Irwin, J. (1992). *The Jail: Managing the Underclass in American Society*. Berkeley, CA: University of California Press.

Kearle, K.E. (1998). *American Jails: Looking to the Future*. Burlington, MA: Butterworth Heinemann.

NOTES

1. Irwin, 1985, 1.
2. Gilliard and Beck, 1999, 5.
3. Zupan, 1991, 48.
4. Thompson and Mays, 1991, 1.
5. Gilliard, 1998; Gilliard 1999, 5.
6. Moynahan and Stewart, 1980, 69.
7. Irwin, 1985, 2.
8. Clear and Cole, 1994, 144.
9. Beck, Karberg, and Harrison, 2002, 7.

10. Sabol and Minton, 2008.

11. Sabol, Minton, and Harrison, 2007.

12. Schwartz, 1991, 216-217.

13. Moynahan and Stewart, 1980, 13.

14. Zupan, 1991, 12.

15. Moynahan and Stewart, 1980, 15.

16. Moynahan and Stewart, 1980, 22.

17. Moynahan and Stewart, 1980, 27.

18. Takagi, 1975, 20.

19. Zupan, 1991, 18.

20. Zupan, 1991, 19.

21. Moynahan and Stewart, 1980, 43.

22. Stephan, 2001, 6; Sabol, Minton, and Harrison, 2007.

23. Bureau of Justice Statistics Internet site, http://www.ojp.usdoj.gov/bjs/jails.htm, retrieved April 21, 2008.

24. Gilliard and Beck, 1999, 7; Beck, Karberg, and Harrison, 2002, 10.

25. Beck, Karberg, and Harrison, 2002, 10.

26. Stephan, 2001, 5.

27. Mays and Thompson, 1991, 13; Cox and Osterhoff, 1991, 237-238.

28. Sabol, Minton, and Harrison, 2008, 1.

29. Sabol and Minton, 2008.

30. Beck, Karberg, and Harrison, 2002, 9.

31. Correctional Association of New York, 2002, 1.

32. Martin, n.d.

33. Jankowski, 1992, 8.

34. American Correctional Association, 1985, 24.

35. Gray, Mays, and Stohr, 1995, 186-202.

36. Gray, Mays, and Stohr, 1995, 199.

37. Sabol and Minton, 2008.

38. Sabol and Minton, 2008.

39. Beck, Karberg, and Harrison, 2002, 9.

40. Bureau of Justice Statistics Internet Site, http://www.ojp.usdoj.gov/bjs/correct.htm, retrieved April 21, 2008.

41. Beck, Karberg, and Harrison, 2002, 8.

42. Beck, Karberg, and Harrison, 2002, 8; Sabol, Minton, and Harrison, 2008.

43. *County of Riverside v. McLaughlin*, 500 U.S. 317 (1992).

44. Reaves and Pierce, 1994; Reaves and Perez, 1994; see also *United States v. Salerno et al.*

45. Maguire and Pastore. 1995, 533.

46. James, 2004, 3.

46. James, 2004, 1.

47. James, 2004, 5.

48. Harlow, 1998, 7.

49. Harlow, 1998, 2.

50. Bureau of Justice Statistics, 1995, 13.

51. Bureau of Justice Statistics, 1995, 13; see also Bureau of Justice Statistics Internet Site, http://ojp.usdoj.gov/bjs/pub/press/pjim03pr.htm, retrieved April 21, 2008.

52. D'Alessio and Stolzenberg, 1995, 282-302.

53. D'Alessio and Stolzenberg, 1995, 283.

54. D'Alessio and Stolzenberg, 1995, 297.

55. Schwartz, 1991, 216-217.

56. U.S. Department of Justice, 1980, 400.

57. Sabol, Minton, and Harrison, 2007.

58. Schwartz, 1991, 225-226.

59. Schwartz, Harris, and Levi, 1988, 146.

60. Schwartz, Harris, and Levi, 1988, 148.

61. Irwin, 1985, 2.

62. The Center on Crime, Communities and Culture, n.d., 1.

63. McEwen, 1995, 66.

64. Goldfarb, 1975, 27.

65. Bureau of Justice Statistics, 1995, 5.

66. Mays and Thompson, 1988, 437.

67. Bureau of Justice Statistics Internet site, http://ojp.usdoj.gov/bjs/pub/press/pjim03pr.htm, retrieved April 21, 2008.

68. Nelson, 1988, 2.

69. Harlow, 1998, 13.

70. Harlow, 1998, 13.

71. West, 1972, 157; as quoted in Zupan, 1991, 20.

72. Gibbs, 1987, 308.

73. Nelson, 1988, 72.

74. Zupan and Menke, 1991, 185.

75. Nelson, 1988, 170.

76. Zupan, 1991, 73.

77. Lansing, Bogan, and Karacki, 1977, 45.

78. Lansing, Bogan, and Karacki, 1977, 44.

79. Nelson, 1988, 6.

80. Nelson, 1988, 4.

81. Nelson, 1988, 4.

82. Nelson and O'Toole, 1983, and Gettinger, 1984; as quoted in Zupan, 1991, 105.

83. Zupan and Menke, 1991, 193.

84. Zupan and Menke, 1991, 193.

85. Mays and Thompson, 1991, 15.

86. American Correctional Association, 1981; National Advisory Commission on Criminal Justice Standards Goals, 1973.

87. Mays and Thompson, 1991, 3-21.

88. Mays and Thompson, 1991, 15.

89. Mays and Thompson, 1991, 15.

90. Mays and Thompson, 1991, 16.

91. Champion, 1991, 205.

92. Champion, 1991, 206.

93. Champion, 1991, 206.

94. Champion, 1991, 206.

95. Sechrest and Collins, 1989, ix.

96. Sechrest and Collins, 1989.

97. Champion, 1998, 211.

98. Guynes, 1988.

99. Poole and Pogrebin, 1991, 163.

100. Mays and Thompson, 1991, 10.

101. Champion, 1998, 173.

102. National Sheriffs' Association 1982, 151.

103. Peterson and Pierce, 1999.

104. *Sourcebook of Criminal Justice Statistics, 2001*, 2002, 3.

105. Harris County, Texas Sheriff's Department Internet site, http://www.hcso.hctx.net/recQualify.asp, retrieved April 21, 2008.

106. Fulton County Sheriff Internet Site, http://www.fultonsheriff.org/misc/Personnel/career_opportunity.asp, retrieved April 21, 2008.

107. Poole and Pogrebin, 1991, 164.

108. Nelson, 1988, 4.

109. Beck, Karberg, and Harrison, 2002, 10.

110. Beck, Karberg, and Harrison, 2002, 10.

111. Beck, Karberg, and Harrison, 2002, 11.

112. *Sourcebook of Criminal Justice Statistics*, 2001, 2001, 497.

113. Welch, 1991.

114. Welch, 1991, 151.

115. Sabol and Minton, 2008.

116. Reaves and Perez, 1994.

117. Zupan, 1991, 28.

118. Harlow, 1998, 1.

119. James, 2004, 1.

120. Harlow, 1998, 1.

121. James, 2004, 1.

122. James, 2004, 1.

123. James, 2004, 1.

124. Harlow, 1998, 1.

125. The Center on Crime, Communities, and Culture, n.d., 1.

126. The Center on Crime, Communities, and Culture, n.d., 1.

127. James and Glaze, 2006.

128. Gibbs, 1987.

129. The Center on Crime, Communities, and Culture, n.d., 1.

130. Kalinich, Embert, and Senese, 1991, 86.

131. Zupan, 1991, 161-162.

132. Winfree, 1988, 641-659.

133. The Center on Crime, Communities, and Culture, n.d., 4.

134. Mumola, 2005.

135. Mumola, 2005.

136. DuRand et al., 1995, 1077.

137. Kennedy and Homant, 1988, 452.

138. Kennedy and Homant, 1988, 453.

139. Kennedy and Homant, 1988, 453.

140. Bureau of Justice Statistics, 1990, 5.

141. Lightfoot, Zupan, and Stohr, 1991, 50.

142. Miller, Sexton, and Jacobsen, 1991, 2.

143. Miller, Sexton, and Jacobsen, 1991, 2.

144. Miller, Sexton, and Jacobsen, 1991, 2.

145. Thompson and Mays, 1991, 244.

146. Thompson and Mays, 1991, 244.

147. Thompson and Mays, 1991, 244.

148. Thompson and Mays, 1991, 244.

149. Thompson and Mays, 1991, 245.

150. Thompson and Mays, 1991, 245.

151. Thompson and Mays, 1991, 245.

152. Thompson and Mays, 1991, 245.

153. Thompson and Mays, 1991, 245.

154. Thompson and Mays, 1991, 245.

155. Thompson and Mays, 1991, 246.

156. Mattick, 1974, 825.

157. Mattick, 1974, 827-828.

REFERENCES

American Correctional Association (1985). *Jails in America: An Overview of Issues.* College Park, MD: American Correctional Association.

American Correctional Association (1981). *Standards for Adult Local Detention Facilities.* Rockville, MD: American Correctional Association.

Beck, A.J., and J.C. Karberg (2001). "Prison and Jail Inmates at Midyear 2000." *Bureau of Justice Statistics Bulletin.* Washington, DC: U.S. Government Printing Office.

Beck, A.J., J.C. Karberg, and P.M. Harrison (2002). "Prison and Jail Inmates at Midyear 2001." *Bureau of Justice Statistics Bulletin.* Washington, DC: U.S. Government Printing Office.

Bureau of Justice Statistics. Internet site. Available at http://www.ojp.usdoj.gov/bjs/jails.htm.

Bureau of Justice Statistics (2002). "Federal Prison Population Increases a Record Amount; State and Local Inmate Growth Moderates." Press release. Available at: http://www.ojp.usdoj.gov/bjs/pub/press/psimo1pr.htm

Bureau of Justice Statistics (1995). "Jail and Jail Inmates, 1993-1994." *Bureau of Justice Statistics Bulletin.* Washington, DC: U.S. Government Printing Office.

Bureau of Justice Statistics (1990). "Census of Local Jails 1988." *Bureau of Justice Statistics Bulletin.* Washington, DC: Government Printing Office.

Champion, D.J. (1998). *Corrections in the United States: A Contemporary Perspective,* 2nd ed. Upper Saddle River, NJ: Prentice Hall.

Champion, D.J. (1991). *Corrections in the United States: A Contemporary Perspective.* Englewood Cliffs, NJ: Prentice Hall.

Champion, D.J. (1991). "Jail Inmate Litigation in the 1900s." In J.A. Thompson and G.L. Mays (eds.), *American Jails: Public Policy Issues,* 197-215. Chicago: Nelson-Hall.

Clear, T.R., and G.F. Cole (1994). *American Corrections,* 3rd ed. Belmont, CA: Wadsworth.

Correctional Association of New York (2002). *Women in Prison Project: The Effects of Imprisonment on Families.* Available at: http://www.correctionalassociation.org/images/Children-of-IncarceratedParents.pdf

Cox, N.R., Jr., and W.E. Osterhoff (1991). "Managing the Crisis in Local Corrections: A Public-Private Partnership Approach." In J.A Thompson and G.L. Mays (eds.), *American Jails: Public Policy Issues,* 227-239. Chicago: Nelson-Hall.

D'Alessio, S.J., and L. Stolzenberg (1995). "The Impact of Sentencing Guidelines on Jail Incarceration in Minnesota." *Criminology* 33:282-302.

DuRand, C.J., G.J. Burtka, E.J. Federman, J.A. Haycox, and J.W. Smith (1995). "A Quarter Century of Suicide in a Major Urban Jail: Implications for Community Psychiatry." *American Journal of Psychiatry* 152:1077.

Fulton County, Georgia Sheriff's Internet Site. Available at http://www.fultonsheriff.org/misc/Personnel/career_opportunity.asp, retrieved April 21, 2008.

Gettinger, S.H. (1984). *New Generation Jails: An Innovative Approach to an Age-Old Problem.* Washington, DC: National Institute of Corrections.

Gibbs, J.J. (1987). "Symptoms of Psychopathology among Jail Prisoners: The Effects of Exposure to the Jail Environment." *Criminal Justice and Behavior* 14:299-310.

Gibbs, J.J. (1986). "When Donkeys Fly: A Zen Perspective on Dealing with the Problem of the Mentally Disturbed Jail Inmate." In D. Kalinich and J. Klofas (eds.), *Sneaking Inmates Down the Alley: Problems and Prospects in Jail Management*, 149-166. Springfield, IL: Charles C Thomas.

Gilliard, D.K. (1999). "Prison and Jail Inmates at Midyear 1998." *Bureau of Justice Statistics Bulletin.* Washington, DC: U.S. Government Printing Office.

Gilliard, D.K. (1998). "Prison and Jail Inmates at Midyear 1997." *Bureau of Justice Statistics Bulletin.* Washington, DC: U.S. Government Printing Office.

Gilliard, D.K., and A.J. Beck (1999). "Prison and Jail Inmates at Midyear 1998." *Bureau of Justice Statistics Bulletin.* Washington, DC: U.S. Government Printing Office.

Goldfarb, R. (1975). *Jails.* New York: Anchor.

Gray, T., G.L. May, and M.K. Stohr (1995). "Inmates Needs and Programming in Exclusively Women's Jails." *The Prison Journal* 75(2):186-202.

Guynes, R. (1988). *Nation's Jail Managers Assess Their Problems.* Rockville MD: National Institute of Justice.

Harlow, C.W. (1998). "Profile of Jail Inmates 1996." *Bureau of Justice Statistics Bulletin.* Washington, DC: U.S. Government Printing Office.

Harris County, Texas Sheriff's Department Internet Site. Available at http://www.hcso.hctx.net/recQualify.asp, retrieved April 21, 2008.

Harrison, P.M., and J.C. Karberg (2003). "Prison and Jail Inmates at Midyear 2002." *Bureau of Justice Statistics Bulletin.* Washington, DC: Government Printing Office.

Irwin, J. (1985). *The Jail.* Berkeley: University of California Press.

James, D.J. (2004). "Profile of Jail Inmates, 2002." *Bureau of Justice Statistics Special Report.* Washington, DC: U.S. Government Printing Office.

James, D.J., and L.E. Glaze (2006). "Mental Health Problems of Prison and Jail Inmates." *Bureau of Justice Statistics Special Report.* Washington, DC: U.S. Government Printing Office.

Jankowski, L.W. (1992). "Jail Inmates 1991." *Bureau of Justice Statistics Bulletin.* Washington, DC: U.S. Government Printing Office.

Kalinich, D., P. Embert, and J. Senese (1991). "Mental Health Services for Jail Inmates: Imprecise Standards, Traditional Philosophies, and the Need for Change." In J.A. Thompson and G.L. Mays (eds.), *American Jails: Public Policy Issues*, 79-99. Chicago: Nelson-Hall.

Kennedy D.B., and R.J. Homant (1988). "Predicting Custodial Suicides: Problems with the Use of Profiles." *Justice Quarterly* 5(3):441-456.

Lansing, D., J.B. Bogan, and L. Karacki (1977). "Unit Management: Implementing a Different Correctional Approach." *Federal Probation* 41:45.

Leibowitz, M.J. (1991). "Regionalization in Virginia Jails." *American Jails* 5(5):42-43.

Lightfoot, C.A., L.L. Zupan, and M.K. Stohr (1991). "Jails and the Community: Modeling the Future in Local Detention Facilities." *American Jails* 5(4):50-52.

Maguire, K., and A.L. Pastore (eds.) (1995). *Sourcebook of Criminal Justice Statistics*. Washington, DC: U.S. Government Printing Office.

Martin, J. (n.d.). *Inside Looking Out: Perceptions of Jailed Fathers Regarding Separation from Children*. (Ph.D. diss., Indiana University of Pennsylvania).

Mattick, H.W. (1974). "The Contemporary Jails of the United States: An Unknown and Neglected Area of Justice." In Daniel Glaser (ed.), *Handbook of Criminology*, 777-848. Chicago: Rand McNally.

Mays G.L., and J.A. Thompson (1991). "The Political and Organizational Context of American Jails." In J.A. Thompson and G.L. Mays (eds.), *American Jails: Public Policy Issues*, 3-21. Chicago: Nelson-Hall.

Mays, G.L., and J.A. Thompson (1988). "Mayberry Revisited: The Characteristics and Operation of America's Small Jails." *Justice Quarterly* 5(3):421-440.

McEwen, T. (1995). *National Assessment Program: 1994 Survey Results*. Washington, DC: U.S. Government Printing Office.

Miller, R., G.E. Sexton, and V.J. Jacobsen (1991). *Making Jails Productive*. Washington, DC: U.S. Government Printing Office.

Moynahan, J.M., and E.K. Stewart (1980). *The American Jail: Its Development and Growth*. Chicago: Nelson-Hall.

Mumola, C.J. (2005). "Suicide and Homicide in State Prisons and Local Jails." *Bureau of Justice Statistics Special Report*. Washington, DC: U.S. Government Printing Office.

National Advisory Commission on Criminal Justice Standards and Goals (1973). *Report on Corrections*. Washington, DC: U.S. Department of Justice.

National Sheriffs' Association (1982). *The State of Our Nation's Jails, 1982*. Washington, DC: National Sheriffs' Association.

Nelson, W.R. (1988). *Cost Savings in New Generation Jails: The Direct Supervision Approach*. Washington, DC: U.S. Government Printing Office.

Nelson, W.R., and M. O'Toole (1983). *New Generation Jails*. Boulder, CO: Library Information Specialists.

Peterson, R.S., and B. Pierce (1999). "Institution Financial Operations." In P.M. Carlson and J.J. Garrett (eds.), *Prison and Jail Administration: Practice and Theory*, 141-148. Gaithersburg, MD: Aspen.

Poole, E.R., and M.R. Pogrebin (1991). "Changing Jail Organization and Management: Toward Improved Employee Utilization." In J.A. Thompson and G.L. Mays (eds.), *American Jails: Public Policy Issues,* 163-179. Chicago: Nelson-Hall.

Reaves, B.A., and J. Perez (1994). "Pretrial Release of Felony Defendants, 1992." *Bureau of Justice Statistics Bulletin*. Washington, DC: U.S. Government Printing Office.

Reaves, B.A., and B. Pierce (1994). "Pretrial Release of Federal Felony Defendants, 1992." *Bureau of Justice Statistics Bulletin*. Washington, DC: U.S. Government Printing Office.

Sabol, W.J., and T.D. Minton (2008). "Jail Inmates at Midyear 2007." *Bureau of Justice Statistics Bulletin*. Washington, DC: U.S. Government Printing Office.

Sabol, W.J., T.D. Minton, and P.M. Harrison (2007). "Prison and Jail Inmates at Midyear 2006." *Bureau of Justice Statistics Bulletin*. Washington, DC: U.S. Government Printing Office.

Schwartz, I.M. (1991). "Removing Juveniles from Adult Jails: The Unfinished Agenda." In J.A. Thompson and G.L. Mays (eds.). *American Jails: Public Policy Issues*, 216-226. Chicago: Nelson-Hall.

Schwartz, I., M.L. Harris, and L. Levi (1988). "The Jailing of Juveniles in Minnesota: A Case Study." *Crime & Delinquency* 34(2):133-149.

Sechrest, D.K. , and W.C. Collins (1989). *Jail Management and Liability Issues*. Miami, FL: Coral Gables.

Sourcebook of Criminal Justice Statistics, 2002 (2004). Washington, DC: U.S. Government Printing Office.

Sourcebook of Criminal Justice Statistics, 2001 (2003). Washington, DC: U.S. Government Printing Office.

Sourcebook of Criminal Justice Statistics, 1997 (1999). Washington, DC: U.S. Government Printing Office.

Sourcebook of Criminal Justice Statistics, 1995 (1997). Washington, DC: U.S. Government Printing Office.

Sourcebook of Criminal Justice Statistics, 1994 (1996). Washington, DC: U.S. Government Printing Office.

Stephan, J.J. (2001). "Census of Jails, 1999." *Bureau of Justice Statistics Bulletin*. Washington, DC: U.S. Government Printing Office.

Takagi, P. (1975). "The Walnut Street Jail: A Penal Reform to Centralize the Power of the State." *Federal Probation* 39:18-26.

The Center on Crime, Communities and Culture (n.d.). *Mental Illness in U.S. Jails; Diverting the Nonviolent, Low-level Offender*. Available at http://www.soros.org

Thompson, J.A., and G.L. Mays (1991a). "Paying the Piper but Changing the Tune: Policy Changes and Initiatives for the American Jail." In J.A. Thompson and G.L. Mays (eds.), *American Jails: Public Policy Issues*, 240-246. Chicago: Nelson-Hall.

Thompson J.A., and G.L. Mays (1991b). "The Policy Environment of the American Jail." In J.A. Thompson and G.L. Mays (eds.), *American Jails: Public Policy Issues*, 1-2. Chicago: Nelson-Hall.

U.S. Department of Justice (1980). *Indexed Legislative History of the Juvenile Justice Amendments of 1977*. Washington, DC: U.S. Government Printing Office.

U.S. Department of Labor (2002). *National Compensation Survey: Occupational Wages in the United States, January 2001*. Washington, DC: author.

U.S. Department of Labor (1994). *Occupational Outlook Handbook*. Washington, DC: U.S. Government Printing Office.

Welch, M. (1991). "The Expansion of Jail Capacity: Makeshift Jails and Public Policy." In J.A. Thompson and G.L. Mays (eds.), *American Jails: Public Policy Issues*, 148-162. Chicago: Nelson-Hall.

West, D. (1972). "I Was Afraid to Shut My Eyes." In D.M. Petersen and M. Truzzi (eds.), *Criminal Life: Views From the Inside*. Englewood Cliffs, NJ: Prentice Hall.

Winfree, L.T. (1988). "Rethinking American Jail Death Rates: A Comparison of National Mortality and Jail Mortality, 1978, 1983." *Policy Studies Review* 7:641-659.

Zupan, L. (1991). *Jails: Reform and the New Generation Philosophy*. Cincinnati: Anderson.

Zupan, L., and B.A. Menke (1991). "The New Generation Jail: An Overview." In J.A. Thompson and G.L. Mays (eds.), *American Jails: Public Policy Issues*, 180-194. Chicago: Nelson-Hall.

COURT CASES

Coffin v. Reichard, 143 F.2d 443 (6th Cir. 1944).

Cooper v. Pate, 378 U.S. 546 (1964).

County of Riverside v. McLaughlin, 500 U.S. 44 (1991).

Monroe v. Pape, 365 U.S. 167 (1961).

United States v. Salerno et al., 431 U.S. 739 (1987).

Wyatt v. Stickney, 325 F.Supp. 781 (M.D. Ala. 1971).

Community Corrections

CHAPTER 5

What You Need to Know

▶ The rationale for community corrections is multifaceted: the avoidance of overly harsh sentences, an emphasis on treatment, and an attempt to reduce costs.

▶ A common complaint about community corrections is that offenders might not be properly supervised and might commit new crimes.

▶ Probation is the release of convicted offenders into the community under a conditional suspended sentence.

▶ Probation began in Massachusetts and has undergone several changes in philosophy throughout its history.

▶ The probation officer's role includes investigation and supervision.

▶ There has been debate over the effectiveness of probation. Some have called for abandoning probation.

▶ Parole developed out of the practices of transportation, mark system, and ticket of leave.

▶ Like probation, parole includes investigation and supervision. Halfway houses, furloughs, and work release programs also exist to help parolees.

▶ Some have called for the abolition of parole. Despite such calls, more than three-quarters of a million adults were on parole at yearend 2006.

▶ Intermediate punishments include community service, intensive supervision, electronic monitoring, and boot camp prisons.

INTRODUCTION

The term "community corrections" refers to a range of programs, supervision, and punishments aimed at the criminal offender. In its broadest sense, community corrections simply involves any treatment or punishment outside the institution of the prison or jail. However, some types of community corrections occur in places most of us would deem a prison (e.g., the boot camp), so the term is used in an imprecise manner. In this chapter, community corrections will refer to traditional probation and parole, diversion programs at various stages of the criminal justice system, and a more recent range of sanctions called intermediate punishments.

• Why Community Corrections? •

Many students have a difficult time understanding the rationale behind the concept of community corrections. To them, the process is simple. If you commit a crime, you should go to prison. If you commit a serious crime, you should go to prison for a very long time. To a small extent, the system does work that way, but there are a number of philosophical, economic, and practical reasons why the criminal justice system is much more complex.

RATIONALE FOR COMMUNITY CORRECTIONS PROGRAMS

The rationale behind community corrections programs is multifaceted. Three major justifications for them include the avoidance of inordinately harsh sentencing, the increased capability of providing treatment, and reduced costs as compared to institutionalized corrections.

Avoidance of harsh sentencing. While many people may believe that the criminal justice system is too lenient on offenders, one of the reasons for community corrections is to limit the severity of sentences given to offenders of minor crimes. If prison is the only option available to a judge, then the judge has no leeway within which to make an appropriate decision. When it comes to sentencing, a "one size fits all" practice is not deemed to be in the best interests of either the offender or society.

Treatment. One of the primary reasons that community corrections has become such a large part of the criminal justice system is the recognition of the fact that rehabilitation is difficult to accomplish in a maximum-security prison. Therefore, most offenders are diverted to some other type of correctional setting. When an offender remains in the community, it is possible to enlist the support of already existing programs. Schools, mental health centers, jobs, and families all can contribute to the treatment goals of an offender.

Cost. Maximum-security prisons are too expensive to use on the majority of offenders. With the cost of building a prison at more than $40,000 per bed, plus the additional expenses of staffing and security, maximum-security prisons are a luxury that can be used only for the most serious of offenders. Moreover, this precious resource is not always used wisely; a large number of inmates in the nation's prisons are not dangerous and have committed nonviolent crimes. Community corrections, particularly probation and parole, provide a certain level of treatment and supervision for the offender and security for the community at a greatly reduced cost from the maximum-security prison. While medium- and, particularly, minimum-security prisons may be less costly to build than maximum-security institutions, they are still substantially more expensive than community corrections programs.

It should be clear that the rationale behind community corrections is complex. In the present political and economic circumstances, community corrections is necessary: the criminal justice system simply cannot function without the contribution of community corrections. This is not to say that there are not problems and dangers associated with the practice. Examples of these difficulties are mistakes in classification and net-widening. These examples occupy the extreme ends of a continuum of concerns about community corrections.

CONCERNS ABOUT COMMUNITY CORRECTIONS

• Mistakes in Classification •

The most common complaints lodged against programs in community corrections are those claiming that dangerous offenders are not properly supervised and may use the less restrictive surveillance to commit further serious crimes. Each time a parolee or a probationer commits a rape or homicide, the entire field of community corrections is questioned. The public's perception is that there are thousands of offenders on probation and parole who should be in prison because they are committing new crimes.

Certainly, there are some offenders who do commit crimes while under the supervision of community corrections programs. However, the vast majority do not, and are in fact making contributions to society by holding down a job, supporting their families, and paying taxes. It is the exception that the public hears about, especially the violent offender who hurts someone. These types of cases are reported by the media and often elicit editorials in the newspaper.

How does someone capable of committing a rape or homicide end up on probation, parole, or in some other type of community corrections program after the criminal justice system has already had a chance to put the person in prison? Why aren't dangerous offenders locked away where they can't hurt further innocent victims? The answers to these questions lie at the heart of community corrections. The simple truth is that the prediction of future dangerousness is an inexact science.[1] Sentencing and parole decisions are made by judges and parole boards who must work under very specific guidelines that cannot always ascertain how dangerous each individual offender may become. The pickpocket of today may become the rapist of tomorrow, and the seemingly well-adjusted child molester may reoffend. Given that there are not enough prison beds for all the convicted felons in a community, the decisionmakers have to use their judgment in deciding who will be incarcerated and who will be placed in a community corrections program. It may be a testament to how well the criminal justice system works that there are not more of these sensational cases in which someone under community supervision commits a new serious offense.

• Net-Widening •

The opposite problem of placing the "dangerous" offender in a community corrections program is placing a "harmless" offender in a restrictive program. Historically, decisionmakers have used discretion in determining who is brought into the criminal justice system. Many offenders of minor crimes are simply warned and released. Why expend valuable resources on people who made a mistake but pose no real threat to the community? Many people, at some time in their lives, engage in behaviors that, if detected by the criminal justice system, could land them in jail, but it has usually been the case that the vast majority are simply released. Because many community corrections programs are measured by their recidivism rates, there is an inherent temptation to select for these programs those offenders who are likely to be successful. Therefore, instead of relieving prison overcrowding and providing services for the marginal offender who might benefit from a community correctional program, the net of social control is widened to encompass the least serious offender.[2] Eventually, this widening of the net can pull the less serious offender into the depths of the criminal justice system. When placed in a community corrections program, the offender is subject to a number of rules and requirements that require attention. Failure to report to a probation officer, missing a drug test, and refusing to go to mandatory counseling are all reasons that could land a relatively minor offender in prison. Such cases may result in a self-fulfilling prophecy for some minor offenders. Being placed in a community corrections program can have the unintended consequence of accelerating the offender's involvement in the system.[3] Sometimes the best policy for these offenders may be to do nothing at all.[4]

DIVERSION

Diversion programs have been introduced at several steps along the criminal justice process. Probation and parole, which are discussed in greater length later in this chapter, are means for diverting the offender out of the traditional prison. Diversion programs can also operate before the offender even goes to court. The prosecutor's office can channel offenders into treatment programs in lieu of going before a judge. Typically, the prosecutor will hold the criminal charge against the offender in abeyance, pending the successful completion of a diversion program. This program might include drug treatment, restitution, school, or simply staying out of trouble for a certain period of time. Failure to complete the diversion program successfully means that the case is reinstituted and the offender must face the judge for a disposition of the case.

Technically, the term "diversion" refers to cases in which the offender has not been convicted of a crime. Realistically, diversion programs are simply one type of community corrections practice designed to limit the impact of the criminal justice system on the offender's life.

PROBATION

• Probation Defined •

Probation refers to the release of convicted offenders into the community under a conditional suspended sentence, avoiding imprisonment.[5] The word "probation" is derived from the Latin term *probatio*, which means a period of proving or trial. If offenders comply with the conditions of their probation, they may be forgiven and released from further involvement with the criminal justice system. Their criminal records may not be expunged or forgotten, but at least incarceration is avoided. Some states (e.g., California) allow expungement under certain conditions after probation has been served satisfactorily.

Every state or federal criminal statute carries statutory sanctions for the length of time an offender can be supervised under probation. These sanctions always provide for the possibility of incarceration and/or a fine, depending on the seriousness of the offense. In Tennessee, for example, a convicted shoplifter is punished by "a fine of not more than three hundred dollars ($300) or imprisonment for not more than six (6) months, or both."[6] A conviction for violating a federal criminal law such as the willful destruction of U.S. government property not exceeding the sum of $100 is punishable by "a fine of not more than $1,000 or by imprisonment for not more than one year, or both."[7] If U.S. government property damage exceeds $100, the punishment escalates to "a fine of not more than $10,000 or imprisonment for not more than ten years, or both."[8] The important phrase in these statutes is "not more than." The judges have the discretionary power and authority to sentence offenders to the maximum penalties provided by the law or as outlined in the criminal statutes.

• The History and Origins of Probation •

Probation is an American invention; however, its origins can be traced to English common law through four judicial practices. The first practice was a form of a suspended sentence that evolved from right of sanctuary.[9] The right of sanctuary was a biblical practice in which holy places and certain cities were traditionally set aside as places for sanctuary. This right was written into Mosaic law. To escape the blood vengeance of a victim's family, a killer would go to specified cities and find refuge. During the Middle Ages, some churches would offer sanctuary for those hiding from secular law.

The benefit of the clergy replaced the right of sanctuary and was a religious practice initially reserved only for the wrongdoing of clerics. This special plea was a part of the feudal power struggle between Church and State in England as Henry II sought to expand his power over the Church by subjecting clerics to the King's Court. The benefit of the clergy was a mechanism through which Church functionaries escaped potential persecution. Ordained clerks, monks, and nuns accused of crimes could claim the benefit and have their cases transferred to the Bishop's Court.[10] It originally protected violators from the clergy, usually members of the upper social class. It would eventually be extended to protect the ordinary citizen. The benefit of the clergy involved appealing to an ecclesiastical judge for leniency in exchange for reading the 51st Psalm. The reading of this biblical passage became known as the "neck verse" (because if one did not know it, he or she was hanged, or if an offender was hanged, those may have been his or her last words) and required that its benefactor be literate. This practice was, of course, discriminatory in nature, because those who could not read (usually the poor) were unqualified. To overcome this disparate treatment, common thugs eventually learned how to circumvent the system by memorizing the verse so that they could pretend to read it before the court. As a result, judges began to apply the benefit arbitrarily, resulting in sentencing discrimination. Benefit of clergy was practiced in the American colonies. After the United States gained its independence, benefit of clergy eventually fell into disuse because of its unequal application by judges.

Judicial reprieve, or the suspended sentence, was another English common law practice. During this process, the convicted offender would ask the judge to suspend the imposition or execution of a sentence in exchange for his or her "good behavior." The judge could elect to do so, and at the end of the suspension, the offender could apply to the king for a pardon. This worked well in England, but when this practice was adopted in the United States, it became controversial. The problem was that offenders could be under the purview of the court for an indefinite period. The indefinite sentence allowed the judge to suspend the sentence and punish the reprieved offender if he or she violated the law. In 1916, the Supreme Court declared this practice unconstitutional because it subjected offenders to lengthy sentences beyond those established by law. Today, we still use the suspended sentence, but judges must adhere to the penal code regarding the length of time an offender's sentence can be held in abeyance by the court.

The last inception of probationary practices was recognizance. Unlike the recognizance as we know today (i.e., release on recognizance), this practice involved the offender's posting a sum of money or surety in exchange for refraining from further criminal behavior. It also did not provide official supervision by an official of the court. This practice, also called "binding over," required the offender to remain law-abiding for a stipulated period and to appear in court on a specified date for trial or for final disposition of the case.[11] In England, it was frequently used with petty offenders; if the offender violated the terms of the agreement, the bond would be claimed by the state and the offender incarcerated.

• John Augustus: The Father of Probation in United States •

John Augustus is commonly recognized as the "father of probation." He was a philanthropist, temperance advocate, and Boston bootmaker who was a frequent observer in the Boston courts. His visits to the courts led him to focus on offenders charged with public drunkenness or prostitution. A devoutly religious man and a fervent opponent of alcohol consumption, Augustus believed that exposure to religious influence and abstention from alcohol were the keys to rehabilitation for many offenders. One morning, while appearing in a municipal court to observe offenders charged and sentenced with various crimes, Augustus intervened on behalf of a man charged with being a "common drunkard."[12] Augustus convinced the judge to allow him to "stand bail" for the offender who was later released into his custody. Augustus offered to supervise the man's behavior for a three-week period and guaranteed his subsequent reappearance in court. Knowing Augustus's reputation for philanthropy and trusting his motives, the judge agreed.

When Augustus returned within the three weeks with the "reformed" drunkard, the judge was so impressed that he reduced the fine and suspended the man's sentence of incarceration. This would be the beginning of Augustus's role as a probation officer. His efforts to implement probation were met with much resistance from his fellow Bostonians. He was often faced with skeptical and hostile public officials. However, between 1841 and 1859, the year he died, it is estimated that he saved nearly 2,000 men and women from incarceration by bailing them out and supervising them for a fixed probationary period.

• The Birth of American Probation •

Even though community corrections options are older than institutional corrections, the birth of American probation is generally attributed to the volunteer efforts of John Augustus. Actually, Augustus's work was more akin to modern pretrial supervision than probation.

Augustus would return offenders to court within 30 to 60 days of their discharge to his custody and report their progress to the court. If the court was satisfied with Augustus's report on the offender's progress, it would usually suspend sentence or impose a small fine and court cost. What Augustus brought to community corrections were the elements of interviewing, assessment, and supervision. He also generated attention to the needs of petty street criminals in big cities, so much so that his friends took over his work after financial and health problems forced him to curtail his activities.

In 1878, 20 years after Augustus's death, the city of Boston hired a police captain named Edward Savage as a probation officer. Although Augustus is regarded as the patriarch of American probation, Savage

John Augustus, often credited as the "father of probation," convinced judges to release individuals who suffered with alcoholism into his care in lieu of jail.

was actually the first paid probation officer.[13] Over the next quarter of a century, other states followed Massachusetts' lead, authorizing probation services and hiring officers. Most early probation programming targeted young first-time offenders and those convicted of minor crimes.

• The Philosophy of Probation •

In 1878, Massachusetts was the first state to pass a law authorizing probation for adults and juveniles. By 1923, this concept was implemented in virtually every state and juvenile court system, including the federal jurisdictions. Probation has experienced tremendous transitions since the days of John Augustus. During the 1940s, the field of psychology and the work of Sigmund Freud influenced probation. There was a shift in the philosophy of punishment from focusing on the crime that was committed to focusing on the criminal. Emphasis was placed on the "medical model" and identifying psychological problems of the offender. Rehabilitation was the goal of the medical model. Under this concept, a treatment plan would be tailored to meet the needs of the offender and to "effect a cure" in his or her behavior.

The medical model remained popular until the 1960s, when it began losing its appeal to community corrections. This shift occurred during the Civil Rights Movement, when the country was experiencing unrest in social, economic, and political spheres. Many professionals came to believe that crime was attributed to poverty, racism, inequality, and unemployment. Probation was seen as a central correctional method because it was the primary existing means of working with the offender in the problem's context: the offender's community. The goal of the community corrections model was reintegration. Under this model, criminal justice agencies began relying on the community to help them fight crime. They also began relying on the community in their efforts to help offenders become productive and law-abiding citizens. The methods of probation began to change from direct service through psychological counseling to "service brokerage."

Service brokerage involves the probation officer becoming familiar with the available community resources and using these services to meet the needs of the probationers. In this approach, the probation officer is viewed as a "community resource manager." The primary function of the community resource manager is to assess the probationer's needs and identify the resources that are available in the community to meet those needs. After the referral is made, the community resource manager will follow up on the referral to make sure the probationer received the services. The community resource manager's role is also to act in the capacity of an advocate for the probationer. For example, many probationers experience some frustration when they seek help from institutions (e.g., schools, welfare, and mental health agencies) that are supposed to treat them. When this happens, the community resource manager's role is to intervene and provide assistance to the probationer. The community resource manager should refer the probationer to other programs that may better address the probationer's needs. Service brokerage programs have been heralded by government studies.

By the late 1970s and 1980s, there was yet another shift in the philosophy of probation. Risk management began to take priority over rehabilitation and reintegration programs because public officials were becoming concerned about the increasing recidivism rates of offenders.

Some government officials and the general public also began criticizing the current correctional practices, which they felt were failures. Emphasis was now being diverted to a "just deserts" model of punishment, by which offenders would be accountable for their criminal behavior. Focus shifted from the "treatment of the offender" to the "protection of the community." Because correctional officials had failed at treating offenders effectively, they recognized the need to develop strategies to control the offenders' behaviors while they were being supervised by the probation department.

During the 1990s, correctional officials continued using the risk-management philosophy. However, despite this shift, some continue to believe that rehabilitation remains the overriding goal of probation. This position remains debatable. For example, developments such as intensive supervision, house arrest, and electronic monitoring do not seem to be rehabilitation-oriented. Critics attribute the uncertainties that underlie the goals of probation to the absence of a clear "mission" of what community supervision should be. Fitzharris lists several reasons for probation's continued state of "vulnerability":

1. An unclear mission;

2. Overstated, unspecified, and unmeasurable objectives;

3. Undemonstrated expertise and inadequate standards and training;

4. Unsubstantial results;

5. A history of inadequate funding;

6. Isolation from the public (noninvolvement) and a lack of public awareness;

7. Lack of strategic planning and effective management techniques; and

8. A weak constituency.[14]

In essence, some have argued that most of these criticisms are logistical, organizational, financial, and/or political. Nothing in this listing states that the "idea" of probation as an alternative to incarceration is bad. Champion[15] believes most of these concerns will disappear with better staffing, better funding, better planning from administration (including specific forms of probation for particular offenders), and greater communication with the public about existing probation programs and aims.

• The Administration of Probation •

Today, probation is administered by more than 2,000 separate agencies in the United States, with some adult probation agencies being located in the executive branch of state government and others in the judiciary branch. There is an ongoing debate on who should administer probation services. The three issues concerning how probation should be administered are: (1) should probation be centralized or decentralized?, (2) should probation be administered under the executive branch or the judicial branch of government?, and (3) should it be combined with parole? These three issues may also contribute to the confusion and vulnerability regarding the mission and goals of probation.

• Centralized vs. Decentralized Probation Services •

Centralization places authority for a state's probation activity with a single administrative body. Proponents of centralization argue that it creates consistency and uniformity of policies across jurisdictions. In the decentralized model, each jurisdiction has its own sets of policies that create inconsistency and disparity in sentencing. States that utilize the centralized model are larger and can train a staff to take on a variety of roles. For example, under the centralized model, probation officers are also trained to be parole officers. Therefore, if there is a shift in program needs (e.g., more parole officers are needed than probation officers), the probation officer can be transferred to parole services. Under the centralized model, there is likely to be greater equality in supervision. They can implement more program services because the tax base is broader and not as restrictive as one would find under a decentralized model. Under the decentralized model, probation services are administered by the city or county instead of the state. These agencies are usually smaller, and their policies, unlike centralized models, are inclined to be more flexible and responsive to the needs of the community.

• Executive vs. Judicial Administration of Probation •

The next issue concerns whether probation should be administered by the executive branch (e.g., the Department of Corrections, which also administers parole) or the judicial branch of government. Most organizations administer probation services under the executive branch of government. If probation is structured under the executive branch, it usually is a centralized or statewide system as described above. One advantage of probation's being under the executive branch is that program budgeting can be better coordinated. The courts are at an advantage to manipulate and allocate resources according to need. Some, however, maintain that probation should be administered by the judiciary because probation provides services to offenders (e.g., placements in employment, education, drug treatment programs) that can be monitored. If the judiciary administers the program, failure to comply with the court can be promptly brought to the attention of the sentencing judge. In such a case, the relationship between the probation staff and the courts creates a direct feedback mechanism.

When probation is administered by the judiciary, courts have a greater awareness of the resources needed by the probation agency. Judges also tend to have greater confidence in an agency for which they are responsible. If probation is administered on a centralized or state-wide basis, it is usually incorporated into a department of corrections. Under such circumstances, probation services might be assigned a lower priority than they would have as part of the judicial branch.

• *Probation and Parole: Should They Be Combined Services?* •

If probation is administered under the executive branch of government, it will most often be combined with parole services. Some believe the two should be combined because they have similar investigative and supervision functions. This approach takes advantage of efficiencies in hiring, training, and developing staff. Others believe the two should remain separate because they handle different types of offenders. Offenders who are placed on probation do not require the same close supervision and surveillance as parolees who are still at "inmate status." Probationers also do not pose the same threats to the community as do parolees, and the type of offenses they commit are not as serious. However, there are some cases in which the crime of conviction may have been plea-bargained to a lesser charge, which allows the judge to grant probation. In other instances, offenders may be placed on probation for subsequent offenses after they have served a prison term. In any event, probationers do not usually experience the same "re-entry to the community" problems as do parolees who have been incarcerated before they are granted parole. Because of these differences, opponents would argue that probation services should not be combined with parole.

• The Dual Role of Investigation and Supervision in Probation •

• *The Probation Officer's Role* •

The role of the probation officer is to investigate offenders who are being sentenced before the court. In doing so, officers must complete a presentence investigation and report the findings of their investigation to the judge. In most states, there is a legal mandate that a presentence investigation report be submitted to the court for offenses that can result in imprisonment for more than a year. It is also used to assist the judge in determining the appropriate sentence for the offender. If the offender is granted probation, then the probation officer's role involves supervision. Here the probation officer advises and counsels offenders according to the conditions set forth in the order of probation. Probation officers essentially have a dual role: investigation and supervision.

• *The Investigation Function* •

As stated, one of the probation officer's roles is to conduct a presentence investigation (PSI) report. Also assisting judges are privately commissioned presentence investigation reports as well as local agencies[16] that prepare individualized client-specific sentencing plans that stress nonincarceration sanctions.[17] The PSI helps the judge select an appropriate sentence for the offender. If the offender is granted probation, then information from the report will be used to develop the treatment plan for his or her supervision in the community. If the offender is sentenced to prison, the report will be used as a classification tool for decisions made about the offender while he or she is institutionalized in the prison and when he or she becomes eligible for parole.

The presentence investigation report includes information on the offense committed, the offender's prior criminal history, history on relationship with family and the family's personal assessment of offender, educational history, information on physical and mental health, drug addiction history (if applicable), risk assessment, and summary and recommendations. The recommendation can be for or against probation. If the probation officer does not feel the offender is a suitable candidate for community supervision, the officer can make a recommendation to the judge that probation not be granted. Research shows that judges tend to accept the presentence recommendation of probation officers at a rate of about 83 percent for probation and 87 percent for incarceration. In some jurisdictions, defendants and their attorneys are entitled to see the entire presentence report so they can rebut the report's contents; in other jurisdictions, they have limited or no access to the report.[18]

• *The Supervision Function* •

If granted probation, the offender will be placed in a caseload and supervised in the community by a probation officer. Supervision includes the monitoring and surveillance of the offender during the course of his or her sentence. The probationer, depending on the severity of the offense committed, will be monitored through either minimum (low or administrative), medium (average), or maximum (high) supervision levels. Under minimum or administrative supervision, the probationer may only be required to report to the probation department once a month in person, by phone, or by mail. Probationers at this supervision level have committed minor offenses (e.g., shoplifting) and are sometimes placed on suspended sentences. The typical probationer will be placed on medium supervision. Under medium supervision, offenders are usually required to report to the probation department once a month. The probation officer will also visit the probationer at home on a monthly basis. Probationers on maximum supervision require the most surveillance and control. These offenders are usually under intensive supervision, and may be serving a split sentence, which means a portion of their time is spent incarcerated.

• Caseload Size and Officer Effectiveness •

The caseload of a probation or parole officer is considered by many authorities to affect the quality of supervision that officers can provide their clients. Caseloads refer to the number of offender-clients supervised by the officer. Caseloads vary among jurisdictions.[19] Because most caseloads are high (e.g., 100 to 200 cases per officer), probation officers cannot always provide their clients with supervision needs. In those cases, monthly visits to probation departments are usually brief, and the probation officer's major concerns are to make sure authorities know the correct location of the probationer's place of residence and to ensure that the probationer has not committed any new offenses. Theoretically, the larger the caseload, the poorer the quality of supervision and other services. Intensive probation or parole supervision (IPS), for example, is based on the premise that low offender caseloads maximize the amount of attention the officer can give their clients, including counseling, employment, and social and psychological assistance. The success of such IPS programs suggests that lower caseloads contribute to lower recidivism rates among parolees and probationers.

No one knows the ideal caseload because the actual caseloads of probation and parole officers vary greatly, ranging from a low of five or 10 clients to a high of 400 clients.[20] The earliest work outlining optimal caseloads for professions was done by Chute, who advocated that caseloads for probation officers be no larger than 50.[21] Edwin Sutherland made a similar endorsement in 1934, followed by the American Prison Association in 1946, the Manual of Correctional Standards in 1954, and the National Council of Crime and Delinquency in 1962.[22] After evaluating caseloads of officers in a variety of jurisdictions, researchers have concluded that "it may be said with assurance . . . that (1) no optimal caseload size has been demonstrated, and there is (2) no clear evidence that recidivism will decrease, simply by reducing one's caseload size." It has been suggested that 30 clients per probation or parole officer would be the ideal caseload size.[23]

BOX 5.1

The Eve Carson Tragedy

Eve Carson was an attractive, immensely popular and ambitious 22-year-old student at the University of North Carolina at Chapel Hill. A native of Athens, Georgia, she was a member of the Phi Kappa Phi Honor Society, a political science and biology major with intentions of attending medical school, and was elected president of the student body for the 2007-08 academic year. Carson was murdered on March 5, 2008. Carson's murder received widespread media coverage, in large measure because of her accomplishments and status as UNC student body president, and her murder happened to coincide with the approaching Atlantic Coast Conference basketball tournament, always a high-profile event in North Carolina.

Two suspects, Laurence Alvin Lovette (age 17) and Demario James Atwater (age 21), were subsequently arrested and charged with Carson's murder. Lovette was also charged with the January 18, 2008, murder of Abhijit Mahato, a Duke University graduate student. The outrage over Carson's and Mahato's murders was compounded when it was discovered that both murder suspects were on probation at the time of the killings. Lovette was serving a 24-month probation sentence for breaking and entering, and Atwater was serving a 36-month sentence for breaking and entering and larceny. The more the press reported on the story, the more the outrage grew, and much of it was directed at the North Carolina Department of Correction, based on reports that both men's cases had allegedly been mishandled by probation officials. The required contacts with officers had not been made, and one of the defendant's cases was in the course of being revoked but the revocation effort was thwarted by bureaucratic and courtroom mixups. One of the probation officers involved was accused of violating department policy by not keeping accurate records and not doing enough to supervise the offender. This same officer was contesting a second drunk-driving charge of her own. North Carolina probation officials ordered an investigation into the handling of both cases as well as a review of the practices of the officers involved. It was alleged that the case of one of the accused was transferred to several officers within a very short period of time, making the local probation office appear the picture of bureaucratic ineptitude.

The Carson and Mahato cases reinforced existing prejudices against probation and community corrections in general. Once again, community corrections suffered a public black eye. Much of the public blames probation officers for crimes committed by probationers even when the officers follow proper procedure, but the blame is compounded when officers are found to be delinquent in their job.

BOX 5.1 *(continued)*

The media coverage in the Carson and Mahato cases also demonstrates one of the problems community corrections has in the area of public relations. Some media outlets reported that the two suspects were on probation, which was true, but others erroneously reported that the pair were on parole, which was untrue. Such mistakes may seem inconsequential to many, but when the public calls for the abolition of parole because of cases involving probation, it contributes to the misinformation that commonly exists with respect to community corrections.

Sources: (Raleigh) *News and Observer* Internet site, http://www.newsobserver.com; University of North Carolina Relations Internet Site, http://universityrelations.unc.edu/alert/carson/, retrieved April 21, 2008.

• *Case Management Styles* •

Probation and parole officers have four basic management styles they may use while supervising their clients. These styles usually reflect their personal views toward crime. The first is the punitive/law enforcement officer, who places an emphasis on surveillance. His or her primary concern is the protection of society through controlling the behavior of the probationer. The welfare/therapeutic officer emphasizes the social worker role. His or her primary concern is to improve the welfare of the probationer through the use of supportive social services and counseling to meet the needs of the offender.[24]

The protective/synthetic officer attempts to combine the welfare/therapeutic and punitive/law enforcer roles. This probation officer will change roles according to how the probationer responds to probation. If the probationer's adjustment to supervision is good, then the probation officer's role will be more treatment-oriented. If the probationer's adjustment is poor, the probation officer will once more be oriented toward surveillance and control. The final role is passive/time server. Officers who adopt this style have little concern for the welfare of the community or the client. They are usually cynical, apathetic, and have experienced a tremendous amount of stress and burnout on the job. Probation officers who are older and close to retirement may fall within this category.

• Is Probation Effective? •

One of the positive aspects of probation is the financial savings associated with its operation. However, some have argued that probation, especially felony probation, presents a societal protection dilemma.

Advocates of incapacitation focus on the recidivism rates of probationers in order to defend their position that probation does little to deter criminal behavior. As such, they maintain that correctional agencies should rely much less on probation and more on punitive measures to prevent future crimes. Petersilia and her colleagues, who conducted a 40-month follow-up study of felony probationers in California, found that 65 percent were rearrested, 51 percent were reconvicted (one-third of these for serious violent crimes), and 18 percent were sent on to institutions. Those centering attention on societal protection find these statistics important in criticizing the actual effect of probation.[24]

Such pessimistic statistics were, however, countered by more optimistic findings.[25] Some researchers believe it is possible to not only reduce the use of incarceration but to maintain public safety in the process. For instance, Vito evaluated a shock probation program in Ohio during the 1970s. Shock probation involves incarcerating convicted offenders for periods ranging from 90 to 130 days and then releasing them on probation by the sentencing judge. The goal of shock incarceration is to make most offenders want to avoid future imprisonment that would result from the commission of new offenses.[26]

There is an ongoing debate about whether correctional authorities should abandon probation in favor of incapacitation for those offenders who do not benefit from community supervision. Reactions by professionals remain controversial, with some favoring probation[27] and others opposing it.[28] Vito, based on his research findings, argues that we should not abandon probation. His study showed that when the recidivism

---

BOX 5.2

Probation/Parole Management Style

1. *Punitive/law enforcement:* focus is on surveillance, client control, and enforcing conditions of probation

2. *Welfare/therapeutic:* focus is on counseling clients, providing social services, and helping clients to succeed vocationally and interpersonally

3. *Protective/sympathetic:* attempts to combine, in a flexible manner, both client control and treatment in a balanced approach in order to enforce the conditions of supervision and to help the client to succeed

4. *Passive/timeserver:* exhibited by pessimistic and apathetic officers who are often experiencing stress-related burnout; minimal concern for the welfare of community or client

rates of offenders who did not participate in treatment programs are compared with those who do, the treatment programs appeared to be of some value in deterring crime and reducing recidivism. Some researchers have argued that no program is going to function perfectly as a crime deterrent or rehabilitative tool. Therefore, the effectiveness of probation or any other form of community supervision will depend on how the offender is controlled and monitored while free in the community.[29]

• Revocation and Termination of Probation •

Probation can end in one of two ways—the successful completion of the probation term or the commission of a new offense or some other form of misbehavior. If the probationer fails to comply with the conditions set forth in the order of probation, the result can be a revocation of probation. The revocation of probation can arise from "technical violations," which include such acts as the failure to report to the probation department, the failure to participate in drug rehabilitation, or the failure to seek gainful employment.

In most revocation proceedings involving technical violations, the probationer appearing before the sentencing judge could have his or her probation status continued. The probability is that probation will not be revoked because technical violations, although unacceptable, are not ordinarily illegal. They usually do not result in incarceration unless there are some other factors related to the probationer's behavior that may be viewed as unacceptable by the court (e.g., the probationer failed to report to the probation department as instructed, the probationer continued to use drugs, etc.). Another rationale for continuing probation for offenders in cases involving technical violations is because overcrowding in jails and prisons limits judges from incarcerating violators. The limited spaces in correctional facilities are usually reserved for more serious offenders.

Although patterns vary across the nation, the most common reason for a revocation of probation is the commission of a new offense. Sometimes the court will wait until the probationer is convicted of the new offense before his or her probation status is revoked. In other instances, if the new offense is serious, probation is revoked immediately.[30]

Because the revocation of probation is a serious matter, the probationer who is subjected to such a change has some constitutional safeguards. The court must adhere to certain procedures under the due process clause (Fourteenth Amendment) because the revocation of probation involves a "loss of liberty" for the probationer. A major case that addressed the probation revocation process was *Mempa v. Rhay*. In 1967, Rhay was given a deferred sentence for two years by a Spokane, Washington, judge for a joyriding charge. Several months later, his probation status was revoked after he admitted to new charges of burglaries while he was under the supervision of the court. Rhay was then sentenced to 10 years in a Washington penitentiary. Six years later, he filed a writ of habeas corpus, alleging he was denied the right to an attorney at the revocation hearing.

While the court did not question the state's authority to defer sentencing in the probation matter, it said that any indigent probationer is entitled to be represented by counsel at every stage of a criminal proceeding when "substantial rights of a criminal may be affected." In essence, the Supreme Court considered a probation revocation hearing to be a "critical stage" that falls within the due process provisions of the Fourteenth Amendment. In subsequent years, several courts applied this decision to parole revocation hearings.

Probationers' due process rights were extended further in the 1972 U.S. Supreme Court decision of *Morrissey v. Brewer*. At the start, this case protected the rights of parolees; later, it was extended to probation revocation proceedings. The significance of *Morrissey* was that it set forth minimum due process rights, including a preliminary hearing that must be held at the time of arrest and detention. When it is determined that probable cause exists and the probationer actually committed the new offense, a second hearing takes place. This second hearing is more extensive and establishes whether the probationer's status should be revoked and a punishment imposed relating to the violation of probation.

The Court did not address the question of whether probationers or parolees should have the right to a court-appointed counsel during these proceedings. Nor did it require parole or probation proceedings to be identical, because probationers are "convicted" offenders and do not possess the same rights as criminal defendants. The minimum rights passed down in *Morrissey v. Brewer* are:

1. There must be written notice of offender's alleged violations.

2. Offenders are to receive full disclosures of the evidence against them.

3. When facing possible revocation, offenders have the right to present their cases in person and to present witnesses on their behalf.

4. The decisions about whether to revoke offenders' probation are to be made by neutral and detached hearing bodies.

5. Once decisions are made, those making the decisions are to prepare and file written statements explaining the evidence on which they based their decision and the specific reasons for deciding to revoke the offenders' probation.[31]

The significance of the *Morrissey* case was that it set forth minimum due process rights for probationers and parolees. It also created a two-stage proceeding in which the violation of probation or parole is examined first, and then a full hearing is held to determine the most appropriate decision for the offender.

The issue of representation by counsel was addressed a year later in the *Gagnon v. Scarpelli* case. In 1965, Gerald Scarpelli pleaded guilty to the charge of robbery and was sentenced to prison for 15 years. The judge, however, suspended his sentence and placed him on probation for a seven-year period. A day later, Scarpelli was arrested and charged with burglary. His probation status was revoked without a hearing, and he was placed in a Wisconsin reformatory and given a 15-year sentence. Shortly before his parole, Scarpelli filed a habeas corpus petition alleging that his probation status was revoked without the benefit of counsel. He claimed that he was denied the right to due process. The Supreme Court agreed and ruled in his favor. The Court, referring to *Morrissey v. Brewer*, held that Scarpelli's due process rights were violated because there was no revocation hearing.

PAROLE

• Parole Defined •

Parole comes from a French term *parole d'honneur* ("word of honor"), which characterized the French efforts to establish parole release. The term "parole" was originally applied to war prisoners who were released from captivity upon promise not to take up arms again. Prisoners would be released after showing good behavior and industry in prison, and on their word of honor that they would obey the law. The term "parole," rather than "parolee," was used in the United States during and just after the American Civil War when discussing freed prisoners, especially those from the defeated confederacy who signed an oath vowing not to resume fighting against the Union. In the United States, parole is defined as the conditional release of a prisoner from incarceration after a portion of the sentence has been served. The distinguishing feature between parole and probation is that the parolee is still on inmate status.

Unlike the probationer, the parolee has served a period of time in jail or prison before being released into the community under the supervision of a parole officer. Parolees serving split sentences will usually serve a shorter period of time in jail. This is reserved for sentences under a year or less. Parolees who commit more serious offenses serve some of their sentence in prison. Parolees also have more stringent conditions to adhere to than probationers (e.g., curfews, bans against associations with ex-convicts, requirements to report to the parole department more often, etc.). Because the parolee has "inmate status," his or her parole status can be easily revoked if he or she fails to comply with the conditions set forth in the parole contract.

• The History and Origins of Parole •

• Transportation •

Parole evolved during the nineteenth century out of such English, Australian, and Irish practices as conditional pardon, apprenticeship by indenture, and "ticket of leave." Parole also evolved from a process called transportation, which entailed sending the offender away to live in exile. Initially, transportation was chosen by English prisoners to replace the gallows or the whipping post. The Vagrancy Act of 1597, however, prescribed transportation for the first time. England relied on transportation as one of its major sanctions until the middle of the nineteenth century. Upon the independence of United States, Australia and other Pacific colonies became the outlets for England's overcrowded prisons; offenders were given conditional pardons known as tickets-of-leave and were sent to those outposts of the empire. Transportation seemed such a successful policy that in 1717 a statute was passed allowing convicts to be given over to private contractors, who then shipped them to the colonies and sold their services.

Transportation was the standard sanction during this period for about 90 percent of convicted felons. It is estimated that from 1596 to 1776, up to 2,000 convicts a year were shipped to American colonies.[32] Transportation began to lose its popularity during the American Revolution. At that point, the labor done by prisoners was replaced with the labor of African slaves. The importation of African slaves proved to be more economically feasible for planters in the United States. This shift led to overcrowded prison conditions in England. In about 1787, transportation was shifted to other countries. The termination of the Revolutionary War ended transportation to the United States, and England then sent convicts to Australia until 1879.[33] Criticism about the ineffectiveness of transportation continued to mount. In 1837, a committee of Parliament was appointed to study the effects of transportation. In its report, the committee concluded that transportation did not reform prisoners and recommended its abolition. This recommendation was only partially adopted; it was not until 1868 that all transportation from England ceased.[34]

• The Mark System •

In 1840, Alexander Maconochie was appointed superintendent of the penal colony at Norfolk Island, located 900 miles off the coast of Australia. He was known as a social reformer, and his personal views for humanitarianism and a lenient administrative style toward prisoners made him unpopular in many circles. Maconochie believed that confine-

BOX 5.3

The Mark System

Norfolk Island's horrid reputation changed after Maconochie implemented his mark system, which brought tranquility to the colony. The "mark system," also known as the "marks of condemnation," was established by Maconochie so prisoners could accumulate marks for good work performed and for complying with prison rules. Thus, Maconochie pioneered what later came to be known as the "good time" credits that are used today in American prisons.

The mark system resulted in the early release of prisoners. Release was earned according to the following principles:

- Early release should not be computed on the amount of time served, but rather upon the amount of work completed.

- Prisoners can earn marks by hard work, better conduct, and industrious working habits. Prisoner release determined on the basis of the number of marks accumulated.

- Prisoners must earn everything they receive. Food and other indulgences were charged against the marks they had acquired.

- Prisoners should work in small groups; the entire group would be held accountable for the conduct of individual members.

- Prisoners would move through various stages of progressively less discipline; eventually, they would be given more rights in their own labor to prepare them for release into society.

Although his experiment at Norfolk was successful from the standpoint of penology, the experiment was opposed by authorities back in Australia, who viewed it as "coddling criminals" while incurring extra costs on the government. Maconochie was relieved of his position in 1844 and returned to England, where he campaigned for penal reforms as a writer and speaker. In 1853, he successfully lobbied for the passage of the English Penal Servitude Act that established several rehabilitation programs for inmates and abolished transporting prisoners to Australia. Because of these significant improvements in British penal policy and institutionalization of early-release provisions throughout England's prison system, Maconochie is credited as being the Father of Parole.

Source: Adapted from Barnes, H., and N. Teeters (1959). *New Horizons in Criminology*, 3rd ed., 419, 422. Englewood Cliffs, NJ: Prentice Hall.

ment should be rehabilitative, not punitive. He believed that prisoners ought to be granted early release from custody if they behaved well and did good work while confined.[35] In essence, his philosophy of punishment was based on reforming the individual criminal. The convict was to be punished for the past and trained for the future.

Because the amount of time needed to instill self-discipline and train a criminal could not be estimated in advance of sentencing, Maconochie advocated sentences that were open-ended—what is known today as the indeterminate sentence. He set up a system of marks to be earned by each inmate based on good behavior; a sentence could not be terminated until a certain amount of marks had been achieved. The five stages of his system were based upon an accumulation of marks in which each carried increased responsibility and freedom, leading to a ticket-of-leave or parole resulting in a conditional pardon and, finally, to full restoration of liberty.[36]

• *The Irish System: The Ticket of Leave* •

In 1853, England's Parliament enacted the Penal Servitude Act, which enabled prisoners to be released or paroled on a ticket of leave and supervised by the police. In this same year, Sir Walter Crofton was commissioned to investigate conditions in Irish prisons; in 1854, he became the director of the Irish prison system. Crofton was familiar with Maconochie's work, and their views on the reformation of criminals were similar. Impressed with Maconochie's work, Crofton copied Maconochie's three-stage intermediate system whereby Irish prisoners could earn their early conditional release. However, he modified Maconochie's plan in such a way that prisoners would be subject to:

1. strict imprisonment for a time;

2. transferred to an "intermediate" prison for a short period, where they could participate in educational programs and perform useful and responsible tasks to earn good marks; and

3. given a ticket-of-leave and released from prison on license under the limited supervision of local police.

Crofton developed what came to be called the Irish system of penal administration. Central to that system was a process of graduated release that gave prisoners the responsibility for how short or long their actual time in prison would be. Under the Irish system, the ticket-of-leave was a form of conditional release. According to the ticket, prisoners were required to report to the constable of their home town as soon as they arrived, and once a month thereafter until the expiration of their sentence. Conditions were attached to the ticket. Any violations (e.g., idle or dissolute living, association with notoriously bad characters, and lack of visible means of support) could lead to immediate arrest and return to prison.[37]

During the 1850s, a study of 559 prisoners showed that only 17 had their tickets of leave revoked for various infractions. The concepts of the intermediate prison, assistance, and supervision were Crofton's contributions to the modern system of parole. In essence, Crofton pioneered what later came to be known as several major functions of parole officers: employment assistance to released prisoners, regular visits by officers to parolees, and the general supervision of their activities.[38]

Maconochie and Crofton had similar needs to make their systems of parole work. However, the determinate sentence restricted them from effectively implementing their programs. Maconochie wanted to base the eligibility for a ticket of leave on the prisoner's behavior rather than on certain amount of time. However, he needed some level of control over how long the prisoners could be kept in the penal colony. Crofton believed that his system, which was based on a graduated release, would have no meaning if prisoners were released at a certain date regardless of their stage at the time. The indeterminate sentence would satisfy the needs of both parole systems because it would allow them to carry a threat over the prisoner's head of returning to prison if they failed to comply with the terms of their conditional release. As good time, the ticket-of-leave system, and indeterminate sentencing came together, they provided the essential ingredients of parole.[39]

• The Development of Parole in the United States •

By 1870, a new generation of American penal reformers had arisen. The U.S. connection with the European use of parole allegedly occurred in 1863 when Gaylord Hubbell, the warden at Sing Sing Prison, New York, visited Ireland and conferred with Crofton about his penal innovations and parole system. In 1870, the National Association of Prisons (later to become known as the American Correctional Association) met in Cincinnati, Ohio, and established the Declaration of Principles, which embraced the philosophy of inmate change through reformation. Fixed sentences would be replaced by sentences of indeterminate length. Proof of reform, rather than lapse of time (a requirement under the determinate sentence), would now be required. In addition, a classification system would be utilized on the basis of the prisoner's character and improvement. The goal of parole would be the treatment of criminals through their moral regeneration, not the infliction of pain.[40]

Zebulon Brockway became the new superintendent of the New York State Reformatory at Elmira in 1876 and was instrumental in the passage of the first indeterminate sentencing law in the United States.[41] He is also credited with introducing the first good-time system, whereby an inmate's time to be served is reduced by the number of good marks earned. Once this system was in operation and shown to be moderately effective, several other states patterned their early-release standards after it. Brockway and the Elmira Reformatory are important because they are credited with originating the good-time release system for prisoners in 1876, but the practice of using early release for inmates occurred in the United States much earlier (though authorities dispute its true origin).

Dressler claims that parole was officially established in Boston by Samuel G. Howe in 1847. From 1790 to 1817, convicts were obligated to serve their entire sentences in prison.[42]

The extension of the parole idea in the United States was linked to the indeterminate sentence. As states adopted indeterminate sentencing, parole followed. By 1900, 20 states had parole systems, but it was not until the 1920s that parole really caught on. Starting in 1910, each federal prison had its own board composed of the warden, the medical office, and the superintendent of prisons of the Department of Justice. The U.S. Board of Parole was created by Congress in 1930. By 1932, 44 states and

A historical marker in Cincinnati, Ohio, commemorates the 1870 First Congress of the National Association of Prisons. The meeting endorsed the philosophy of inmate change through reformation and produced the association's Declaration of Principles.

the federal government had established the parole system. Until recently, all jurisdictions had some mechanism for release of felons into the community under supervision.[43] Some states, however, have since abolished parole due to criticism that parolees were committing new crimes and represented a threat to society.

• The Decision to Release: The Parole Process •

However parole may be given, the decision is usually made through a parole board that reviews information from a prerelease investigation report, which is similar to the presentence investigation report. The difference between the two is that the prerelease investigation report will make the recommendation whether the prisoner should be granted parole, while the presentence investigation report recommends either incarceration or community supervision in lieu of incarceration.

• The Organization of the Parole Board •

The powers of the parole board are extensive. Statutes and (in a few cases) state constitutions determine the size and the basic qualifications of parole board membership. For example, parole board members are usually appointed by the government. Who sits on the board plays a

BOX 5.4

Probation versus Parole

Probation

- Probation is a sentence imposed by a judge

- Probation is a judicial action

- Probation allows the offender to remain in the community under the supervision of the court while being supervised by a probation officer

- Probation can be administered by the county or state (usually through the Department of Corrections) agencies

- Probationers usually commit crimes that are not as serious as parolees

- Caseloads in probation can be high because the majority of offenders are under the supervision of the court

- Probation may be granted and terminated by the courts

Parole

- Parole is a status imposed by a parole board

- Parole is an action carried out by the Department of Corrections

- Parole follows incarceration and is a conditional release from prison

- The parolee who is released from prison is on "inmate status" until he or she is discharged from parole

- The parolee is supervised by a parole officer

- Parolees usually have committed more serious crimes that have resulted in their incarceration

- Caseloads are not as high as probation because parolees are monitored more closely due to "inmate status"

- Parole may be granted and terminated by a parole board

large role in how parole is administered. Most jurisdictions provide for five- to seven-member parole boards who may serve from four to six years. The average length of actual service on parole boards is a little more than four and one-half years.[44]

States using discretionary parole must decide who will make up the parole board's membership, what organizational structure the board will have, and what criteria the board will use to decide who gets released on parole. Parole board members are seldom required to have specific qualifications. When qualifications are indicated, they tend to be general, such as "of good character" or "judicious temperament." However, some states are more concerned with the character of the board than the character of the individual members.[45] Parole boards function under three major parole structures: the institutional model, the autonomous model, and the consolidation model.

Under the institutional model, parole release decisions are made primarily within the institution by the staff members. This model is most prevalent in the juvenile justice system and best reflects the rehabilitative expectations of the indeterminate sentence. Because institutional staff members are most familiar with the prisoner's progress, they are often in the best position to make the release decision. The parole board is an independent unit under the autonomous model, and therefore their decisions whether to release a prisoner are not influenced by the correctional institution. This board is not affiliated with the other criminal justice agencies and is most frequently found in the adult system. Advocates of this system believe that the parole board can be more objective because it is less influenced by problems in other parts of the justice system. Critics of parole boards point out that because members are typically appointed by the governor, they may primarily serve his or her interests. Moreover, such appointees often have no criminal justice or correctional qualifications, or understanding of the justice and corrections process.

The consolidation model is a combination of the two models. Here, the parole board is an independent unit; however, it is located in the department of corrections. This model is becoming increasingly popular as jurisdictions move toward consolidating all correctional services into a single department. Proponents of consolidation tout the benefit of taking into account the parole system's connection to the various corrections agencies.[46]

Most parole boards operate by assigning cases to individual board members who review the cases in detail and then make recommendations to the board as a whole. In most instances, the recommendation of the individual member is accepted. However, from time to time, the assembled board will request more information. At this point, the prisoner often will be asked to appear. Some states send individual board members to the institutions to interview the inmate and prison staff; others convene the entire board at the various institutions on a regular schedule. If inmates do not meet the standards the board has established for parole, their sentences are continued and they are denied parole. However, if they are accepted, they are prepared for turnover to the adult parole authority for a period of supervision determined by the parole board.

• *Types of Release Decisions* •

Earlier studies show that the main factor considered in the selection process was the seriousness of the crime for which the offender was originally convicted.[47] However, in 1979, a national study of parole boards determined that the specific factors were considered evidence of parole readiness. The five most important criteria used to make release decisions were participation in prison programs, good prison behavior, change in attitudes, increased maturity, and development of insight.[48] There are four ways in which all prisoners can obtain their release: discretionary release, mandatory release, expiration release, and a pardon or clemency.

Discretionary release involves a decision by parole boards, who determine the date of release from prisons within the limits of maximum, minimum, and good-time set by statutes. The parole eligibility date is calculated from an indeterminate sentence, by which the offender has been given a minimum and a maximum sentence range to be served. The inmate has usually served a portion of the minimum term before he or she is eligible, and the calculation for release will include any earned good-time credits, earned jail time, and earned meritorious good time. Under this form of release, prisoners are given conditions to which they must adhere, and they remain in state custody until the expiration of their full sentences.

Under mandatory release, parolees are released conditionally into the community by provisions of determinate sentencing laws or fixed sentence and parole guidelines. Legislatures and judges, not correctional authorities, determine sentences. In states where determinate sentences have been legislated, inmates are released when their sentences have been served, with adjustments made for good time. Unlike discretionary release, parole is not contingent on the inmate's behavior and institutional adjustment. In essence, parolees remain in state custody until the expiration of their terms.

Parole guidelines place inmates into categories according to two criteria—the seriousness of the offense and the Salient Factor Score (SFS). The Salient Factor Score is a risk assessment tool by which a number is computed that determines the probability a parolee will succeed on parole. Supporters of parole guidelines contend that they bring objectivity and fairness to the decision-making process. Opponents focus on the legal problems they create.[49] There may be errors in computing salient factor scores. There may also be complaints about placements in offense severity levels. There are also claims that parole examiners either illegally elevate cases of aggravation or fail to consider mitigating factors.

Conditional release (also known as expiration release) is used in a few states where parole has been abolished, such as Maine and Connecticut. In these jurisdictions, parolees are released unconditionally at the end of their terms, less good time. They are released not only from incarceration, but also from state custody at the time they leave prison.[50] A pardon or executive clemency is another way in which an offender can be released from prison. It also serves to excuse an offender from suffering all the consequences of a conviction for a criminal act, and is most commonly used to expunge the records of first-time offenders. A pardon can be granted only at the executive branch of the state or federal level of government.

• The Terms and Conditions of Parole •

If an inmate is granted parole, he or she is released to the community, subject to compliance with various rules and regulations. The parolee has to sign a parole contract or order of parole, which is an agreement between the state and the offender. As a part of the contract, the state promises to release the offender on specific conditions. If the offender fails to keep any of the conditions in the agreement or commits a new crime, the offender is in breach of the parole contract and the state can revoke his or her parole status. The conditions of the parole contract are usually set out specifically in the contract or the certificate of parole. Each jurisdiction determines its own conditions, and each individual agreement may have its own special conditions. However, most conditions resemble those included in the U.S. Parole Commission's certificate of discharge.[51] The most commonly stated conditions are:

1. You must directly report to your parole officer within three days.

2. If you are unable to report to the office in where you have been assigned within the specified time, then you shall report to the nearest office.

3. You shall not leave the state without prior permission of the parole officer. . . .

• Revocation and Termination of Parole •

A person on parole is not considered a free person, despite the fact that he or she has been released from prison. Therefore, parole is said to be granted on three principles. It can be granted through an act of grace or privilege. If this is the case, the government extends a privilege of release. Parole can also be granted through a contract of consent, which is most often the case. Here, the government enters into an agreement with the prisoner whereby he or she promises to abide by certain conditions in exchange for being released. Finally, parole can be granted through retained custody by the government. This means the prisoner, although released, retains his or her "inmate status" and is still the responsibility of the government. If the conditions of parole are not met, the offender's parole status can be revoked.

If parole is revoked, it is usually revoked for the technical violation of a condition or the commission of a new offense. Parole officers possess considerable discretion in reporting violations and in calling for the revocation when they occur. However, revocation rarely occurs for a single technical violation. From what is known, a parolee is likely to have his or her parole revoked if they do one or more of the following: carry a weapon, fail to report to the parole office as instructed, abuse alcohol or other drugs, or commit a new crime.

As discussed in previous chapters, until the 1970s, the courts had a hands-off policy on matters concerning the correctional process. This was partly because they felt correctional officials were in the best position to make decisions regarding the rehabilitation of criminals. Because of the arbitrary procedures used in earlier revocation hearings, the Supreme Court, in 1971, defined the basic rights of parolees at a parole revocation hearing in *Morrissey v. Brewer* (which, as you may recall, was applied to probation revocation as well, see page 171 in this chapter). Parolees must be notified in writing of the charges they face at least 24 hours before the preliminary hearing in which "probable cause" will be established. Second, the parolee will then have a full hearing in which he or she has a right to hear the evidence against him or her, to cross-examine, and to refute the testimony. Furthermore, parolees can present their own evidence and have the right to a written report from the hearing that must be held before a neutral third party. Some states mandate legal counsel at this stage.

• The Supervision and Control of Inmates in the Community •

Once the inmate has been granted parole, he or she is considered a parolee. Like probation, parole officers are responsible for the supervision and control of parolees during their release from prison. However, a major difference between the two is that parole officers have more control over the behavior of parolees because of their retained custody status. For example, because the parolee remains in "retained custody of the state," any violation of the terms of parole can result in his or her being returned to prison. Second, parolees are usually more serious offenders than probationers, and because they have served a portion of their sentence in prison, they have been exposed to the prison's subculture, have the stigma associated with having been a convict, and are returning to a family life that has been disrupted.[52] Failure to adhere to the conditions of parole can result in a revocation of parole and the return to prison.

• The Parole Officer's Role •

Parole officers are responsible for the supervision, assistance, and control of parolees during the period of their conditional release. Parole officers, like probation officers, are mainly assigned to field offices. However, they can also work in correctional facilities or temporary units. Abadinsky identifies three types of assignments they can fulfill: treatment agent, broker/advocate, and law enforcement agent.[53] Parole officers in correctional facilities counsel and prepare inmates for release to the community. Parole officers in temporary release programs combine both field and institutional functions. A few can also be assigned to special programs. The investigative role of the parole officer involves conducting a pre-release investigation, which yields a report similar to the presentence investigation used in probation. The pre-release investigation report is used by the parole board to assist in making a decision on whether an inmate is eligible for parole.

The literature on parole practices reveals that parole officers tend to act as "street-level bureaucrats."[54] In this role, parole officers use their discretion to deal differentially with individuals in their caseloads. The laws and the formal agency policies set broad parameters for the actions and judgments of parole officers. Elliot Studt's famous study of parole officers in California revealed that their individual styles were so varied that each could be thought of as almost a separate agency.[55] Michael Lipsky first used the term "street-level bureaucrats" to describe parole officers, meaning that while parole officers at times use their discretion to deal differentially with individuals in their caseloads, the actual thrust of their use of discretion is more toward agency "ways of doing business."[56] In other words, laws and formal agency policies set broad parameters for the actions and judgments of parole officers. What one is more likely to find is a group of 10 officers most often acting in a similar fashion, occasionally manifesting differences, while basing their similarities in discretionary authority.

Culbertson and Ellsworth point out that the roles adopted by probation and parole officers are determined by a variety of issues, ranging from the personality of the officer to the political-social-legal philosophy of the agency administering the supervision.[57] Finally, McCleary's classic study on parole officers in Cook County, Illinois, disclosed that decisions about individual parolees are influenced by the organization's definition of the situation, the officer's own perception of the parolee, and the officer's professional reputation. Certain parolees are viewed as threatening to the status quo because they make trouble for their officers and for the officer's superiors. Those individuals elicit special responses from their officers. By typecasting each parolee from the start, the officer neutralizes potential trouble. This is usually done by reviewing the parolee's files, initial interviews, and home visits. The parolees are categorized as sincere, criminally inclined, or dangerous—and they are supervised and handled accordingly.

• The Investigation Function •

The parole officer is not as extensively involved in the investigative process as a probation officer, but they may be called on by the parole board to conduct investigations for pre-release decisions. The pre-release investigation provides a report on the inmate that includes information on the offense that led to the inmate's incarceration, where the inmate will reside upon release from prison, employment status, special treatment programs, and recommendation for release. Changes made since the inmate was first received at the prison are also included. In addition, parole officers may be called upon to investigate incidents that may lead to the revocation of parole for those who violate the conditions of their parole status. McCleary, in his study, found that parole officers use preparole investigations as part of a "typing" process, categorizing offenders generally in terms of "control" and developing reports in a routine manner by focusing on a few key issues. Accordingly, parole officers understand that offenders will be released to different environments. Therefore, the parole officer's main focus is to control the offender's behavior while he or she adjusts to the new environment.[58]

• *The Supervision Function* •

Like probation officers, parole officers experience conflict between two basic roles: social worker and law enforcer. Supervising parolees has always meant both surveillance in order to protect society and treatment in order to rehabilitate individual parolees. However, since the 1970s, with the tougher attitude toward crime and the accompanying shift in emphasis from rehabilitation to incarceration and punishment, the law enforcement role of parole officers has taken precedence.[59] Parole supervision often has more of a control function than does probation. This is because the parolee presents a more difficult case and may be a greater danger to the community. As such, a parole officer may put the needs of the community ahead of the needs of the offender.

Depending on the organization of parole departments, some states may have field officers (or agents) and institutional parole officers. Field officers provide supervision, guidance, and control over an assigned caseload of parolees. The tasks vary depending on the type of offender. They guide and direct parolees during their period of adjustment from incarceration to normal community life. In addition, they investigate and take appropriate action concerning possible parole violations, new crimes, and other unacceptable behavior, and represent the agency in hearings concerning alleged violations. The parole officer is probably more likely to take on the role of law enforcer because the main concern is to make sure the parolee does not involve himself or herself in further criminal activity.[60]

The institutional parole officer has the primary responsibility for helping parole-eligible inmates prepare a reasonable parole plan. They prepare pre-release and other reports on inmates for the parole board and help inmates secure furloughs, work release, or halfway house placement. The institutional parole officer is likely to be utilized in states that have abolished parole or that use determinate sentencing structures. States that have abolished parole do not need field agents because inmates are released to the community at the expiration of the offender's sentence.

• Parole Programs •

Because reintegration is the primary goal of parole, there are different programs that help the parolee with this process. They include halfway houses, furloughs, work release programs, and intermediate sanction releases.

Halfway houses are transitional residences for inmates who are released from prison.[61] The halfway-house concept probably originated in England during the early 1800s, but the first formal recommendation for the creation of a halfway house in the United States was made in 1817 in Pennsylvania.[62] A Pennsylvania prison riot had stirred the legislature to think of various prison reforms, including housing provisions for ex-convicts who were often poor and could not find employment or adequate housing. The proposals were never implemented, however, because the public feared "criminal contamination." It was believed that if ex-offenders lived together, they would spread their criminality like a disease.

During the 1960s, correctional reform shifted to the community corrections approach. During earlier times, halfway houses were used to house the homeless, unemployed men or women released from prison. Today, these facilities house felony offenders in need of a brief residency. The housing is usually a structured environment that offers treatment services to the offenders. These offenders often need basic education, job skills training, and treatment for the abuse of alcohol or other drugs.

These facilities offer a homelike atmosphere with minimal security measures. Residents are classified according to their individual needs and assigned to a treatment regimen (which usually includes counseling, educational classes, and vocational training). They also share in the housekeeping responsibilities. As residents advance in the program, they are allowed to check in and out of the facility to go to work or receive training in the community. If unemployed, they may be assigned to do community service work. When residents have advanced to an acceptable level in their treatment plan, they are released from the center and placed under regular probation or parole supervision.[63]

Furloughs are authorized leaves from confinement for specified time periods and for specific purposes. The major mission of furloughs, as with halfway houses, is to aid in the reintegration of prisoners into society. Furloughs originated in 1918 in Mississippi. In those days, prisoners who had completed two or more years of their original sentences were considered eligible for furloughs. These furloughs usually involved conjugal visits with families or holiday activities for brief, 10-day periods. The purpose of this program then, as now, was to prepare offenders for permanent re-entry into their respective communities.[64] Furloughs are an outgrowth of work release programs, for which select inmates are chosen, usually through application for participation. Typically, inmates have served a significant portion of their originally prescribed sentences and are eligible for parole consideration. The success of inmate furlough experiences figures prominently in early release decisions by parole boards. Thus, offenders who are granted furloughs and who successfully comply with furlough requirements have an advantage over those not otherwise considered for such special consideration.[65]

Work release programs have been a part of American corrections since the nineteenth century.[66] Work release refers to programs that allow selected prisoners to be released from jail or prison during certain hours for the purpose of private employment.[67] In this sense, work release and educational release are forms of furlough because the release is authorized for a specific amount of time and for a particular purpose. Because inmates on work release are still in prison rather than having been conditionally released, prison officials are selective abut placing offenders in the program. Eligibility may be restricted to prisoners within a few months of release or to those who have attained trustee status.

The need for work release programs to ease the overcrowded situations in prisons also aids in the reintegration process of prisoners preparing to be released on parole. However, reliance on these programs makes correctional authorities vulnerable to instances of highly publicized failure. This happened in the case of Willie Horton. Willie Horton was a prison inmate in the Massachusetts correctional system who was sentenced to life without parole. Horton was released on weekend passes on furloughs nine times without incident. On the tenth pass, he broke into a Maryland home, twice raped a woman who lived there, and stabbed her husband. After this offense, he was convicted and sentenced to two life sentences in Maryland.

In the 1988 presidential campaign, this incident was used against Michael Dukakis, the Democratic Presidential nominee. In a debate with some of his fellow Democrats, Senator Al Gore brought up the Horton incident and asked Dukakis if he planned to implement such a furlough program at the federal level. The question caught Dukakis off-guard, but it did not stop him from getting the nomination. His Republican opponent, George H.W. Bush, used the Horton incident in one of his campaign advertisements, highlighting the dangers of the liberal furlough policy in Massachusetts.

Some believe the publicity given to the Horton and other cases may have affected furlough programs. In 1988, the number of furloughs declined, despite empirical evidence that most furloughed inmates commit fewer crimes while on furlough.[68] By 1990, however, the number of furloughs granted in some areas increased. In Florida, for example, prison furloughs were up 73 percent over the previous year.[69]

• Abolishing Parole •

For the last three decades of the twentieth century, parole became a target in the attack on the rehabilitative philosophy. The major criticisms focused on the unfettered discretion of parole boards to determine time served, and the ineffectiveness of parole's treatment component.[70] The indeterminate sentence, which is tied in with the concept of parole, was to provide prisoners with an opportunity for early release. This early release was contingent on a positive institutional adjustment. Positive changes in the prisoner's behavior were also an indication that the treatment was effective, and that the prisoner was ready for reintegration back into society. The authority to make release decisions was given to parole boards during the rehabilitation era. However, when the philosophy of punishment shifted from rehabilitation to retribution and punishment, the discretion given to parole boards came under attack.

Some critics believed that because parolees did not serve the entire sentence imposed by the judge, early release programs under parole did not hold prisoners accountable for their misdeeds to society. Another criticism of parole centered on a perceived lack of effectiveness in treating those prisoners who were given an early release. Moreover, evaluation studies of parole supervision offered little evidence that it was effective in reducing further offenses by the parolee, and at best, served only to delay re-offending behavior.[71] As a result, some states moved toward abolishing the institution of parole.

Abolishing parole removes the parole board, which makes the release decision based on information and knowledge of the offender's performance in prison. When parole is abolished, victims are not provided the opportunity to give their side of the story in a parole eligibility hearing to determine if the offender is ready for release. The abolition of the parole review and the ability of parole boards to decide who will be released (and when) also significantly undercuts post-release supervision. Abolishing parole is also referred to as automatic or determinate sentencing, meaning that the time of release is determined at the time of sentencing—unless it is shortened without cause.[72]

The Quakers were the first organization to call for abolishing parole.[73] In 1972, the New York State Special Commission on Attica was the next organization to follow suit, along with academicians who associated with the "just deserts" rationale.[74] These critics struck a chord with the public and the legislators and by the mid-1980s, all 50 states, including the District of Columbia and the federal government, revised or considered replacing indeterminate sentencing with determinate sentencing.[75] Despite the call for change, the majority of jurisdictions retained indeterminate sentencing, but several others passed determinate sentencing legislation and moved away from the rehabilitation philosophy.

In 1976, Maine was the first state to abolish parole. Between 1976 and 1979, other states—California, Colorado, Illinois, Indiana, and New Mexico—followed, eliminating or severely limiting the discretionary powers of their parole boards. Another five states—Connecticut, Florida, Minnesota, North Carolina, and Washington—followed suit from 1980 to 1984. Since this time, the pace has slowed down, with Delaware abolishing parole in 1990 and Virginia in 1995.[76] Ironically, some states that abolished parole have reversed the trend and reinstated discretionary parole. Colorado abolished parole in 1985 and reinstated it in 1993, while Florida provided a parole function under a new name: Controlled Release Authority. In Maine, the legislature enacted certain good-time provisions for the prison population in 1983.

In 1995, the American Probation and Parole Association and the Association of Paroling Authorities International formed a joint committee to counteract some of the blatant and damaging misconceptions about criminal sentencing in the United States. Realizing that the topic of parole abolition was again working its way onto legislative agendas around the nation, the joint committee commissioned a report as one way to begin to clear up these misconceptions. The report, in support of parole contends the following:

- Parole abolition has been tried and failed.

- Parole can actually make a sentencing system tougher.

- Parole is one of the strongest, most far-reaching weapons the system has to control violent and dangerous criminals.

- Parole is the one part of the system that has, as its foremost concern, the safety of community.

- Parole is an important ally within the system for the victims of crime. The public wants a system that protects its safety and peace of mind.

- Parole can be an effective, tough weapon to defend both of these.[77]

In essence, the report seeks to clarify some of the important lessons that have been learned by states that have retained, abolished, or reinstated parole.

• Probation and Parole Populations: A New Demographic Record •

In 2006, the total federal, state, and local adult correctional population—incarcerated or in the community—grew to reach a new high of nearly 7.2 million (versus 6.4 million in 2000). About 3.2 percent of the U.S. adult population, or about one in every 31 adults, was incarcerated or on probation or parole at yearend 2006. At the end of 2006, a total of 4.1 million adult men and women were on probation in the United States, representing a growth of 2.3 percent during the year. The adult parole population rose to a total of more than 780,000 by December 31, 2006 (see Table 5.1).[78]

The adult probation population grew 1.7 percent in 2006, an increase of more than 70,000 probationers. Forty-nine percent of all probationers had been convicted of a felony, 49 percent of a misdemeanor, and 2 percent of other infractions. Twenty-seven percent were on probation for a drug law violation, and 16 percent for driving while intoxicated. Three states registered an increase of 10 percent or more in their probation population in 2006, led by California with a 19 percent increase. Fifteen states reported a decrease in their adult probation population during 2006, with Alabama and Vermont experiencing the largest

TABLE 5.1
Persons Under Adult Correctional Supervision, 1995, 2000-2006

Year	Total estimated correctional population[a]	Community Supervision		Incarceration	
		Probation	Parole	Jail	Prison
1995	5,342,900	3,077, 861	679,421	507,044	1,078,542
2000	6,445,100	3,826,209	723,898	621,149	1,316,333
2001	6,581,700	3,931,731	732,333	631,240	1,330,007
2002	6,758,800	4,024,067	750,934	665,475	1,367,547
2003	6,924,500	4,120,012	769,925	691,301	1,390,279
2004	6,995,100	4,143,792	771,852	713,990	1,421,345
2005	7,051,900	4,166,757	780,616	747,529	1,448,344
2006	7,211,400	4,237,023	798,202	766,010	1,492,973
% change 2005-06	2.3%	1.7%	2.3%	2.5%	3.1%
Average annual % change 1995-2006	2.5%	2.4%	1.5%	3.8%	3.0%

Note: Counts are for December 31, except for jail counts, which are for June 30. Jail and prison counts include inmates held in private facilities. Totals through 2001 exclude probationers held in jail or prison.

Source: Glaze, L.E. (2007). "Probation and Parole in the United States, 2006." *Bureau of Justice Statistics Bulletin*. Washington, DC: U.S. Government Printing Office.

drops. Finally, Georgia had the highest rate of probationers per 100,000 (6,059), while New Hampshire had the lowest (450).[79]

In 2006, 58 percent of all adults on probation had received a direct sentence to probation from court, up from 48 percent in 1995. Twenty-three percent received suspended sentences, while 10 percent of probationers received a split sentence, which includes a short period of incarceration combined with a period of probation.[80] Fifty-seven percent of the 2.2 million adults discharged from probation in 2006 had successfully met the conditions of their supervision. On the other hand, approximately 18 percent of probationers who were discharged from supervision in 2006 were incarcerated because of a rule violation or new offense.[81]

Overall, the nation's parole population grew by 15,000 in 2006, a sudden surge relative to slow growth in past years.[82] Mandatory releases from prison as a result of sentencing statute or good-time provision comprised 52 percent of those entering parole in 2006.[83] Thirteen states registered double-digit increases in their parole population in 2006. North Dakota led the way with a 22 percent increase. Oklahoma experienced the largest decrease at 29 percent.[84]

About one out of every eight adults on parole in 2006 was a woman. Women represented a larger percentage of the parole population in 2006 (12%) than in 1990, when they comprised 8 percent of the population. Thirty-nine percent of adults on parole were African-American, while 41 percent of the parole population were white. Eighteen percent were Hispanic, and about 1 percent of parolees were of other races.[85]

Of the more than 519,000 parolees discharged from supervision in 2006, 44 percent had successfully met the conditions of their supervision, while 39 percent had been returned to incarceration either because of a rule violation or a new offense. Absconders (parolees who flee or fail to report to the parole officer as instructed) accounted for an additional 11 percent of those discharged from parole.[86]

INTERMEDIATE PUNISHMENTS

One of the practical realities of corrections today is that there simply are not enough prison beds to accommodate all the offenders the public and judges would like to send to prison. Because traditional probation is considered too mild a sentence for some of these offenders, a new and more politically palatable practice called intermediate punishments has been instigated.[87] What is pertinent about intermediate punishments is the emphasis on the word "punishment." The public does not want the offender to "get off easy" for his or her crime; therefore, the criminal justice system must demonstrate that the offender is paying a heavy price.

Intermediate punishment programs are designed to increase the amount of surveillance of the offender while he or she is in the community. They are meant to protect the community to the greatest possible extent short of incarceration in a prison. Some of these intermediate punishments, such as the boot camp prison, are actually mini-prisons themselves but are considered community corrections programs because of their small size and location in the community. Intermediate punishments include, but are not limited to, intensive supervision probation, boot camp prisons, home confinement, and day-reporting centers. Some of the techniques designed to increase the quality of supervision include drug testing, increased reporting requirements, and electronic monitoring. Intermediate punishment programs may include a combination of these practices. They may sanction different types of offenders with different types of reporting requirements and rules. It is instructive to consider each of these programs and techniques in context.

• Community Service •

A sanction that has grown in usage since the 1980s is community service work. Sometimes referred to as an intermediate sanction, and sometimes merely a condition of probation or parole supervision, community service work obligates an offender to work for a charity, government agency, or nonprofit agency without compensation. Examples of community service assignments include trash collecting near public roads, working at animal shelters, or washing school buses, police cars, or other government vehicles.

Although community service is imposed for a myriad of offenses, the crime that has done more than any other to generate an increase in community service work is drunk driving. One of the positive aspects of community service work is that, unlike monetary sanctions for which an offender's family often bears the brunt of the punishment, community service does not allow the offender to pass the burden of the sanction on to anyone else. In addition, offenders who cannot afford to pay fines may be ordered to perform community service work as an alternative. Although some community service work results in negligible benefits to the agency or the public, many community service projects serve the dual purpose of sanctioning (along with perhaps assisting in the rehabilitation of) offenders and serving the public.

• Intensive Supervision Probation and Parole •

With the increase in overcrowding of the prison system has come an increase in probation caseloads. Depending on the jurisdiction, it is possible to find probation officers with caseloads of 300 or more assorted misdemeanants and felons. In theory, this is not what probation was designed to do. Probation officers should have the time to get to know each of their clients and spend some time each month monitoring their behavior and helping them with their employment, families, and the goal to remain crime free. It is simply not possible for a probation officer to give the desired level of service to 300 cases. The probation officer saddled with this type of caseload is tied to his or her desk dealing with the paperwork required by the courts.

Intensive supervision probation involves greatly reduced caseloads for the officers and increased reporting requirements for the probationers. In some jurisdictions, a team of probation officers and aides work together to ensure that the offenders are maintaining law-abiding behavior. In conjunction with increased reporting requirements, the probationer may undergo random drug testing and/or some form of electronic monitoring. Intensive probation supervision is a program with special resources devoted to protecting the community from probationers who would be in a prison if there were adequate space.

• Electronic Monitoring •

Electronic monitoring is a recent and controversial technique in the supervision of probationers and parolees. It involves placing a device on the ankle of the client that sends a signal to the probation office if the client strays from home. There are several different types of electronic monitors, which work according to various technologies. Some work better than others. Given the rate of technological change, we can expect the technical proficiency and sophistication to improve. For instance, correctional systems may soon require offenders to have a tiny microchip placed under the skin rather than wearing an electronic anklet. The microchip would be monitored from a geosynchronous satellite that reveals the exact location of the offender. A device marketed by LoJack Corp. currently exists that allows cars to be tracked by the police. The electronic monitoring device would work in a similar way.

There are many companies that produce and market electronic monitoring devices. All of these companies offer a significant amount of information about their product. Go to the web sites and find some information on how these devices operate.

Regardless of the type of technology used, electronic monitoring is a technological solution to a human problem. Because probation and parole officers have such high caseloads and cannot adequately supervise everyone, they resort to using electronic monitoring to help them determine the location of their clients. Electronic monitoring, though, cannot tell the officer what the offender is doing. The offender may legitimately be at home but may be engaging in the use of illegal drugs or molesting children. As such, a home visit by the officer would be the optimal method of supervision. However, lacking the time and resources necessary to visit everyone on the caseload, electronic monitoring can be a useful supplement.

There are individuals who criticize electronic monitoring as being invasive of the offender's privacy. They liken it to the situation in the novel *1984* in

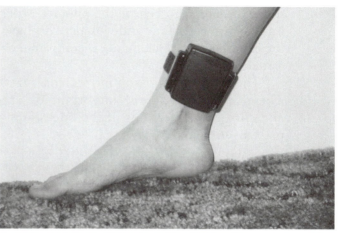

A person models an electronic anklet that functions as a transmitter. The anklet is tracked electronically by a receiver that is installed in the participant's home. The receiver is monitored via a telephone line by a computer in a central monitoring unit.

which the state watched over everyone with television cameras in their bedrooms. This "Big Brother" specter is disturbing because it keeps individuals under constant surveillance. To the offender, whose alternative is incarceration in a prison, this technological babysitter may not seem so draconian. The freedom to live with their families, eat their own food, keep their job, and enjoy the relative luxuries of television, a private bathroom, and solitude may outweigh the inconveniences imposed by electronic monitoring.

• Boot Camp Prisons •

Boot camp prisons have become a recent addition to many correctional jurisdictions, but it remains to be seen whether they become a permanent part of intermediate punishments. Patterned after military basic-training boot camps, these prisons aim to establish self-discipline, respect for authority, and fear of the criminal justice system in the offender. The ideal profile of an offender sent to the boot camp prison is a young, first-time offender who has committed a relatively minor crime. The boot camp program typically lasts from 90 to 120 days, during which offenders are subjected to physical training, work, and military-type discipline such as marching and constant inspection.

The boot camp prison answers several demands. First, to the public, boot camp prisons appear to be tough on crime. Young men and women are subjected to a harsh and Spartan lifestyle, not some seemingly "country club" prison. Another reason the boot camp prison is appealing is the fact that its short duration makes it economical for the state. For every prisoner in the traditional prison, three or four can be sent to the boot camp prison. Finally, the boot camp prison is attractive to individuals who believe the military experience is a positive influence on young men. Many individuals who have been in the military credit the experience with changing them from a child to an adult—almost like a rite of passage.

The boot camp prison movement is not without its critics, though. There are at least three important differences between the military and corrections versions of the boot camp that render the boot camp prison problematic.

> *Mission.* The military has a very different mission than the correctional system. The ultimate goal of the military is to train people to kill the enemy. It does not make a great deal of sense to many people that the correctional system should adopt a method that demands blind obedience and gets the prisoners in excellent physical shape. If the goal were to develop drug dealers and gang members, the military-style boot camp might make more sense.

> *Dominance and Humiliation.* The way the offender is treated in the boot camp prison is also a matter of concern. From a simple cultural patterning model, does it make sense to systematically train inmates in the techniques of dominance and humiliation? When they are released into society, what lessons have they learned that they can use to be productive citizens?

> *The Boot Camp Myth.* In the military, the real training and development of self-worth does not occur until after basic training. The boot camp breaks down the identity of the recruits; then further training builds it back up in the ideals of the military. In the prison boot camp, offenders are released back into society with little or no guidance or supervision.

As an intermediate punishment, the boot camp prison practice has great appeal to many people. As part of the community corrections concept, however, it does not emphasize treatment and integration back into the community. Some of the newer boot camp prisons are stressing more of the rehabilitative concerns of the community corrections ideal.

CONCLUSION

Despite the rhetoric of many politicians, the future of community corrections is bright. Calls for the abolishment of parole, mandatory prison sentences for many types of crimes, and a get-tough "war on crime" philosophy are mitigated by the sheer expense of the prison system. In truth, society simply cannot afford to incarcerate everyone who commits a felony. The numbers are so great that we cannot build enough prisons to accommodate the demand.[88] Because prison space is so expensive, it would drain needed resources of the state from other essential services such as schools and hospitals.

The fact that prisoners must be released at the end of their sentences is also becoming a critical concern. About 600,000 prisoners are now being released each year.[89] There is concern about the crimes that some of these released offenders might commit as well as about the readiness of these offenders to take a productive role in their communities. On the positive side, there are initiatives underway to help returning offenders, and research is being conducted to promote community safety and to devise better methods for assisting offenders as they leave prison. The exploding prison population may finally have some positive impact on community corrections.

Intermediate punishments will be modified and improved. More sophisticated technology will enable parole and probation officers to supervise the offender in the community. Drug-testing procedures will

---

▶ At the Movies . . . .

Tough Guys, 1986.

This comedy features Burt Lancaster and Kirk Douglas as Harry Doyle and Archie Long, two recently released inmates who have just served prison sentences that spanned practically half of their lives. The two career prison inmates have a difficult time adjusting to a much changed society, but they receive assistance from their young, idealistic, naïve parole officer, named Richie Evans. Officer Evans, portrayed by Dana Carvey, is somewhat fascinated by the two parolees, whose crime made them folk heroes—so fascinated that he resists his supervisor's instructions to treat the two celebrity criminals the same as he does his other charges.

Sherry Baby, 2007.

In this somber examination of the life of a parolee, Maggie Gyllenhaal portrays Sherry Swanson, who has just completed a three-year sentence for a drug conviction. Swanson struggles with her addiction to narcotics and adapting to life in the community, while trying to re-establish a relationship with her young daughter, who is being raised by Sherry's brother and sister-in-law. The latter resents Sherry's attempts to rebuild her maternal relationship.

Giancarlo Esposito plays Sherry's parole officer, Hernandez. He is honest, but also brutally blunt and needlessly profane and confrontational. Along with a female colleague, he employs use of force against Sherry merely as a threat, something that would not be tolerated in a real parole office. Officer Hernandez tries to help Sherry adjust to life in the community and with her drug problem.

continue to be developed to a point at which offenders cannot hide their drug use. Additionally, increasingly more offenders will be handled through some form of community corrections.

Nevertheless, the future holds more controversy for community corrections. No matter how well-conceived the programs or how well-trained the officers, there will be offenders who fail. Murder, rape, and child molestation will occur, and these sensational cases will prompt more demands to incarcerate more offenders. It is unlikely that we will ever solve the problems associated with community corrections. We can only hope to limit the damage done to individuals and society from the recalcitrant offender.

DISCUSSION QUESTIONS

1. What are the differences between probation and parole? What are the most important functions of each?

2. Identify three important cases associated with probationer and parolee rights. What is the significance of each case?

3. What is the relationship between indeterminate sentencing and parole?

4. What is a presentence investigation (PSI)? Who prepares the PSI?

5. Describe the different types of parole boards. Are parole board members experts in the field of corrections?

6. What are the major reasons for the revocation of probation? Parole?

7. What correctional activities are included in the term intermediate sentencing?

8. Are boot camp prisons successful? What problems can you see with them?

9. What is meant by net-widening? How does community corrections contribute to this problem?

FURTHER READING

Morris, N., and M. Tonry (1991). *Between Prison and Probation: Intermediate Punishments in a Rational Sentencing System.* New York: Oxford University Press.

Petersilia, J. (2002). *Reforming Probation and Parole in the 21st Century.* Lanham, MD: American Correctional Association.

NOTES

1. Walker, 1998.
2. Austin and Krisberg, 1981. See also, Blomberg, 1977.
3. Blomberg and Lucken, 1994.
4. Schur, 1973.
5. Black, 2004, 1240.
6. T.C.A. 39-3-1124, 1994.
7. 18 U.S.C. § 1361, 1995.
8. 18 U.S.C. § 1361, 1995.
9. Johnston, 1973, 8. The concept of imprisonment as a substitute for death or mutilation of the body was derived in part from a custom of the early Church whereby asylum or sanctuary was granted to fugitives and criminals.
10. Dressler, 1962, 7.
11. Dressler, 1962, 9.
12. Augustus, 1852.
13. Augustus, 1852.
14. Fitzharris, 1984, 338.
15. Champion, 1996, 96-97.
16. Donnelly and Clark, 1990.
17. Dickey, 1979, 28-39.
18. Allen et al., 2007.
19. Davis, 1990b, 16.
20. Davis, 7.
21. Chute, 1922.
22. Gottfredson and Gottfredson, 1988, 182.
23. Champion, 2008, 475-476.
24. Glaser, 1969, 292-293.
25. Petersilia et al., 1985.
26. Vito, 1984, 22-27; Vito, 1983; Fichter et al., 1987.
27. Vito, 1978, 123-132.
28. Austin and Krisberg, 1982, 374-409; Scull, 1977; Travis, 1985.
29. Edna McConnell Clark Foundation, 1982; Coffey, 1986; Huskey, 1984.
30. Vito, 1983, 66-67; Clear and O'Leary, 1983.
31. *Morrissey v. Brewer*, 408 U.S. 471 (1972).

32. de Beaumont and de Tocqueville, 1964, 146. Originally published in 1833.

33. Hughes, 1987.

34. Teeters and Shearer, 1957.

35. Erikkson, 1976.

36. Barnes and Teeters, 1959, 419.

37. Abadinsky, 2009.

38. Cole, 1986, 595.

39. Erikkson, 1976.

40. Clear and Cole, 2003, 372.

41. Smykla, 1981, 139-140.

42. Dressler, 1969.

43. Clear and Cole, 1994, 406-407.

44. Samaha, 1997, 626.

45. Riechel, 1997, 474.

46. Cromwell and Killinger, 1994, 225-226.

47. Scott, 1972; Metchik, 1992, 135-137.

48. Carlson, 1979, 105.

49. The Florida Parole Commission reported that civil litigation by adult male prisoners rose 450 percent following this change.

50. Cohen, 1995; Glaze, 2002.

51. U.S. Department of Justice, 1991.

52. Inciardi, 1993; Senna and Siegel, 1993.

53. Abadinsky, 2009.

54. Lipsky, 1980.

55. Studt, 1972.

56. Lipsky, 1980.

57. Culbertson and Ellsworth, 1985, 131.

58. McCleary, 1978.

59. Samaha, 1997, 637.

60. Abadinsky, 2009.

61. Wilson, 1985, 152.

62. Chamberlain, 1977; McCarthy and McCarthy, 1984, 204.

63. Abadinsky, 2009.

64. Marley, 1973.

65. Champion, 1996, 353.

66. Reichel, 1997, 487.

67. Goldfarb and Singer, 1973.

68. "Study of 53,000 Inmates in '87 Finds Few Did Harm." *The New York Times*, October 12, 1988; "Tough Talk Cuts Prison Furloughs," *Tampa Tribune*, November 27, 1988, 12.

69. "Prison Furloughs Up 73 Percent From Last Year," *Tallahassee Democrat*, November 12, 1990, 2C.

70. Bottomley, 1990; Rhine, Smith and Jackson, 1991.

71. Bottomley, 1990.

72. American Probation and Parole Association, 1995.

73. American Friends Service Committee, 1971.

74. Fogel, 1975; von Hirsch and Hanrahan, 1979.

75. Rhine et al., 1991.

76. Rhine et al., 1991; Allen, 1995.

77. American Probation and Parole Association, 1995.

78. Glaze, 2007, 2.

79. Glaze, 2007, 3-4.

80. Glaze, 2007, 2.

81. Glaze, 2007, 2.

82. Glaze, 2007, 6.

83. Glaze, 2007, 5.

84. Glaze, 2007, 5.

85. Glaze, 2007, 6.

86. Glaze, 2007, 6.

87. Morris and Tonry, 1990

88. Irwin and Austin, 1997.

89. Travis, Solomon, and Waul, 2001.

REFERENCES

Abadinsky, H. (2009). *Probation and Parole: Theory and Practice*, 10th ed. Upper Saddle River, NJ: Prentice Hall.

Allen, G. (1995). "The Courage of Our Convictions." *Policy Review* Spring:4-7.

Allen, H., E.J. Latessa, B.S. Ponder and C. Simonsen (2007). *Corrections in America: An Introduction*, 11th ed. Upper Saddle River, NJ: Prentice Hall.

American Friends Service Committee (1971). *Struggle for Justice.* New York: Hill and Wang.

American Probation and Parole Association (1995). *Abolishing Parole: Why the Emperor Has No Clothes.* Lexington, KY: APPA.

Augustus, J. (1852). *A Report of the Labors of John Augustus for the Last Ten Years: In Aid of the Unfortunate.* New York: Wright and Hasty.

Austin, J., and P. Hardyman (1991). *The Use of Early Parole with Electronic Monitoring to Control Prison Crowding: Evaluation of the Oklahoma Department of Corrections Pre-Parole Supervised Release with Electronic Monitoring.* Unpublished report. Washington, DC: National Institute of Justice.

Austin, J., and B. Krisberg (1982). "The Unmet Promise of Alternatives to Incarceration." *Crime & Delinquency* 28:374-409.

Austin, J., and B. Krisberg (1981). "Wider, Stronger, and Different Nets: The Dialectics of Criminal Justice Reform." *Journal of Research in Crime and Delinquency* 18:165-196.

Barnes, H., and N. Teeters (1959). *New Horizons in Criminology*, 3rd ed. Englewood Cliffs, NJ: Prentice Hall.

Baumer, T.L., and R.I. Mendelsohn (1991). "Comparing Methods of Monitoring Home Detention: The Results of a Field Experiment." Paper presented at the annual meeting of the American Society of Criminology, San Francisco, CA, 1991.

de Beaumont, G., and A. de Tocqueville (1964). *On the Penitentiary System in the United States and Its Application in France*, 146. Carbondale, IL: Southern Illinois Press; also originally published in 1833.

Black, H. (2003). *Black's Law Dictionary*, 8th ed. St. Paul, MN: Thomson West.

Blomberg, T.G. (1977). "Diversion and Social Control." *Journal of Criminal Law and Criminology* 68:274-282.

Blomberg, T.G., and K. Lucken (1994). "Stacking the Deck by Piling Up Sanctions: Is Intermediate Punishment Destined to Fail?" *Howard Journal* 33:62-80.

Bottomley, A.K. (1990). "Parole in Transition: A Comparative Study of Origins, Developments, and Prospects for the 1990's." In M. Tonry and N. Morris (eds.), *Crime and Justice: A Review of Research* 12:319-374. Chicago: University of Chicago.

Carlson, E. (1979). *Contemporary United States Parole Board Practices.* San Jose, CA: San Jose State University Foundation.

Chamberlain, N.F. (1977). "Halfway Houses for Nondangerous Offenders: What Are They? What Part Do They Play in Crime Control and Correctional Management?" *Center for Information on America* 26:1-6.

Champion, D. (2008). *Probation, Parole and Community Corrections*, 6th ed. Upper Saddle River, NJ: Pearson Prentice Hall.

Chute, C.L. (1992). "Probation and Suspended Sentence." *Journal of American Institute of Criminal Law and Criminology* 12:558.

Clear, T., and G. Cole (2003). *American Corrections*, 6th ed. Belmont, CA: Wadsworth.

Clear, T., and V. O'Leary (1983). *Controlling the Offender in the Community*. Lexington, MA: Lexington.

Coffey, B. (1986). "Community Corrections: An Equal Partner." *Corrections Today* 48:44-46.

Cohen, R.L. (1995). "Probation and Parole Violators in State Prison, 1991." *Bureau of Justice Statistics Special Report*. Washington, DC: U.S. Department of Justice.

Cole, G. (1986). *The American System of Criminal Justice*. Belmont, CA: Wadsworth.

Cromwell, P.F., and G.G. Killinger (1994). *Community-Based Corrections: Probation, Parole and Intermediate Punishments.* Minneapolis: West.

Culberton, R., and T. Ellsworth (1985). "Treatment Innovations in Probation and Parole." In L. Travis (ed.), *Probation, Parole, and Community Corrections.* Prospect Heights, IL: Waveland Press.

Davis, S. (1990). "Survey: Parole Officers' Roles Changing in Some States." *Corrections Compendium* 15:7.

Dickey, W. (1979). "The Lawyer and the Accuracy of the Presentence Report." *Federal Probation* 43 (June).

Donnelly, L., and S. Clark (1990). North Carolina's Community Penalties Program: *An Evaluation of Its Impact on Felony Sentencing in 1987-88.* Chapel Hill: University of North Carolina Press.

Dressler, D. (1974). *Practice and Theory of Probation,* 2nd ed. New York: Columbia University Press.

Dressler, D. (1962). *Practice and Theory of Probation.* New York: Columbia University Press.

Edna McConnell Clark Foundation (1982). *Overcrowded Time: Why Prisons Are So Crowded and What Can Be Done.* New York: The Edna McConnell Clark Foundation.

Erikkson, T. (1976). *The Reformers: An Historical Survey of Pioneer Experiments in the Treatment of Criminals.* New York: Elsevier.

Fichter, M., P. Hirschburg, and J. McGaha (1987). "Increased Felon Probation: Is It the Answer to Overcrowded Prisons?" Unpublished paper presented at the annual meeting of the Academy of Criminal Justice Sciences, St. Louis, MO.

Fitzharris, T.L. (1984). "The Federal Role in Probation Reform." In P.D. McAnany, D. Thomson and D. Fogel (eds.), *Probation and Justice.* Cambridge, MA: Oelgeschaler Gunn and Haig.

Fogel, D. (1975). We Are the Living Proof: The Justice Model for Corrections. Cincinnati: Anderson.

Glaser, D. (1969). *The Effectiveness of a Prison and Parole System.* Indianapolis: Bobbs-Merrill.

Glaze, L.E. (2007). "Probation and Parole in the United States, 2006." *Bureau of Justice Statistics Bulletin.* Washington, DC: U.S. Government Printing Office.

Glaze, L.E. (2002). "Probation and Parole in the United States, 2001." *Bureau of Justice Statistics Bulletin.* Washington, DC: U.S. Government Printing Office.

Goldfarb, S., and L. Singer (1973). *After Conviction.* New York: Simon and Schuster

Gottfredson, S., and D. Gottfredson (1988). *Decision-Making in Criminal Justice: Toward the Rational Exercise of Discretion,* 2nd ed. New York: Plenum Press.

Huffey, B.L. (1984). "Community Corrections Acts Help Promote Community-Based Programming." *Corrections Today* 46:45.

Hughes, R. (1987). *The Fatal Shore.* New York: Alfred Knopf

Huskey, B.L. (1984). "Community Corrections Acts." *Corrections Today* 46:45.

Inciardi, J.A. (1993). "Drug-Involved Offenders." *Prison Journal* 73:253-422.

Irwin, J., and J. Austin. (1997). *It's About Time: America's Imprisonment Binge*, 2nd ed. Belmont, CA: Wadsworth.

Johnston, N. (1973). *The Human Cage: A Brief History of Prison Architecture*: New York: Walker.

Lipsky, M. (1980). *Street-Level Bureaucracy: Dilemmas of the Individual in Public Services*. New York: Russell Sage Foundation.

Marley, C.W. (1973). "Furlough Programs and Conjugal Visiting in Adult Correctional Institutions." *Federal Probation* 37:19-25.

McCarthy, B., and B. McCarthy (1984). *Community-Based Corrections*. Belmont, CA: Brooks/Cole.

McCleary, R. (1978). *Dangerous Men*. Beverly Hills: Sage.

McLeod, M. (1989). "GettingFree." *Criminal Justice* (Spring):13

McLeod, M. (1986). "Victim Precipitation at Sentencing." *Criminal Law Bulletin* 22:501-517.

Metchik, E. (1992). "Judicial Views of Parole Decision Processes: A Social Science Perspective." *Journal of Offender Rehabilitation* 18:135-137.

Morris, N., and M. Tonry (1990). *Between Prison and Probation: Intermediate Punishments in a Rational Sentencing System*. New York: Oxford

Petersilia, J., S. Turner, J. Kahan, and J. Peterson (1985). *Granting Felons Probation: Public Risks and Alternatives*. Santa Monica, CA: RAND.

"Prison Furloughs Up 73 Percent from Last Year." *Tallahassee Democrat*, November 12, 1990, 2C.

Reichel, P. (1997). *Corrections*. Minneapolis: West.

Rhine, E.E., W.R. Smith, and R.W. Jackson (1991). *Paroling Authorities: Recent History and Current Practice*. Laurel, MD: American Correctional Association.

Samaha, J. (1997). *Criminal Justice*. Minneapolis: West.

Schur, E.M. (1973). *Radical Nonintervention: Rethinking the Delinquency Problem*. Englewood Cliffs, NJ: Prentice Hall.

Scott, J. (1972). "An Examination of the Factors Utilized by Parole Boards in Determining the Severity of Punishment." Ph.D. dissertation, Indiana University, 57-59.

Scull, A. (1977). *Decarceration: Community Treatment and the Deviant—A Radical Overview*. New York: Spectrum.

Siegel, L.J., and J.J. Senna (2005). *Introduction to Criminal Justice*, 10th ed. Belmont, CA: Thomson Wadsworth.

Smykla, J. (1981). *Community-Based Corrections: Principles and Practices*. New York: Macmillan.

Studt, E. (1972). *Surveillance and Service in Parole: A Report of the Parole Action Study*. Los Angeles: UCLA Institute of Government and Public Affairs.

"Study of 53,000 Inmates on Furlough in '87 Finds Few Did Harm," *The New York Times*, October 12, 1988, 12.

Teeters, N.D., and J. Shearer (1957). *The Prison at Philadelphia Cherry Hill: The Separate System of Penal Discipline:1829-1913*. New York: Columbia University Press.

"Tough Talk Cuts Prison Furloughs," *Tampa Tribune*, November 27, 1988, 12.

Travis, J., A.L. Solomon, and M. Waul (2001). *From Prison to Home: The Dimensions and Consequences of Prisoner Reentry*. Washington, DC: The Urban Institute.

Travis, L. III (1985). *Probation, Parole, and Community Corrections*. Prospect Heights, IL: Waveland.

U.S. Bureau of Justice Statistics (1997). *Nation's Probation and Parole Population Reached New High Last Year*. Washington, DC: U.S. Government Printing Office.

U.S. Department of Justice (1991). *U.S. Parole Commission, Parole Commission Rules* 28 C.F.R., 2.39, 2.40.

Vito, G. (1984). "Developments in Shock Probation: A Review of Research Findings and Policy Implications." *Federal Probation* 48:22-27.

Vito, G. (1983). "Reducing the Use of Imprisonment." In L. Travis, M. Schwartz, and T. Clear (eds.), *Corrections: An Issues Approach*, 2nd ed. Cincinnati: Anderson.

Vito, G. (1978). "Shock Probation in Ohio: A Re-Examination of the Factors Influencing the Use of an Early Release Program." *Journal of Offender Rehabilitation* 3:123-132.

von Hirsh, A., and K.J. Hanrahan (1979). *The Question of Parole: Retention, Reform or Abolition?* Cambridge: Ballinger.

Walker, S. (1998). *Sense and Nonsense about Crime and Drugs: A Policy Guide,* 4th ed. Belmont, CA: Wadsworth.

Wilcox, C. (1927). *Parole from State Penal Institutions*. Philadelphia: Pennsylvania State Parole Commission, 5-6.

Wilson, G.P. (1985). "Halfway House Programs for Offenders." In L. Travis III (ed.), *Probation, Parole, and Community Corrections*. Prospect Height, IL: Waveland.

COURT CASES

Gagnon v. Scarpelli, 411 U.S. 778 (1965).

Mempa v. Rhay, 389 U.S. 128 (1967).

Morrissey v. Brewer, 408 U.S. 471 (1972).

Community Justice and Corrections

CHAPTER 6

What You Need to Know

▶ Community justice involves a partnership between criminal justice professionals in law enforcement, the courts and corrections, and members and organizations from local communities.

▶ Goals of community intervention are to prevent crime and respond to victim and community needs when a crime is committed. Part of these needs include holding offenders accountable, determining appropriate sanctions, and looking for ways to reintegrate offenders into the community as productive and law-abiding members.

▶ Community justice is more focused on what occurs prior to criminal conduct, while restorative justice focuses more on its effectiveness in repairing harm and restoring victims and offenders to community life.

▶ Four approaches to community justice are victim-offender mediation, family group conferencing, community reparative boards, and peacemaking circles.

▶ The three key stakeholders in the community justice process are victims, offenders, and the community.

▶ Challenges to community justice include engaging communities, government net-widening, protecting individual rights, remaining aware that structural inequities may work against the community justice model, and remembering that community justice is not the solution to all problems in criminal justice.

INTRODUCTION

Community justice is a vision for criminal justice based on the idea of partnership between criminal justice agencies and the community. While the idea is not entirely new, the last decade has witnessed increasing government and community attention to this model as a viable alternative to more formal, state-run justice system strategies. In the community justice model, responsibility for public safety no longer rests solely with justice professionals. It is also generated from active working partnerships between justice professionals, community members, and local organizations and institutions. According to one definition, community justice includes:

> . . . All variants of crime prevention and justice activities that explicitly include the community in their processes. Community justice is rooted in the actions that citizens, community organizations, and the criminal justice system can take to control crime and social disorder.[1]

Examples of community-oriented justice initiatives are appearing in law enforcement, prosecutor's offices, correctional agencies, and judicial institutions. Community courts, community prosecution, community defense, community mediation, community corrections, and a range of preventive initiatives are included under the community justice umbrella.

The goal of this chapter is to explore the key concepts upon which the community justice ideal rests. Our objective is to give you a general sense of the intention, character, and potential impact of the community justice model. To do so, we will define the characteristics of community justice, place them in contrast to the current retributive model, present some examples of community justice practices, and explore some of the challenges to the community justice vision.

As you read this chapter, however, it is important to remember that the function of a "model" is to represent a depiction of reality, not necessarily the reality itself. The description of community justice presented here represents an ideal type. It does not necessarily present the reality of what is possible to achieve under the current conditions of poverty, racism, economic, and social inequality that beset our criminal justice system. These are important concerns that must also be considered when examining the viability of any approach that challenges traditional notions of how the government should do what it does. This approach does, however, suggest a standard to consider when thinking about the type of world in which you would like to live, what it would take to get there, and the role that we all play in achieving that outcome. After first explaining what community justice is, we will examine the key components of the community model noted in Box 6.1.

By the end of this chapter, you should have a basic understanding of what community justice is and is not, how realistic it is given

> **BOX 6.1**
>
> *Five Components of Community Justice*
>
> 1. Principles and core values
> 2. Practices
> 3. Stakeholder involvement—new roles for victims, communities, and offenders
> 4. Decision-making structures
> 5. Government (or criminal justice system) role

current conditions of the criminal justice policy environment, its key components, and how it compares to the traditional retribution model that currently guides the criminal justice system. You should also have enough information to decide whether you think the current model or the community justice approach holds the most promise for the future of the criminal justice system in general and corrections in particular.

WHAT IS COMMUNITY JUSTICE?

Community justice is fundamentally based on the notion of partnership between the criminal justice system and the community. Broadly speaking, community justice focuses on enhancing neighborhood stability, improving the quality and nature of community social networks, and expanding the community's capacity to manage its own problems.[2] Community justice suggests that responses to crime, and to the conditions believed to foster crime, should seek to empower crime victims, offenders, other citizens, and community groups to work with government in justice decisionmaking. These same groups should be involved in collaborative efforts to build community capacity, repair harm, and strengthen weak or damaged relationships. Carey defines community justice as "a community-led decisionmaking process to address interpersonal conflict which is marked by a problem-solving orientation, decentralized authority, accountability to each other [government and the community], and a consensus driven process."[3] According to Clear and Karp:

> . . . the ideal of community justice is that the agents of criminal justice should tailor their work so that their main purpose is to enhance community living, especially through reducing the paralysis of fear, the indignities of disorder and the agony of criminal victimization.[4]

The goal of community justice is, first, *preventive*. Community justice interventions seek to strengthen the ability of the community, community groups, and socializing institutions to control and prevent crime.[5] From this perspective, efforts to control crime concentrate less on "after the fact" responses and services and more on proactive efforts to change conditions in neighborhoods and institutions believed to contribute to crime. The idea is not simply to identify and target individual delinquents and those at risk of criminal involvement but rather to cultivate institutional change that promotes positive youth development and personal growth for all people.[6]

A second goal of community justice is to be *responsive*. In community justice, the response to crime should primarily address victim and community needs. Community members should be involved in the decision-making processes that both hold offenders accountable as well as determine appropriate sanctions. Responses to crime are designed to consider the best interests of the victim and the community as well as explore possibilities for reintegrating the offender into the community as a productive and useful member.

In responding to crime, there is some similarity between the values and concepts relating to what is known as restorative justice and those described as community justice. While there is significant overlap between the two, the simplest way to distinguish between them may be to remember that community justice approaches the justice process from the perspective that social problems engender justice system problems, and that separating pre-crime conditions from criminal events is unproductive. Restorative justice focuses primarily on the aftermath of the crime—now that it has already happened, what can we do about it?[7] While restorative justice focuses on its effects and looks to create outcomes that promote restoration and harmony, community justice is interested in what occurs prior to crime commission. In this chapter, we often refer to "restorative community justice" because that best characterizes what we are discussing—the integration of values from two models as they relate to prevention, consequences, and opportunities for healing and reparation resulting from criminal behavior.

In the traditional retributive model, the focus (or "target") of attention is the offender. Justice system activities are designed to determine guilt while protecting against rights violations and to punish for misdeeds. In the restorative community justice paradigm, goals shift from being solely concerned with conviction, incapacitation, and reduced recidivism to enhancing community capacity, reparation, and fear reduction.[8] In this model, the "target" of intervention is broadened from addressing only the offender to transforming communities, individual victims, other citizens, and interpersonal relationships.[9] Moreover, decisionmaking changes from having a primary focus on formal court hearings carried out by justice professionals to nonadversarial dispute resolution and mediation encounters. These new processes are designed to achieve sanctioning and preventive objectives while also emphasizing strengthening or rebuilding relationships.[10]

Community justice does not include just any program that exists outside an institution. There is an important distinction between community-based corrections and community-oriented corrections.[11] Community-based strategies refer to correctional projects that are located in the community. Government or nonprofit programs that are located in the community but do not involve community members in decisionmaking or offender reintegration are not examples of community justice. Community-based programs that focus solely on changing the behavior of the offender do little to enhance community capacity for problem-solving and conflict resolution.

Community-oriented interventions, however, are not only located in the community but are driven by the needs and interests of the community, and consider equally the needs of the victim, the community, and the offender when determining an appropriate response to criminal behavior. Community justice is a community-oriented strategy that begins with the premise that the community, not the offender, is the ultimate customer of the system.[12] The community justice paradigm also presumes a continuum of interventions ranging from less to more incapacitative. When community safety is at risk, it may be appropriate to incarcerate; when an offender can reasonably be supervised in the community without risking community well-being, there may be an opportunity for simultaneously strengthening the community and reintegrating the offender into a useful and productive social role. The primary difference between this approach and the current retributive model is that the community is fundamentally involved in the decision-making processes that will affect its members' well-being.

Broadly speaking, what is "new" about community justice is the movement toward systematic reform in criminal justice. Such reform includes a different set of values and principles to inform justice system activities and outcomes. In addition, there is a different set of goals for the system as well as different targets of intervention, decision-making processes, intervention practices, and finally, new roles for government and community participants.

PRINCIPLES AND CORE VALUES

• The Traditional Retributive Approach •

Core values in the traditional retributive model highlight offender culpability and responsibility, determination of proper punishment, and an adversarial process. Due process, preservation of individual rights, and following proper procedures are the cornerstones of this model. As a reactive strategy, the system responds after a crime has been committed; it does not address conditions that may result in crime, and it is not formally expected to do so. In this model, precipitating conditions that may lead to criminal activity are the domain of other social welfare systems, such as social services, health and mental health care systems, or drug treatment agencies.

Legal due process requirements structure this process to ensure that offender rights are protected from potential government abuse.[13] Establishing legal guilt (as proven in a court of law) takes precedence over determining factual guilt (as given by evidence, confession, witnesses, or other details). As a result, cases may take more than a year to reach trial and subsequent adjudication. Plea bargaining ensures the steady flow of cases into and out of the system, and caseload management considerations dominate the behavior and priorities of justice system practitioners.

The retributive approach considers individuals solely responsible for their actions, and thus they are individually sanctioned for their behavior. Societies and communities, although comprised of individuals, are not held accountable for the actions of their members. There is only a general sense of social responsibility for other individuals, although this predominantly refers to the "good" ones; the government is responsible for dealing with the "bad" ones. Criminal incidents are seen to impact only the particular victim(s) against whom the act was committed. The impact of an incident or crime on a community that diminishes the quality of life in that neighborhood is considered irrelevant. In this model, the central purpose of the justice system is to respond only to criminal incidents. Individual, or social, environmental, and economic conditions are, for the most part, considered to be outside the realm of the criminal justice system.

• The Community Justice Model •

The key difference between the community justice model and the traditional approach is the shift in focus. In the traditional model, the offender is at center stage; in the new community model, the community is the focus of attention.[14] As Box 6.2 suggests, community justice hinges on community engagement, community and victim involvement, and partnerships for action between the formal justice system and community members and organizations. Crime is seen as a symptom of broken relationships and disharmony rather than a cause of it, and the community is thus the primary resource for problem-solving. This design shifts the strategy from a competitive, adversarial model to one that works based on cohesion and harmonious relationships.

In this model, the community and the formal criminal justice system work together as partners to produce "justice." The goal of such a partner-

BOX 6.2

Principles of Community Justice

- The community, including victims and offenders, is the ultimate customer and full partner of the formal justice system.

- Partnerships for action, among justice components and citizens, strive for community safety and well-being.

- The community is the preferred source of, and resource for, problem-solving.

- The primary goal is harmony of the system components and the community.

- Community-based sanctions are worthy responses to the problem of crime.

- Work efforts must focus on the underlying causes of crime rather than simply responding to criminal behavior; crime is confronted by addressing social disorder, criminal activities, and behavior, and by holding offenders accountable to victims and the community

Source: *Working Group on Restorative Justice* (1996). Cited in Karp, D. (ed.) (1998). *Community Justice: An Emergency Field.* Lanham, MD: Rowman and Littlefield.

ship is for individuals to feel safe and protected in their own communities. It is based on the premise that this cannot occur without the active involvement and coordination of criminal justice professionals and community members alike. This model recognizes that there are some problems that the government is not equipped to manage, and the best resources are available outside of the formal justice system. In some instances, the community not only has the best resources but also has the most knowledge about where, how, and when to best confront crime and criminals.

Community justice stresses the importance of coordination of activities at the neighborhood level.[15] Community justice does not concentrate on individual incidents; rather, it examines and responds to patterns of incidents that affect neighborhoods and serve to create disharmony and disorder. Although determining community boundaries can be challenging, this model takes a rather broad view of "community"—it might be a neighborhood, a social or spiritual organization, a school district, or a group united by a purpose that brings them together. In the case of a criminal event, the community might be represented by those individuals or groups affected by the particular crime at hand. While the borders of community may be geographic, this is not necessarily the only means by which to identify a community.

Community justice presumes that community-based sanctions and interventions are an appropriate and meaningful way to deal with criminal behavior. While incarceration may be appropriate in severe cases, the preferred option should first be to see if the offender can remain in the community where he or she can both compensate the victim and the community for the harm done, as well as establish relationships that help him or her to remain a part of the community. The idea is that allowing the community to be involved in decisionmaking is the best way both to respond to a criminal event and to prevent future offending. Sanctions should be designed to serve the needs of victim and the community rather than just the system. Opportunities for earning restitution should be developed as well as programs to learn important skills that are valued by other community members. Such efforts enable offenders to compensate the victim, develop competence in an area valued by other community members, and develop relationships in their own neighborhoods.

It is important to remember that there are some significant challenges to this approach. Many people do not want to be involved in the justice system. Despite complaints about its inadequacies, most people are too busy living their own lives to worry about the lives of others, particularly strangers who are not "playing by the rules" and whose actions harm others. It is doubtful that those who can insulate themselves from the impacts of most street-level crime are apt to become involved. Those who are economically well-off, who live in secure gated communities, or whose resources enable them to navigate (and often completely avoid) the current system are most likely to be content with allowing government and the criminal justice system to do the work for them. In other words, they may not find sufficient incentive to change the way things are in favor of the way things could be—especially if that means giving up some of what they have in order to produce a more equitable and just system.

COMMUNITY JUSTICE PRACTICES

Illustrations of community justice permeate all levels of the justice system. Community policing, community prosecution, community courts, and community defender services are all examples of community justice processes that occur prior to adjudication.[16] There are also a variety of community sanctioning and decision-making models emerging throughout North America and the world that may be invoked at different stages in the process. Examples include Vermont's reparative boards; various models of family group conferencing used in New Zealand, Australia, and North America; numerous victim-offender dialogue programs; and circle sentencing and peacemaking approaches.[17] What some have generically described as "restorative community conferencing models" are now being implemented in environments ranging from schools and neighborhoods to residential facilities.[18] These strategies represent important nonadversarial sanctioning and dispute resolution alternatives to formal court sentencing or dispositional processes. They also serve as important case studies in increasing the direct involvement of crime victims, offenders, families, and other citizens as active participants in decisionmaking about the response to crime. Below are descriptions of several of the more well-known models operating in and around the United States.

• Victim-Offender Mediation (VOM) •

Throughout North America, as well as in many cities in Europe and other parts of the world, crime victims and offenders meet with trained mediators in victim-offender mediation (VOM) programs to allow the victim to tell his or her story to the offender, express feelings about the victimization, make the offender aware of the harm caused by his or her crime, and gather information about the offender and the offense. At the conclusion of most of these sessions, both victim and offender work with the mediator to develop a reparative plan that ensures that the offender provides appropriate restoration and restitution to the victim and/or the community based on direct input from the victim. Originally and still frequently referred to as Victim Offender Reconciliation Programs (VORPs), VOM programs are still unfamiliar to some mainstream criminal justice audiences and marginal to the court process in many jurisdictions where they do operate. However, VOM programs now have a long and respectable 25-year track record, and more than 300 programs now serve victims and offenders in Canada and the United States.[19]

• Family Group Conferencing (FGC) or Community Conferencing •

In cities and towns in the United States and Canada, as well as in Australia and New Zealand, family members and other citizens acquainted with a young offender or victim of a juvenile crime gather to determine what should be done in response to the offense. Often held in schools, churches, or other facilities, family group conferences (FGCs) are facilitated by a community justice coordinator or police officer. These conferences are aimed at ensuring that offenders face community disapproval of their behavior, that an agreement is developed for repairing the damage to victim and community, and that community members recognize the need for reintegrating the offender once he or she has made amends. Based on the centuries-old sanctioning and dispute resolution traditions of the Maori, a New Zealand Aboriginal band, the modern FGC was adopted into national juvenile justice legislation in New Zealand in 1989. Conferencing is now widely used in modified form as a police-initiated diversion alternative in Australia, and is being rapidly introduced in communities in Minnesota, Pennsylvania, Montana, other American states, and parts of Canada.

• Community Reparative Boards (CRBs) •

In a number of juvenile court jurisdictions in the United States, non-violent offenders meet with local citizen community reparative boards (CRBs) or "neighborhood panels" whose members recommend a plan that generally requires that offenders complete community service, make restitution to the victim, and become involved in educational activities or treatment. At the end of the session, the offender signs an agreement or contract to complete the plan within a specified time period. Community boards, which may be formally coordinated by probation, court, or diversion personnel, are generally composed of five or more local citizens who make recommendations for eligible cases referred by courts, intake departments, schools, or police officers.

• Circle Sentencing (CS) or Peacemaking Circles •

In Canadian towns and First Nation communities, and in two communities in Minnesota, residents sit, sometimes for hours, in a circle listening to citizens, offenders, victims, their advocates, and other community members speak about the impact of their crimes. When the feather or "talking stick" is passed to them and it is their turn to speak without being interrupted, circle participants may comment favorably on rehabilitative efforts already begun by the offender, who may be a chronic and sometimes violent perpetrator well known to the community. Speakers in these circle sentencing (CS) sessions also express concerns for the victim or about the continuing threat posed by the offender. At the end of the session, an attempt is made to come to consensus about a rehabilitative plan for the offender and an approach to "healing" the victim and the community. A recently updated version of ancient sanctioning and settlement practices adapted from the traditions of Canadian aboriginals[20]—as well as those of indigenous people in the Southwestern United States[21]—circle sentencing was resurrected in 1991 by supportive judges and community justice committees in the Yukon and other northern Canadian communities. These committees and community members are now working with judges, police, justices of the peace, and other supportive criminal justice officials to assume increasing responsibility for offender sentencing and supervision.

The four sanctioning models vary significantly on the extent to which community members participate in the process, make decisions about case outcomes, and are involved in policy decisions for the program. The degree to which programs are operated in partnership with or in isolation from government agencies will also vary. This may reflect either government or community preferences in a given locality, and it may also depend on the community's knowledge of the program and desire to become involved based upon the relationship with local justice professionals.

BOX 6.3

Case Studies of Restorative Justice Techniques

Case 1—After the offender, his mother and grandfather, the victim, and the local police officer who had made the arrest had spoken about the offense and its impact, the Youth Justice Coordinator asked for any additional input from other members of the group of about 10 citizens assembled in the local school (the group included two of the offender's teachers, two friends of the victim, and a few others). The Coordinator then asked for input into what should be done by the offender to pay back the victim, a teacher who had been injured and had a pair of glasses broken in an altercation with the offender, and pay back the community for the damage caused by his crime. In the remaining half hour of the approximately hour-long conference, the group suggested that restitution to the victim was in order to cover medical expenses and the costs of a new pair of glasses and that community service work on the school grounds would be appropriate.

Case 2—The victim, a middle-aged man whose parked car had been badly damaged when the offender, a 16-year-old, who had crashed into his car and also damaged a police vehicle after joyriding in another vehicle, talked about the emotional shock of seeing what had happened to his car and his costs to repair it. Following this, an elder leader of the First Nations community where the circle sentencing session was being held, and an uncle of the offender, expressed disappointment and anger with the boy. The elder observed that this incident, along with several prior offenses had brought shame to his family—noting that in the old days he would have been required to pay the victim's family a substantial compensation as a result of such behavior. After he had finished, the feather was passed to the next person in the circle, a young man who spoke about the contributions the offender had made to the community, the kindness he had shown toward the elders, and his willingness to help others with home repairs. Having heard all this, the judge asked the Crown Council (Canadian prosecutor) and the public defender, who were also sitting in the circle, to make statements and then asked if anyone else in the circle wanted to speak. An RCMP (Royal Canadian Mounted Police) officer, whose police car had also been damaged, then took the feather and spoke on the offender's behalf, proposing to the judge that in lieu of statutorily required jail time for the offense, the offender should be allowed to meet with him on a regular basis for counseling and community service. After asking the victim and the prosecutor if either had any objections, the judge accepted his proposal. In addition, he ordered restitution to the victim and asked the young adult who had spoken on the offender's behalf to serve as a mentor for the offender. After a prayer in which the entire group held hands, the circle disbanded and everyone retreated to the kitchen area of the community center for refreshments.

BOX 6.3 (continued)

Case 3—In a recent reparative board hearing in Vermont, a young man sat before the board members for a DWI conviction. In such cases, board members generally ask the offender how he is managing without a license (which is invariably suspended by the judge) after such convictions. While pursuing this line of inquiry, one board member found his chance to find common ground:

BM1:	How do you get to work?
Offender:	My friend, we both work up at Middlebury.
BM2:	Who are you working for up in Middlebury?
Offender:	[Name of contractor.] They're out of Boston.
BM2:	Yeah, what are you doing up there?
Offender:	Slate roofing.
BM2:	Which building do you work on now?
Offender:	On the college. It's a huge building.
BM2:	Yeah, I'm working on the same building.
Offender:	You are?
BM2:	Yeah. The science building.
Offender:	Yup! That's where it is.
BM2:	I thought I'd seen you before.

Two consequences seemed to follow from this brief interaction. First, the offender immediately relaxed, smiling for the first time in the hearing, feeling like he could identify with at least one person on the board. Second, there was an implication that his future behavior could be monitored. He might, in fact, see this board member again soon on the job.

Source: Adapted from Karp, D. (1997). "Community Justice." Research Seminar on Community, Crime, and Justice. Monograph. George Washington University/National Institute of Justice, 15.

Notably, eligibility varies from rather minor first offenders to violent, chronic offenders. While each model claims some discretion for citizens, only circle sentencing has allowed citizens control over admission (through community justice committee discretion). In VOM, the victim is in one sense the primary gatekeeper because the process is totally voluntary and depends on the victim's participation in order to proceed. The New Zealand juvenile justice system legislatively requires FGCs for adjudicated delinquents or those admitting guilt in all offenses except homicide, rape, and aggravated assault. Circle sentencing, VOM, and the New Zealand conferences all may admit more serious offenders.

Following a restorative decisionmaking process, the two most common community sanctions are restitution and community service. When implemented in a restorative community context, these sanctions offer the opportunity for offenders to both "make things right" with their victims and provide some service of value to the community. There are a variety of restitution programs operating in the United States and elsewhere that offer offenders the possibility of making reparation to the victim for the damage done. Some programs are designed so that offenders may perform some community service in order to earn the money to repay the victim. When implemented as a truly restorative program, both

Go to www.restorativejustice.org to learn more about the latest developments in restorative/community justice.

restitution and community service can enable offenders to repay their debt while also learning skills that are valued by the community. The offender can then offer something back to the community and become a truly responsible and productive member of that community.

STAKEHOLDER INVOLVEMENT: THE ROLES OF VICTIM, COMMUNITY, AND OFFENDER

• The Traditional Model •

As described previously, the traditional model focuses almost exclusively on the offender, with little attention paid to either the victim or the community. Government actors, in the form of prosecutors and defense attorneys, act on behalf of both victims and offenders. The victim and the offender may never actually see one another or interact on any level. The state provides attorneys for both parties, and the prosecutor is even empowered to proceed in the absence of a participating client (i.e., the victim). Acting as the injured party, the state can prosecute on its own behalf, and if the prosecutor thinks it is in the best interest of the case, the victim's voice may never actually be heard.

In this model, the needs of the "working group"—comprised of the judge, the prosecutor, the defense attorney, the court clerk, and sometimes the probation and police officers—dominate the justice process.[22] The adjudicatory process is controlled by the interests of the prosecutor and the defense attorney, who typically have too many cases and too few resources. If there is a conviction, the judge then determines the sanction based on the offender's current charge and prior criminal history. Sometimes, the probation officer may have input into the sentence by virtue of the presentence investigation (PSI) report. Victim and community concerns are at best considered secondary, and at worst disruptive to moving cases through the system efficiently. In fact, victims and communities are not defined as stakeholders in the process, but rather are peripheral to the "real" focus of the action—the offender and his or her crime. The victim might have a small role as a witness for the prosecution, but there is little opportunity to present the material, psychological, or social effects the crime may have had on the victim's well-being.

In states that permit it, victim participation is generally limited to giving input in the form of a victim impact statement (VIS). This is the only opportunity for the victim to present information about the impact of the crime on his or her life. The VIS can be in written or oral form and may or may not be considered by the judge in imposing the sentence. Because such a statement generally occurs after legal guilt has been established, it is not fundamental to the core system values of due process and establishing offender culpability. While it is relevant to the value of imposing punishment, its "nonexpert" quality often diminishes its significance. The sentence (and sometimes even the charge itself, as a result of plea bargaining) generally bears little relationship to the harm caused. In addition, the victim is rarely compensated for his or her loss. Sentences are considered separate from the criminal act—they are linked only in determination of severity, not in terms of relevance to the damage done or harm caused to the victim.

Communities have little or no role in the current justice process. Although they provide the context within which crime occurs, they are generally perceived as made of stone and concrete rather than being flesh-and-blood entities. Because crime is often not seen as directly impacting those living in the immediate area, the justice system may ignore those other than the parties directly involved in a criminal event. Think, though, of how you might feel if your neighbor's car were vandalized. Would such an act make you fear for the safety of your own vehicle? What about if a neighbor's house were burglarized? Would you feel less safe in your own home at night? These are the types of impacts crime can have on the surrounding community and on the individuals who live close by. It becomes even more threatening if the crime is a violent one in which a neighbor or other community member is assaulted.

The Community Model

There are three key stakeholders in the community justice process—the victim, the offender, and the community.[23] The community justice model depends on the full involvement of all stakeholders.[24] Because there is a great deal of overlap between community justice and restorative justice, we will use the term "restorative community justice," since it best characterizes the model we are discussing.[25]

The role of the victim is especially important in the restorative community justice model. Crimes are seen as inflicting harm on victims, not the state, and thus it is victims who should be compensated and whose interests should be considered when determining the method and severity of sanction. It should be clear here that there is a difference between the interests a victim may have in the outcome of the process and the rights that victims have won (through the victim rights movement) that allow them to be seen and heard and to be supported by the community and the formal justice process. In the community model, victims are integral to the process both in terms of respecting their rights as delineated by statute as well as in honoring their interests in expressing themselves and participating in the justice process. While the traditional approach may view victim rights as necessarily antithetical to those of offenders, the restorative community justice model promotes an approach by which victims may gain rights and the ability to express their interests without offenders sacrificing their rights. This model does not require lawmakers to "choose sides" between victim and offender but rather promotes a more holistic approach.[26]

Through community-oriented options such as victim-offender mediation and community conferencing, victims have an opportunity to meet "their" offender face-to-face and to discuss the impact of the crime on their lives.[27] Victims also participate in determining the appropriate response to the crime, as well as how they would like to see the offender make compensation for the damage wrought or harm inflicted. The process itself elevates the role of the victim and focuses attention on victim needs, while allowing for victim, offender, and community input. Although not the only dimension of restorative community justice, it is the victim's central role in the justice process that perhaps most distinguishes this model of sanctioning from traditional approaches.

The role of the offender is altered considerably in the restorative community justice model. First, the offender moves out of center stage, while the victim and the community gain importance. The offender thus becomes accountable to the real targets of his or her criminal actions rather than to the state acting on behalf of the victim or as "pseudo-victim." Second, there is a shift from proving legal guilt as the focus of justice system activity to determining an appropriate response to the crime. The idea is that the breakdown in relationships evidenced by the crime itself can be used to further a positive and healing experience rather than one devoted to blame and meting out punishment. In a restorative community justice model, the offender will either be adjudicated guilty and then given the opportunity to participate in a restorative process, or he or she may admit responsibility and the process will move on to the real heart of the problem—what should be done about it. Less time is spent on adversarial "bargaining" between paid "experts" (i.e., the prosecutor and the defense attorney) and more on developing a meaningful response to the event through stakeholder input. Determining what constitutes a "meaningful response" is gauged by the satisfaction of the key parties. Is the outcome, or sanction, satisfactory to the victim, the offender, and the community or its representatives, whenever possible and appropriate?

In a truly restorative community model, the offender will be held accountable to the victim and/or the community by performing some work that simultaneously helps develop his or her own skills while at the same time repaying those affected by the crime. This shift allows the crime to become an opportunity for: (1) helping the offender develop skills that are valued in the community and that can facilitate his or her reintegration as a productive member of the community; (2) compensating the victim and/or the community for the harm and/or damage inflicted; and (3) furthering the possibility of healing and reparation between the offender, the victim, and the community. An important element is that the offender gets the opportunity to lose the permanent stigmatizing label of "offender" and regain status as spouse, sibling, student, child, parent, employee/employer, and community member.

There is the possibility that certain stakeholders, particularly some victims, will not be interested in "repairing harm," "rebuilding relationships," "developing offender competencies," or other assorted purported benefits of the restorative community justice model. Some victims simply want to be left alone. Some victims simply want the offender put somewhere where he or she cannot cause future harm. Sometimes the power structure that surrounds the event and the stakeholders is so unequal that restorative values cannot be enacted (e.g., when an offender of a different racial or ethnic or financial background

AP Photo/West Central Tribune, Bill Zimmer

Kenny Turck, coordinator of the circle-sentencing program in the Willmar, Minnesota, region, says the volunteers who work with juvenile offenders as part of their sentence bring a "realness" that changes kids lives and gets results. Several counties in Minnesota have circle-sentencing programs.

is confronted in a bigoted and/or intolerant community, or when a less influential person is victimized by a powerful community member). These structural considerations need to be taken into account when implementing this approach, and it is important to recognize that there may be some very basic work to accomplish in the community before any of these strategies can become even remotely effective. Even in the face of these concerns, it is also important to recognize the value each stakeholder brings to the process and the importance of both the governmental and community roles. It is the concept of partnership that is central to the community justice ideal, and the way this becomes meaningful is through the active involvement of all the relevant stakeholders.

THE PROCESS OF DECISIONMAKING

In community justice, the focus is on long- and short-term problem-solving at the community level.[28] Community justice is preventive and focuses on areas that are likely to create potential problems for residents, rather than only responding to problems once they have already occurred. Attention is paid to crime as a symptom of an unhealthy and disconnected society rather than as a unique and isolated occurrence. While the traditional model sees the crime problem as a "war" to be waged, the problem-solving approach of community justice relies on information, deliberation, and mutual interest to bring peace to a community. Its premise is dispute resolution and satisfaction of the parties as opposed to an adversarial structure where "winners" triumph over "losers." In this model, there are no "enemies" to be conquered, but rather problems to be solved.

Community justice also requires decentralization of authority and accountability. In this way, communities can take more responsibility for, and ownership of, their own problems.[29] This requires transferring justice system authority whenever possible to the local level, where problems are most evident and solutions most likely to occur. In this model, criminal justice professionals are responsible to community members in addition to professional superiors. Members of one justice subsystem (e.g., police) may be linked with members of another subsystem (e.g., probation) to work together in the community. Problems are not isolated to one or another branch of the system, but rather can be cross-referenced for better coordination and idea-sharing. This tends to encourage innovative problem-solving that reflects the priorities and issues of the locality. Community justice requires that more authority and accountability be held at lower levels of the criminal justice organization as well as within community associations.

Citizen participation is critical in the community model, as citizens are most likely both to know the problems with which the community is confronted and to be most invested in fostering safety and peacefulness in their own neighborhoods. Citizens need to work with local justice professionals to identify resourceful solutions that are practical, creative, and direct. Citizen participation is necessary for developing informal ways to censure antisocial behavior and reintegrate offenders as productive members of the community. Moreover, active citizen participation will help victims feel connected with a broader sense of community of support. Citizens may become active through a variety of means, such as citizen advisory panels, volunteer associations, and community meetings.[30] In these capacities, they may interact work with justice professionals whose work will be triggered in response to citizen-identified needs.

Again, not all citizens want or are able to become involved. This model rests on the assumption that there are community members who are willing and able to take responsibility for generating and partici-pating in restorative community justice processes. At first glance, this scenario may seem unlikely and too idealistic, because only a handful of particularly motivated individuals in any given community might be willing to cooperate. There are, however, increasingly more examples of citizen involvement in justice processes. In Vermont, for example, community members support and participate in that state's Department of Probation–sponsored community reparative boards where a panel of community members participate in determining appropriate probation-ary sanctions. Colorado is also having some success with this approach. In addition, there are many examples of family group and community conferencing programs that have been developed and generated by com-munity members. To some extent, the key seems to lie in educating residents about the potential of such efforts and actively engaging their participation. This may be easier in some places than in others.

THE ROLE OF GOVERNMENT AND COMMUNITY

In the last several decades, there has been a profound change in the role and responsibility of government in the response to crime. Indeed, most "baby boomers" and older generations can recall a time when adults in their neighborhoods or small towns took responsibility for looking after and imposing informal controls on neighborhood children other than their own. Moreover, there were numerous informal means of resolving disputes and disturbances peacefully as well as "sanction-ing" behaviors that went beyond normal tolerance without resorting to formal court processes. In effect, community members—with the encouragement and support of police, schools, churches, and other socializing institutions—often "took care of" problems that now end up in juvenile and criminal justice courts. Although not all of these informal approaches were as sensitive to diversity in culture and lifestyle as we would now expect, it seems that perhaps something is missing as com-munities have lost their capacity to respond to many of the problems that now find their way into court dockets.

Table 6.1 suggests some of the fundamental differences between the role of government in the traditional retributive justice system response to crime and the community justice model.

• The Traditional Model •

As suggested by Table 6.1, there are several important distinctions as to how each model sees the role of government in the criminal justice system. In the traditional model, the government is the primary deci-sionmaker who determines what is best for all parties. This model sees

TABLE 6.1
Role of Government in Traditional and Community Justice Models

Traditional	Community
Primary government role is to prosecute offenders while ensuring protection of thier rights and consideration of their needs. Offender is, in effect, the primary customer of the system; the community is irrelevant.	The community, which includes both victims and offenders, is the ultimate customer, as well as a full partner with government in producing "justice."
Government's central job is to establish guilt and punish wrong behavior by imposing sanctions proportionate in severity to the crime committed. Type of sanction imposed need not be related to type of crime committed.	Role of formal system is to work with and empower the community in holding offenders accountable to those harmed. Community input helps assure that sanctions reflect harm done and encourage "making things right" whenever possible. Proportionality is determined by the extent to which both victims and offenders feel satisfied with the outcome.
Government is the expert decisionmaker in determining appropriate responses to criminal behavior. The community is best served by delegating responsibility for "justice" to government professionals.	Community members should be active participants in problem-solving, preventing criminal victimization, and conflict resolution. The best way to ensure community safety and well-being is to create partnerships for action between the community and the government.
Government is responsible for maintaining order, securing peace, and sanctioning offenders.	Government is responsible for ensuring order; community is responsible for maintaining peace through promoting harmonious relationships.
Primary justice responses must remain within the context of the formal criminal justice system; informal community-based initiatives should remain marginal to the "real" work of the system.	Informal community-oriented programs are critical to maintaining peace and harmony in the community; community and victim involvement is crucial to resolving and preventing crime.

victims and communities as being largely outside the process and hence less important to the fundamental goals of the criminal justice process. The government is responsible for ensuring that the punishment is equal in severity to the crime committed. Yet, there is no requirement or intention that the type of sanction itself be related to the harm caused. In addition, sanctions need not necessarily bring compensation or satisfaction to the victim, nor harmony and peace to the community.

Holding the offender accountable to the state ensures that government needs and activities dominate the process; these are dictated, for the most part, by the interests of the offender and of the state. Overall, the process is predominantly driven by system needs—for example, to reduce court dockets or divert offenders—rather than by the combined needs of citizens, victims, and offenders.[31] In this model, there is no question that government "experts" are the ultimate decisionmakers and are those ultimately responsible for determining and authorizing justice outcomes.

• The Community Model •

What is most important here is not the specific tasks practiced by either the government or the community but rather the nature of their relationship to one another. One practitioner, Kay Pranis, has suggested that the relationship between justice systems and communities evolves as the government slowly changes in relation to the community role.[32] The goal of shifting the role of the system from "expert" crisis manager to "partner" with the community occurs as citizens take on more responsibility and provide more input in an emerging collaborative process.

The concept of transferring decision-making authority to the local level is a key element here.[33] Efforts to centralize, professionalize, and expand criminal justice and social services have, over time, sent messages to communities to "leave it to the experts." In doing so, justice agencies may have inadvertently undercut the role and responsibility of citizens, institutions, and community groups in responding to crime and disorder, leaving communities more helpless and hapless. The community model presumes that decisionmaking is best confronted at the local level where problems actually occur. The presence of creative solutions derived from community members' own ideas is a basic component of the community justice model.[34]

Traditionally, the formal system has maintained a tight hold on justice initiatives and has labeled those outside the traditional menu of choices as "alternatives."[35] In the community justice model, however, such options are not considered alternatives but rather integral parts of the justice process itself. Community justice presumes that the community is capable of making informed decisions about individual cases as well as about what is best for harmonious relationships and community-building.[36] Here, government should provide guidance when necessary and serve as a fallback when the community is unable to achieve consensus or is unwilling to voluntarily participate; it is only at this point that legal authority should represent the larger community.[37] In this way, the job of maintaining order can be left to government, while the job of preserving peace can at least initially remain in the community.[38]

There is an important distinction here between community involvement and community engagement.[39] When the community is "involved," the government, while valuing community input in an advisory role, still dominates and controls the process. Community engagement, on the other hand, suggests partnership between criminal justice agencies and the community. When communities are engaged, they are central to accomplishing the job of "doing justice." They have helped design the processes that will impact their lives and communities. In order for communities to "own" their own justice problems, they must be intimately engaged in identifying, analyzing, and resolving them.[40] When communities are engaged, they are no longer outsiders sitting in the stands while the main action takes place on the court before them. Rather, they are on the court as key players in the game. An example of this might be community policing, which, if successfully implemented, requires the input and full partnership of the community. There are numerous examples of situations in which community policing has missed the intent of the community justice approach by mistaking the goal as being "community involvement" instead of community engagement.[41]

The community justice model contends that vital resources exist within the community to which government does not have direct access. Without access to these resources, crime and its related problems cannot be as effectively addressed. For example, informally supporting victims and reintegrating offenders into productive social roles can often be best handled by the community, not the government. There are also other important resources that may lie outside the scope of governmental role, such as identifying mentoring adults who can help youths develop skills or perform schoolwork, locating spiritual or religious organizations that involve youths and community members in activities designed for and

---

▶ Ethics Focus: "An Eye for an Eye?"

You are in charge of the Governor's "community empowerment" task force, which has involved community representatives from each county in your state. The task force is charged with making recommendations to the Governor regarding how the state could improve the justice process within the community. The representatives seem to fall into one of two groups: those who advocate a more retributive approach and those who support a more restorative approach. The retributive group wants offenders to be punished within the community. They offered suggestions such as publishing their names in the paper, performing community service while wearing old-fashioned prison uniforms, and a one-strike program by which they would be sent to the state prison after one violation. The restorative group is more concerned with reconciling victims and offenders whenever possible, which would include financial restitution and counseling in many cases. Your role is to bring the two factions together and come up with a useful recommendation to the Governor's office.

What are some of the ethical issues regarding the retributive and restorative factions? How can you balance the concerns of the two factions? What will you recommend?

about the community, or engaging small businesses dedicated to improving the quality of life in the neighborhood by employing local youths. The community justice model sees strength in empowering the community to resolve its own conflicts at the local level without involvement of the formal justice system.

CHALLENGES TO THE COMMUNITY JUSTICE APPROACH

There are a variety of concerns about the community justice model raised by advocates and critics alike. These revolve around issues of defining and engaging communities, governmental versus community authority, individual rights and the encroachment of personal liberties, societal structural inequities, and overly optimistic expectations of the community model. Some of these issues are briefly detailed below. As with any new model, this one must be challenged and refined as it experiences its own growing pains. In fact, the absence of such critique would more likely signal a useless intellectual exercise rather than a serious possibility for transforming the nature of the criminal and juvenile justice systems.

• Defining and Engaging Communities •

One of the most difficult problems in engaging the community is locating it.[42] As individual neighborhoods have disintegrated in concept and in practice, community members often tend to insulate themselves both for self-protection as well as because they feel disconnected from neighbors and local businesses. The urban sprawl has resulted in dispersion of the city centers that once held common gatherings. Communities are thus more likely to be defined through religious and spiritual centers, schools, professional organizations, or other means by which people from diverse areas are brought together. Moreover, while geographic communities have become more insular, interconnectedness through other media such as computers has become more commonplace.

Communication by telephone, fax, the Internet, e-mail, and other modes of modern telecommunications simultaneously expands global relationships while potentially diminishing local ones. One can now communicate with hundreds of individuals and never have to leave the house or actually talk out loud to another person. Moreover, as people increasingly tend to work in home businesses and virtual offices, the workplace gets lost as a common meeting ground wherein individuals share stories and become related. An unfortunate side effect of this technology is that as people lose reasons to interact on a personal level, their fear of and isolation from one another tend to increase.

As a result of these trends toward seclusion and virtual communication, encouraging community members to take responsibility for their own environments can be a laborious task for justice professionals. Likewise, as community members lose their sense of connectedness to one another, it becomes increasingly difficult for disenfranchised members (i.e., victims and offenders) to reconnect and find support with their own immediate surroundings. This creates special problems for youths from troubled neighborhoods who are unable to form bonds with conventional adults who might mentor them through challenging periods of adolescent peer pressure and frustration with lack of opportunity.[43] Corrections and other justice professionals are often faced with resistant community residents who are doing their best to hold on to what they have without being asked to contribute more in the best interests of the community.[44] Hence, it may appear to many that the best alternative is to lock "them" away, enabling the rest of "us" to move on. The challenge here is to create a vision whereby community members see more possibility in creating a viable, vibrant environment wherein all members are included and cared for, rather than one in which disorderly individuals are simply shipped off somewhere else.

• Governmental vs. Community-Based Net-Widening •

Another concern often voiced in the literature of restorative and community justice is the danger of expanding government "nets" where marginal offenders who might otherwise be released are caught up in the web of governmental control. An important distinction is made in restorative community justice between governmental versus community-based net-widening.[45] While expansion of "government nets" may have detrimental implications for juvenile offenders, strengthening "community nets" may be beneficial and serve to (re)integrate the offender into the community. Diverting first-time offenders to community sanctioning processes such as mediation may reduce future offending as community groups and citizens become more aware of the needs and risks presented by such offenders. This may in turn encourage the community to take responsibility for preventive action at the neighborhood and institutional levels.[46]

• Individual Rights •

There is a continuing debate about the extent to which sacrificing individual rights is in the interest of the common good.[47] Some citizens are willing to sacrifice an amount of freedom in the interest of personal security (e.g., gun control); others prefer individual liberty at any cost and see any governmental intrusion as unjustified state tyranny. There is no simple formula by which to evaluate the preferences of a community and then to provide precisely the right balance of control, protection, and liberty. According to Clear and Karp, the problem is not in striking the right balance but rather lies in misunderstanding the roles played by individuals and the state.[48] Government actions may create the conditions that allow individuals to grow and develop; this enables them to make contributions benefiting the public good. It is possible that by increasing social control, government fosters those conditions that allow us to live with a certain degree of freedom and autonomy. "City air may make men and women free, but it also paralyzes many behind dead-bolted doors. Individuals need a certain amount of security in order to pursue their own happiness."[49]

The balance between these competing demands may naturally occur as the community begins to assume more responsibility for public safety and the government role shifts from that of "justice provider" to "justice facilitator." The adversarial relationships that characterize today's justice system need not also characterize the relationship between the state and the community. It is possible to envision the two as equal partners in creating safe and peaceful communities. The outcomes are beginning to speak for themselves. Some of the more progressive states pursuing the community justice model include Vermont's Reparative Community Boards sponsored by the Department of Probation, or Minnesota's model conferencing and circle programs inspired by leaders in that state's Department of Corrections. There is no question that what people want is to be able to pursue their own livelihoods and dreams without threat of physical harm or financial ruin. The government has an important role to play in facilitating that goal, but it cannot successfully do so without the collaboration of the community.

• Structural Inequities in Society •

It should not go unnoticed that there are certain structural inequities that often work against the community model ideal. For instance, poor people (the "have nots") do not have a lot of power. Everyone is not equal in our present social and economic structure. Moreover, some of the "haves" may devise rather solid structures to maintain the imbalances that preserve their interests. These imbalances can cross social, economic, racial, ethnic, and gender lines and create significant obstacles for implementing a model such as the one presented here. In addition, when considering that most people chiefly just want to be left alone to live their lives, the idea of creating an integrated, harmonious society in which individuals take responsibility for one another seems a bit unrealistic.

The challenge is in overcoming the notion that it is primarily the poor and disempowered who most benefit from a community justice model. In fact, although the powerful may seem less in need of the benefits offered by a model like this, it is hard to argue that we would not all be better off with less fear, better relationships with those in our communities and neighborhoods, and a more productive citizenry. The trick is how to get there. It is important to recognize that the problem is not simply crime but rather the antecedent conditions that beget criminal antisocial behavior. Government and communities must be willing to devise new approaches that are capable of generating change at the structural level.

• Community Justice as a Panacea •

Community justice is not a solution to all the ills of the current justice system, and it should not be held to standards that unrealistically expect zero crime and neighbors hugging each other on the street while exchanging family photos. There are clearly conditions in which a community approach may be inappropriate at best, and harmful at worst. Amitai Etzioni, a leader in developing the communitarian ideal, suggests that:

- Not all criminals can or should be subject to community justice. There are some psychopaths, serial murderers, and hard-core sex offenders for whom these processes are not appropriate and for whom the idea of "reintegration" into peaceful communities is abhorrent even to the most generous of community members.

- Community justice may work best for nonviolent and first-time offenders.

- Community justice works best for communities that have accepted the moral values of reconciliation and forgiveness, as well as the nonpunitive approach.

- Community justice will be hampered if it is implemented in social settings in which there are no or very weak communal bonds or where the community is divided along racial, ethnic, religious, or other divisive lines. In these environments, community building will have to precede, or at least accompany, community justice.[50]

While some experts in the field would disagree that the community or restorative justice model cannot work with serious offenders, it is certainly important to screen candidates carefully for participation and to ensure that such cases are handled by individuals well-trained in community and restorative methods. For example, Umbreit has been doing victim-offender mediation in cases of severe violence in Minnesota and has had positive results.[51] He cautions that such cases require longer case preparation, extreme sensitivity, and advanced training on the part of the mediator, but that mediation can produce positive and healing results in such cases.

Etzioni's caution that community building must first occur in jurisdictions already divided by intolerance and bigotry cannot be overstated. Communities long divided by prejudice and racism cannot be expected to embrace a concept such as community or restorative justice overnight. A community is unlikely to work harmoniously together when neighbors see each other as enemies and see their own liberation coming only at the cost of the others' demise or expulsion. Implementers of community justice must be sensitive to preexisting conditions in communities where justice professionals are seen as "outsiders" with little sense of the daily realities of neighborhood life.

Etzioni also cautions against overselling or overhyping the approach such that its values and possibilities become endangered.[52] We must learn more about how communities work, the conditions under which such an approach is most viable, and the extent to which programs implemented in various circumstances can actually be labeled "community justice." Programs implemented in the name of community or restorative justice that become coopted by retributive values do a disservice to both philosophies. Worse, they will interfere with the possibilities of the community model by misdirecting program goals and confusing program values. Without clarifying some of these important issues, some invaluable opportunities may be lost in the tendency to "throw the baby out with the bath water."

CONCLUSION

When considering the possibilities of community justice, perhaps the concept of balance is most important. In our desire to furnish complete and incontrovertible answers to difficult social questions, we tend to forget that the world does not exist in black and white but rather in a variety of colors, forms, shapes, sizes, and textures. Thus, while some societies might need to consider more autonomy in terms of rights and freedom of expression, others might better be served by curtailing some of the privileges that have come to be taken for rights in the name of independence and individuality.

The movement toward community and restorative justice is, in an important sense, an effort to rediscover a collective community response to crime at a time when the citizen role in sanctioning and social control has been greatly diminished. After at least three decades of justice system expansion and professionalization of tasks once handled by families, neighbors, teachers, clergy and others, a reinvention of practical neighborhood responses will not be easy. Communities may not only be resistant to taking on increased responsibility after being told for years to "leave it to the experts" but may be so blinded to other possibilities that the mere idea of community engagement may appear quite threatening.

There are many ways to view the community justice model. It might be seen as an encroachment on civil liberties, as a thinly veiled attack on due process and individual rights, or as a threat to a system of justice wherein the ideal of punishment is dominant. On the other hand, it might also be seen as an opportunity to transform our communities into ones in which inclusion and involvement are honored, respect for others is the norm rather than the exception, and individuals see more possibilities in working together than in remaining isolated.

▶ At the Movies . . . .

Life as a House, 2001.

A divorced father reenters his delinquent son's life. With the help of friends and family, the two of them tear down an old house and end up rebuilding their broken lives.

The Straight Story, 1999.

Based upon a true story, an old man suffering from a variety of disabilities, rides an ancient John Deere lawnmower 260 miles to make things right with his estranged brother. Along the journey, he helps others and is himself helped through shared experiences.

DISCUSSION QUESTIONS

1. What are the fundamental differences between community justice and traditional retributive justice? Name at least three.

2. Who are the key stakeholders in restorative community justice? How is this different from the current criminal justice system model?

3. What is the difference in the relationship between government and the community in the community justice model as compared with the traditional retributive model?

4. The community justice approach may not be appropriate for all offenders and communities. Discuss Etzioni's suggestions regarding the conditions and limitations of community justice. Do you agree or disagree with his suggestions?

5. Discuss circle sentencing and peacemaking circles, which are derived from ancient aboriginal practices. Can you think of any other ancient practices that may be relevant to a community justice approach?

6. You have just been named the community justice planner in your state's Department of Corrections. How will you promote the idea of community justice in your state? What will you do to engage communities in participating in community restorative justice practices? Who would you need to talk to, and why? What key community members would you involve?

FURTHER READING

Dass, R., and P. Gorman (1985). *How Can I Help? Stories and Reflections on Service*. New York: Knopf.

Lozoff, B. (1999). *Deep and Simple*. Durham, NC: Human Kindness Foundation.

Sullivan, D., and L. Tifft (2005). *Restorative Justice*. Monsey, NY: Willow Tree Press.

Van Ness, D., and K.H. Strong (2006). *Restoring Justice*, 3rd ed. Newark, NJ: LexisNexis Matthew Bender.

Wozniak, J., M. Braswell, R. Vogel, and K. Blevins (eds.) (2008). *Transformative Justice*. Lanham, MD: Lexington Books.

NOTES

1. Karp, 1997.

2. Clear and Karp, 1998.

3. Carey 1998, 217.

4. Clear and Karp 1998, 4-5.

5. Barajas, 1995; Bazemore and Schiff, 1996.

6. Polk and Kobrin, 1972; Pittman and Fleming, 1991.

7. Pranis (1998) describes the difference between restorative and community justice as a difference in goals; community justice does not always hold as its goal repair of the harm and healing for all. While both processes are located in the community, community justice tends to focus more on preventive pre-crime interventions, while restorative justice is more geared to outcomes that result after a crime has been committed. In restorative justice, the parties' satisfaction with the outcome of the event is paramount, and crime is seen as an opportunity to mend broken relationships that have been fragmented by the criminal event.

8. Young, 1995; Bazemore and Schiff, 1996; Chavis, 1998; Van Ness and Strong, 2006.

9. Byrne, 1989; Bazemore, 1999.

10. Van Ness and Strong, 2006.

11. Barajas, 1998.

12. Barajas, 1998.

13. Packer, 1968.

14. Barajas, 1998.

15. Clear and Karp, 1998.

16. Goldstein, 1987; Trojanawicz,1990; Boland, 1998; Anderson, 1996; Stone, 1996.

17. Dooley, 1995; Bazemore, 1997b; Stuart, 1996; Melton, 1995; McElrae, 1993; McElrae, 1996; Umbreit and Stacy, 1996; Bazemore, 1997a; Umbreit, 1999.

18. Braithwaite and Parker, 1999.

19. Umbreit, 1999; Umbreit and Coates, 1993.

20. Stuart, 1996.

21. Melton, 1995.

22. Eisenstein and Jacobs, 1977.

23. Bazemore and Schiff, 1996; Bazemore, 1997b.

24. Bazemore and Schiff, 1996.

25. Bazemore and Schiff, 1996.

26. Elias, 1993; Karmen, 1996.

27. Umbreit, 1999; Maxwell and Morris, 1993; Morris and Maxwell, 1998.

28. Clear and Karp, 1998.

29. Clear and Karp, 1998.

30. An excellent example of this is the Takoma Orange Hats, a voluntary group of neighbors in the District of Columbia who took to patrolling the streets at night in order to demonstrate a strong community presence to unwanted drug dealers and prostitutes. The presence of the group's loud orange baseball caps, night after night, helped to deter dealers and prostitutes from that area and increase the quality of life in that neighborhood (for a full description, see "Takoma Orange Hats: Fighting Crime and Building Community in Washington, DC," by Suzanne Goldsmith-Hirsch, in David Karp's *Community Justice*, New York: Rowman and Littlefield, 1998).

31. Van Ness, 1993.

32. Pranis, 1996.

33. Bazemore and Griffiths, 1997.

34. Clear and Karp, 1998.

35. Bazemore and Griffiths, 1997.

36. Carey, 1998.

37. Carey, 1998; Van Ness and Strong, 2006.

38. Van Ness and Strong, 2006.

39. Barajas, 1998.

40. Pranis, 1998.

41. Grinc, 1994.

42. Bazemore and Schiff, 1996.

43. Currie, 1993.

44. Grinc, 1994.

45. Braithwaite and Mugford, 1994; Polk, 1994.

46. Bazemore, 1997b.

47. Etzioni, 1993.

48. Clear and Karp, 1998.

49. Clear and Karp, 1998, 22.

50. Etzioni, 1998.

51. Umbreit, 1999.

52. Etzioni, 1998.

REFERENCES

Alder, C., and J. Wundersitz (1994). *Family Group Conferencing and Juvenile Justice: The Way Forward or Misplaced Optimism?* Canberra: Australian Institute of Criminology.

Anderson, D. (1996). "In New York City, a 'Community Court' and a New Legal Culture." *National Institute of Justice Program Focus.* Washington, DC: U.S. Department of Justice.

Barajas, E. (1998). "Community Justice: An Emerging Concept and Practice." *Community Justice Concepts and Strategies.* Lexington, KY: American Correctional Association.

Barajas, E. (1995). "Moving Toward Community Justice." *Topics in Community Corrections.* Washington, DC: National Institute of Corrections.

Bazemore, G. (1999). "After the Shaming, Whither Reintegration: Restorative Justice and Relational Rehabilitation." In G. Bazemore and L. Walgrave (eds.), *Restoring Juvenile Justice.* Monsey, NY: Criminal Justice Press.

Bazemore, G. (1997a). "What's New about the Balanced Approach?" *Juvenile and Family Court Journal* 48:1:1-23.

Bazemore, G. (1997b). "The Community in Community Justice: Issues, Themes and Questions for the New Neighborhood Sanctioning Models." *The Justice System Journal,* 19(2):193-228.

Bazemore, G. (1996). "Three Paradigms for Juvenile Justice." In J. Hudson and B. Galaway (eds.), *The Practice of Restorative Justice.* Monsey, NY: Criminal Justice Press.

Bazemore G., and S. Day (1996). "Restoring the Balance: Juvenile and Community Justice." *Juvenile Justice Journal* (December):3-14.

Bazemore, G., and C. Griffiths (1997). "Circles, Boards, Conferences and Mediation: Scouting the New Wave in Community Justice Decision-Making." *Federal Probation* LXI(2):25-37.

Bazemore, G., and M. Schiff (1996). "Community Justice/Restorative Justice: Prospects for a New Social Ecology for Community Corrections." *International Journal of Comparative and Applied Criminal Justice* 20(2):311-335.

Bazemore, G., and M. Umbreit (1995). "Rethinking the Sanctioning Function in Juvenile Court: Retributive or Restorative Responses to Youth Crime." *Crime & Delinquency* 41(3):296-316.

Belgrave, J. (1995). *Restorative Justice*. Discussion paper. Wellington, NZ: New Zealand Ministry of Justice.

Braithwaite, J. (1989). *Crime, Shame, and Reintegration*. New York: Cambridge University Press.

Braithwaite, J., and S. Mugford (1994). "Conditions of Successful Reintegration Ceremonies." *British Journal of Criminology* 34(2):139-171.

Braithwaite, J., and C. Parker (1999). "Restorative Justice Is Republican Justice." In G. Bazemore and L. Walgrave (eds.), *Restorative Juvenile Justice: Repairing the Harm of Youth Crime*. Monsey, NY: Criminal Justice Press.

Boland, B. (1998). "Community Prosecution: Portland's Experience." In D. Karp (ed.), *Community Justice: An Emerging Field*, 253-278. Lanham, MD: Rowman and Littlefield.

Byrne, J.M. (1989). "Reintegrating the Concept of Community into Community-Based Corrections." *Crime & Delinquency* 35:471-499.

Carey, M. (1998). "Building Hope Through Community Justice." *Community Justice Concepts and Strategies*. Lexington, KY: American Correctional Association.

Chavis, D. (1998). "Building Community Capacity to Prevent Violence through Coalitions and Partnerships." In D. Karp (ed.), *Community Justice: An Emerging Field*, 81-95. Lanham, MD: Rowman and Littlefield.

Clear, T., and D. Karp (1998). "The Community Justice Movement." In D. Karp (ed.), *Community Justice: An Emerging Field*, 3-28. Lanham, MD: Rowman and Littlefield.

Currie, E. (1993). *Reckoning Drugs, Cities and the American Future*. New York: Hill and Wang.

Dooley, M.J. (1996). *Restoring Hope Through Community Partnerships: The Real Deal in Crime Control*. Monograph. American Probation and Parole Association.

Dooley, M.J. (1995). *Reparative Probation Program*. Monograph. Vermont Department of Corrections.

Eisenstein, J., and H. Jacobs (1977). *Felony Justice: An Organizational Analysis of Criminal Courts*. Boston: Little, Brown.

Elias, R. (1993). *Victims Still*. Newbury Park: Sage.

Etzioni, A. (1998). "Community Justice in a Communitarian Perspective." In D. Karp (ed.), *Community Justice: An Emerging Field*, 373-378. Lanham, MD: Rowman and Littlefield.

Etzioni, A. (1993). *The Spirit of Community: Rights, Responsibilities and The Communitarian Agenda*. New York: Crown.

Goldstein, H. (1987). "Toward Community-Oriented Policing: Potential, Basic Requirements and Threshold Questions." *Crime & Delinquency* 33:6-30.

Griffiths, C., and R. Hamilton (1996). "Spiritual Renewal, Community Revitalization and Healing Experience in Traditional Aboriginal Justice in Canada." *International Journal of Comparative and Applied Criminal Justice* 20(1).

Grinc, R. (1994). "Angels in Marble: Problems in Stimulating Community Involvement in Community Policing." *Crime & Delinquency* 40:437-468.

Karmen, A. (1996). *Crime Victims*. Belmont, CA: Brooks/Cole.

Karp, D. (1997). "Community Justice." *Research Seminar on Community, Crime, and Justice*. Monograph. George Washington University/National Institute of Justice.

Kelling, G., and C. Coles (1998). "Disorder and the Court" In D. Karp (ed.), *Community Justice: An Emerging Field*, 233-251. Lanham, MD: Rowman and Littlefield.

Maxwell, G., and A. Morris (1993). *Family Participation, Cultural Diversity and Victim Involvement in Youth Justice: A New Zealand Experiment*. Wellington, NZ: Victoria University.

McElrae, F.W.M. (1996). "The New Zealand Youth Court: A Model for Use with Adults." In B. Galaway and J. Hudson (eds.), *Restorative Justice: International Perspectives*, 69-83. Monsey, NY: Criminal Justice Press.

McElrae, F.W.M. (1993). "A New Model of Justice." In B.J. Brown (ed.), *In the Youth Court in New Zealand: A New Model of Justice*. Auckland, NZ: Legal Research Foundation.

Melton, A. (1995). "Indigenous Justice Systems and Tribal Society." *Judicature* 70(3):126-133.

Morris, A., and G. Maxwell (1998). "Restorative Justice in New Zealand: Family Group Conferences as a Case Study." *Western Criminology Review*, 1. Available at http://wcr.sonoma.edu/vlnl/morris.html

Packer, H. (1968). *Limits of the Criminal Sanction*. Stanford, CA: Stanford University Press.

Pittman, K., and W. Fleming (1991). "A New Vision: Promoting Youth Development." Testimony to House Select Committee on Children, Youth and Families. Academy for Education Development, Washington, DC (September).

Polk, K. (1994). "Family Conferencing: Theoretical and Evaluative Questions." In C. Alder and J. Wundersitz (eds.), *Family Conferencing and Juvenile Justice: The Way Forward or Misplaced Optimism?* 155-168. Canberra: Australian Institute of Criminology.

Polk, K., and S. Kobrin (1972). *Delinquency Prevention Through Youth Development*. Washington, DC: Office of Youth Development.

Pranis, K. (1998). "Promising Practices in Community Justice: Restorative Justice." *Community Justice Concepts and Strategies*. Lexington, KY: American Correctional Association.

Pranis, K. (1996). "Communities and the Justice System—Turning the Relationship Upside Down." Paper presented before the Office of Justice Programs, U.S. Department of Justice.

Stone, C. (1996). "Community Defense and the Challenge of Community Justice." *National Institute of Justice Journal* 231:41-45

Stuart, B. (1996). "Circle Sentencing—Turning Swords into Ploughshares." In B. Galaway and J. Hudson (eds.), *Restorative Justice: International Perspectives*, 193 -206. Monsey, NY: Criminal Justice Press.

Trojanowicz, R.C. (1990). "Community Policing Is Not Police-Community Relations." *FBI Law Enforcement Bulletin*, October: 6-11.

Umbreit, M. (1999). "Restorative Justice Through Juvenile Victim Offender Mediation." In G. Bazemore and L. Walgrave (eds.), *Restoring Juvenile Justice: Repairing the Harm of Youth Crime*. Monsey, NY: Criminal Justice Press.

Umbreit, M., and R. Coates (1993). "Cross-Site Analysis of Victim-Offender Conflict: An Analysis of Programs in These Three States." *Juvenile and Family Court Journal* 43 (1):21-28.

Umbreit, M., and S. Stacy (1996). "Family Group Conferencing Comes to the US: A Comparison with Victim Offender Mediation." *Juvenile and Family Court Journal* 29-39.

Van Ness, D. (1993). "New Wine and Old Wineskins: Four Challenges of Restorative Justice." *Criminal Law Forum* 4(2):251-276.

Van Ness, D., and K.H. Strong (2006). *Restoring Justice*, 3rd ed. Newark, NJ: LexisNexis Mathew Bender.

Young, M. (1995). "Restorative Community Justice: A Call to Action." Report for the National Organization of Victim Assistance. Washington, DC.

Zehr, H. (1990). *Changing Lenses: A New Focus for Crime and Justice*. Scottdale, PA: Herald Press.

Prisoners and Prison Life

CHAPTER 7

What You Need to Know

▶ More than one-half (52%) of the prisoners in state prisons are in prison for a violent offense, approximately 20 percent are in for a property offense, and another one-fifth are in for a drug offense. More than one-half of federal prisoners are in prison for a drug offense, and less than 10 percent are in for a violent offense.

▶ All prisoners suffer the deprivations of imprisonment, including loss of freedom, loss of autonomy, and reduced possessions. Some prisoners suffer even more by being sexually victimized in prison.

▶ At yearend 2006, more than 3,000 offenders were on death row. The year 2006 saw 66 executions, 19 fewer than in 2000.

▶ Prisoners have problems with both substance abuse and mental illness. Approximately one-half of all prisoners are drug-dependent or have substance abuse problems. The 2004 Survey of Inmates indicated that 56 percent of state inmates, 45 percent of federal prisoners, and 64 percent of jail inmates had a mental health problem.

▶ Although the percentage of black prisoners has declined, blacks still make up more than 40 percent of state prisoners. Racial tension continues to be a problem in prisons.

▶ Women make up a little more than 7 percent of prisoners. Women are less violent than men, and their prisons have less violence than men's prisons.

INTRODUCTION

As Chapter 2 noted, reformers like the Quakers thought that prisons would be quiet places where offenders could reflect on their lives as they spent their days praying and working. They thought that prisons would be like monasteries where prisoners would reform. Later prison leaders were not as clearly religious as the Quakers, but they still believed in rehabilitation. In fact, rehabilitation continued as a stated goal of prison life well into the twentieth century. In the last 20 years, however, prisons have emphasized punishment, deterrence, and incapacitation.

Whatever the particular prison philosophy of the day, prisoners adjust and cope. They manage to live their days inside prison walls or fences in ways that allow them to complete their sentences. This chapter will examine how prisoners cope with the deprivations of prison such as loss of freedom and loss of possessions and security. We will look at long-term inmates and supermax prisons. We will review what is known about victimization in prison, including sexual victimization and victimization by guards. In addition, we will consider some special issues such as death row, women in prison (although Chapter 8 covers this topic in more detail), and racial adjustment. We will also discuss some of the problems of probationers and parolees, such as the abuse of alcohol and other drugs.

THE PRISON POPULATION

At the end of 2006, prisons were bursting at the seams, with 1,570,891 prisoners under federal or state jurisdiction, an increase of 2.8 percent over the number in 2005. The prison population was 93 percent male and 7 percent female. Of state prisoners, it is estimated that 35 percent were white, 38 percent black, 21 percent Hispanic or Latino, 4 percent "other," and 3 percent of two or more races.[1]

In 2004, more than one-half (52%) of the prisoners in state prisons were in prison for a violent offense (murder, manslaughter, rape, other sexual assault, robbery, assault, or other violent crime).[2] One-fifth (21%)

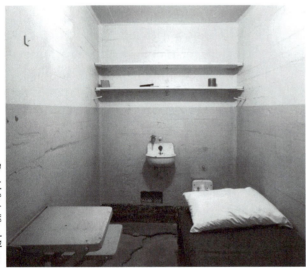

Daniel Stein/iStockPhoto

While there is much disagreement as to whether prisons are too harsh or too lenient, Gresham Sykes offered a list of five deprivations that all prisoners experience: loss of liberty/freedom, loss of goods and services, loss of autonomy, loss of heterosexual contact, and loss of security.

were in prison for a property offense (burglary, larceny, motor vehicle theft, fraud, or other property offense), 20 percent were in for a drug offense, and 7 percent were in for a public order offense.[3]

In 2006, the largest group (53%) of federal prisoners were in prison for a drug offense. Less than 10 percent (9.4 %) of federal prisoners were incarcerated for a violent offense. These figures represent a major change compared to 1985, when 28 percent of federal prisoners were in prison for a violent offense, and only 34 percent were incarcerated for a drug offense.[4]

An important concern is the differential incarceration rates for whites and blacks. For males, whites have an incarceration rate of 487 per 100,000 in the population, but blacks have a rate of more than 3,000 per 100,000 in the population, and Hispanics/Latinos have a rate of more than 1,200 per 100,000 in the population. In other words, about one in every 33 black men in the country was a sentenced prisoner in 2006, compared to one in every 205 white men.[5]

As the prison population was increasing, the crime rate was decreasing. For example, the violent crime rate decreased 22.5 percent from 1997 to 2006 and 4.2 percent from 2002 to 2006. (Note: The violent crime rate did increase by 1 percent from 2005 to 2006).[6] Some criminologists argue that this crime drop was at least partially the result of putting more offenders in prison. In other words, some claim a deterrent and

> For further statistics on prisons and prisoners, go to www.ojp.usdoj.gov/bjs and look for *Prisoners in 2006*. A more up-to-date report on prison statistics may be available, as this report is issued every year by the Bureau of Justice Statistics.

incapacitative impact of putting more offenders in prison. Others, however, argue that the crime drop was due to other factors.

• Are We Imprisoning the Wrong Offenders? •

A number of prison critics argue that prisons contain too many offenders who do not need to be incarcerated. These critics argue that we are using too many scarce prison beds for either property offenders or drug offenders. Austin and Irwin, for example, did an ethnographic study of 154 males sentenced to prison in Washington, Nevada, and Illinois. Their interviews with these male offenders led them to conclude that a little more than one-half of the persons being admitted to prison are actually being admitted for petty crimes. These are "crimes with no aggravating features—that is, no significant amount of money, no injury, or any other feature that would cause ordinary citizens to view the crime as particularly serious."[7] Austin and Irwin argue that some crimes generally considered "serious" may not be as serious as they appear. They note a particular robber, for example, who robbed convenience stores with a BB gun tucked in his belt. He showed the gun in his belt to the clerk but did not take it out of his belt or point it at the clerk.

Austin and Irwin are probably correct that not every criminal labeled "dangerous" by offense type is as dangerous or threatening as the name of the offense implies. It seems, however, that these critics may have gone a bit too far. Even if a robber uses only a BB gun and keeps it tucked in his belt, that scenario is filled with the potential for violence. Surely some convenience store clerks would interpret a gun—real, BB, or even toy—as threatening. One possible response is for the clerk to pull a gun from under the counter and shoot the robber. Thus, to dismiss such a robbery situation as not serious or violent is potentially misleading.

It is also noteworthy that approximately 11 percent of the offenders admitted to state prisons each year were convicted of burglary.[8] Although prison critics may label burglary as a "property" crime, many average citizens regard this crime as more serious than other property crimes such as shoplifting. Burglary involves trespass into one's personal space (one's home) and also involves a very real potential for violence. Either the burglar or the victim may have a weapon at hand and resort to using it. Indicating the seriousness with which some people regard burglary is the criminal law allowance in at least one state of deadly force against burglary.[9] Moreover, many burglars are looking for guns.[10] Clearly, there is some probability that stolen guns will be fenced or otherwise transferred to other criminals directly engaged in violent crime. Therefore, while Austin and Irwin may be correct that some "violent" crimes are not as threatening as claimed, it is also correct that some crimes labeled "property" or "nonviolent" crimes may be more threatening than claimed.

Much stronger is the evidence that U.S. prisons, especially federal prisons, house more drug offenders than necessary. Changes in federal sentencing policies have resulted in a dramatic increase in the percentage of federal prisoners convicted of drug crimes. When the costs of incarceration continue to increase, it is imperative to question the wisdom of incarcerating such a high percentage of drug offenders.

PRISON ADJUSTMENT

Some people claim that prisons today are too easy or comfortable for prisoners. Such objections often follow stories of prisoners being able to watch cable television, attend a concert, or participate in a sports event (such as a baseball game against a team from another prison). In one presidential campaign, for instance, candidate and magazine publisher Malcomb "Steve" Forbes criticized a Connecticut women's prison for being "plush" because it had "airy courtyards," a shuffleboard court, and oak bunk beds (instead of less expensive metal frame beds).[11]

Others contend that prison is too harsh. Some of these critics point to prisons in other countries where sentences are much shorter in length and where housing units resemble college dormitories more than the cell bars and prison walls that many have in mind when they think of a "prison."

Both types of charges may ignore prison reality. Prison life involves many discomforts and problems that the "too soft" critics often forget or do not consider. On the other hand, the "too harsh" critics may not be aware of the adjustments prisoners create to make their lives as comfortable as possible.

DEPRIVATIONS OF PRISON LIFE

Gresham Sykes[12] provides a useful starting point in discussing prison conditions with a list of deprivations that all prisoners experience. The first such deprivation is the deprivation of liberty. Prisoners are deprived of their liberty or freedom. They are locked up and confined. Such confinement may be total: 24-hour lockup in solitary confinement or in a new supermaximum facility. Alternatively, it may be minimal: a federal prisoner may be in a prison camp that has dormitories rather than cells and a painted white line rather than a wall or a fence around the institution. In either case, however, the prisoner is expected to stay within a certain area and may not travel about as a free citizen.

One aspect of confinement that many people forget is that confinement often translates into few visitors. If a prisoner is locked up even 100 miles from home, distance alone may make visits by relatives quite difficult. The prisoner's family may simply not have transportation to the prison.

A second deprivation is that of goods and services. Prisoners are limited in their access to possessions and services. One aspect of this depri-

---

BOX 7.1

Deprivations of Prison Life

- Deprivation of Liberty/Freedom
- Deprivation of Goods and Services
- Deprivation of Autonomy
- Deprivation of Heterosexual Contact
- Deprivation of Security

Source: Sykes, G. (1958). *The Society of Captives: A Study of a Maximum Security Prison.* Princeton, NJ: Princeton University Press.

vation that is ignored by many critics is that Americans define themselves to a great extent by their possessions. Most are concerned about their clothes, cars, residences, and the "stuff" (as the late comedian George Carlin would say) possessed within their homes and cars. Americans live in a materialistic society and tend to value having increasingly more and better-quality possessions (e.g., one may be proud of having a late-model car or designer blue jeans or a particular brand of shoes rather than a $15 pair of shoes from a discount store). Prisoners are issued a uniform with no permission for individualizing differences and are allowed only certain things—a few books, magazines, and pictures for their cells. Even necessities may be in short supply. One prison, for example, allowed inmates only two rolls of toilet paper per week (they were able to get more only if they had the money to buy it).

A third deprivation is that of autonomy. Free persons can make all sorts of everyday choices—when to get up, when to go to bed, when to eat, what to eat, when to schedule activities, and when to take some time to relax. Prisoners are regimented. They are told when to get up, when to eat, when to work, when to recreate, and when to go to bed. Their choices are minimal. Sykes contends that part of this regimentation is intended to treat prisoners like children. Adults choose; children are directed. So the message to prisoners is that they are like children who need to be told what to do and when to do it.

A fourth deprivation is that of sexual contact and expression—at least legitimate heterosexual contact. Adults on the outside can engage in sexual activity essentially when and where they choose. Except in rare circumstances, prisoners are forbidden heterosexual contact, let alone intercourse. Prisons are usually same-gender facilities with little or no opposite-sex presence. One exception is conjugal visitation, such as an overnight visitation program at San Quentin in California for prisoners who are legally married. Interestingly, women partners who are not legally married feel discriminated against.[13] (For a discussion of coed prisons, see Box 7.2.)

Some homosexual sex does occur in prisons. One study of federal prisoners reported that 12 percent of all federal inmates reported participation in homosexual sexual activity in their current prison. The percentage was higher for those inmates in penitentiaries, as opposed to less secure facilities such as camps.[14] Such homosexual activity, however, is contrary to prison rules and regulations. What is sometimes forgotten is that humans define themselves to a considerable extent by contact with the opposite sex. As anyone who has attended an all-male or all-female college can confirm, the absence of one gender from an environment can lead to behaviors that would not occur when both genders are present.

A fifth deprivation is deprivation of security. Prisons are not always safe places. Many of the offenders are violent; some are disturbed. Many prisoners note that the worst thing about prison is the company they

BOX 7.2

Coed Prisons

One suggestion to improve prisons is to offer more coed facilities. Smykla, for example, contends that single-sex imprisonment "exacerbates the sexual abnormality of offenders by fostering development of homosexual and often violent subcultures, ignores the fact that much criminal behavior stems, directly or indirectly, from the absence of healthy relationships with the opposite sex, or the inability to explore problems of sexual identification, impedes postrelease adjustment, engenders continued criminality, and caricaturizes traditional sex-role stereotypes" (Smykla and Houston, 1999:204). Houston, on the other hand, argues that women often do better in segregated environments where they do not fall under the sway of negative male influence and where they may enter programs that are geared to their special needs rather than to male needs. Houston argues that in coed prisons women often enter programs dictated by their walk partner (the term for relationships in such prisons) rather than their own needs. In addition, coed prisons often result in pregnancies and abortions (Smykla and Houston, 1999:215). One woman prisoner noted that she developed some relationships with male inmates at a coed prison that were harmful to her adjustment and rehabilitation (Parker-Jimenez, 1997).

What do you think? Should we attempt to have more coed prisons? Is the debate over coed prisons similar to the debate over single-gender colleges versus coed colleges? How so?

are forced to keep. For example, a recent study of three Ohio prisons showed that about 25 percent of the inmates studied were victimized by either assault or theft during the six months prior to their interviews. Adding robbery, simple assault, and property damage to the definition of victimization increased the victimization percentage to almost one-half (48%).[15] Official statistics showed that in 1997 there were 4,095 inmate assaults on other inmates—1,860 in New York, 1,499 in Texas, and 394 in Ohio.[16]

Outside of prison, given adequate resources, one can avoid living in a violent section of a city or town. Prisoners, though, must live in their assigned cells, and their neighbors may be undesirable. (A later section of this chapter will examine prison victimization in greater detail.)

Guenther has added to Sykes's list of deprivations.[17] One addition is pain involving visits, even visits by spouses. Guenther notes that fellow prisoners or guards can be very callous about such visits, using the occasion to suggest to a prisoner that his wife is free and can be seeing a lover while the prisoner is counting the years until release. Related to this, letters to prisoners from family members are not always pleasant and uplifting. Letters can remind a prisoner of problems back home when he or she has no way to help resolve those problems due to being miles away and unable to intervene. A letter can even include negative comments such as a son expressing anger at his father for things his father (the prisoner) did or failed to do.

Still another problem in prison life is holiday time such as Thanksgiving and Christmas. Guenther notes that prisoners tend to watch television during the holiday season just like the rest of us.[18] Programs and commercials remind the prisoner that he or she is locked up during a time of year when most people are busy planning parties and family gatherings that celebrate the occasion. In plain terms, the prisoner is exposed to a media barrage of images of family togetherness while he or she might experience only a few holiday cards or some canned turkey on Thanksgiving and Christmas. Time passes slowly in prison, and this sense is exacerbated during holidays. In view of this, the Angola prison in Louisiana has volunteers that come in over the holidays to help prevent suicide attempts.

Most prisoners experience these problems or deprivations. This makes it difficult to say that prisons are "country clubs" and are too soft. Even if a prisoner has access to some amenities that might seem luxurious, such as a jogging track or a tennis court, the deprivations of freedom, autonomy, possessions, heterosexual sex, and security are constant reminders that one is being punished for a crime. One prisoner remarked, for example, that even though the dining hall at her federal prison looked more like a popular restaurant chain than a prison cafeteria, it only covered up the repressive atmosphere that was very much the daily reality.[19]

On the other hand, some writers contend that prisons are not as negative as others claim. In a study of the federal prison at Lompoc, California, anthropologist Mark Fleisher notes that many inmates do not see prison as very intimidating or unpleasant:

> Lompoc inmates claim that doing time isn't punishment. They hasten to add that when they're released to the street the high risk of returning to federal or state prison by committing new crimes will not prevent them from doing so. For these high-risk criminals, crime is a way of life and going to prison isn't a burden. . . . Many inmates say, too, that daily life in Lompoc, and in other prisons where they have done time, is easier, less frustrating, and more secure than life on the street. For many of them, in fact, prison has become their preferred lifestyle. . . .[20]

One problem with this assessment is that it may be out of date. Recent changes in prisons (e.g., cutbacks in opportunities for education) have made the prison experience more negative.[21] The assessment also ignores the negative environments that many prisoners come from and return to after release. A major reason some prisoners say prison is not so bad is that their home environments are problematic. Therefore, their assessment of the prison environment is made in reference to the environment in which they were living, not in comparison to a desirable home environment. If these prisoners had grown up in more positive environments, they probably would not rate prison so highly. More importantly, if they had grown up in more positive surroundings, they might not have become criminals.

One danger in labeling prisons as "not that bad" or as "comfortable" is that such labels can make it easier to build more prisons and to send more offenders to prison. If prison is not so terrible, then there will be less reluctance on the part of prosecutors and judges to send offenders to prison. Perhaps the most accurate way to assess prison environments is to note that they are varied. Some are negative with high rates of victimization. Some, especially federal minimum-security facilities, are probably not that different from many college environments. Some prisons may be "luxurious" or even be places where heroin or other drugs are available to prisoners, but such prisons are often deviant cases in which the administration has lost control of the facility.[22] Many more are in between the extremes.

One of the most detailed and rigorous studies of a prison environment concluded that prison is often a place where not much happens. Prisoners endure the prison environment and come out roughly the same persons they were when they entered. To emphasize this point, the study authors called prison "the deep freeze."[23] The good news about the "deep freeze" nature of prisons is that most prisoners do not come out worse than they entered. The bad news is that most prisoners had either inadequate or maladaptive coping skills when they entered prison. Rather than improving those skills, prison has little or no impact: the offenders come out with the same inadequate or maladaptive skills. This is a major reason for the discouraging recidivism statistics. The released prisoner is no better prepared to avoid crime on release than he or she was on the day he or she entered the facility.

Another prison expert notes that often prisoners try to find niches in prison.[24] Niches are places or situations that provide something that a particular prisoner may be seeking. For example, a prisoner who believes he is weak might seek confinement in a segregated cellblock with 24-hour lockdown so that he feels safe. He wants security and does not want to defend himself against assaults. Other prisoners, though, need more social interaction and would hate such total confinement.

For example, *The New Yorker* magazine once printed a New York state prisoner's diary that shows how the prisoner created such a niche for himself.[25] This prisoner preferred privacy and security and took steps to achieve those goals as much as possible. He managed to get coffee and donuts and other food supplies from a friend in the kitchen so he could eat in his cell instead of in the cafeteria. He managed to get a job with another inmate in the clothing office for inmates being released or going to court. Besides their official chores, their responsibilities apparently centered on making themselves coffee, listening to the radio, and chatting about everyday topics. At night, he would either go to a Jaycees (Junior Chamber of Commerce) meeting or work on art (glass pictures) in his cell, as well as fixing himself an evening meal or snack. In this fashion, he was able to avoid most other inmates and achieve relative privacy and security in an unsafe world.

Carroll offers a more systematic account.[26] He notes that on a typical morning in Rhode Island's largest prison, about 400 inmates out of approximately 700 are working and that about 150 are in educational or therapy programs. Many of these programs are run by private vendors who contract with the state to provide the programs. Minimum-security inmates may be working outside the prison in either public or nonprofit agencies. Rhode Island allows these agencies to purchase inmate labor at $3.00 per hour. Maximum-security inmates are most likely to be idle, as they cannot go outside the prison to work, and security issues may prevent them from going to work or programs inside the prison. (For further discussion of prison labor, see Box 7.3.)

In recent years, some states have tried to make prison even more painful. In response to criticisms that prisons are too soft, many prisons have opted to curtail amenities. Thus, some prisons have cut back on such amenities as exercise equipment and cable television. One concern in response is that some helpful amenities, such as college courses, are being eliminated. To discontinue college courses is to take away a major chance for the inmate to improve himself or herself. This lessens the chances of success once released from prison. Another legitimate concern is that amenities reduce the frustration in prison and lessen the odds of violence and riots in prison. A female prisoner noted that exercise equipment helped her to both "pass the time" and to relieve stress.[27] This is important for staff and inmate safety. If "frills" reduce the chances of injury to staff and inmates, they may well be worth the price of some critics calling the prison too soft.

LONG-TERM INMATES

Long-term inmates can and do perceive prison quite differently than short-term prisoners. Long-term prisoners are more concerned about privacy and stability than are younger, short-term prisoners. All inmates must cope with the loss of relationships with family and friends, but long-term inmates face the additional problem of complete cut-off of relationships. If a prisoner is going to serve only two

BOX 7.3

Prison Labor

Prison labor has a long history, including the infamous road gangs of the South after the Civil War. In one sense, Southern prison camps were an extension of slavery after it had been outlawed.

The ideal of prison labor is a job in which the inmate is involved in activity that contributes to the welfare of the prison or the community. The labor can be service-oriented or product-oriented. Prisoners can make license plates, furniture, and other goods, or do such things as take hotel or airline reservations for national companies.

As has been the case throughout the history of prison labor, a major objection to the practice is its possible effect of taking jobs away from free-world citizens. A privately operated prison in Texas, for example, recently opened a circuit board assembly operation in its prison. The private company running the circuit board operation got a brand new facility for which it pays rent of only $1 per year. It pays its workers minimum wage. The company closed its free-world plant and moved the entire operation to the prison, laying off 150 workers (Erlich, 1997).

Do you think any prison industry should be allowed to exist if it takes jobs away from law-abiding citizens? One problem is that you could argue that every prison job takes a job away from someone outside prison. For example, although the manufacture of license plates has been a long-standing prison industry, it could be set up outside prisons and create jobs for law-abiding citizens. Instead of using prisoners to clean up prisons, outside cleaning companies could be paid to come in and clean up prisons just like they clean other sorts of buildings in the outside world. So do we run prison industries that give prisoners something to do and perhaps a chance to learn responsibility and other positive work habits, or do we keep all prisoners idle? Where do we draw the line of what jobs are appropriate for prisoners and which are not?

years, he or she expects to re-establish relationships upon release. A 20-year or life stay makes it likely that many relationships will never be re-established. Likewise, young, short-term prisoners do not have to establish friendships in prison. They can pass time until they are released back to their friends in the community. Long-term prisoners have less in common with younger prisoners, so they may not want to establish ties with them. Establishing relationships with fellow long-term prisoners can be difficult because transfers and releases can end any friendships built.[28]

Program planning for long-term inmates, especially those with extreme-ly long sentences or life sentences, can be very difficult:

> They have too much time to fill, too remote a future, and too little hope. How many correspondence courses can a man take, how many vocational programs can he complete? And what is the point of it all, when the time for learning is indefinite, and the time to apply learning is limited? And . . . how can one learn among noisy young inmates playfully filling in a few painless days in a brief interlude of captivity?[29]

Toch offers the suggestion that prisons consider career planning for long-term inmates.[30] By this, he means that prisons take into account the fact that long-term inmates will be in prisons for periods long enough to plan a career. Rather than just teach an inmate how to repair a car and become an auto mechanic, for example, teach him or her how to become first an auto repair instructor's helper and then an auto repair instructor. If an inmate is going to be in prison for a long time, it does not make sense to treat him or her as if he or she is going to be released tomorrow. This career planning and training helps the inmate as well as helping the prison in its service delivery to all inmates.

PRISON VICTIMIZATION

The previous section on prison adjustment discussed the depriva-tions that prisoners experience, including the deprivation of security. As noted in that section, 25 to almost 50 percent of prisoners report assault, theft, robbery, or property damage in the previous six months of their incarceration. Clearly, prison is a dangerous place. Sexual victimization and victimization by guards are two issues that deserve special attention.

• Sexual Victimization •

Scientific studies of sexual victimization have been hindered due to the sensitive nature of the subject. Men, especially, are not very forthcom-ing about their sexual victimization in prison. Many men would rather lie or say nothing about a victimization experience in confinement.

In an early study of sexual victimization in New York, Lockwood found that 28 percent of male inmates had been targets of sexual aggres-sion at least once while in custody. Only one inmate, however, stated that he had been sexually assaulted.[31] In a study of 330 federal male inmates, Nacci and Kane reported that only one inmate had been "raped" (sod-omized) in a federal prison. Defining being "targeted" as being forced (or someone had attempted to force them) into performing sexual acts against one's will, they found that only 2 percent of the respondents had been targets of sexual aggression in a federal prison, but that 9 percent had been targets in either a federal or a state prison taken together.[32] In line with Lockwood's study, however, 29 percent of the inmates reported having been "propositioned' for sex.[33] In still another study, of 101 prisoners in Delaware, again only one inmate reported having been raped during his lifetime incarceration history, but five inmates reported that others had attempted to rape them in prison. Respondents reported that they thought the incidence of rape had decreased in prison because of greater guard vigilance and because of fear of contracting HIV/AIDS.[34]

One indication that more than one male prisoner was in fact a victim of sexual victimization in the studies just noted is the recent investigation of Human Rights Watch.[35] Human Rights Watch reported numerous cases of such sexual violence behind bars based on court cases, prison records, and testimony from family members.

In a more recent study, Struckman-Johnson and Struckman-Johnson studied both male and female victimization, thus offering the first direct male-female comparisons. These researchers found that about 20 percent of both genders reported sexual victimization and that, in worst-case incidents, men were much more likely to report that the perpetrator of sexual violence against them was another inmate (72%). Women, however, reported that staff were the perpetrators in 41 percent of the worst-case incidents, and inmates were perpetrators in less than one-half (47%) of the worst-case incidents. Moreover, higher percentages of males answered that their worst-case incident resulted in "oral, vaginal, or anal sex" compared to women (70% of the men, compared to 29% of the women). Finally, more

than one-half of the male prisoners reported an incident classified as rape compared to less than one-third (28%) of the women. The research indicated that women are often concerned about inap-

> For further statistics on sexual victimization in prison, go to www.ojp.usdoj.gov/bjs and find the Bureau of Justice Statistics report titled *Sexual Victimization in State and Federal Prisons Reported by Inmates, 2007.* You can find, for example, the 10 prisons with the highest victimization prevalence and the six prisons with the lowest prevalence.

propriate touching as well as more serious acts of sexual victimization and that staff are often perceived as problematic in women's prisons.[36]

Prior research has indicated a number of correlates of male victimization. Specifically, victimization is related to the following characteristics: young, small size, physically weak, white, homosexual, first offender, having so-called "feminine characteristics" such as hair or voice tone, lack of assertiveness or aggression, shyness, lacking "street smarts," or a record that includes a sexual offense against a minor.[37]

The seriousness of the problem was highlighted by the Prison Rape Elimination Act, enacted in 2003. This Act has prompted a federally sponsored investigation into the issue, including the first national survey of prison inmates concerning sexual victimization. This survey found that 2.1 percent of prisoners reported an incident involving another inmate, 2.9 percent reported an incident involving staff, and 0.5 percent reported having been sexually victimized by both other inmates and staff. While the overall prevalence of sexual victimization was approximately 4.5 percent, some prisons had rates as high as 13 to 15 percent.[38]

Based on the sensitive nature of this topic and the difficulty of conducting research about it, we will never have a completely accurate picture of the extent of sexual victimization in prison. It is clear, however, that some victimization does occur and that prison authorities need to take steps to prevent as much victimization as possible.

• Victimization by Guards •

The victimization of prisoners by guards is covered in depth in Chapter 11. Here we simply note that it is a problem of prison life.[39] Jerome Washington was a prisoner in the state of New York. His prison stories recount several guard actions against prisoners that could be considered forms of victimization. For example, on one New Year's Eve night, a 21-year-old prisoner was gang-raped in the bathhouse while a guard smoked a cigarette and "took his time responding to the screams that [were] soon gagged away with a bar of prison soap."[40] On one occasion, a prisoner befriended a pigeon, and a guard responded by killing the bird and cutting out the head, heart, wings, and legs. When the prisoner complained to the guard captain, the captain threatened the prisoner with 30 days in the hole (solitary confinement) for violating the rule against pets. Still another prisoner was allegedly beaten to death. When the prison doctor refused to sign the death certificate, a prison official had to drive 25

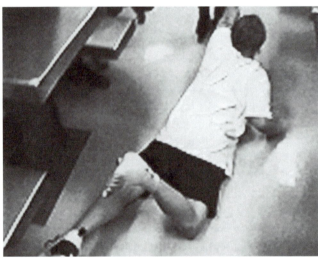

AP Photo/via St. Louis Post Dispatch, HO

This video image shows a prisoner with a broken ankle apparently being dragged from his cell at a detention facility in Texas. Missouri prisoners housed in rented cells as part of a lease agreement with Texas made claims of abuse, sparking an investigation into possible civil rights violations.

miles to find a doctor who would sign a death certificate attesting that the prisoner had hanged himself. These stories, although not proven true, suggest that guards do engage in behaviors that range from insensitive to inhumane and that on some occasions they escape accountability for such actions.

As noted above, Struckman-Johnson and Struckman-Johnson found that 20 percent of Midwestern women prisoners reported being sexually victimized and that staff were the perpetrators in 41 percent of the worst-case victimizations.[41] Similarly, Rathbone's research on women prisoners in Massachusetts found that guards frequently victimized women prisoners or pressured them into so-called consensual sex.[42]

It is difficult to obtain accurate data. Guard victimization of prisoners is criminal, and guards are reluctant to divulge such information. Prisoners, especially women prisoners, may be so afraid and powerless that they are reluctant to report any victimization. It is safe to conclude that victimization occurs at some times in some prisons. The complete extent of such victimization will never be known exactly.

• Summary on Prison Life and Victimization •

We have now looked at the conditions of daily life in prison and at the special problems of prisoner victimization by fellow prisoners and guards. One must remember that prisons vary. Some are relatively problem-free, some are problem-ridden, and some are in between these extremes. With this qualification in mind, a key question persists: What do prisoners (many of whom have committed horrible crimes and thus may not deserve much) deserve from society while they are in prison?

One prison expert, John Conrad, argues that the "undeserving" deserve safety, lawfulness, industriousness, and hope.[43] Safety and lawfulness go together. If the inmates and guards are following the laws and rules, there will be a minimum of assaults and other victimizations in prison. Conrad defines industriousness as "a full day of work at jobs that are worth doing and [getting] paid accordingly."[44] By hope, he means that the prisoners have some confidence that things can get better. Educational and vocational programs allow prisoners such a sense of hope.

To those who would argue that even these four factors are too much, Conrad contends that denying safety, lawfulness, industriousness, and hope will have disastrous consequences:

> If there is only a system in which prisoners are interchangeable units, that system will degenerate into pernicious anarchy in which terror imposes its own values. No criminal is so undeserving as to deserve consignment to such a condition. I have seen such prisons. . . . The society that maintains them deserves what it gets.[45]

SUPERMAX PRISONS

A recent development in prisons is the supermax (or maxi-maxi or administrative segregation) facility. Intended for the "worst of the worst" offenders, these prisons are designed for prisoners who have broken the rules in a regular prison (perhaps by assaulting other prisoners or guards). These prisons are designed to maximize security and surveillance. Guard booths are constructed so that visual and auditory monitoring of every cell is easy. Prisoners may be fed through a slot in the door, forbidden to speak with other prisoners or to have pictures of family members in their cells, or kept in their cells 23 hours a day and allowed out only into an exercise "cage" where they have a few square yards to walk. Two examples of supermax prisons are Pelican Bay in California and the Federal Penitentiary at Marion, Illinois. A recent estimate put the number of prisoners in these facilities at approximately 25,000 inmates.[46]

One disturbing element of supermax prisons is the sensory deprivation experienced by prisoners. This deprivation was considered so severe in Indiana that it sparked an inquiry from Amnesty International, a class action lawsuit by the Indiana Civil Liberties Union, and a 37-day hunger protest from the prisoners.[47]

Psychological research indicates that sensory deprivation leads to increased symptoms of psychological trauma and disturbance. Nine of 10 supermax prisoners reported anxiety compared to 4.5 persons out of 10 in the general population. Eighty-four percent of supermax prisoners reported lethargy, and 77 percent reported depression, compared to 17 percent and 23.5 percent, respectively, for populations outside prison.[48] In Colorado, testing revealed that prisons with administrative segregation had a disproportionately high rate of prisoners with mental health needs and more prisoners with personality disorders.[49] On the other hand, some inmates do actually volunteer for supermax confinement due to fear of injury, a desire to be alone rather than share a cell, or as a way to get out of a work assignment.[50]

Another problem is that inmates may not receive appropriate mental health services. In Pelican Bay, for example, in 1990, one master's degree-level psychologist was responsible for the care of 3,500 prisoners. Prisoners needing psychiatric treatment were literally bussed to another prison (Vacaville) and back if they needed more than the counselor could provide at Pelican Bay.[51]

Prison officials argue that prisoners in supermax facilities have proven how difficult they are to manage in a traditional prison and that their rule violations in traditional settings justify the drastic measures in the supermax prisons.

There is little empirical evidence proving that supermax prisons are effective. A study of the opening of supermax prisons in three states did not find any reduction in the levels of inmate-on-inmate violence in those jurisdictions.[52] In addition, some correctional officers report greater job dissatisfaction where no interaction is allowed with inmates.

DEATH ROW

At the end of 2006, 3,228 offenders were on death row, 17 fewer than at yearend 2005. The year 2006 saw 66 executions, 19 fewer than in 2000. California led the nation with 656 death row inmates, followed by Texas (391), Florida (374), and Pennsylvania (219).[53] (For further information on the death penalty, see Chapter 14.)

After interviewing 35 men on Alabama's death row, Johnson concluded that life on death row often involved two "deaths": the death from the execution itself and the extra "death" of living on death row.[54] The prisoner's time on death row is marked by anticipation of death in the electric

For further statistics on the death penalty, go to the web site of the Death Penalty Information Center to find their Death Penalty Fact Sheet at www.deathpenaltyinfo.org.

chair (which was the method of execution in Alabama at the time of the study) and by a dulling, meaningless routine. At the time of the research, death row inmates spent most of their time in their cells and had little to do but read, listen to the radio, and chat with the men in adjoining cells. Thus,

> Many condemned prisoners lead palpably empty lives. They feel isolated and lonely. Visits are scarce or nonexistent. Exercise provides little relief, and may become, instead a burdensome departure from inactivity. Alone and uncared for, some condemned prisoners are consumed by apathy, emerging as stuporous, inert figures who do little more than survive each day.[55]

Further, Johnson contends that guards create death anxiety by such means as taking every newly arrived inmate on a tour of the execution chamber and taunting them whenever the electric chair needs to be tested.

The aptly titled book *Welcome to Hell*[56] contains letters of death row prisoners documenting problems such as noise, vermin, annoying fellow prisoners, unappetizing and insect-laden meals, deprivation of privacy and human contact, and lack of cleansers to clean one's cell.

However, there are some indications that death row is not always as stupefying as Johnson found in Alabama. In some states, death row prisoners work just like other prisoners. For example, Tennessee death row inmates entered data into computers for a state agency and Texas death row inmates were employed in prison industries just like other inmates.

One Texas inmate was even able to sell his artwork over the Internet. As the book and movie *Dead Man Walking* showed, Louisiana allows its death row prisoners to meet with spiritual advisors, such as Sister Helen Prejean, who can help the inmate prepare spiritually for death.[57] Going even further, Missouri has "mainstreamed" death-eligible prisoners, that is, mixed them in with the general prison population.[58]

There are conflicting pieces of information. While Johnson's study of one death row paints a disturbing picture of mind-deadening inactivity and guard behavior that approaches psychological torture and a collection of inmate letters details numerous problems, it nevertheless appears that some prisons' inmates are working and appear to be treated humanely. Research is needed to obtain a more complete picture of the current status of death rows across the nation.

OFFENDER NEEDS

Offenders are multi-problem individuals. It is likely that many street criminals will have such problems as below-average intelligence, less than a high school education, a history of alcohol and other drug abuse, few (if any) job skills, and a lack of family attachments. In addition, a number of offenders have children for whom they are legally responsible, mental or emotional difficulties, and/or a history of abuse in their childhoods. The approximately one-half of prisoners that are African-American face the problems that confront all blacks in the United States: prejudice and discrimination. Whether on probation or in prison, the typical offender has one or more of these needs.

• Alcohol-Drug History •

Offenders often have alcohol and other drug problems. The 2004 Survey of Inmates in State and Federal Correctional Facilities showed that more than one-half (56%) of state prisoners had used illegal drugs in the month before their offense, one-third (32%) had used an illegal drug at the time of their offense, and more than one-half (53%) were dependent on or were abusing drugs. The percentages for federal prisoners were just slightly lower. Fifty percent of federal prisoners had used illegal drugs in the month before their offense, 22 percent used illegal drugs at the time of their offense, 26 percent used alcohol at the time of their offense, and 45 percent reported being drug-dependent or that they were abusing drugs.[59] After admission to prison, more than 40 percent of prisoners who used drugs in the month before their offense had participated in drug treatment or programs.[60] (For information on the drug problems of probationers, see a later section of this chapter.)

In their study of armed robbers in St. Louis, Wright and Decker noted that two-thirds (40 of 59) of their respondents who told them what they did with their money used the money for gambling or alcohol or other drugs. The researchers concluded that giving robbers money would not end their need to steal but instead would just "set off a round of drinking and drug taking that would plunge them deeper into financial desperation and thereby *increase* their lawbreaking" (emphasis in original).[61]

• Mental Health Needs •

The 2004 Survey of Inmates shows that 56 percent of state inmates, 45 percent of federal prisoners, and 64 percent of jail inmates had a mental health problem. These percentages were higher for women than for men. For example, approximately three-quarters of female inmates in state prisons and jails had mental health problems.[62] More than one-third of state prisoners and one in six jail inmates with a mental problem had received treatment after admission.[63] (See Box 7.4 for information about the related problem of prisoner suicide, and Chapter 9 for information on the mental health problems of juveniles.)

Educational attainment was also a problem. Forty percent of state prisoners and more than one-fourth (26.5%) of federal prisoners had not finished high school. About another one-fourth of prisoners had a General Equivalency Diploma (GED) instead of a regular high school diploma.[64]

• Prison Responses to Prisoner Needs •

As noted in Chapter 1, one current trend in corrections is punitiveness. Part of this punitive trend is an unwillingness to address prisoner needs. For example, programs offering college courses and degrees to inmates are now considered by many to be "coddling." Counseling programs are considered unnecessary "frills." All that is considered necessary is a punishment regime. There are many people who consider Angola State Penitentiary in Louisiana to be an ideal prison because it sends most of its prisoners to work in agricultural fields that are actually part of the prison complex.

Prisons like Angola do keep prisoners busy. In that sense, they are probably better than prisons that do little to combat idleness. In fact, it could even be argued that legitimate labor such as farm labor at Angola is more humane than forced idleness that does nothing to uplift the human spirit and encourages such negative outcomes as boredom, depression, and even riots.

A problem with the contemporary trend toward eliminating amenities and so-called frills is that farm labor or its equivalent does little or nothing

BOX 7.4

Suicide in Prison

According to the most recent available data, 168 inmates in state prisons and 314 jail inmates nationwide committed suicide in 2002. Both numbers are about the same as the numbers for 2001. Suicides accounted for 5.8 percent of state prison inmate deaths, and almost one-third of local jail inmate deaths (Mumola, 2005).

When standardized to comparable proportions according to gender, age, and race in the whole United States, the prison suicide rate, 14 suicides per 100,000 inmates, is lower than the resident population rate of 18 suicides per 100,000 United States residents. Even after standardization, however, the jail suicide rate—47 suicides per every 100,000 jail inmates—is considerably higher than the national resident rate (again, 18 suicides per 100,000 residents) (Mumola, 2005).

Risk factors include alcohol and other drug problems, a history of previous suicide or self-injury attempts, and previous self-injury in custody. Hanging at night is the frequent mode, with slightly disproportionate numbers taking place on weekends and in the early phases of custody. "The most common emotion in suicides is hopelessness or helplessness, intense anguish, or 'ennui'" (Liebling, 1999:297-298).

Liebling argues that it is helpful to distinguish three distinct profiles of suicides in prison: life or long-sentence prisoners, psychiatrically ill prisoners, and poor copers. Each group has its own motivation and features. Poor copers constitute the highest proportion of prison suicides, accounting for about 30 to 45 percent of prison suicides. In general, though, prison suicide attempters had important coping problems. Many felt less able to pass time in their cells and thus were especially vulnerable to committing suicide (Liebling, 1999).

Suggested interventions include transfer to a shared cell, courses on coping and problem-solving skills, and psychological support. Prisoner support in the form of listener schemes or "buddy" schemes has been used in both Great Britain and the United States (Liebling, 1999).

to deal with the real needs that offenders have. When a man leaves Angola, he may know something about farming sugar cane, which could possibly help him get a job and stay out of crime, but more than likely, he will go back to an urban environment (in Louisiana, this would be in New Orleans or Baton Rouge) where there will be no opportunity to farm. Without an adequate education or vocational skills appropriate for his urban home environment, and without treatment for any substance abuse problems he might have, the prisoner will be much more likely to recidivate. Even a factory job in prison may not provide much in the way of vocational training. The job might be available in prison because the wages are extremely low—below prevailing market rates—and if the prison labor were not available the manufacturer would probably take the operation to a third-world country for a similar below-market wage rate.[65]

Offering substance abuse treatment, college courses, or job training programs in prison may seem to make prison too soft because such programs detract from the punitive character of prisons. Perhaps it is reasonable to say that prisoners can get into treatment or college courses or vocational programs after prison. However, a critical opportunity may be missed by taking such an approach. Offering substance abuse treatment and educational and vocational programs in prison may be "coddling" society more than the inmates. It may help inmates to avoid criminal activity after release, thereby insulating society from such criminal activity.

Lack of treatment could also translate into a constitutional violation. California's lack of mental health treatment, for example, occasioned Magistrate-Judge John F. Moulds of the Eastern District of California court to describe the system as inflicting cruel and unusual punishment, contrary to the Eighth Amendment. For example, a report found that California prison over-relied on medication and did not use proper monitoring of such medications.[66]

RACE IN PRISON

Until about 30 years ago, blacks were a minority in America's prisons. Whites dominated the prisons numerically and in terms of power. From then until the year 2000, there was a dramatic increase in the number of blacks in prison, and then a decline among black prisoners between 2000 and 2006. Overall, African Americans, male and female, make up approximately 40 percent of the prisoner population (41.6%) under state jurisdiction, and Hispanic or Latino persons make up approximately 20 percent.[67]

There has been little research on the interaction of black inmates and white inmates in prisons today, and most of the research that does exist is dated. Despite the lack of current studies, it is obvious that racial tension is a key aspect of current prison life.

One of the basic issues concerning race in prison is the perception that the criminal justice system discriminates unfairly in law enforcement and sentencing, resulting in the disproportionate number of blacks in prison. One writer argues that the "war on crime" is simply a disguise for a war on his race:

> It's respectable to tar and feather criminals, to advocate locking
> them up and throwing away the key. It's not racist to be against
> crime, even though the archetypical criminal in the media and

the public imagination almost always wears "Willie" Horton's [a black criminal's] face. Gradually, "urban" and "ghetto" have become code words for terrible places where only blacks reside. Prison is rapidly being re-classified in the same segregated fashion.[68]

Criminologists debate the extent to which race unfairly enters in as a factor in arrest, prosecution, and sentencing decisions. Many African-American prisoners conclude that racism is a prominent factor and, as a result, come to prison with resentment. That resentment affects their daily interactions with both prisoners and guards. Prison officials must deal with this issue every day.

WOMEN IN PRISON

Women still represent only a small percentage—approximately 7.2 percent—of the prison population, but their numbers have been increasing.[69] In 1980, women made up 4.1 percent of the prison population and in 1990 made up 5.7 percent.[70] The many important differences between women's and men's prisons are addressed fully in Chapter 9. Here we simply note a few important points about women in prison.

First, there are fewer women's prisons than men's prisons. There may be only one or two women's prisons in a state, and because of this, women prisoners may have to serve their sentences at greater distances from their homes than males who have more prisons available to them. This may make it difficult for women prisoners to have visitors as frequently as they would like.

Women are typically less violent and aggressive than men, and thus their prisons provide more of a sense of security than do men's prisons and female prisoners can be less fearful of assaults than male prisoners. However, women's prisons can include minor violence[71] and sexual abuse of prisoners by guards (see Chapter 11 for more details), and they may be more nitpicking in rule enforcement. Society still has somewhat of a double standard for behavior. Women are expected to be more obedient and docile than men. What might pass in a men's prison as normal behavior might be cited as a rule violation in a women's prison. Guards will cite women for improper language or jostling, behaviors ignored by guards in male prisons.

Women's prisons may look more appealing than men's prisons. The cells or dormitory areas often look less like stark cellblocks than men's. However, also stemming from societal notions about appropriate gender roles, educational and vocational programs in women's prisons are often more limited. Cosmetology and food service might be the main vocational training programs in a women's prison whereas such options as auto mechanics and television repair might be available for male prisoners.

Part of the problem with women's prisons is that the smaller number of prisoners means that less money is allocated for women's prisons, including training programs, than for men's prisons.

As we can see, there is a mixture of elements that makes women's prisons better than men's prisons in some respects and worse in others. They have less serious violence and probably look better to the uninformed eye, but they can also be rather harsh in terms of strict rule enforcement based on societal expectations of gender-appropriate behavior. A woman prisoner may not fear a physical assault but she may well fear a guard citing her for

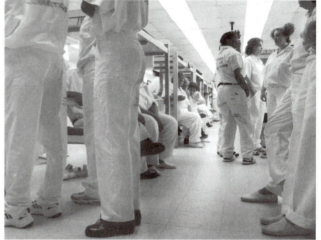

Inmates at Tutwiler Women's Prison in Wetumpka, Alabama, stand around and sit on bunks in a dorm that holds 250 women. At the time of this photo, 986 prisoners were being held at Tutwiler, the state's only women's prison.

AP Photo/Kevin Glackmeyer

a rule violation for what many would consider relatively harmless language or behavior. Few programs exist for the myriad of problems facing women, such as unemployment or underemployment, drug addiction, unresolved issues relating to childhood sexual and physical abuse, and difficulties associated with being a mother in prison.

SPIRITUAL ADJUSTMENT IN PRISON

If spiritual adjustment is mentioned in connection with prison life, usually this refers to the provision of chaplains and official religious services. Traditional religious services and chaplains are helpful for prisoners as they attempt to adjust to the pains of imprisonment and as they try to change their lives while inside in preparation for release. A relatively recent development is faith-based programming and even some faith-based prisons, including two in Florida.

Faith-based prison initiatives are based on the premise that religion can be a powerful force for change. The hope is that offering faith-based programs to prisoners will help them to re-orient their lives to positive values and goals. Recall that, as noted in Chapter 2, America's prisons were founded by religious people such as the Quakers who wanted to reform criminals with religion.

Research is being conducted on the effectiveness of contemporary faith-based programs. One problem with the research is that prisoners who volunteer for such programs are motivated individuals, so any evaluation of a program must take into account the positive motivation of such prisoners and distinguish any effect of the program from the effect of having motivated subjects. A related point is that faith-based programs need to be compared to nonreligious programs that are high-quality programs. Because a great deal of effort appears to be going into faith-based programs, it would be unfair to compare them to mediocre or less substantial nonreligious programs.

Some critics worry that faith-based initiatives may divert resources from traditional, non-faith-based programs such as educational and vocational programs. These critics caution that many prisoners have significant problems that need to be addressed. There is even concern that some states want to reduce the number of state-paid chaplains and replace them with faith-based volunteers.[72]

Another issue is providing access to all religions, not just Christianity. Perhaps more important than providing access to all religions, however, is providing access to the spiritual in whatever guise the prisoner may pursue it. Jean Harris, notorious for killing Dr. Herman Tarnower (the creator of the "Scarsdale Diet") served 12 years in New York's Bedford Hills Correctional Facility for women. She found meaning by reading Viktor Frankl's account of his suffering in a Nazi concentration camp and was inspired by his decision during the Holocaust that "he, and not they, would decide how he would react to what they did to him."[73] Such a simple thing as reading helped Harris come to grips with her life behind bars. Just as prisons need to offer education and vocational training programs, there should be opportunities for prisoners to do what they can do to make their lives as meaningful as possible despite the fact of their incarceration.

Go to www.humankindness.org to learn more about the Human Kindness Foundation, the Prison Ashram Project, and the writings of Bo Lozoff.

Bo Lozoff has been doing prison ministry work for about a quarter of a century. He teaches prisoners how to meditate and do other spiritual practices including spiritual reading. He is eclectic and uses the sacred texts and teachers of Christianity, Judaism, Hinduism, Islam, Buddhism, and other religions to help prisoners develop the spiritual dimension of their lives. In addition to going to prisons, he also prints a newsletter and has written several books that he offers to prisoners at no charge.

Some prisons offer life skills programs such as moral reconation therapy, a cognitive-behavioral treatment for offenders that is intended to raise moral reasoning.[74] Offering such programs is one possible approach. For many inmates, however, it may not be a particular program that awakens in them the desire to find deeper meaning in their lives; it may simply be a guard or prison counselor who takes an interest in them and shows by

BOX 7.5

Some Findings on Faith-Based Prison Programs

Research on the ability of faith-based programs to reduce recidivism has produced some interesting results. Five studies that all promoted Christianity as a way to reduce recidivism failed to do so. However, a program that involved prison chaplains and faith-based volunteers connecting high-risk sex offenders with a community support group of faith-based persons who wanted to help offenders did reduce recidivism by about one-third. A possible inference from this is that the effective program used the principles of effective correctional treatment such as focusing on criminogenic needs (O'Connor, Duncan, and Quillard, 2006), while the other programs did not use those principles. A second point is that faith-based programs may be more effective in helping prisoners cope with the many losses (deprivations) of prison life and thereby help them to counteract the dehumanizing tendencies of prisons than in reducing recidivism (Clear et al., 2000). A third lesson is that perhaps the government's concern for reducing recidivism, while completely legitimate, is quite distinct from religion's interest in saving one's soul. As Hewitt argues, "Rebirth is only the start of learning about grace and how faith may work in one's life. Although the inmate has accepted forgiveness and begins to walk down the path of change, it could be years before there is sufficient clarity in his or her salvation to notice measurable change in behaviour [such as reduced recidivism]" (Hewitt, 2006: 554). Both faith-based programming and research on such programs are still relatively new. Current research should be reporting additional findings in the next few years.

What do you think? Is it essential that faith-based programs reduce recidivism? Or is it enough that we think that faith-based programs are affecting prisoners spiritually and that it may take years for that spiritual change to show results?

Sources: O'Connor, T.P., J. Duncan, and F. Quillard (2006). "Criminology and Religion: The Shape of an Authentic Dialogue." *Criminology & Public Policy* 5:559-570. Clear, T.R., P.L. Hardyman, B. Stout, K. Lucken, and H.R. Dammer (2000). "The Value of Religion in Prison: An Inmate Perspective." *Journal of Contemporary Criminal Justice* 16: 53-74. Hewitt, J.D. (2006). "Having Faith in Faith-Based Prison Programs." *Criminology & Public Policy* 5:551-558.

his or her actions that there can be meaning in the inmate's life. To paraphrase one prison authority, the example of one guard or counselor who shows by example that he or she is in touch with a deeper dimension of life and that he or she cares for the prisoners encountered every day may be worth more than any life skills program costing hundreds of thousands of dollars.[75] (For more about religion in prison, see Box 7.5.)

CONCLUSION

This chapter has looked at prisoners and prison life. We have seen that some criticize prison life for being too soft while others argue that it is too harsh. The current trend is to remove some of the amenities of prison life and return prisons to more Spartan circumstances. Prison victimization was also discussed, including both sexual assaults and victimization of prisoners by guards. Often those who criticize prisons for being too soft neglect to consider the problems of prison adjustment. The issues of death row prisoners, race in prison, supermax prisons, and women in prison were examined. The issues covered in this chapter show that prison life is difficult in many ways and can have long-term effects on prisoners. Those effects continue in other areas, especially on the release experience.

In subsequent chapters, we will devote additional attention to women prisoners, correctional officers, juvenile correctional interventions, special populations, and the administration and management of correctional institutions. Those chapters will complement the material covered in this chapter.

▶ Ethics Focus: How Far Should We Go in Protecting Inmates from Each Other?

Consider the following situation:

You are a correctional officer at a maximum-security prison. Recently, an inmate who was considered a bully and sexual predator was raped in the cellblock shower by four other inmates. The victim had himself participated in several previous sexual assaults on younger or weaker inmates. You heard about this assault through the prison grapevine and had confirmed that it had taken place through some reliable sources. The victim had not come forward and more than likely would not. Some of the other officers had indicated that if anyone ever deserved such an assault, it was the inmate in question. In addition, an investigation would require a lot of paperwork and a lot of your time.

What should you do?

▶At the Movies......................

The Farm: Life Inside Angola Prison, 1998.

This is a documentary about Angola, the Louisiana State Penitentiary. One highlight of this film is the segment that filmed an actual parole hearing that indicates to everyone except the three parole board members hearing the case that the prisoner requesting parole did not in fact commit the rape for which he was convicted.

The Shawshank Redemption, 1994.

This movie is about a wrongly imprisoned prisoner and a corrupt warden and how both get justice in the end.

DISCUSSION QUESTIONS

1. A friend learns you are taking this corrections course and studying prisons. She remarks that "those prisoners have it made and should be put to work more and suffer more for the crimes they committed." Keeping Sykes's deprivations of prison life in mind and noting statistics on sexual victimization, how would you respond?

2. Discuss victimization in prison. How and to what extent do prisoners victimize other prisoners? How do guards victimize prisoners?

3. What is life like on death row? What would a humane death row look like?

4. What do prisoners deserve? Even though offenders may have injured others, what does society owe prisoners?

5. Imagine you are the commissioner of corrections in a state that has only one prison for males. What would your prison be like? What amenities would you provide for prisoners? What would a typical day's schedule be like? Justify your ideal prison.

6. How far should society go to help parolees or prisoners who have completed their sentences? When a prisoner leaves prison, what does society owe that offender as he or she tries to readjust to life outside of prison?

FURTHER READING

Bergner, D. (1998). *God of the Rodeo: The Quest for Redemption in Louisiana's Prison*. New York: Ballantine Books.

Carceral, K.C. (2006). *Prison, Inc.: A Convict Exposes Life Inside a Private Prison*. New York: New York University Press.

Lozoff, B. (1985). *We're All Doing Time: A Guide for Getting Free*. Durham, NC: Human Kindness Foundation.

Ross, J.I., and S.C. Richards (2002). *Behind Bars: Surviving Prison*. Indianapolis: Alpha.

NOTES

1. Sabol, Couture, and Harrison, 2007. For periodically updated statistics, consult the Bureau of Justice Statistics, available at http://www.ojp/usdoj.gov/bjs/

2. Sabol, Couture, and Harrison, 2007.

3. Sabol, Couture, and Harrison, 2007.

4. Sabol, Couture, and Harrison, 2007.

5. Sabol, Couture, and Harrison, 2007.

6. FBI, Uniform Crime Reports, Crime in the United States, 2006.

7. Austin and Irwin, 2001, 26.

8. Austin and Irwin, 2001.

9. See, e.g., Alabama Code, 13A-3-23.

10. Wright and Decker, 1994.

11. Forbes, 1994.

12. Sykes, 1958.

13. Comfort et al., 2005.

14. Nacci and Kane, 1983.

15. Wooldredge, 1998.

16. U.S. Department of Justice, 1998.

17. Guenther, 1978.

18. Guenther, 1978.

19. Parker-Jimenez, 1997.

20. Fleisher, 1989, 131.

21. Austin and Irwin, 2001.

22. Carroll, 1998.

23. Zamble and Porporino, 1988.

24. Toch, 1977.

25. Sheehan, 1977.

26. Carroll, 1998.

27. Parker-Jimenez, 1997.

28. Flanagan, 1995.

29. Toch, 1995, 246.

30. Toch, 1995.

31. Lockwood, 1980.

32. Nacci and Kane, 1983.

33. Nacci and Kane, 1983.

34. Saum et al., 1995.

35. Human Rights Watch, 2001.

36. Struckman-Johnson and Struckman-Johnson, 2006.

37. Human Rights Watch, 2001.

38. Beck and Harrison, 2007.

39. Marquart, 1986.

40. Washington, 1994, 72.

41. Struckman-Johnson and Struckman-Johnson, 2006.

42. Rathbone, 2006.

43. Conrad, 1982.

44. Conrad, 1982.

45. Conrad, 1982, 329.

46. Pizzaro and Narag, 2008.

47. Larson, 1993.

48. Haney, 2003.

49. O'Keefe, 2008.

50. Pizzaro and Narag, 2008.

51. Specter, 1994.

52. Pizzaro and Narag, 2008.

53. *Capital Punishment, 2006*—Statistical Tables. Available at http://www.ojp.usdoj.gov.

54. Johnson, 1998.

55. Johnson, 1998.

56. Arriens, 1997.

57. Prejean, 1993.

58. Cunningham et al., 2005.

59. Mumola and Karberg, 2006.

60. Mumola and Karberg, 2006.

61. Wright and Decker, 1997, 59-60.

62. James and Glaze, 2006.

63. James and Glaze, 2006.

64. Harlow, 2003.

65. Erlich, 1997.

66. Specter, 1994.

67. Sabol, Couture, and Harrison, 2007.

68. Wideman, 1995, 503.

69. Sabol, Couture, and Harrison, 2007

70. Beck et al., 2000.

71. Bottoms, 1999.

72. O'Connor et al., 2006.

73. Anderson, 1995.

74. Finn, 1998.

75. Lozoff and Braswell, 1989.

REFERENCES

Alabama Code, 13A-3-23.

Anderson, G.M. (1995). "Women and Criminal Justice: An Interview with Jean Harris." *America* 172 (March 18, 1995):10-17.

Arriens, J. (ed.) (1997). *Welcome to Hell: Letters and Writings from Death Row*. Boston: Northeastern University Press.

Austin, J., and J. Irwin (2001). *It's About Time: America's Imprisonment Binge*, 3rd ed. Belmont, CA: Wadsworth.

Beck, A.J., T.P. Bonczar, P.M. Ditton, D.K. Gilliard, L.E. Glaze, C.W. Harlow, C.J. Mumola, T.L. Snell, J.J. Stephan, and J.W. Wilson (2000). "Correctional Populations in the United States, 1997." *Bureau of Justice Statistics Bulletin*. Washington, DC: U.S. Government Printing Office.

Beck, A.J., and P.M. Harrison (2007). "Sexual Victimization in State and Federal Prisons Reported by Inmates, 2007." *Bureau of Justice Statistics Bulletin*. Washington, DC: U.S. Government Printing Office.

Bottoms, A.E. (1999). "Interpersonal Violence and Social Order in Prisons." In M. Tonry and J. Petersilia (eds.), *Prisons*, 205-281. Chicago: University of Chicago Press.

Capital Punishment, 2006—Statistical Tables. Available at http://www.ojp.usdoj.gov

Carroll, L. (1998). *Lawful Order: A Case Study of Correctional Crisis and Reform*. New York: Garland.

Comfort, M., O. Grinstead, K. McCartney, P. Bourgois, and K. Knight (2005). "'You Can't Do Nothing in this Damn Place": Sex and Intimacy among Couples with an Incarcerated Male Partner." *Journal of Sex Research* 42(1):3-12.

Conrad, J.P. (1982). "What Do the Undeserving Deserve?" In R. Johnson and H. Toch (eds.), *The Pains of Imprisonment*, 313-330. Beverly Hills: Sage.

Cunningham, M.D., T.J. Reidy, and J.R. Sorensen (2005). "Is Death Row Obsolete: A Decade of Mainstreaming Death-Sentenced Inmates in Missouri." *Behavioral Sciences and the Law* 23:307-320.

Erlich, R. (1997). "Inmate Labor May Not Be Beneficial." In C.P. Cozic (ed.), *America's Prisons: Opposing Viewpoints*, 102-110. San Diego: Greenhaven Press.

Federal Bureau of Investigation (FBI) (2007). *Uniform Crime Reports, Crime in the United States, 2006.* Available at www.fbi.gov/ucr/cius2006/

Finn, P. (1998). "The Delaware Department of Correction Life Skills Program." *Bureau of Justice Statistics Bulletin.* Washington, DC: U.S. Government Printing Office.

Flanagan, T.J. (1995). "Correctional Policy and the Long-Term Prisoner." In *Long-Term Imprisonment: Policy, Science, and Correctional Practice*, 249-257. T.J. Flanagan (ed.), Thousand Oaks, CA: Sage.

Fleisher, M.S. (1989). *Warehousing Violence.* Newbury Park, CA: Sage.

Forbes, S. (1994). "Can You Believe This?" *Forbes* 154 (3):21.

Guenther, A. (1978). "The Impact of Confinement." In N. Johnston and L.D. Savitz (eds.), *Justice and Corrections*, 596-603. New York: John Wiley & Sons.

Haney, C. (2003). "Mental Health Issues in Long-Term Solitary and 'Supermax' Confinement." *Crime & Delinquency* 49:124-156.

Harlow, C.W. (2003). "Education and Correctional Populations." *Bureau of Justice Statistics Special Report.* Washington, DC: U.S. Government Printing Office.

Human Rights Watch (2001). "No Escape: Male Rape in U.S. Prisons." Available at http://www.hrw.org/reports/2001/prison/report4.html

James, D.J., and L.E. Glaze (2006). "Mental Health Problems of Prison and Jail Inmates." *Bureau of Justice Statistics Special Report.* Washington, DC: U.S. Government Printing Office.

Johnson, R. (1989). *Condemned to Die: Life under Sentence of Death.* Prospect Height, IL: Waveland.

Larson, J.K. (1993). "Society Behind Bars: Race, Rights and Religion." *The Christian Century* 110 (32):1123.

Liebling, A. (1999). "Prison Suicide and Prisoner Coping." In M. Tonry and J. Petersilia (eds.), *Prisons*, 283-359. Chicago: University of Chicago Press.

Lockwood, D. (1980). *Prison Sexual Violence.* New York: Elsevier.

Lozoff, B., and M. Braswell (1989). *Inner Corrections: Finding Peace and Peace Making.* Cincinnati: Anderson.

Maguire, K., and A.L. Pastore (eds.) (1999). *Sourcebook of Criminal Justice Statistics 1998.* Washington, DC: U.S. Department of Justice.

Maitland, A.S., and R.D. Sluder (1996). "Victimization in Prisons: A Study of Factors Related to the General Well-Being of Youthful Inmates." *Federal Probation* 60 (2):24-31.

Marquart, J.W. (1986). "Prison Guards and the Use of Physical Coercion as a Mechanism of Prisoner Control." *Criminology* 24:347-366.

Mumola, C.J. (1999). "Substance Abuse and Treatment, State and Federal Prisoners, 1997." *Bureau of Justice Statistics Special Report*. Washington, DC: U.S. Government Printing Office.

Mumola, C.J. (2005). "Suicide and Homicide in State Prisons and Local Jails." *Bureau of Justice Statistics Bulletin*. Washington, DC: U.S. Government Printing Office.

Mumola, C.J., and J.C. Karberg (2006). "Drug Use and Dependence, State and Federal Prisoners, 2004." *Bureau of Justice Statistics Bulletin*. Washington, DC: U.S. Government Printing Office.

Nacci, P.L., and T.R. Kane (1983). "The Incidence of Sex and Sexual Aggression in Federal Prisons." *Federal Probation* 47 (4):31-36.

O'Connor, T.P., J. Duncan, and R. Quillard (2006). "Criminology and Religion: The Shape of an Authentic Dialogue." *Criminology & Public Policy* 5:559-570.

O'Keefe, M.L. (2008). "Administrative Segregation From Within: A Corrections Perspective." *The Prison Journal* 88:123-143.

Parker-Jimenez, J. (1997). "An Offender's Experience with the Criminal Justice System." *Federal Probation* 61 (1):47-52.

Pizzaro, J.M., and R.E. Narag (2008). "Supermax Prisons: What We Know, What We Do Not Know, and Where We Are Going." *The Prison Journal* 88:23-42.

Prejean, H. (1993). *Dead Man Walking: An Eyewitness Account of the Death Penalty in the United States*. New York: Vintage Books.

Rathbone, C. (2006). *A World Apart: Women, Prison, and Life Behind Bars*. New York: Random House Trade Paperbacks.

Sabol, W.J, H. Couture, and P.M. Harrison (2007). "Prisoners in 2006." *Bureau of Justice Statistics Bulletin*. Washington, DC: U.S. Government Printing Office.

Saum, C.A., H.L. Surratt, J.A. Inciardi, and J. Bennett (1995). "Sex in Prison: Exploring the Myths and Realities." *The Prison Journal* 75:413-430.

Sheehan, S. (1977). "Annals of Crime." *The New Yorker*, October 31, 1977:48-55.

Smykla, J.O., and J. Houston (1999). "Coed Prison: Should We Try It (Again)?" In C.B. Fields (ed.), *Controversial Issues in Corrections*, 203-218. Boston: Allyn & Bacon.

Snell, T.L., and L.M. Maruschak (2002). "Capital Punishment 2001." *Bureau of Justice Statistics Bulletin*. Washington, DC: U.S. Government Printing Office.

Specter, D. (1994). "Cruel and Unusual Punishment of the Mentally Ill in California's Prisons: A Case Study of a Class Action Suit." *Social Justice* 21:109-117.

Struckman-Johnson, C., and D. Struckman-Johnson (2006). "A Comparison of Sexual Coercion Experiences Reported by Men and Women in Prison," *Journal of Interpersonal Violence* 21:1591-1615.

Sykes, G. (1958). *The Society of Captives: A Study of a Maximum Security Prison*. Princeton, NJ: Princeton University Press.

Toch, H. (1995). "The Long-Term Inmate as a Long-Term Problem." In T.J. Flanagan (ed.), *Long-Term Imprisonment: Policy, Science, and Correctional Practice*, 245-248. Thousand Oaks, CA: Sage.

Toch. H. (1977). *Living in Prison: The Ecology of Survival*. New York: Free Press.

U.S. Department of Justice (1998). *State Efforts to Manage Violent Long-Term Offenders*. Washington, DC: U.S. Department of Justice.

Washington, J. (1994). *Iron House: Stories from the Yard*. New York: Random House.

Wideman, J.E. (1995). "Doing Time, Marking Race (Incarceration and Racism)." *The Nation*, October 30, 1995, 503.

Wooldredge, J.D. (1998). "Inmate Lifestyles and Opportunities for Victimization." *Journal of Research in Crime and Delinquency* 35:480-502.

Wright, R.T., and S.H. Decker (1997). *Armed Robbers in Action: Stickups and Street Culture*. Boston: Northeastern University Press.

Wright, R.T., and S.H. Decker (1994). *Burglars on the Job: Streetlife and Residential Break-Ins*. Boston: Northeastern University Press.

Zamble, E., and F.J. Porporino (1988). *Coping, Behavior, and Adaptation in Prison Inmates*. New York: Springer-Verlag.

Women Offenders and Correctional Workers

What You Need to Know

▶ There are now more than 110,000 women in jail or prison.

▶ The average yearly increase in women prisoners has been greater than the increase in male prisoners.

▶ The history of women in prison has been one of unequal and inadequate resources and programs compared to men prisoners.

▶ Women in prison tend to be young, single, economically disadvantaged, and disproportionately minority.

▶ Female prisoner subcultures are distinct from male prisoner subcultures and are more relationship-based.

▶ It is estimated that 60 to 85 percent of women prisoners are mothers.

▶ In the past, programs for women offenders have suffered from gender stereotypes. Today there is greater attention being paid to gender-specific programming.

▶ Two important issues concerning women prisoners are cross-sex supervision and health care.

▶ Recent statistics show that there are more than 1 million women probationers and almost 100,000 women on parole.

▶ Recent figures show that about 20 percent of correctional officers and 50 percent of probation and parole officers are women.

INTRODUCTION

Women have never been a visible presence in the field of corrections. Because of their small numbers and a perception that they pose less risk, they have tended to be overlooked by researchers and practitioners. For instance, it is rare to find more than a few pages on female offenders in most corrections, criminology, or criminal justice textbooks. Some books offer special chapters, like this one, devoted to women's issues. The reason that it is hard to integrate their "story" into an account of corrections in general is that they are different from men, their history is distinct, and their problems are not always the same.

In the last 20 years or so, the number of women sentenced to some form of correctional sentence has increased dramatically. With these larger numbers has come the growing realization that even though women may have been overlooked in the past, they no longer can be ignored. States are scrambling to build new facilities for women, evaluate women's programming, and address the unique problems of women—sometimes in response to court orders to do so. This chapter will explore these problems and others, starting with a presentation of what has occurred in the sentencing and treatment of women offenders in recent years. It then explores the history of corrections for women—a history that is quite different from that of men's. Women who are sentenced to some form of community corrections sanctions are also described, although there is little information available concerning their problems. Finally, a few issues concerning women workers in corrections are discussed.

• Increasing Numbers: Increasing Problems •

Although women have never comprised a large segment of the United States' prison population, their numbers are increasing alarmingly. In 2001, there were more than 93,000 women in jail or prison.[1] In 2006, their numbers increased to 112,498.[2] Although the total number of women incarcerated is dwarfed by the number of men in prison, the percentage increase of women sentenced to prison over the last decade has been higher than men's. As can be seen in Table 8.1, between 2000 and 2006, the average yearly increase for women was 2.9 percent, compared to a 1.8 percent increase for men.[3] Although the lower percentage increase for men represents thousands more inmates than the percentage increase for women, it is troubling to note that sentencing practices seem to be impacting female offenders even more dramatically than their male counterparts.

While women historically have comprised about 5 percent of the total prison population in this country, today the percentage of women is about 7.2 percent of the total prison population—still small, but increasing.[4] There is still a huge difference in the numbers and likelihood of imprisonment for women and men. The national incarceration rate for women sentenced to more than one year is 68 per 100,000, while the rate for men is 943 per 100,000.[5]

TABLE 8.1
Women's and Men's Imprisonment

	2000	2006	Average Annual Growth Rate 2000-2005
Women	93,234	112,948	2.9%
Men	1,298,027	1,458,363	1.8%
Total	1,391,261	1,570,861	1.9%

Source: Sabol, W.J., H. Couture, and P.M Harrison (2007). "Prisoners in 2006." *Bureau of Justice Statistics Bulletin*. Washington, DC: U.S. Government Printing Office.

This pattern of increase is present in jail and community corrections populations as well. Today, women comprise about 24 percent of the probation population, about 12 percent of the parole population, and 12 percent of jail inmates.[6] In fact, it can no longer be said (as it has in the past) that because there are so few women in the corrections system, it is understandable that the system does not respond very well to their needs.

An obvious question is whether the pattern of increase in correctional sentencing is a reaction to an increase in women's criminal behavior. Are we sentencing more women to prison because they are committing more crime and more violent crime? The answer is mixed. While women's contribution to violent crime has not risen substantially, women have increased their participation in property crimes and drug crimes.[7]

Women continue to commit a consistently small percentage (about 11%) of violent crimes.[8] While there are certainly women in prison for violent crime, including gang violence, few studies conclude that women as a whole are becoming increasingly violent.[9] The problem of the "new violent female criminal" seems to be a recurring myth in criminal justice and popular literature— one that may well have contributed to harsher prison sentences imposed on female offenders. If one looks at arrest rates, conviction rates, or other objective evidence of violent crime, there is great consistency over time in women's violent crime rates.[10] It should also be noted that the 1998 homicide rate for women was less than 40 percent of the 1976 homicide rate.[11] Several studies find that 50 percent or more of the number of women who are in prison for homicide killed or injured an

> For more details about the numbers of women in corrections, go to www.ojp.usdoj.gov. In December of each year the Bureau of Justice Statistics releases annual bulletins on prisoners and probation and parole.

BOX 8.1

Karla Faye Tucker

For 15 years, Karla Faye Tucker led an exemplary life. She was strong of faith and supportive of those around her. She fell in love and married. But there was a problem. She was a resident on the Texas death row.

When she was 23 years old, Tucker, along with her live-in boyfriend, Danny Garrett, pick-axed to death Jerry Lynn Dean and his acquaintance, Deborah Thornton. The murders were committed after a long weekend of shooting crystal meth, drinking tequila, and downing an assortment of pills. The motivation was never clear: something about stealing a motorcycle and paying back past grudges. A few weeks later, Tucker told a friend that killing the two victims excited her sexually. It took a Houston jury an hour to find her guilty. Under Texas law, for the jury members to impose the death penalty, they had to find Tucker a "continuing threat to society." They did.

The heinous nature of the crime overshadowed any possible mitigating factors. By most anyone's standards, Karla Faye Tucker had lived a rough life. Growing up in Houston, Texas, at age eight she was using drugs regularly. Two years later, she was using heroin. When she was 11, her mother introduced her to prostitution. Tucker was on her own. She continued in the ways she knew best. Drugs were always close at hand. Along with her sister, Shawn, she made a living servicing men out of motels. She was a survivor. Tough, cocky, and hot-headed, she had a "draw-a-line-in-the-sand-and-I'll-show-you" personality. Thrills were what kept her going.

But going to prison for murder had a profound effect on Tucker. She experienced a religious conversion. She said it was what changed her. Something did. She became a model prisoner. Fifteen years later, as her execution date approached, she wanted to live, even if it meant remaining in prison for the rest of her life. Through the media, she appealed to the public. "Larry King Live." "60 Minutes." "The Charles Grodin Show." Public support for her cause grew. Pat Robertson, a leader of the "religious right" and a strong advocate of the death penalty, publicly opposed her execution. The responses were understandable. Gone was the hard, street-tough. In her place was a far gentler person, convincingly remorseful. It didn't hurt that she was attractive, her appearance much softer now than years earlier during her trial. Dressed in crisp prison whites, her brown hair pulled back in a ponytail and her eyes sparkling, she looked younger than her age of 38. She had an engaging smile and an intelligent presence. It was a terrible thing she had done, she admitted. She was deeply sorry and was willing to spend the rest of her life trying to make up for it.

BOX 8.1 (continued)

Expressions of support came from around the world. The United Nations, the Parliament of the European Union, and the Pope asked that her life be spared. On February 2, 1998, the Texas Board of Pardons and parole voted unanimously, 16-0, against clemency. The Governor, George W. Bush, had already made it clear where he stood. If she did the crime and was found guilty and sentenced to death, and if she had exhausted all her appeals, she must be executed. According to Bush, it was the right thing to do.

Tucker's last words were for her husband, a minister whom she had met during her tenure in prison, and for her friends: "I love all of you very much," she said. "I will see you all when you get there. I will wait for you." When the lethal injection was started, she closed her eyes. Half a minute later, she sighed. At 6:45 P.M., February 3, 1998, Karla Faye Tucker was pronounced dead, the first woman to be executed in Texas since the Civil War.

Source: Adapted from Taylor, R.L., *End of the Death Penalty*. Unpublished draft.

intimate partner after years of battering.[12] While still a violent act, this type of crime is arguably different than an assault or homicide perpetrated against a stranger.

There has been an increase in women's arrest rates for assault.[13] In 1965, women accounted for 13.5 percent of all arrests for aggravated assault, and in 2006, they comprised 21 percent of such arrests.[14] What this increase means, however, is unclear. One possible explanation is that mandatory arrest policies for domestic violence have led to police officers arresting both parties, creating this increase in reported crime.

For greater detail and annual updates on women and crime, go to www.fbi.gov/ucr to find the FBI Uniform Crime Reports. This source gives data on male and female arrests every year. Much of the FBI data is also available in the *Criminal Justice Sourcebook* available at www.albany.edu/sourcebook.

There is no doubt, however, that women's contributions to various property crimes are increasing. Women's participation rates in property crime are roughly double what they were in 1965, with the largest arrest increases in fraud and embezzlement (see Table 8.2).[15]

Explanations for the increased participation of women can be categorized into the general explanations of "opportunity theory" or "economic necessity." Opportunity theories speculate that women are in the workplace and involved in public life more so than in the past, so they are utilizing that opportunity for illegitimate as well as legitimate

TABLE 8.2
Females Arrested as Percentage of Total: Selected Crime Categories

Crime	Percentage of total arrests (female)/year					
	1965	1975	1985	1995	2000	2006
Homicide	15.4	14.9	12.4	9.5	10.6	10.9
Robbery	5.2	7.0	7.6	9.3	10.1	11.3
Aggravated Assault	13.5	13.1	13.5	17.7	20.1	20.7
Burglary	3.7	5.4	7.4	11.1	13.3	14.5
Larceny	22.1	30.7	31.0	33.3	35.9	37.7
Auto Theft	4.2	7.0	9.3	13.1	15.8	17.7
Embezzlement	17.2	31.1	35.6	43.6	50.0	52.7
Fraud	20.3	34.2	42.6	41.0	44.9	44.5
Forgery/Counterfeiting	19.8	28.9	33.2	35.9	39.0	39.1
Offenses Against Family	8.8	11.7	12.7	20.2	22.4	24.5
Drug Laws	13.4	13.8	13.8	16.7	17.6	18.9
Prostitution	77.5	74.3	69.5	61.1	62.1	64.2

Source: Adapted from Simon, R., and J. Landis (1991). *The Crimes Women Commit, The Punishments They Receive*, 46, 52. Lexington, MA: Lexington Books. Years 1995, 2000, and 2006 added from *Uniform Crime Reports*. Washington, DC: Federal Bureau of Investigation.

activities. Economic necessity theories speculate that because of no-fault divorce, abysmal child support enforcement, and reduced national and state public assistance, women and their children form the largest poverty class. Some of these women commit property crimes to survive.[16] Neither theory is inconsistent with the observation that drug use is correlated with participation in crime.

Several authors have argued that the increase of female offenders is largely due to the increased number of women arrested for drug crimes. Whether women are using more drugs today than in the past or whether they are more likely to be arrested today is somewhat unclear. However, what we do know is that drugs account for a large proportion of women entering prisons. About one in 10 women in prison were there for drug crimes in 1979.[17] In 2004, 29 percent of sentenced women state prisoners were in prison for a drug offense, and more than one-quarter of sentenced women federal prisoners were in prison for a drug offense.[18]

There is also some evidence to indicate that women involved in crime are using and abusing drugs to a greater extent than their male counterparts. Drug Use Forecasting (DUF) figures indicate that female arrestees are more likely than male arrestees to have drugs in their system and self-report more drug use. Needs assessment studies of prisoners also indicate that women self-report more drug use. However, it does not seem to be true that women are playing increasingly more powerful roles in drug distribution systems. Evidence indicates that women continue to have fairly minor participation in drug dealing, acting as "mules" or low-level dealers.[19]

The increasing numbers of women in prison and other correctional populations is most probably due to a combination of increased participation in criminal activities and changing patterns of sentencing. Determinate sentencing systems, drug laws, and a more punitive sentencing culture all account for the increased numbers of women in corrections.

In early jails and other places of confinement in England and the colonies, men and women were housed together. In these squalid and wretched facilities, women were sexually assaulted and exploited, or sold themselves for small comforts that jailers or other prisoners could provide. They were extremely outnumbered by men. Often, they were in prison for prostitution, thus garnering little sympathy for their plight.

Only in the late 1700s did reformers and enlightened practitioners succeed in separating women from men. However, even then, their guards were men, and women were typically housed in one room or building on the grounds of a prison for men. They were given no opportunity to exercise and often were still subject to sexual exploitation. Part of the reason for their ill treatment was the fact that there were so few of them. Only women who committed crimes that shocked or enraged the public or those women who were chronic offenders were placed in confinement. The indignities of prison were reserved for those females who were considered to be evil and irredeemable. Courts managed to find any number of other solutions for most women who committed crimes.[20]

In the 1800s, the number of female prisoners increased, and some prison administrators began hiring female wardens to run the women's wing or section. There was also a growing perception that women were not evil but misguided and could benefit from the influence of proper "ladies" who could teach them how to be good housewives and mothers. This involved teaching them to read, cook, clean, and sew. Even music and art were added to the curriculum of some prisons. These early female wardens faced opposition from male administrators for their attempts to introduce the "gentle arts" into the environment of the prison. They were supported, at least in the northeast, by various women's reform groups, who took up the cause of their "fallen" sisters.[21]

In 1873, the first completely separate prison for women was built in Indiana. Several states followed suit in short order. However, even as late as the 1950s, many states only had a wing or building on the grounds of a prison for men. Between 1930 and 1950, only three or four women's prisons were built in each decade; however, in the 1980s alone, 34 prisons were built for women.[22] In the 1990s, the building trend accelerated. Historically, there simply were not enough women sentenced to prison in most states to justify a separate prison for them. That, of course, has changed.

The late 1800s has been called the "reformatory era" because after the 1870 Prison Congress, many states built reformatories in addition to penitentiaries. While older, chronic, and violent offenders were sent to penitentiaries, younger and first-time offenders may have been sent to a reformatory. In these institutions, prisoners were expected to reform through education and strict discipline. Women's institutions also were divided into reformatories and "custodial prisons." While some new facilities that were built followed a reformatory model, the state usually kept open the wing or building at the prison for men for chronic or older female offenders. Minority offenders were also usually sent to custodial institutions.[23]

The agenda for women's reformatories was a bit different than that for men's reformatories. Instead of a vocation, women learned to be good housewives or domestic servants. The architecture of such places reflected the expectation that inmates' needs lay in the acquisition of domestic skills. Instead of large tiers or dormitories, women were often housed in cottages, each with its own kitchen, living room, and private rooms for sleeping. Women often also helped in the operation of the reformatory, cleaning as well as sometimes engaging in farm work and other maintenance tasks. These early reformatories were noteworthy for their "maternal" approach to offenders. "Matrons" replaced guards, and their role was less guard than role model. The female offenders who were sent to reformatories were not the same type of offender as those found in prisons for men. Because of extremely flexible and broad sentencing authority, they might have been young girls whose parents thought they were promiscuous, women who lived "in sin," or wives who ran away from their husbands.[24]

Thus, in the early 1900s, women who were incarcerated ended up either in a reformatory or custodial prison. While both institutions bore some similarities to their male-oriented counterparts, they were very different. The Southern pattern of incarceration followed a different path. Because the South followed an agricultural model, most prisoners were either leased to landowners or performed agricultural labor for the state. Able-bodied male prisoners were economically useful, but women were not. The few women that were incarcerated were most often minority women, and they worked in small garden plots for the prison staff's use or did domestic labor in the homes of the wardens and other staff.[25] Very few white women were sentenced to prison. To a great extent this was because of the belief that prison was just not an appropriate place for a "lady" and due to a racist reluctance to house white women with black women.

By the 1960s, most states had some type of facility for female offenders. Programming was a product of the beliefs regarding women's place in society. While some type of basic educational programming was common, other opportunities were extremely limited. College classes or educational release programs were much less common in women's prisons than in men's. Typing classes, food service, and beautician training might have been offered, but that was the extent of vocational programs. There was an unfounded belief that women would exit prison to take on roles as wife and mother, dependent on another as breadwinner. This has never been the case. Women leaving prison are almost always economically independent. They do not have a husband or other relative to support them, and therefore it is essential that they have the skills to support themselves. Throughout the 1960s and 1970s, the idealized role of domesticity bore little relation to the lives of women leaving prison. It was only in the 1980s and 1990s that prisons began in earnest to provide programs that had some chance of helping women achieve economic success.

WOMEN IN PRISON

All studies indicate that women in prison are young, single, economically disadvantaged, and disproportionately minority. Women in prison are there most often for drug offenses and/or property crimes—usually larceny. There are some notable differences between women and men in prison. Women tend to be slightly older, have slightly more education, and they do not have as extensive criminal histories as do men in prison. They are also less likely to have been employed before incarceration. They are more likely to have come from dysfunctional families (with histories of sexual and physical abuse) and report more illegal drug use (while men report more alcohol use). They are also more likely to have been custodial parents of children before incarceration, and more likely to plan on being primary providers for their children upon release.[26]

Inmates take part in a group therapy session, which is part of a substance abuse program at the Iowa Correctional Institution for Women in Mitchellville, Iowa. Studies of female prisoners show that women prisoners are often in need of intensive programming for their drug problems.

AP Photo/Steve Pope

Needs assessment surveys of female prisoners have been done in California,[27] Oklahoma,[28] and Texas.[29] Findings from these state studies are consistent with a national study of female prisoners.[30] What these studies show is that because of their criminal history, fewer women than men present much risk to the public. Because of their family and drug backgrounds, women may need more intensive programming. Because of their status as primary caregiver, imprisoning women often results in far-reaching negative effects on their innocent children.

Information about the needs of female prisoners corresponds to the crimes that get women into prison. For prisoners in state prisons, higher percentages of women than men are incarcerated for property and drug offenses. Thirty-one percent of women prisoners in state facilities were in prison for a property offense in 2004, and 29 percent were incarcerated for drug offenses, compared to 20 percent of men incarcerated for property offenses and 19 percent of men incarcerated for drug offenses. More men (53%) are in prison for a violent offense than women (34%).[31] (For incarceration rates for men and women, see Table 8.3.)

TABLE 8.3
Incarceration Rates for Prisoners under State or Federal Jurisdiction Sentenced to more than One Year (per 100,000 U.S residents)

	2000	2005	2006
Total	473	491	501
Male	904	929	943
Female	59	65	68

Source: Sabol, W.J., H. Couture, and P.M Harrison (2007). "Prisoners in 2006." *Bureau of Justice Statistics Bulletin*. Washington, DC: U.S. Government Printing Office.

There is clear evidence to indicate that women are more heavily impacted by federal and state drug sentencing that reduces judicial discretion and imposes heavy sanctions on users as well as distributors. For instance, the federal drug sentencing statute is interpreted to mean that mothering responsibilities are not "ordinarily relevant" to the sentencing decision. This is interesting when one considers that other factors are considered relevant, such as whether the offender cooperates with authorities.[32]

In response to a request from Representative Eleanor Holmes Norton, the General Accounting Office conducted a study of the issues of women in prison and reported the following findings:

- There has been tremendous growth in the number of women in prison, and this increase can be attributed to changes in sentencing laws, particularly sentencing laws for drug offenders.

- The typical female offender is over age 30 and a member of an ethnic or racial minority, with a drug abuse history and a history of sexual and physical victimization. She is likely to be unmarried with at least one minor child.

- Jurisdictions have conducted an active building plan to accommodate increasing numbers of sentenced women. Women are unlikely to be housed near their home communities.

- Few jurisdictions utilized gender-specific training or programming.

- More than one-half of women never receive visits from their children, primarily because of travel costs. Few jurisdictions provide anything but parent education classes to help in increasing parenting skills or maintaining contact with children.

- Programs for substance abuse are not offered in sufficient quantity to meet the demand.[33]

• Prisoner Subcultures •

Women's social interactions and subcultural norms have not been examined as closely as male prisoner subcultures, but research indicates that they are quite distinct.[34] For instance, while men in prison are likely to form gang structures and have social organizations that are more political, women tend to form small cliques and dyads (friendship pairs). If they do organize in larger groups, communication patterns tend to be less political and more familial. One of the interesting differences, for instance, between men and women in prison is women's tendency to form "pseudo-families" or play families. These social structures involve several or many women who take on familial roles (i.e., mother, father, daughter, sister, and so on). Women will play male roles fairly stereotypically, so that those who are "fathers" will be authoritarian yet protective; those who are "husbands" will be jealous and domineering.[35]

Earlier researchers were very interested in the sexual practices of women in prison. Indeed, one of the most obvious differences of men's and women's relationship patterns is that homosexuality in women's prisons tends to be consensual while homosexuality in men's prisons is often coerced. For most women, prison homosexuality is a transitory adaptation to the deprivations of prison. Women who play the male role in "the game" may, at times, drop their male persona and switch to a female role if they are attracted to another woman who is also playing the male role. While the superficial indices of a homosexual relationship are fairly apparent (women acting like men, hugging, handholding, kissing), these relationships may or may not actually involve sexual contact. Many women admit that they engage in such activity just to have someone to "love them." Such relationships may cause trouble for the woman when she is released. For instance, it is a fairly common practice for women to tattoo their lover's name on their body. This is a challenge to overcome when the woman returns to her roles as mother and daughter (and perhaps wife or girlfriend) on the outside.

Women whose sexual orientation was homosexual before prison often do not engage in any relationships in prison and usually express scorn for "jailhouse turnouts." Those women who are engaged in a committed lesbian relationship will take great pains to hide their relationship from others and from staff. In most prisons, women are punished for any sexual contact, and in some prisons, any form of physical contact, including handholding, is against the rules in an effort to control and suppress homosexuality. These absolute prohibitions against any physical affection are as unsuccessful as they are unnatural.

There is not as much violence in prisons for women, but there is always the threat of violence. Women have been known to rape (with an object) a prison "snitch," although the more common sanction is ostracism. There is fighting—usually caused by jealousy or hurt feelings. Because women do not have as organized a black market or as extensive a drug market as one finds in prisons for men, the fighting that ensues from business activities is relatively rare. Weapons are also not as prevalent in women's prisons.

Another interesting difference between men and women in prison is that women rarely express or exhibit any racial violence. While men in prison form racial gangs and a good proportion of violence is directly or indirectly attributed to racial tension and hostility, women do not show the same pattern. In fact, many sexual dyads and pseudo-family structures are interracial. While there is some voluntary racial segregation while eating and in recreational activities, women tend not to form the distinct and extreme patterns of segregation and hostility that one finds in prisons for men.

While most studies of prisoner subcultures were completed in the 1960s and 1970s, an ethnography by Barbara Owen offers a more current view of life in a women's prison.[36] In her study, she finds that the earlier descriptions of prison life hold true today with a few changes. While pseudo-family structures are somewhat more diffuse, they still exist. "Homegirls" (those who lived in the same neighborhood) also exist as a network of friends and supporters in prison. In California prisons, some young women have belonged to gangs on the outside, and so fellow gang members also provide companionship and share resources.

Drugs are more prevalent than in the past. In Owen's description of a very large California prison, "the mix" was the term used for the subcultural activity of those comfortable in prison. The "drug mix" involved those who sold, traded, and used drugs; the "homosexual mix" involved those who were involved in pseudo-families and homosexual dyads; the "fighting mix" involved those who established themselves as fighters. Inmates who wanted to do their time quietly avoided the "mix" by avoiding the yard.

"Programming" meant volunteering and participating in prison programs. Some women entered into programming enthusiastically; some did not. Old-timers or "convicts" avoided officers as well as programming. As in the earlier studies, Owen found that the relationships between staff and inmates could be cordial, even helpful, if the staff members interacted with the women with fairness and kindness. Women who were ready to change entered into programs, sought out good jobs in prison, and avoided the "mix."[37]

• Prisoners as Mothers •

Women in prison are usually property or drug offenders with relatively nonserious criminal histories. They are also very often mothers of small children.[38] A large number of these women were the primary caregivers of their children before their imprisonment. Many expect to regain custody upon their release. Of those who retained custody during imprisonment, most placed their children with relatives, usually the maternal grandmother. Estimates of the number of women prisoners who have children range from 60 percent to about 85 percent.[39] There seems to be consensus that about 70 percent of women in prison have at least one child under 18, and women have an average of two or three children.[40] If one uses the figure of 112,000 women imprisoned, then a conservative estimate of the number of children under 18 with mothers in prison is 150,000.[41]

What happens to these children when their mother is imprisoned? Surprisingly, only about 10 percent enter foster care.[42] Many are cared for by relatives of the female offender, usually the maternal grandmother.[43] It is also true, however, that the children are moved around several times during the prison sentence. Placement and arrangements for guardianship of the children is often informal, ad hoc, and without resources. The lack of intervention by state protection agencies is largely because of the woman's fear that she will have difficulty regaining custody of her children after release from prison. However, this means that there are no financial resources to help care for the children, necessitating already overburdened families with few resources to care for them. Most states do not keep records on children's placement in the community, so we have very little knowledge about what happens to these children.

Some women in prison never see their children.[44] Visits are difficult because of the long distances between the prison and home and the expense of traveling. There also may be hesitancy on the part of caregivers to take the children to the prison and/or anger at the mother for her actions that led to the situation. Many social workers may feel it is traumatic for the child to see his or her mother in prison and resist accommodating such visits. Finally, the mother herself may not want her children to see her in prison, or subject them to the search and admission procedures required for visitation. She may feel guilty and ashamed about her imprisonment and refuse to let her children see her in such a setting. Furthermore, visits necessarily include saying goodbye—an experience that is so painful to both mother and child that many prefer to avoid it.[45]

In 1993, Bloom and Steinhart found that 54 percent of mothers in a national sample reported no visits; this compares to only 2 percent of those surveyed in a similar study in 1978 who reported no visit.[46] The increase in the number of women who never receive visits has been attributed to a restriction of prison telephone privileges to collect calls only,

AP Photo/Kathy Willens

Children of inmates in the maximum-security women's prison at Bedford Hills, New York, are escorted to the main gate for a visit with their mothers. Through this summer program, children are housed with local families and are brought to the prison for daily visits with their mothers to maximize the visiting time inmates have with their children.

the construction of new women's prisons in rural areas, and a lack of financial support from social service agencies for travel. Bloom and Steinhart report that the pre-prison care-giving arrangements were correlated with visitation frequency. While 46 percent of those who lived with children prior to imprisonment received no visits, 72 percent of those who did not live with children prior to prison or jail received no visit.[47]

There are some models of successful programs. Bedford Hills Correctional Facility in New York, for instance, has a prison nursery for women who give birth during their prison term. There is also a foster home for the children of incarcerated women fairly close to the facility. Managed by Catholic nuns, this allows the children to have frequent and consistent contact with their mother during the period of incarceration. The prison also runs "day camps" for children during the summer. Children stay with volunteer families close to the prison and enter the prison each day for scheduled activities and free time with their mother for a week. These week-long "camps" run all summer long, and there are also "weekend camps" during the school year. Bedford Hills has a parenting center that runs a range of programs and classes for inmate mothers—many of which are conducted by inmates.

About 10 percent of women in prison on any given day are pregnant.[48] This percentage may mean a few women a year in those states with small prison populations, but it could mean close to 100 women in larger states. These pregnancies are often high-risk because women in prison may have been drug users, have avoided or neglected medical treatment, and/or have had difficult previous pregnancies.[49]

One report indicated that 77 percent of imprisoned women had exposed their fetus to drugs.[50] Some research indicates a higher-than-average rate of miscarriages for women in prison. Part of the reason for this is attributed to the fact that women must be transported to outside hospitals for delivery and for medical emergencies.[51]

Amnesty International published a critical report on the imprisonment of women in the United States. One of the major criticisms was the way in which pregnant women were treated. Prison policies provided for no prenatal care even when there were medical problems with the pregnancy and allowed the shackling of inmates to the hospital bed during labor, delays in transporting a woman in labor to an outside hospital, and immediate separation from the infant with no opportunity to bond.[52]

• Prison Programs for Women •

Historically, correctional policies and practices have been influenced by gender stereotypes. While stereotypes involve preconceived ideas of women's needs, issues, and problems, gender-specific programming recognizes the real issues and needs of female offenders. Making program and policy decisions using gender stereotypes ignores the current realities in the lives of women offenders; making such decisions ignoring gender differences, however, creates a lack of fit between programs and offender needs.[53]

There has been at least one national survey of women's correctional programs.[54] There also have been several national surveys of parenting programs.[55] These projects have begun the task of identifying and implementing effective gender-specific programs for female offenders. What emerges from these studies is that women's programming in prisons is improving but does not currently meet the many needs of female offenders.

Female offenders, at least those sentenced to prison, may face even greater challenges than men in prison. Needs assessment surveys have found that more than one-half of women in prison have grown up in a household without both parents and are more likely than male prisoners to have relatives incarcerated and/or with alcohol or other drug problems. They also report abuse—estimates range from one-third to three-fourths of women in prison have been victims of childhood abuse (either physical or sexual). Even higher numbers of women report physical or sexual victimization as adults. Women in prison are also more likely than men in prison to have encountered such abuse.[56] Such victimization may be related to an increased propensity to commit crimes of violence.[57] This prior victimization has been cited as a factor in women's drug use and their often destructive relationships with men. Many women express the desire for programming to help them understand and come to terms with childhood abuse, but few prisons offer programming directly related to such victimization.

Women in prison are generally amenable to treatment. In needs assessments, women indicate that they appreciate all forms of programming and specifically ask for more programs that will help them overcome drug addiction, obtain a job upon release, and become better parents to their children.[58] Correctional administrators who responded to national surveys see the need for programs in vocational training, work skill development, family development, substance abuse, domestic violence, and physical and sexual victimization.[59] Many states however, do not screen for such things as childhood abuse or battering. Further, many states do not know how the female offender has arranged for her children to be cared for during her imprisonment. Some states do not even collect information on whether incoming female inmates have children.

As discussed earlier, women's vocational programming has historically been gender-stereotyped; in the early part of this century, women in prison were taught housekeeping and cooking because they were expected to be housewives or domestic servants upon release. Later, they were offered food service, cosmetology, and clerical programs because those were the vocations in which they were expected to pursue employment. More recently, "nontraditional" programming (such as auto mechanics, heavy machinery operation, and carpentry) has been offered in some state systems. However, many women have the mistaken impression that these programs are merely "leftovers" from facilities for men and that the programs are offered because of a neglect or ignorance of the needs of women. In actuality, they have been proposed and implemented to help women make a living wage upon release. Some women who enter such programs do so unwillingly and report that they plan to ignore their training and get a job as a beautician or nurse's assistant upon release because they "like helping people."[60] The lesson to be learned from this example is that programming must match women's interests and needs, or at least there must be an effort to educate participants about the benefits of nontraditional vocational programming.

There is a need to develop gender-specific treatment programs. It has been found that drug treatment programs designed for men do not necessarily work as well for women. For instance, while women tend to be more open and have less resistance to introspection, this advantage can be circumvented by forcing them into treatment groups with men. In addition, women respond less well to confrontational tactics common in some group therapy programs directed to male offenders.[61]

If it is true that women are more likely than male offenders to have dysfunctional family backgrounds, then it is important to create gender-specific programming that responds to this fact. Programs that deal with incest, sexual abuse, and the like are in demand when they are offered, and they often have waiting lists, despite the inmate subcultural prohibition against self-disclosure. However, these programs are not often evaluated. Further, few, if any, such programs exist to meet the needs of female offenders under other forms of correctional supervision (jail, parole, probation, or in community correctional facilities).

Studies of correctional programs have typically either ignored programs for women or included them in general findings in which they have been eclipsed by the much larger samples of programs for men. It may be that certain characteristics of female offenders make them especially amenable to particular types of programs and not so amenable to others. Research from other disciplines leads to intriguing questions regarding

BOX 8.2

Blocks to Treatment: Reasons Why Treatment Programs for Men May Not Be Effective for Women

1. **Stereotyped as caregivers**—Female offenders may use this role to ignore their own problems, or may be prevented by others to engage in self-discovery and improvement.

2. **Sexual abuse**—Women who are victims of sexual abuse may have trouble discussing their reasons for drug use, especially in mixed-sex groups.

3. **Anger suppression**—Women are socialized to suppress anger in our culture; this may be a block to treatment. Anger is often sublimated into depression and acts as an instigator of drug use.

4. **Co-dependency**—For some women, drug use is part of a cycle of co-dependency.

Source: Adapted from Murphy, J., N. Johnson, and W. Edwards (1992). *Addicted Mothers, Imprisonment and Alternatives.* Albany, NY: New York State Coalition for Criminal Justice/ Center for Justice Education.

the effect of certain programs on female offenders as compared to male offenders.[62] There has been virtually no work in corrections that uses gender as an independent variable when evaluating correctional programming.[63] It has been found that cognitive and behavioral programs work better than other types of programming,[64] but no study has looked at the relative effectiveness of such programs for women separately.[65] Only if we isolate and evaluate programs for women separately from larger evaluation efforts will we be able to test whether programs impact men and women differently.

The body of research exploring correctional programs for female offenders is extremely small. Meta-analyses of correctional programs have not studied programs for female offenders, and if such programs were included in the sample, the findings from such evaluations have not been presented in a gender-specific manner.[66] Morash and Bynum's[67] survey of correctional programming for women is perhaps the only study available that specifically evaluates women's programming. In their study, they found that their sample of programs most often offered drug treatment (54.9%), and the programs sampled also offered "life skills" (40.3%), parenting skills (40%), information on relationships (30.6%), and basic education (29%).[68] This study concludes that there are very few innovative programs for women across the country, and those that might be described as innovative are gender-specific and individualized.[69]

BOX 8.3

Elements of Successful Programs

1. Caring and qualified staff.

2. Specific and multiple needs are met.

3. Program participation is high.

4. Inmates take part of the responsibility to help run the program.

5. There is a positive peer influence.

6. There is an individualized, structured program.

7. Sufficient resources are available.

8. Inmates acquire real job skills.

9. Program has good atmosphere and a safe, small size.

10. Program addresses self-esteem.

11. Program addresses domestic violence.

12. Program teaches self-sufficiency.

13. There is adequate administrative support.

14. Program staff use a nonaggressive management style.

15. Program enjoys assistance from outside the prison.

Source: Adapted from Morash, M., and T. Bynum (1995). *Findings from the National Study of Innovative and Promising Programs for Women Offenders* (Final Report). Washington, DC: U.S. Department of Justice.

A few published studies exist that evaluated parenting programs in women's prisons. A reduction of recidivism is rarely stated as a goal or objective of such programs. However, there is some evidence to indicate that family ties and frequent visitation are correlated with a reduction of recidivism.[70] Camp Retreat in New Jersey is an extended visitation program in which qualified female inmates camp with their children over a weekend with prison staff and volunteers. In a 1991 study of Camp Retreat, it was found that not one of the 70 women who participated thus far had returned to prison.[71]

Another evaluation of a parenting program was conducted in a Pennsylvania jail.[72] The goals of the program were to foster an individual's awareness of her parenting style and an understanding of the significant factors in developing her parenting style.[73] Information was collected on the participants' self-evaluations (Self Evaluation Inventory, SEI), including locus of control, efficacy, self-esteem, self-control, and self-criticism. Also collected was information on the participant's parenting expectations and attitudes (Adult-Adolescent Parenting Inventory, AAPI), including any knowledge of child development, empathetic awareness of children's need, parental belief in corporal punishment, and whether the parent looked to the child for emotional satisfaction. Comparison of pretest and posttest results indicated that of the 20 women who finished the program, scores were within normal or average range on a parenting scale (with the exception of the subscale regarding being aware of child's needs). There was an improvement in self-esteem scores and some improvement in the locus of control and self-control, but no real changes in parenting scores.[74] The author speculates that changes might have occurred if the women had been given a chance to practice their knowledge and new skills with their children in a supervised setting.

Girl Scouts Behind Bars is a program that exists in several state prisons and jails. This program allows girls to meet with their imprisoned mothers once a month as part of the organized activity of a specialized Girl Scout troop. An evaluation of the program was conducted in Maryland.[75] The number of mothers who participated ranged from 23 at the beginning to 12 women two years later. The average time in the program was 6.3 months. The program served a total of 42 mothers and 47 daughters in the study period.[76] The program review interviewed 35 mothers and 32 daughters and caregivers, using a Parent Rating Scale, a Children's Self-Concept Scale,[77] a Parent-Child Attachment Scale, and a Worry Scale. It was found that the daughters fell within normal range on most items of the Self-Concept Scale, but some had low self-esteem. The parents' rating scale (of the daughters) fell within normal range, except for slightly elevated scores for impulsive-hyperactive and problem behavior.[78] There were highly positive scores for attachment between mothers and daughters. More mothers (70%) than guardians (52%) perceived that daughters were affected negatively by their imprisonment or reported daughters having problems with incarceration. The study found that program participants were more likely to receive visits from daughters than those not in the program (64.4% vs. 49% of a matched group not in the program). Program participants averaged more visits per month, and had them more consistently over the course of a prison stay. However, it was not evident that the program increased visitation; the patterns remained similar before and during the program.[79]

A study of another parenting program, the AIM (Aid to Children of Imprisoned Mothers) program in Georgia, found that one-third of the children who participated in individual or group counseling experienced significant improvement in attitudes toward their educational activities, their relationships with others, and/or their general demeanor; however, a majority remained at risk due to ongoing behavioral problems.[80]

BOX 8.4

Prisoners as Parents: Camp Celebration and Girl Scouts Behind Bars

Two programs that help female prisoners maintain ties with their children are Camp Celebration in Illinois and Girl Scouts Behind Bars, a federally supported program that exists in several state prisons.

Camp Celebration is a program that allows 12 mothers per weekend for 13 weekends each summer to "camp" with their children during summer months on the prison grounds. The female prisoners have to meet certain qualifications—including type of crime and no prison disciplinary history. They participate in preliminary program and planning meetings before the weekend occurs. Caregivers in the community must agree to bring the children to the prison on Friday afternoon and come back for them at the end of the camping weekend. Camp Celebration is within the perimeter of the prison, and is a semi-permanent camping facility with a mess tent, pavilion, bathroom and shower facilities, and several smaller tents for sleeping. For those women who qualify and who are able to have their children participate, the camping weekend is a chance to have uninterrupted and extended time with their children. After check-in, no security staff are visible during the camping weekend. There are scheduled activities for children, such as campfires and games, but mothers and children also have quiet time to talk and do activities together. Staff members cook some meals, but women also cook some meals for their children over individual campfires. On Sunday afternoon, women escort their children back to the visiting room and say goodbye. The major problem with the program has been transportation for the children, and securing permission from the children's caregivers.

Girl Scouts Behind Bars is a program pioneered in Maryland, but now existing in Florida, Arizona, Ohio, South Carolina, Texas, and several other states. In this program, the daughters of incarcerated women belong to their own Girl Scout Troop. They meet once or twice a month with their mothers in prison for scheduled activities and extended visitation. They also meet together outside the prison once or twice a month like a regular troop.

The program allows the daughters of incarcerated women to share their experiences with sponsors and each other, and also spend more time with their mothers than regular visitation would allow. Mothers meet together inside the prison in the alternate weeks and are able to talk about their problems and experiences as well. The troop completes projects and engages in activities, such as aerobics, mini-science fair, and arts and crafts. Sessions on such things as coping with family crises, anatomy and physiology of the reproductive system, and teenage pregnancy are also experienced.

The program has certain requirements for participation, such as no history of child abuse and the female prisoners must have had no infractions for at least six months and during the entire time they participate in the program.

Sources: Moses, M. (1993). "Girl Scouts Behind Bars: New Program at Women's Prison Benefits Mothers and Children." *Corrections Today*, 132-135; Stumbo, N., and S. Little (1991). "Campground Offers Relaxed Setting for Children's Visitation Program." *Corrections Today*, 136-144; Janie Magruder (May 8, 2006). "Girl Scouts Connects Daughters, Imprisoned Mothers." *The Arizona Republic*.

Martin examined mothers who were incarcerated in the Minnesota Correctional Facility at Shakopee in 1985 five years after their release.[81] She found that their "commitment to parenthood is tenacious and most had sustained continuous primary parenting from within prison." Most were reunited with their children after release. This study establishes the fact that frequent contact with children in a child-centered institution supports future reunification with children. Nearly two-thirds of the women studied who were imprisoned in Shakopee in 1985 emerged five years later as "primary, highly involved parents to at least one of their children."[82] One-third of the women were no longer connected with their children; the difficulties were too great to overcome and too complex to allow them to care for children. There was no relationship between seriousness of crime and ongoing connection with children. Mothers who were "connected" with their children were three times more likely than nonconnected mothers to be drug-free and have no history of chemical abuse. Connected mothers were more likely to be married. While 80 percent of connected mothers had no new crimes, only 57 percent of nonconnected mothers had not committed subsequent crimes. However, 28 percent of the mothers were still in prison.[83]

The mothers described as unconnected did not parent well; they let children control interactions and had histories of drug use, erratic contact, and repeated criminal activity. Connected mothers had legal custody, emotional connection, and a mature grasp of their children's needs. Martin compared the liberal overnight visitation policy at Shakopee to a National Council on Crime and Delinquency (NCCD) study of programs nationally.[84] Mothers in Shakopee saw their children twice a month. Nationally, only 10 percent of mothers saw children more than once a month, and only 12 percent were allowed overnight or weekend visits. The frequency of visitation was related to whether the mother was described as connected five years later.[85]

Good programs for female offenders should address a number of different but related issues. First, the program should address the woman's specific needs, including the cycles of poverty, violence, poor parenting, marital discord, parental psychopathology/mental illness/depression, lack of education, parenting issues, addictions, childhood incest or physical abuse, criminal behavior, and survival strategies.[86] A parenting program should address the children's needs, including the provision of a safe, nonintimidating location to visit the mother in prison—and preferably a long, uninterrupted time for such a visit to take place. In addition, there should be support for children outside of prison in the form of either counseling or support groups.

Vocational programs should offer opportunities for inmates to acquire skills that have the potential to draw a decent wage. If such skills are nontraditional, program staff may have to convince women that the programs are valuable. However, if women acquire nontraditional skills only to discover they cannot find work outside, then such programs are a waste of time and money.

• Special Issues •

The differences between male and female offenders that lead to different program outcomes arguably also impact on policies and procedures within prisons. Among other things, there are differences in uniform requirements, supplies, and healthcare items approved to have in the cell. One of the most hotly debated issues regarding the different needs of women in prison is whether there should be limits and restrictions on the use of cross-sex supervision.

• Cross-Sex Supervision •

Lori Girshick makes the point that strip-searching, whether done by a male or female guard, is "the number-one humiliation inmates experienced." She writes that ". . . for many women strip searching was the worst aspect of prison, something they had to endure again and again. Several prisoners did not go out on CV [community volunteer] passes or have visits because they would be strip-searched afterward, quite a sacrifice to make in order to avoid what they felt was a very degrading act."[87] A strip search by anyone is humiliating; when it is done by a male officer, there is even a greater intrusion on personal privacy.

When female inmates have challenged such treatment utilizing right-to-privacy arguments, some courts have agreed that women and men are different and experience different realities. In this instance, the fact that so many women in prison have experienced sexual abuse by men arguably makes them different from male prisoners who do not share that history and, therefore, do not experience the same level of anxiety or violation as do women when undergoing a search conducted by a guard of the opposite sex.[88]

The negative reaction of some female prisoners to their male guards is supported by recent findings that indicate that sexual abuse and exploitation of women in prison is occurring across the country. In the last 20 years, there has been a shift from women's prisons having very few male correctional officers to a situation in which male officers are the majority. Evidence of sexual exploitation and abuse has emerged in Hawaii, Texas, Michigan, New York, Georgia, and other states.[89]

Rathbone had to sue the state of Massachusetts for access to women prisoners in the Framingham Correctional Institution. Her interviews revealed that sex between guards and inmates was commonplace. Some of it was due to gifts like pizza or Chinese takeout; some of it was due to the difficulty of proving claims of abuse and retaliation for filing such claims.[90]

While some state officials faced with such scandals have responded with proposed policies that completely bar male officers from working with female inmates, the more efficacious solution might be to improve screening and training, and instruct supervisors in how to identify potential abusers.

• Health Care •

In addition to pregnancy and prenatal needs, women face a range of healthcare needs that are different from those of men. While some state systems meet these needs appropriately, arguably other systems do not. Typical complaints include the lack of medical staff, the use of inmates or officers as "screeners" before an inmate can get in to see a doctor or healthcare professional, the lack of follow-up when a woman has been diagnosed and treatment has been prescribed, and ignoring serious medical problems and telling inmates that it is "all in their heads." There is a greater percentage of women than men in prison diagnosed with HIV and/or AIDS, yet there is less intervention and education for female inmates to prevent and contain the transmission of the disease.[91]

Because most prisons for women are generally smaller than prisons for men, the medical facilities are usually not as extensive. This necessitates transportation to outside hospitals for even minor surgical procedures, and doctors may be available only on a part-time or "on call" basis. This means that women may have to wait for treatment, and in some emergency situations, waiting may endanger health.

A recent successful court challenge to the California Department of Corrections persuaded the court that California was deficient in a range of areas in its medical services for female inmates. Such cases are usually only won when the court recognizes egregious lapses in the state's duty to provide minimal health care. Some women gave birth in the prison because prison staff refused to order transportation to an outside hospital. Moreover, several women died after they complained about health-related problems. These situations contributed to the court's decision finding medical services for female prisoners deficient.

• Other Issues •

Female inmates have never been as litigious as male prisoners. When suits have been filed, they have typically concerned equal protection challenges to the lack of programming or the lack of adequate medical services. In several groundbreaking cases, courts have agreed with women in prison that the state must provide roughly equal program opportunities to men and women, and that the small numbers of women are not reason enough to deny them opportunities.[92] As some writers have noted, the only court mandate is that equal opportunities be provided for men and women; to meet such a mandate, the state can choose to increase program offerings for women or reduce program offerings for men.[93] In some more recent decisions, it seems that courts are retreating to a position that finds men and women in prison are not "similarly situated." This makes it unnecessary for the prison system to equalize program offerings or make other services equally available. Apparently the courts are accepting the prison authorities' argument that the small numbers of women make such equalization impossible.

Women in prison face many challenges. They have usually encountered hardships and abuse as children, been exposed to alcohol and other drugs very early, and engaged in self-destructive behavior and relationships. Their children are typically experiencing the same type of lifestyle that the woman herself endured as a child, continuing an intergenerational cycle of poverty, abuse, and drug use as self-medication.

Prison offers a break from the streets, but many women re-create the street life in prison—fighting, engaging in destructive relationships, and using drugs. Others use the time in prison to reflect on their lives, take advantage of educational and therapeutic opportunities, and make plans to do better when they are released. Many of these women will tell interviewers that if it were not for prison, they would probably be dead. Unfortunately, prisons do not always have the resources to offer enough programs to all of the women who desire them. Vocational, educational, and therapeutic programs often have waiting lists. Many women are idle because the prison staff cannot create enough job slots for the burgeoning prison population. States are building more prisons for women and adding new beds to existing facilities.

WOMEN AND COMMUNITY CORRECTIONS

Community correctional sanctions are for individuals who have committed crimes but do not pose serious or extreme risk to the public. Historically, women were more likely to receive some form of community correctional sanction because they were not perceived as presenting much risk to the public. Zebulon Brockway originally developed the concept of graduated liberty with female prisoners. Only later in his career did he apply the principles to men at Elmira Reformatory. Some of the earliest halfway houses were for "fallen women"—prostitutes who needed help to change their lives. Early paroles were used for women from reformatories who were placed with "good" families as domestic servants.

Rafter described these early parole arrangements from Albion Reformatory for women in New York in the late 1800s and early 1900s. The parole to domestic service was extremely restrictive for the girls and women. Their wages were held by their employer except for a small allowance, and they were given free time only for one afternoon a week but were not allowed to socialize with their own family members or anyone else not approved by the employer or the reformatory. They were expected to write monthly reports to the reformatory and were visited by a parole officer.[94] Still, the opportunity allowed them to leave the reformatory and make a small amount of money that was given to them upon their release from parole. Thus, female offenders played a role in the early history of community corrections.

The profile of women who are sentenced to prison is not necessarily the same as that of the total population of female offenders. Women who end up in prison are more likely than those under other forms of correctional supervision to be members of a minority group, more likely to have a history of drug use, and more likely to come from family backgrounds characterized by alcoholism, illegal drug use, and a criminal history. They are also more likely to be without skills or education.[95] Women in jail and under community supervision represent those who may not have as extreme problems as those who are sentenced to prison; however, still relevant are the issues of poverty, lack of skills, alcohol and other drug problems, and so on.

• Jail •

Chapter 4 provides a discussion of both male and female jail prisoners. As noted, women comprise 12.9 percent of the jail population. In 2006, more than 98,000 women were incarcerated in American jails. The female jail population increased 4.9 percent from mid-year 2005 to mid-year 2006, while the male prison population only increased about 2 percent.[96]

In the 1990s, about one-half of the increase in jail populations could be accounted for by drug arrests. More than one in three women were jailed for drug violations (compared to one in eight in 1983).[97] The average length of stay in jail is about seven months.[98]

About two-fifths of jailed women reported that they committed their first crime under the influence of drugs, and about 40 percent reported daily drug use before arrest. About 25 percent reported that they committed their current crime because of drugs. About 40 percent of the female inmates grew up with a single parent, and 17 percent had no parent living with them. About one-third reported that a parent abused alcohol or other drugs, and about 40 percent reported that a sibling or parent was also incarcerated.[99]

About 50 percent of the female jail inmates (compared to 13% of male inmates) reported that they had been sexually or physically abused sometime in their life.[100] A study in Chicago found that in a sample of jail inmates, about 80 percent met the criteria for at least one life-time psychiatric disorder, most commonly alcohol or other drug dependence. Rates of all psychiatric illnesses were higher for the jail sample than a comparable general population sample. The study also found that most needs went unmet because the jail simply did not have the resources.[101] Another study found that 64 percent of female jail detainees had symptoms of depression. The same researcher also found that about 22 percent of a female jail population suffered post-traumatic stress disorder symptoms, including hypervigilance, startle reflex, phobias, and auditory and visual flashbacks due to earlier childhood sexual and physical victimization.[102]

One study of five women's jails found that programming for women was inadequate. Especially needed were vocational programs, drug treatment, and "self-help programming" (including classes on stress management, self-esteem, and parenting).[103]

It appears that women and men in jail don't necessarily react similarly to administrative and architectural changes. In one study, it was found that women reacted negatively to a "new generation" jail while male detainees expressed more positive reactions.[104] In fact, just as in prison, it seems that differences are found in the subcultures, stressors, and needs of women in jail as compared to men.[105]

• Probation •

In 2006, there were more than 4 million (4,237,023) offenders on probation: a little more than 1 million of them were women. Women make up almost one-quarter (24%) of the adult probation population, up from one-fifth in 1995.[106]

Women on probation are disproportionately minorities, but the disparity is not as extreme as in prison populations. Women on probation are less likely than men to have committed a violent offense. While almost 20 percent of men on probation in 1995 had committed a violent offense (usually assault), only 9.5 percent of women had done so (also usually assault). Women were much more likely to be on probation for a property offense; 42.8 percent of those on probation had committed a property offense (usually fraud), compared to 25.3 percent of men (usually larceny/theft). About equal percentages of men and women were on probation for drug offenses (20.1% of women and 21.7% of men).[107] Some evidence indicates that women are less likely to be revoked and sent back to prison while on probation.[108]

A study in Illinois compared male and female probationers on a number of indices. They found that there were substantial differences between the two populations. The survey included 1,834 probationers (459 of them women). The average age of the women was slightly higher than that of men, but there were no differences found in the proportion of minorities in the two groups. Women were more likely to come from households with lower incomes and were significantly more likely than men to be unemployed before arrest. There were no significant differences between male and female probationers in educational achievement. Women were less likely to have prior criminal histories (33% vs. 41%) and less likely to have committed violent crimes in the past five years (13% vs. 23%). Men were more likely to report substance abuse histories (65% vs. 57%), but the difference seems to be largely due to alcohol abuse. When alcohol is excluded, the abuse histories between men and women were similar.[109]

The Illinois researchers also looked at conviction records and sentence characteristics. Women were more likely to be on probation for property or drug offenses, whereas men were more likely to be on probation for violent crimes or driving while under the influence of alcohol. Few significant differences were found between men's and women's lengths of sentence, when controlling for offense. Only in certain property crime areas did men receive slightly longer probation terms. Women were, however, less likely to be assessed court costs, supervision fees, or fines. Women were also less likely to be ordered into some form of treatment. Men were more likely to be rearrested on probation; however, no significant differences were found between the two groups on committing technical violations or revocations. One interesting finding of the researchers was that women were compelled to undergo significantly more drug tests, even after controlling for the crime of conviction. While male drug offenders were required to undergo an average of 4.1 tests, female drug offenders completed 9.8 tests. Women were slightly more likely to drop out of drug treatment before completion.[110] This study illustrates the importance of further research on the differences between men and women on probation and parole.

Community corrections in Florida is divided into traditional probation and "community control," a type of intensive probation that is available as an alternative to prison. Research indicates that the childcare responsibilities of female "controllees" are sometimes hard to reconcile with the stringent conditions of community control. Women must present a schedule of movement and activities to their community control officer every week. Few deviations are allowed, so child-centered activities such as taking children to sports events or meeting with school officials are considered violations.[111] Earlier researchers have found that probation officers considered female clients to be more "troublesome" because of their greater need for support and advice concerning their care-giving responsibilities.[112] Similarly, correctional personnel in one study considered the female client's role as caregiver to be incompatible at times with her role as correctional client, and personnel assumed that the family should make adjustments rather than have the system make accommodations for the responsibilities of parenthood.[113] Recognition of such responsibilities does not have to be gender-based, but to ignore the fact that childcare falls disproportionately on women, including female correctional clients, is to ignore reality.

• Parole •

Women comprise about 12 percent of those on parole; in 2006, there were approximately 96,200 women parolees.[114] Not much is known about the women on parole. Evidence indicates that men are more likely to be placed on parole than women, but women do better (in terms of recidivism) on parole than men. Female property offenders are more likely to recidivate than women who commit other crimes, as are those who use alcohol, while first-time offenders are less likely to recidivate.[115]

Historically, women have shown lower recidivism rates than men after a prison term. In one study, while 58 percent of the women successfully completed their parole term, only 49 percent of the men in the sample were successful.[116] One New York study showed that 36 percent of a sample of men failed on parole, compared to only 12.1 percent of a comparable sample of women. Another New York study reported that 37.3 percent of men failed, compared to 16.9 percent of women.[117]

In one study of 85 female parolees in the greater Boston area, it was found that use of community service referrals was correlated with a lower level of recidivism. Those who completed community programs in employment, drug treatment, and other social service programs were significantly less likely to recidivate. About one-third of the women did not recidivate, one-third were reported to have "low recidivism," and the final one-third had "high recidivism" during a two-year follow-up period. It was also found that minority, older women, with few or no children, and who had committed a personal offense with a low number of prior arrests were least likely to recidivate. Women who had a low rate of recidivism were white, slightly younger, with slightly more children, and had a slightly higher number of prior arrests with a slightly longer sentence than the no-recidivism group. Women with high levels of recidivism were much younger, had the most children, were white, and were arrested much more often, had a longer sentence, and were less likely to have committed a personal offense.[118]

Women on probation or parole face similar problems. The major issue is how to survive economically while caring for young children. Because drugs present an opportunity to make fast, easy money, and also provide an escape from the troubles of everyday life, it is no wonder that involvement in drugs is so prevalent in the lives of women in the criminal justice system. When presented with programs to help them overcome personal and pragmatic problems, however, women can succeed. In one Pennsylvania study on the effectiveness of a community program for female offenders, it was reported that in a sample of 1,000 women, only 3.2 percent were rearrested.[119] Another program description reported that women who were discharged from a comprehensive multi-services program were unlikely to recidivate (only 7% were convicted of a new offense within one year, and 13% were rearrested after two years of discharge).[120]

• Other Programs •

While probation and parole are, arguably, equally available to women and men, other community programs are not. In a national study of community sanctions, it was found that 68 percent of the intensive probation programs, 41 percent of electronic monitoring programs, 33 percent of home confinement programs, and 26 percent of split sentence/boot camp programs accepted women.[121]

Just as with prison programs, community programs that are developed for men may not be appropriate for women. This is especially true when considering boot camps. Boot camps have become a popular correctional alternative, despite evaluations that show that they are not appreciably more successful in reducing recidivism than standard alternatives. In fact, the only boot camp programs that have shown any moderate success are those programs that have enriched program offerings. Yet, the prospect of having offenders do push-ups, have their head shaved, and march seems to have great popular appeal. So much so, in fact, that boot camps for women exist in several states. It is hard to think of a more classic example of male programming being blindly applied to women than boot camps. There is nothing in theory or research to support the idea that women need or profit from the experience of militaristic discipline and environment. In fact, some authors note that women may be especially traumatized from the experience if they have male drill masters and have been the victims of battering and emotional abuse.[122] The benefits promoted, such as completion of educational programs, could be achieved without the trappings of the boot camp model.

In a 1990 survey, it was found that community programs for women were small (average size: 24) and privately run. The typical client was an African-American woman between the ages of 25 and 30 who was not married and had young children. Service needs involved alcohol or other drug treatment, domestic violence or sexual abuse counseling, and employment, education, housing, and legal assistance. Services offered (in descending order) were "counseling," living skills, alcohol or other drug treatment, parenting, and job-seeking.[123]

Programs for women in the community almost always address drug abuse. One national survey identified programs for both men and women in prison and in the community. Researchers reported that programs that provided services only to women were more likely to provide the services that women needed, such as child care and family planning. They found that there was a great need for treatment beds for women who are pregnant, have children, are mentally ill, are homeless, or have a history of violence.[124]

Some drug treatment programs provide the opportunity for women to live with their infants in a halfway-house setting. There are 65 residential treatment facilities around the country for women and their children that are funded by the U.S. Department of Health and Human Services and administered by the Center for Substance Abuse Treatment.[125] There are others that are privately funded. Providing facilities that allow women to live with their children is important because often the woman is faced with a choice of entering a drug treatment program and losing her children or not entering any treatment program at all and risking her probation or parole status. In community mother-infant programs, women have a chance to bond with their babies and engage in treatment groups while the children are being cared for in a safe environment. The women learn about child care and child development at the same time that they are helping themselves. These programs should include a therapeutic nursery; developmentally appropriate infant activities; pediatric medical services; parent education; individual, group, and/or family counseling for mothers and children; physical conditioning and nutrition services; emotional/behavioral interventions when appropriate; life skills training; substance dependency education; treatment and/or self-help activities; general education, especially high school equivalency; job training and placement; child custody/placement advocacy; and aftercare.[126]

Very little is known about women in community correctional settings. They are arguably more in need of counseling and vocational services. The programs available do not serve their needs. Program models developed for men do not take into consideration child care or childhood victimization issues. Community models that are individualized, gender-specific, and comprehensive show the most success. Considering that the female offender population is, for the most part, nonviolent and low-risk, it is a shame that community correctional alternatives are not more available and more responsive to their unique problems.

More recently, there has been some attention to developing "gender-specific" programming for women in the community. Policymakers, researchers, and advocates have promoted the idea that female correctional clients are more successful with "empowerment" models that focus on a multitude of issues, such as victimization, substance abuse, domestic violence, pregnancy and parenting, and relationships.[127]

WOMEN CORRECTIONAL WORKERS

Historically, women have been restricted to working with other women and juveniles in the corrections system. Women entered into corrections in the 1800s after female offenders were separated from male offenders and state officials were convinced that it would be better for all concerned to have women, rather than men, guard female prisoners. As mentioned earlier, the first female jail matron was appointed in Maryland in 1822; about 10 years later, women were hired to supervise female prisoners in women's wings of prisons for men.[128] By the end of the 1800s, almost all prisons and jails for women employed exclusively female supervisors of female offenders.

For many years, women in corrections had a very limited occupational sphere—they could only work with other women and juveniles. Today, this is no longer the case. In the 1960s and 1970s, Title VII of the Civil Rights Act opened the door for women to demand entry into previously all-male occupations. Lawsuits were won concerning the right to be hired, promoted, or assigned in a non-gender-discriminatory manner. Law enforcement patrol was integrated by the end of the 1970s so that instead of having a separate and distinct job title as "policewoman," women were hired as police officers and had the same opportunities and assignments as their male counterparts. Women in corrections also pushed for equal opportunities. New York voluntarily employed women in prisons for men in 1973, and in 1974, California merged the job titles of men and women, placing women into facilities for men. By the mid-1980s, female correctional officers could be found in most prisons for men. Today, about 20 percent of the state correctional officer force and 30 percent of the federal correctional officer force are comprised of women. Women work in prisons for men in 46 states.[129] There is great variability, however, in how many women work in prisons for men. In some states, only about 1 percent of the force in prisons for men are women, while in others the percentage is closer to 10 percent.[130]

Women enter corrections largely for the same reasons that men do: security and pay. Women report that they "drifted" into corrections after exploring other jobs. There are few differences between men and women in job satisfaction and attitudes toward inmates; however, some studies report that women experience more stress.[131] Evaluations of female officers in prisons for men have found that they perform their job duties as well as men. Attitude surveys among male co-workers and inmates show that male co-workers exhibit more resistance to female officers than male inmates do. In addition, male inmates rate female officers more highly on "listening" capability but feel that female officers are less able to protect them against physical threats.[132]

A correctional officer patrols the corridor during lockdown. While for many years female correctional officers were limited to working with juveniles and women, today's prisons employ a large number of women officers in many different roles.

Mark C. Ide

Some authors contend that women may perform their job functions differently than their male colleagues. One hypothesis is that women employ a more nurturing, "listening" style of supervision, while male staff members are more likely to employ an authoritarian, formal mode of interaction. However, evidence to support such an assertion tends to be anecdotal and phenomenological. Paper-and-pencil tests of attitudes toward inmates fail to uncover any differences between male and female correctional staff.[133] Other research indicates that women fall into several different adaptational styles: while some adopt a more masculine orientation, emphasizing the custodial and authoritarian aspects of the job, others adapt by adopting other roles emphasizing feminine characteristics.[134]

Equal opportunity has ensured that men have now entered women's institutions in great numbers as well. In fact, in some state systems, men comprise more than 50 percent of the guard force in prisons for women. While there are reports of inappropriate relationships between female officers and male inmates, and women have been disciplined, fired, and charged with crimes because of their relationships with male inmates, even more common are reports and lawsuits arising from sexual exploitation and even rape of female prisoners by male guards. Because so many allegations of abuse across the country have been raised, Amnesty International published a report condemning the practice of having female prisoners guarded by male officers because of the potential and increasing incidence of sexual abuse.[135]

Women have also entered corrections as probation and parole officers. In the same way that prisons were sex-segregated, so too were community corrections caseloads. Probation caseloads were divided so that women supervised women and men supervised men. This meant that women's job opportunities in probation and parole were limited, because not nearly the number of women are on probation and parole as men. It has only been within the last 30 years or so that all states abandoned sex-specific caseloads.

▶ Ethics Focus: What Do Women Prisoners Deserve?

Because women comprise a much smaller percentage of persons who are imprisoned in a given state, they are often the last to receive any resources for facilities improvement, new programs, or staffing needs. Incidents of exploitation and sexual coercion by male corrections officers have also been documented on occasion. Should the quality of care and services female offenders receive be based solely on their numbers? Taking into consideration the differences between male and female offenders as well as their respective subcultures, what would a just and responsible women's prison look like? How would it be different from its male counterpart?

There has been very little research on any differences that might exist between male and female probation and parole officers. Early studies found that there were no significant differences found between men and women on presentence recommendations.[136] Whitehead studied job burnout among both male and female probation and parole workers through a questionnaire mailed to officers in several states. He found that only two scales showed marginal significant differences between men and women. Women scored higher on emotional exhaustion and lower on depersonalization. There were no significant differences in intrinsic job satisfaction or role conflict scores, nor were there any differences found in probation workload.[137] Whitehead hypothesized that so few differences were found because women in probation and parole are well represented and not just present in token numbers, and there are few differences between men and women in work environment factors. However, he points out that self-selection on the part of male officers may also play a role in why male and female officers appear so similar on a variety of scales.

Today, about 20 percent of correctional officers, 24 percent of jail officers, and close to 50 percent of probation and parole officers, are women.[138] Not much attention has been paid to their growing numbers in corrections, and there is very little effort to explore whether they have issues or concerns distinct from those of their male colleagues.

CONCLUSION

Imprisonment has become the sentence of choice for many offenders. In looking at female offenders, in particular, it is clear that convictions for drug crimes account for many women's involvement in the criminal justice system. The criminalization of drug use has resulted in huge increases in the number of women imprisoned and the number of children who are impacted by their mothers' imprisonment. While many women admit that drugs have been a negative influence in their lives, community correctional alternatives, if combined with appropriate and effective treatment, may offer the opportunity for the female offender to maintain ties with her children and avoid the experience of prison.

▶ At the Movies . . . .

A Hard Straight, 2004.

A documentary by Goro Toshima about parolees in California, including one woman who faces the difficulties of drug addiction and trying to fit in with her children after a long absence.

DISCUSSION QUESTIONS

1. Describe how women have been perceived and treated in the corrections system for the last several hundred years.

2. Explain the factors that contribute to increasing numbers of women in the corrections system.

3. Describe the typical female offender. How is the demographic profile of a female prisoner (or probationer) different from that of a male offender?

4. Describe the differences between male and female prisoner subcultures.

5. Describe the different program needs of women.

6. What do we know about women on probation and parole?

7. Describe the entry of women into traditionally male occupations in corrections.

8. What do evaluations show regarding the performance of female corrections officers?

FURTHER READING

Johnson, R., and H. Toch (2000). *Crime and Punishment: Inside Views*. Los Angeles: Roxbury.

Rathbone, C. (2005). *A World Apart: Women, Prison, and Life Behind Bars*. New York: Random House.

NOTES

1. Sabol, Couture, and Harrison, 2007.

2. Sabol, Couture, and Harrison, 2007.

3. Sabol, Couture, and Harrison, 2007.

4. Sabol, Couture, and Harrison, 2007.

5. Sabol, Couture, and Harrison, 2007.

6. Glaze and Bonczar, 2007.

7. See Pollock, 1999, or Chesney-Lind, 1997, for a discussion of women's crime rates.

8. Uniform Crime Reports, 2006.

9. Pollock, 1999. Those that do typically utilize case studies or small samples to come to such a conclusion.

10. Chesney-Lind, 1997; Pollock, 1998, 1999.

11. Greenfeld and Snell, 1999.

12. Pollock, 1998; Browne, 1987; Ewing, 1987.

13. Uniform Crime Reports, 2000, 221.

14. Uniform Crime Reports, 2006. Also, see Pollock, 1999, 83, for expanded discussion of crime rates.

15. Pollock, 1999, 83.

16. Pollock, 1999.

17. Greenfeld and Snell, 1999, 10.

18. Sabol, Couture, and Harrison, 2007.

19. Pollock, 1999, 54. See also Wellisch et. al., 1994.

20. Pollock, 1990; Rafter, 1990; Freedman, 1986.

21. Rafter, 1990; Freedman, 1986.

22. Rafter, 1990.

23. Rafter, 1990.

24. Rafter, 1990.

25. Pollock, 1990.

26. Owen and Bloom, 1994, 1995; Fletcher et al., 1993; Snell, 1994; Pollock, 1998.

27. Owen and Bloom, 1994, 1995.

28. Fletcher et al., 1993.

29. Pollock, 1998.

30. Snell, 1994.

31. Sabol, Couture, and Harrison, 2007

32. See Pollock, 1998.

33. General Accounting Office, 1999.

34. Most of the discussion that follows is from Pollock, 1990; also see Giallombardo, 1966, and Ward and Kassebaum, 1965.

35. See Pollock, 1990.

36. Owen, 1998.

37. Owen, 1998.

38. McGowan and Blumenthal, 1978; Hungerford, 1993; Pollock, 1998.

39. McGowan and Blumenthal, 1978; Datesman and Cales, 1983; Baunach, 1984; Bloom and Steinhart, 1993; Pollock, 1998; Henriques, 1996; Hungerford, 1993.

40. Immarigeon (1994) estimates that two-thirds of women had at least one child who was under 18. Henriques (1996:86) and Bloom and Steinhart (1993) presented a much higher estimate that nine out of 10 mothers have children under 18. Blakely reported in 1995 that of the 8,600 women incarcerated in California, 2,500 had small children, but "small" was not defined, so it may mean pre-school or elementary school-age children. Gaudin (1984:279) estimated that two-thirds of the children of imprisoned mothers are under 10. Pollock (1998) found an average of 70 percent of women in prison had children under 18, but this number varied from state to state.

41. Seventy percent of 112,000 is 78,400; multiplied by two (the average number of children), the number is 156,800. So an estimate of 150,000 is very conservative. See Johnston (1995a,b,c) for more details.

42. Immarigeon (1994) estimates that about 11 percent were in foster care. Beckerman (1994) looked at 53 inmate-mothers and their experience with foster care in New York State. She found that 36 percent of these mothers had no telephone contact with the caseworker, did not know of hearings regarding child custody even though New York has a law mandating such notice, and only 30 percent of the women had ever received a copy of the child's case plan. The conclusion of the author was that there needed to be a better effort to involve the mother in permanency planning with better communication between caseworkers and inmate-mothers.

43. Block and Potthast (1997) reported that in their Maryland study, 60 percent of the children were cared for by grandparents or other relatives, 19 percent by fathers; 9 percent by nonrelatives, and 5 percent were in foster care. Bloom and Steinhart (1993:80) reported that maternal grandmothers were the most frequent placement. The tendency to place children with relatives is problematic because grandparents are unlikely to receive financial support from the state, even if they need it to care adequately for the children. In fact, both the California and Oregon Supreme Courts ruled it was not unconstitutional to bar grandparents from receiving foster care payments (Gabel and Johnston, 1995).

44. Immarigeon (1994) reports that only 9 percent of women in prison received visits from children. Courturier (1995) uses the NCCD figure of 54 percent of women who never receive visits.

45. Henriques (1996:82). Gaudin (1984:280) summarized the problems with visitation as: remote location of prison, restrictive visiting regulations, and resistance and lack of cooperation on the part of the family or social services.

46. Bloom and Steinhart, 1993.

47. Bloom and Steinhart, 1993.

48. Muse (1994) estimated that 8 to 10 percent of women are pregnant. Gable and Johnston (1995:vii) report that somewhere between 7 and 10 percent of women enter jail or prison pregnant. Pollock (2002) found that about 10 percent was the average for most states in her study. Henriques (1996) reports that 6 percent of women were pregnant in her study.

49. Wooldredge and Masters (1993:195-203) explored the special issues presented by pregnant inmates. They reported that pregnant inmates had special needs, including attention to their physical and emotional needs. They required special diets, lighter work assignments, separate and less crowded living quarters, prenatal care, and counseling. A survey to all wardens of prisons housing women in 1991 (100) resulted in a 61 percent return rate. Responses indicated that 48 percent offered any type of prenatal care; 15 percent offered special diets or nutritional allowances; and only 9 percent had full-time nurses or midwifes for pregnant inmates.

50. Johnston, 1995(c), 67.

51. Bloom, 1995, 23.

52. Amnesty International, 1999.

53. One example of this is classification devices that were designed for male offenders being applied to female offenders. Typically, what occurs is that women are classified into higher security levels in error considering their background and likelihood of future violence. Such classification systems also are unable to identify unique needs of female offenders (Pollock, 1998).

54. Morash and Bynum, 1995.

55. Boudouris, 1998; Clement, 1993; Pollock, 2003.

56. Owen and Bloom, 1994, 1995; Fletcher et al., 1993; Snell, 1994; Pollock, 1998.

57. Harlow, 1999.

58. Owen and Bloom, 1994, 1995; Fletcher et al., 1993; Snell, 1994; Pollock, 1998.

59. Morash and Bynum, 1995.

60. Pollock, 1998.

61. Pollock 1998.

62. Gilligan (1982) and others have speculated that women are more likely to voice a "different morality" from men—one that emphasizes personal relationships over rules. If so, perhaps programs that encourage the offender to think about the victim (i.e., sentencing circles, victim-offender meetings, and restitution programs) have more impact on female offenders than they do on male offenders.

63. For a discussion of moral development differences and implications for corrections, see Pollock, 1999, 227-257.

64. Pollock (1997) offers a discussion of evaluating correctional programming. In this discussion, findings from various studies are cited to support the view that cognitive and behavioral programs tend to be more effective than analysis, group therapy, or other types of correctional programs.

65. For instance, it may be that cognitive programs work well for female offenders because they encourage moral development growth. Behavioral programs may not work as well for women as for men because they place an emphasis on rules and rewards, and these may not be motivators for women.

66. See, for instance, Palmer, 1994.

67. Morash and Bynum, 1995

68. Morash and Bynum, 1995.

69. Morash and Bynum, 1995.

70. Block and Potthast (1997) and Hairston (1991) cite studies finding such a relationship. Hairston's study was with all male samples, but she found that increase in family visitation or use of furlough programs was associated with lower recidivism. She points to social support literature to explain the relationship. Releasees receive both emotional and pragmatic support from family, as well as the motivation to change.

71. Driscoll, 1991; no subsequent follow-up for the program is known.

72. Browne (1989) reports on the Parent Education Project implemented in 1984 by the Program for Female Offenders, Inc., in Pittsburgh, Pennsylvania. The curriculum was developed and field tested by the Community Mental Health/Mental Retardation Center of St. Francis Hospital.

73. Curriculum included Maslow's needs hierarchy with the understanding that needs are motivations of behavior. Also included were units on the emotional needs at each stage of development of the child, the development of individual personalities within a family setting, life scripts, and the importance of self-esteem in the development of a healthy child. The classes met twice a week for two hours for 24 weeks with a group of women incarcerated in the Allegheny County Jail. Both a pretest and posttest were conducted and data collected.

74. Browne, 1989.

75. Block and Potthast, 1997.

76. Block and Potthast, 1997.

77. This scale (Piers-Harris Children's Self-Concept Scale) included the following global self-concept measure (filled out by daughters). Six clusters: behavior (problem behaviors), intellectual and school status (satisfaction and expectations re: school); physical appearance and attributes (assessment of physical appearance, expressive and leadership skills); anxiety (sense of emotional problems including depression, worry, sadness, and fear); popularity (with friends, classmates); happiness; and satisfaction.

78. Interestingly, the mothers and guardians scores did not match in this scale (Block and Potthast, 1997, 21).

79. Block and Potthast, 1997, 22.

80. Dressel and Barnhill, 1994.

81. Martin, 1997.

82. Martin, 1997, 3. She explains that 70 women were in the mother's program in 1985; 55 of those women were interviewed in 1985. Of those women, 39 were reinterviewed in 1990-91. No statistical differences existed between these 39 and those not interviewed again. The sample subjects were less likely to be minority, less likely to be convicted of drug crimes, and more likely to be convicted of homicide than the national profile of women incarcerated.

83. Martin, 1997, 4-9.

84. Bloom and Steinhart, 1993.

85. Martin, 1997, 18.

86. Bedell, 1997.

87. Girshick, 1999, 95, 97.

88. Pollock, 1990; Chesney-Lind and Pollock, 1994.

89. Amnesty International, 1999.

90. Rathbone, 2006.

91. Acoca, 1998; see also Ross and Lawrence, 1998 and Barry, 1996.

92. *Glover v. Johnson,* 1979. Recently the state of Michigan was released from court monitoring after a finding that the state had met all required conditions of the original court order to improve programming for women.

93. Chesney-Lind and Pollock, 1994.

94. Rafter, 1985/1990.

95. Owen and Bloom, 1994, 1995; Fletcher et al., 1993; Snell, 1994; Pollock, 1998.

96. Sabol, Minton, and Harrison, 2007.

97. Beck, 1995; Snell, 1992

98. James, 2004.

99. Beck, 1995; Snell, 1992.

100. Beck, 1998.

101. Teplin, Abrams, and McClelland, 1996.

102. Veysey, DeCou, and Prescott, 1998.

103. Gray, Mays, and Stohr, 1995.

104. Jackson and Stearns, 1995.

105. Gray, Mays, and Stohr, 1995.

106. Glaze and Bonczar, 2007.

107. Bonczar, 1997, 2.

108. Brennan, 1999.

109. Olson, Lurigio, and Seng, 2000.

110. Olson, Lurigio, and Seng, 2000.

111. Ansay and Benveneste, 1999.

112. Norland and Mann, 1984.

113. Ansay and Benveneste, 1999, 131.

114. Glaze and Bonczar, 2007.

115. Findings reported in Latessa and Smith, 2007.

116. Reported in Reichel, 1997, 403.

117. Study findings reported in Samaha, 1997, 566-557.

118. Pearl, 1998, 46-48.

119. Reported in Samaha, 1997, 566.

120. Prichard, 2000, 28.

121. Robinson, 1992.

122. Reichel, 1997, 404.

123. Austin, Bloom, and Donahue, 1992.

124. Prendergast, Wellisch, and Falkin, 1995.

125. Chapple, 2000, 31.

126. Johnston, 1995c, 210.

127. Bloom, 2000.

128. Pollock in Merlo and Pollock, 1995; Reichel, 1997.

129. Reichel, 1997, 379.

130. Reichel, 1997, 379.

131. Zupan, 1992.

132. Pollock in Merlo and Pollock, 1995.

133. Pollock in Merlo and Pollock, 1995.

134. Zimmer, 1986.

135. Amnesty International, 1999.

136. Frazier et al., 1983.

137. Whitehead, 1986.

138. "Women in the Criminal Justice System," 1998.

REFERENCES

Acoca, L. (1998). "Defusing the Time Bomb: Understanding and Meeting the Growing Health Care Needs of Incarcerated Women in America." *Crime & Delinquency* 44:53-73

Amnesty International (1999). *"Not Part of My Sentence": Violations of the Human Rights of Women in Custody*. London: Amnesty International.

Ansay, S., and D. Benveneste (1999). "Equal Application or Unequal Treatment: Practical Outcomes for Women on Community Control in Florida." *Women & Criminal Justice* 10, 3:121-135.

Austin, J., B. Bloom, and T. Donahue (1992). *Female Offenders in the Community. An Analysis of Innovative Strategies and Programs*. Report prepared by the National Council on Crime and Delinquency. Washington, DC: National Institute of Corrections.

Barry, E. (1996). "Women Prisoners and Health Care." In K. Moss (ed.), *Man-Made Medicine*, 250-272. Durham, NC: Duke University Press.

Baunach, P. (1984). *Mothers in Prison*. New Brunswick, NJ: Rutgers/Transaction.

Beck, A. (1998). "Profile of Jail Inmates, 1996." *Bureau of Justice Statistics Bulletin*. Washington, DC: U.S. Government Printing Office.

Beck, A. (1995). "Profile of Jail Inmates, 1989." *Bureau of Justice Statistics Bulletin*. Washington, DC: U.S. Government Printing Office.

Beckerman, A. (1994). "Mothers in Prison: Meeting the Prerequisite Conditions for Permanency Planning." *Social Work* 39, 1:9-14.

Bedell, P. (1997). *Resilient Women*. Master's Thesis. Unpublished. Vermont College of Norwich University.

Blakely, S. (1995). "California Program to Focus on New Mothers." *Corrections Today*, December: 128-130.

Block, K., and M. Potthast (1997). "Living Apart and Getting Together: Inmate Mothers and Enhanced Visitation through Girl Scouts." Paper presented at the annual meeting of the Academy of Criminal Justice Sciences, March 1997.

Bloom, B. (2000). "Gender-Responsive Supervision and Programming for Women Offenders in the Community." In National Institute of Corrections, *Topics in Community Corrections: Responding to Women Offenders in the Community*, 11-19. Longmont, CO: NIC Information Services.

Bloom, B. (1995). "Imprisoned Mothers." In K. Gabel and D. Johnston (eds.), *Children of Incarcerated Parents*, 21-30. New York: Lexington Books.

Bloom, B., and D. Steinhart (1993). *Why Punish the Children? A Reappraisal of the Children of Incarcerated Mothers in America*. San Francisco: National Council on Crime and Delinquency.

Bonczar, T.P. (1997). "Characteristics of Adults on Probation, 1995." *Bureau of Justice Statistics Special Report*. Washington, DC: U.S. Government Printing Office.

Boudouris, J. (1996/1998). *Prisons and Kids*. College Park, MD: American Correctional Association.

Brennan, P. (1999). "Male and Female Prison Populations: Differential Effects of Technical Violations of Probation and Parole." Paper presented at the annual meeting of the American Society of Criminology, November 1999.

Browne, A. (1987). *When Battered Women Kill*. New York: Free Press.

Browne, D. (1989). "Incarcerated Mothers and Parenting." *Journal of Family Violence* 4, 2:211-221.

Chapple, K. (2000). "Community Residential Programming for Female Offenders and their Children." In National Institute of Corrections, *Topics in Community Corrections: Responding to Women Offenders in the Community*, 31-36. Longmont, CO: NIC Information Services.

Chesney-Lind, M. (1997). *The Female Offender: Girls, Women and Crime*. Thousand Oaks, CA: Sage.

Chesney-Lind, M., and J. Pollock (1994). "Women's Prisons: Equality with a Vengeance." In A. Merlo and J. Pollock (eds.), *Women, Law and Social Control*, 155-177. Boston: Allyn & Bacon.

Clement, M. (1993). "Parenting in Prisons: A National Survey of Programs for Incarcerated Women." *Journal of Offender Rehabilitation* 19, 1:89-100.

Couturier, L. (1995). "Inmates Benefit from Family Services Program." *Corrections Today* (December):100-107.

Datesman, S., and G. Cales (1983). "I'm Still the Same Mommy: Maintaining the Mother/Child Relationship in Prison." *The Prison Journal* 63, 2:142-154.

Dressel, P., and S. Barnhill (1994). "Reframing Gerontological Thought and Practice: The Case of Grandmothers with Daughters in Prison." *The Gerontologist* 34, 5:685-691.

Driscoll, D. (1985). "Mother's Day Once a Month." *Corrections Today* (August):18-24.

Ewing. C. (1987). *Battered Women Who Kill*. Lexington, MA: Lexington Books.

Federal Bureau of Investigation (FBI) (2007). *Uniform Crime Reports, 2006*. Washington, DC: U.S. Department of Justice. Available at http://www.fbi.gov/ucr

Fletcher, B., L. Shaver, and D. Moon (1993). *Women Prisoners: A Forgotten Population*. Westport, CT: Praeger.

Frazier, C., W. Bock, and J. Henretta (1983). "The Role of Probation Officers in Determining Gender Differences in Sentencing Severity." *Sociological Quarterly* 24 (Spring):305-318.

Freedman, E. (1981/1986). *Their Sisters' Keepers: Women's Prison Reform in America, 1830-1930*. Ann Arbor: University of Michigan Press.

Gabel, K., and D. Johnston (1995). *Children of Incarcerated Parents*. New York: Lexington Books.

Gaudin, J. (1984). "Social Work Roles and Tasks With Incarcerated Mothers." *Social Casework* 53:279-285.

General Accounting Office (1999). *Women in Prison: Issues and Challenges Confronting U.S. Correctional Systems*. Washington DC: U.S. Government Printing Office.

Giallombardo, R. (1966). *Society of Women: A Study of Women's Prison*. New York: Wiley.

Gilligan, C. (1982). *In a Different Voice: Psychological Theory and Women's Development*. Cambridge, MA: Harvard University Press.

Girshick, L. (1999). *Stories of Women in Prison*. Boston: Northeastern University Press.

Glaze, L.E., and T.P. Bonczar (2007). "Probation and Parole in the United States, 2006." *Bureau of Justice Statistics Bulletin*. Washington, DC:U.S. Government Printing Office.

Gray, T., L. Mays, and M.K. Stohr (1995). "Inmate Needs and Programming in Women's Jails." *The Prison Journal* 75 (2):186-202.

Greenfeld, L.A., and T.L. Snell (1999). "Women Offenders." *Bureau of Justice Statistics Special Report*. Washington, DC: U.S. Government Printing Office.

Hairston, C. (1991). "Family Ties During Imprisonment: Important to Whom and For What?" *Journal of Sociology and Welfare* 18, 1:87-104.

Harlow, C.W. (1999). "Prior Abuse Reported by Inmates and Probationers." *Bureau of Justice Statistics Selected Findings*. Washington, DC: U.S. Department of Justice.

Harrison, P.M., and A.J. Beck (2002). "Prisoners in 2001." *Bureau of Justice Statistics Bulletin*. Washington, DC: U.S. Government Printing Office.

Harrison, P.M., and A.J. Beck (2002). "Prisoners in 2001." *Bureau of Justice Statistics Bulletin*. Washington, DC: U.S. Government Printing Office.

Henriques, Z. (1996). "Imprisoned Mothers and Their Children: Separation-Reunion Syndrome Dual Impact." *Women & Criminal Justice* 8, 1:77-97.

Hungerford, G. (1993). *The Children of Incarcerated Mothers: An Exploratory Study of Children, Caretakers and Inmate Mothers in Ohio*. Ph.D. dissertation, Ohio State University.

Immarigeon, R. (1994). "When Parents Are Sent to Prison." *National Prison Project Journal* 9(4):5, 14.

Jackson, P., and C. Stearns (1995). "Gender Issues in the New Generation Jail." *The Prison Journal* 75, 2:203-221.

James, D.J. (2004). "Profile of Jail Inmates, 2002." *Bureau of Justice Statistics Special Report*. Washington, DC: U.S. Government Printing Office.

Johnston, D. (1995a). "Parent-Child Visitation in the Jail or Prison." In K. Gabel and D. Johnston (eds.), *Children of Incarcerated Parents*, 135-143. New York: Lexington Books.

Johnston, D. (1995b). "Effects of Parental Incarceration." In K. Gabel and D. Johnston, *Children of Incarcerated Parents*, pp. 259-263. New York: Lexington Books.

Johnston, D. (1995c). "Intervention." In K. Gabel and D. Johnston (eds.), *Children of Incarcerated Parents*, 199-232. New York: Lexington Books.

Latessa, E., and P. Smith (1999). *Corrections in the Community*, 4th ed. Newark, NJ: LexisNexis Matthew Bender.

Martin, M. (1997). "Connected Mothers: A Follow-Up Study of Incarcerated Women and Their Children." *Women & Criminal Justice* 8, 4:1-23.

McGowan, B., and K. Blumenthal (1978). *Why Punish the Children? A Study of Children of Women Prisoners*. Hackensack, NJ: National Council on Crime and Delinquency.

Merlo, A., and J. Pollock (1995). *Women, Law and Social Control*. Boston: Allyn & Bacon.

Morash, M., and T. Bynum (1995). *Findings from the National Study of Innovative and Promising Programs for Women Offenders*. Washington DC: Department of Justice, National Institute of Justice.

Muse, D. (1994). "Parenting from Prison." *Mothering* (Fall) 72:99-105.

Norland, S., and P. Mann (1984). "Being Troublesome: Women on Probation." *Criminal Justice and Behavior* 11, 1:114-135.

Olson, D., A. Lurigio, and M. Seng (2000). "A Comparison of Female and Male Probationers: Characteristics and Case Outcomes." *Women & Criminal Justice* 11, 4:65-81.

Owen, B. (1998). *"In the Mix": Struggle and Survival in a Women's Prison*. Albany, NY: State University of Albany Press.

Owen, B., and B. Bloom (1995). "Profiling Women Prisoners: Findings from National Surveys and a California Sample." *The Prison Journal* 75, 2:165-185.

Owen, B., and B. Bloom (1994). "Profiling the Needs of California's Female Prisoners: A Study in Progress." Paper presented at the annual meeting of the Western Society of Criminology.

Palmer, T. (1994). *A Profile of Correctional Effectiveness and New Directions for Research*. Albany, NY: SUNY Press.

Pearl, N. (1998). "Use of Community-Based Social Services to Reduce Recidivism in Female Parolees." *Women & Criminal Justice* 10(1):27-52.

Pollock, J. (2002). *A National Survey of Parenting Programs in Women's Prisons*. Available from author.

Pollock, J. (1999). *Criminal Women*. Cincinnati: Anderson.

Pollock, J. (1998). *Counseling Women in Prison*. San Francisco: Sage.

Pollock, J. (ed.) (1997). *Prisons: Today and Tomorrow*. Philadelphia: Aspen.

Pollock, J. (1995). "Custody and the 'Caring Ethic.'" In A. Merlo and J. Pollock (eds.), *Women, Law and Social Control*, pp. 97-116. Boston: Allyn & Bacon.

Pollock, J. (1990). *Women, Prison and Crime*. Belmont, CA: Wadsworth.

Prendergast, M., J. Wellisch, and G. Falkin (1995). "Assessment of and Services for Substance Abusing Women Offenders in Community and Correctional Settings." *The Prison Journal* 75, 2:240-256.

Prichard, D. (2000). "Project ReConnect Responds to Women Offenders on a Personal Level." In National Institute of Corrections, *Topics in Community Corrections: Responding to Women Offenders in the Community*, pp. 26-31. Longmont, CO: NIC Information Services.

Rafter, N. (1985/1990). *Partial Justice: Women in State Prisons, 1800-1935*. Boston: New England University Press.

Rathbone, C. (2006). *A World Apart: Women, Prison, and Life Behind Bars*. New York: Random House Trade Paperbacks.

Reichel, P. (1997). *Corrections*. Minneapolis: West.

Robinson, R.A. (1992). "Intermediate Sanctions and the Female Offender." In J. Byrne, A. Lurigio, and J. Petersilia (eds.), *Smart Sentencing: The Emergence of Intermediate Sanctions*, 245-260. Newbury Park, CA: Sage.

Ross, P., and J. Lawrence (1998). "Health Care for Women Offenders." In T. Alleman and R. Gido (eds.), *Turnstile Justice: Issues in American Corrections*, 176-191. Upper Saddle River, NJ: Prentice Hall.

Sabol, W.J, H. Couture, and P.M. Harrison (2007). "Prisoners in 2006." *Bureau of Justice Statistics Bulletin*. Washington, DC: U.S. Government Printing Office.

Sabol, W.J, T.D. Minton, and P.M. Harrison (2007). "Prisoner and Jail Inmates at Midyear 2006." *Bureau of Justice Statistics Bulletin*. Washington, DC: U.S. Government Printing Office.

Samaha, J. (1997). *Criminal Justice*. Minneapolis/St. Paul: West.

Snell T. (1994). "Women in Prison. Survey of State Prison Inmates, 1991." *Bureau of Justice Statistics Special Report*. Washington, DC: U.S. Government Printing Office.

Snell, T. (1992). "Women in Jail: 1989." *Bureau of Justice Statistics Special Report*. Washington, DC: U.S. Department of Justice.

Teplin, L., K. Abrams, and G. McClelland (1996). "Prevalence of Psychiatric Disorders among Incarcerated Women." *Archives of General Psychiatry* 53(2):505-512.

Veysey, B., K. DeCou, and L. Prescott (1998). "Effective Management of Female Jail Detainees with Histories of Physical and Sexual Abuse." *American Jails* 12 (May/June):50-54.

Ward, D.A., and G.G. Kassebaum (1965). *Women's Prison: Sex and Social Structure*. Chicago: Aldine.

Wellisch, J., M.L. Prendergast, and M.D. Anglian (1994). *Drug Abusing Women Offenders: Results of a National Survey*. Washington, DC: U.S. Department of Justice.

Whitehead, J. (1986). "Gender Differences in Probation: A Case of No Differences." *Justice Quarterly* 3(1):51-65.

Women in Criminal Justice: A Twenty Year Update (1998). Available at: http://www. ojp.usdoj.gov/reports/98Guides/wcjs98

Wooldredge, J., and K. Masters (1993). "Confronting Problems Faced by Pregnant Inmates in State Prisons." *Crime & Delinquency* 39(2):195-203.

Zimmer, L. (1986). *Women Guarding Men*. Chicago: University of Chicago Press.

Zupan, L. (1992). "The Progress of Women Correctional Officers in All-Male Prisons." In I. Moyer (ed.), *The Changing Roles of Women in the Criminal Justice System*, 2nd ed., 323-343. Prospect Heights, IL: Waveland.

COURT CASE

Glover v. Johnson, 478 F. Supp 1075 (ED Mich. 1979).

Juvenile Corrections

What You Need to Know

▶ Almost 100,000 juvenile offenders were in public, private, or tribal residential placement on the date of the most recent census. In addition, about 4,000 juveniles were placed in adult prisons according to recent data.

▶ Traditionally, juvenile court and corrections have claimed to seek "the best interests of the child," but critics question to what extent juvenile correctional interventions actually achieve that objective.

▶ Recent statistics indicate that 55 percent of juveniles released from state facilities are rearrested. On the other hand, effective programs can reduce recidivism significantly.

▶ The most prevalent problem in the juvenile justice system is the presence of mental disorders. Studies show that more than two-thirds of juveniles in the juvenile justice system experience mental disorders.

▶ Estimates of victimization, including sexual victimization, in juvenile facilities vary. Some estimates indicate that almost two-thirds of youths are victimized. A government report noted 2,821 allegations of sexual violence in juvenile facilities in 2004.

▶ Racial tension has been a problem in juvenile facilities. In 2003, minorities constituted 60 percent of the committed juveniles in custody in public and private facilities nationwide. Blacks comprised about 37 percent of both public and private placement populations.

▶ In 2004, probation handled more than 650,000 youths who were processed in some way for delinquency or a status offense by the juvenile court.

▶ Blended sentencing allows for youths to serve sentences in adult prisons. Restorative justice, on the other hand, emphasizes community-based programs that are more victim- and offender-oriented.

INTRODUCTION

This chapter will examine juvenile corrections, including both institutional corrections and community corrections such as juvenile probation. Although juvenile correctional programs share many features and problems with adult corrections, they also have unique concerns that justify a separate chapter.

We will discuss types of institutional placements, including training schools and boot camps. We will consider what life in an institution is like, including the prevalence of mental disorders, the extent of victimization, racial tension, the inmate code, and the deprivation of sexual relationships. We will discuss recent developments such as deinstitutionalization, blended sentencing, and wilderness programs. We will provide an overview of probation as well as recent trends such as the balanced approach, a more punitive approach to probation, and restorative justice. We will also discuss the effectiveness of both institutional placements and juvenile probation.

INSTITUTIONAL CORRECTIONS FOR JUVENILES

Almost 100,000 (96,655) juvenile offenders were in public, private, or tribal residential placement in October of 2003.[1] The latest information indicates that the average length of stay was approximately four months and the average yearly cost of custody ranged from $41,000 to $71,000 in three states for which information was available.[2]

In addition, some juvenile offenders who were transferred to adult criminal court were tried as adults and sent to adult prisons. While we do not have the precise number of such youths, we do know that in 2002 an estimated 4,100 youths younger than 18 were committed to state adult prison systems. Some of these youths had been transferred out of juvenile court to adult court;

You can access Office of Juvenile Justice and Delinquency Prevention (OJJDP) reports at www.ojp.usdoj.gov/ojjdp. They publish reports periodically on juvenile arrests, juvenile court statistics, and the number of juveniles in custody.

some were from states where the age of adult court jurisdiction is 16 or 17 or from states that gave jurisdiction over certain crimes to the adult court. The 2002 figure of more than 4,000 such admissions is down from the peak years of 1995 and 1996, when more than 7,000 youths under 18 were admitted to adult prisons.[3]

Although probation handles many more youths, institutions involve a significant minority of the offenders who go through the juvenile justice system. They are the costliest part of the system. One public facility in New York was reported to cost more than $80,000 a year.[4]

Correctional managers contend that these facilities seek to serve the "best interests of the child," which means that they attempt to provide educational, therapeutic, and recreational programs staffed by concerned caregivers. Critics argue that, at best, the facilities are warehouses or holding tanks where little, if any, positive change takes place. Past critics have contended that juvenile facilities harbor as many horror stories as they do children: tales of neglect, abuse, and even death.[5]

This chapter examines various types of institutional and residential interventions with juveniles, including state training schools, youth camps, private placements, and group homes. After describing these various placements, the chapter will examine some of the current issues about their operation, such as the determination of appropriate targets for intervention, effectiveness in reducing recidivism, and client and worker adaptations to the pressures of institutional life. The chapter material on institutional corrections concludes with information on innovative trends in this area, such as deinstitutionalization and wilderness programs.

• State Training Schools •

State training schools are the juvenile justice system's equivalent of adult prisons; they house the delinquents whom juvenile court judges consider unfit for probation or some other lesser punishment. Some training schools actually resemble adult prisons in terms of their architecture: high walls or fences, locked cell blocks, self-sufficiency (they have their own laundry, hospital, and maintenance facilities), and solitary confinement for the recalcitrant. Other training schools utilize the so-called cottage system of architectural design. The cottage system, however, is often a far cry from the homelike atmosphere intended by its founders. Cottages are often deteriorating dormitories with decrepit plumbing, heating, and lighting, as well as an accompanying host of social-cultural problems.

• Training School Programs for Residents •

The programming at state training schools is often a combination of academic and vocational education and behavior modification. Residents attend school much of the day just like their noninstitutionalized counterparts, but the school run by the prison educates youths who are usually two to three years below their appropriate grade level in both reading and mathematics. (For a list of the school rules in one training school, see Box 9.1; for a typical daily schedule, see Box 9.2.)

The behavior modification system usually involves the grading of youths at one of several levels. The system includes the daily awarding of points for almost every possible action of the youth's day, from getting up on time to getting to bed quietly and on time. The points earned each

BOX 9.1

Sample of One Training School's Rules

Below is an actual set of rules and a list of minor rule violations from a southeastern training school:

Rules:

1. There will be no misuse of any property.
2. There is to be no use of vulgar or profane language.
3. There will be no gambling.
4. There will be no tampering with fire and safety equipment.
5. Students will remain in their assigned areas.
6. Students may not borrow, sell, lend, or trade their property.
7. Students are expected to always be courteous.
8. Students are expected to respect privacy and property of others.
9. Students are expected to follow all dress codes.
10. Students are expected to follow instructions of staff.

Minor Rule Violations:

1. Disruptive behavior
2. Failure to follow institutional rules
3. Horseplay
4. Out of assigned area
5. Racial slurs
6. Refusal of a direct order
7. Self-mutilation
8. Sexual slurs
9. Use of obscene language

Source: Student handbook from a southeastern state.

day can be spent on various privileges, ranging from games, television time, and telephone calls home to off-campus group outings and visits home. The higher the youth's level, the more extensive the privileges available. (Box 9.3 gives an actual list of opportunities for earning and spending points at a southeastern training school.)

In addition to qualifying for daily privileges, such as television, the points earned also count toward movement from one level to another

BOX 9.2

Typical Weekday Daily Schedule at a Residential Placement for Delinquents

6:30 A.M.	Wake up: dress and clean room
7:00 A.M.	Calisthenics
7:30 A.M.	Hygiene (showers, etc.)
8:00 A.M.	Clean dormitories
8:30 A.M.	Breakfast
9:00 A.M.	Start school
10:30 A.M.	"Rap" half-hour
11:00 A.M.	Return to school
12:00 P.M.	Lunch
12:30 P.M.	"Rap" half-hour
1:00 P.M.	School
3:30 P.M.	Group therapy
5:00 P.M.	Dinner
5:30 P.M.	Work details (kitchen clean-up and dormitory clean-up)
6:00-7:00 P.M.	TV news
7:00-9:00 P.M.	Activities (vary by day: Example: Values Clarification; Occupational Therapy; Recreational Therapy, etc.)
9:00 P.M.	Bedtime for Phase 1 (9:30 P.M. in the summertime)
10:00 P.M.	Bedtime for Phase 2 and above

Source: Manual from a midwestern residential facility. Note: In this context, to "rap" is to talk freely and frankly.

with additional privilege possibilities. One training school employee characterized the point system as working both as a behavioral control device and as a device to monitor progress within the institution.

Concern for the victim and for crime control has translated into some program additions in juvenile institutions. In California, for example, the Impact of Crime on Victims program combines an educational curriculum with presentations by victims and victims' advocates. In Texas, juvenile murderers receive group psychotherapy and role-playing sessions to help them learn responsibility for their crimes and to understand what they put their victims through.[6]

BOX 9.3

Typical Institutional Point System

Responsibilities	Points[a]	
1. Get self up on time (6:00 A.M.)	+25	-50
2. Locker neat, orderly, clean room or area with bed made	+50	-100
3. Appropriately dressed	+25	-50
4. Brush teeth and comb hair	+25	-50
5. Daily bath and use deodorant	+25	-100
6. Exercise	+25	-50
7. Acts appropriately: a: Breakfast	+10	-20
b: Lunch	+10	-20
c. Dinner	+10	-20
8. School	+40 per hour	
9. Study hour or watching news	+25 per hour	
10. Daily chores	+50	-100
11. Volunteer work	+60 per hour (120 maximum per day)	
13. See counselor	+25 per hour	
14. Attend group	+50	-100 per hour
15. Attend church or Sunday school services	+25	
16. Bonus points	+100 maximum per day	

Note: A +25 indicates that a resident can earn up to 25 points for performing the specified behavior. A -100 indicates that a resident can have as many as 100 points deducted if the behavior is not performed or not performed properly.

Spending Opportunities

1. Swimming	25 points
2. Recreation room	25 points
3. Parlor games (checkers, cards, etc.)	25 points
4. Telephone calls	20 points
5. Use of television room	25 points
6. Play outside	25 points
7. Group outing off campus	300 points
8. Group outing on campus	200 points
9. Living room	25 points
10. Movies in dorm	100 points
11. Home Pass	350 points

Source: Student manual from a southeastern training school.

• Other Placements •

Traditional training schools are not the only means states use for housing delinquents. In some years, almost 10,000 youths are held in long-term open facilities that allow greater freedom for residents within the facilities and more contacts with the community. The open facilities category of placements includes shelters, halfway houses, group homes, and a few ranches. Group homes are residential facilities for relatively small numbers of youths (perhaps one or two dozen youngsters). The residents often attend regular public schools but participate in group counseling sessions and recreational activities at the group home.

Juvenile court judges sometimes commit juvenile delinquents to detention centers for a short period of time. Youths are placed on probation, with one condition of probation being a short stay in the local detention facility.

States also utilize private residential placements to house delinquents and some status offenders. The October 2003 census showed 30,321 juveniles in private residential placement, representing 31 percent of all juveniles in placement.[7] Private facilities, like state facilities, range from relatively large institutions to small group homes and even wilderness programs in which juveniles camp. Many were originally started by churches as charitable institutions but have evolved into nonsectarian operations that charge the state thousands of dollars each year for each child they handle.

AP Photo/Waterloo Courier, Rick Chase

Students participating in the Four Oaks Day Treatment Program held at the Oelwein (Iowa) National Guard Armory stand at attention with their chairs under one arm and notebooks under the other, as they await instructions from the program overseer. The Oelwein School District, the Fayette Juvenile Courts, and Four Oaks Day Treatment Program jointly established the school, which mixes tough discipline with constant one-on-one counseling.

• Boot Camps •

A continuing trend is the use of boot camps (also called shock incarceration). Boot camps are short-term facilities (90-day/120-day/six-month) that are intended to resemble basic training facilities for the military. There is considerable emphasis on discipline and physical training such as marching, running, calisthenics, and other types of conditioning. Usually a "drill instructor" is assigned to each group of offenders. Many boot camp programs also involve aftercare supervision for program graduates. Box 9.4 shows the daily schedule at one boot camp. In 2003, boot camps held about 7 percent of committed juveniles.[8]

BOX 9.4

Daily Schedule for Offenders in a New York Boot Camp

A.M.

5:30	Wake up and standing count
5:45-6:30	Calisthenics and drill
6:30-7:00	Run
7:00-8:00	Mandatory breakfast/cleanup
8:15	Standing count and company formation
8:30-11:55	Work/school schedules

P.M.

12:00-12:30	Mandatory lunch and standing count
12:30-3:30	Afternoon work/school schedule
3:30-4:00	Shower
4:00-4:45	Network community meeting
4:45-5:45	Mandatory dinner, prepare for evening
6:00-9:00	School, group counseling, drug counseling, prerelease counseling, decision-making classes
8:00	Count while in programs
9:15-9:30	Squad bay, prepare for bed
9:30	Standing count, lights out

Source: Clark, C.L., D.W. Aziz, and D.L. MacKenzie (1994). *Program Focus: Shock Incarceration in New York: Focus on Treatment*. Washington, DC: National Institute of Justice.

The rationale behind boot camps is multifaceted. It is claimed that boot camps can protect the public, alleviate prison crowding, reduce costs, punish offenders, hold offenders accountable, deter additional crime, and rehabilitate (provide counseling and education).[9]

For both adult and juvenile offenders, the effectiveness of boot camps is mixed. There is some indication that boot camps can reduce state correctional costs and that participants rate their experience in camp as positive, but the evidence shows that boot camps have little or no effect on recidivism (new crimes).[10] It does appear clear, however, that "the military atmosphere alone does not reduce recidivism and increase positive activities during community supervision."[11] Although many politicians favor boot camps because they appear to be "tough," it appears that the educational and rehabilitative programming is what helps the offenders.

An evaluation of three boot camps in Cleveland, Mobile, and Denver offers insights about their advantages and disadvantages. Eligible youths for these camps were those ages 13 to 17 who had been adjudicated by the juvenile court and were awaiting disposition. Youths considered eligible could not have any history of mental illness or involvement in violent crime but were rated at "high risk" of chronic delinquency and minimal risk of escape.

The graduation rates were positive, ranging from a low of 65 percent at Denver to 87 percent at Mobile and 93 percent at Cleveland. There was significant academic progress at the Cleveland and Mobile boot camps. From one-half to two-thirds of the youths at Cleveland improved at least one grade level in various academic skills. In Mobile, about 80 percent of the youths improved at least one grade level.[12]

The findings on recidivism, however, were discouraging. There were no significant differences in recidivism between boot camp offenders and the control group offenders at Denver or Mobile. In Cleveland, the experimental youths did worse than the controls. Moreover, at all three sites, survival times—time to the commission of a new offense—were shorter for the youths who went through the boot camps than for control cases.[13]

Concerning cost-effectiveness, the costs per day of the boot camps were similar to one day of institutionalization but more expensive than a day of probation. Costs per offender were lower than controls because boot camp offenders spent less time in the boot camps. Sample boot camp costs are $64 per day in South Dakota and $96 per day ($35,000 per year) in Maine.[14]

Peters and his colleagues concluded that boot camps are not a panacea but they do offer some advantages:

> As an intermediate sanction, boot camps are a useful alternative for offenders for whom probation would be insufficiently punitive, yet for whom long-term incarceration would be excessive. As such, under certain conditions, boot camps can free bed space for more hardened offenders, thereby reducing the financial burden on correctional budgets.[15]

A final word on boot camps is that they were part of a more general trend (as noted in Chapter 1) in society to "get tough" on crime. One author (Todd Clear) called this trend the "penal harm movement";[16] another team of authors called it "the punishment paradigm."[17] These authors contended that since 1980 the United States has operated on the premise that more punishment is needed to deter crime and incapacitate offenders. Boot camps are one component of the movement, which includes increased use of prisons and jails, lengthier sentences, determinate sentences, career criminal sentencing provisions, increased use of capital punishment, and harsher community sanctions (intensive supervision, house arrest, and electronic monitoring). For juveniles, the punishment paradigm has translated into greater prosecution of juveniles in adult court and blended sentences involving the adult correctional system. Thus, boot camps are not an isolated phenomenon but are part of a broader trend in criminal justice focusing on retribution, deterrence, and incapacitation.

The trend may be changing, however. At least concerning boot camps, there has been considerable concern about their lack of effectiveness and about abuses in some camps. The death of a 14-year-old youth in a boot camp in Panama City after eight guards hit and kicked him led the state of Florida to close that particular boot camp and to limit the use of physical and psychological intimidation in the four boot camps still in operation in the state. Florida also decided to rename the camps "training and respect programs."[18]

PROGRAM EFFECTIVENESS

One of the most critical issues facing residential interventions is effectiveness: Do the interventions have any impact on the criminal behavior of their charges? Although most of what follows pertains most directly to publicly run placements, the problems also affect private placements.

• Reviews of Multiple Studies •

In the last decade a number of states have reported recidivism rates for youths released from state juvenile correctional facilities. When rearrest is the measure, on average, 55 percent of released youths recidivate. That figure drops to 33 percent failure when the measure is reconviction or readjudication. With reincarceration as the measure, the failure rate drops to between 12 and 25 percent.[19] These statistics give no information on what sort or what quality of rehabilitation programs took place in these states.

While much of the effectiveness research has focused on specific programs, some researchers have tried to summarize individual program research into a global conclusion on effectiveness. Most of these studies have used meta-analysis. Meta-analysis is a technique that allows researchers to re-analyze individual studies and arrive at a summary statistic of effectiveness for each individual study that can then be compared to the summary statistics from the other studies.

A meta-analysis of 443 studies published between 1970 and 1987 focused on formal contact with the juvenile justice system as an outcome measure. It reported that approximately two-thirds of the study outcomes favored the treatment group over the control group. Behavioral, skill, and multimodal treatment programs resulted in greater effects than other approaches. Deterrence-based programs were not effective.[20]

Lipsey and Wilson conducted a meta-analysis of 83 studies of institutional programs for serious offenders. They found that there were many instances of programs that had positive effects. The most effective treatment types had an impact on recidivism that was equivalent to reducing a control group baseline recidivism rate of 50 percent to around 30 or 35 percent. If the recidivism rate for these juveniles would have been 50 percent without treatment, the most effective programs reduced it to 30-35 percent. They concluded that this represents a "considerable decrease, especially in light of the fact that it applies to institutionalized offenders, who can be assumed to be relatively serious delinquents."[21] Successful interventions included aggression replacement training, behavior modification, and a stress inoculation program that helped youths to define anger, analyze recent anger episodes, review self-monitoring data and construct an individualized six-item anger hierarchy.

• Conclusions about Program Effectiveness •

Several cautious conclusions about the effectiveness of institutional programs for delinquents are in order. First, research such as an evaluation of the Provo program indicates that community programs are at least as effective as traditional training schools.[22] Second, research such as the evaluation of the Silverlake Project suggests that an innovative and less repressive residential program can be at least as effective as a traditional training school.[23] Third, even training schools may have an effect in suppressing the average number of crimes youths commit after release, but such institutions may not be able to deter their charges from committing any crimes after release. Fourth, this alleged suppression effect may be the result of such factors as regression toward the mean, simple maturation, or the rehabilitation programs in the training schools instead of the deterrent effect of a punitive regime in the training school.[24] Finally, the effectiveness literature suggests that certain interventions can be effective in reducing recidivism from about 50 percent to 30-35 percent. It is imperative, however, that these interventions follow the principles that research has identified as effective.[25]

Before moving on to other current issues in juvenile institutions, it is important to note that the measurement of the effectiveness of treatment programs in such settings assumes that the programs are in fact carried out as originally intended. Unfortunately, that is not always true. Wooden contended that institutions were using behavior modification techniques "to manipulate and control the child for the convenience of the custodians."[26] In a New York facility, "education" actually meant watching movies on the VCR, especially on Friday.[27] In what was intended to be a model facility in Arizona, treatment quickly deteriorated. Staff appeared inconsistent and capricious in such matters as scoring youths' behaviors, staff were disrespectful and interrupted youths in group meetings, a few staff made racially insensitive remarks, and youths were shackled when transported to medical treatment. A key educational program did not accomplish its objectives and did not provide substance abuse treatment. In short, there was a "repeated and systematic violation of the program's fundamental principles and spirit."[28] Although Wooden did this research many years ago, his observations on this matter apply today. What it shows is that impressive terms such as "behavior modification," "model program," or "education" do not necessarily translate into humane and progressive interventions. If such interventions are implemented in negative ways, it is hardly possible to know what results an evaluation study will find or what sort of confidence can be placed in the results.

INSTITUTIONAL LIFE

An important concern in juvenile justice is the effect of institutional life on youths. The theory of institutional placements is that they will provide a caring and nurturing environment that will allow the delinquents to change to prosocial behavior in the institution. This then will carry over into future behavior after release. As we shall see, however, the practice often falls far short of the theoretical ideal.

• Mental and Substance Disorders •

Research shows that the most prevalent problem in the juvenile justice system is mental disorders. Studies show that more than two-thirds of juveniles in the juvenile justice system experience mental disorders. In fact, a study that looked at more than 1,400 youths in three states found that 70 percent of youths in the system met the criteria for at least one mental health disorder. The most common disorders found were disruptive disorders such as conduct disorder, then substance abuse disorders such as alcohol abuse, then anxiety disorders (e.g., obsessive-compulsive disorder), and then mood disorders (e.g., depression).[29]

High rates of disorder persist even if conduct and substance abuse disorders are removed from the equation. With conduct disorders removed, 66 percent of youths still met the criteria for a mental health disorder. With substance abuse disorders removed, 62 percent of youths still met the criteria for a mental health disorder. With both disorders removed, almost half (45.5%) of youths still met the criteria for having a mental health disorder.[30]

Girls involved in the juvenile justice system have higher rates of mental disorders than boys. More than 80 percent of girls met the criteria for at least one mental health disorder, compared to 67 percent of boys. Girls were more likely to exhibit internalizing disorders such as anxiety and mood disorders.[31]

Most importantly, 27 percent of boys and girls in the juvenile justice system had a disorder serious enough to require "significant and immediate treatment."[32] In short, many juvenile offenders are suffering from mental health disorders, many need immediate attention, and many others need some type of treatment.

• Victimization •

As is true of adult prisons, probably the most dramatic example of a negative effect of the institution on incarcerated youths is the problem of victimization, which ranges from the relatively insignificant act of taking a boy's dessert to forcing a boy to take the "female" role in oral sodomy. Such victimization knows no geographic boundaries. In one northern training school, 53 percent of the boys exploited others, and 65 percent were exploited at least on occasion.[33] In a study of six southeastern training schools, more than one-third of the whites but less than 25 percent of the blacks reported frequent victimization. In addition, 61 percent of the whites but less than 50 percent of the blacks reported that other residents "took advantage of them" in the institution.[34] It appears that institutionalized girls are less subject to forceful sexual attacks but that "attacks sometimes occur, usually involving adolescent inmates who have expressed an unwillingness to participate in homosexuality and who are zealous in ridiculing inmates who engage in this behavior."[35] In one New York facility, some guards formed a "wake-up club" that administered regular beatings to misbehaving or disrespectful youths.[36] Although it is difficult to get an accurate and up-to-date picture of the victimization that takes place across the country, it is safe to say that the institutionalized youngster is deprived of the security that teenagers in positive home environments take for granted.

The Prison Rape Elimination Act of 2003 requires facilities to report statistics on sexual violence in both adult and juvenile correctional facilities to the federal Bureau of Justice Statistics. In 2004, juvenile facilities reported 2,821 allegations of sexual violence. Almost 60 percent (59%) involved charges of youth-on-youth violence, and the rest (41%) were staff-on-youth incidents. One-third of these incidents occurred in state-operated facilities, and two-thirds took place in privately operated facilities. The overall rate of sexual violence was 18.1 incidents per 1,000 beds.[37] It must be emphasized that these numbers are based on what officials reported to the federal government. Surveys of residents have been going on in the last few years, and those statistics will be available in the future to give us a more complete picture of sexual victimization in youth facilities.

Statistics on incident rates in juvenile facilities from one report are summarized in Table 9.1. As the table shows, it is estimated that about 24,200 juvenile-on-juvenile injuries and approximately 7,000 juvenile-on-staff injuries take place every year. Every year there are about 17,600

TABLE 9.1
**Incident Rates per 100 Juveniles and Annualized Estimates
of Incidents in Juvenile Facilities**

Type of Incident	Rate per 100 juveniles (last 30 days)	Estimated incidents (per year)
Injuries		
Juvenile-on-juvenile	3.1	24,200
Juvenile-on-staff	1.7	6,900
Staff-on-juvenile	0.2	106
Escapes		
Completed	1.2	9,700
Unsuccessful attempts	1.2	9,800
Acts of suicidal behavior	2.4	17,600
Incident requiring emergency health care	3.0	18,600
Isolation incidents		
Short-term (1-24 hrs.)	57.0	435,800
Longer-term (more than 24 hours)	11.0	88,900

Source: Abt Associates (1994). "Conditions of Confinement: Juvenile Detention and Corrections Facilities: Research Report." *Bureau of Justice Statistics Bulletin*. Washington, DC: U.S. Department of Justice.

acts of suicidal behavior and more than 18,000 incidents requiring emergency health care.[38] In 2002, however, juvenile facilities reported that only 26 youths died while in custody.[39] Subjectively, approximately 20 percent of confined youths report not feeling safe when in custody.[40] This may be a conservative estimate, however, because youths compare their safety in an institution with their safety on the outside. For some youths, life in the institution may be perceived as safer than life on the streets. For example, one institutionalized youth reported that he only had to fear a punch or being hit with furniture in the institution. On the outside, he had to fear being shot. Thus, in the institution "he felt perfectly safe."[41] (For further discussion of living conditions in juvenile prison, see Boxes 9.5 and 9.6.)

Girls may face special problems in juvenile institutions. For instance, when girls undergo strip searches and cavity searches in the presence of male guards, it tends to reinforce the belief that they do not have control over their own bodies. Moreover, some facilities have not given girls clean clothes, towels, and washcloths, and some have provided limited hygiene supplies. These abuses and deprivations can be especially traumatic to girls as they make the transition to womanhood.[42]

• Racial Tension •

The statistics on victimization also suggest that racial tension is a problem in juvenile institutions. For example, a study in the 1980s by Bartollas

BOX 9.5

Making Juvenile Prisons Spartan

Many state legislatures have passed laws to make adult prisons as Spartan as possible. Responding to alleged citizen displeasure with "soft" prisons, politicians have passed laws forbidding cable television and physical training equipment (weightlifting and other body-building equipment) in adult prisons.

To date, this movement has affected only juveniles placed in adult facilities via transfer, direct file, or blended sentencing. However, the call for amenity-free prisons raises the issue of what level of "comfort" is appropriate for offenders—adult or juvenile. Is television all right but premium cable services such as Home Box Office (HBO) inappropriate? Is weightlifting equipment inappropriate because inmates can use the equipment to get in better shape and then assault other inmates or staff?

Years before this controversy erupted, prison authority John Conrad (1982) addressed this question of "What do the undeserving deserve?" His answer was that there are four essentials needed in prison: safety, lawfulness, industriousness, and hope (Conrad, 1982).

What do you think? Can prisons be too soft? Can they be too tough? Are Conrad's four essential ingredients a good guideline? Why or why not? What are your suggestions for juvenile prisons? For adult prisons?

and Sieverdes found African-American youths to be both more dominant and more aggressive than white inmates: "Twice as many black as white residents were classified by staff members as highly aggressive toward others; over 40 percent of whites were defined by staff as passive."[43] They attributed this situation to role reversal in the institution, whereby white Southern youths found themselves in the novel position of being in the minority. About 60 percent of the inmates were black, and about one-half of the staff members were black. The white youths felt threatened because they were in an environment very different from "the Southern culture, [where] whites are used to a position of greater superiority in the free society relative to minority groups than are youth elsewhere in the United States."[44] A model youth prison in Arizona also experienced some racial tensions. One staff member called one youth a "taco bender," and another staff member called an African-American youth "colored."[45]

The fact that training schools continue to be places with significant proportions of several ethnic groups suggests that racial/ethnic tensions will continue into the foreseeable future. In 2003, minorities constituted 60 percent of the committed juveniles in custody in public and private facilities nationwide. Blacks made up about 37 percent of both public

BOX 9.6

Abuses in One Juvenile Facility

In 2000, the U.S. Justice Department won a lawsuit to gain custody of juvenile inmates at the Jena Juvenile Justice Center in Jena, Louisiana, from a private corrections company (the Wackenhut Corrections Corporation). The following are some of the allegations that led to the lawsuit:

- Staff used force against a youth with a colostomy, which caused his intestines to go out of the colostomy hole.

- One nurse accused another nurse of forcing youths against the wall, tossing water on them, and refusing them medication if they were not obedient.

- One youth attempted suicide twice (tied a sock tightly around his neck) to avoid sexual victimization and racial tension.

- Nine juveniles accused a guard of taking food off their trays and snacks.

- One youth damaged his testicles and inflicted other injuries to get to the medical treatment ward to avoid victimization by peers.

- One youth wrote his mother that a female guard forced him to take off his shirt and move like a snake.

Source: "I Know Why the Cajun Bird Sings." *Harper's Magazine*, July 2000, 301, 29.

and private placement populations; Hispanics accounted for 18 percent of those in custody; and American Indians, Asians, and others accounted for 4 percent of committed juveniles in placement.[46] Hopefully, such tension will decrease as the twenty-first century continues, but the painful truth is that even 50 years after the Supreme Court ruled against segregated schools, race is still problematic in the juvenile justice system.

• The Inmate Code •

Another negative effect of institutions is that youths may develop or maintain allegiance to peer norms that run counter to staff efforts to rehabilitate the youngsters. This is the problem of the inmate code, which can stress such maxims as "exploit whomever you can," "don't play up to staff," "don't rat on your peers . . .," and "be cool."[47] In other words, juvenile inmates develop feelings of distrust and resentment toward staff. These feelings operate in opposition to staff efforts to build trust and openness. There has been some indication that the inmate code is moving away from minding one's own business ("do your own time") to greater exploitation of others:

> In other words, the "old con" who did his/her own time has disappeared from the juvenile correctional system and from most adult correctional systems. Inmates are now more likely to show certain allegiances to other prisoners, especially those in the same racial group or social organization. But, at the same time, this inmate is scheming to manipulate staff and to take advantage of weaker peers.[48]

As might be expected, research indicates that organizational structure affects the norms and behavior of youthful prisoners. In other words, "[t]he more custodial and punitive settings had inmate cultures that were more violent, more hostile, and more oppositional than those in the treatment-oriented settings.[49] This finding on the impact of organizational structure on inmate culture suggests that it is possible for administrators to reduce the negative environments in juvenile prisons by opting for an organizational structure that emphasizes treatment over custody. One specific option that administrators can take is to limit the size of juvenile residential placements. Larger populations are more susceptible to custodial climates than smaller populations. Another option is to facilitate communication between treatment staff and custodial staff so that staff members do not exacerbate potential treatment-custody conflicts.[50]

• Deprivation of Heterosexual Contact •

Another negative effect of institutions is that incarcerated youths are deprived of heterosexual relationships at a time when such relationships are critical in helping the teenager to define himself or herself as a mature sexual adult. Although written about incarcerated girls, Giallombardo's comments on this matter apply equally well (with the appropriate adjustments) to imprisoned boys:

> They are developing images of themselves as adult women, and they are beset with many anxieties concerning their sexuality and acceptance by males. The exclusion of males in their own age group is a source of confusion for adolescent girls. . . . Their confusion is compounded by virtue of the fact that during incarceration they are socialized to view other women as legitimate sex objects.[51]

In response to this deprivation, many of the girls adjust by participating in kinship role systems and/or homosexual alliances. In the training schools Giallombardo studied, for example, the girls had

Female juvenile offenders at the Missouri Division of Youth Services' Rosa Parks Center in Fulton, Missouri, "circle up" to resolve a problem. Part of their rehabilitation involves learning anger management and peaceful ways to resolve disputes.

affectionate nicknames for one another, wrote love letters to other girls, picked their own special songs, "went steady," and even got married in formal ceremonies (out of staff view).[52] Another study reported that only about 17 percent of the institutionalized girls reported at least one homosexual experience (ranging from kissing to intimate sexual contact), but about one-half of the girls reported taking a "make-believe family" role.[53] Such behavior was clearly not intended by the authorities and has been labeled a "secondary adjustment."[54] The problem with secondary adjustments is that they divert the youths' attention away from the main aspects of the supposedly rehabilitative programs, such as education and counseling, and direct that attention to making life within the training school as pleasant as possible.

Other problems faced by incarcerated youths include loss of liberty, deprivation of personal possessions, and boredom. Particularly important in terms of possessions is the loss of clothing articles. This is important because it entails a loss of the opportunity to explore various clothing styles. According to Giallombardo, such exploratory behavior is directly related to a girl's sense of identity and also her popularity.[55]

An important national study on living conditions in juvenile facilities found "substantial and widespread deficiencies" in four matters: living space, security, control of suicidal behavior, and health care.[56] Many institutions experience problems concerning crowding, safety, prevention of escapes, suicidal behavior, and health screening. That same report also expressed a need to collect systematic data on confined youths' educational and treatment needs. Further evidence that problems continue to exist in juvenile institutions is the publication of a recent American Bar Association manual that offers suggestions for litigation strategies to contest problematic conditions.[57] It is unfortunate but true that often a lawsuit is the only way that problems in youth prisons become known. For example, it took a lawsuit in Arizona to make it known that one of the state youth prisons maintained "harsh conditions, arbitrary and capricious decision making, and an unduly punitive, unrehabilitative environment."[58]

NEW DIRECTIONS IN INSTITUTIONAL INTERVENTIONS

• Deinstitutionalization of Status Offenders •

Since the mid-1970s, there has been a movement away from placing status offenders and delinquents in the same state-operated institutions. It is felt that any mixing of status offenders and delinquents can have harmful consequences on the status offenders. In fact, much of this movement has been one of deinstitutionalization: trying to avoid any involuntary placements of status offenders (some states' practice of deinstitutionalization of delinquents and status offenders will be discussed later in this chapter). The strength of this movement is indicated by the fact that 95 percent of the juveniles in residential placement in October of 2003 were delinquents, and only 5 percent were status offenders. This is a decrease from the 7 percent figure in 1985.[59]

• Deinstitutionalization: Closing Training Schools •

Several states, including Massachusetts, Maryland, Pennsylvania, and Utah, have decreased dramatically their use of training schools by closing some of these facilities. In Massachusetts, for example, only about 15 percent of the approximately 800 youths committed to the State Department of Youth services each year are first placed in a locked treatment program. The other 85 percent of the committed youths are placed in community-based programs such as group homes, forestry camps, day treatment programs, outreach-tracking programs, or foster care. Most of the programs have been privatized; private agencies run the programs on a contract basis with the state. In addition, the residential programs are small in size, with no more than 30 youths housed in a facility.[60] What this means for most youths is that they spend only about four weeks in secure placement and then are placed in nonsecure treatment programs. In states with heavy reliance on traditional training schools, most youths spend several months in secure confinement and then are placed on aftercare (parole).

The National Council on Crime and Delinquency evaluated the Massachusetts reform and found it to be successful. Compared to other states still relying on traditional training schools, Massachusetts had similar recidivism results, and the effort was cost-effective. More specifically, depending on how long Massachusetts would incarcerate youths in traditional training schools, it would have to spend $10 to $16.8 million more per year than it was spending in its deinstitutionalization mode.[61]

An evaluation of the closing of one institution in Maryland, however, found contrary results. Almost three-quarters (72%) of the youths committed to the State Department of Juvenile Services after the institution's closing were rearrested during the one-year follow-up period, whereas only about 45 percent of the youths who had been institutionalized at the training school prior to its closing were rearrested. In a two-and-one-half year follow-up period, 83 percent of the post-closing group were rearrested compared to 66 percent and 69 percent of the two groups that had been incarcerated at the training school under study. The authors concluded that "the alternatives available when Montrose [the state training school] was closed were less effective in reducing crime than institutionalization would have been."[62] The authors suggest that their findings support the conclusion that "neither institutional nor community-based programs are uniformly effective or ineffective. The *design* of the intervention rather than its location appears important." [emphasis in original][63] In other words, simply closing traditional training schools is only half of a strategy. The other half is to devise effective programs for the youths that would have been committed to the training schools. It appears that Massachusetts was able to devise such effective alternative programming for its delinquent commitments. Because Maryland did not come up with effective alternative programming, the recidivism rates for the group not sent to the training school were disappointing.

• Blended Sentencing •

The creation of blended sentencing allows either the juvenile court or the adult court to impose a sentence that can involve either the juvenile correctional system, the adult system, or both. The adult sentence may be suspended pending either a violation or the commission of a new crime. Texas, for example, allows juveniles convicted of certain violent crimes or of habitual offender status to be sentenced to terms of up to 20 years for a second-degree felony and up to 10 years for a third-degree felony. One result of blended sentencing will be a growing number of youthful offenders in adult prisons. Note that juvenile offenders in adult prisons may still be considered "minors" for other purposes. In Wisconsin, for example, 17-year-olds in adult prisons are still subject to mandatory education and require parental consent for medical treatment.

Go to www.ojp.usdoj.gov/ojjdp and examine *Juvenile Offenders and Victims: 2006 National Report* to see what blended sentencing provisions, if any, exist in your state.

At the end of 2004, 15 states had blended sentencing laws allowing juvenile courts to impose adult criminal sanctions on juvenile offenders. Seventeen states had blended sentencing laws allowing the adult criminal court to impose either juvenile or adult sanctions or a combination sentence.[64]

A study on victimization among youthful inmates in adult prisons is important in light of the development of blended sentencing. Maitland

and Sluder interviewed 111 inmates ages 17 to 25. They found that less than 1 percent reported that they had been forced to engage in sexual activity, 3 percent had been forced to give up their money, and 5.5 percent had had a weapon used on them. Less serious victimization experiences, however, were much more frequent. Fifty-nine percent had been verbally harassed, approximately 50 percent had had their property stolen, and 38 percent had been hit, kicked, punched, or slapped. The authors concluded that "young, medium-security prison inmates are most likely to be subjected to less serious forms of victimization by peers during their terms of incarceration."[65] Putting delinquents in adult prisons when they are 17 or 18 can be expected to produce such victimization results for the youthful offenders so incarcerated.

Another negative aspect of blended sentencing and putting juveniles into criminal court and adult institutions is that the youths may have negative perceptions of how they were processed. In research on criminal court processing of youths in Florida, it was found that the court message to the youths was that their behavior was bad and they were bad. Prison staff also communicated a similar negative message; the youthful prisoners heard that "they were lost causes who could never redeem themselves or return to normal personhood."[66] For a discussion of "life without parole" sentences for juvenile murderers, see Chapter 14.

• Wilderness Programs •

Another relatively recent direction in residential placements is the use of various types of wilderness experiences, ranging from relatively short stays in outdoor settings to rather long wagon train or ocean ship trips. Private operators as well as some states have used this type of programming, which places delinquents in settings where they are taught survival skills, limits, and self-esteem. The youths are put in natural settings in which they must learn to cook, obtain shelter from the elements, tell directions (read a compass), start fires, and so forth. In the process of accomplishing such tasks, the youths learn to depend on themselves and others. The theory is that a successful survival experience in a natural setting will then transfer to the youth's normal environment and he or she will turn to more constructive activities than delinquency.

AP Photo/Douglas C. Pizac

Basics such as food, clothing, and shelter are some of the required criteria for wilderness treatment programs such as RedCliff Ascent's outing in the Wah Wah Mountains of southwestern Utah. Troubled youths from around the world are sent to such programs in hope that they will straighten out their lives.

In earlier research, Lipsey and Wilson concluded that wilderness programs generally had weak effects or no effects on the recidivism rates of the youths who went through the programs compared to control groups.[67] But in a more recent analysis of wilderness and challenge programs for juveniles, they found that programs with more intense physical activities or greater therapeutic enhancements reduced recidivism from 37 percent down to 29 percent. It appears that a therapeutic component is critical.[68]

In conclusion, simply putting teens through a "survivor's" experience as depicted on television is not enough to reduce delinquency. It appears that the wilderness program must have a therapeutic aspect to be effective.

• Summary on Institutional Placements •

This section has examined state and private residential placements, ranging from training schools to wilderness experience programs. An examination of the effectiveness of institutional placements indicates that many children do not really need to be in training schools. Instead, they can be handled in less restrictive settings without any increase in recidivism. This part of the chapter also examined several problematic factors in residential placements, such as victimization, racial tension, and homosexual behavior. Unfortunately, residential placements often translate into horror stories for the children rather than therapeutic havens. Sexual assaults and racial tension have been well-documented components of placements in the past, and they are unlikely to disappear completely. Because of these and related problems, states such as Massachusetts, Maryland, Pennsylvania, and Utah have turned to noninstitutional approaches to delinquency, by which fewer youngsters are placed in state training schools. Blended sentencing and increased processing of juvenile offenders in adult court, however, may translate into significant numbers of youthful offenders being incarcerated in adult prisons and youths serving longer sentences than in the past.

In the next section of the chapter, we will examine community interventions such as traditional probation and innovations such as intensive supervision. As will be shown, there are important developments taking place in this often neglected component of the juvenile justice system.

COMMUNITY INTERVENTIONS

Even before the founding of the first juvenile court in Illinois at the turn of the twentieth century, community interventions had been a central weapon of those seeking to fight delinquency. This section of the chapter will examine both traditional and nontraditional community interventions and focus on some of the problems with these approaches to the delinquency problem. The section will describe probation and aftercare for juveniles, highlight some of the current trends in community interventions, and look at some of the concerns in the field. One of the key issues examined in this part of the chapter is the effectiveness issue: Do community interventions have any impact on recidivism? In other words, do community interventions help to reduce the number of offenses committed by the juveniles exposed to the programs, or are the programs ineffective in reducing delinquent activity?

• Probation •

Statistics demonstrate that probation continues to be a critical part of the juvenile justice system. In 2004, 393,100 youths who were adjudicated delinquent in juvenile court were placed on probation. This represents almost two-thirds (63%) of the more than 600,000 youths who were adjudicated delinquent. Another 14,700 youths who were not adjudicated delinquent agreed to some form of probation, and another 194,100 youths who were not petitioned agreed to some form of voluntary probation. Further, 51,800 youths were adjudicated status offenders and placed on probation, while another 1,700 petitioned but nonadjudicated status offenders were placed on probation. Altogether,

TABLE 9.2
Offense Profile of Cases Adjudicated Delinquent That Resulted in Probation

Most serious offense	1985	2005
Person	17%	26%
Property	60%	36%
Drugs	7%	13%
Public order	16%	26%
Total	100%	100%
Cases resulting in formal probation	191,500	373,400

Offense Profile of Adjudicated Status Offense Cases That Resulted in Probation

Most serious offense	1995	2005
Runaway	15%	12%
Truancy	37%	39%
Curfew	4%	4%
Ungovernability	16%	20%
Liquor law	23%	19%
Miscellaneous	5%	6%
Total	100%	100%

Note: Totals may not equal 100% due to rounding.

Source: Puzzanchera, C., and M. Sickmund (2008). *Juvenile Court Statistics 2005*. Pittsburgh: National Center for Juvenile Justice. Reprinted by permission.

probation handled more than 650,000 youths who were processed in some way for delinquency or a status offense by the juvenile court in 2004.[69] (Table 9.2 shows the offenses for which delinquents and status offenders were placed on probation in 1985 and 2005.) It is fair to call probation the workhorse of the juvenile court.[70]

• Social History (Predisposition) Investigations •

When a child has been adjudicated as either a delinquent or a status offender, a probation officer usually conducts a social history investigation (predisposition report) of the youngster and his or her family. Similar to the presentence investigation report in adult courts, the social history report offers judges legal and social information. Legal information includes descriptive material about the delinquency or status offense, including the child's, the victim's, and the police officer's (if a delinquent act) version of the offense, and verified data on the child's prior contacts, if any, with the juvenile court and the police department's juvenile bureau. Social history information includes verification of the child's age (a critical legal condition for court action) and information on the child's development, family, education, and possible problems such as the abuse of alcohol or other drugs.

Probation officers gather such information by interviewing the youth; the youth's family, teachers, and other school personnel; the victim; and the police. They also check various police, court, and school records. They usually collect information on previous arrests from police and court files. Likewise, they may obtain a copy of the child's cumulative school record, which contains information on the child's grades, attendance, disciplinary history, and intelligence testing scores. If necessary, in probation departments that have the resources, the officer may also see to it that a psychologist and/or a psychiatrist examines the child for any suspected emotional problems and to determine the child's intelligence quotient (IQ) more accurately (by an individual IQ test rather than a group test). The probation officer then summarizes all of this information in a report that provides the judge with a more informed basis for the disposition decision.

• Probation Supervision •

Youths who are placed on formal probation supervision in court must follow various conditions, such as reporting regularly to a probation officer, obeying the law, attending school, and remaining within the geographical jurisdiction of the court. Judges may also order specific conditions, such as restitution to the victim(s) of the delinquent act or community service restitution (e.g., performing cleanup work at the local park or playground). Another special condition might be to attend counseling sessions with a social worker, psychologist, or psychiatrist, or require the parents to attend the counseling sessions. A judge might also order a short stay (about one month) in detention as a condition of probation.[71]

If a juvenile follows the conditions of the probation disposition and is adjusting favorably at home, in school, and in the community, then the probation officer can request an early discharge from supervision. If a youngster is not abiding by the conditions and is not adjusting well, then the probation officer may request that the judge order that the youth is in violation of the probation agreement. In that case, the judge can either order the probation to continue (perhaps with additional conditions such as more frequent reporting to the probation officer) or can terminate the probation and place the youth under the supervision of the state youth correctional authority for placement in a public facility or a private residential setting.

• Aftercare •

Many states also have aftercare or parole programs for youths released from state training schools, group homes, or forestry camp placements. Aftercare supervision is very similar to probation supervision. In fact, in some states, probation officers also perform aftercare supervision duties. Just as with probation, youths on aftercare status must follow specific conditions and report on a regular basis to a parole officer. If they do not, parole can be revoked and they can be sent back to an institutional placement.

Recent evaluations of aftercare programs have shown mixed findings.[72] In light of the interest in controlling violent juveniles, however, the federal government has been testing a new model of aftercare for serious, chronic juvenile offenders in several jurisdictions throughout the United States. The new model is a mix of intensive surveillance and services. Research to date indicates that the pilot programs are delivering more services and more surveillance (especially on nights and weekends) than what is being given to control groups. Recidivism has not yet been examined, however.[73]

• Supervision and Counseling •

Probation and aftercare (parole) officers working with juveniles use various combinations of assistance and control[74] to help youthful offenders avoid further trouble. Some officers act like social workers or counselors as they try to understand the youth and his or her problems and assist the youngster in gaining greater self-insight and self-esteem. Officers also might attempt some family counseling to help parents better understand the family interaction patterns that have contributed to the child's misbehavior. Other officers assume a tougher role: a quasi-police officer who first threatens the youth with punishment and then monitors the compliance of the child to the court conditions. This "surveillance"[75] type of officer typically believes that deterrence and incapacitation are more important goals than rehabilitation.

Whether oriented toward assistance or control, probation and parole officers tend to use one of several counseling techniques—including reality therapy, client-centered (nondirective) therapy, rational emotive therapy, or behaviorism. Assistance-oriented officers utilize these counseling techniques to a greater extent than control-oriented officers, but even the latter use some of the basic principles of these approaches to interview probationers and establish some rapport.[76] Both cognitive techniques[77] and behavior modification have proved effective in community interventions with juveniles.[78]

• Current Trends in Community Supervision •

Several developments are taking place in community corrections. Many people are calling for a tougher community corrections with greater attention on punishment and controlling offender risk. Other voices, however, continue to insist that probation and other community interventions need to be more than just strict punishment for crime.

• The Balanced Approach •

One current approach in juvenile corrections is the balanced approach. "This philosophy requires the system to provide balanced attention to the need for competency development, accountability, and community safety and requires efforts to restore, to the greatest extent possible, the victim and community to their pre-crime status."[79] It is thought that restitution and community service send out a message that the offender is responsible for his or her crime and is being held accountable for it. It is considered important that the offender come to realize the harm he or she has caused the victim(s). As a result of this philosophy, 17 states amended their legislation (juvenile court purpose clauses) to include the balanced approach.[80] In actuality, the balanced approach is a combination of traditional rehabilitation, restorative justice, and classical criminology.

One example of the balanced approach is Utah's juvenile restitution program, which includes a restitution work fund. Juveniles without jobs or money can perform community service tasks and thereby earn money for their restitution orders. In Boston, Operation Night Light has police and probation officers together on street patrol checking to ensure that probationers are complying with their probation conditions. A similar program in Maryland has the probation officers and police targeting selected crime "hot spots."[81]

Another example is the Gang Violence Reduction Program in Chicago, which combines surveillance of violent or potentially violent gang members and the provision of services. Police and probation officers increase their supervision of target youths and provide education, employment, employment training, and some counseling. Evaluation has found decreased serious gang violence and improved perceptions among residents concerning gang crime and police effectiveness in targeting such crime.[82]

• The Punitive Model: Attack Probation •

One concern about the balanced approach is whether it in fact "balances" the concerns for competency development, accountability, and community safety or whether it simply places emphasis on accountability. If the balanced approach is not actually balanced, then it might be considered a punitive model. This philosophy is quite direct; the offender, even if a juvenile, deserves to be punished.

Miller, for one, argues that the toughening of probation has gone too far. He contends that probation has lost much of its original mission of helping the offender. He argues that probation officers have abandoned any pretense at a social work role and have become "ersatz" (imitation) cops. He says that in this new "attack probation" style (a term developed by British criminologist Andrew Rutherford) officers see "their role as one in which to search out any means possible to get the probationer into prison. The motto of this practice was mounted on the office wall of one of California's chief probation officers: 'Trail 'em, Surveil 'em, Nail 'em, and Jail 'em.'"[83] In other words, if probation officers are out on the streets at night in "hot spots" (areas with high rates of crime), they are there as quasi-police officers looking for trouble and not as friendly social workers.

A critical question about getting tough is whether such tactics are effective in reducing recidivism. That issue is discussed in the next major section of this chapter. Another interesting question posed by this "get tough" movement is whether it is appropriate to use shame tactics in probation. For a discussion of this issue, see Box 9.7.

• Renewed Emphasis on Status Offenses •

Emphasis on status offenses (e.g., truancy) is making a comeback in some circles. Kern County, California, for example, has instituted a truancy program that uses two deputy probation officers to work with students and families. If initial efforts to resolve truancy fail, the truant youth is referred to one of the deputy probation officers who then meets with

BOX 9.7

Shame Tactics in Probation and Community Corrections

Shame strategies take several forms. One form of shame penalties is apology. For example, one school vandalizer was forced to apologize in front of the student bodies at the 13 schools he vandalized. Some shame penalties, however, are much more negative, and objections arise that they are stigmatizing rather than reintegrative. For example, some offenders have been required to wear t-shirts or to display signs on their cars or residences proclaiming their offense ("I am a convicted shoplifter" or "Convicted Drunk Driver"). Karp (1998) contends that such dramatic strategies are ineffective or worse: "Shame penalties that emphasize humiliation are likely to be counterproductive, as they drive a wedge between offenders and conventional society" (p. 291). Thus, shame penalties can isolate the offender rather than assist him or her to rejoin the community. Karp also questions whether shame penalties are effective in modern society, which has an anonymous aspect compared to the potentially more effective informal small-group setting (Karp, 1998). In other words, modern America is so big that we do not know our neighbors and thus we do not really experience shame when others (who are strangers) learn that we have done wrong. Shame only has meaning in a small community in which people know one another.

Andrew von Hirsch argues against shaming tactics based on an ethical position that such tactics violate the respect that the offender as a human deserves. Von Hirsch argues that punishments should not demean the dignity of the offender. If they destroy the dignity of the offender, they are unacceptable:

> Acceptable penal content, then, is the idea that a sanction should be devised so that its intended penal deprivations are those that can be administered in a manner that is clearly consistent with the offender's dignity. If the penal deprivation includes a given imposition, X, then one must ask whether that can be undergone by offenders in a reasonably self-possessed fashion. Unless one is confident that it can, it should not be a part of the sanction (von Hirsch, 1990:167).

Thus, von Hirsch is opposed to t-shirts or bumper stickers that make drunk drivers advertise their offense because there "is no way a person can, with dignity, go about in public with a sign admitting himself or herself to be a moral pariah" (1990:168).

Proponents of identifying labels for offenders would argue that they enhance the punishment value of community corrections. Such marks make probation or parole tougher rather than a more lenient "slap on the wrist." Supporters would also argue that there may be deterrent value in the measures. Because it is embarrassing to wear such markings, this could serve to deter others from drunk driving or whatever offense results in the added penalty.

What do you think? What kinds of shaming might be effective for juvenile offenders? What are the limits of acceptable strategies?

the family at least four times. The officer also makes unannounced home visits, monitors attendance, counsels the youth and his or her parents, and refers the family to appropriate service providers. Tracking continues for one year. If unsuccessful, the case is referred back to the school for possible referral to the district attorney for court action.[84] Status offenses such as truancy are receiving increased attention because of research that indicates that they are risk factors for serious and violent delinquency. There is a fear that if these troublesome behaviors are not dealt with, then there is a definite possibility of much worse behavior in the future.

• *Restorative Justice* •

Bazemore and Maloney argue that restorative justice should be the theme in a new paradigm for criminal justice and juvenile justice in general and probation in particular. In contrast to retributive justice, which focuses on vengeance, deterrence, and punishment, restorative justice "is concerned with repairing the damage or harm done to victims and the community through a process of negotiation, mediation, victim empowerment, and reparation."[85] As another commentator put it, "restorative justice is about relationships—how relationships are harmed by crime and how they can be rebuilt to promote recovery and healing for people affected by crime."[86]

Contrary to much community service at present, which is unsupervised, unplanned, and performed individually, Bazemore and Maloney argue that community service should be creatively planned, well supervised, and group-oriented. In addition, it should be relevant to the offense, such as requiring teen vandals to clean up or repair a vandalized school.[87] One jurisdiction had juveniles grow food and then give it to an agency feeding the homeless.[88] The service obligations should also contribute to the offender's sense of competency. In other words, the service assignments should offer "positive, productive roles in the community which allow them [offenders] to experience, practice, and demonstrate ability to do something well that others value."[89] This focus on competence is related to a concern for rehabilitation, which is seen as "the development and application of productive skills or 'competencies' that provide the basis for conventional ties or 'bonds' with community institutions."[90]

Restorative justice practices include victim-offender mediation, family group conferencing, sentencing circles, and reparative probation boards. One indication of the popularity of such programs is that in 1998 reparative boards (citizen volunteers) processed 1,200 adult criminal cases in Vermont.[91] Most boards, however, handle juvenile cases.

Mediation programs (meetings between victims and offenders) have been very effective in terms of satisfaction, agreement, and completion rates (usually between 75% and 100%). There are problems, however.

For instance, the general conclusion is that mediation does not decrease recidivism. Moreover, restorative programs do not necessarily provide procedural safeguards, and they often deal with trivial matters such as shoplifting. Restorative programs also tend to develop in middle-class or rural areas; disadvantaged urban areas tend to be neglected.[92] Restitution payments are not always completed, and perhaps most importantly, restorative justice programs do not necessarily control crime and criminals, especially serious and chronic offenders.[93]

Despite its problems, this model is attractive because it offers a plausible alternative to the get-tough attitude that is currently popular. It focuses on the victim as well as the offender and the community. It seeks to make the offender more competent and productive in an effort to bond the offender more closely to the community. Finally, the public looks more favorably on such programs dealing with juvenile offenders than those handling adults. (For more information, see Chapter 6, "Dimensions of Community Justice.")

• *Peacemaking* •

Like restorative justice, peacemaking is a positive philosophy that seeks to go beyond simply criticizing the status quo and beyond a simple focus on recidivism reduction. The peacemaking perspective supports efforts of corrections workers, whether prison counselors or probation officers, to help offenders find greater meaning in their lives. Two proponents, Bo Lozoff and Michael Braswell, contend that all great religions teach four classic virtues: honesty, courage, kindness, and a sense of humor. In this perspective, reductions in recidivism and programs such as counseling or vocational training are still important but they are more external. The deeper goal is internal personal change: "The primary goal is to help build a happier, peaceful person right there in the prison [if working with prisoners], a person whose newfound self-honesty and courage can steer him or her to adjust to the biases and shortcomings of a society which does not feel comfortable with ex-offenders."[94]

In a peacemaking perspective, both personal transformation and institutional change are critical. Personal change is seen as the basis of social change. It is critical to begin with yourself. It is also a lifetime task that needs constant work.[95]

WHAT DOES THE FUTURE HOLD?

It is difficult to predict where community corrections will go from here. One possible path is to continue down the get-tough road. A grim reality is that further financial cutbacks will force probation to do less and less. Another path is to attempt to return probation to a more traditional focus on trying to rehabilitate offenders. An important issue in deciding which direction to take is the effectiveness of community corrections. The next two sections will discuss some important findings from the effectiveness literature. The first section will review major findings on the effectiveness of community sanctions such as probation. The second section will review the research on effective treatments. Together, these findings give some assistance in thinking about the most appropriate future direction for community corrections.

THE EFFECTIVENESS OF JUVENILE PROBATION

Although national recidivism statistics on juvenile probationers are not readily available and though the research on juvenile probation has not been as extensive as the research on adult probation, there are considerable research findings available to illuminate the effectiveness issue for juvenile probation. Based on research on both juveniles and adults, several conclusions about the effectiveness of community correctional interventions for juveniles seem sound.

One implication of the research is that simply making probation tougher does not work.[96] The cumulative research on such get-tough measures as Scared Straight programs, boot camps, and intensive supervision has demonstrated that harsher measures, without additional features, do not reduce recidivism. Experimental evaluations of such programs have shown that these tough measures do not reduce recidivism (new arrests or convictions).

Related to this is the finding that often community supervision may be at least as effective as incarceration.[97] In fact, Lipsey and Wilson found that among programs that produced consistent evidence of positive effects for serious offenders, noninstitutional programs showed greater reductions in recidivism than institutional programs.[98] Although offenders released to community supervision commit some new crimes, the fact that they do no worse (and may do better) than offenders sentenced to training schools and then released on traditional aftercare suggests that society can use community supervision knowing that it is not more harmful than incarceration.

Another clear lesson is that the effectiveness of probation varies from place to place. An initial report on the effectiveness of adult felony probation found that the failure rate (new arrests) was 65 percent.[99] Subsequent studies found some rates as low as 22 percent and others in between those two rates.[100] There are several explanations for such variation. Some locations may be under budgetary pressures and may not have the financial resources to provide much treatment or surveillance of offenders. Some locations may be implementing treatment programs that have proved to be effective. (For a discussion of such principles, see the next section.) Juvenile probation, then, may be quite effective in some locations but likely to experience serious problems in other locations.

Still another lesson is that intensive supervision can lead to easier detection of technical violations.[101] In other words, intensive supervision offenders are more likely to be detected violating the rules of probation such as not reporting to the probation officer, leaving the jurisdiction without permission, breaking curfew, testing positive on a urine drug test, and skipping school. This explains why intensive supervision can be ineffective if the goal is to reduce prison or training school populations. Detection of technical violations often results in revocations of probation. When this happens, the offender is incarcerated as punishment for breaking the conditions of probation. Therefore, a sanction intended to reduce the number of persons being institutionalized (intensive supervision) can in fact increase the number being institutionalized. This problem can be avoided, however, if a court and correctional agency put in place a system of graduated penalties for technical violations.[102]

A discouraging finding is that some studies have shown that simply being on probation supervision without any officer contacts sometimes is just as effective as being on probation and being seen by an officer.[103] This finding questions whether probation officers have much impact on their clients. One explanation is that perhaps officers are not doing much for their clients. Another explanation is that some offenders do not need much supervision. Being caught and being placed on probation may have sent a clear message to these probationers. They have learned their lesson and will not reoffend.

Perhaps the most encouraging finding in recent research is that intensive supervision that includes treatment components can reduce recidivism.[104] This suggests that although being tough is not enough, addressing offender needs can make a difference. (Contrary to this claim, a recent study of aftercare with treatment did not show any effectiveness. The study, however, involved a sample of all substance-abusing offenders.)[105]

Because research indicates that treatment is critical, the next section will review the treatment research to show which types of treatment appear to offer promise and which seem to be ineffective.

EFFECTIVE AND INEFFECTIVE TREATMENT INTERVENTIONS WITH OFFENDERS

Although several well-publicized reports claimed that little seemed to be effective in changing offenders and reducing recidivism, there now appears to be considerable consensus that there is knowledge about effective and ineffective interventions. This section will discuss both types of interventions.

Gendreau and his colleagues have spearheaded much of the treatment research. They have concluded that there are several principles of effective interventions. First, interventions need to be intensive and behavioral. Intensive means that the intervention takes up at least 40 percent of the offender's time and goes on for three to nine months. Behavioral interventions are based on the principles of operant conditioning, especially reinforcement. In simple terms, there must be rewards for desirable behaviors. Some examples are token economies, modeling, and cognitive behavioral interventions such as problem-solving, reasoning, self-control, and self-instructional training. Successful programs target criminogenic needs such as antisocial attitudes, peer associations, substance abuse problems, and self-control issues rather than noncriminogenic needs such as low self-esteem, anxiety, or depression. The responsivity principle means that attention needs to be paid to matching offenders, therapists, and programs. For example, offenders who prefer structure do better in a more structured program such as a token economy. More anxious offenders do better with therapists who show more interpersonal sensitivity. Programs need to enforce their rules in a firm but fair manner, and positive reinforcers should outnumber punishers by a ratio of at least four to one. Therapists need to be sensitive and to be adequately trained and supervised. Relapse prevention and advocacy and brokerage with other community agencies are also necessary.[106]

This brief summary of the effectiveness literature gives an outline of effective intervention principles. It is also important, however, to note what has been found to be ineffective. Freudian psychodynamic therapy is ineffective with offenders, as is Rogerian nondirective (person-centered) therapy.[107] Freudian therapy seeks to uncover and resolve unconscious conflicts stemming from the failure to resolve critical developmental crises in childhood. It can be looked at as something of a blessing that it is not appropriate for offenders because it is both expensive and time-consuming. Nondirective counseling assumes that clients have the potential to change and can do so if the therapist offers unconditional positive regard and a listening forum so that the client can explore options and achieve his or her full potential. It is probably more appropriate for other populations, such as college students, in which the clients are more mature and independent. It should be noted, however, that certain principles of nondirective therapy such as positive regard and empathy still apply in other counseling strategies.

• Additional Factors Related to Effectiveness •

The effectiveness research is critical. It is imperative to know what works and what does not work. It is also important, however, to recall some additional factors about successful intervention with offenders.

One point to note is that often programs are simply not available for offenders. For example, in 1990, the estimate was that 26 percent of all probationers needed drug abuse treatment. At the same time, the average wait for entry into outpatient programs was 22 days.[108] So although research indicates that resolving criminogenic needs such as substance abuse problems is critical in changing offenders and reducing recidivism, the programs that change such offenders are not always readily available. Another problem is that the public and politicians are reluctant to increase government spending even for worthy projects.

Another factor to consider is that interventions that would appear to offer benefits for offenders do not always do so. For example, many people assume that part-time employment for teens would reduce their chances of committing delinquent acts. Some recent research, however, shows that employment is not always beneficial. Wright and his colleagues found that the "number of hours employed had an indirect effect in increasing delinquency across the sample."[109] In fact, much of the delinquency of working teens is occupationally related.[110] Therefore, it may not always be productive for probation officers to help teenage probationers obtain part-time jobs. Instead, it may be productive to provide teens with "modest" cash incentives to graduate. In one study, such incentives prevented approximately the same amount of crime as a three-strikes law at one-tenth the cost.[111]

This issue is complex. Several programs for older adolescents that included an emphasis on employment or advanced skills training had very positive effects. Krisberg and his colleagues argue that such programs are effective for older teens.[112]

One study confirmed the oft-repeated observation that workers perceive working with delinquent girls to be more difficult than working with delinquent boys. Baines and Alder interviewed youth workers in Victoria, Australia, and found that perceptions of girls were that they were "more 'devious,' 'full of bullshit,' and 'dramatic' contrasted with their understanding of young men as 'open' and 'honest' and therefore easier to engage."[113] A distressing implication of this study is that workers dislike working with girls. Thus, female offenders who have very real and serious needs are not getting the attention and treatment that they need. This is especially distressing given that this "may be a last chance opportunity for many of the young women who are clients of these services."[114]

Another popular idea is that alternative education programs that have distinct school schedules intended for students not doing well in traditional classrooms would be beneficial for delinquents. A recent meta-analysis of alternative schools found that they could have positive effects on school performance and attitude but that they did not reduce delinquent behavior.[115]

Perhaps the most important cautionary note in any discussion of effectiveness is that financial cutbacks often make any debate about effectiveness moot. When state legislators reduce probation budgets, it is simply impossible for probation officers to implement research findings on effective interventions. In California, for example, a report indicated that cutbacks caused caseloads to mushroom to 200 probationers per officer. In response, some offices resorted to computer monitoring of probationers. As a result, the probationers were not receiving any personal contacts or supervision. When there are no funds for probation supervision, all the research on effective interventions becomes meaningless. As one youth told Humes, "Probation isn't worth shit."[116] As noted above, a recent national survey of probation agencies confirmed that declining budgets are a reality for many agencies.[117] On the positive side, the state of Ohio has had success in using financial incentives to encourage counties to send only the most serious offenders to state training schools and to treat less serious youths without committing them to state training schools.[118]

CONTINUING CONCERNS IN COMMUNITY CORRECTIONS

As juvenile court and probation enter into their second century of formal existence since the historic founding of the Illinois juvenile court in 1899, several concerns continue. The concerns discussed in this section include: goal confusion, the no-fault society, restitution, and community service.

• Goal Confusion •

Goal confusion means that judges, probation and aftercare officers, probation directors, state legislators, and juvenile justice experts disagree about the purposes and objectives of juvenile court and community supervision. Part of the reason for such goal confusion is that we have conflicting images of juvenile offenders. At times, we see them as "kids gone wrong"—as victims who are not completely evil. At other times, we see them as "hostile predators" and "full-fledged" criminals.[119] These conflicting images influence how we treat juveniles. Thus, what was once a rather clear institution for supplementing parental concern by means of adult advice and psychological/social work skill has become a matter of controversy. Some courts, officers, and experts still advocate a *parens patriae* and rehabilitation philosophy. In Glaser's (1964) terminology, the emphasis is on assistance to the probationer rather than on controlling the offender.[120] As noted above, however, developments such as "attack probation" treat the juvenile as hostile predator. They indicate that many no longer adhere to a pure assistance model. Advocates of restorative justice argue that it is time to go beyond the stale debates of the past and place new attention on the concerns of the victim. Proponents of the balanced approach would second that suggestion and add that community safety should also be a prime concern.[121]

• Restitution •

Restitution occurs when juvenile offenders pay for all or part of the damage inflicted on crime victims or property. Restitution can take the form of either the payment of money or the performance of work for the victim. Restitution may be part of a victim-offender reconciliation in which the offender and victim meet to express their concerns and feelings. In some cases, probation officers or restitution officers help juveniles find jobs so that they can afford to make restitution payments.

The costs of victimization show the importance of restitution to victims. The average dollar loss for robberies in 2000 was $1,170; the average loss in residential burglaries was $1,381.[122] Although restitution has many positive features, especially concern for the victim, there are some problems. As with adults, some critics think that it is unfair to law-abiding juveniles to help law-breaking youths find jobs. From this viewpoint, job assistance seems like a reward for delinquency. Second, claims made about the amounts of money paid back to victims are often exaggerated. While victims may be told that all of their losses will be recouped, actual restitution often falls short. One study, for example, found that the percentage of youths paying all of the restitution ordered by the judge varied from 40 percent to 88 percent and that judges did not always order full restitution.[123] Another study (of adults) found that 48 percent of the offenders ordered to pay restitution paid it in full, 35 percent paid some, and 17 percent paid none. Moreover, 41 percent paid either nothing or less than half of the restitution ordered in their case.[124] Third, restitution advocates often neglect to consider all of the costs involved in administering a restitution program, such as the salaries of those who oversee the program.

Some evaluation research on restitution has been promising. In one study, in two of four sites, about 10 percent fewer offenders sentenced to restitution recidivated than offenders not ordered to pay restitution.[125] Restitution also resulted in clear suppression effects. Juveniles who were ordered to pay restitution had lower arrest rates in the year after their sentences compared to the year prior to their sentences.[126] A study of more than 7,000 cases handled informally and more than 6,000 cases placed on formal probation in Utah showed that "the use of restitution is associated with significant reductions in recidivism among certain juvenile offenders."[127] In a New Hampshire program cited as a model program by the Office of Juvenile Justice and Delinquency Prevention, more than 80 percent of the offenders completed their community service and restitution obligations. The recidivism rate was below 30 percent.[128] In general, however, restorative justice programs do not appear to have recidivism rates significantly better or worse than traditional criminal justice programs.[129]

Some juveniles have been unable to pay restitution because they could not find jobs or because of family circumstances. To deal with such problems, Utah established a restitution work fund that allows juveniles to work in community service projects. Victims receive restitution from the state fund. Youths have cleaned buses, removed graffiti, cleaned up parks, and worked in public libraries.[130]

• Community Service •

Community service is similar to restitution. It means that offenders perform unpaid work for government or private agencies as payment for crimes without personal victims (e.g., vandalism of public property). Community service could include cutting grass at local parks, doing volunteer work in hospitals, or painting the clubhouse of a Boys Club. Advocates argue that community service helps delinquents realize the extent of the damage they have done and feel as if they have paid their debt to society. Proponents also argue that cost benefits result from the "free" labor of the youths. Critics argue that extensive use of community service could take away jobs from law-abiding citizens and that the actual cost benefits of community service are not as impressive as claimed. More specifically, critics contend that the work done is not always necessary (e.g., the clubhouse did not really need a new coat of paint) and that many hours of community service labor included such nonproductive activities as learning the job, work breaks, and dawdling if an adult supervisor is not constantly watching over the work. These criticisms do not mean that restitution or community service is worthless but that claims about their worth should be realistic rather than exaggerated.

As noted in the earlier discussion of restorative justice, an important question is whether the community service is simply busy work or has some relationship to the delinquent's offense. If a delinquent can see the connection between his or her community service order and the harm done or can see that the community service is a meaningful contribution to the community where he or she lives, then he or she is more likely to see the importance of such service. The youth is more likely to learn something positive from his or her community service assignment rather than see it as a boring burden to finish as quickly as possible. Therefore, community service needs to be taken seriously by both the juvenile justice system and the juvenile so that it is a teaching tool and not just something to keep a youth busy for a few hours a week.

CONCLUSION

The founding of the first juvenile court in Illinois in 1899 marked an era of optimism about our country's ability to deal with juvenile misbehavior. More than a century later, much of that optimism has turned to despair. There are still remnants of paternal and maternal judges and parental probation officers. Juvenile corrections, though, now includes such previously unthought-of programs as blended sentences, boot camps, and tough probation. There are even some who call for the end of the juvenile justice system so that adult criminal court and adult corrections can deal with all offenders.[131]

The direction of juvenile corrections is at a crossroads. It is conceivable that juvenile corrections as we have known it—training schools and social work–oriented probation officers—will soon be relics of history. Developments such as increasing reliance on transfer of violent juveniles to adult court and blended sentencing could be just the first phase of the demise of juvenile justice. On the other hand, rehabilitation researchers have demonstrated that when done right, interventions can be effective and can reduce recidivism significantly. The implementation of the effectiveness literature could mean new life for the rehabilitative ideal with juvenile offenders. Alternatively, the restorative justice movement, already well established in many locales such as Minnesota and Vermont, could expand and perhaps be the new dominant model in juvenile corrections.

The only safe prediction is that juvenile corrections will not be the same as it was 25 years ago. It is likely that changes will continue to multiply as society attempts to minimize youth crime.

▶ Ethics Focus: "Who's There?"

You are a prosecutor in a state that allows juveniles to be tried as adults for crimes such as murder and to be sentenced to an adult prison. A 15-year-old talked two other boys, ages 15 and 14, respectively, into burglarizing the home of a 72-year-old woman who lived alone. The woman woke up during the burglary and shouted "Who's there?" Then she got out of bed and saw the three youths and called out the name of the youth who planned the burglary. She knew him because he had been her paperboy for more than a year and regularly collected payment from her. Panicking, he picked up a fireplace tool and hit her on the head several times. She died almost instantly.

How do you handle this case? Would you prosecute all three youths in juvenile court? In adult court? Would you seek life without parole (the most severe possible penalty for a juvenile) for any of the youths? What possible mitigating factors would lead you to be more lenient in this case? What aggravating factors would influence you to be more severe?

►At the Movies ....

Bad Boys, 2001.

This movie, starring Sean Penn and Esai Morales and directed by Rick Rosenthal, tells the story of life in a juvenile prison. It deals with youths hardened by a life of crime, especially drug abuse and sales, at a young age.

Orphans, 1987.

This film, starring Albert Finney, Matthew Modine, and Kevin Anderson, is about how a gangster saves two orphaned juvenile delinquents by becoming a father figure for both of them.

DISCUSSION QUESTIONS

1. Many are calling for harsher punishment for juvenile offenders, especially violent juvenile offenders. Do you think that persons holding that position are aware of the information on victimization in juvenile training schools (prisons)? Would knowledge of victimization risks in juvenile prisons affect calls for tougher measures for juveniles?

2. Do juveniles deserve prisons that are different from adult offenders? Should we continue to model juvenile prisons after schools? Should we drop any pretense of lesser punishment for juveniles and make juvenile facilities similar to adult prisons?

3. Would you consider a career in juvenile corrections, either prisons or community corrections? Why or why not?

4. What measures should community corrections take to best serve juveniles? Give specific suggestions.

5. Should community corrections for juveniles go back to its roots and try to emphasize rehabilitation, or should it attempt to incorporate more punitive dimensions? Do advocates of restorative justice or the balanced approach have the answer to the question of how can we make juvenile probation better? What would the ideal probation program for juveniles look like?

6. How do you envision the future of juvenile corrections? What will juvenile prisons and probation look like a decade from now?

FURTHER READING

Kozol, J. (1995). *Amazing Grace: The Lives of Children and the Conscience of a Nation*. New York: Harper Perennial.

Kozol, J. (2005). *The Shame of the Nation: The Restoration of Apartheid Schooling in America*. New York: Crown.

NOTES

1. Snyder and Sickmund, 2006
2. McGarvey, 2005. The three states for which information was available were Maryland, Missouri, and California.
3. Snyder and Sickmund, 2006.
4. Singer, 1996.
5. Wooden, 1976.
6. Bilchik, 1998.
7. Snyder and Sickmund, 2006.
8. Snyder and Sickmund, 2006.
9. Cronin, 1994.
10. Cronin, 1994.
11. MacKenzie, 1994, 66.
12. Peters, Thomas, and Zamberlan, 1997.
13. Peters, Thomas, and Zamberlan, 1997.
14. National Association of State Budget Officers, 1999.
15. Peters, Thomas, and Zamberlan, 1997.
16. Clear, 1994.
17. Cullen and Wright, 1995.
18. *U.S. News and World Report*, 2006, 18.
19. Snyder and Sickmund, 2006.
20. Lipsey, 1992.
21. Lipsey and Wilson, 1998, 336.
22. Lundman, 1993.
23. Lundman, 1993.
24. Lundman, 1993.
25. Lipsey and Wilson, 1998.
26. Wooden, 1976, 101.
27. Singer, 1996.
28. Bortner and Williams, 1997, 112.

29. Shufelt and Cocozza, 2006.

30. Shufelt and Cocozza, 2006.

31. Shufelt and Cocozza, 2006

32. Shufelt and Cocozza, 2006, 4.

33. Bowker, 1980, 47.

34. Bartollas and Sieverdes, 1981, 538.

35. Giallombardo, 1974, 160.

36. Singer, 1996.

37. Snyder and Sickmund, 2006. (*Juvenile Offenders and Victims: 2006 National Report*, 230)

38. Abt Associates, 1994.

39. Sickmund, 2006.

40. Abt Associates, 1994.

41. Abt Associates, 1994, 111.

42. Acoca, 1998.

43. Bartollas and Sieverdes, 1981, 538.

44. Bartollas and Sieverdes, 1981, 541.

45. Bortner and Williams, 1997.

46. Snyder and Sickmund, 2006.

47. Sieverdes and Bartollas, 1986, 137.

48. Sieverdes and Bartollas, 1986, 143.

49. Feld, 1981, 336.

50. Feld, 1981.

51. Giallombardo, 1974, 244.

52. Giallombardo, 1974.

53. Propper, 1982.

54. Goffman, 1961, 199.

55. Giallombardo, 1974, 242.

56. Abt Associates, 1994.

57. Puritz and Scali, 1998.

58. Bortner and Williams, 1997, 3.

59. Snyder and Sickmund, 2006.

60. Sickmund, 2002.

61. Krisberg and Austin, 1993.

62. Krisberg, Austin and Steele, 1989.

63. Gottfredson and Barton, 1993, 604.

64. Snyder and Sickmund, 2006.

65. Maitland and Sluder, 1998, 68.

66. Bishop, 2000, 153.

67. Lipsey and Wilson, 1998.

68. Wilson and Lipsey, 2003; MacKenzie, 2006.

69. Puzzanchera et al., 2000.

70. Torbet, 1996.

71. Schwartz et al., 1987.

72. Altschuler, Armstrong, and MacKenzie, 1999.

73. Wiebush, McNulty, and Le, 2000.

74. Glaser, 1964.

75. Studt, 1973.

76. For more information on counseling techniques, see Van Voorhis, Braswell, and Lester, 2007.

77. Chavaria, 1997.

78. Gendreau, Cullen, and Bonta, 1994.

79. Kurlychek, Torbet, and Bozynski, 1999.

80. Bilchik, 1998.

81. Kurlychek, Torbet, and Bozynski, 1999.

82. Howell and Hawkins, 1998.

83. Miller, 1996, 131.

84. Garry, 1996.

85. Bazemore and Maloney, 1994, 28.

86. Kurki, 2000, 266.

87. Bazemore and Maloney, 1994, 29.

88. Hsia, 1997.

89. Bazemore and Maloney, 1994, 29.

90. Bazemore and Maloney, 1994, 29.

91. Kurki, 2000.

92. Kurki, 2000.

93. Levrant, Cullen, and Wozniak, 1999.

94. Lozoff and Braswell, 1989, 2.

95. Braswell, Fuller, and Lozoff, 2001.

96. Cullen, Wright, and Applegate, 1996.

97. For a list of studies showing this, see Krisberg and Howell, 1998, 361.

98. Lipsey and Wilson, 1998.

99. Petersilia et al., 1985.

100. Whitehead, 1991.

101. Petersilia, 1997.

102. Altschuler, 1998.

103. National Council on Crime and Delinquency, 1987.

104. Petersilia, 1997.

105. Sealock, Gottfredson, and Gallagher, 1997.

106. Gendreau, 1996.

107. Gendreau, 1996.

108. Duffee and Carlson, 1996.

109. Wright, Cullen, and Williams, 1997, 215.

110. Wright and Cullen, 2000.

111. Wright, Cullen, and Williams, 1997; see also Ploeger, 1997.

112. Krisberg et al., 1995.

113. Baines and Alder, 1996, 481.

114. Baines and Alder, 1996, 483.

115. Cox, Davidson, and Bynum, 1995.

116. Humes, 1996, 18.

117. Lindner and Bonn, 1996.

118. Moon, Applegate, and Latessa, 1997.

119. Morse, 1999.

120. Glaser, 1964.

121. Umbreit, 1986.

122. Federal Bureau of Investigation, 2000.

123. Schneider and Schneider, 1984.

124. Outlaw and Ruback, 1999.

125. Schneider, 1986.

126. Schneider, 1990.

127. Butts and Snyder, 1992, 4.

128. Allen, 1994.

129. Kurki, 2000.

130. Kurlychek, Torbet, and Bozynski, 1999.

131. Feld, 1993.

REFERENCES

Abt Associates (1994). "Conditions of Confinement: Juvenile Detention and Corrections Facilities: Research Report." *Bureau of Justice Statistics Bulletin.* Washington, DC: U.S. Government Printing Office.

Acoca, L. (1998). "Outside/Inside: The Violation of American Girls at Home, on the Streets, and in the Juvenile Justice System." *Crime & Delinquency* 44:561-589.

Allen, P. (1994). "OJJDP Model Programs 1993." *Bureau of Justice Statistics Bulletin.* Washington, DC: U.S. Government Printing Office.

Altschuler, D.M. (1998). "Intermediate Sanctions and Community Treatment for Serious and Violent Juvenile Offenders." In R. Loeber and D.P. Farrington (eds.), *Serious and Violent Juvenile Offenders: Risk Factors and Successful Interventions,* 367-385. Thousand Oaks, CA: Sage.

Altschuler, D.M., T.L. Armstrong, and D.L. MacKenzie (1999). "Reintegration, Supervised Release, and Intensive Aftercare." *Juvenile Justice Bulletin.* Washington, DC: U.S. Department of Justice.

Baines, M., and C. Alder (1996). "Are Girls More Difficult to Work With? Youth Workers' Perspectives in Juvenile Justice and Related Areas." *Crime & Delinquency* 42:467-485.

Bartollas, C.L., and C.M. Sieverdes (1981). "The Victimized White in a Juvenile Correctional System." *Crime & Delinquency* 27:534-543.

Bazemore, G., and D. Maloney (1994). "Rehabilitating Community Service: Toward Restorative Service Sanctions in a Balanced Justice System." *Federal Probation* 58(1):24-35.

Bilchik, S. (1998). "A Juvenile Justice System for the 21st Century." *Bureau of Justice Statistics Bulletin.* Washington, DC: U.S. Government Printing Office.

Bishop, D.M. (2000). "Juvenile Offenders in the Adult Criminal Justice System." In M. Tonry (ed.), *Crime and Justice: A Review of Research* (Vol. 27), 81-167. Chicago: University of Chicago Press.

Bortner M.A., and L.M. Williams (1997). *Youth in Prison: We the People of Unit Four.* New York: Routledge.

Bowker, L.H. (1980). *Prison Victimization.* New York: Elsevier.

Braswell, M., J. Fuller, and B. Lozoff (2001). *Corrections, Peacemaking, and Restorative Justice.* Cincinnati: Anderson.

Butts, J.A., and H.N. Snyder (1992). "Restitution and Juvenile Recidivism." *Bureau of Justice Statistics Bulletin.* Washington, DC: U.S. Government Printing Office.

Chavaria, F.P. (1997). "Probation and Cognitive Skills." *Federal Probation* 61:57-60.

Clear, T.R. (1994). *Harm in American Penology: Offenders, Victims, and Their Communities.* Albany, NY: SUNY Press.

Cox, S.M., W.S. Davidson, and T.S. Bynum (1995). "A Meta-Analytic Assessment of Delinquency-Related Outcomes of Alternative Education Programs." *Crime & Delinquency* 41:219-234.

Cronin, R.C. (1994). *Boot Camps for Adult and Juvenile Offenders: Overview and Update.* Washington, DC: National Institute of Justice.

Cullen, F.T., and J.P. Wright (1995). "The Future of Corrections." In B. Maguire and P. Radosh (eds.), *The Past, Present, and Future of American Criminal Justice,* 198-219. New York: General Hall.

Cullen, F.T., J.P. Wright, and B.K. Applegate (1996). "Control in the Community: The Limits of Reform?" In A.T. Harland (ed.), *Choosing Correctional Options That Work: Defining the Demand and Evaluating the Supply*, 69-116. Thousand Oaks, CA: Sage.

Duffee, D.E., and B.E. Carlson (1996). "Competing Value Premises for the Provision of Drug Treatment to Probationers." *Crime & Delinquency* 42:574-592.

Federal Bureau of Investigation (2000). *Uniform Crime Reports: Crime in the United States*. Available at http://www.fbi.gov/ucr/00cius.htm

Feld, B. (1993). *Justice for Children: The Right to Counsel and the Juvenile Courts*. Boston: Northeastern University Press.

Feld, B.C. (1981). "Legislative Policies Toward the Serious Juvenile Offender: On the Virtues of Automatic Adulthood." *Crime & Delinquency* 27:497-521.

Garry, E.M. (1996). "Truancy: First Step to a Lifetime of Problems." *Bureau of Justice Statistics Bulletin*. Washington, DC: U.S. Government Printing Office.

Gendreau, P. (1996). "The Principles of Effective Intervention with Offenders." In A.T. Harland (ed.), *Choosing Correctional Options That Work: Defining the Demand and Evaluating the Supply*, 117-130. Thousand Oaks, CA: Sage.

Gendreau, P., F.T. Cullen, and J. Bonta (1994). "Intensive Rehabilitation Supervision: The Next Generation in Community Corrections?" *Federal Probation* 58(1):72-78.

Giallombardo, R. (1974). *The Social World of Imprisoned Girls*. New York: Wiley.

Glaser, D. (1964). *The Effectiveness of a Prison and Parole System*. Indianapolis: Bobbs-Merrill.

Goffman, E. (1961). *Asylums: Essays on the Social Situation of Mental Patients and Other Inmates*. New York: Anchor.

Gottfredson, D.C., and W.H. Barton (1993). "Deinstitutionalization of Juvenile Offenders." *Criminology* 31:591-611.

Howell, J.C., and J.D. Hawkins (1998). "Prevention of Youth Violence." In M. Tonry and M.H. Moore (eds.), *Youth Violence*, 189-261. Chicago: University of Chicago Press.

Hsia, H.M. (1997). "Allegheny County, PA: Mobilizing to Reduce Juvenile Crime." *Bureau of Justice Statistics Bulletin*. Washington, DC: U.S. Government Printing Office.

Humes, E. (1996). *No Matter How Loud I Shout: A Year in the Life of Juvenile Court*. New York: Simon and Schuster.

Karp, D.R. (1998). "The Judicial and Judicious Use of Shame Penalties." *Crime & Delinquency* 44:277-294.

Krisberg, B., and J. Austin (1993). *Reinventing Juvenile Justice*. Newbury Park, CA: Sage.

Krisberg, B., J. Austin, and P.A. Steele (1989). *Unlocking Juvenile Corrections: Evaluating the Massachusetts Department of Youth Services*. San Francisco: National Council on Crime and Delinquency.

Krisberg, B., E. Currie, D. Onek, and R.G. Wiebush (1995). *Unlocking Juvenile Corrections: Evaluating the Massachusetts Department of Youth Services*. San Francisco: National Council on Crime and Delinquency.

Krisberg, B., and J.C. Howell (1998). "The Impact of the Juvenile Justice System and Prospects for Graduated Sanctions in a Comprehensive Strategy." In R. Loeber and D.P. Farrington (eds.), *Serious and Violent Juvenile Offenders: Risk Factors and Successful Interventions*, 313-345. Thousand Oaks, CA: Sage.

Kurki, L. (2000). "Restorative and Community Justice in the United States." In M. Tonry (ed.), *Crime and Justice: A Review of Research* 27:235-303.

Kurlychek, M., P.M. Torbet, and M. Bozynski (1999). "Focus on Accountability: Best Practices for Juvenile Court and Probation." *Bureau of Justice Statistics Bulletin*. Washington, DC: U.S. Government Printing Office.

Levrant, S., F.T. Cullen, and J.F. Wozniak (1999). "Reconsidering Restorative Justice: The Corruption of Benevolence Revisited?" *Crime & Delinquency* 45:3-27.

Lindner, C., and R.L. Bonn (1996). "Probation Officer Victimization and Fieldwork Practices: Results of a National Study." *Federal Probation* 60(2):16-23.

Lipsey, M.W. (1992). "Juvenile Delinquency Treatment: A Meta-Analytic Inquiry into the Viability of Effects." In T. Cook, H. Cooper, D. Corday, H. Harman, L. Hedges, R. Light, T. Louis, and F. Mosteller (eds.), *Meta-Analysis for Explanation: A Casebook*, 83-127. New York: Russell Sage Foundation.

Lipsey, M.W., and D.B. Wilson (1998). "Effective Intervention for Serious Juvenile Offenders: A Synthesis of Research." In R. Loeber and D.P. Farrington (eds.), *Serious and Violent Juvenile Offenders: Risk Factors and Successful Interventions*, 313-345. Thousand Oaks, CA: Sage.

Lozoff, B., and M. Braswell (1989). *Inner Corrections: Finding Peace and Peace Making*. Cincinnati: Anderson.

Lundman. R.J. (1993). *Prevention and Control of Juvenile Delinquency*, 2nd ed. New York: Oxford.

MacKenzie, D.L. (1994). "Results of a Multisite Study of Boot Camp Prisons." *Federal Probation* 58(2):60-66.

MacKenzie, D.L. (2006). *What Works in Corrections: Reducing the Criminal Activities of Offenders and Delinquents*. New York: Cambridge University Press.

Maitland, A.S., and R.D. Sluder (1998). "Victimization and Youthful Prison Inmates: An Empirical Analysis." *The Prison Journal* 78:55-73.

McGarvey, A. (2005). "A Culture of Caring." *Prospect* (September):A12-A14.

Miller, J.G. (1996). *Search and Destroy: African-American Males in the Criminal Justice System*. New York: Cambridge University Press.

Moon, M.M., B.K. Applegate, and E.J. Latessa (1997). "RECLAIM Ohio: A Politically Viable Alternative to Treating Youthful Felony Offenders." *Crime & Delinquency* 43:438-456.

Morse, S. (1999). "Delinquency and Desert." *Annals of the American Academy of Political and Social Science* 564:56-80.

National Association of State Budget Officers (1999). "State Juvenile Justice Expenditures and Innovations." Available at http://www.nasbo.org/Publications/information_briefs/juvenile_expend_1999.html

National Council on Crime and Delinquency (1987). *The Impact of Juvenile Court Sanctions: A Court That Works: Executive Summary*. San Francisco: National Council on Crime and Delinquency.

Outlaw, M.C., and R.B. Ruback (1999). "Predictors and Outcomes of Victim Restitution Orders." *Justice Quarterly* 16:847-869.

Peters, M., D. Thomas, and C. Zamberlan (1997). "Boot Camps for Juvenile Offenders: Program Summary." *Bureau of Justice Statistics Bulletin*. Washington, DC: U.S. Government Printing Office.

Petersilia, J. (1997). "Probation in the United States." In M. Tonry (ed.), *Crime and Justice: A Review of Research* (Vol. 22), 149-200. Chicago: University of Chicago Press.

Petersilia, J., S. Turner, J. Kahan, and J. Peterson (1985). "Executive Summary of Rand's Study, 'Granting Felons Probation: Public Risks and Alternatives.'" *Crime & Delinquency* 3:379-392.

Ploeger, M. (1997). "Youth Employment and Delinquency: Reconsidering a Problematic Relationship." *Criminology* 35:659-675.

Propper, A.M. (1982). "Make-Believe Families and Homosexuality among Imprisoned Girls." *Criminology* 20:127-138.

Puritz, P., and M.A. Scali (1998). *Beyond the Walls: Improving Conditions of Confinement for Youth in Custody*. Washington, DC: U.S. Department of Justice.

Puzzanchera, C., A.L. Stahl, T.A. Finnegan, H.N. Snyder, R.S. Poole, and N. Tierney (2000). *Juvenile Court Statistics 1997*. Pittsburgh: National Center for Juvenile Justice.

Schneider, A.L. (1990). *Deterrence and Juvenile Crime: Results from a National Policy Experiment*. New York: Springer-Verlag.

Schneider, A.L. (1986). "Restitution and Recidivism Rates of Juvenile Offenders: Results from Four Experimental Studies." *Criminology* 24:533-552.

Schneider, A.L., and P.R. Schneider (1984). "A Comparison of Programmatic and Ad Hoc Restitution in Juvenile Courts." *Justice Quarterly* 1:529-547.

Schwartz, I.M., G. Fishman, R. Rawson Hatfield, B.A. Krisberg, and Z. Eisikovits (1987). "Juvenile Detention: The Hidden Closets Revisited." *Justice Quarterly* 4:219-235.

Sealock, M.D., D.C. Gottfredson, and C.A. Gallagher (1997). "Delinquency and Social Reform: A Radical Perspective." In L. Empey (ed.), *Juvenile Justice*, 245-290. Charlottesville: University of Virginia Press.

Shufelt, J.S., and J.C. Cocozza, (2006). *Youth with Mental Health Disorders in the Juvenile Justice System: Results from a Multi- State Prevalence Study*. Delmar, NY: National Center for Mental Health and Juvenile Justice.

Sickmund, M. (2002). *Juvenile Offenders in Residential Placement: 1997-1999*. Washington, DC: U.S. Department of Justice.

Sickmund, M. (2006). *Juvenile Residential Facility Census, 2002: Selected Findings*. Washington, DC: U.S. Department of Justice, Office of Juvenile Justice and Delinquency Prevention.

Sieverdes, C., and C. Bartollas (1986). "Security Level and Adjustment Patterns in Juvenile Institutions." *Journal of Criminal Justice* 14:135-145.

Singer, S.I. (1996). *Recriminalizing Delinquency: Violent Juvenile Crime and Juvenile Justice Reform.* New York: Cambridge University Press.

Smith, B. (1998). "Children in Custody: 20-Year Trends in Juvenile Detention, Correctional, and Shelter Facilities." *Crime & Delinquency* 44:526-543.

Snyder, H.N., and M. Sickmund (2006). *Juvenile Offenders and Victims: 2006 National Report.* Washington DC: Office of Juvenile Justice and Delinquency Prevention.

Studt, E. (1973). *Surveillance and Service in Parole: A Report of the Parole Action Study.* Washington DC: National Institute of Corrections.

Torbet, P.M. (1996). "Juvenile Probation: The Workhorse of the Juvenile Justice System." *Bureau of Justice Statistics Bulletin.* Washington, DC: U.S. Department of Justice.

Umbreit, M.S. (1986). "Victim/Offender Mediation: A National Survey." *Federal Probation* 50(4):53-56.

U.S. News and World Report, "Florida Boots Harsh Tactics." (May, 8, 2006):18.

Van Voorhis, P., M. Braswell, and D. Lester (2007). *Correctional Counseling and Rehabilitation,* 6th ed. Newark, NJ: LexisNexis Matthew Bender.

von Hirsch, A. (1990). "The Ethics of Community-Based Sanctions." *Crime & Delinquency* 36:162-173.

Whitehead, J.T. (1991). "The Effectiveness of Felony Probation: Results from an Eastern State." *Justice Quarterly* 8:525-543.

Wiebush, R.G., B. McNulty, and T. Le (2000). "Implementation of the Intensive Community-Based Aftercare Program." *Bureau of Justice Statistics Bulletin.* Washington, DC: U.S. Government Printing Office.

Wilson, S.J., and M.W. Lipsey (2003). "Wilderness Challenge Programs for Delinquent Youth: A Meta-Analysis of Outcome Evaluations." *Evaluation and Program Planning,* 23:1-12.

Wooden, K. (1976). *Weeping in the Playtime of Others: America's Incarcerated Children.* New York: McGraw-Hill.

Wright, J.P., and F.T. Cullen (2000). "Juvenile Involvement in Occupational Delinquency." *Criminology* 38:863-896.

Wright, J.P, F.T. Cullen, and N. Williams (1997). "Working While in School and Delinquent Involvement: Implications for Social Policy." *Crime & Delinquency* 43:203-221.

Special Populations in Prisons

CHAPTER 10

What You Need to Know

▶ Approximately half of state and federal inmates have some sort of mental illness. Mental illness is more prevalent among jail and prison populations than the rest of society.

▶ There are distinctions concerning mental illness, insanity, and incompetence. Mentally ill prisoners are prisoners diagnosed with a mental illness; the focus is on dealing with their adjustment in prison. Insanity is a legal term that refers to the offender's mental status and criminal responsibility at the time of the crime. Incompetence r efers to a defendant's ability to stand trial.

▶ A major reason for the increase in the number of mentally ill persons in jails and prisons is the closing of state mental hospitals.

▶ Mentally challenged inmates may have problems with other prisoners, along with personal hygiene and coping problems.

▶ About half of both state and federal prisoners used drugs in the month before their crime. About one-third of state inmates and one-quarter of federal inmates used drugs at the time of their offense.

▶ Outcomes for drug treatment in criminal justice settings have been positive.

▶ Medical problems that are especially problematic in prison are tuberculosis and HIV/AIDS.

▶ Most states mainstream inmates with HIV/AIDS. Screening is an important issue in this area.

▶ One estimate is that 33 percent of prisoners will be older than age 50 in the next few years. As a result, prison officials will need to respond to the special needs of elderly offenders.

▶ Prison officials must also cope with terminally ill offenders.

▶ Sex offenders make up about 10 percent of the state prison population but only about 1 percent of the federal prison population.

▶ Psychological therapy and biomedical treatment are two main forms of therapy used for sex offenders.

INTRODUCTION

While there have always been inmates with special needs, increasing rates of incarceration and longer sentences have created a substantial percentage of the prison population with a diverse set of problems and challenges. How correctional professionals meet these challenges will set the tone for the success of the correctional system in the coming years. The prison population is aging, and more women are going to prison. Medical and mental health problems such as HIV and tuberculosis are confronting correctional institutions. While often ignored, the challenges of special populations will require greater investment in training and resources for correctional institutions.

In this chapter, we confront the challenges that special populations pose for the correctional system. These special populations include inmates who are medically ill, mentally retarded or developmentally disabled, mentally ill, elderly, terminally ill, or substance-abusing, as well as sex offenders. Each of these groups poses its own set of challenges for corrections in the twenty-first century.

MENTALLY ILL OFFENDERS

The growth in the number of jail detainees and inmates with mental disorders is receiving greater attention. Torrey suggests that jails and prisons now hold twice the number of mentally ill individuals as do state mental hospitals.[1] The 1970s movement to deinstitutionalize mentally ill individuals from state psychiatric hospitals in favor of community treatment programs is often cited as a factor behind the growth in numbers of mentally ill in jails and prisons. Beds in psychiatric facilities have decreased while the number of mentally ill housed in jails and prisons has increased. This shift from mental institutions to jails and prisons has been termed "transinstitutionalization."[2] According to the Bureau of Justice Statistics (BJS), 56 percent of all state prison inmates, 45 percent of all federal inmates, and 64 percent of all jail inmates as of June 30, 2005, had some sort of mental health problem.[3] Similar findings have been reported by others.[4]

Determining an accurate census of mentally ill inmates housed in our jails and prisons is not an easy task because results are impacted by the various definitions of the behavior being considered and the criteria used. Different perspectives may evolve over differences between a diagnosis of mental illness, estimates of prevalence of such disorders, or consideration of those who are criminally insane. Mental disorders are determined by assessments made through the use of psychological tests and clinical interviews that result in a diagnosis conforming to the criteria outlined in the Diagnostic and Statistical Manual of Mental Disorders-IV (DSM-IV).[5] DSM-IV, the "Bible" of mental health diagnosis,[6] provides a multiaxial framework for the diagnosis of mental illness along several dimensions. The 16 major diagnostic groups it provides are used by mental health personnel to classify an individual's behavior and, therefore, determine the appropriate treatment plan. Carbonell and Perkins provide an excellent overview of DSM-IV diagnoses of interest to corrections.[7]

The public sometimes becomes confused about the terminology used in the criminal justice system when dealing with mental illness and issues of insanity. Insanity is not a medical nor a psychiatric concept. It is a creation of our criminal justice system by which courts determine the status of an offender. "Insanity" is a legal term describing an offender who meets specified criteria that vary by jurisdiction. The use of insanity as a defense is a rare occurrence in our criminal justice system.[8] The use of the defense occurs at the rate of about one in every 200 cases, and its success is even less likely, as only one in four of insanity defenses meets with success.[9]

Competency to stand trial is sometimes an issue with the mentally disordered offender. Offenders who are retarded, psychotic, or suffering other mental conditions that prevent them from assisting in their defense, or those who do not understand their criminal charges, may be deemed incompetent to stand trial. While information from mental health professionals may be used in determining whether an offender is incompetent to stand trial, the determination of that status rests with the court. The finding of "not guilty by reason of insanity" (NGRI) also rests with the court, and it generally means that the offender lacks the mental capacity to understand that the behavior was wrong. The individual does not deny the behavior in question; instead, the behavior is explained as occurring because of mental illness. It is important, however, to recall that NGRI pleas are seldom successful.[10]

"Guilty but mentally ill" (GBMI) is a verdict that addresses public concern that NGRI offenders will avoid sanctions for their crimes. A GBMI verdict provides for a finding of guilty while recognizing the need for mental health treatment. If ruled GBMI, the offender receives a prison sentence, and, depending on the jurisdiction and his or her mental status, may receive treatment in a mental health unit within a prison or at a forensic hospital. Callahan and her associates found that those who pleaded insanity but were found GBMI actually received harsher sentences when compared to those found guilty at trial, thereby leading to the conclusion that reform efforts in Georgia to bring about change in the NGRI defense by implementing the GBMI verdict will become a less-than-desirable option for the mentally ill in the criminal justice system.[11]

Recent studies now contradict earlier findings suggesting that the prevalence of mental disorders occurring among inmate populations was less than that for the general population.[12] Studies now reveal that "individuals with major mental disorders are far more prevalent within correctional facilities than had been previously assumed."[13] For example, in a review of studies on mental illness and violent behavior, Monahan reported that "the prevalence of schizophrenia is approximately 3 times higher in the jail and prison samples than in the general population samples, the prevalence of major depression 3-4 times higher, [and] the prevalence of mania or bi-polar disorder 7-14 times higher."[14] Hodgins reported that among male schizophrenic inmates the prevalence of antisocial personality disorder was approximately 63 percent, more than twice the percentage (27%) found in a similar sample discharged from psychiatric hospitals.[15] The prevalence of mental disorders among juveniles has been reported to be higher than that of the general population.[16] Link, Andrews, and Cullen have also reported that mental patients had higher rates of illegal behavior, as compared to a community sample.[17]

The difference in the prevalence of mental disorders among men and women is also striking. In a study of 7,039 women and 7,362 men, Hodgins looked at the criminal behavior of those with and without mental disorders.[18] Compared to those without a mental disorder, men with a mental disorder were two and one-half times as likely to have a criminal record, and women were five times as likely to have a criminal record. In Hodgins's study, criminal behavior generally preceded the identification of a mental disorder. Higher rates of mental illness in female inmate populations also have been reported.[19] Levels of depression among female inmates, as measured by the Center for Epidemiologic Studies' Depression Scale,[20] have been found to be twice the levels reported for samples of women in the general population.[21] Such a finding may be related to the incarceration status of the women. In addition, Fogel and Martin found that the mental health status, in terms of levels of anxiety, differed between female inmate mothers and nonmothers.[22] Nonmothers' levels of anxiety dropped significantly after six months of incarceration whereas the level of anxiety for inmate mothers changed very little. Thus, the mental health status of women may be impacted by their role as well as by the prison environment.

Some investigators have looked at the prevalence of mental disorders among those committing homicide. In a comparison of those convicted of homicide and those convicted of other types of crimes, Cote and Hodgins found a higher prevalence of major mental disorders among those convicted of homicide, and the disorder was present prior to the criminal behavior.[23] Contrary to his earlier conclusions, Monahan reported that mental illness may be a risk factor in violent behavior.[24]

The prediction of dangerousness has long been an issue in corrections. The concern about accurately predicting violent behavior among releasees who are mentally disturbed presents additional challenges.[25]

Identifying variables that impact violent recidivism has not met with much success.[26] However, recent efforts at creating statistical prediction instruments for violent recidivism by mentally disordered offenders have shown some promise.[27]

The issue of co-occurring disorders has generated recent interest. Multiple disorders were present more often among those convicted of criminal homicide than among other types of offenders.[28] Furthermore, inmates with mental illness experienced co-occurring disorders, and those combined disorders were related to the inmate's criminality.[29] Hodgins and Cote reported that among male offenders with a diagnosis of a major mental disorder, many had a concurrent antisocial personality disorder (APD) with a history of childhood criminal acts and antisocial behavior.[30]

BOX 10.1

The National GAINS Center for People with Co-occurring Disorders in the Justice System

Created in 1995, the GAINS Center is a federal partnership between the two centers of the Substance Abuse and Mental Health Services Administration (the Center for Substance Abuse Treatment and the Center for Mental Health Services) and the National Institute of Corrections. It is operated by Policy Research Inc. in conjunction with the Florida Mental Health Institute at the University of South Florida. The GAINS Center collects information on mental health and substance abuse activities in the criminal justice system and provides technical assistance to local jurisdictions in implementing programs. The acronym GAINS translates into the following: *Gathering* information, *Assessing* what works, *Interpreting* the facts, *Networking* the key stakeholders, and *Stimulating* change. The Center maintains a database and provides information to assist in implementing programs for those who have several mental health issues occurring simultaneously, including those coming into contact with the criminal justice system who are substance abusers and who have a mental illness or who have multiple mental health diagnoses. For example, the Center assists with developing alternatives to jail diversion for those with mental illnesses by bringing together key personnel, analyzing costs, creating liaisons, and creating databases for managing this population. In addition, the GAINS Center looks at the issue of co-occurring disorders of women who may have histories of trauma and violence; health issues such as STDs, HIV, or pregnancy; and mental illness and substance abuse. They have proposed a model for involving families of those with co-occurring disorders in addressing the needs of this special population. For additional information, contact: The GAINS Center, 262 Delaware Avenue, Delmar, NY 12054. E-mail: gains@prainc.com

Those with APD initiated their criminal activities earlier in their lives than mentally disordered offenders without APD. There is an increasing risk of crime for those with mental disorders and a co-occurring antisocial personality disorder.[31] The GAINS Center is a federal partnership that provides technical assistance and research on treating people in the criminal justice system who have co-occurring disorders (see Box 10.1).[32]

While the data indicate that prisons and jails are housing more people with mental disorders, there are challenges to making accurate diagnoses of those with a disorder. The possibility of improperly identifying those inmates with mental disorders was noted in a British study of adult male prisoners at the reception center. Researchers found that 26 percent ($n = 148$) of a sample of 569 had one or more psychiatric disorders, excluding substance abuse but including 24 prisoners who were found to be acute psychotics.[33] When substance abuse or dependency was included, the percentage with current mental disorders rose to 62 percent ($n = 354$). However, prison personnel's assessments were not consistent with these numbers. Personnel identified only 34 as having a mental disorder (about one-fourth of those identified by the researchers). Moreover, of the 24 identified as acutely psychotic by the research team, prison officials identified only six. Additionally, prison officials diagnosed a mental disorder in 18 inmates who the researchers found to be without mental illness. Thus, prison officials did not properly identify mental illness in inmates, and according to the researchers, attributed mental illness to inmates who were not mentally ill.[34] It appears that in prison settings abnormal behavior was tolerated and at times ignored.

The problem of feigning mental illness has also been raised as an issue in prison settings. Fauteck suggested using of a battery of assessment instruments, versus relying on a single instrument, if malingering is a question.[35] Additionally, when treatment is the objective, timing of the assessment is an important consideration. Hodgins suggested that proper screening at intake is needed in order to provide proper mental health services because studies indicate that prior mental health treatment is not a good indicator of who currently needs assistance.[36] Likewise, assessment after apprehension would not meet the objectives of determining the need for services once the offender is sentenced to imprisonment. Distinguishing the truly disturbed inmate who needs treatment from the malingerer may present challenges to traditionally trained correctional workers. Separating issues of confinement (such as inmate-to-inmate conflict) from reactions evolving from emotional problems such as depression or other mental illness will enable mental health counselors to use institutional resources properly.[37]

Another issue faced by correctional institutions is the increase in the number of individuals in jail who are mentally ill. Jails have become the alternative to state mental health hospitals that faced deinstitutionalization of their clientele with a national movement sponsored by the 1974

Mental Health Act. Communities seem to be relying on the criminal justice system, especially jails, as a source of beds for the mentally ill.[38] Palermo, Gumz, and Liska found that between 1955 and 1985 the average number of mentally ill in state hospitals decreased by two-thirds while the number of mentally ill in jails increased two-and one-half times.[39] Solomon and Draine reported that approximately 50 percent of those with a mental disorder are arrested at least once.[40]

Teplin, in studies of jail detainees in an urban jail, reported that 6.1 percent of the males and 15 percent of the females had serious mental disorders at the time of admission to the jail.[41] Morris, Steadman, and Versey estimated that 700,000 new arrivals annually at jails have severe or acute mental illness.[42] O'Sullivan reported that the Los Angeles County Jail houses approximately 3,600 individuals who are mentally ill, a number that exceeds the total population of California's four state psychiatric hospitals.[43] It should be kept in mind that, in 1998, 57 percent of jail detainees were in pretrial status. While many jails provide at least some mental health services, there is a lack of comprehensive mental health services in jails.[44] Frequently, a lack of proper budgeting, or perhaps a lack of understanding of the issues facing jails, impedes the proper delivery of services. In spite of the current dilemmas facing jails due to the growth in mental health detainees, Morris and her colleagues, have identified some innovative programs in the areas of mental health services.[45] They include:

1. Screening, evaluation, and classification (e.g., use of multitiered screening and evaluation at Summit County Jail, in Akron, Ohio, and the use of Fairfax County Jail deputies working in classification who were specially trained in mental health and in making referrals);

2. Crisis intervention and short-term treatment practices (e.g., use of intervention specialists at Shelby County Jail, in Memphis, Tennessee, and participatory suicide prevention in which inmate observers are used to monitor inmates at the Jefferson County Jail, in Louisville, Kentucky, under a private contractor's program);

3. Discharge planning, the weakest element of all programs (e.g., Fairfax County Jail, which aids detainees in maintaining family ties and has utilized the well-trained staff members of the county's Offender Aid and Restoration program to provide assistance to detainees from intake to discharge);

4. Court liaison mechanisms (e.g., Pinellas County Jail in Clearwater, Florida, which has a doctoral-level forensic social worker supervisor and three masters-level forensic social workers who identify detainees who need short-term civil commitment in lieu of incarceration, thereby diverting from the criminal justice system those who need treatment);

5. Contracting mental health services (e.g., contracting with the community psychiatry program at nearby medical universities for rotations in the jail as was done at Henrico County, Virginia, or using a private national healthcare provider for services and for ensuring compliance with accreditation and staffing requirements.[46]

Successful diversion of mentally ill patients from jails has been found when the following elements were in place:

1. community-level coordination of services with regularly occurring meetings

2. leadership by one of the staff members involved to see that agencies come together

3. early identification of those needing service, usually in the first two days of confinement

4. case managers who understand mental health and criminal justice and who understand cultural diversity.[47]

Given the mental status of these individuals, family members are generally the only advocates for services for the mentally ill in jails.[48]

The challenge of coordinating mental health services between community mental health clinics and jails was illustrated in a study by Muzekari, Morrissey, and Young.[49] The authors reported that while programs by community mental health clinics were in place to serve jails, staff at the respective facilities had divergent views on level of satisfaction with services. Likewise, Kalinic, Embert, and Senese point to the challenges surrounding the issues of security and authority when providing mental health services to those in jails,[50] and as might be expected, jail size is related to the number of services available for mentally ill detainees in jail.[51] The mental health status of jail detainees impacts the time incarcerated: those experiencing serious mental illness generally spend more time detained in jail than those without signs of mental illness.[52]

The prevalence of mental disorders among inmate populations is increasing. Meeting the needs of those individuals can be challenging. Studies indicate that mentally ill prisoners are more submissive than those prisoners who are not mentally ill; thus, these individuals may be easily influenced or abused by other inmates.[53] Issues such as the severity of the disorder, as well as the problem of co-occurring disorders and the proper identification of those with disorders, present real challenges to correctional workers. Questions related to mainstreaming, creating psychiatric wards in prisons, cost of treatment, and constitutionally acceptable levels of care will all need to be addressed by policymakers.[54] Philosophical differences over treatment versus punishment may impede progress in addressing the needs of the mentally ill.[55] Correctional managers and workers need to be sensitive to the complexities of providing services to the mentally disordered offender, especially in view of the

Americans with Disabilities Act and judicial activism. The courts have intervened to ensure proper treatment of mentally ill inmates;[56] however, the courts do not require due process considerations (e.g., a hearing) prior to the forcible administration of psychotropic medication.[57]

Proper training of staff and coordination of community services will be essential for those working with the mentally ill in jails.[58] Likewise, in prisons, the efficient use of correctional staff in inmate stress reduction and mental illness prevention will be necessary in order to deal with the stress and mental illness that evolve from confinement,[59] especially in view of research indicating that jail environments can impact symptom levels.[60] It is important to note that the level of fear can be related to numerous psychophysiological problems among inmates in prison.[61]

Many believe that our jails and prisons have become the dumping ground for the mentally ill as social services were curtailed in the mental health arena. Correctional personnel and mental health personnel must collaborate their research efforts in order to provide policymakers with information to ensure proper resolution of the problems facing adult and juvenile mentally ill offenders in the criminal justice system. Correctional personnel also must understand the dynamics of the interaction between prison jail environments and the mentally ill and their resulting behavior. Proper evaluation of mental health programs in prisons should look at outcome measures. Frequently, these programs have been evaluated along traditional adjustment indicators that may not be related to the impact of the mental health program on symptomology.[62] Information on model programs and efforts at diversion need broad dissemination and evaluation for suitability in different correctional settings.[63]

MENTALLY RETARDED AND DEVELOPMENTALLY DISABLED OFFENDERS

Mentally challenged inmates present a variety of challenges for prison managers. These inmates may be easily influenced by others, experience difficulty with personal hygiene, and/or have problems coping with prison life. Developmentally delayed inmates may experience communication problems during their contact with the criminal justice system.[64] Additionally, many may experience difficulty in understanding the meaning of "guilty."[65] The mentally deficient receive probationary sentences less frequently than other offenders,[66] perhaps, because of their rapid recidivism rates.[67] Laski suggests that mental retardation be considered a mitigating factor by the sentencing court[68] and that probation become the disposition of choice (a recommendation of the President's Committee on Mental Retardation).[69] In Georgia, those with mental retardation can be found guilty but mentally retarded; in Indiana, guilty but mentally ill.[70] Concerning the issue of competency to stand trial, the rates for offenders with a recommendation of incompetence to stand trial due to mental retardation vary by jurisdiction, with Virginia at 34.5 percent,[71] Michigan at 33 percent, Missouri at 17 percent,[72] and Connecticut at 12.5 percent.[73] Petrella provides an excellent discussion of the variables impacting recommendations for incompetence to stand trial due to mental retardation (e.g., jurisdiction and level of severity),[74] while the issue of competency of those with retardation to assist in their defense has been discussed by Bonnie.[75]

In an institutional setting, efforts are often directed toward exercising some degree of control over the mentally retarded offender (MRO),[76] often because the MRO is easily influenced and often victimized,[77] exploited, and injured more than other inmates.[78] They are apt to steal from others or injure others[79] and cause management problems,[80] including being participants in violent acts.[81] These inmates characteristically have little concern for personal hygiene.[82] The MRO is more likely to be considered a poor parole risk than other offenders, and thereby serves a greater portion of his or her sentence than do other inmates.[83]

A variety of terms are now being used for those who are mentally retarded, such as "mentally deficient" or "developmentally disabled." The American Association on Mental Retardation defines mental retardation as a "significantly sub-average general intellectual functioning existing concurrently with deficits in adaptive behavior and manifested during the developmental period."[84] The developmental period is considered to be prior to an individual's eighteenth birthday. Deficits in adaptive behavior include limitations in personal independence, social responsibility, learning, and maturation. Petersilia describes those with mental retardation as "having a childlike quality of thinking, coupled with slowness in learning new material . . . with little long-term perspective and little ability to think in a causal way to understand the consequences of their actions."[85]

To be classified as mentally retarded, a person must have an IQ of about 70 or below and have deficits in adaptive behavior that interfere with the demands of life.[86] However, there are several issues worth noting regarding intelligence testing and IQ scores (e.g., cultural bias, individual versus group testing),[87] and with regard to testing the mentally retarded offender soon after arrival to the prison, often a time of unpleasant feelings.[88] There are concerns about the validity of some of the indices used in prison settings to gauge the various levels of functioning among those with mental retardation. Hall recommends a review of the mentally retarded offender's diagnostic results by institutional mental retardation specialists because of potential validity issues when testing this inmate "subpopulation."[89] Moreover, the "typical" inmate's attributes of being marginalized (i.e., poorly educated, of lower social economic status, and being a minority) present additional assessment challenges for the MRO.[90]

There have been several investigations to determine the prevalence of mental retardation among the inmate population, some at the national level[91] and others at the state level.[92] Studies conducted on selected states found the prevalence of inmates with mental retardation to range from 1.1 to 23.4 percent,[93] while several national studies reported a range from 1.5 to 19.1 percent. Veneziano, Veneziano, and Tribolet found a wide range for estimates of those inmates with mental retardation (.05 to 35 percent) in various jurisdictions.[94] In a replication of that study, the prevalence rate for mentally retarded inmates was reported to be 4.2 percent.[95] Thus, some 50,000 inmates would be classified as mentally retarded.[96] Prevalence rates for mental retardation seem to be impacted by the definition used, the type of IQ test used, and jurisdiction. As a corollary, Veneziano and Veneziano reported that 10.7 percent of the inmates in their sample of inmates had learning disabilities.[97]

• Programs •

The Lancaster County, Pennsylvania, Office of Special Offenders Services was created in 1980 to serve those adult and juvenile offenders with mental retardation in an effort to increase their chances of success on probation or parole.[98] Using behavioral approaches that provide incremental successes, the program also addresses variables related to the mentally retarded offender's contact with the criminal justice system: self-esteem, peer influence, and understanding the legal consequences of their behavior. The program includes training of criminal justice personnel and prevention efforts through educational programs for special education students on criminal justice processes and the legal ramifications of one's behavior. The recidivism rate for the program is 5 percent.[99] A similar community-based program, the Developmentally Disabled Offender Project, exists in Monroe County, New York.[100]

Petersilia provides additional examples of efforts to provide developmentally disabled/mentally retarded inmates with services:

- New Jersey's Association of Retarded Citizens provides a plan to the court for MROs to serve probation through a Developmentally Disabled Offenders Program, and it provides monitory services while the MRO is in the community.

- New York provides community residential halfway houses to transition MROs into the community, as a diversion or as a probation diversion.

- The Boston Mass CAPP (Community Assistance Parole Program) uses volunteers as advocates, tutors, and role models for parolees with mental retardation. Professionals provide group counseling services.[101]

Noble and Conley list several prison-based programs for the mentally retarded offender;[102] however, only 10 percent of the MROs receive specialized services while incarcerated.[103] Given the nature of the MRO, the provision of services for this group sometimes requires additional staffing and other resources, thereby resulting in the diversion of services to other inmate poulations.[104] Nevertheless, as noted by Hall,[105] the recent increase in services for the MRO can sometimes be attributed to judicial intervention by federal district court judges (e.g., Georgia[106] and Texas[107]). In addition to constitutionally based issues impacting treatment of the MRO in prison (e.g., Eighth Amendment prohibitions against cruel and unusual treatment or deliberate indifference standards), additional federal legislation can become the basis for challenges to the type of care and treatment afforded to MROs in juvenile and adult correctional facilities (e.g., the Education of the Handicapped Act, the Individuals with Disabilities Education Act, Section 504 of the 1973 Vocational Rehabilitation Act, and more recently, the Americans with Disabilities Act).

Hall has provided an excellent overview of programs for MROs in three states: South Carolina, Georgia, and Texas.[108] The Habilitation Unit at Stevenson Correctional Institution in Columbia, South Carolina, provides services for inmates with developmental disabilities, including mental retardation. A multidisciplinary team determines placement and, likewise, a similar group of psychologists, educators, and vocational rehabilitation specialists provides a comprehensive program that includes "special education, life skills and vocational training, recreation, counseling, and pre-release services."[109] With the goal of improving socialization skills, work programs are centered on obtaining and retaining a job. Participants work on horticulture projects and piecework contracted with a sheltered workshop. Values clarification and conflict resolution are elements of the counseling programs, while interpersonal skill development and proper use of leisure time are components of the recreational programs of team sports and arts and crafts. The Habilitation Unit uses inmate aides as a paraprofessional staff, assisting MROs with activities and serving as role models.

Hall, the Mental Retardation Specialist at Georgia State Prison (GSP), describes the Mental Retardation Program as emphasizing institutional adjustment and social skills development.[110] Mentally retarded inmates have access to counseling and special education in supportive living units (SLUs) or in the general population in this maximum-security prison. Programs are similar to those at the Habilitation Unit in South Carolina, such as vocational education coupled with on-the-job training in furniture assembly, groundskeeping, and activities focusing on socialization skills. These inmates participate in a behavioral program in which they earn the privilege to move from lock-down to less restrictive housing arrangements. The correctional staff is trained to work with this atypical population. A team consisting of correctional officers, consulting clinical psychologists, mental retardation specialists, mental retardation counselors, and special education teachers determines the types of services to be provided. MROs may be assigned to one of two units, one for long-term care and the other for transitional care prior to entering the general population. The Habilitation Unit in South Carolina is classified as minimum-security, and thus, provides a less restrictive prison environment than does the Mental Health/Mental Retardation Program at Georgia State Prison, a maximum-security prison. Therefore, the South Carolina Program participants have access to greater socialization and skill development opportunities than do the inmates at GSP. Offenders are assigned to GSP because of their security status, and their diagnostic results from a reception center are reevaluated at GSP with respect to adaptive behavior and intellectual functioning. Hall notes that some of these MROs will have sentences exceeding 10 years; therefore, they may spend years in the long-term supportive living unit.[111] The program has been expanded to additional prisons, and aftercare is available through the services of Georgia's Department of Human Resources.

The Mentally Retarded Offender Program (MROP) of the Texas Department of Corrections evolved from judicial intervention.[112] The MROP differs from the South Carolina and Georgia examples in that all inmates are screened, and those classified with mental retardation are assigned to specialized, separate units. Programming includes vocational training, life skills development, and special education services in a combination of applied and classroom activities.[113] Social support, a component of the program, is provided through case management in which a professional serves as an advocate for the MRO. Correctional officers involved with the MROP receive specialized training and are designated as rehabilitation aides. Aftercare is provided through interagency agreements with the human resources agency and with the Board of Pardons and Paroles.[114]

All three programs are similar in their programming emphasis, educational curriculum incorporating academic and living skills, vocational training, staff expertise and training, and continuity of care through release, all of which are elements recommended as components of correctional special education programs.[115]

The MRO's level of functioning, adaptive behavior deficits, and related behaviors create challenges at each stage of the criminal justice system from arrest through incarceration, including post release.[116] As illustrated above, there are programs at the community and institutional level that provide varying levels of service to the MRO. While the retardation will not be cured, these programmatic efforts offer some hope that the criminal justice system will provide some sense of justice and fairness for this special population of inmates. Additional hope in this area may be provided by an increase in advocacy programs for the MRO—for example, the efforts of the Association for Retarded Citizens of the United States in several states (ARC, New Jersey's Developmentally Disabled Offender's Project; Cuyahoga County Ohio's Mentally Retarded Offender Team Project; Project CHANCE in Austin, Texas; National Association of Protection and Advocacy Systems; Developmental Disabilities Assistance, and Bill of Rights Act of 1978). Related state councils on developmental disabilities and university-affiliated programs may help as well.[117]

The success of correctional programming for the MRO depends on proper screening and assessment, proper training of staff, the use of correctional staff as "aides," interagency agreements, and proper aftercare.[118] Given the current philosophy associated with sentencing, which results in three-strikes or two-strikes laws and mandatory sentences, the number of MROs in the correctional system will likely increase. As Petersilia has noted, the MRO population, while being more prevalent in prisons than other special populations (e.g., AIDS inmates) receives very little interest from scholars and policymakers.[119] With 42 to 50 percent of jail inmates being described as "functionally illiterate,"[120] and with an increased understanding of learning disabilities and attention deficit hyperactivity disorders (ADHDs), the already-taxed correctional system faces some unique challenges in the future. Proper jail services, improved diversionary programs, and specialized resources in prisons will be needed to address the needs of mentally disabled offenders.

SUBSTANCE-ABUSING OFFENDERS

According to the Bureau of Justice Statistics data, the United States is experiencing an increase in the number of inmates abusing alcohol and other drugs. In 2004, approximately 56 percent of state prisoners and 50 percent of federal prisoners reported having used drugs the month prior to their offense.[121] Chaiken reported that more than one-half of the inmates in state prisons used drugs on a regular basis prior to incarceration, but these inmates did not participate in drug-related treatment during their prison stay.[122] Drug abuse treatment for those in prison and jails is important for three reasons: (1) institutional management is enhanced as problems decrease, (2) drug-seeking behavior diminishes, and (3) drug users become involved in the rehabilitation process (and this is often the only involvement with treatment processes encountered by these drug-abusing individuals).[123] Treatment approaches should consist of pre-release treatment, transitional intervention, and ongoing post-institutional treatment.[124]

Contrary to the belief of many critics, the outcomes for drug treatment in criminal justice settings have been positive.[125] Group counseling approaches appear to be the most widely used intensive treatment method in correctional institutions[126] and in jails.[127] Successful outcomes have been reported for drug treatment programs with offenders,[128] including lower rates of recidivism and relapse in several programs (e.g., Stay'n Out,[129] CHOICE,[130] and Cornerstone[131]).

Brown describes five program models for drug-abusing offenders:

1. incarceration without specialized drug programs

2. imprisonment that includes drug education and/or counseling

3. incarceration that includes specialized residential units for drug treatment in a correctional facility (e.g., New York's Stay'n Out, Wisconsin's Drug Abuse Treatment Unit, or programs outside of the prison that are secure, such as Cornerstone in Oregon).

4. self-help groups in prison (e.g., Narcotics Anonymous)

5. imprisonment with specialized programs that do not directly target the offender's drug abuse (e.g., education programs).[132]

Programs for drug-abusing offenders external to prisons include probation, intermediate sanctions such as house arrest or electronic monitoring, and diversion that combines supervision and treatment to lessen jail and prison overcrowding (e.g., Treatment Alternatives to Street Crime, TASC).[133] Such community-based alternatives based on TASC (e.g., Wisconsin's Treatment Alternative Program) have had a positive impact on recidivism.[134]

> See the Bureau of Justice Statistics web site at www.ojp.usdoj.gov/bjs; specifically, see two reports on prisoners and drug use: Christopher J. Mumola and Jennifer C. Karberg (2006), "Drug Use and Dependence, State and Federal Prisoners, 2004," and Doris J. James and Lauren E. Glaze (2006), "Mental Health Problems of Prison and Jail Inmates."

A joint Bureau of Justice Assistance–American Jail Association study of drug treatment in jails found that only 28 percent of the jails responding offered treatment other than detoxification to drug-abusing offenders.[135] The absence of drug treatment programs in jails represents a lost opportunity to prevent relapse, especially in light of the amount of idle time for jail detainees. Likewise, the almost nonexistence of transition and aftercare activities in jails increases the potential for relapse.[136]

An example of an in-jail program that considers relapse prevention is the Hillsborough County (Tampa) Florida program. Female and male inmates participate in an in-jail, six-week program that emphasizes cognitive-behavioral treatment and relapse prevention. Program evaluation measures indicated significant improvements in the ability to respond to situations that result in drug use after treatment. Additionally, improvement was found in the ability to recognize high-risk personal situations, to identify coping skills related to urges, and to identify methods for dealing with irrational beliefs associated with drug abuse.[137] Compared to those released early and those terminated from the program (program noncompleters), 70 and 79 percent of whom were rearrested, respectively, only 39 percent of those completing the program were arrested after one year.[138]

The Federal Bureau of Prisons (FBOP) has offered drug rehabilitation programs since the mid-1960s. According to Murray, prior to 1966, some inmates with a history of narcotics abuse were treated at a U.S. Public Health Service hospital in Lexington, Kentucky, or in Fort Worth, Texas. However, after the passage of the Narcotic Addict Rehabilitation Act (NARA), which required in-prison treatment units that were segregated from general population inmates, FBOP used specialized treatment units staffed by professionals in five federal correctional institutions (FCIs).[139] The therapeutic community (TC) was used as the modality model.[140] Success resulted in an expansion of the program to include non-NARA-sentenced inmates, and aftercare continued to be an element of the program. Thirty-three programs were in FCIs by 1978. FBOP drug treatment has been expanded to a layered multi-tiered approach including:

1. Mandatory Drug Education Program (standardized curriculum) for inmates meeting specified criteria (e.g., evidence that alcohol or other dugs contributed to the offense or is related to revocation of probation or parole) under the auspices of the Psychology Service and conducted by a Drug Treatment Specialist.

2. Voluntary drug abuse counseling services that include individual counseling, self-help groups (AA and NA), group therapy, stress management, personal development, vocational training, and pre-release planning.

3. Comprehensive residential drug abuse treatment programs for those volunteering and meeting specific criteria (e.g., within 18–24 months of release). Group and individual treatment (treatment staff-to-inmate ratio of 1:24) programs are cognitive-behaviorally based, address criminal thinking patterns, and also include relapse prevention, personal development, and aftercare at an FBOP community center or provider contract service.

4. Pilot drug abuse treatment units have a research focus and higher levels of resources, both fiscal and staff. This 12-month program consists of 1,000 hours of treatment services with a treatment staff-to-inmate ratio of 1:12.

5. Community reentry is a two-step, 12-month program consisting of individual and group counseling, relapse prevention planning, and family/work issues resolution. Step One consists of six months in an FBOP community corrections center with specialized drug treatment. After that, the offender has six months of FBOP and U.S. Probation Service jointly coordinated community services.[141]

The therapeutic community model has met with success in the treatment of drug-abusing offenders. Amity Return, a nine- to-12-month, prison-based TC in California, which provides the possibility for transitional care during a four-month period of parole, uses a multifaceted approach of counseling (individual and group), vocational training, expressive therapy, leisure planning, academic assistance, and transition-into-the-community preparation through three phases:

> **Phase I (2 to 3 months):** The inmate is assimilated into the program through full participation in activities designed to enhance social, therapeutic, and vocational abilities, including encounter groups and a prison industry job. Inmates provide support to new arrivals.

> **Phase II (5 to 6 months):** The emphasis is on improved personal, social, and psychological functioning as inmates increase responsibilities, including becoming a group facilitator.

> **Phase III (1 to 2 months):** The inmate will exit the program and reenter the community. Relapse prevention and discharge planning are emphasized.[142]

A goal of the program is to strengthen the relationship between corrections personnel and treatment personnel, some of whom are ex-addicts/offenders; this has been successful at the County Jail of Tucson, Arizona, Amity program.[143]

The Florida Department of Corrections uses a multi-tiered residential program for its drug offenders.[144] Although designed to provide a continuum of care through a three-tier TC, some offenders experience only portions of the multi-tiered program because of their sentences. The first tier consists of a 40-hour educational program that also provides an introduction to group counseling. Tier II, an intensive eight-week residential program, consists of individual and group counseling. While designed for those inmates who are described as serious abusers, it provides much-needed services for those whose sentences do not permit extensive treatment. Inmates participating in the program are isolated from the general population as they progress though three phases: (1) orientation—sets the parameters for recovery, (2) treatment—addiction education, life management, skill development, and relapse prevention, and (3) reentry—preparation for release or return to general population. Tier III is a six- to-12-month, full-service residential program based on the TC concept. In addition to counseling for anticriminal thinking and personal development, therapeutic communities are available at this stage through contracted services. Thus, inmates nearing the end of their sentences can make a transition into the community. The Department of Corrections utilizes a variety of post-release supervision programs designed to enhance reentry (e.g., provisional release, controlled release, conditional release, and Tier IV community correctional centers). Evaluation of the program indicates that participants had knowledge of the effects of drugs, improvement on various indices of psychological function (e.g., paranoid ideation, psychoticism, depression, anxiety), and reduction in rates of recommitment.[145]

According to one study, Stay'n Out, an in-prison therapeutic community in New York, was effective in reducing recidivism for participants, compared to those not receiving treatment.[146] Additionally, the longer the inmates were in the TC, the greater their success after release. Moreover, the TC program was more effective in reducing recidivism than such treatment approaches as milieu therapy and counseling. The authors' conclusions held for both male and female inmates.

Oregon also uses a multi-phase treatment approach in the widely known Cornerstone TC program,[147] Correctional Residential Treatment Programs, Correctional Institution Treatment Services, and a variety of community programs.[148] Of those efforts directed toward the reduction of criminal activities of drug-abusing offenders, the Cornerstone program is often cited as a model of success.[149]

Designed to address criminal behavior, addictive behavior, and institutionalization, treatment at Cornerstone consists of four phases, two of which are in-patient and two transitional. In the "Orientation" (30 days) and the "Intensive" (four to eight months) phases, emphasis is on personal development (i.e., assertiveness training, values clarification, self-help, and self-talk) and personality development (i.e., confronting criminal thinking patterns and barriers to recovery). The "Transition" and "Aftercare" phases include volunteer community work, 12-step participation, recovery planning, giving and receiving support at Cornerstone, and eventually becoming members of the Cornerstone Alumni Association. Field has reported that Cornerstone has an impact on the reduction of criminal activity, that the amount of time in intensive treatment correlates positively with reduction in criminal activities, and involvement in criminal activity by participants is at reduced levels compared to nonparticipants.[150]

According to Giuliani and Schnoll, a comprehensive treatment system for substance abusers would include these elements:

1. Uniform assessment processes

2. Emphasis on abusers' characteristics that goes beyond consideration of severity of the substance being abused

3. Differential application of treatment approaches

4. Varying levels of treatment[151]

The treatment of substance-abusing offenders is not straightforward. As Van Voorhis and Hurst state, "there is no consensus about what should be the underlying philosophy of treatment, particularly whether we should consider substance abuse a disease or learned behavior."[152] From the model programs described in this section, it seems that certain approaches hold promise (e.g., cognitive behavioral counseling and therapeutic communities) even though confusion over the use of the term "therapeutic community" is developing.[153] Relapse prevention must be an integral component of a comprehensive program of treatment for the substance-abusing offender, and community care (post-institutionalization) is an important element of such treatment. Such continuity of care will require cooperation among many community agencies. Suggesting a greater level of cooperation among criminal justice agencies, drug treatment groups, and other support agencies in the community, Prendergast, Anglin, and Wellisch made the following policy recommendations:

- Acceptance of drug abuse treatment. Because we know that drug treatments do work, the challenge becomes implementing cost-effective treatments for specific types of offenders.

- Realization that supervision by itself is not sufficient. Long-term treatment that is intensive and comprehensive can be successful for hard-core offender addicts. Supervision from intermediate sanctions and low-intensity treatment such as educational and 12-step-type programs will not have a long-term impact of offenders with severe dependence.

- Interventions should have realistic treatment outcomes. For example, an overnight, long-term cure is not practical. A more reasonable expectation would be to reduce the number of offenders requiring high-level security and/or intensive treatment interventions and reducing the need for costly, long-term imprisonment or residential treatment, thereby increasing the use of community progress.[154]

The number of offenders arrested for drug offenses and/or drug-related offenses is likely to continue to increase in the current political climate of "get tough on crime" and the "war on drugs." However, we know we can reduce reoffending among this group of offenders with proper programs such as cognitive behavioral approaches that include relapse prevention.[155]

MEDICALLY ILL OFFENDERS

As Coleman noted in his discussion of issues facing corrections in the twenty-first century, corrections will be faced with demands to move beyond institutional safety and security to the notion of responsibility for community safety and security, a proposition that takes on great importance when looking at the prevalence of physical illness found among prisoners.[156] In correctional settings, there is a higher rate of such illnesses as HIV/AIDS, sexually transmitted diseases, and tuberculosis than found in the general population. In addition, given the at-risk behavior of those found in prisons, these diseases are more prevalent among the offender population.[157] Once released from confinement, many inmates return to their pre-incarceration lifestyle, thereby increasing the risk of transmitting these diseases to others.

The resurgence of tuberculosis (TB) in the United States presents correctional personnel with another serious health issue.[158] Since 1985, this country has seen a 20 percent increase in TB cases,[159] and concern has developed about the onset of multiple-drug-resistant TB.[160] According to Smith, there are three factors impacting the increase in TB: (1) HIV, (2) the immigration of people from countries with high rates of TB, and (3) diminished federal funding for TB prevention.[161]

Correctional facilities—jails and prisons—are settings that are conducive to the spread of this communicable disease. Smith suggests that the constant movement of inmates from jails to prisons, coupled with the overcrowding and poor ventilation found in jails and prisons, enhances the spread of TB.[162] Although the spread of TB in jails can be addressed by placing infected inmates in units with rooms with negative air pressure, a recent study in Indiana by Kane and Dotson found that only one jail among 24 utilized negative air pressure.[163] With inmate populations three times more likely to have TB than the general public, the potential for the spread of the disease among inmates is frightening.

According to Hammett and Harrold, research since the 1950s has found the incidence of TB to be higher among inmates than among the general public.[164] As early as 1984-85, a Centers for Disease Control and Prevention (CDC) study of 29 states revealed that the incidence of TB among prisoners was three times that of the general population, and between 1985 and 1989, the CDC reported 11 TB outbreaks in correctional institutions in eight states.[165]

In addition to implementing preventive measures such as facility design and screening, effective coordination between community corrections and community health agencies is necessary to ensure continuity of care in the treatment and prevention of TB. Braithwaite, Braithwaite, and Poulson, in noting that local public health officials tend to ignore institutionalized groups such as inmates, call for a nontraditional outreach emphasis by state and local health department staff in providing education and prevention programs in jails, prisons, and juvenile facilities.[166] Wilcock, Hammett, and Parent provided some examples of collaboration to address continuous care for offenders and staff protection.

- In New York, discharge planning and follow-up procedures for release with TB include referrals with an appointment at a public health or private care provider and a supply of medications; incentives such as vouchers for food or transit tokens that are redeemable after phases of treatment are used.

- In Arkansas, parolees with TB have a condition of parole requiring that they report to their county health department within seven days of release. Releasees receive a supply of medication, and the public health department receives a notice. The health department provides free medication and counseling. Prospective correctional employees are tested for TB, and a mandatory TB screening program for staff is now in place.

- Texas has enacted laws requiring inmates, staff, and volunteers who are detained, or who work in, jails, prisons, or community correctional facilities to be screened for TB. However, parolees are excluded from the screening. Inmates must be tested if confinement exceeds 14 days. The state health department and the state criminal justice department share the cost.[167]

Thus, some jurisdictions have collaborated in discharge planning and treatment following incarceration. The continuity of care is important in addressing the increasing incidence of TB. Additionally, correctional staff need to be aware of the risks they face in working with TB offenders.

The relationship between HIV and TB has been made clear. That relationship has resulted in court action for one disadvantaged group, the homeless. In New York, a court order required that homeless persons who were HIV-positive but had yet to develop AIDS must be housed in properly ventilated rooms of four or less inhabitants, in beds at least eight feet apart from other residents, and have separate bathroom facilities.[168] Given the known relationship between HIV and TB, and the increased risk presented by overcrowding, the potential for court intervention in prison is heightened under the Court's notion of "deliberate indifference" in *Estelle v. Gamble*. Deliberate indifference was found to exist in Texas' failure to address inmates' medical needs.[169] The design of jails and prisons must address the issues surrounding the spread of communicable diseases.

According to the Bureau of Justice Statistics in 2002, the rate of confirmed AIDS cases among the U.S. prison population was 3.5 times the rate in the general U.S. population.[170] Of those in jails tested in 1999 for HIV, 1.7 percent were positive.[171] The changes in the number of HIV-positive inmates in recent years have been interesting. From 1993 to 1995, the number of inmates in state custody who were infected with HIV increased by 14 percent while the number of federal prisoners who were HIV-positive decreased by the same percentage for the same period.[172] The percentage of the total inmate population testing HIV-positive remained relatively unchanged over the three-year period from 1997 to 1999 (1%) and experienced a decrease until 2002.[173] In 2002, HIV-positive inmates comprised 1.9 percent of the state prison population, down from 2.4 percent in 1995.[174]

The data regarding AIDS-related deaths is more positive. In 1995, 100 inmates died of AIDs-related causes for every 100,000 state-held inmates,[175] but in 1999, that rate decreased to 20 for every 100,000 state prisoners (but increased to 22 percent by 2002).[176] From 1995 to 2002, the number of deaths from AIDS among prisoners decreased by 72 percent.[177] Approximately 11.2 percent of state prisoners' deaths were attributed to AIDS-related causes in 1999, about twice the percentage for the general population ages 15-54.[178]

In a study of prison inmates in Florida, Mutter, Grimes, and Labarthe reported a high rate of HIV infection among those who had been incarcerated continuously since the HIV/AIDS outbreak.[179] Thus, as the authors concluded, there might be a high risk of becoming HIV-infected while in prison. However, before generalizing these findings to all jurisdictions, one should understand that among HIV-positive inmates, rates vary dramatically among jurisdictions. In 1999, New York, Florida, and Texas had the highest number of HIV-positive inmates, accounting for almost 50 percent of all HIV-positive prisoners in the United States. The northeastern section of the nation had the most HIV-positive inmates.[180]

In noting the evidence on the relationship between unprotected sex among jail detainees and the spread of gonorrheal infections, as well as the spread of the AIDS virus, Richard Koehler approved the distribution of condoms to inmates by health officials when he led New York City's jail system.[181] To address the problem presented in the relationship between HIV, tuberculosis, multidrug-resistant tuberculosis, and conditions of confinement, Koehler recommended:

- alternatives to incarceration for drug abusers who have no history of violence
- residential drug treatment outside the correctional system
- new educational programs and condom distribution to inmates.[182]

Alternatives to prison placement would be more cost-effective, especially if medical intervention and treatment reduced the risky behavior of injecting drug use. Such alternative treatment placement would need to ensure public safety. Educational initiatives concerning reducing the spread of communicable diseases would reduce at-risk behaviors.[183]

However, we do not know the impact that AIDS educational programs have had on inmates.[184] While programs may exist in prisons and jails, specific information on risk reduction is often missing from brief educational programs.[185] It would seem that a meaningful educational and counseling program would be an effective use of incarceration, whether in jail or prison. However, the type of program and its delivery method is important. Keeton and Swanson found that while HIV/AIDS knowledge might be high among inmates, there is a major limitation in that programs failed to provide learning tools to assist inmates in discriminating between various risky situations.[186] Olivero suggested that educational information on transmission of AIDS be included.[187]

A therapeutic community (TC) can be effective in changing HIV risk behaviors of offenders. Those offenders who successfully completed a five-phase TC, when compared to a control group and to those failing to complete the program, reported reduction in such behaviors as injecting drugs, trading sex for drugs, and inconsistent condom use.[188] Clark and Boudin have reported on the challenges of implementing an AIDS peer counseling and educational program in a women's prison.[189] When fully implemented, the program, which was started by female inmates, reduced fear of transmission by casual contact and reduced the stigmatization of people with AIDS. Another benefit of the program was the development of an environment of caring among the inmates.

Some correctional officers and others suggest that inmates should be subjected to mandatory HIV screening.[190] However, only 19 states test all entering inmates, and only two states (Missouri and Nevada) and the Federal Bureau of Prisons (FBOP) test upon release.[191] Of 52 jurisdictions (50 states, Federal Bureau of Prisons, and the District of Columbia), 45 test inmates if they make a request or if they have HIV-related symptomology, 16 test inmates belonging to high-risk groups, 39 test inmates who are involved in an incident, and six states and the FBOP have a program of random testing.[192]

Blumberg and Laster have clearly articulated the pros and cons of mandatory HIV screening of inmates.[193] They note that the information obtained from screening can be used to:

- specifically target education and prevention programs to those with a need
- better supervise those with HIV to prevent the spread of the virus
- better predict programs and, thus, budget needs
- provide medical treatment.

On the other hand, some suggest that HIV education programs should be for all inmates because segregation of HIV inmates creates a false sense of security, epidemiological investigations conducted anonymously will reveal valid data for planning, and the labeling process may negatively impact inmates while in prison and upon release.[194]

Another issue often raised concerning inmates who are HIV-positive or have AIDS is the notion of segregation. Should those inmates confirmed as being HIV-positive or having AIDS be isolated? Proponents of the segregation approach use some of the same arguments used to promote mandatory screening (e.g., supervision is enhanced) and also claim that it protects inmates from sexual attacks and homosexual relationships. Critics of segregation suggest that such a practice restricts program opportunity and work assignments, encroaches upon privacy, conveys the incorrect public health message concerning risk and transmission, subjects inmates to the dangers associated with having such a public label (harassment and post-incarceration discrimination), and creates a false impression of safety among general population inmates.[195]

Most states mainstream inmates with HIV/AIDS; that is, those with AIDS or who are HIV-positive are not segregated from the general prison population. In 1996, Braithwaite, Hammett, and Mayberry found that only two states isolated HIV-positive inmates.[196] According to Jacobs, segregation "does not clearly reduce the spread of the HIV/AIDS virus."[197]

Corrections officials' actions toward HIV/AIDS inmates have generated numerous legal issues. The major legal issues center on mandatory HIV/AIDS screening, segregating HIV/AIDS-infected inmates, and level of care.[198] The level-of-care issue revolves around the question of deliberate indifference as espoused in *Estelle v. Gamble*,[199] that is, the inmate must show intentional deprivation.[200] The courts have permitted mandatory HIV screening, mandatory testing after an incident, the absence of testing by correctional officials, the practice of correctional officials determining placement of inmates (mainstreaming or segregation), officials disclosing an inmate's HIV status, and prison officials excluding inmates from programs (community work programs) and certain work assignments.[201] In 2000, the U.S. Supreme Court let stand lower court rulings that permitted the state of Alabama to segregate HIV-positive inmates by barring their participation in programs.[202]

To address the problems associated with the spread of HIV/AIDS, Mahon suggests a public health response, much like programs in other countries.[203] However, the conservative, get-tough approach to corrections now found in the United States does not seem congruent with the public health efforts found in other countries (e.g., availability of condoms, methadone maintenance, and needle exchange programs).

The changing demographics of the prison population will certainly impact healthcare services in corrections. The increase in the number of elderly inmates and the graying of the prison population because of longer prison sentences will create problems in adjustment,[204] a demand for specialists in gerontology and geriatrics to work with this population, and specialized health facilities, including hospice care[205] and increased costs of care and medication.[206] Women's health issues,[207] including care of pregnant offenders,[208] will increase the costs of medical correctional care, as will increased concern over contagion.[209] In a period of correctional conservatism, there may be reluctance to implement programs such as discharge planning and primary care for high-risk groups such as intravenous drug users and HIV/AIDS-positive inmates; however, such programs have reduced recidivism in such at-risk groups.[210]

Some state systems have attempted to recover some of the escalating costs of health care for inmates by charging a copayment fee. Some inmates have challenged those fees, but in general, the courts have upheld the charging of inmates for copayments if programs are reasonable (e.g., indigent inmates are not charged and chronically ill inmates are not denied care because of repeated charges).[211] However, the imposition of such fees may discourage inmates from seeking medical care, thereby resulting in postponed care that may be more costly to the institution in the long run.[212] Offenders entering the correctional system bring a history of poor health care, numerous at-risk behaviors, and a poor understanding of the relationship between these behaviors and the spread of infectious diseases, and long-term health outcomes to an already burdened system.

BOX 10.2

Web Sites with Information on HIV/AIDS

Correctional HIV Consortium
http://www.sicom.com/~chc

Human Rights Watch: HI/AIDS in Prisons
http://www.hrw.org/advocacy/prisons/hiv-aids.htm

The Body: An AIDS and HIV Information Resource
http://www.thebody.com

ELDERLY OFFENDERS

Combine longer prison sentences, truth-in-sentencing, and three-strikes laws with longer life expectancies and you have the recipe for an aging inmate population. While younger people disproportionately commit crimes, newer sentencing laws will make these offenders stay in prison longer, many until old age. According to Department of Justice reports, of the state and federal prison population in 1998, 10 percent will serve 20 or more years, and 5 percent will never be released.[213] In fact, according to one estimate, by the year 2010, 33 percent of the prison population will be over the age of 50.[214] This figure stands in stark contrast with the mere 3 percent of the prison population that was over age 55 in 1991. This rapid growth of the aging inmate population will require corrections professionals to develop new programs and procedures to assist this special population.

The first issue to confront when addressing the topic of elderly prisoners is how to define this group. In prison, an offender is considered "elderly" at the chronological age of 50.[215] The reason for using this early age is because many offenders may have had inadequate access to health care, including preventive medicine, and/or have been involved in risky lifestyles (e.g., drug abuse, unprotected sex).

Elderly individuals end up in prisons primarily from one of four different paths.[216] First, there are those who are first-time offenders who commit their crimes when elderly. It is estimated that 61 percent of that group are incarcerated for sexual crimes. This group, then, has all of the problems that confront sexual offenders as well as those that affect elderly offenders. The second type of elderly prisoner is a chronic offender who is incarcerated for the first time. The third type, the prison recidivist, has a relatively easy time adjusting to incarceration. However, inmates age 55 and above have a very low percent of recidivism[217] (see Table 10.1). Lastly, there are those who were incarcerated while young and have grown old in prison. For prisoners who are serving their second or third sentence or for those who have grown old in prison, the adjustments to old age in prison are easier than for those serving their first sentence. When addressing the problems of elderly prisoners, then, correctional staff members need to be aware of which path the inmate has taken to get there.

The most important adjustment that correctional institutions have to make in accommodating elderly prisoners is an increased demand for health services. Because health problems are more frequent and potentially severe among the elderly, prisons will have to respond. Front-line prison staff such as correctional officers will carry most of the burden of seeing to the healthcare needs of elderly inmates. This is because prisons have limited medical resources and the health of elderly inmates can deteriorate quickly.[218]

Another issue regarding the health of elderly prisoners involves the accommodation of traditional aging problems such as hearing and sight problems as well as difficulty with mobility. In order to address these concerns, prisons should be modified or constructed with ramps, handrails, and the like. In addition to potential health problems, elderly prisoners have more extensive maintenance needs for good health. For example, the dietary needs of elderly prisoners require special attention as compared to the general prison population.

Aside from the physical health of elderly inmates, correctional staff will also have to attend to a host of special mental health needs. While the elderly population can be expected to have similar mental health problems as the general prison population, the aging condition of elderly prisoners can lead to particular problems. The most common age-related mental health difficulties faced by elderly prisoners are Alzheimer's disease and dementia. To address these problems, prisons will need to employ professionals accustomed to treating mental health problems in the elderly. Correctional staff members should be attuned to issues such as the elderly inmates' feelings of vulnerability, the need for slower-paced activities, possible abrasive interactions between older and younger inmates, and the need for passive-type recreational activities.[219]

In many cases, elderly prisoners do not need the same programs as younger prisoners. The most common programs aim at preparing young offenders for reintegration into society. Educational and occupational development programs fall into this category. The elderly population, however, does not need these programs to the same extent.[220] Even if an elderly prisoner is likely to be released, he or she is not likely to use educational or occupational training. It is more important for these individuals to receive assistance with adjustment to prison life.[221]

One of the proposals to deal with the elderly population is to segregate them into special wings of existing prisons or into entirely separate facilities. For example, Louisiana developed the Dr. Martin L. Forcht Jr. Clinical Treatment Unit as a satellite of the David Wade Correctional Center near Shreveport as a special needs facility for those inmates who are elderly and physically impaired.[222] Johnson points out the possible positive and negative consequences of segregation. Segregation "may increase self-respect, diminish feelings of loneliness, stimulate social interaction, encourage identification with peers, and if available, generate treatment programs oriented to the age group."[223] In other words, segregation can make the experience of incarceration more productive and useful for the elderly inmate. On the other hand, segregation may have its potential downside. It may result in certain types of work assignments being denied, limited access to treatment programs that are provided to younger prisoners, and may violate the preferences of those older inmates who do not identify with members of their own age group.[224] Segregation, then, can lead to situations in which a given population is too small to warrant the expense for special programs to assist the elderly.

One of the chief worries regarding the aging prison population is that many prisons will effectively become nursing homes. As these changes take place, the procedures and personnel of correctional institutions will have to adjust accordingly. Refitted facilities, retrained staff, and reworked programming will all be necessary. In addition, an increased attentiveness to health concerns will be required.[225] All of these adjustments will cost money. The Coalition for Federal Sentencing Reform estimates that the cost of incarcerating elderly prisoners can be as much as four times the amount needed to imprison the average inmate.[226] As Neeley, Addison, and Craig-Moreland point out, "correctional facilities will have to stretch their budgets to accommodate this mushrooming number of aging inmates. A growing elderly prison population will be more costly to accommodate than a younger one because elderly inmates require more medical and mental health services in special settings."[227]

The case of elderly prisoners provides an interesting example of the relationship between public policy and correctional administration. The presence of this population with its special needs is most clearly the result of public policy decisions. Prisons will deal with an increased number of elderly prisoners not because of an elderly crime wave but because of changes in sentencing procedures. In the not-so-distant past,

TABLE 10.1
Recidivism by Age Group

	Percent of released prisoners who, within 3 years, were—				
Prisoner characteristic	Percent of all released prisoners	Rearrested	Reconvicted[a]	Returned to prison with a new prison sentence[b]	Returned to prison with or without a new prison sentence[c]
All released prisoners	100.0%	67.5%	46.9%	25.4%	51.8%
14-17	0.3	82.1	55.7	38.6	56.6
18-24	21.0	75.4	52.0	30.2	52.0
25-29	22.8	70.5	50.1	26.9	52.5
30-34	22.7	68.8	48.8	25.9	54.8
35-39	16.2	66.2	46.3	24.0	52.0
40-44	9.4	58.4	38.0	18.3	50.0
45 or older	7.6	45.3	29.7	16.9	40.9

[a] Because of missing data, prisoners released in one state (Ohio) were excluded from the calculation of "Percent reconvicted."

[b] "New prison sentence" does include new sentences to State or Federal prisons but does not include sentences to local jails. Because of missing data, prisoners released in 2 States (Ohio and Virginia) were excluded from the calculation of "Percent returned to prison with a new prison sentence."

[c] "With or without a new prison sentence" includes both prisoners with new sentences to State or Federal prisons plus prisoners returned for technical violations. Because of missing data, prisoners released from 6 States (Arizona, Delaware, Maryland, New Jersey, Ohio, and Virginia) were excluded from the calculation of "Percent returned to prison with or without a new prison sentence." New York State custody records did not always distinguish prison returns from jail returns. Consequently, some persons received in New York jails were probably mistakenly classified as prison returns. Also, California with a relatively high return-to-prison rate affects the overall rate of 51.8%. When California is excluded, the return-to-prison rate falls to 40.1%.

Source: Langan, P.A., and D.J. Levin (2002). "Recidivism of Prisoners Released in 1994." *Bureau of Justice Statistics Special Report.* Washington, DC: U.S. Government Printing Office.

many prisoners would be released before they reached elderly status or they would be paroled when their age reduced their threat to society. The increased use of incarceration as a means of addressing crime has led to the graying of the prison population. Our public policymakers must address these new issues and the added costs regarding elderly prisoners as the prison population continues to age.

TERMINALLY ILL OFFENDERS

Another growing problem for the nation's correctional institutions is the large number of prisoners dying behind bars. In recent years, reports indicate that an increasing number of prisoners are in the advanced stages of incurable diseases such as cancer and AIDS.[228] Reports also indicate that many correctional facilities are ill-equipped to deal with these inmates.[229] In 2005, a total of 3,179 inmates died in state prisons. The causes of deaths in state prison for 2001-2005 are contained in Table 10.2.[230] According to Warden Burl Cain of Angola Prison, approximately 85 percent of the 5,200 inmates currently housed at Angola will die while incarcerated. He states that, "[Angola] prison has become nothing more than an oversized nursing home; it is an 18,000 acre graveyard."[231]

As a result of the rising number of terminally ill inmates and increasing medical costs, many states have enacted medical-parole laws, also known as "compassionate release," which allow for the early release of terminally ill offenders.[232] All states have a variety of methods for early release that include the reduction of the inmate's sentence by a judge, parole or clemency hearing, administrative release, or even commutation of sentence.

Many victim advocates are opposed to any kind of special consideration for terminally ill offenders. For example, the Nevada legislature was criticized for sponsoring Assembly Bill 298, which would allow for the early release of terminally ill inmates.[233] Judy Jacoboni, a victim

TABLE 10.2
Number of State Prisoner Deaths, by Cause of Death

Cause of Death	2001	2002	2003	2004	2005
All Causes	2,878	2,946	3,167	3,138	3,179
Illness	2,303	2,379	2,633	2,645	2,670
AIDS	270	245	210	145	153
Suicide	169	168	200	200	215
Homicide	39	48	50	51	56
Drug/alcohol intoxication	36	37	23	23	37
Accident	23	31	26	37	30
Other/unknown	38	38	25	37	18

Executions not included.

Source: http://www.usdoj.gov/bjs/DCRP/tables/dcst06sptl.htm.

advocate with Mothers Against Drunk Driving, said to the Senate panel, "Why should we give this undue consideration to offenders? Plus, some terminally ill offenders could pose a greater threat to the community."[234] However, Assemblywoman Christina Giunchigliani, the bill's sponsor, noted that several safeguards are incorporated into the bill. First, only offenders who are physically incapacitated or sick and expected to die within 12 months could qualify for consideration. Second, any inmates released under this provision would be under electronic supervision and monitored while on parole. Third, death row inmates and prisoners serving life-without-parole sentences are ineligible for early release. Finally, the Department of Prisons would be required to notify the offender's victim(s), the Division of Parole and Probation, and the county within which the offender would be released.

Connecticut also allows for the early release of inmates by the Board of Parole if the inmate has a terminal condition and is physically incapable, because of his or her illness, of presenting a danger to society.[235] A terminal condition includes but is not limited to any prognosis by a licensed physician stating that the inmate has six months or less to live. Any terminally ill prisoner except one convicted of a capital felony is eligible. This authorization applies despite other statutes precluding release. The parole board must base the "medical-parole" decision on a detailed diagnosis by a licensed physician. If the physician is not one employed or used by the Department of Correction (DOC), a DOC physician can review the diagnosis. As a condition of release, the board must require that the parolee agree to placement in a hospital, hospice, or other suitable housing accommodation, which may include his or her family's home. The board has the option to require a periodic rediagnosis and order a return to custody for any inmate who improves to a point where he or she no longer meets the criteria for release. The board can appoint a special panel to review and decide on requests for medical parole.

Like state inmates, federal prisoners can seek release in a number of ways. A prisoner can petition the Federal Bureau of Prisons to file a motion in court to end his or her confinement. If an inmate committed a crime prior to November 1, 1987, he or she can petition the court for early medical release within 120 days of sentencing when there is new evidence not known at the time of sentencing.[236] The President of the United States can also grant a reduction or commutation of sentence.[237]

Some members of the public fear that compassionate release will result in the mass release of potentially violent offenders. However, very few inmates are actually granted this type of release. In 1997, across the United States, only 96 inmates received parole or other forms of compassionate release.[238] Additionally, when an inmate does qualify, his or her release is not guaranteed. The rigorous standards set forth by many states result in some inmates dying while awaiting the release decisions of parole boards or other officials.[239]

Another solution for the treatment of terminally ill prisoners is the use of separate facilities designed specifically to address their needs. Tennessee, for example, houses its chronically and terminally ill inmates at the Lois Deberry Special Needs Facility in Nashville.[240] In addition, any inmate within the Tennessee Department of Corrections (TDOC) who needs special medical services such as surgery will be temporarily housed at this facility until their treatment is completed. Housing special-needs inmates in one central location has improved the quality of care these inmates receive and lowered medical costs for the TDOC.[241]

Another option implemented by many correctional facilities is hospice care. The primary philosophy of hospice is to allow seriously ill and dying patients to "live and die with dignity and humanity and with as little pain as possible."[242] Some of the services provided by hospice include pain management, spiritual support, psychological counseling, and grief counseling for surviving family members. Prior to the implementation of hospice, many inmates died alone in their cells. Many people see hospice as a more humane treatment alternative.

Hospice recognizes that pain often goes beyond the physical realm and extends to the emotional and spiritual areas as well. Therefore, a team effort is used to respond to the needs of dying inmates. Doctors, nurses, social workers, and chaplains each make significant contributions to the success of the program. While correctional line staff can also play a key role in the success of hospice, they are often overlooked or underutilized. Correctional officers have more contact with inmates than other staff members. They control inmate movement, the degree of interaction between inmates, and inmate property. Therefore, the inclusion of correctional personnel in the multidisciplinary team and recognition of their contribution are necessary ingredients for a viable program.

Volunteers are a central component of hospice care, and the use of volunteers is actually written into federal and state Medicare regulations.[243] Cheryl Price, a Licensed Social Worker and the Hospice Coordinator of the Dixon Correctional Center in Dixon, Illinois, recommends the following screening and training procedures for inmate-volunteers:

- Volunteers should be subject to a thorough interview and receive approval from the hospice coordinator, the counselor, security personnel, and the warden. Inmates should not be considered if they have violated an institutional rule in the last six months.

- From day one, either in pre-training interviews or on the first day of training, the inmates' responsibility as a volunteer is emphasized: they are special, they are chosen. One rule infraction can result in suspension or removal from the program.

- The inmate volunteer should receive a minimum of 40 hours of training. The inmate's responses in class and his or her attitude and demeanor should be evaluated. The training is designed to identify what situations the inmate-volunteer may find difficult to handle by probing his or her own inner experiences and knowing how those experiences will influence his or her caring. The leaders should make pairings of inmate-volunteers and patients based on these strengths and weaknesses.[244]

According to 1997 figures, most inmates who are terminally ill are receiving treatment in non-hospice settings. Nationally, 824 terminally ill inmates were placed in regular DOC infirmaries or prison hospitals.[245] During that same year, formal hospice settings within the correctional system were available to 152 terminally ill inmates.[246] As of 1998, 11 states and the Federal Bureau of Prisons had formal hospice programs. It is the goal of hospice advocates to eventually implement hospice programs in all correctional facilities across the country.[247]

See the web site of The National Prison Hospice Association at www.npha.org. The Association provides a network for the exchange of information between corrections facilities, community hospices, and other concerned agencies about existing programs, best practices, and new developments in the prison hospice field.

Prison systems across the country are experiencing a rapid growth in the number of aging and chronically/terminally ill prisoners in their custody. The increasing occurrence of substance abuse, infectious disease, and long histories of poor nutrition, as well as longer, mandatory sentencing and the depopulation of large mental health institutions, are all contributing factors to this phenomenon. The challenge of providing for the safety and treatment of terminally ill inmates has become more arduous given the difficulty and the great expense this prison population requires. In addition, the geriatric and infirm population suffers from limited mobility and includes many individuals who are especially vulnerable or are unable to care for themselves in a mainline prison environment. The group also commonly needs frequent medical interventions and special dietary regimes requiring significant time and attention from the staff. Therefore, correctional administrators should implement innovative programs in order to meet the needs of the growing number of terminally ill prisoners in their custody.

SEX OFFENDERS

Much like other correctional approaches, dealing with sexual offenders has been cyclical. The approach to sex offenders from the 1930s through the 1960s was one of indefinite hospitalization and treatment instead of imprisonment. As correctional philosophies changed, states began to repeal or not use hospitalization for sex offenders. Seeking retribution or punishment, states opted to sentence sex offenders to prison under criminal statutes as opposed to civil confinement in psychiatric hospitals. As sentencing philosophies changed and prison overcrowding became an issue, states began to implement laws that permitted officials to use civil law to commit dangerous sex offenders to psychiatric hospitals after completion of their prison sentences. The sexual predator laws required that sex offenders have a mental disorder that would result in the commission of additional crimes upon release from prison.

There is a general scientific consensus that sex offenses are very likely the result of psychosexual disorders.[248] It is for this reason that sex offenders should be considered a special population requiring special attention and services. While many inmates face mental health difficulties, most if not all sex offenders are considered mentally ill. The difficulties arise in identifying the source of the mental problems and treating them. While the sex offender population in federal prisons is only about 1 percent, sex offenders make up nearly 10 percent of the prisoners under state jurisdiction,[249] and many of them require extensive mental health resources.

The first step in addressing the mental health problems of sex offenders is assessment of the nature of their sexual deviance. Marsh and Walsh suggest the use of a plethysmograph to measure sexual arousal.[250] This device measures penile erection of sex offenders after the presentation of a variety of sexual stimuli such as pictures depicting various sex acts. By determining what types of acts arouse the offender, the particular deviance can be identified. In order to avoid false results, Marsh and Walsh suggest that this approach be supplemented with the use of sexual history surveys accompanied by the use of a polygraph.

Assessment of the nature of the deviance is crucial for treatment. For example, personality differences exist between child molesters and rapists.[251] Child-molesting offenders tend to be characterized as anxious and depressed, as well as being conforming, passive, submissive, and insecure. They tend to lack initiative and give in to strong adult authority figures. This personality pattern inhibits these individuals from having sexual relations with adults, and treatment becomes a challenge because of the passive-aggressive nature of their personality. The personalities of adult rapist offenders tend to be more similar to nonsexually aggressive offenders than to those of child molesters.[252] Adult rapists and nonsexually aggressive felons are higher in narcissism but less anxious and depressed than child molesters.[253]

There are two main forms of treatment of sex offenders: psychological therapy and biomedical treatment. Psychological treatment can include individual, group, or family therapy and can target psychoanalytic, cognitive, behavioral, social learning, or family systems. Biomedical treatments generally include drug treatments but may include surgery in some cases. Research indicates that rapists generally have poor empathy skills.[254] Because rapists tend to experience little, if any, empathy for their victims,[255] empathy training for rapists seems worthwhile. In one empathy study, Pithers reported that sex offenders completing a comprehensive five-step group therapy program exposing offenders to cognitive, emotional, and behavioral experiences of sexually abused survivors increased their levels of empathy and reduced approval of cognitive distortions of abuse, an important aspect of relapse prevention.[256] Empathy enhancement has been shown to be an important aspect of relapse prevention.

Denial of responsibility for one's inappropriate behavior is a major barrier to therapy. O'Donohue and Letourneau reported on the success of a brief, structured group treatment program for probationers in denial of their sexual abuse of children.[257] Undergoing cognitive restructuring, victim empathy, sex education, assertiveness and social skills training, and discussions of the consequences of denial, 76 percent of the participants in two group therapy programs moved from denial to being at least partially out of denial.

Quinsey has found that effective programs include a "skill-based training approach; the modeling of prosocial behaviors and attitudes; a directive but nonpunitive orientation; a focus on modifying antecedents to criminal behavior; a supervised community component in order to assess and teach the offender relevant skills; and a high-risk clientele."[258] Programs that do not work include "confrontation without skill building; a nondirective approach; a punitive orientation; a focus on irrelevant factors; and the use of highly sophisticated verbal therapies, such as insight-oriented psychotherapy."[259]

Prison counselors have a difficult job in treating sex offenders. Priest and Smith note that counselors must be aware that (1) they will have to work with pedophiles and other deviant sex offenders, (2) their personal feelings, emotions, and biases might negatively impact treatment, and (3) they will need a belief in rehabilitation as an acceptable and proper approach to sex offenses.[260]

In addition to therapeutic techniques, correctional treatment of sex offenders can include biomedical procedures. Biomedical techniques are utilized in order to address the physiological root of the offender's sex drive. These techniques can include physical castration, so-called "chemical castration," and stereotactic brain surgery.[261] Physical castration, the removal of the testicles, aims at the elimination of the production of testosterone, thereby reducing the sex drive. This procedure as a form of treatment for sex offenders is used mainly in Europe where studies have shown that it is an effective procedure in reducing recidivism rates.[262] In the United States, there has been an increased call for physical castration despite the fact that the history of the practice in the United States has been associated with racist practices in the earlier part of the twentieth century in the South.

More popular has been the use of drug treatment to "chemically castrate" sex offenders. There are a variety of drugs that can be administered to lower the sex drive of individuals. In most cases, these drug treatments are administered in conjunction with therapeutic treatments.

One of the most daunting tasks involving special offenders is dealing with those on probation and parole. Treatment programs in correctional facilities or psychiatric hospitals are fairly easy to administer, compared with keeping track of the paroled and probationary population of sexual offenders. According to the Department of Justice, approximately 60 percent of sex offenders under the control of correctional officials are on probation or parole.[263] Given the size of this population, special techniques and substantial follow-up are necessary for sex offenders under community supervision.[264] One attempt to deal with the paroled and probationary population of sex offenders is public registration and notification of sex offenders. The registration of sex offenders with law enforcement agencies is not new, but the additional requirement of community notification evolved in 1990. California enacted a registration system in 1947, and the first community notification statute was enacted by Washington state in 1990.[265] Currently, all states have a system requiring the registration of sex offenders.[266] These laws are commonly referred to as "Megan's Laws" after Megan Kanka, who was murdered by Jesse Timmendequas, a neighbor and—unbeknownst to the Kanka family—a repeat sex offender, in New Jersey in 1994. Megan's Laws were enacted with the belief that community awareness would reduce future sexual criminal acts. This rests on two assumptions: first, that sex offenders have high recidivism rates; second, that rapes are likely to occur in neighborhoods where the offender is likely to become close to the child. In fact, according to the Department of Justice, in 90 percent of the rapes of children under age 12, the child knew the rapist. The constitutionality of these laws have been challenged on three grounds.[267] First, the notification can serve as an ex post facto punishment on those convicted before the statute went into effect. Second, notification violates the privacy rights of those released. Third, the stigma associated with notification is a form of cruel and unusual punishment.

In some cases, states are hesitant to release sex offenders even when their sentence has been completed. Kansas, for instance, passed a law permitting psychiatric detention under civil law after an offender has completed his or her criminal sentence. In a 5–4 decision, the U.S. Supreme Court upheld Kansas' statute based on the view that the "commitment" was civil as opposed to criminal and that treatment was the goal of the confinement.[268] Thus, a set of circumstances can occur in which offenders subjected to this post-imprisonment confinement are mentally fit for trial and imprisonment but are not deemed mentally suitable for release from prison—and therefore are sent to a psychiatric facility. Zonana raises several issues surrounding the use of civil commitment after incarceration of sex offenders: sexual criminal behavior is being cast as mental illness for the purpose of preventive detention, not treatment; definitions of mental abnormalities in these statutes are extremely vague; an inappropriate and costly demand will be put on the healthcare system; and problems initiated by criminal justice system sentencing approaches are being transferred to psychiatric hospitals.[269]

There are many important and difficult issues to confront regarding the incarceration, treatment, and reintegration of sex offenders. Traditionally, sex offenders are the least liked among their fellow inmates; therefore, the management of the sex offender becomes a concern in the institution. The placement of sex offenders on probation can create public relations problems for the criminal justice system, especially in the current political climate regarding offenders in general and sex offenders in particular. As correctional officials and public policymakers confront these issues, they have to weigh the safety of the general population against the high costs of psychiatric treatment and detention.

▶ Ethics Focus: Justice or Mercy?

You are a member of a state parole board. You and the other members have the power to grant medical parole or compassionate release. You have a decision to make. Doctors have declared that an inmate is in the final stages of brain cancer. This inmate is a virtual invalid. He is bedridden, barely conscious, and presents no threat to staff or the other inmates. The only liability he seems to pose at this time is the cost to the prison system for his medical care, which is enormous.

The inmate is serving a long prison sentence for rape. Although he has served several years, he has several more years to serve before his sentence has been completed, and he will not live to complete his sentence. The inmate's family is begging you and the other parole board members to allow his release so he can spend his dying days in their home. You are also besieged with the same request from prisoners' rights groups. However, the victim, still traumatized even years after the rape occurred, is urging you to deny his release. That sentiment is shared by victims' rights groups in your state who maintain that the inmate deserves to die in prison, and that he showed no compassion for his victim while raping her. Prison authorities want to rid themselves of the cost and labor required to care for this inmate who poses no threat to society if released. You are feeling pressure from all sides. What do you do?

▶At the Movies . . . .

One Flew Over the Cuckoo's Nest, 1975.

In this film, Nicholson portrays R.P. McMurphy, an incorrigible prison inmate in a Northwestern state. The film, set in the 1960s, is based on a 1962 novel by Ken Kesey. The novel is laced with anti-establishment themes that were common to films and writings of that decade. Prison officials, unable to deal with McMurphy's continued disruptive behavior, decide that he is in need of medical assistance, and he is transferred to a mental hospital. McMurphy finds that the hospital staff, especially Nurse Ratched, is more intent on maintaining an iron grip of control over the patients than actually helping them. One of the many messages of the film is that a government can do its greatest harm to its citizens when it declares them to be ill rather than simply criminal.

CONCLUSION

The way special-needs populations will be dealt with in our correctional institutions in the future depends on the effort and resources committed to serving the needs of these populations in the present. Sufficient medical care must be provided for sick, elderly, and dying inmates in our prisons. The mental health problems of those persons who are incarcerated must also be attended to. Sexual offenders, one of the most difficult offender populations to change, cannot be treated as if they were guilty of property crimes. Reoffending among substance abusing inmates can be reduced if the offenders are placed in appropriate programs.

The Russian novelist Dostoevsky, himself a political prisoner under Czar Nicholas I, pointed out that the mark of a civilization can be measured based on how it treats its prisoners. As we measure our civilization, we will have to watch closely how we treat not only our general prison population but particularly those with special needs.

DISCUSSION QUESTIONS

1. Mentally ill and developmentally disabled inmates present some unique challenges to correctional staff. Discuss some of those challenges and some possible solutions for dealing with these special-needs inmates.

2. Many states laws allow for the "compassionate release" of terminally ill inmates. Discuss the advantages and disadvantages of compassionate release.

3. Some states have passed laws permitting psychiatric detention of sex offenders even after the offender has completed his or her criminal sentence. What are some of the reasons for these laws? Do you see any potential problems associated with this practice?

4. What are some of the advantages and disadvantages to segregating inmates who are chronically or terminally ill?

5. Should HIV/AIDS prisoners be segregated from other prisoners? Why or why not?

6. Discuss what you think can and should be done with elderly offenders.

FURTHER READING

Brown, T.J. (1998). *Dorothea Dix: New England Reformer*. Cambridge, MA: Harvard University Press.

Pollock, J.M. (1999). *Criminal Women*. Cincinnati: Anderson.

Terry, C.M. (2003). *The Fellas: Overcoming Prison and Addiction*. Belmont, CA: Wadsworth Thomson.

Zimbardo, P. (2007). *The Lucifer Effect: Understanding How Good People Turn Evil*. New York: Random House.

NOTES

1. Torrey, 1995.
2. Adams, 1992.
3. James and Glaze, 2006.
4. Guy et al., 1985; Steadman, McCarty, and Morrissey, 1989; Teplin, 1990.
5. American Psychiatric Association, 1994.
6. Carbonell and Perkins, 2007.
7. Carbonell and Perkins, 2007.
8. Hans, 1986.
9. Wrightsman, 1991.
10. See Callahan et al., 1991; Cirincione, Steadman, and McGreevey, 1995; Rice, Harris, and Lang, 1990.
11. Callahan et al., 1992.
12. See Hodgins (1995) for a review. Powell, Holt, and Fondacaro (1997) suggest that among jail detainees, rates of mental illness may not be as high in rural jails as in urban jails.

13. Hodgins, 1995, 16.

14. Monahan, 1992, 518.

15. Hodgins, 1995; Hodgins and Cote, 1990.

16. Briscoe, 1996.

17. Link, Andrews, and Cullen, 1992.

18. Hodgins, 1992.

19. See Novick et al., 1977; Scott, Hannum, and Gilchrist, 1982; Washington and Diamond, 1985.

20. Radloff, 1975.

21. Fogel and Martin, 1992.

22. Fogel and Martin, 1992.

23. Cote and Hodgins, 1992.

24. Monahan, 1992.

25. See Monahan and Steadman (1996) for issues surrounding this topic.

26. Monahan, 1981.

27. Harris, Rice, and Quinsey, 1993.

28. Abram, 1990.

29. Abram, 1990; Cote and Hodgins, 1990.

30. Hodgins and Cote, 1993a.

31. Hodgins and Cote, 1993b.

32. The National GAINS Center for People with Co-Occurring Disorders in the Justice System is a federal partnership involving two centers of the Substance Abuse and Mental Health Services Administration, The Center for Substance Abuse Treatment and the Center for Mental Health Services, and the National Institute of Corrections.

33. Birmingham, Mason, and Grubin, 1996.

34. Also see Toch and Adams, 1987.

35. Fauteck, 1995.

36. Hodgins, 1995.

37. Clymer, 1992.

38. Teplin and Pruett, 1992; Torrey et al., 1992.

39. Palmero, Gumz, and Liska, 1992.

40. Solomon and Draine, 1995.

41. Teplin, 1994; Teplin, 1996.

42. Morris, Steadman, and Veysey, 1997.

43. O'Sullivan, 1992.

44. Morrissey et al., 1984; Steadman, Barbara, and Dennis, 1994.

45. Morris, Steadman, and Veysey, 1997.

46. Steadman and Veysey, 1997.

47. Morris and Steadman, 1994.

48. Walsh and Bricout, 1997.

49. Muzekari, Morrisey, and Young, 1997.

50. Kalinich, Embert, and Senese, 1988.

51. Morris, Steadman, and Veysey, 1997.

52. Belcher, 1988; Steadman, McCarty, and Morrisey, 1989.

53. Blackburn, 1998.

54. Alexander, 1991.

55. Schultz-Ross, 1993. Several resources on treatment and counseling for offenders are available, Van Voorhis, Braswell, and Lester, 2000; Alexander, 2000; Hodgins, 1993.

56. Cohen, 1996; Scott and O'Connor, 1997.

57. Floyd, 1990.

58. Hartwell et al., 1999.

59. Lombardo, 1985.

60. Gibbs, 1987.

61. McCorkle, 1993.

62. Alexander, 1992.

63. Johnson and Hoover, 1988; Steadman and Veysey, 1997; Briscoe, 1996; Rogers and Bagby, 1992.

64. See Ellis and Luckasson (1985) for issues facing mentally retarded defendants. Giagiari (1981) provided an account of the mentally retarded offender.

65. Smith, 1993.

66. Wolford, Nelson, and Rutherford, 1996.

67. Coffey, Procopiow, and Miller, 1989.

68. Laski, 1992.

69. President's Committee on Mental Retardation, 1991.

70. Fitch, 1992.

71. Petrella, 1992.

72. Petrila et al., 1981.

73. Reich and Wells, 1985.

74. Petrella, 1992.

75. Bonnie, 1992.

76. Austin and Duncan, 1988.

77. Santamour, 1986.

78. Ellis and Luckasson, 1985.

79. Noble and Conley, 1992.

80. Petersilia, 1997.

81. Finn, 1992.

82. Walsh, 1997.

83. Lampert, 1987.

84. American Psychiatric Association, 1994; Carbonell and Perkins, 2007.

85. Petersilia, 1997, 37.

86. McGee and Menolascino, 1992; Spruill and May, 1988.

87. Noble and Conley, 1992.

88. Denkowski, Denkowski, and Mabli, 1983; Hall, 1985.

89. Hall, 1985.

90. MacEachron, 1979.

91. Brown and Courtless, 1971; Denkowski and Denkowski, 1985; Veneziano and Veneziano, 1996; Veneziano, Veneziano, and Tribolet, 1987.

92. Prescott and Van Houten, 1982; Lampert, 1987; Santamour and West, 1982; Spruill and May, 1988.

93. Noble and Conley, 1992.

94. Veneziano, Veneziano, and Tribolet, 1987.

95. Veneziano and Veneziano, 1996.

96. Petersilia, 1997.

97. Veneziano and Veneziano, 1996.

98. White and Wood, 1986; 1988.

99. Wood and White, 1992.

100. Rockowitz, 1986.

101. Petersilia, 1997.

102. Noble and Conley, 1992.

103. Wolford, 1987.

104. Smith et al., 1988.

105. Hall, 1992.

106. *Guthrie v. Evans*, 1981.

107. *Ruiz v. Estelle*, 1980.

108. Hall, 1992.

109. Hall, 1992, 182.

110. Hall, 1992.

111. Hall, 1992.

112. Pugh, 1986.

113. Hall, 1992.

114. Hall, 1992; Pugh, 1986.

115. Rutherford, Nelson, and Wolford, 1985.

116. Santamour and Watson, 1982.

117. DeMoll, 1992. Also see Bowker and Schweid (1992) for information on the programs in Cuyahoga County.

118. Hall, 1992.

119. Petersilia, 1997.

120. Jones, 1995.

121. Mumola and Karberg, 2006.

122. Chaiken, 1989.

123. Tims and Leukefeld, 1992.

124. Tims and Leukefeld, 1992.

125. See Leukefeld and Tims, 1990, Anglin and McGlothlin, 1984; Lipton, Falkin, and Wexler, 1992.

126. Lipton, Falkin, and Wexler, 1992.

127. Peters and May, 1992.

128. See DeLeon, 1984.

129. Wexler and Williams, 1986; Wexler et al., 1992; Anglin and Maugh, 1992.

130. Wexler et al., 1992.

131. Field, 1985; Field, 1989.

132. Brown, 1992.

133. Weinman, 1992.

134. Van Stelle, Mauser, and Moberg, 1994. For information on Wisconsin's Department of Corrections program that includes coordination with parole for alcohol and other drug offenders, see Vigdal and Stadler, 1992.

135. Peters and May, 1992.

136. Peters and May, 1992.

137. Peters and May, 1992.

138. Peters and May, 1992.

139. Murray, 1992.

140. See Lipton (1998) for a history of therapeutic communities. For a review of the effectiveness of therapeutic communities with substance-abusing inmates, see Wexler's 1995 review.

141. Murray, 1992. For information on the evaluation processes utilized for the FBOP's substance abuse programs, see Pelissier and McCarthy, 1992.

142. Winett et al., 1992.

143. See Arbiter, 1988.

144. Bell et al., 1992.

145. Bell et al., 1992.

146. Wexler, Falkin, and Lipton, 1990.

147. Field, 1985; Field, 1989.

148. See Field, 1992.

149. See Lipton, Falkin, and Wexler, 1992; Field, 1992.

150. Field, 1992.

151. Giuliani and Schnoll, 1985.

152. Van Voorhis and Hurst, 2007, 257.

153. Van Voorhis and Hurst, 2007.

154. Prendergast, Anglin, and Wellisch, 1995.

155. Andrews et al., 1990; McGrath, Hoke, and Vojisek, 1998.

156. Coleman, 1999.

157. Hammet, 1998.

158. Cartwell et al., 1994.

159. Smith, 1994.

160. Kerle, 1994

161. Smith, 1994.

162. Smith, 1994.

163. Kane and Dotson, 1997.

164. Hammett and Harrold, 1994.

165. See Wilcock, Hammett, and Parent, 1995.

166. Braithwaite, Braithwaite, and Poulson, 1998.

167. Wilcock, Hammett, and Parent, 1995.

168. Koehler, 1994.

169. Estelle v. Gamble, 1976.

170. Maruschak, 2004, 1.

171. Maruschak, 2001, 1.

172. Maruschak, 1999.

173. Maruschak, 2001, 2.

174. Maruschak, 2004, 2.

175. Maruschak, 2001, 5.

176. Maruschak, 2004, 1.

177. Maruschak, 2004, 1.

178. Maruschak, 2001, 7.

179. Mutter, Grimes, and Labarthe, 1994.

180. Maruschak, 2001, 1, 2.

181. Koehler, 1994

182. Koehler, 1994.

183. Harrison et al., 1998.

184. Martin, Zimmerman, and Long, 1993.

185. Martin and Zimmerman, 1990; Vlahor, 1990.

186. Keeton and Swanson, 1998. Goisman et al. (1991) discusses the challenges of providing educational programming for AIDS patients who have chronic mental illness.

187. Olivero, 1990.

188. Harrison et al., 1998.

189. Clark and Boudin, 1990.

190. Mahaffey and Marcus, 1995.

191. Maruschak, 2001, 8.

192. Maruschak, 2001, 8.

193. Blumberg and Laster, 1999.

194. Blumberg and Laster, 1999.

195. Blumberg and Laster, 1999.

196. Braithwaite, Hammett, and Mayberry, 1996.

197. Jacobs, 1995, 29.

198. See Belbot and del Carmen, 1991; Blumberg and Laster, 1999; Jacobs, 1995.

199. *Estelle v. Gamble*, 1976.

200. *Wilson v. Seiter*, 1991.

201. Blumberg and Laster, 1999.

202. *Davis v. Hopper*, 98-9663.

203. Mahon, 1996.

204. Kratcoski, 1994.

205. Fiske, 1994.

206. Faiver, 1998a.

207. Faiver and Rieger, 1998.

208. Fogel, 1995.

209. Faiver, 1998b.

210. Vigilante et al., 1999.

211. Rold, 1996.

212. Lopez and Chayriques, 1994.

213. Ditton and Wilson, 1999.

214. Neeley, Addison, and Craig-Moreland, 1997.

215. Cromwell, 1994.

216. Neeley, Addison, and Craig-Moreland, 1997.

217. The Coalition for Federal Sentencing Reform, 1998.

218. Booth, 1989. Alday, 1994, in a study of the concerns and programs for the elderly in state prison systems, found that the concerns for rising medical costs and the problems presented by chronic health problems were issues for administrators. For a review of the health care issues facing the aging prisoner, see Faiver, 1998c.

219. Alday, 1994; Booth, 1989.

220. Sabath and Cowles, 1988.

221. Fry, 1988.

222. Wall, 1998.

223. Johnson, 1988, 163.

224. Johnson, 1988, 163. Moore (1989) discusses the impact of the physical prison environment of the aged. Older inmates transferred to a special Michigan facility showed an initial increase in health complaints, but the special facility also reflected an overall improvement in inmate welfare.

225. Alday, 1994.

226. Coalition for Federal Sentencing Reform, 1998.

227. Neeley, Addison, and Craig-Moreland, 1997, 120.

228. Maruschak, 1999.

229. Braithwaite, Braithwaite, and Poulson, 1998.

230. Bureau of Justice Statistics, 2007.

231. Stolberg, 2001.

232. Ratcliff, 2000.

233. *Las Vegas Review-Journal*, 1997.

234. *Las Vegas Review-Journal*, 1997.

235. Connecticut General Statutes § 54-131a et seq.

236. 18 USC § 4205(g).

237. Reinhart, 2000.

238. National Prison Hospice Association, 2003.

239. National Prison Hospice Association, 2003.

240. Lois Deberry Special Needs Facility, 2001.

241. Lois Deberry Special Needs Facility, 2001.

242. The National Prison Hospice Association, 1999.

243. Price, 1998.

244. Price, 1998.

245. National Prison Hospice Association, 1999.

246. National Prison Hospice Association, 1999.

247. National Prison Hospice Association, 1999.

248. Coleman et al., 1996.

249. Harrison and Beck, 2007.

250. Marsh and Walsh, 1995.

251. Chantry and Craig, 1994. See also Miner and Dwyer, 1997.

252. Chantry and Craig, 1994; Ploscue, 1968; Langevin et al., 1988.

253. Chantry and Craig, 1994.

254. See Abel, Mittelman, and Becker, 1985; Deitz et al., 1982.

255. Rice et al., 1994.

256. Pithers, 1999.

257. O'Donohue and Letourneau, 1993. See also Pithers (1994) for a program to enhance the offender's empathy for survivors of sexual abuse.

258. Quinsey, 1998, 417. For a review of sex offender treatment programs, see Sapp and Vaughan, 1991; Thorton and Hogue, 1993; and Lester, 1995. Plaud and Gaither (1997) report success with behavioral interventions.

259. Quinsey, 1998, 417.

260. Priest and Smith, 1992. For a discussion of the pedophile in prisons, see Musk, Swetz, and Vernon, 1997. Keiser (1998) discusses the management of the sex offender in prisons.

261. Schorsch et al., 1990.

262. Meyer and Cole, 1997.

263. Greenfeld, 1997.

264. Quinsey, 1998. See English, 1991.

265. Kabat, 1998.

266. Kabat, 1998; Petrosino and Petrosino, 1999.

267. Petrosino and Petrosino, 1999.

268. *Kansas v. Hendricks*, 1997.

269. Zonana, 1997.

REFERENCES

Abel, G., M. Mittelman, and J. Becker (1985). "Sexual Offenders: Results of Assessment and Recommendations for Treatment." In M. Ben-Aron, S. Hucker, and C. Webster (eds.), *Clinical Criminology: The Assessment and Treatment of Criminal Behavior*, 191-205. Toronto: M.M. Graphics.

Abram, K. (1990). "The Problem of Co-Occurring Disorders among Jail Detainees: Antisocial Disorder, Drug Abuse, and Depression." *Law and Human Behavior* 14:333-345.

Adams, K. (1992). "Who Are the Clients? Characteristics of Inmates Referred for Mental Health Treatment." *The Prison Journal* 72:120-141.

Alday, R. (1994). "Golden Years Behind Bars." *Federal Probation* 58(2):47-54.

Alexander, R. (2000). *Counseling, Treatment and Intervention Methods with Juvenile and Adult Offenders*. Belmont, CA: Wadsworth/Thompson Learning.

Alexander, R. (1992). "Determining Appropriate Criteria in the Evaluation of Correctional Mental Health Treatment for Inmates." *Journal of Offender Rehabilitation* 18:119-134.

Alexander, R. (1991). "The United States Supreme Court and an Inmate's Right to Refuse Mental Health Treatment." *Criminal Justice Policy Review* 5:225-240.

American Correctional Association (1999). "Death Row and the Death Penalty. " *Corrections Compendium* 24 (September):6-18.

American Correctional Association (1990). *The Female Offender: What Does the Future Hold?* Arlington, VA: Kirby Lithographic.

American Psychiatric Association (1994). *Diagnostic and Statistical Manual of Mental Disorders-IV*. Washington, DC: author.

Andrews, D., I. Zinger, R. Hoge, J. Bonta, P. Gendreau, and F. Cullen (1990). "Does Correctional Treatment Work? A Psychologically Informed Meta-analysis." *Criminology* 28:369-404.

Anglin, M., and T. Maugh (1992). "Ensuring Success in Interventions with Drug Using Offenders." *Annals of AAPSS* 521:66-90.

Anglin, M., and W. McGlothlin (1984). "Outcome of Narcotic Addict Treatment in California." In F. Tims and J. Ludford (eds.), *Drug Abuse Treatment Evaluation: Strategies, Progress and Prospects*. Rockville, MD: National Institute on Drug Abuse.

Anonymous (1998). "Health Promotion and Disease Prevention Activities in Federal Penitentiaries in Ontario." *Canadian Journal of Criminology* 40(4):451-452.

Arbiter, N. (1988). "Drug Treatment in a Direct Supervision Jail: Pima County's Amity Jail Project." *American Jails* 2:35-36, 39-40.

Arriens, J. (ed.) (1997). *Welcome to Hell: Letters and Writings from Death Row*. Boston: Northeastern University Press.

Austin, J., B. Bloom, and T. Donahue (1992). *Female Offenders in the Community: An Analysis of Innovative Strategies and Programs*. Washington, DC: National Institute of Corrections.

Austin, R., and A. Duncan (1988). "Handle with Care: Special Inmates, Special Needs." *Corrections Today* 50:13.

Baskin, D., I. Sommers, R. Tresslen, and H. Steadman (1989). "Role Incongruence and Gender Variation in Prison Mental Health Sources." *Journal of Health and Social Behavior*, 305-314

Beck, A., and C. Mumola (1999). "Prisoners in 1998." *Bureau of Justice Statistics Bulletin*. Washington DC: U.S. Government Printing Office.

Bedau, H. (ed.) (1997). *The Death Penalty in America: Current Controversies*. New York: Oxford University Press.

Belbot, B., and R. del Carmen (1991). "AIDS in Prison: Legal Issues." *Crime & Delinquency* 37:135-153.

Belcher, J. (1988). "Are Jails Replacing the Mental Health System for the Homeless Mentally Ill?" *Community Mental Health Journal* 24:185-195.

Belknap, J. (1996). *The Invisible Woman: Gender, Crime, and Justice*. Belmont, CA: ITP/Wadsworth.

Bell, W., J. Mitchell, J. Bevino, A. Darabi, and R. Nimer (1992). "Florida Department of Corrections Substance Abuse Programs." In C. Luekefeld and F. Tims (eds.), *Drug Abuse Treatment in Prisons and Jails*, 110-124. Rockville, MD: National Institute on Drug Abuse.

Bickell, N., S. Vermund, M. Holmes, S. Safyer, and R.D. Burk (1991). "Human Papillomavirus, Gonorrhea, Syphilis, and Cervical Dysplasia in Jailed Women." *American Journal of Public Health* 8 1:1318-1320.

Birmingham, L., D. Mason, and D. Grubin (1996). "Prevalence of Mental Disorder in Remand Prisoners: Consecutive Case Study." *British Medical Journal* 3 13:152.

Blackburn, R. (1998). "Criminality and the Interpersonal Circle in Mentally Disordered Offenders." *Criminal Justice and Behavior* 25(2):155-176.

Blumberg, M., and J. Laster (1999). "The Impact of HIV/AIDS on Corrections." In K. Haas and G. Alpert (eds.), *The Dilemmas of Corrections: Contemporary Readings*, 574-591. Prospect Heights, IL: Waveland.

Bonnie, R. (1992). "The Competency of Defendants with Mental Retardation to Assist in Their Own Defense." In R. Conley, R. Luckasson and G. Bouthilet (eds.), *The Criminal Justice System and Mental Retardation*, 97-120. Baltimore: Paul H. Brookes.

Booth, D. (1989). "Health Status of the Incarcerated Elderly: Issues and Concerns" *Journal of Offender Counseling, Services and Rehabilitation* 13:193-214.

Bowker, A., and R. Schweid (1992). "Habilitation of the Retarded Offender in Cuyahoga County." *Federal Probation* 56:48-52.

Braithwaite, R., T. Hammett, and R. Mayberry (1996). *Prisons and AIDS—A Public Health Challenge*. San Francisco: Jossey-Bass.

Braithwaite, R., K. Braithwaite, and R. Poulson (1998). "HIV and TB in Prisons." *Corrections Today* 60(2):108-110.

Brewer, V., J. Marquart, J. Mullings, and B. Crouch (1998). "AIDS-Related Risk Behavior among Female Prisoners with Histories of Mental Impairment." *The Prison Journal* 78:101-119.

Briscoe, J. (1996). "Examining Juvenile Offenders with Mental Impairments." *Corrections Today* 58(6):106-109.

Brown, B. (1992). "Program Models." In C. Leukefeld and F. Tims (eds.), *Drug Abuse Treatment in Prisons and Jails*, 31-37. Rockville, MD: National Institute on Drug Abuse.

Brown, B., and T. Courtless (1971). *The Mentally Retarded Offender*. Washington, DC: Department of Health, Education and Welfare.

Bureau of Justice Statistics, Department of Justice (2007). Available at http://www.ojp. usdoj.gov/bjs/dcrp/tables/pristab1.htm

Bureau of Justice Statistics, Department of Justice (1999). Available at http://www.ojp. usdoj.gov/bjs/ correct.htm

Burr, R. (1992). "Introduction to Brief of American Association of Mental Retardation et al. as Amici Curiae." In support of petitioner. *In re Johnny Paul Penry, Petitioner, v. James A. Lynaugh*, Director, Texas Department of Corrections. In R. Conley, R. Luckasson, and G. Bouthilet (eds.), *The Criminal Justice System and Mental Retardation: Defendants and Victims*, 245-248. Baltimore: Paul H. Brookes.

Callahan, L., M. McGreevy, C. Cirincione, and H. Steadman (1992). "Measuring the Effects of the Guilty but Mentally II (GBMI): Georgia's 1982 GBMI Reform." *Law and Human Behavior* 16:447-462.

Callahan, L., H. Steadman, M. McGreevy, and P. Robbins (1991). "The Volume and Composition of Insanity Defense Pleas: An Eight State Study." *Bulletin of the American Academy of Psychiatry and the Law* 19:331-338.

Carbonell, J., and R. Perkins (2007). "Diagnosis and Assessment of Criminal Offenders." In P. Van Voorhis, M. Braswell, and D. Lester (eds.), *Correctional Counseling and Rehabilitation*, 6th ed., 113. Newark, NJ: LexisNexis Matthew Bender.

Carp, S., and L. Schade (1992). "Tailoring Facility Programming to Suit Female Offenders' Needs. *Corrections Today* 54:152-159.

Cartwell, M., D. Snider, G. Cauthen, and I. Onorato (1994). "Epidemiology of Tuberculosis in the United States, 1985-1992." *Journal of American Medical Association* 272:535-539.

Chaiken, M.R. (1989). "In-Prison Programs for Drug-Involved Offenders." *National Institute of Justice Research in Brief*. Washington, DC: U.S. Department of Justice.

Chantry, K., and R. Craig (1994). "Psychological Screening of Sexually Violent Offenders with the MCMI." *Journal of Clinical Psychology* 50:430-435.

Chesney-Lind, M. (1995). "Rethinking Women's Imprisonment: A Critical Examination of Trends in Female Incarceration." In B. Price and N. Sokoloff (eds.), *The Criminal Justice System: Offenders, Victims, and Workers*, 105-117. New York: McGraw-Hill.

Chesney-Lind, M. (1992). "Putting the Brakes on the Building Binge." *Corrections Today* 54(6):30, 32-34.

Cieslak, P., M. Curtis, D. Coulombier, A. Hathcock, N. Bean, and R. Tauxe (1996). "Preventable Diseases in Correctional Facilities: Domestic Foodborne Outbreaks in the United States." *Archives of Internal Medicine* 156:1883-1888.

Cirincione, C., H. Steadman, and M. McGreevy (1995). "Rates of Insanity Acquittals and the Factors Associated with the Insanity Plea." *Bulletin of the American Academy of Psychiatry and the Law* 23:399-409.

Clark, J., and K. Boudin (1990). "Community of Women Organize Themselves to Cope with the AIDS Crisis: A Case Study from Bedford Hills Correctional Facility." *Social Justice* 17 (2):90-109.

Clement, M. (1993). "Parenting in Prison: A National Survey for Incarcerated Women." *Journal of Offender Rehabilitation* 19:89-100.

Clymer, P. (1992). "Managing Malingers: Power Stems from Active Involvement, Not Control." *Corrections Today* 54 (6):22-24.

Coalition for Federal Sentencing Reform (1998). "Elderly Prison Initiative: Executive Summary." Available at http://www.sentencing.org/elder.html

Coffey, O., N. Procopiow, and N. Miller (1989). *Programming for Mentally Retarded and Learning Disabled Inmates: A Guide for Correctional Administrators*. Washington, DC: U.S. Department of Justice, National Institute of Corrections.

Cohen, F. (1996). "Ohio's Mentally Ill Prisoners Get Historic Consent Decree: Both Sides Agree." *Corrections Today* 58(2):156-160.

Coleman, E., S. Dwyer, G. Abel, W. Berner, J. Breiling, J. Hindman, F. Honey-Knopp, R. Langevin, and F. Phafflin (1996). "Standards of Care for the Treatment of Adult Sex Offenders." *Journal of Offender Rehabilitation* 23:5-11.

Coleman, R. (1999). "Corrections in the 21st Century." *American Jails* 12 (6):47-49.

Cote, G., and S. Hodgins (1992). "The Prevalence of Major Mental Disorders Among Homicide Offenders." *International Journal of Law and Psychiatry* 15 (1):89-99.

Cote, G., and S. Hodgins (1990). "Co-Occurring Mental Disorders among Criminal Offenders." *Bulletin of the American Academy of Psychiatry and Law* 18(3):271-281.

Cromwell, P. (1994). "The Graying of America's Prisons." *Overcrowded Times* 6:3.

DeLeon, G. (1984). *The Therapeutic Community: Study of Effectiveness*. Rockville, MD: U.S. Department of Health and Human Services.

Dallo, M. "Coping with Incarceration—From the Other Side of the Bars." *Corrections Today* 59:96-98.

Daly, K. (1998). "Gender, Crime, and Criminology." In M. Tonry (ed.), *The Handbook of Crime and Punishment*, 85-108. New York: Oxford.

Death Penalty Information Center (1999). Available at http://www.essential.org/dpic

DeCostanzo, E., and J. Valente (1990). "Designing a Corrections Continuum for Female Offenders: One State's Experience." *The Prison Journal* 64:120-128.

Deitz, S., K. Blackwell, P. Daley, and B. Bentley (1982). "Measurement of Empathy Toward Rape Victims and Rapists." *Journal of Personality and Social Psychology* 43:372-384.

DeMoll, C. (1992). "Advocacy Service Systems for Defendants with Mental Retardation." In R. Conley, R. Luckasson, and G. Bouthilet (eds.), *The Criminal Justice System and Mental Retardation: Defendants and Victims*, 191-207. Baltimore: Paul H. Brookes.

Denkowski, G., and K. Denkowski (1985). "The Mentally Retarded Offender in the State Prison System: Identification, Prevalence, Adjustment and Rehabilitation." *Criminal Justice and Behavior* 12:53-70.

Denkowski, G., K. Denkowski, and J. Mabli (1983). "A Fifty State Survey of the Current Status of Residential Treatment Programs for Mentally Retarded Offenders." *Mental Retardation* 21:197-203.

Ditton, P.M., and D.J. Wilson (1999). "Truth in Sentencing in State Prisons." *Bureau of Justice Statistics Special Report*. Washington, DC: U.S. Government Printing Office.

Downey, G., G. Gabriel, A. Deery, J. Crow, and P. Walker (1994). "Management of Female Prisoners with Abnormal Cervical Cytology." *British Medical Journal* 308:1412-1413.

Dressel, P., J. Porterfield, and S. Barnhill (1998). "Mothers Behind Bars." *Corrections Today* 60:90-94.

Ellis, J., and R. Luckasson (1985). "Mentally Retarded Criminal Defendants." *George Washington Law Review* 53:414-493.

English K. (1991). "Managing Adult Sex Offenders in the Community—A Containment Approach." *National Institute of Justice Research Brief*, I -11.

Faiver, K. (1998a). "What Is Happening in Health?" In K. Faiver (ed.), *Health Care Management in Corrections*, 1-23. Lanham, MD: American Correctional Association.

Faiver, K. (1998b). "Special Issues of Aging." In K. Faiver (ed.), *Health Care Management in Corrections*, 123-132. Lanham, MD: American Correctional Association.

Faiver, K. (1998c). "Preventing Contagion." In K. Faiver (ed.) *Health Care Management in Corrections*, 83-100. Lanham, MD: American Correctional Association.

Faiver, K., and D. Rieger (1998). "Women's Health Issues." In K. Faiver (ed.), *Health Care Management in Corrections*, 133-141. Lanham, MD: American Correctional Association

Farnsworth, B., and R. Teske (1995). "Gender Differences in Felony Court Processing." *Women & Criminal Justice* 6:23-44.

Farr, K. (1997). "Aggravating and Differentiating Factors in the Cases of White and Minority Women on Death Row." *Crime & Delinquency* 43(July):260-278.

Fauteck, P. (1995). "Detecting the Malingering of Psychosis in Offenders." *Criminal Justice and Behavior* 22:3-18.

Feinman, C. (1986). *Women in the Criminal Justice System*. New York: Praeger.

Field, G. (1992). "Oregon Prison Drug Treatment Programs." In C. Luekefeld and F. Tims (eds.), *Drug Abuse Treatment in Prisons and Jails*, 142-155. Rockville, MD: National Institute on Drug Abuse.

Field, G. (1989). "The Effects of Intensive Treatment on Reducing the Criminal Recidivism of Addicted Offenders." *Federal Probation* 63:51-56.

Field, G. (1985). "The Cornerstone Program: A Client Outcome Study." *Federal Probation* 49:50-55.

Finn, M. (1992). "Prison Misconduct among Developmentally Challenged Inmates." *Criminal Justice and Mental Health* 2:287-299.

Fishman, S. (1982), "The Impact of Incarceration on Children of Offenders." *Journal of Children in a Contemporary Society* 15:89-99.

Fiske, D. (1994). "Pennsylvania Department of Corrections Joins with Local Hospital to Meet Needs of Dying Inmates." *CorrectCare* 8:4.

Fitch, W. (1992). "Mental Retardation and Criminal Responsibility." In R. Conley, R. Luckasson, and G. Bouthilet (eds.), *The Criminal Justice System and Mental Retardation*, 121-136. Baltimore: Paul H. Brookes.

Fleisher, M., R. Rison, and D. Heiman (1997). "Female Inmates: A Growing Constituency in the Federal Bureau of Prisons." *Corrections Management Quarterly* 1:28-35.

Floyd, J. (1990). "The Administration of Psychotropic Drugs to Prisoners: State of the Law and Beyond." *Correctional Law Review* 78(5):1243-1285.

Fogel, C. (1995). "Pregnant Prisoners: Impact of Incarceration on Health and Health Care." *Journal of Correctional Health Care* 2:169-190.

Fogel, C., and S. Martin (1992). "The Mental Health of Incarcerated Women." *Western Journal of Nursing Research* 14:30-47.

Fritsch, T., and J. Burkhead (1982). "Behavioral Reactions of Children to Parental Absence Due to Imprisonment." *Family Relations*, 301.

Fry, L. (1988). "The Concerns of Older Inmates in a Minimum Prison Setting." In B. McCarthy and R. Langworthy (eds.), *Older Offenders: Perspectives in Criminology and Criminal Justice*. New York: Praeger.

Furby, L., M. Weinrott, and L. Blackshaw (1989). "Sex Offender Recidivism: A Review." *Psychological Bulletin* 105:3-30.

Giagiari, S. (1981). "The Mentally Retarded Offender." *Crime and Delinquency Literature*, 559-577.

Giallombardo, R. (1966). *Society of Women: A Study of a Women's Prison*. New York: Wiley.

Gibbs, J. (1987). "Symptoms of Psychopathology among Jail Prisoners: The Effects of Exposure to the Jail Environment." *Criminal Justice and Behavior* 14(3):288-310.

Gill, O., A. Noone, and J. Heptonstall (1995). "Imprisonment, Injecting Drug Use, and Bloodborne Viruses." *British Medical Journal* 310:275-276.

Gilliard, D., and A. Beck (1998). "Prison and Jail Inmates at Midyear 1997." *Bureau of Justice Statistics Bulletin*. Washington, DC: U.S. Government Printing Office.

Giuliani, D., and S. Schnoll (1985). "Clinical Decision Making in Chemical Dependence Treatment: A Programmatic Model." *Journal of Substance Abuse Treatment* 2:203-208.

Goisman, R., A. Kent, E. Montgomery, M. Cheevers, and S. Goldfinger (1991). "AIDS Education for Patients with Chronic Mental Illness. " *Community Mental Health Journal* 27:189-197.

Goodstein, L., D. MacKenzie, and R. Shotland (1984). "Personal Control and Inmate Adjustment to Prison." *Criminology* 22:343-369.

Gray, T., G. Mays, and M. Stohr (1995). "Inmate Needs and Programming in Exclusively Women's Jails." *The Prison Journal* 75:186-202.

Greenfeld, L. (1997). "Sex Offenses and Offenders." *Bureau of Justice Statistics Bulletin*. Washington, DC: U.S. Government Printing Office.

Gregrich, J. (1992). "Management of the Drug-Abusing Offender." In C. Leukefeld and F. Tims (eds.), *Drug Abuse Treatment in Prisons and Jails*, 211-231. Rockville, MD: National Institute on Drug Abuse.

Grossman, H. (1983). *Classification in Mental Retardation*. Washington, DC: American Association on Mental Deficiency.

Gunn, J., A. Maden, and M. Swinton (1991). "Treatment Needs of Prisoners with Psychiatric Disorders." *British Medical Journal* 303:338-341.

Guy, E., J. Platt, I. Zwerling, and S. Bulloch (1985). "Mental-Health Status of Prisoners in an Urban Jail." *Criminal Justice and Behavior* 12:29-53.

Gwinn, B. (1992). "Linking Inmate Families Together." *Federal Prisons Journal* 3:37-39.

Hall, J. (1992). "Correctional Services for Inmates with Mental Retardation: Challenge or Catastrophe?" In R. Conley, R. Luckasson, and G. Bouthilet (eds.), *The Criminal Justice System and Mental Retardation: Defendants and Victims*, 167-190. Baltimore: Paul H. Brookes.

Hall, J. (1985). "Identifying and Serving Mentally Retarded Inmates." *Journal of Prison and Jail Health* 5:29-38.

Hammett, T. (1998). "Public Health/Corrections Collaboration: Prevention and Treatment of HIV/AIDS, STDs, and TB." *Research in Brief*. Washington, DC: National Institute of Justice.

Hammett, T., and L. Harrold (1994). *Tuberculosis in Correctional Facilities*. Washington, DC: U.S. Government Printing Office.

Hans, V. (1986). "An Analysis of Public Attitudes Toward the Insanity Defense." *Criminology* 24:393-413.

Harris, G., M. Rice, and V. Quinsey (1993). "Violent Recidivism of Mentally Disordered Offenders: The Development of Statistical Prediction Instrument." *Criminal Justice and Behavior* 20:315-335.

Harrison, P.M., and A.J. Beck (2007). "Prisoners in 2005." *Bureau of Justice Statistics Bulletin*. Washington, DC: U.S. Government Printing Office.

Harrison, L., C. Butzin, J. Inciardi, and S. Martin (1998). "Integrating HIV-Prevention Strategies in a Therapeutic Community Work-Release Program for Criminal Offenders." *The Prison Journal* 78(3):232-243.

Hartwell, S., K. Off, D. Humphrey, and D. Janey (1999). "Taking the Long View: Joint Training of Criminal Justice and Mental Health Professionals in the Assessment of Substance Abuse Problems among the Incarcerated Dually Diagnosed in Massachusetts." *American Jails* 12(6):83-86.

Hefferman, E. (1992). "The Alderson Years." *Federal Prisons Journal* 3:20-26.

Heidensohn, F. (1985). *Women and Crime: The Life of the Female Offender.* New York: New York University Press.

Hodgins, S. (1995). "Assessing Mental Disorder in the Criminal Justice System: Feasibility Versus Clinical Accuracy." *International Journal of Law and Psychiatry* 18:15-28.

Hodgins, S. (1993). "Mental Health Treatment Services in Quebec for Persons Accused or Convicted of Criminal Offenses." *International Journal of Law and Psychiatry* 16:179-194.

Hodgins, S. (1992). "Mental Disorders, Intellectual Deficiency, and Crime: Evidence from a Birth Cohort." *Archives of General Psychiatry* 49(6):476-483.

Hodgins, S., and G. Cote (1993a). "Major Mental Disorders and Antisocial Personality Disorder: A Criminal Combination." *Bulletin of the American Academy of Psychiatry and the Law* 21(2):155-160.

Hodgins, S., and G. Cote (1993b). "The Criminality of Mentally Disordered Offenders." *Criminal Justice and Behavior* 20(2):115-129.

Hodgins, S., and G. Cote (1990). "Prevalence of Mental Disorders among Penitentiary Inmates in Quebec." *Canada's Mental Health* 38(1):1-4.

Houston, J., D. Gibbons, and J. Jones (1988). "Physical Environment and Jail Social Climate." *Crime & Delinquency* 34:449-466.

Hungerford, G. (1993). *The Children of Inmate Mothers: An Exploratory Study of Children, Caregivers, and Inmate Mothers in Ohio.* Unpublished doctoral dissertation, Ohio State University.

Immarigeon, R., and M. Chesney-Lind (1992). *Women's Prisons: Overcrowded and Overused.* San Francisco: National Council on Crime and Delinquency.

Inciardi, J., S. Martin, D. Lockwood, R. Hooper, and B. Wald (1992). "Obstacles to the Implementation and Evaluation of Drug Treatment Programs: Reviewing the Delaware KEY Experience." In C. Luekefeld and F. Tims (eds.), *Drug Abuse Treatment in Prisons and Jails*, 176-191.

Jackson, P., and C. Stearns (1995). "Gender Issues in the New Generation Jail." *The Prison Journal* 75:203-221.

Jacobs, S. (1995). "AIDS in Correctional Facilities: Current Status of Legal Issues Critical to Policy Development." *Journal of Criminal Justice* 23(3):209-221.

James, D.J., and L.E. Glaze (2006). "Mental Health Problems of Prison and Jail Inmates." *Bureau of Justice Statistics Special Report.* Washington DC: U.S. Government Printing Office.

Johnson, E. (1988). "Care for Elderly Inmates: Conflicting Concerns and Purposes in Prisons." In B. McCarthy and R. Langworthy (eds.), *Older Offenders: Perspectives in Criminology and Criminal Justice*. New York: Praeger.

Johnson, R. (1998). *Death Work: A Study of the Modern Execution Process*. Belmont, CA: Wadsworth.

Johnson, S., and J. Hoover (1988). "Mental Health Services Within the Federal Bureau of Prisons." *Psychiatric Annuals* 18:673-674.

Johnston, D. (1995a). "Effects of Parental Incarceration." In K. Gabel and D. Johnson (eds.), *Children of Incarcerated Parents*, 59-88. New York: Lexington.

Johnston, D. (1995b). "Child Custody Issues of Women Prisoners: A Preliminary Report from the Chicas Project." *The Prison Journal* 75:222-239.

Jones, W. (1995). "Developmentally Disabled in Jail." *American Jails*, 16-19

Kabat, A.R. (1998). "Scarlet Letter Sex Offender Database and Community Notification; Sacrificing Personal Privacy for a Symbol's Sake." *American Criminal Law Review* 35:333-370.

Kalinich, D., P. Embert, and J. Senese (1988). "Integrating Community Mental Health Services into Local Jails: A Policy Perspective." *Policy Studies Review* 1(3):660-669.

Kane, S., and C. Dotson (1997). "HIV Risk and Injecting Drug Use: Implications for Rural Jails." *Crime & Delinquency* 43(2):169-185.

Keeton, K., and C. Swanson (1998). "HIV/AIDS Education Needs Assessment: A Comparative Study of Jail and Prison Inmates in Northwest Florida." *The Prison Journal* 78(2):119-132.

Keiser. G. (1998). "Sex Offender Management." *Corrections Today* 60:65.

Kempfner, C. (1995). "Post-Traumatic Stress Reactions in Children of Imprisoned Mothers." In K. Gabel and D. Johnson (eds.), *Children of Incarcerated Parents*, 89-100. New York: Lexington.

Kerle, K. (1994). "Jails: The Growing T.B. Menace." *American Jails* 8(1):5.

Koehler, R. (1994). "FEW Infection, TB, and the Health Crisis in Corrections." *Public Administration Review* 54(1):31-35.

Kratcoski, P. (1994). "Older Inmates: Special Programming Concerns." In P. Kratcoski (ed.), *Correctional Counseling and Treatment*, 505-518. Prospect Heights, IL: Waveland.

Krohn, M., J. Curry, and S. Nelson-Kilger (1983). "Is Chivalry Dead? An Analysis of Changes in Police Dispositions of Males and Females." *Criminology* 2(1):228-244.

Kruttscnitt, C., and S. Krmpotich (1990). "Aggressive Behavior among Female Inmates: An Exploratory Study." *Justice Quarterly* 7:371-389.

Lamontagne, Y., and A. Lesage (1986). "Private Exposure and Covert Sensitization in the Treatment of Exhibitionism." *Justice Behavior Therapy & Experimental Psychiatry* 17:197-201.

Lampert, R. (1987). "The Mentally Retarded Offender in Prison." *Justice Professional* 2:60-69.

Langevin, R., R. Lang, R. Reynolds, P. Wright, D. Garrels, and V. Marchese (1988). "Personality and Sexual Anomalies: An Examination of the Million Clinical Multiaxial Inventory." *Annals of Sex Research* 1:13-32.

Las Vegas Review-Journal (online version), Saturday, June 28, 1997. Available at http://www.reviewjournal.com/lvrj-home/1997/jun-28-Sat-1997/news/5628473.html

Laski, F. (1992). "Sentencing the Offender with Mental Retardation: Honoring the Imperative for Intermediate Punishments and Probations." In R. Conley, R. Luckasson and G. Bouthilet (eds.), *The Criminal Justice System and Mental Retardation*, 137-152. Baltimore: Paul H. Brookes.

Lester, T. (1995). "Sex Offender Facility Committed to Change and Rehabilitation." *Corrections Today* 57:168.

Leukefeld, C., and F. Tims (eds.) (1992). *Drug Abuse Treatment in Prisons and Jails*. Rockville, MD: National Institute on Drug Abuse.

Leukefeld, C., and F. Tims (1990). "Compulsory Treatment for Drug Abuse." *International Journal of Addictions* 25:621-640.

Link, B., H. Andrews, and F. Cullen (1992). "The Violent and Illegal Behavior of Mental Patients Reconsidered." *American Sociological Review* 57:275-292.

Lipton, D. (1998). "Therapeutic Communities: History, Effectiveness and Prospects." *Corrections Today* 60:106-109, 146.

Lipton, D., G. Falkin, and H. Wexler (1992). "Correctional Drug Abuse Treatment in the United States: An Overview." In C. Leukefeld, and F. Tims (eds.), *Drug Abuse Treatment in Prisons and Jails*, 8-30. Rockville, MD: National Institute on Drug Abuse.

Lois Deberry Special Needs Facility. Personal Communication, 2001.

Lombardo, L. (1985). "Mental Health Work in Prisons and Jails: Inmate Adjustment and Indigenous Correctional Personnel." *Criminal Justice and Behavior* 12:17-28.

Lopez, M., and K. Chayriques (1994). "Billing Prisoners for Medical Care Blocks Access." *National Prison Project Journal* 9:1-2, 17.

MacEachron, A. (1979). "Mentally Retarded Offender: Prevalence and Characteristics." *American Journal on Mental Deficiency* 84:168-176.

MacKenzie, D., and L. Goodstein (1986). "Stress and Control Beliefs of Prisoners: Inmate Adjustment and Indigenous Correctional Personnel." *Criminal Justice and Behavior* 12:17-27.

MacKenzie, D., L. Goodstein, and D. Blouin (1987). "Personal Control and Prison Adjustment: An Empirical Test of a Proposed Model." *Journal of Research in Crime and Delinquency* 24:49-68.

Magura, S., A. Rosenblum, and H. Joseph (1992). "Evaluation of In-Jail Methadone Maintenance: Preliminary Results." In C. Luekefeld amd F. Tims (eds.), *Drug Abuse Treatment in Prisons and Jails*, 192-210. Rockville, MD: National Institute on Drug Abuse.

Mahaffey, K., and D. Marcus (1995). "Correctional Officers' Attitudes Towards AIDS." *Criminal Justice and Behavior* 22:91-105.

Mahon, N. (1996). "New York Inmates' THV Risk Behaviors: Implications for Prevention and Policy." *American Journal of Public Health* 86:1211-1215.

Malliori, M., V. Sypsa, M. Psichogiou, G. Toulourni, A. Skoutelis, N. Tassopoulos, A. Hatzakis, and C. Stefaniss (1998). "A Survey of Bloodborne Viruses and Associated Risk Behaviors in Greek Prisons." *Addiction* 93 (2):243-251.

Mann, C. (1984). *Female Crime and Delinquency*. Tuscaloosa, AL: University of Alabama Press.

Marsh, R., and A. Walsh. (1995). "Physiological and Psychosocial Assessment and Treatment of Sex Offenders" *Journal of Offender Rehabilitation* 22:77-96.

Martin, R., and S. Zimmerman (1990). "Adopting Precautions Against MV Infection among Male Prisoners: A Behavioral and Policy Analysis." *Criminal Justice and Policy Review* 4:330-348.

Martin, R., S. Zimmerman, and B. Long (1993). "AIDS Education in U.S. Prisons: A Survey of Inmate Programs." *The Prison Journal* 73:103-129.

Martin, S., and R. Bachman (1998). "The Contribution of Alcohol to the Likelihood of Completion and Severity of Injury in Rape Incidents." *Violence Against Women* 4:694-712.

Maruschak, L. (2004). "HIV in Prisons and Jails 2002." *Bureau of Justice Statistics Bulletin*. Washington, DC: U.S. Government Printing Office.

Maruschak, L. (2001). "HIV in Prisons and Jails 1999." *Bureau of Justice Statistics Bulletin*. Washington, DC: U.S. Government Printing Office.

Maruschak, L.M. (1999). "HIV in Prisons." *Bureau of Justice Statistics Bulletin*. Washington, DC: U.S. Government Printing Office.

McCorkle, R. (1993). "Fear of Victimization and Symptoms of Psychopathology among Prison Inmates." *Journal of Offenders Rehabilitation* 19:27-41.

McGee, J., and F. Menolascino (1992). "The Evaluation of Defendants with Mental Retardation in the Criminal Justice System." In R. Conley, R. Luckasson, and G. Bouthilet (eds.), *The Criminal Justice System and Mental Retardation: Defendants and Victims*, 55-71. Baltimore: Paul H. Brookes.

McGrath, R., S. Hoke, and J. Vojisek (1998). "Cognitive-Behavioral Treatment of Sex Offenders; A Treatment Comparison and Long-Term Follow-Up Study." *Criminal Justice and Behavior* 25:203-225.

Messinger. R., and P. Davidson (1992). "Training Programs and Defendants with Mental Retardation: History and Future Directions." In R. Conley, R. Luckasson, and G. Bouthilet (eds.), *The Criminal Justice System and Mental Retardation: Defendants and Victims*, 221-234. Baltimore: Paul H. Brookes.

Meyer, W., and C. Cole (1997). "Physical and Chemical Castration of Sex Offenders: A Review." *Journal of Offender Rehabilitation* 25:1-18.

Miner, M., and S. Dwyer (1997). "The Psychosocial Development of Sex Offenders: Differences Between Exhibitionists, Child Molesters and Incest Offenders." *International Journal of Offenders Therapy and Comparative Criminology* 4(1):36-44.

Moghissi, K., H. Mack, and J. Porzak (1968). "Epidemiology of Cervical Cancer. Study of a Prison Population." *American Journal of Obstetrics and Gynecology* 100:607-612.

Monahan, J. (1992). "Mental Disorders and Violet Behavior: Perceptions and Evidence." *American Psychologist* 47:511-521.

Monahan, J. (1981). *The Clinical Prediction of Violent Behavior: Crime and Delinquency Issues*. Rockville, MD: National Institute of Mental Health.

Monahan, J., and H.S. Steadman (1996). "Violent Storms and Violent People: How Meteorology Can Inform Risk Communication in Mental Health Law." *American Psychologist* 51:931-938.

Moore, E. (1989). "Prison Environments and the Impact on Older Citizens." *Journal of Offender Counseling, Services and Rehabilitation* 13:175-192.

Morash, M., R. Haarr, and L. Rucker. (1994). "A Comparison of Programming for Women and Men in U.S. Prisons in the 1980's." *Crime & Delinquency* 40:197-221.

Morgan, E. (2000). "Women on Death Row." In R. Muraskin (ed.), *It's a Crime: Women and Justice*, 269-283. Upper Saddle River, NJ: Prentice Hall.

Morgan-Sharp, E. (1992). "Gender, Race, and Law: Elements of Injustice." *The Justice Professional* 6:86-93.

Morris, A., and C. Wilkinson (1995). "Responding to Female Prisoners' Needs." *The Prison Journal* 75:295-306.

Morris, S., and H. Steadman (1994). "Keys to Successfully Diverting Mentally Ill Jail Detainees." *American Jails* 8:47-49.

Morris, S., H. Steadman, and B. Veysey (1997). "Mental Health Service in United States Jails: A Survey of Innovative Practices." *Criminal Justice and Behavior* 24:3-19.

Morrissey, J., H. Steadman, H. Kilburn, and M. Lindsey (1984). "The Effectiveness of Jail Mental Health Programs: An Interorganizational Assessment." *Criminal Justice and Behavior* 11:235-256.

Mumola, C.J., and J.C. Karberg (2006). "Drug Use and Dependence, State and Federal Prisoners, 2004." *Bureau of Justice Statistics Special Report*. Washington, DC: U.S. Government Printing Office.

Mumola, C.J., and A.J. Beck (1997). "Prisoners in 1996." *Bureau of Justice Statistics Bulletin*. Washington, DC: U.S. Government Printing Office.

Murray, D. (1992). "Drug Abuse Treatment Programs in the Federal Bureau of Prisons: Initiatives for the 1990s." In C. Luekefeld and F. Tims (eds.), *Drug Abuse Treatment in Prisons and Jails*, 62-83. Rockville, MD: National Institute on Drug Abuse.

Musk, H., A. Swetz, and M. Vernon (1997). "Pedophilia in the Correctional System." *Corrections Today* 59:24.

Mutter, R., R. Grimes, and D. Labarthe (1994). "Evidence of Intraprison Spread of HIV Infection." *Archives of Internal Medicine* 154:793-795.

Muzekari, L., E. Morrissey, and A. Young (1997). "Community Mental Health Centers and County Jails: Divergent Perspectives." *American Jails* 11(1):50-52.

National Prison Hospice Association. Available at http://www.npha.org/, February 10, 2003

Neeley, C., L. Addison, and D. Craig-Moreland. (1997). "Addressing the Needs of Elderly Offenders." *Corrections Today* 59:120-123.

Nobel, Jr., J., and R. Conley (1992). "Toward an Epidemiology of Relevant Attributes." In R. Conley, R. Luckasson, and G. Bouthilet (eds.), *The Criminal Justice System and Mental Retardation: Defendants and Victims*, 17-53. Baltimore: Paul H. Brookes.

Norton, J., and D. Williams (1998). "Mother/Child Bonding." *Corrections Today* 60:100-105.

Novick, L., R. Penna, M. Swartz, E. Remmlinger, and R. Loewenstein (1977). "Health Status of the New York City Prison Population." *Medical Care* 15:205-216.

O'Donohue, W., and E. Letourneau (1993). "A Brief Group Treatment for the Modification of Denial in Child Sexual Abusers: Outcome and Follow Up." *Child Abuse and Neglect* 17:299-304.

Olivero, J. (1990). "The Treatment of AIDS Behind the Walls of Correctional Facilities." *Social Justice* 17(1):113-125.

Owen, B., and B. Bloom (1995). "Profiling Women Prisoners: Findings from National Surveys and a California Sample." *The Prison Journal* 75:165-185.

O'Sullivan, M. (1992). "Criminalizing the Mentally Ill." *America* 166:8-13.

Palermo, G., E. Gumz, and E. Liska (1992). "Mental Illness and Criminal Behavior Revisited." *International Journal of Offender Therapy and Comparative Criminology* 36:53-61.

Pelissier, B., and D. McCarthy (1992). "Evaluation of the Federal Bureau of Prisons' Drug Treatment Programs." In C. Leukefeld and F. Tims (eds.), *Drug Abuse Treatment in Prisons and Jails*, 261-278. Rockville, MD: National Institute on Drug Abuse.

Peters, R., and R. May II (1992). "Drug Treatment Services in Jails." In C. Leukefeld and F. Tims (eds.), *Drug Abuse Treatment in Prisons and Jails*, 38-50. Rockville, MD: National Institute on Drug Abuse.

Petersilia, J. (1997). "Unequal Justice? Offenders with Mental Retardation in Prison." *Corrections Management Quarterly* 1:36-43.

Petrella, R. (1992). "Defendants with Mental Retardation in the Forensic Services System." In R. Conley, R. Luckasson, and G. Bouthilet (eds.), *The Criminal Justice System and Mental Retardation*, 79-96. Baltimore: Paul H. Brookes.

Petrila, J., I. Selle, P. Rouse, C. Evans, and D. Moore (1981). "The Pretrial Examination Process in Missouri: A Descriptive Study." *Bulletin of the American Academy of Psychiatry and Law* 9:61-84.

Petrosino, A., and C. Petrosino. (1999). "The Public Safety Potential of Megan's Law in Massachusetts: An Assessment from a Sample of Criminal Sexual Psychopaths." *Crime & Delinquency* 45:140-158.

Pithers, W. (1999). "Empathy: Definition, Enhancement and Relevance to the Treatment of Sexual Abusers." *Journal of Interpersonal Violence* 14:257-284.

Pithers, W. (1994). "Process Evaluation of a Group-Therapy Component Designed to Enhance Sex Offenders Empathy for Sexual Abuse Survivors." *Behavior Research and Therapy* 32:565-570.

Plaud, J., and G. Gaither (1997). "A Clinical Investigation of the Possible Effects of Long-Term Habituation of Sexual Arousal in Assisted Covert Sensitization." *Justice Behavior Therapy & Experimental Psychiatry* 28:281-290.

Ploscue, M. (1968). "Rape." In E. Sagarin and D. MacNamara (eds.), *Problems of Sex Behavior*. New York: Cromwell.

Pollock, J. (1986). *Sex and Supervision: Guarding Male and Female Inmates*. New York: Greenwood Press.

Pollock-Byrne, J. (1990). *Women, Prison, and Crime*. Belmont, CA: Wadsworth.

Pollock-Byrne, J. (1992). "Women in Prison: Why Are Their Numbers Increasing?" In P. Benekos and A. Merlo (eds.), *Corrections: Dilemmas and Directions*, 79-95. Cincinnati: Anderson.

Porporino, F., and E. Zamble (1984). "Coping with Imprisonment." *Canadian Journal of Criminology* 26:403-421.

Powell, T., I. Holt & K. Fondacaro (1997). "The Prevalence of Mental Illness among Inmates in a Rural State." *Law and Human Behavior* 21:427-438.

Prendergast, M., M. Anglin, and I. Wellisch (1995). "Treatment for Drug-Abusing Offenders under Community Supervision." *Federal Probation* 59:66-75.

Prescott, M., and E. Van Houten (1982). "The Retarded Juvenile Offender in New Jersey: A Report on Research in Correctional Facilities and Mental Retardation Facilities." In M. Santamour and P. Watson (eds.), *The Retarded Offender*, 168-175. New York: Praeger.

President's Committee on Mental Retardation (1991). *Annual Report to the President: Citizens with Mental Retardation and the Criminal Justice System*. U.S. Department of Health and Human Services, Administration for Children and Families.

Price, C. (1998). "To Adopt or Adapt? Principles of Hospice Care in the Correctional Setting." Paper presented at the American Correctional Association, 128th Congress of Correction, Detroit, MI, August 12, 1998.

Priest, R., and A. Smith (1992). "Counseling Adult Sex Offenders: Unique Challenges and Treatment Paradigms." *Journal of Counseling and Development* 71:27-31.

Pugh, M. (1986). "The Mentally Retarded Offenders Program of the Texas Department of Corrections." *The Prison Journal* 66:39-51.

Quinsey, V. (1998). "Treatment of Sex Offenders. " In M. Tonry (ed.), *The Handbook of Crime and Punishment*. New York: Oxford University Press.

Radloff, L. (1975). "The CES-D: A Self-Report Depression Scale for Use in the General Population." *Applied Psychological Measurement* 1:385-401.

Rafter, N. (1990). *Partial Justice: Women, Prisons, and Social Control*. New Brunswick, NJ: Transaction Books.

Rafter, N. (1983). "Prisons for Women." In M. Tonry & N. Morris (eds.), *Crime and Justice: An Annual Review of Research* 59:129-181. Chicago: University of Chicago Press.

Ratcliff, M. (2000). "Dying Inside the Walls." *Journal of Palliative Medicine* 3:509-511.

Reich, J. , and J. Wells (1985). "Psychiatry Diagnosis and Competency to Stand Trial." *Comprehensive Psychiatry* 26:421-431.

Reinhart, C. (2000). *Court Security Personnel*. Hartford, CT: Connecticut General Assembly.

Rice, A., L. Smith, and F. Janzen (1999). "Women Inmates, Drug Abuse, and the Salt Lake County Jail." *American Jails* 13:43-47.

Rice, M., T. Chaplin, G. Harris, and J. Coutts (1994). "Empathy for the Victim and Sexual Arousal among Rapists and Nonrapists." *Journal of Interpersonal Violence* 9:435- 449.

Rice, M., G. Harris, and C. Lang (1990). "Recidivism among Male Insanity Acquitees." *Journal of Psychiatry and the Law* 18:379-403.

Rockowitz, R. (1986). "Developmentally Disabled Offenders: Issues in Developing and Maintaining Services." *The Prison Journal* 66:19-23.

Rogers, R., and M. Bagby (1992). "Diversion of Mentally Disordered Offenders: A Legitimate Role for Clinicians." *Behavioral Sciences and the Law* 10:407-418.

Rold, W. (1996). "Charging Inmates for Medical Care: A Legal, Practical, and Ethical Critique." *Journal of Correctional Health Care* 3:129-143.

Ruback, R., T. Carr, and C. Hooper (1986). "Perceived Control in Prison: Its Relation to Reported Crowding, Stress, and Symptoms." *Journal of Applied Social Psychology* 16:375-386.

Rutherford, R., C. Nelson, and B. Wolford (1985). "Special Education in the Most Restrictive Environment: Correctional Special Education." *Journal of Special Education* 19:59-71.

Ryan, T., and K. McCabe (1997). "A Comparative Analysis of Adult Female Offenders." *Corrections Today* 59:28, 30.

Sabath, M., and E. Cowles (1988). "Factors Affecting the Adjustment of Elderly Inmates to Prison." In B. McCarthy and R. Langworthy (eds.), *Older Offenders: Perspectives in Criminology and Criminal Justice*. New York: Praeger.

Sack, W., J. Seidler, and S. Thomas (1976). "The Children of Imprisoned Parents: A Psychosocial Explanation." *American Journal of Orthopsychiatry* 46:618-628.

Santamour, M. (1986). "The Offender with Mental Retardation." *The Prison Journal* 66:3-18.

Santamour, M., and P. Watson (1982). *The Retarded Offender*. New York: Praeger.

Santamour, M., and B. West (1982). "The Mentally Retarded Offender: Presentation of the Facts and a Discussion of the Issues." In M. Santamour and P. Watson (eds.), *The Retarded Offender*, 7-36. New York: Praeger.

Sapp, A., and M. Vaughan (1991). "Sex Offender Rehabilitation Programs in State Prisons: A Nationwide Survey." *Journal of Offender Rehabilitation* 17:55-75.

Schorsch, E., G. Galedary, A. Haag, M. Hauch, and H. Lohse (1990). *Sex Offenders: Dynamics and Psychotherapeutic Strategies*. New York: Springer-Verlag.

Schultz-Ross, R. (1993). "Theoretical Difficulties in the Treatment of Mentally Ill Prisoners." *Journal of Forensic Science* 38:426-431.

Scott, N., T. Hannum, and S. Gilchrist (1982). "Assessment of Depression among Incarcerated Females." *Journal of Personality Assessment* 46:372-379.

Scott, R., and T. O'Connor (1997). "Treatment in Transition: The Role of Mental Health Correctional Facilities." *Journal of Contemporary Criminal Justice* 13 (3):264-278.

Shenson, D., N. Dubler, and D. Michaels (1990). "Jails and Prisons: The New Asylum." *American Journal of Public Health* 80:655-656.

Shepard, J. (1997). "Double Punishment." *American Journalist Review* 19:36-41.

Silverman, I., M. Vega, and T. Danner (1993). "The Female Murderer." In A.V. Wilson (ed.), *Homicide: The Victim/Offender Connection*, 175-190. Cincinnati: Anderson.

Smith, C., R. Schmid, L. Clark, W. Crews, and N. Nunnery (1988). "The Mentally Retarded Inmates: Prison Adjustment and Implications for Treatment." *Journal of Offender Counseling* 9:8-17.

Smith, R. (1994). "The TB Crisis in Our Nation's Jails." *American Jails* 8(1):11-12, 14.

Smith, S. (1993). "Confusing the Term 'Guilty' and 'Not Guilty': Implications for Alleged Offenders with Mental Retardation." *Psychological Reports* 73:675.

Sobel, S. (1980). "Women in Prison: Sexism Behind Bars." *Professional Psychology*, 331-338.

Sokoloff, N., and B. Price (1995). "The Criminal Law and Women." In B. Price and N. Sokoloff (eds.), *The Criminal Justice System: Offenders, Victims, and Workers*, 11-29. New York: McGraw-Hill.

Solomon, P., and J. Draine (1995). "Issues in Serving the Forensic Client." *Social Work* 40:25-33.

Spruill, J., and J. May (1988). "The Mentally Retarded Offender: Prevalence Rates Based on Individual Versus Group Intelligence Tests." *Criminal Justice and Behavior* 15:484-491.

Steadman, H., S. Barbara, and D. Dennis (1994). "A National Survey of Jail Mental Health Diversion Programs." *Hospital and Community Psychiatry* 45:1109-1113.

Steadman, H., S. Fabisiak, J. Dvoskin, and E. Holohean (1989). "A Survey of Mental Disability among State Prison Inmates." *Hospital and Community Psychiatry* 38:1086-1090.

Steadman, H., E. Holohean, and J. Dvoskin (1991). "Estimating Mental Health Needs and Service Utilization among Prison Inmates." *Bulletin of the American Academy of Psychiatry and the Law* 19:297-307.

Steadman, H., D. McCarty, and P. Morrissey (1989). *The Mentally Ill in Jail. Planning for Essential Services*. New York: Guilford Press.

Steadman, H., and B. Veysey (1997). "Providing Services for Jail Inmates with Mental Disorders." *American Jails* 11(2):11-23.

Stewart, T., P. Hearne, X. Ping; A. Breschlain, and S. Locarnini (1995). "Spread of Bloodborne Viruses among Australian Prison Entrants." *British Medical Journal* 310:285-288.

Stolberg, S.G. (2001). "Behind Bars: New Effort to Care for the Dying." *The New York Times* (April 1, 2001):A1, 4.

Sykes, G. (1958). *The Society of Captives*. New York: Atheneum.

Teplin, L. (1996). "Prevalence of Psychiatric Disorders among Incarcerated Women." *Archives of General Psychiatry* 53:505-512.

Teplin, L. (1994). "Psychiatric and Substance Abuse Disorders among Male Urban Jail Detainees." *American Journal of Public Health* 84:290-293.

Teplin, L. (1990). "The Prevalence of Severe Mental Disorders among Male Urban Jail. Detainees: Comparison with the Epidemiologic Catchment Area." *American Journal of Public Health* 80:661-669.

Teplin, L., and N. Pruett (1992). "Police as Streetcorner Psychiatrist: Managing the Mentally Ill." *International Journal of Law and Psychiatry* 15:139-156.

Thornton, D., and T. Hogue (1993). "The Large-Scale Provision of Programs for Imprisoned Sex Offenders: Issues, Dilemmas and Progress." *Criminal Behavior and Mental Health* 3:371-380.

Tims, F.M., and C.G. Leukefeld (1992). "The Challenge of Drug Abuse Treatment in Prisons and Jails." In C.G. Leukefeld &F.M. Tims (eds.), *Drug Abuse Treatment in Prisons and Jails*, 1-7. Rockville, MD: National Institute on Drug Abuse.

Toch, H. (1977). *Living in Prison*. New York: Free Press.

Toch, H., and K. Adams (1987). "In the Eye of the Beholder? Assessments of Psychopathology among Prisoners by Federal Prison Staff." *Journal of Research in Crime & Delinquency* 24:119-139.

Torrey, E. (1995). "Jails and Prisons: America's New Mental Hospital." *American Journal of Public Health* 85:1611-1613.

Torrey, E., J. Stieber, J. Ezekiel, S. Wolfe, J. Sharfstein, J. Noble, and L. Flynn (1992). *Criminalizing the Seriously Mentally Ill: The Abuse of Jails as Mental Hospitals*. Washington, DC: Public Citizen's Health Research Group and the National Alliance for the Mentally Ill.

Van Stelle, K., E. Mauser, and D. Moberg (1994). "Recidivism to the Criminal Justice System of Substance-Abusing Offenders Diverted into Treatment." *Crime &Delinquency* 40(2):175-196.

Van Voorhis, P., M. Braswell, and D. Lester (2007). *Correctional Counseling and Rehabilitation*, 6th ed. Newark, NJ: LexisNexis Matthew Bender.

Van Voorhis, P., and G. Hurst (2007). "Treating Substance Abuse in Offender Populations." In Van Voorhis, P., M. Braswell, and D. Lester (eds.), *Correctional Counseling and Rehabilitation*, 6th ed., 257. Newark, NJ: LexisNexis Matthew Bender.

Van Voorhis, P., and K. Spencer (1999). "Planning for Differences among Correctional Clients." *Corrections Today* 61:38-42.

Veneziano, L., and C. Veneziano (1996). "Disabled Inmates." In M. McShane and F. Williams (eds.), *Encyclopedia of American Prisons*, 157-161. New York: Garland.

Veneziano, L., C. Veneziano, and C. Tribolet (1987). "The Special Needs of Prison Inmates With Handicaps: An Assessment." *Journal of Offender Counseling, Services and Rehabilitation* 12:61-72.

Veysey, B. (1998). "Specific Needs of Women Diagnosed with Mental Illnesses in U.S. Jails." In B. Levin, A. Blanch, and A. Jennings (eds.), *Women's Mental Health Sources: A Public Health Perspective*, 368-389. Thousand Oaks: Sage.

Vigdal, G., and D. Stadler (1992). "Comprehensive System Development in Corrections for Drug Abusing Offenders: The Wisconsin Department of Corrections." In C. Luekefeld and F. Tims (eds.), *Drug Abuse Treatment in Prisons and Jails*, 126-141. Rockville, MD: National Institute on Drug Abuse.

Vigilante, K., M. Flynn, P. Affleck, J. Stunkle, N. Merriman, T. Flanigand, A. Mitty, and J. Rich (1999). "Reduction in Recidivism of Incarcerated Women Through Primary Care, Peer Counseling, and Discharge Planning." *Journal of Women's Health* 8:409-415.

Vlahor, D. (1990). "MV Infection in the Correctional Setting." *Criminal Justice Policy Review* 4:306-318.

Vlahor, D. (1992). "IRV-1 Infection in the Correctional Setting." In C. Leukefeld and F. Tims (eds.), *Drug Abuse Treatment in Prisons and Jails*, 51-61. Rockville, MD: National Institute on Drug Abuse.

Wall, J. (1998). "Eldercare: Louisiana Initiates Program to Meet Needs of Aging Inmate Population." *Corrections Today* 60:136-140.

Walsh, A. (1997). *Correctional Assessment, Casework, and Counseling*. Lanham, MD: American Correctional Association.

Walsh, J., and J. Bricout (1997). "Service for Persons with Mental Illness in Jails: Implications for Family Involvement." *Families in Society: The Journal of Contemporary Human Services* 78(4):420-428.

Washington, P., and R. Diamond (1985). "Prevalence of Mental Illness among Women Incarcerated in Five California County Jails." *Research in Community and Mental Health* 5:33-41.

Weilerstein, R. (1995). "The Prison Match Program." In K. Gabel and D. Johnson (eds.), *Children of Incarcerated Parents*. New York: Lexington.

Weinman, B. (1992). "A Coordinated Approach for Drug-Abusing Offenders: TASC and Parole." In C. Leukefeld and F. Tims (eds.), *Drug Abuse Treatment in Prisons and Jails*, 232-245. Rockville, MD: National Institute on Drug Abuse.

Wexler, H., G. Falkin, and D. Lipton (1990). "Outcome Evaluation of a Prison Therapeutic Community for Substance Abuse Treatment." *Criminal Justice and Behavior* 17:71-92.

Wexler, H., and R. Williams (1986). "The 'Stay'n Out' Therapeutic Community: Prison Treatment for Substance Abusers." *Journal of Psychoactive Drugs* 18:221-230.

Wexler, H., G. Falkin, D. Lipton, and A. Rosenblum (1992). "Outcome Evaluation of a Prison Therapeutic Community for Substance Abuse Treatment." In C. Leukefeld and F. Tims (eds.), *Drug Abuse Treatment in Prisons and Jails*. Rockford, MD: National Institute of Drug Abuse.

White, D., and H. Wood (1988). "Lancaster County MRO program." In J. Stark, F. Menolascino, M. Albarelli, and V. Gray (eds.), *Mental Retardation/Mental Health: Classification, Diagnosis, Treatment, Services*. New York: Springer-Verlag.

White, D., and H. Wood (1986). "The Lancaster County, Pennsylvania, Mentally Retarded Offenders Program." *The Prison Journal* 65:77-84.

Wilcock, K., T. Hammett, and D. Parent (1995). "Controlling Tuberculosis in Community Corrections." *NIJ Research in Action*. Washington, DC: U.S. Department of Justice.

Wilson, M., and M. Daly (1992). "Who Kills Who in Spouse Killing? On the Exceptional Sex Ratio of Espousal Homicides in the United States." *Criminology* 27:251-271.

Winett, D., R. Mullen, L. Lowe, and E. Missakian (1992). "Amity Righturn: A Demonstration Drug Abuse Treatment Program for Inmates and Parolees." In C. Luekefeld and F. Tims (eds.), *Drug Abuse Treatment in Prisons and Jails*, 84-98. Rockville, MD: National Institute on Drug Abuse.

Wolford, B. (1987). "Correctional Education: Training and Education Opportunities for Delinquent and Criminal Offenders." In C. Nelson, R. Rutherford Jr., and B. Wolford (eds.), *Special Education in the Criminal Justice System*, 53-82. Columbus, OH: Merrill.

Wolford, B., C. Nelson, and R. Rutherford (1996). "Developmentally Disabled Offenders." In M. McShane & F. Williams III (eds.), *Encyclopedia of American Prisons*, 149-151. New York: Garland.

Wood, H., and D. White (1992). "A Model for Habilation and Prevention for Offenders with Mental Retardation: The Lancaster County (PA) Office of Special Offenders Services." In R. Conley, R. Luckasson, and G. Bouthilet (eds.), *The Criminal Justice System and Mental Retardation*, 153-165. Baltimore: Paul H. Brookes.

Wooldredge, J. (1999). "Inmate Experiences and Psychological Well-Being." *Criminal Justice and Behavior* 26:235-250.

Wrightsman, L.S. (1991). "HIV in Prisons, 1977." *Bureau of Justice Statistics Bulletin*. Washington, DC: U.S. Government Printing Office.

Yang, S. (1990). "The Unique Treatment Needs of Female Substance Abusers in Correctional Institutions: The Obligation of the Criminal Justice System to Provide Parity." *Medicine and Law* 9:1018-1027.

Zonana, H. (1997). "The Civil Commitment of Sex Offenders." *Science* 278:1248-5341.

Zupan, L., and A Stohr-Gillmore (1988). "Doing Time in the New Generation Jail: Inmate Perceptions of Gains and Losses." *Policy Studies Review* 7:626-640.

COURT CASES

Coker v. Georgia, 428 U.S. 584 (1977).

Davis v. Hopper, No. 98-9663.

Estelle v. Gamble, 429 U.S. 97 (1976).

Furman v. Georgia, 408 U.S. 238 (1972).

Gregg v. Georgia, 428 U.S. 158 (1976).

Guthrie v. Evans, 815 F.2d 626 (11th Cir. 1987).

Kansas v. Hendricks, 117 S. Ct. 2072, 138 L.Ed.2d 501 (1997).

McClesky v. Kemp, 481 U.S. 279 (1987).

Penry v. Lynaugh, 492 U.S. 302 (1989).

Roberts v. Louisiana, 428 U.S. 325 (1976).

Ruiz v. Estelle, 679 F.2d 115 (5th Cir.) opinion amended in part and vacated in part, 688 F.2d 266 (5th Cir. 1982).

Sumner v. Shuman, 483 U.S. 66 (1987).

Wilson v. Seiter, 501 U.S. 294 (1991).

Woodson v. North Carolina, 428 U.S. 280 (1976).

Correctional Officers

CHAPTER 11

What You Need to Know

▶ The role of the correctional officer has changed along with changes in the mission and objectives of the prison itself.

▶ Other factors affecting the role of the correctional officer include unionization, professionalization, and bureaucratization.

▶ There are more than one-half million correctional officers; the majority are working in state prisons.

▶ Female officers have become a significant and accepted portion of the correctional officer force.

▶ Some officers have abused their authority by engaging in physical force, sexual abuse, or manipulation of female inmates.

▶ There is an officer subculture that dictates that officers aid other officers and maintain distance from inmates.

▶ Management can reduce corruption by improving hiring practices, instituting training, and using supervisory practices that reduce temptation and punish wrongdoers.

INTRODUCTION

In the prison world, correctional officers are the symbol of state power. Like the bars and fences that surround the prison, they represent the power to incarcerate. Even in the most enlightened, treatment-oriented prison, officers represent loss of freedom and state power. Thus, there is an inherent conflict between inmates and officers. Stereotypes of correctional officers as sadistic brutes are present in books and movies, and reinforced by some works written by inmates.[1] The reality, of course, is much more complex. At times, the power and authority all officers possess by virtue of their uniforms is abused. Other officers, however, go out of their way to instill a bit of humanity in the prison world of violence and depersonalization. This chapter will explore the changing role of the correctional officer over the last 50 years, as well as demographic characteristics and structural factors that influence the correctional officer subculture, stress, and working conditions.

TRANSFORMATION

The role of the correctional officer is obviously tied to the mission and objectives of the prison itself. As noted in an earlier chapter, the history of prisons involves cycles of despair and optimism.[2] The early utopias perceived by the architects of the Walnut Street Jail and other institutions soon gave way to places where violence and corruption prevailed. More recent histories of American prisons illustrate the effects of social and political changes on those who live and work within the prison.

The pre–World War II "big house" emphasized order and security. In the South, prison farms, although following a different economic and production model, also maintained an order in which inmates had no rights. A small number of officers were able to control large numbers of inmates through intimidation and with the assistance of prisoner trustees. Brutality was present but perhaps not frequent because inmates lived and understood hierarchies of power. It is hard to know exactly how much brutality was present because records were not kept and the histories of such institutions are fragmented.

In the 1960s, the mission of prisons changed, characterized by their new name: "correctional institutions." As treatment supplanted custody as the theme in many prisons, older methods of control hierarchies were challenged and abandoned. Legal challenges and court holdings eliminated the unquestioned authority of prison management. Inmates utilized court action to secure some civil rights and liberties, but this came at a heavy price. In some prisons, curtailing "official intimidation" opened the door to gangs and inmate cliques who filled the power vacuum and used violence to get what they wanted. Inmates had less to fear from guards but more to fear from each other, as racial gangs and other powerful cliques or individuals solidified their control over prison black markets. For a time in the 1970s and 1980s, officers described some prisons as "out of control"—places where guards were afraid to walk into living units and inmates controlled the prison.[3]

The Texas experience is illustrative. The vacuum left by court action in the *Ruiz v. Estelle*[4] decision created an environment in which individual officers felt compelled to enforce their own individual authority. Inmates vied for power in a free-for-all in which inmate-to-inmate violence increased at an incredible rate, as did reports of officer brutality. In 1984, for instance, 200 disciplinary actions were taken against officers who had used excessive force. There were also 25 inmate homicides. This was double the rate that had occurred before or immediately following *Ruiz*.[5]

A correctional officer at the Arkansas Department of Correction's Wrightsville Unit closes the entry gate as she arrives for her shift. To settle a 1997 Justice Department lawsuit, Arkansas agreed to hire 400 more female guards for some of its toughest jobs at its all-male prisons.

Carroll described a similar situation in Rhode Island in the 1970s:

> Feeling betrayed by the court, sold out by their superiors who—in their view—had negotiated a settlement rather than defend what was right and intimidated by inmates who seemingly knew the rules better than they did, the officers abandoned any effort to maintain order through rule enforcement. Instead they sought to maintain control while minimizing their personal trouble through cultivating close personal ties with inmates. The result was a pervasive corruption of authority, on the one hand, and a rebellion against the courts and the administration, on the other.
>
> Assaults and stabbings became almost everyday events. On just one weekend near the end of May 1973 two officers were assaulted with a pipe, and another suffered a fractured foot when he was pushed down a flight of stairs; two inmates were likewise assaulted with pipes, and two others were stabbed, all requiring hospitalization. And on Saturday afternoon of the following weekend, an inmate was stabbed over 100 times, his body stuffed in a trash can and set on fire.[6]

Taylor, in an exhaustive history of Parchman Farm and the Mississippi prison system, observed similar disruptions as the Southern prison slowly and reluctantly accommodated court orders to integrate, get rid of the trustee system, and improve physical conditions. During this period of change, however, officers felt as if they were left powerless and vulnerable:

> Below wardens, employees voice confusion, negativism, and fear. None of them, it seems, are quite sure of what is expected of them, or if they can depend on the support of their superiors. "Nobody knows what to do," claims one young correctional officer. They [middle managers] tell you one thing one day, something else the next, and all the while you know they'll cut your balls off and save their own asses if someone in Jackson gets embarrassed or pissed off by something you do or don't do.[7]

Silberman proposes that much of the violence escalation in the 1980s and early 1990s has been eliminated or reduced and that "legally imposed professionalism," where it occurs, has done a lot to quell prison violence.[8] He compared prisons with grievance procedures to those without and found that those jurisdictions that had improved their response to civil rights complaints had lower rates of violence.

Crouch, in a discussion of the changes throughout the 1970s and 1980s that affected the guard force, noted that three factors combined to change the prison world for inmates and officers alike.[9] First was a new emphasis on rehabilitation that led to a loosening of the tight controls that characterized prisons in early years, as well as an expectation that officers would do more than just "lock and unlock" doors. Second were changes in the size and composition of inmate populations. There were more inmates entering the system, and more of them had serious drug problems. Finally, judicial intervention eventually affected every policy and procedure, leading to a belief that "the courts ruled the prison." Crouch examined how these three events created role conflict and ambiguity, danger, loss of control, stress, racial and sexual integration, and deviant behavior among officers. Other factors that have been discussed by various authors as affecting the correctional officer role include: unionization, professionalization, and bureaucratization.[10]

• Unionization •

Unions are a more powerful force in the Northeast and on the west coast (especially, California) than they are in the South. Where they exist, they have developed into a powerful political body that affects policy as management struggles to accommodate union demands for pay, benefits, and the bidding system. Correctional officer unions tend to act as a resistant force to treatment initiatives. Sometimes the interests of the officers are not necessarily the same interests of the prison managers. For instance, unions fight vigorously to defend the "bidding" system whereby senior officers get first choice on assignments. Because many, if not most, officers prefer posts away from inmates, what occurs is that those officers with the least experience are left with posts that have the most inmate-officer interaction. The consequence is conflict between young, inexperienced officers and inmates. However, those officers that are not protected by unions find that they have little bargaining power and have a difficult task convincing the legislature that pay raises are a top priority.

• Professionalization •

In the last 30 years, the trend has been to increase hiring qualifications, standards, and training of correctional officers. Although the overcrowding problem of the 1980s limited and slowed the trend toward professionalization, most states now have quite extensive training academies. In these academies, officers experience training somewhat similar to that given law enforcement personnel—a combination of practical "how to" courses and a sampling of sociological and psychological offerings such as communication, cultural sensitivity, criminology, and legal rights of prisoners. One list of subjects in a training curriculum included: relevant legal knowledge, rules of the institution, administrative policies and procedures, elementary personality development, methods of counseling, self-defense tactics and use of firearms, report writing, inmate rules and regulations, inmates' rights and responsibilities, race relations, basic first aid and CPR techniques, radio communication, substance abuse awareness, and how to deal with special inmate populations (i.e., mentally ill).[11] Many of those who have been in the correctional system for a long time observe that it is different from the "old days" when officers were given their stick and told to "do their best."

In the 1970s and 1980s, another goal of correctional administrations was diversification of the guard force. As was the case with law enforcement in the 1960s, prison guard forces were integrated with minorities, women, and college-educated individuals in response to problems and complaints.[12] These changes led to a more professional role for corrections officers, with more formal hiring, training, and promotion practices.

• Bureaucratization •

Bureaucratization describes the situation occurring when formal procedures and policies supplant more ad hoc decisionmaking. Hiring and firing, assignments, and discipline for both officers and inmates became more formal during the 1980s and 1990s. To some extent, this limited the widespread patronage, discrimination, and favoritism that characterized earlier prison management, but officers also lost some level of personal autonomy and control. Because of bureaucratization and greater civil liberties ensured by court order, prisoners no longer relied on guards for everything (e.g., favors like phone calls or permission slips to see a counselor). This led to guards having less ability to control inmates through discretionary favors. Silberman argues that this might have, in turn, led to officers resorting to more coercive controls contributing to the increased numbers of officer-to-inmate incidents.[13] Other authors have also noticed that in recent years, officers seem more willing to use excessively firm and even "extreme" force to keep prisoners in line, arguably because courts have been less likely to find prisoner legal claims justified.[14]

DEMOGRAPHICS

There are more than 500,000 correctional officers in the United States working in state and federal prisons, and county facilities. About six out of 10 work in state prisons.[15] Of these officers, a growing percentage are minority or female.[16]

BOX 11.1

Women Correctional Officers in Massachusetts

Women made up more than 20 percent of correctional officers nationwide in 2002. Massachusetts, however, employed approximately 400 women correctional officers, about 11 percent of its correctional force as of 2007. Many women have advanced to key administrative posts, including the top three administrative posts at Bridgewater State Hospital.

A female officer at the Souza-Baranowski Correctional Center noted that she rarely had problems with inmates and believes that many of the male prisoners appreciated having women officers. Women officers, who comprise about 7 percent of the guard force at this maximum-security prison, do everything the male officers do, except strip searches. This particular officer reported that she had never been physically assaulted and could always talk her way out of difficulty.

Source: Adapted from Preer, R. (June 7, 2007). "New Guards on the Block—Female Officers in Men's Prison Face Danger, Command Respect." *The Boston Globe*, p. 1.

Officers find jobs in either the public-sector or private corrections. Salaries for correctional officers have never been a strong attraction to the job. In some areas (especially those areas with strong unions), however, it provides a good alternative to other occupations requiring only a high school diploma. In 2006, the median salary was $35,760.[17] In the state of New York, correctional officers start at approximately $34,300 and earn more than $41,000 after one year. Unionized guards in Ohio start at a salary of more than $32,800. Some states, especially non-unionized states, pay considerably less. Texas starts its officers at only $23,000 and pays $27,000 after nine months on the job. Tennessee starts at approximately $24,500 a year. In Arizona, state correctional officer starting pay is just over $31,800; after training and one year of experience, the pay is just over $34,100.[18] However, the Maricopa County Sheriff's Department pays officers $36,000 to start, and the top of the pay range is $50,000, compared to a salary of $39,664 for an Arizona state correctional officer with eight years of experience.[19] Even though some states pay low wages, salaries are a significant part of correctional operating expenses. In 2007, states spent more than $49 billion on corrections, and wages made up a significant proportion of the average per-prisoner operating cost of $23,876.[20]

Officers usually also have the opportunity to make substantial overtime pay, sometimes up to double their salary. For instance, a recent report noted that in 2006 California spent more than one-half billion dollars in overtime, and 15 percent of the state's correctional employees earned at least $25,000 in overtime for the year.[21] Problems arise because of abuse of sick time. When officers call in sick, their posts must be filled by others, even if it means keeping an officer who has finished his or her shift and paying him or her overtime.

To see how much various states are paying correctional officers, simply go to a search engine and type in the names of the states you are interested in and "department of corrections." Then click on employment opportunities or correctional officer pay.

Qualifications for correctional officers usually include only a high school diploma or a GED, but the federal Bureau of Prisons requires a college degree. About 24 percent of states use psychological testing to screen out inappropriate job candidates.[22] About 80 percent of states use a written civil service exam to hire correctional officers. Training of new officers ranges from a low of 17 days to a high of 16 weeks, but the average number of training hours for new hires is about 221 hours. About 75 percent of the states also require about 40 hours of in-service training for all officers.[23]

Freeman reports that there is about 20 percent turnover in this occupation every year.[24] In addition to fairly low pay in most of the United States, there are other disadvantages to the job that contribute to a high degree of turnover, including the nature of the job, long hours, stress, and a poor fit between the person and the job.

• Female and Minority Officers •

As mentioned previously, larger numbers of women and minorities entered the correctional officer workforce in the 1980s and 1990s. Freeman[25] reviewed the literature documenting the entry of women into correctional institutions for men and detailed the fears held by some management and fellow male officers that women would not be able to handle aggressive inmates, would be subject to harassment and assault, and would be co-opted by inmates. Evaluations indicated, however, that women officers did their jobs adequately. By most measuring gauges, there were few differences between male and female officers. When surveyed, inmates indicated a generally positive regard for the entry of women as officers. Evidently, female officers were perceived as "sexual objects" and made the day more interesting by being there. Another factor noted by inmates, however, was that the female officers were more communicative and exhibited a more humane style of intervention. This tendency for female officers to engage inmates in more communication and utilize other methods of control rather than pure coercion has been noted by other authors.[26] It should be noted that other researchers have found few differences in the methods of control used by male and female officers. Jenne and Kersting,[27] for instance, used hypothetical situations and asked male and female officers to respond. They discovered few differences between the sexes in the use of aggression in resolving the hypothetical situations. When differences were observed, they were in the opposite direction from that predicted; that is, it was female officers who were more likely to use aggressive responses.

Zimmer[28] saw three role types emerge among female officers: the institutional role (rule-oriented, professional stance), the modified role (feared inmates, avoided contact, relied heavily on male workers for backup), and the inventive role (looked to inmates for support, expressed little fear, preferred work that involves direct inmate contact). Later observations indicated that these adaptations were not necessarily unique to women—male officers also have a variety of adaptations to the role: some avoided inmates, while others sought them out and participated fully in the more complex nature of the treatment role offered.

Thinly veiled racism and sexism have prevailed and still exist in some prisons. Ironically, by some accounts, women were especially resented by other officers—even more so than were African-American officers. Speculation as to why male officers were so hostile to women entering the workforce included the idea that it destroyed the "macho" character of job.[29] One study conducted in a midwestern prison discovered that there is still a degree of male resistance to the presence of women officers. In a sample of men and women, male officers were less likely than their female counterparts to agree with a statement that "male staff accepted women as corrections officers" (47% versus 67%). Men were also less likely to agree with the statement "most inmates accept women as corrections officers" (44% versus 74%). Interestingly, however, 80 percent agreed that women "should be hired as corrections officers." Male officers were more likely than female officers to believe that female officers were in more danger than male officers (61% versus 32%) and that male officers' safety is endangered when working with a female officer (37% versus 16%). Only 44 percent of male officers believed that women could control a fight between inmates (compared to 96% of the responding female officers), and only 52 percent of the male officers agreed that the presence of women officers improved the prison environment (compared to 89% of the women).[30] These results indicate that there is still a good deal of hostility and cynicism regarding the presence of female officers in prisons for men.

Findings reviewed by Freeman[31] indicated that women COs respond equally aggressively as male COs given similar situations. There is no statistical evidence to indicate that they are more subject to assault, and they write approximately the same number of misconduct reports. Other researchers report that female officers do not experience more stress than male officers, as was previously believed. They do, however, exhibit significantly less intense feelings of cynical attitudes that depersonalize inmates.[32]

Today, female officers are in virtually all maximum-security institutions for men. They have job assignments that place them in all areas of the prison. Because they are still fewer in number than male guards, however, women still experience some features of tokenism. They still also experience some forms of sexual harassment. McMahon described some types of harassment that occurred in a Canadian prison from the mid-1980s through the mid-1990s.[33] She described minor forms of discrimination (called "microinequities"), such as receiving a much smaller amount of money in advance than male officers for a work-related trip. She also described an almost constant focus on and search for mistakes by female officers, as well as "nitpicking" about how they did their job or their activities on the job (e.g., their entries in logbooks). Further, there were disparities in job assignments and shift rotations, and women were passed over for overtime duty and sent to the control room when there were emergency situations. She also described how some female officers were directed to do laundry or wash windows with inmates, activities that male officers were never ordered to do.[34] Women also experienced sexual harassment that included sexual propositions, unwanted and sexual touching, and routine use of vulgar language. For instance, in one incident, "He poked me in the behind with keys, and made a comment about my behind. . . ."[35] In another, "Larouche liked to grab his groin in front of female correctional officers. He would stand up against the wall and grab his groin—it was deliberate. He would see if we would look, and he would snigger—it was disgusting . . ."[36]

Although the amount and kind of sexual harassment that female officers are exposed to is much different today than it was in the past, it has not entirely gone away and probably will not do so without a concerted effort on the part of administrators for organizational change.[37] Prisons for men are a largely male environment, with women still playing largely token roles. Moreover, they are hidden from public scrutiny. These elements combine to make it extremely difficult to completely eliminate forms of sexual harassment.

Objections to female officers in prisons for men also revolved around the fact that inmates would lose a certain amount of privacy by having opposite-sex guards watching them shower and perform other private body functions. In most court cases, there was little sympathy for this challenge, at least when presented by male inmates arguing against the entry of female officers. Courts were more sympathetic to arguments against the entry of male correctional officers into prisons for women. However, most states interpreted equal opportunity to mean that if they could not bar women from entering institutions for men, they also could not bar men from working in institutions for women. The consequence has been a complete reversal of the trend of same-sex guards in women's institutions. In some states, men comprise more than 50 percent of the guard force in prisons for women. There has been a steady stream of allegations, exposures, and court action involving sexual harassment and abuse. This issue is covered more fully in Chapter 9.

A less studied but no less important development was the entry of African-American and other minority officers into the ranks of correctional officers in large rural prisons in the 1970s. There was a difficult adjustment for the first minority officers who may have been subjected to racial slurs and other forms of discrimination. Initially, white officers mistrusted minority officers, believing them to be sympathetic to inmates and, therefore, not to be trusted. African-American officers felt completely unprotected by white colleagues and depended on inmates to keep them safe.[38]

There is little research available on black or other minority guards. Some research indicates that neither race nor ethnicity is related to job satisfaction, although minority officers report more feelings of effectiveness in working with inmates.[39] In another study of 2,979 correctional officers, using the Prison Social Climate Survey, it was found that race and sex did influence the officers' perception of their work environment.[40]

In an interesting study on officers' perceptions of job opportunities, it was discovered that there was a wide gap between African-American and white officers in their perceptions of the available opportunities for advancement of minority officers. The white officers perceived greater advancement opportunities for minority officers than did minority officers themselves.[41]

It is probably true that the blatant racism that correctional officers experienced in the 1960s and 1970s has been largely eliminated; however, more subtle evidence of discrimination may still be present in corrections. There is no indication that minority officers perform their job differently from white officers, but it would be helpful to have more information on how they perceive their job, their advancement, and their interactions with inmates.

WORKING IN PRISON

Officers often say they are doing time just like the inmates—only in eight- or 10-hour installments. There is some truth to the idea that officers are the "other inmates." They spend a great deal of time inside the prison walls and must adapt to the prison world just as surely as do the inmates who live there. This section will explore officers' relationships with inmates as well as their interactions with management. One of the most fearsome elements for both officers and inmates alike is the ever-present threat of violence.

• Violence •

According to some authors, there is little state-sanctioned violence in prison anymore, but informal violence continues to exist. Prison is a world in which violence and the threat of violence is more the norm than the aberration, and officers are affected by the reality of this world just as surely as inmates. Thus, we need to discuss two forms of violence: inmates assaulting officers, and officers assaulting inmates.

The rate of inmate-on-officer assaults has decreased from a high experienced in the 1980s. Silberman[42] is one author who reports that violence from inmates to guards is still present and continuous but may be decreasing from the number of incidents in the 1980s and 1990s. He reports situations in which some guards have been killed or severely beaten during hostage-taking incidents or

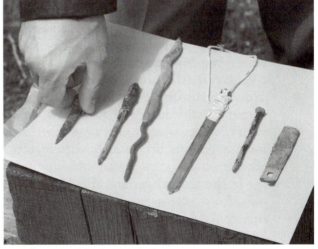

A collection of knives made by inmates at Attica Correctional Facility in Attica, New York. The presence of such weapons is one indication of the informal violence that continues to exist in prison environments and one of many reasons the job of correctional officer is stressful.

AP Photo/David Duprey

individual attacks, as well as rapes of both male and female guards by inmates.[43] Ross reports that there were 6,850 assaults on officers in 1994; that figure is lower than the reported 9,269 reported assaults in 1988.[44] On the other hand, some sources indicate that assaults on guards nationwide have more than doubled in recent years.[45]

Light discussed findings from an analysis of 694 incidents of assaults on guards in New York.[46] The analysis indicated that much of violence directed toward officers is unplanned and unpredictable. Fully 25 percent of incidents fell into the category of "unexplained." The next most frequent category was violent retaliation in response to an officer's command (13%).[47] Another study found that conduct (or an order) by an officer that was perceived to be inconsistent, arbitrary, spiteful, or unnecessary was often the stated cause of the assault. The authors go on to say that the deprivations of imprisonment compel inmates to resist attempts to deprive them of perceived rights.[48]

In one study of inmate attacks, it was found that there was an association between inmate alienation and expressions of hostility toward staff. Those who expressed hostility toward staff (and engaged in actual incidents of assault against officers) were also more likely to assault other inmates.[49] A British study found a correlation between a number of variables and the frequency of assaults on staff. Prisons that reported higher numbers of staff assaults were more likely to be those with open designs, those that had a high percentage of black prisoners and young, inexperienced staff, and those with a high percentage of sex offenders.[50] An American study collected information on 604 assaultive incidents in 21 state and federal prisons. After analyzing the incidents, the authors concluded that the typical assaulter was 26 years old and was 10 years younger than the victimized officer. The prisoner was almost as likely to be African-American as white, and was likely to have had prior incarcerations, be incarcerated for a violent crime, and be serving a long sentence. The typical assault took place during the course of basic job tasks, such as enforcing institutional rules, giving orders, conducting searches, and supervising. Officers were likely to be assaulted with hands (e.g., punch, slap, kick), and the most common injury was a back injury or a fracture. The most frequent victims of inmate assaults are officers with five to eight years of experience and between the ages of 30 and 45.[51]

In the federal system, the AIMS classification system (Adult Internal Management System) is used to reduce the risk of violence. In this system, "heavies" are those who are aggressive and independent. Members of this group, not surprisingly, are more likely to assault officers than the moderate or victim group members identified by the classification system.[52] By identifying the group members and utilizing the unit management system to house them separately, violence can be reduced.

BOX 11.2

Guard Predators

Guard abuse of prisoners, including sexual abuse of women prisoners, is a serious problem in prisons. Less serious, but still a problem, is prisoner abuse of guards. One specific form of this problem involves inmates who establish inappropriate relationships with prison staff.

Worley, Marquart, and Mullings interviewed 32 inmate "turners" who had been investigated for having inappropriate relationships with prison staff in the Texas prison system. They identified three types of "turners": heart-breakers, exploiters, and hell-raisers. Heart-breakers tried to establish romantic relationships, culminating in a physical relationship. Most intended to manipulate the guards, but a few insisted they wanted a genuine relationship. Exploiters aggressively sought out inappropriate relationships to make money in the underground prison economy, such as by bringing in cigarettes or drugs. The third type, hell-raisers, simply wanted to cause trouble. One hell-raiser, for example, bragged about having sex with two wardens' wives and thought it was hilarious.

The authors note that one contributing factor, especially for the exploiters, was the low pay in Texas prisons. At the time (the late 1990s), Texas guards started at only $1,716 a month, so bringing in cocaine and making an extra $1,000 a week was quite attractive to some guards.

Source: Adapted from Worley, R., J.W. Marquart, and J.L. Mullings (2003). "Prison Guard Predators: An Analysis of Inmates Who Established Inappropriate Relationships with Prison Staff, 1995-1998." *Deviant Behavior: An Interdisciplinary Journal* 24:175-194.

Officers also assault inmates. All officers may at times have to use force to subdue a violent inmate, separate two fighting inmates, or move a recalcitrant prisoner by legitimate force. It becomes assault and unlawful when the officer uses violence beyond what is necessary to accomplish the legitimate goal, or when the violence is gratuitous and/or undertaken for extralegal punishment or harassment rather than legitimate control.

In the prison world, officers have historically used physical coercion against those inmates who disrespected or assaulted officers. Crouch and Marquart[53] described Texas "tune-ups"—abuse administered to those inmates who did not show proper respect. These incidents involved profanity, shoving, kicks, and slaps. Violence toward inmates was more severe depending on the level of disrespect. Serious beatings were reserved for those who attacked officers. A beating was also the common response to an inmate who hurt an officer. There is some evidence to indicate that these "lessons" continue to occur in today's prisons.

A Florida news article reported that prison guards were more than twice as likely as police officers to violate state standards of conduct. An analysis of the state records for disciplinary actions showed that from January 1998 to June 1999, 769 corrections officers (29.6 per 1,000) were brought up on disciplinary charges, including sexual assault, shoplifting, and excessive force. During the same period, 559 law enforcement officers from city, county, and state police forces were sanctioned (14 per 1,000).[54]

In an earlier study conducted in 1994, 424 use-of-force reports were examined from 27 Florida prisons. The authors of the study found that most use-of-force incidents were in response to inmate fights (36%) or inmate disobedience (35%). Inmates physically resisted the guards in 42 percent of the cases. The authors then undertook a national survey and found that 60 percent of use-of-force incidents were in response to inmates fighting or disobeying orders. Note that these incidents were almost always determined to be legitimate use of force.[55] Information on those incidents in which guards' use of force was illegitimate and illegal is harder to come by.

Silberman[56] reports that officers respect those who can "dish it out" to inmates and are not afraid to utilize violence to obtain compliance. The use of violence has been seen as a rite of passage for officers.[57] "War stories" are told to indoctrinate new officers. They are also informed of various homicides of officers by inmates to emphasize the point that the inmates are the "enemy."[58]

State-sanctioned violence has been ruled violative of the Eighth Amendment protection against cruel and unusual punishment. In *Jackson v. Bishop*,[59] the Supreme Court ruled that the prison's use of a whip to administer punishment was against the evolving standards of decency and, thus, was cruel and usual. In a more recent case, the Court also held that any slaps, punches, or kicks, if done for the purpose of inflicting pain as punishment and not as part of a legitimate use of force, were also violative of the Eighth Amendment, whether or not serious injury resulted.[60] There is no question that officer-to-inmate violence, undertaken to teach a lesson to a disrespectful inmate, is not only unethical but also illegal. Silberman surveyed 96 inmates; none reported being abused by officers, although they did report threats and believed that such beatings occurred in segregation.[61] These results led Silberman to conclude that officer-to-inmate violence is much less prevalent today than in years past.

However, Hamm and his colleagues[62] found evidence that times have not changed very much. They first describe the history of violence against prisoners, including beatings, whippings, use of "the hole" or "doghouse," and the "Tucker telephone" (an electrical device attached to earlobes, genitals, and other sensitive parts of the body to administer shocks). The authors reported on a study of officer abuse that utilized a survey questionnaire. First, they noted severe problems with distribution, partly because of active resistance and repression on the part of some state prison management. The survey was printed in prison news-papers, but many states confiscated all copies of the newspaper and pun-ished inmates for having copies of the questionnaire. In addition, guards read the surveys before they were mailed, which reduced the likelihood of inmates accurately reporting the incidence of officer assaults. Despite these problems, the researchers received 605 surveys back from 41 dif-ferent states (for a return rate of 10%).[63]

BOX 11.3

Use-of-Force Allegations in California and Maryland

▶ **California**—Former guards at Corcoran State Prison implicated other guards in a series of allegations that involved such activities as setting up "gladiator"-type fights be-tween inmates and encouraging or allowing prisoner rapes. One former guard testified that when he asked why a prisoner was housed with a known prison rapist known as the "Booty Bandit," he was told that the inmate was a staff assaulter and loudmouth punk. The prisoner was subsequently viciously raped by the cellmate and the same officers de-nied knowledge of the risk. In subsequent court action, the accused guards were found not guilty of almost all charges brought against them.

▶ **Maryland**—In April 2008, Maryland Correctional officials fired a total of 17 correc-tional officers as a result of an investigation into charges of excessive force. One inmate alleged that he was made to put his face against a wall. Then an officer jumped off a bunk and kicked the inmate in the head and continued to kick the prisoner.

Source: Arax, M. (1999). "Ex-Guard Says 4 Men Set Up Rape of Inmate." *Los Angeles Times*, October 14, 1999; State Prison Officers Under Investigation: Eight Accused of Assault in Western Maryland," *Baltimore Sun*, March 28, 2008; "17 Corrections Officers Fired," *The New York Times*, April 10, 2008, A23.

According to inmate respondents, abuse seemed uniform across the country. About 62 percent of the sample had observed physical beatings (almost 50% said they occurred routinely).[64] Inmates reported that the two most frequently mentioned reasons for the abuse were being ver-bally abusive to guards and not following orders.[65] The survey respon-dents also indicated that a pattern of abuse occurred in relationship to "jailhouse lawyers"—those inmates who were vocal and confrontational in their challenges to prison authority. Some may argue that inmates may not be the most accurate and unbiased source for such informa-tion. However, the trends and patterns that seemed to exist, as well as the reinforcing information from other sources (such as officers), lends credibility to the proposition that officer-on-inmate violence is neither rare nor unsupported by the officer subculture.

One particular aspect of use of force in prisons has been described with special bitterness by inmate writers. Special Response Teams or Disturbance Teams are the prison world's version of law enforcement SWAT teams. Following the model of the federal system, which was developed in Leavenworth in early 1980s, Texas was one of first states to develop a team in 1984.[66] Some advantages of such teams are that their use results in reduced injury to officers, the action is videotaped for the protection of both inmates and officers, and highly trained officers are less likely to hurt inmates. However, others allege that abuses continue to occur.

The training, uniforms, and practices of the team create a mystique among officers and inmates. In some prisons, inmates have such antipathy for team members that members' identities are kept secret. This safeguard may be necessary because it has been noted in some hostage-taking situations that officers on such squads are often on the "hit lists" of inmates. When professionally run, this approach probably reduces injury for both inmate and officer. However, as stated earlier, we have very little information on incidents of abuse from special response teams or individual officers.

For official government statistics on staff sexual misconduct and staff sexual harassment, go to www.ojp.usdoj.gov/bjs/ and look for the report on sexual violence reported by correctional authorities.

• Interactions with Inmates •

The relationship between officers and inmates is one of "structured conflict."[67] This term refers to the inherent tension between the two groups arising from the role conflict of the keepers and the kept. This "structured conflict" permeates the prison and the relationship between officers and inmates. It is present even in the most cordial of relationships and influences every interaction between the two groups. It is why officers say, "you can be friendly with inmates, but you can't trust them," and why inmates, despite their surface friendliness, could never look upon an officer as a friend.

Officers are outnumbered and usually unarmed, and live with the constant knowledge that they may be assaulted, taken hostage, and/or killed. Because of this, inmates are perceived with suspicion, distrust, cynicism, and bitterness—especially by those officers who have been tricked and/or threatened.

Just as one can observe a prisoner subculture consisting of values sometimes antithetical to dominant society, there is also an observable correctional officer subculture. As with the prisoner subculture, the officer subculture is formed by the needs and realities of the officers. Kauffman provides the most detailed description of this culture. According to Kauffman's descriptions, the norms of the officer culture include:

- always go to the aid of an officer in distress;
- never make a fellow officer look bad in front of inmates,
- always support an officer in a dispute with an inmate,
- always support another officer's sanctions against an inmate,
- show concern for fellow officers,
- don't lug drugs, and
- don't "be a white hat" (be sympathetic to inmates).[68]

These norms promote safety and a unified front but also encourage a curtain of secrecy against those officers who exceed their authority.

In a more recent study of the correctional officer subculture, Farkas found that many of the principles mentioned by Kauffman were still salient. In her study at two medium-security prisons, she found important principles to include:

- always go to the aid of an officer in real or perceived physical danger,
- do not get too friendly with inmates,
- do not abuse your authority with inmates,
- keep your cool,
- back your fellow officers in decisions and actions,
- do not stab a coworker in the back,
- do not admit to mistakes,
- carry your own weight,
- defer to the experience and wisdom of veteran officers, and
- mind your own business.[69]

According to Farkas, the code engenders solidarity among officers, provides meanings for their actions, and supports the officer through relationships and shared values.

Some argue that the officer culture is not monolithic. Klofas and Toch propose that only some officers uphold the pure custody and anti-inmate values of the officer subculture.[70] In their view, officers are divided into the "subculture custodians," who are anti-treatment and place high value on security and control; the "supported majority," who are pro-treatment and professional; and the "lonely braves," who are pro-treatment, but feel the custodians overwhelm the institution and have trouble expressing support for pro-treatment initiatives. Freeman[71] also discusses the types of roles played by corrections officers. He notes the differences between "custody-oriented" officers and "professional" officers in their use of control (custody officers use more formal means), affective ties, informal relationships, social distance (social distance is greater between inmates and custody officers), and use of discretion.

Gilbert[72] parallels correctional officers and police officers by using Muir's[73] typology of "professional," "enforcer," "reciprocator," and "avoider." These types are described on the basis of their use of discretion, coercion, and human relations. The professional is reasonable, innovative, and able to make exceptions when necessary. The enforcer is aggressive, allows no exceptions to rules, and is cynical. The reciprocator has a counseling orientation, has difficulty using coercion even when called for, and is easily frustrated. The avoider uses means to avoid confrontations or even interaction with clients. While acknowledging that some adaptations are necessary to apply these police types to correctional officers, Gilbert goes on to note that they help in understanding the role of the correctional officer and the part discretion plays in their interactions with inmates. He notes that although the prison is viewed as a militaristic bureaucracy and officers are viewed as having little discretion in day-to-day decisionmaking, it is actually a social service organization. Therefore, officers employ discretion daily. Rather than ignore the discretion officers have, a better management approach would be to guide them to use it ethically.

Despite the inherent "structured conflict" between inmates and officers, and despite the presence of some officers who abuse their power, there is a good deal of positive interaction that occurs between officers and inmates. Because officers are the prison staff who spend the most time with inmates, some inmates report that it is an officer who has helped them by acting as a role model or informally talking about life's problems. Johnson described the type of officer who performs an expanded role and discussed their role in rehabilitation.[74] Silberman reported in his study that inmate-respondents described surprisingly positive interactions with correctional officers.[75] Good officers are invaluable in running a safe and secure facility. Their careful observations of inmates can avert riots, suicides, and assaults.

There are differences in the nature of officers' interactions with female inmates and those with male inmates. Female inmates seem to be more open to interactions with officers. Girshick, in her study of one women's prison, noted that female inmates were often asked if "anything was wrong" by an officer. While some perceived this as prying, others appreciated the concern.[76]

In a study of pre-service officers, it was found that officers today hold significantly more negative views toward treatment than officers did in the 1970s, but there is still a good deal of positive regard for treatment initiatives for inmates. Variables that affect attitudes toward treatment in a positive direction included age, the size of town from which an officer came, and race. Younger officers, officers coming from larger cities, and African-American and Hispanic officers were more positively oriented toward treatment. Gender was not found to be significant in views toward treatment.[77]

An officer's interactions with inmates will depend on his or her type of job assignment. Some assignments have direct, all-day contact with inmates. Some have almost none at all (such as the tower officer). One list of job assignments includes: block officers, work detail officers, industrial shop and school officers, yard officers, administration building assignment officers, wall post officers, and relief officers.[78]

Hepburn's[79] typology of power is useful for understanding the interactions between inmates and officers. In this typology, there are several kinds of power an officer might employ to perform the functions of the role. Legitimate legal authority is what comes with the uniform. In other words, every officer, just by wearing his or her uniform, has this type of authority. Coercive power is the implicit power behind the uniform. If an inmate does not follow orders because the officer says so, then coercive power is always the next potential alternative. It includes segregation, loss of good time, or removal of privileges, as well as the power to use brute force to move the inmate or compel him or her to comply. Reward power is the ability of officers to provide inmates with things in order to gain compliance. Expert power is the officer's ability to depend on some special skill, ability, or expertise. For instance, an officer supervising a work detail might possess this power because of a superior knowledge of carpentry or some other skill. Finally, referent power is personal authority that comes from the officer's individual personality, especially his or her ability to deal with inmates fairly and with respect. Having referent power means that inmates will comply not because of the uniform but specifically because of who the guard is.

Officers vary in their ability to employ these types of power, and some officers give up some of the authority that they have through "corruption of authority." First discussed by Sykes,[80] and reviewed and discussed by Crouch,[81] this interaction between inmates and officers describes the close relationship that develops at times between inmates and some officers. Some officers become so dependent on certain inmates to help them conduct the tasks of the job (e.g., paperwork, count, etc.) that they, in effect, give up a certain amount of their power to the inmates. It also occurs when officers accept goods and gifts from the inmate. Although the gift-giving may be innocuous at first (for instance, a cold soda on a hot day), it may result in the officer doing "favors" for the inmate. Over time, the power balance shifts between officer and inmate because the officer knows the inmate could report him or her for numerous rule violations. Although officers are taught to avoid this type of manipulation in the training academy, the process is so slow and insidious that many officers still get trapped by it.

Most often, inmates complain that officers put their own needs first and do little to help inmates. This reaction results from small things (like officers turning the television to a program they want to watch instead of what the inmates are watching) as well as larger issues (officers not sending down inmate's slips to see a counselor or forgetting to replenish supplies on a tier). Inmates also complain that officers take out their domestic troubles on the inmates and that they have a "negative attitude."[82] Although these particular observations come from a sample of female inmates, they are similar to complaints that male inmates have.

One of the most well known psychological experiments in a prison setting is the Zimbardo experiment. In this experiment, conducted at Stanford University, young male college students were randomly assigned to the role of guards or inmates. The experiment was abandoned after only six days because of the transformation of the young men into brutal, sadistic "guards" who took pleasure in cruelty. About one-third of the "guards" became "tyrannical in their arbitrary use of power."[83] The experiment illustrates the potential of the "power corrupts" truism. Although many argue that the experiment was different from real prisons in that prisons today are governed by a panoply of laws, regulations, policies, and procedures, the specter of college men turning into the worst stereotype of brutal guards is a cautionary lesson in the danger of power and how easy it is for some people to abuse that power.

• Interactions with Management and Administration •

The management of correctional institutions is patterned after the military. The chain of command is largely militaristic and bureaucratic, and management ranks are borrowed from the military—officer, sergeant, lieutenant, and so on. Many officers feel as controlled as if they were inmates and believe that they are treated unfairly by management. In fact, in many studies, officers report more dissatisfaction arising from management than from dealing with inmates.[84] Officers are both managers and line workers. As the lowest line in the pyramid, they have many supervisors above them but, unlike factory workers, they are also managers of inmates and are expected to handle inmates and achieve compliance on a daily basis. Officers often feel emotionally isolated, whether they work alone or as part of a small group.[85] They have the same feeling of isolation and separateness from the rest of society as do law enforcement officers. However, their work is less respected than law enforcement, so they get less satisfaction from belonging to the occupational group.

Management in prisons follows traditional bureaucratic patterns. Discipline follows the progression of: verbal instruction, verbal warning, written memo of instruction, letter of reprimand, disciplinary reduction in pay, disciplinary suspension without pay, demotion, and discharge.[86]

Yet, as in many organizations, officers often feel unfairly treated and observe that certain officers "get away" with more than others.

The perceived failure of managers to support line staff has been noted as contributing to the stress officers feel from the job. Corrections evidently does create a good deal of stress. There are higher-than-average rates of stress-related illnesses such as hypertension and alcoholism among correctional officers.[87] Some of the major reasons for disability leave are stress-related alcoholism, cardiac problems, and emotional disorders.[88] Kamerman notes that little attention is given to the problem of correctional officer suicides, even though the evidence indicates that they are at least as great a problem as law enforcement officer suicides.[89]

Freeman reviewed the literature on correctional officer stress. He found that some reports showed higher-than-normal levels of stress, while others indicated that stress may be related to the period of time on the job.[90] It is possible that those individuals not suited for a corrections job leave their positions (as older officers report lower levels of stress). However, other reports indicate that divorce, hypertension, alcoholism, and the like are all elevated in correctional officer populations. Stress is caused by potential danger; lack of predictability; feeling trapped in the job; low salaries; inadequate training; absence of standardized policies, procedures, and rules; lack of communication with management; and little participation in decisionmaking. Management can alleviate or exacerbate many of these elements.

In a survey analysis looking at management approaches and social climate, Stohr and her colleagues inadvertently found that jail officers reported higher levels of stress-related symptomology than did the psychiatric patient group for which the instrument was designed.[91] Although there are differences in the working conditions and management of jails versus prisons, these results should be viewed as important and possibly reflective of prisons as well. Jail officers scored higher than normal in five jails on obsessive-compulsive, anxiety, hostility, phobic anxiety, and psychoticism scales. The authors concluded that workers in those jails that employed personnel investment strategies (training, benefits, etc.) had higher job satisfaction levels, and officers in them reported less psychosomatic stress symptoms. These jails also boasted more organizational identification and a reduction in turnover.[92]

Another study conducted in the federal prison system studied the effects of job autonomy and participation on job satisfaction, commitment, stress, and efficacy in working with inmates.[93] Contrary to DiIulio's[94] argument that the best management approach for a prison was a bureaucracy with little input from staff, these authors found that indices of job satisfaction and commitment were positively correlated with a feeling of autonomy and participation in management decisions.

• Unions •

As mentioned previously, corrections professionals' unions became increasingly powerful in the 1980s in the northeast and California. Carroll noted their power in Rhode Island:

> Over the twenty years since its establishment in 1971, the Brotherhood of Correctional Officers (RIBCO) had developed into a shadow government at the ACI [Adult Correctional Institute], exerting a profound influence upon the organizational culture and day-to-day events.[95]

In California, the correctional officer union has become so powerful that it has become a real political force in gubernatorial races and other political contests. In fact, in the 1994 political race, the union contributed more than any other donor to Governor Pete Wilson's campaign. One source reports that only the California Medical Association spent more than the correctional officer union.[96]

The political power of unions is important because, unlike unions in the private sector, the power of guard unions to call for a strike is limited by legislative or executive action making strikes by public employees illegal. The unions that can dispense large monetary contributions to members of the legislature do not need the power of the strike to affect raises and other benefits because a legislative vote is what determines these benefits for its members.

So far, researchers have seen unions as a resistant force to rehabilitation, concerned with individual benefits for members rather than the mission or goal of corrections. Unions provide legal assistance to officers. They often support officers who, many would argue, should not be working in corrections. In California, for instance, unions provide legal assistance to officers who have been accused of assaulting inmates, having sex with inmates, giving drugs to inmates, and setting up gladiator fights between inmates.[97] Taxpayers may end up paying for both the prosecution of errant officers and their defense (through special legislative funds).

• Unit Management •

Unit management was developed in the federal system and has been quite successful in its stated objectives. It has been described as a way to alleviate the alienation of both inmates and officers, give more control to officers, and enrich job descriptions by reducing the anonymity of relations in prison living units.[98] Unit management involves creating fairly small living units and rearranging traditional management structures so that the living unit becomes almost self-sufficient in services and decisionmaking. A small number of inmates (50-120), usually of some similar type (e.g., MMPI profile), are permanently assigned to live together with a multidisciplinary staff placed within the housing unit. The unit manager has administrative authority and supervisory responsibility, and the staff have expanded authority over inmates. Treatment staff work evenings and weekends along with correctional officers, thus there is less distance between counselors and inmates, and correctional officers and staff have a closer working relationship. The frequency and stability of contact increases safety and decreases alienation, and decisionmaking is more immediate.[99]

Officers and inmates report increased levels of satisfaction and safety. The disadvantages of this system of management are that some individuals must share their authority (e.g., captains, assistant wardens), and there is less uniformity in decisionmaking across the units. Some prisons cannot employ unit management because of architecture, but it has been so successful in the federal system that there continues to be expansion of the concept.

ETHICS AND THE GOOD OFFICER

Pollock describes the ethical issues of correctional officers as relating to their use of discretion and authority.[100] Abuses occur either in the form of personal favors and inappropriate relationships with inmates or inappropriate use of power to harass certain inmates. Unfortunately one does not need to look hard to find examples of unethical and illegal behavior on the part of correctional workers.

Contraband trafficking, theft, warehouse sabotage, sexual relations with inmates, bartering with inmates, assisting in escape, theft of weapons, and brutality are a partial list of the types of unethical behaviors that occur.[101] Souryal, in another typology, describes the types of corruption as falling into the following categories: arbitrary use of power (e.g., treating workers or inmates preferentially or in a biased fashion), use of oppression or extralegal methods, failure to demonstrate compassion/caring, and abuse of authority for personal gain (e.g., extortion, smuggling, theft).[102]

Houston discussed a 1990 investigation of wide-scale corruption involving smuggling drugs into Florida's Martin Correctional Institution.[103] Fifteen arrests of corrections officials resulted. Pollock presented a number of examples in which investigations uncovered abuses ranging from sexual abuse of inmates to bribery at the highest levels of corrections departments.[104] Carroll detailed some of the problems that emerged during a rapid hiring of large numbers of officers in the early 1990s in Rhode Island. Brutality and corruption charges resulted from this cadre who were believed to be underqualified by management and older officers.[105]

Carroll noted other factors involved in corruption scandals associated with the growing importance and potential profits of drugs as well

BOX 11.4

American Correctional Association—Code of Ethics

Preamble

The American Correctional Association expects of its members unfailing honesty, respect for the dignity and individuality of human beings and a commitment to professional and compassionate service. To this end, we subscribe to the following principles:

1. Members shall respect and protect the civil and legal rights of all individuals.

2. Members shall treat every professional situation with concern for the welfare of the individuals involved and with no intent to personal gain.

3. Members shall maintain relationships with colleagues to promote mutual respect within the profession and improve the quality of service.

4. Members shall make public criticism of their colleagues or their agencies only when warranted, verifiable, and constructive.

5. Members shall respect the importance of all disciplines within the criminal justice system and work to improve cooperation with each segment.

6. Members shall honor the public's right to information and share information with the public to the extent permitted by law subject to individuals' right to privacy.

7. Members shall respect and protect the right of the public to be safeguarded from criminal activity.

8. Members shall refrain from using their position to secure personal privileges or advantages.

9. Members shall refrain from allowing personal interest to impair objectivity in the performance of duty while acting in an official capacity.

10. Members shall refrain from entering into any formal or informal activity or agreement which presents a conflict of interest or is inconsistent with the conscientious performance of duties.

11. Members shall refrain from accepting any gifts, service, or favor that is or appears to be improper or implies an obligation inconsistent with the free and objective exercise of professional duties.

12. Members shall clearly differentiate between personal views/statements and views/statements/positions made on behalf of the agency or Association.

13. Members shall report to appropriate authorities any corrupt or unethical behaviors in which there is sufficient evidence to justify review.

BOX 11.4 *(continued)*

14. Members shall refrain from discriminating against any individual because of race, gender, creed, national origin, religious affiliation, age, disability, or any other type of prohibited discrimination.

15. Members shall preserve the integrity of private information; they shall refrain from seeking information on individuals beyond that which is necessary to implement responsibilities and perform their duties; members shall refrain from revealing nonpublic information unless expressly authorized to do so.

16. Members shall make all appointment, promotions, and dismissals in accordance with established civil service rules, applicable contract agreements, and individual merit, rather than furtherance of personal interests.

17. Members shall respect, promote, and contribute to a work place that is safe, healthy, and free of harassment in any form.

Source: American Correctional Association. Revised August 1994 at the 124th Congress of Correction.

as issues relating to cross-sex supervision (leading to charges of sexual harassment and abuse).[106] He observed that because of the large number of complaints in the women's unit, it is now fitted with powerful cameras to deter any such activity from occurring.[107] Similar to police, correctional officers cannot "rat" on each other without encountering extreme social sanctions that include not receiving backup when in danger.

> If an incident went down, there was no one to cover my back. That's a very important lesson to learn. You need your back covered and my back wasn't covered there at all. And at one point I was in fear of being set up by guards. I was put in dangerous situations purposely. That really happened to me.[108]

Thus, as in law enforcement, in corrections, even if only a small number of officers are engaged in illegal or unethical practices, they are protected by the large silent majority who are afraid to come forward because of the powerful subcultural prohibitions against exposing fellow officers.

To reduce corruption in corrections, there must be a concerted effort to improve hiring practices (e.g., background checks and psychological testing), institute training, and employ supervisory devices to reduce temptation and punish wrongdoers. By most accounts, law enforcement seems to be ahead of corrections in ethics training for its officers. Law

BOX 11.5

Money Laundering and Drug Dealing by Guards

In an *Austin American Statesman* article, it was reported that four state prison guards faced felony bribery charges after agreeing to "launder" money for inmates. One guard received $60,000; his understanding was that he was supposed to "launder" $50,000 and keep $10,000 for himself. The other officers acted as lookouts in the transaction. The guards were arrested as a result of a sting operation by the Department of Criminal Justice internal affairs office and Sheriff's Deputies.

Source: Adapted from Associated Press (2000). "Prison Guards Suspected of Money Laundering." *Austin American Statesman*, January 27, 2000, B3.

One New York State Correctional officer sometimes made drug deals, including selling cocaine, on his cell phone while he was working in the guard tower at Wende Correctional Facility (near Buffalo, NY). Although his customers included nine other correctional officers, the officer denied selling drugs to inmates. The officer lost his job and served two years in a federal prison. His brother, also an officer, was arrested for conspiring to buy and sell cocaine. He received a sentence of probation and was forced to resign.

New York State correctional officials report that on average 20 employees a year are disciplined or resign because of alleged drug activity in and out of prison. Pennsylvania fired three officers from 2001 to 2004. Michigan fired five employees from 2003 to 2006.

Source: Adapted from L. Michel and S. Schulman (2008, Sept. 18). "Dealer in the Guard Tower." *Buffalo News*, September 18, 2008.

BOX 11.6

Death of Inmate—Guards Investigated

A grand jury is investigating the death of an inmate. Nine guards are expected to be indicted. Prosecutors say obtaining evidence is difficult because guards refuse to testify—they present a "wall of silence." A nurse did testify as to the extensive injuries sustained by the inmate. An autopsy revealed that Valdes died from a beating in which all his ribs were broken, his testicles swollen, and many cuts and bruises were sustained. Guards insist he killed himself by flinging himself against the concrete wall of his cell. Valdes was on death row for killing a prison guard in a botched escape attempt in 1983.

Source: Adapted from Cox, D. (2000). "Grand Jury Inquiry Into Death of Inmate Extended." *Sun-Sentinel*, January 5, 2000, B1.

enforcement also has the benefit of a greater pool of interested applicants.[109] The "trickle down" theory of ethical management holds that officers will treat inmates the way they perceive they are being treated—with fairness, compassion, and respect—or not. It becomes easier to justify unethical actions if one feels victimized.[110]

BOX 11.7

Corruption Reduction Policy

1. Upgrade quality of correctional personnel.

2. Establish quality-based supervisory techniques.

3. Strengthen fiscal controls.

4. Emphasize true ethical training.

Source: Adapted from Souryal, S. (1999). "Corruption of Prison Personnel." In P. Carlson and J. Garrett (eds.), *Prison and Jail Administration: Practice and Theory*, 171-177. Gaithersburg, MD: Aspen.

The job of the correctional officer is not an easy one. Supervising inmates who are held in captivity against their will on a daily basis requires a good deal of human relations skills. If one also aspires to help in the process of reformation, or even make the experience less debilitating, it is an even more difficult task.

A good officer is described as one who treats all inmates fairly with no favoritism, but who does not always follow rules to the letter. Discretion is used judicially; when a good officer makes a decision to bypass rules, all involved tend to agree that it is the right decision. A good officer is not quick to use force, nor afraid of force if it becomes necessary. A good officer treats inmates in a professional manner and gives them the respect they deserve as human beings.[111]

As Robert Johnson notes, the best guards go even further. The best officers try to expand their roles to be human service providers and problem solvers. As a consequence, these officers improve their own working conditions and the living conditions of the inmates:

> These officers discover that in the process of helping inmates and thereby giving them more autonomy, security, and emotional support, they gain the same benefits: more control over their environment; more security in their daily interactions with prisoners; and a sense of community, however inchoate or ill-defined, with at least some of the inmates under their care.[112]

CONCLUSION

Corrections has a long way to go to provide officers with the needed training, supervision, and rewards for doing a good job. In the past several decades, officers have seen their role and responsibilities changed and changed again. Their world has been virtually turned upside down by court orders, inmate population changes, and the pressures of overcrowding. They continue to struggle to control an increasingly frustrated inmate population with inadequate programming and little innovation. Moreover, in some states, they do so with abysmal salaries and expectations for advancement. Despite these handicaps, though, some officers do make a difference and the prison becomes, for some at least, a place to effect change.

▶ Ethics Focus: "It's Only a Birthday Card"

You have worked at the state prison for five years. There is an inmate you have known for four of those five years who works in the security office. He has asked you to mail a birthday card to his niece, Sarah, who is not on his approved mailing list. You have observed other correctional officers mailing cards and letters on occasion for inmates to persons not on their approved mailing list. You really don't see the harm in a birthday card for a niece. Still, she isn't on the approved mailing list.

What should you do? What is the best possible outcome of such an action? What is the worst possible consequence?

▶ At the Movies . . . .

The Green Mile, 1999.

This movie portrays novelist Stephen King's fictional account of how guards treated inmates on death row more than 50 years ago. Although fictional, this movie raises issues about the ethical way to treat prison inmates.

The Shawshank Redemption, 1994.

This classic movie is about life in a Big House prison with a corrupt warden.

DISCUSSION QUESTIONS

1. Describe the transformation of the correctional officer role from World War II to the present. Explain why such changes may have caused alienation and stress among correctional officers.

2. Discuss the impacts of unionization, professionalization, and bureaucratization on the role of the correctional officer.

3. Describe in a general way the qualifications, salary range, and occupational outlook for correctional officers.

4. Utilizing the information provided in the text, evaluate the performance of female correctional officers in prisons for men.

5. Discuss the experience of female and minority officers in prison.

6. Explain how the relationship between officers and inmates is one of "structured conflict."

7. Describe Hepburn's typology of power, and give examples of how they might be used by correctional officers.

8. Describe corrupt practices of correctional officers. Explain what steps might be done to prevent it.

FURTHER READING

Johnson, R. (2002). *Hard Time: Understanding and Reforming the Prison*. Belmont, CA: Wadsworth.

Masters, J.J. (1997). *Finding Freedom: Writings from Death Row*. Junction City, CA: Padma.

NOTES

1. Freeman, 1997b.

2. Johnson, 1997.

3. See, for instance, Kauffman, 1988.

4. *Ruiz v. Estelle*.

5. Martin and Eckland-Olson, 1987, 38.

6. Carroll, 1998, 55, 82.

7. Taylor, 1993, 217.

8. Silberman, 1995, 121.

9. Crouch, 1995, 184.

10. Crouch, 1995; Silberman, 1995; Johnson, 1997; Irwin, 1980; Crouch and Marquart, 1989.

11. Josi and Sechrest, 1998, 37.

12. Freeman, 1997a.

13. Silberman, 1995, 119.

14. Irwin and Austin, 1997, 68.

15. Bureau of Labor Statistics, Occupational Outlook Handbook, 2008-09 Edition, *Correctional Officers*, available at http://www.bls.gov/oco/ocos156.htm

16. American Correctional Association, 2007.

17. Bureau of Labor Statistics, Occupational Outlook Handbook, 2008-09 Edition, *Correctional Officers*, available at http://www.bls.gov/oco/ocos156.htm

18. Respective state web sites.

19. See http://www.mcso.org, the web site for the Maricopa County, AZ Sheriff's Office.

20. Pew Center on the States, 2008.

21. Pew Center on the States, 2008.

22. Josi and Sechrest, 1998, 7, 24.

23. Josi and Sechrest, 1998, 28, 34.

24. Freeman, 1999, 59.

25. Freeman, 1999.

26. Pollock, 1986.

27. Jenne and Kersting, 1996.

28. Zimmer, 1986.

29. Freeman, 1997b, 324.

30. Lawrence and Mahan, 1998.

31. Freeman, 1997b.

32. Gross et. al., 1994.

33. McMahon, 1999.

34. McMahon, 1999, 71-73.

35. McMahon, 1999, 83

36. McMahon, 1999, 79.

37. McMahon, 1999, 135.

38. Owen, 1985.

39. Wright and Saylor, 1992.

40. Britton, 1997.

41. Camp et. al., 1997.

42. Silberman, 1995.

43. Silberman, 1995.

44. Ross, 1996, 6.

45. Associated Press, 2000a, B3.

46. Light, 1999.

47. Light, 1999, 211-212.

48. Light, 1991.

49. Silberman, 1995, 85.

50. Ditchfield and Harries, 1996.

51. Ross, 1996.

52. Silberman, 1995, 92.

53. Crouch and Marquart, 1989.

54. Kleindienst, 1999.

55. Henry, Senese, and Ingley, 1994.

56. Silberman, 1995.

57. Marquart and Crouch, 1985.

58. Silberman, 1995.

59. *Jackson v. Bishop*, 404 F.2d 571 (8th Cir. 1968).

60. *Hudson v. McMillian*, 503 U.S. 1 (1992).

61. Silberman, 1995, 222.

62. Hamm et al., 1994.

63. Hamm et al., 1994, 181.

64. Hamm et al., 1994, 185

65. Hamm et al., 1994, 187

66. Silberman, 1995.

67. Jacobs and Kraft, 1978.

68. Kauffman, 1988.

69. Farkas, 1997.

70. Klofas and Toch, 1982; also see Toch, 1981.

71. Freeman, 1997b.

72. Gilbert, 1997.

73. Muir, 1977.

74. Johnson, 1981.

75. Silberman, 1995.

76. Girshick, 1999, 93

77. Paboojian and Teske, 1997.

78. Freeman, 1997b.

79. Hepburn, 1985.

80. Sykes, 1958.

81. Crouch, 1995.

82. Girshick, 1999, 94.

83. Zimbardo, 1982, 196.

84. Freeman, 1997a.

85. Freeman, 1997a.

86. Wright, 1999.

87. Williamson, 1990, 149; Kauffman, 1988.

88. Gross et al., 1994.

89. Kamerman, 1995.

90. Freeman, 1999.

91. Stohr et al., 1994, 489.

92. Stohr et al., 1994, 495.

93. Wright et. al., 1997.

94. DiIulio, 1987.

95. Carroll, 1998, 269.

96. Josi and Sechrest, 1998, 160.

97. Josi and Sechrest, 1998, 161.

98. Houston, 1999, 189.

99. Houston, 1999.

100. Pollock, 1998.

101. McCarthy, 2008.

102. Souryal, 1999.

103. Houston, 1999, 360.

104. Pollock, 1998.

105. Carroll, 1998.

106. Carroll, 1998.

107. Carroll, 1998, 284.

108. Reported by Kauffman, 1988, 207.

109. Houston, 1999, 365.

110. Souryal, 1999; Pollock, 1998.

111. Pollock, 1998, 300.

110. Johnson, 1981, 256.

REFERENCES

Arax, M. (1999). "Ex-Guard Says 4 Men Set Up Rape of Inmate." *Los Angeles Times*, October 14, 1999.

American Correctional Association (2007). *2007 Directory of Adult and Juvenile Correctional Departments, Institutions, Agencies, and Probation and Parole Agencies.* Alexandria, VA: American Correctional Association.

Associated Press (2000a). "Prison Guards Send Plea to Bush." *Austin American Statesman*, January 11, 2000, B3.

Associated Press (2000b). "Prison Guards Suspected of Money Laundering." *Austin American Statesman*, January 27, 2000, B3.

Britton, D. (1997). "Perceptions of the Work Environment among Correctional Officers: Do Race and Sex Matter?" *Criminology* 35(1):85-105.

Bureau of Labor Statistics, Occupational Outlook Handbook, 2008-09 Edition, *Correctional Officers*, available at http://www.bls.gov/oco/ocos156.htm.

Camp, S., T. Steiger, K. Wright, W. Saylor, and E. Gilman (1997). "Affirmative Action and the 'Level Playing Field': Comparing Perceptions of Own and Minority Job Advancement Opportunities." *The Prison Journal* 77(3):313-334.

Carroll, L. (1998). *Lawful Order: A Case Study of Correctional Crisis and Reform*. New York: Garland Press.

Cox, D. (2000). "Grand Jury Inquiry into Death of Inmate Extended." *Sun-Sentinel*, January 5, 2000.

Crouch, B. (1995). "Guard Work in Transition." In K. Haas and G. Alpert (eds.), *The Dilemmas of Corrections*, 3rd ed., 183-203. Prospect Heights, IL: Waveland.

Crouch, B., and J. Marquart (1989). *An Appeal to Justice: Litigated Reform of Texas Prisons*. Austin, TX: University of Texas Press.

DiIulio, J., Jr. (1987). *Governing Prisons: A Comparative Study of Correctional Management*. New York: Free Press.

Ditchfield, J., and R. Harries (1996). "Assaults on Staff in Male Local Prisons and Remand Centres." *Home Office Research and Statistics Directorate Research Bulletin*, Issue 38, 1996, 15-20.

Farkas, M. (1997). "Normative Code among Correctional Officers: An Exploration of Components and Functions." *Journal of Crime and Justice* 20(1):23-36.

Freeman, R. (1999). *Correctional Organization and Management: Public Policy Challenges, Behavior, and Structure*. Boston: Butterworth/Heinemann.

Freeman, R. (1997a). "Management and Administrative Issues." In J. Pollock (ed.), *Prisons: Today and Tomorrow*, 270-299. Gaithersburg, MD: Aspen.

Freeman, R. (1997b). "Correctional Officers: Understudied and Misunderstood." In J. Pollock (ed.), *Prisons: Today and Tomorrow*, 306-332. Gaithersburg, MD: Aspen.

Gilbert, M. (1997). "The Illusion of Structure: A Critique of the Classical Model of Organization and the Discretionary Power of Correctional Officers." *Criminal Justice Review* 22(1):49-64.

Girshick, L. (1999). *No Safe Haven: Stories of Women in Prison*. Boston: Northeastern University Press.

Gross, G., S. Larson, G. Urban, and L. Zupan (1994). "Gender Differences in Occupational Stress among Correctional Officers." *American Journal of Criminal Justice* 18, 2:219-234.

Hamm, M., T. Coupez, F. Hoze, and C. Weinstein (1994). "The Myth of Humane Imprisonment: A Critical Analysis of Severe Discipline in U.S. Maximum Security Prisons, 1945-1990." In M. Braswell, R. Montgomery, Jr., and L. Lombardo (eds.), *Prison Violence in America*, 167-200. Cincinnati: Anderson.

Henry, P., J. Senese, and G. Ingley (1994). "Use of Force in America's Prisons: An Overview of Current Research." *Corrections Today* 56(4):108-110.

Hepburn, J. (1985). "The Exercise of Power in Coercive Organizations: A Study of Prison Guards." *Criminology* 23(1):146-164.

Houston, J. (1999). *Correctional Management: Functions, Skills, and Systems*. Chicago: Nelson-Hall.

Irwin, J. (1980). *Prisons in Turmoil*. Boston: Little, Brown.

Irwin, J., and J. Austin (1997). *It's About Time: America's Imprisonment Binge*. Belmont, CA: Wadsworth.

Jacobs, J., and L. Kraft (1978). "Integrating the Keepers: A Comparison of Black and White Prison Guards in Illinois." *Social Problems* 25:304-318.

Jenne, D., and R. Kersting (1996). "Aggression and Women Correctional Officers in Male Prisons." *The Prison Journal* 76(4):442-460.

Johnson, R. (1997). "Race, Gender, and the American Prison: Historical Observations." In J. Pollock (ed.), *Prisons: Today and Tomorrow*, 26-52. Gaithersburg, MD: Aspen.

Johnson, R. (1981). "The Complete Correctional Officer: Human Service and the Human Environment of Prison." *Criminal Justice and Behavior* 8(3):343-373.

Josi, D., and D. Sechrest (1998). *The Changing Career of the Correctional Officer: Policy Implications for the 21st Century*. Boston: Butterworth-Heinemann.

Kamerman, J. (1995). "Correctional Officer Suicide." *The Keepers' Voice* 16(3):7-8.

Kauffman, K. (1988). *Prison Officers and Their World*. Cambridge, MA: Harvard University Press.

Kleindienst, L. (1999). "Florida Prison Guards Twice as Likely as Police to Commit Violations." *Sun-Sentinel*, August 25, 1999.

Klofas, J., and H. Toch (1982). "The Guard Subculture Myth." *Journal of Research in Crime & Delinquency* 19(2):238-254.

Lawrence, R., and S. Mahan (1998). "Women Corrections Officers in Men's Prisons: Acceptance and Perceived Job Performance." *Women and Criminal Justice* 9(3):63-86.

Light, S. (1999). "Assaults on Prison Officers: Interactional Themes." In M. Braswell, R. Montgomery, Jr., and L. Lombardo (eds.), *Prison Violence in America*, 207-223. Cincinnati: Anderson.

Light, S. (1991). "Assaults on Prison Officers: Interactional Themes." *Justice Quarterly* 8, 2:242-261.

Martin, S., and S. Eckland-Olson (1987). *Texas Prisons: The Walls Came Tumbling Down*. Austin, TX: Texas Monthly Press.

Marquart, J., and B. Crouch (1985). "Judicial Reform and Prisoner Control." *Law and Society Review* 16:557-586.

McCarthy, B. (2008). "Keeping an Eye on the Keeper: Prison Corruption and Its Control. " In M. Braswell, B. McCarthy, and B. McCarthy (eds.), *Justice, Crime, and Ethics*, 6th ed., 299-318. Newark, NJ: LexisNexis Matthew Bender.

McMahon, M. (1999). *Women on Guard: Discrimination and Harassment in Corrections*. Toronto: University of Toronto Press.

Muir, W. (1977). *Street Corner Politicians*. Chicago: University of Chicago Press.

Owen, B. (1985). "Race and Gender Relations among Prison Workers." *Crime & Delinquency* 31 (January):147-159.

Paboojian, A., and R. Teske (1997). "Pre-Service Correctional Officers: What Do They Think about Treatment?" *Journal of Criminal Justice* 25(5):425-433.

Pew Center on the States (2008). *One in 100: Behind Bars in America, 2008*. Available at http://www.pewcenteronthestates.org

Pollock, J. (1998). *Ethics in Crime and Justice: Dilemmas and Decisions*, 3rd ed. Belmont, CA: West/Wadsworth.

Pollock, J. (1986). *Sex and Supervision: Guarding Male and Female Inmates*. New York: Greenwood.

Ross, D. (1996). "Assessment of Prisoner Assaults on Corrections Officers." *Corrections Compendium* 21(8):6-10.

Silberman, M. (1995). *A World of Violence: Corrections in America*. Belmont, CA: Wadsworth.

Souryal, S. (1999). "Corruption of Prison Personnel." In P. Carlson and J. Garrett (eds.), *Prison and Jail Administration: Practice and Theory*, 171-177. Gaithersburg, MD: Aspen.

Stohr, M., N. Lovrich, B. Menke, and L. Zupan (1994). "Staff Management in Correctional Institutions: Comparing DiIulio's 'Control Model' and "Employee Investment Model' Outcomes in Five Jails." *Justice Quarterly* 11(3):471-497.

Sykes, G. (1958). *The Society of Captives*. New York: Atheneum.

Taylor, W. (1993). *Brokered Justice: Race, Politics, and Mississippi Prisons, 1798-1992*. Columbus, OH: Ohio State University Press.

Toch, H. (1981). "Is a 'Correctional Officer,' by Any Other Name, a 'Screw?'" In R. Ross (ed.), *Prison Guard/Correctional Officer*, 87-103. Toronto: Butterworth.

Williamson, H. (1990). *The Corrections Profession*. Newbury Park, CA: Sage.

Wright, K., and W. Saylor (1992). "Comparison of Perceptions of the Work Environment Between Minority and Non-minority Employees of the Federal Prison System." *Journal of Criminal Justice* 20(1):63-71.

Wright, K., W. Saylor, E. Gilman, and S. Camp (1997). "Job Control and Occupational Outcomes among Prison Workers." *Justice Quarterly* 14(3):525-546.

Wright, R. (1999). "Governing—The Human Side of Personnel Management." In P. Carlson and J. Garrett (eds.), *Prison and Jail Administration: Practice and Theory*, 151-157. Gaithersburg, MD: Aspen.

Zimbardo, P. (1982). "The Prison Game." In N. Johnston and L.D. Savitz (eds.), *Legal Process and Corrections*, 195-198. New York: Wiley and Sons.

Zimmer, L. (1986). *Women Guarding Men*. Chicago: University of Chicago Press.

COURT CASES

Hudson v. McMillian, 503 U.S. 1 (1992).

Jackson v. Bishop, 404 F.2d 571 (8th Cir. 1968).

Ruiz v. Estelle, 679 F.2d 1115 (5th Cir. 1982). Opinion amended in part and vacated in part, 688 F.2d 266 (5th Cir. 1982).

Correctional Counselors and Other Treatment Professionals

CHAPTER 12

What You Need to Know

▶ Correctional counseling and treatment has evolved over the years through both prison and community-based settings.

▶ Correctional counseling includes education and vocational programs, healthcare, recreation, and religion.

▶ Correctional counseling and treatment programs use a variety of intervention strategies, including cognitive, group work, and family therapy approaches.

▶ Antisocial, substance abuse, and sex offenders are often involved in correctional treatment programs. "Special needs" offenders including the developmentally disabled, HIV/AIDS-infected offenders, and the elderly and terminally ill are also a part of correctional counselors' caseloads.

▶ Concerns of correctional treatment professionals include prison overcrowding, increasing caseloads, racial/ethnic conflict, lack of institutional support, confidentiality issues, and stress and burnout.

INTRODUCTION

What does it mean to be a correctional counselor or other treatment professional? What do you have to do? How does it feel?

There is some public and political sentiment that supports the idea that "once a criminal, always a criminal." In addition, there are some persons who believe that offenders and inmates do not deserve counseling, adequate health care, and other appropriate treatment services. However, because the majority of offenders who are incarcerated in correctional institutions and community-based programs will eventually be released back into society, it would seem to make sense for corrections to at least increase the odds that offenders live reasonably normal and law-abiding lives upon release from the criminal justice system. It is true that while corrections cannot make an offender change against his or her will, dedicated helping professionals can become a positive catalyst for those who do want to become law-abiding and productive citizens.

The counseling and treatment of criminal and delinquent populations involve a variety of mental health professionals and other related helping professionals. These professionals may be found in various correctional settings, including human services programs that contract with correctional agencies, probation, parole, community-based residential dwellings such as halfway houses, and correctional institutions.

Working in a correctional treatment setting requires human relations skills, knowledge, and experience. A combination of these attributes helps shape the professional style and attitude of the correctional worker. Unique challenges and counseling situations occur with each offender.

The term "correctional counseling" may be somewhat inaccurate in describing what are often conflicting objectives present when working with offenders. For example, should the primary goal of the correctional counselor be to help the inmates adjust to life in prison or to prepare the inmate for successful reintegration into the community? Should probation/parole counselors be more concerned with case management and enforcement of probation/parole conditions or with therapeutically helping the offenders under their supervision? More fundamentally, one might ask whether there is any evidence that counselors are able to "correct" offenders in the first place. Perhaps the most appropriate way to view these counselors is as helping professionals who seek to apply their skills in correctional settings. The primary goal of such helping professionals would then seem to be to one of intervening therapeutically with various clients, the majority of whom happen to be offenders. This intervention may take the form of prison adjustment, prerelease and postrelease adjustment issues including family issues, drug counseling, or dealing with any of the numerous crises and problems that may be present in the lives of offenders.

In some correctional agencies, a greater emphasis has been placed upon managing resources and supervising clients than on more traditional counseling and casework duties. In such instances, the correctional counselor becomes involved in a wide range of responsibilities, including assessment and evaluation of offenders and matching offender needs with appropriate community and institutional resources. In addition, on occasion, case management may include the counselor acting as an advocate on behalf of a particular offender.

On many occasions, case management becomes the function of probation and parole officers. These professionals are not simply resource brokers, although they do help offenders obtain the appropriate drug, mental health, or other types of counseling. Case managers also consider informal counseling a vital component of their relationship with a client.[1] Developing employment opportunities for the offender is often another goal of case management.

THE HISTORICAL CONTEXT OF TREATMENT

Historically, correctional counseling has evolved through several phases and periods. The Quakers inspired the earliest efforts at treatment, which included religious instruction and reform in order to influence the offender. Following the Civil War, efforts revolved around teaching offenders to read the Bible and exposing them to vocational and educational training.

In the 1950s, the medical model was the primary approach to criminal behavior. Criminal behavior was treated as a disorder or disease in the same manner that medical professionals treated physical illnesses and disease. First, the disorder had to be diagnosed. Next, as in medicine, a proper treatment needed to be prescribed and administered to obtain a cure. Just as a physically ill person was to be cured of his or her illness, an offender was to be cured of his or her criminality.

The behavioral science movement followed the era of the medical model. Behavioral scientists believed criminal behavior could be modified and shaped into positive and law-abiding behavior through the use of reinforcement, psychological conditioning, and other behavioral principles and technologies.

In the 1970s, therapeutic communities became a popular treatment approach, particularly in dealing with substance abusers. These "communities" typically stressed common goals and personal responsibility. More recently, many correctional counselors have had to assume greater supervision and resource management roles regarding offenders under their care. Get-tough programs such as juvenile "boot camps" (see Chapter 9) have come into fashion on one end of the treatment spectrum, while restorative and community justice programs that bring together victims and offenders (see Chapter 6) have emerged on the other end of the continuum.

Each treatment approach has started with high levels of enthusiasm and promise. As time passed, the initial promise of each new movement faded and was often overwhelmed by the business and politics of corrections. In the end, what was claimed about each new treatment approach often bore little resemblance to what was actually done. In many instances, political and social fashion have shaped our correctional efforts more than serious long-term program commitments and research. Many people continue to believe that society can isolate offenders in the abnormal world of prisons and teach them how to cope in the outside, relatively normal world. However, many offenders learn how to cope—not to the outside world, but to the realities of life in prison.

In general, there is currently a trend toward reducing treatment and education programs as well as restricting recreational activities in some state prison systems. Yet, there are also a number of other community- and institution-based corrections programs that are implementing innovative treatment and rehabilitation strategies.

CORRECTIONAL TREATMENT AND HEALTH CARE

While the duties of correctional counselors and treatment professionals overlap to some extent, all must work together, particularly in an institutional setting, in order to maintain as calm and positive a working and living environment as possible. This includes a prison's medical and healthcare unit. Physicians, nurses, dentists, and other health professionals provide essential health-related services, dispense medicines, and monitor and manage potential infectious diseases such as HIV/AIDS and tuberculosis.

In 1972, the American Medical Association (AMA) surveyed the nation's jails and found that medical services were lacking in three major areas: adequacy, access, and availability. In the 1976 decision of *Estelle v. Gamble*, the court ruled that correctional facilities could be liable if they acted with "deliberate indifference to the serious medical needs" of inmates.[2] As a result, the AMA developed a set of standards to address these deficiencies. Because of the *Estelle* decision and the newly adopted standards of the AMA, sweeping changes occurred in the prison healthcare system.

Today the National Commission on Correctional Health Care (NCCHC) is the leading authority on correctional health care. The NCCHC sets the standards for jails, prisons, and juvenile facilities. The NCCHC standards include administrative and personnel issues as well as environmental and preventive health care, routine and emergency health services, and medical-legal concerns.[3]

However, in 1979, the U.S. Supreme Court ruled in *Bell v. Wolfish* that standards developed by professional associations were only advisory and do not necessarily define what is minimally required by correctional facilities.[4] Nevertheless, the courts and correctional administrators frequently set healthcare guidelines in accordance with the standards of the AMA and NCCHC.

In 1995, the American Correctional Health Services Association (ACHSA) adopted a Code of Ethics for treating patients in correctional facilities. The ACHSA noted that the correctional focus of discipline, deterrence, and punishment often runs contrary to the concerns of health professionals, which include curing, healing, and relieving suffering. The ACHSA also recognized the importance of medical autonomy—that correctional health professionals should be afforded the opportunity to carry out their duties.[5]

The majority of people who are incarcerated are poor and a member of a minority group. As a result, many inmates may not have had access to preventive medical care when they were not in prison. The majority of inmates use tobacco and abuse alcohol. Inmates also have a higher rate of intravenous drug use and tend to have histories of multiple sexual partners.[6] All of these behaviors contribute to a higher incidence of serious illness and debilitating diseases among the prison population. It is important for these inmates to undergo a thorough medical evaluation and examination in order to determine their medical needs.

Inmates typically use medical services more often than people do in the outside community. In part, this happens because inmates are required to use official medical services in order to receive over-the-counter medications for minor complaints that noninmates would normally treat themselves. Moreover, some inmates also use the correctional health system to avoid work details, to socialize with friends, or to obtain drugs for recreational purposes. Therefore, the medical staff must be able to discern the legitimate medical needs of the inmate.[7]

Although vast improvements have been made in the healthcare services provided to inmates, several areas need additional improvements. Box 12.1 includes some suggestions for needed improvements.

Healthcare services need to be coordinated between prisons and jails and the community. The prison medical staff should be aware of an inmate's previous medical treatment and history. Familiarity with inmate medical histories is essential to providing quality medical care. Failure by the prison staff to consider an inmate's prior health care can lead to an overuse of some medical services and an insufficient use of others. Therefore, it is important to provide inmates with the care they need while utilizing scarce healthcare resources effectively.[8] (For further details, see Chapter 10.)

BOX 12.1

Suggestions for Improving Correctional Healthcare Services

1. Containing health care costs

2. Improving the quality of care

3. Improving staff-inmate relationships

4. Controlling infectious diseases

5. Increasing the professionalism of the staff through continuing education

6. Promoting data collection and research efforts for future planning and management strategies

Source: Anno, B.J. (1992). *Prison Healthcare: Guidelines for the Management of an Adequate Delivery System.* Longmont, CO: National Institute of Corrections Information Center.

TYPES OF CORRECTIONAL COUNSELING AND RELATED TREATMENT

Although the term "correctional counseling" is relatively new, the use of counseling services has been in evidence from the beginning of corrections. The 1800s saw correctional counseling duties being performed by ministers and, later, by probation and parole officers. In the twentieth century, social workers, sociologists, psychiatrists, and psychologists began to provide counseling services. The increased popularity of counseling after World War II and the rehabilitation emphasis of the 1960s and early 1970s served to make more commonplace the use of the term "correctional counseling." Counseling and treatment services are still provided by a variety of professionals.

Correctional counselors can be grouped into two categories: community-based and institutional. Many community-based counselors work as probation or parole officers. However, community counselors can also be found in a variety of other settings, including employment agencies, schools, private counseling agencies, mental health centers, hospitals, halfway houses, and churches. Institutional counselors and helping professionals include psychologists, social workers, chaplains, educators, vocational instructors, and recreation specialists.

• Education and Vocational Programs •

Education has long been viewed as an essential part of preparing inmates for a more productive, noncriminal lifestyle. A popular notion has been that an educated prisoner will have more law-abiding options for gainful employment upon release than an illiterate or semi-literate inmate.

In 2003, the National Center for Education Statistics found that approximately one in three inmates performed at the lowest literacy level.[9] People functioning at this level would have problems reading newspapers, filling out job applications, or working in all but the lowest-paid jobs. This finding was not surprising to many correctional educators and counselors because inmates are one of the most educationally disadvantaged groups in the United States. Correctional educators have to work with individuals who have typically experienced failure in traditional school systems. Many have either dropped out or been pushed out of public schools for a variety of reasons. In addition, these individuals often have learning problems, problems with substance abuse, histories of violence, and emotional difficulties. Few have had positive educational experiences, and many inmates lack the necessary family support and study skills for traditional education programs.

Correctional education can take many forms. The majority of prisoners are enrolled in adult basic education (ABE) and general equivalency diploma (GED) programs. These programs help inmates catch up with the education level of the general population. Furthermore, basic education and high school diplomas help make inmates more marketable to employers. Other programs offered in correctional institutions include job readiness training and prerelease education. These programs are designed to help the inmate's transition to life outside the prison go as smoothly as possible. These courses teach skills such as how to set up and maintain a budget, how to fill out a job application correctly, and how to manage one's time.

Some state and federal institutions offer opportunities to earn advanced degrees. Inmates may access college education courses through live instruction, correspondence courses, television and Internet courses, and release time to attend local colleges and universities. However, obtaining an advanced degree while in prison is becoming more difficult. Higher education opportunities appear to be diminishing. For example, Pell grants for prisoners were eliminated in the mid-1990s.[10]

Research suggests that educational programs affect the ability of inmates to succeed outside of prison. Ryan and Mauldin found that of 97 studies, 85 percent reported a positive relationship between participation in correctional education and reduction in recidivism.[11] Harer reported similar findings in a study of federal prisoners: Inmates who participated in educational programs exhibited better institutional adjustment, were more likely to become employed upon release, and were less likely to return to prison.[12]

Many inmates lack regular work experience or any useful vocational skills. Vocational programs teach inmates practical skills and positive work habits in order to prepare them for employment after prison. Criminological research has linked unemployment with crime. The goal of vocational education is to reduce unemployment as a way of helping to reduce crime. Vocational programs are diverse, ranging from air conditioning repair to restoring antique cars. Prisons in Michigan and Ohio, for example, teach inmates how to raise service dogs for disabled individuals. The number of inmates in the prison system far exceeds the number of openings in vocational programs. Many inmates who desperately need job training do not have access to vocational education and training. Those inmates who manage to complete a vocational program often face employers who are reluctant to hire ex-convicts.

Several factors have shown promise in improving vocational training. Technology such as the use of videos and interactive television has allowed instructors to train larger numbers of inmates at one time. The current trend toward accreditation of correctional facilities may also help improve the quality of individual vocational programs.

Educators in correctional settings often perform a variety of duties. Correctional teachers may be responsible for developing individualized curricula for ABE programs or providing group instruction for the GED program. Other instructor duties may include teaching in vocational training programs, counseling students regarding academic problems, participating in in-service training, and serving on various institutional boards.

Correctional educators are expected to have at least a bachelor's degree in education from an accredited college or university. Instructors must also be certified in the state in which the prison is located. A vocational teacher must have relevant work and/or teaching experience in his or her specialty area. Coursework in psychology, criminal justice, and special education may be beneficial for those who plan to work in a correctional environment.

Correctional education can be both rewarding and frustrating. Teachers must be prepared for all skill levels of students. Some students will refuse to take part, while others will require nontraditional methods to be able to participate in the education process successfully. Adaptability is one of the key traits for success in correctional education. As one educator stated, "Each day can be viewed as a lifetime . . . I will have experienced many ups and downs, accomplishments and failures, laughter and tears."[13]

Because resources for education are limited, correctional educators often turn to community and professional resources when developing programs. Examples of groups that may be available are literacy organizations, college and university groups (e.g., service clubs, fraternities, sororities, and religious groups), senior and retiree organizations, and labor organizations. Community resources may provide support through donations of money and other resources, staff training, and volunteer mentors and teachers. Professional organizations are also available to support correctional educators. The Correctional Education Asso-

To become acquainted with correctional education programs and the issues that face correctional educators, go to the Correctional Education Association web site at www.ceanational.org.

ciation (CEA), for example, publishes a journal that advises members concerning the education of prisoners.

• Religion •

The practice of religion in correctional settings is probably as old as the use of prisons. Some of the earliest known records of religion in prison are found in Bible stories of imprisoned disciples and prophets such as Paul, Peter, and John the Baptist. Early Christian churches had the power to grant asylum to criminals as a substitute for corporal and capital punishment.[14] An accepted correctional practice of the eighteenth century was to isolate prisoners from their fellow inmates, give them a Bible to read and contemplate, and require them to perform manual labor. The purpose of the isolation was to allow the prisoners time to reflect upon and repent their crimes. The term "penitentiary" was used to describe this type of imprisonment. During the nineteenth century, prisons continued the use of solitary confinement for such purposes.

The chaplain has been a central figure in the care and treatment of inmates throughout the history of corrections in America. Because historically prisons have often been plagued with overcrowding and less than adequate budgets, chaplains have often served as ministers, counselors, and educators. Until the twentieth century, religious training was the only source of treatment and rehabilitation in most prisons.[15]

Today, a chaplain may perform many duties, including conducting religious services and funeral services, counseling troubled inmates, conveying news of family tragedies to prisoners, helping link parolees and probationers to community religious resources, and advising staff about the doctrines of nontraditional religious groups. Correctional chaplains must be able to minister to inmates, families, and staff members from a variety of religious faiths. However, the primary focus is often on helping inmates survive the stresses of prison life.

Currently, prisoners in the United States are afforded certain legal rights pertaining to the practice of religion by the U.S. Constitution. Prisoners in state and federal correctional institutions have the right to assemble for religious services, attend different denominational programs, receive visits and correspond with religious ministers, observe dietary laws, and wear appropriate religious paraphernalia. However, security considerations continue to retain priority over the exercise of these rights.

In most jails and prisons in the United States, the practice of religion is a common event. Four traditional denominations are supported by nearly all state and federal correctional institutions: Catholic, Jewish, Muslim, and Protestant. Many variations of these denominations and other religious traditions also exist in American prisons; for example, Native American religions, Buddhism, Christian Science, Espiritismo, Santeria, and Mormonism all have followers who reside in American correctional institutions.

During the 1960s and 1970s, court cases contributed many of the current guidelines for the practice of religion in correctional institutions. In the late 1970s and 1980s, the courts began to side more with correctional administration regarding religious rights issues. This shift of

BOX 12.2

Selected Religious Organizations for Inmates and Correctional Staff

American Catholic Correctional Chaplains Association

American Jewish Chaplains Association

Bill Glass Ministries

Christian Prison Ministries

Clinical Pastoral Education

Federal Bureau of Prisons, Religious Services Department

Institute for Prison Ministries

Match-2

Moorish Science Temple of America

Nation of Islam

Native American Prison Ministry Project (Denver Colorado)

Prison Fellowship International (Reston, Virginia)

The Salvation Army

Spanish Evangelical Literature Fellowship Inc. (Ft. Lauderdale, Florida)

Tahrike Tarile Quar'an Inc. (Elmhurst, New York)

Victory Ministries (San Antonio, Texas)

Source: McShane, M.D., and F.P. Williams (1996). *Encyclopedia of American Prisons*. New York: Garland.

court attitudes and rulings away from the religious rights of prisoners and toward the security priorities of prison security may reflect, to some extent, the current pessimistic attitudes of some of the public toward the sincerity of "jailhouse religion."

The question is often asked: Why do inmates become involved in religious activities? Many people believe that inmates "find" religion in order to gain sympathy from the public or influence parole board decisions. While this may be true in some cases, in other instances, prisoners may turn to religion for the same reasons nonprisoners do in times of difficulty—to try to find some sense of purpose and direction in their lives. According to Dammer, reasons for religious involvement can be grouped into two broad categories: personal and pragmatic.[16] Personal reasons include a search for meaning in life, a source of hope, a way to improve oneself, and a way to change personal behavior. More pragmatic reasons for inmate religious involvement include a need for protection, a way of meeting other inmates, a means of making contact with outside volunteers, and a method to obtain prison resources.

• Recreation •

Correctional recreation is an important but often overlooked facet of institutional programming. Much of the American public currently appears to favor policies supporting longer sentences, three-strikes laws, and indeterminate sentencing. As a result, recreation programs are often viewed as being "soft" on criminals. One popular belief is that prisons are too much like "country clubs." As noted in Chapter 1, discussion has centered on making prison less pleasant by eliminating educational, recreational, and treatment programs. Advocates of this position argue that prisons are supposed to be places of punishment, not places to learn how to do crafts, participate in sports, or watch television. Some state legislatures have responded to such public sentiment by reducing and restricting prison recreation programs. For example, Arizona, California, Georgia, Mississippi, North Carolina, Ohio, South Carolina, and Wisconsin have banned weightlifting equipment and restricted other recreational activities.[17] The "No Frills Prison Act," also known as the Zimmer Amendment,[18] is another example of a state legislative response to the perception of corrections being too "soft" on criminals. This bill calls for prohibiting the purchase and replacement of weightlifting equipment and musical instruments.

It is important to note that two of the most serious problems for the prison system are overcrowding and idleness. Eliminating recreational opportunities in overcrowded prisons may create a "powder keg" situation for prison officials. Idle time must be filled with institutionally approved activities; otherwise, inmates may fill time with less desirable activities and more frequent occurrences of violence. The combination of overcrowding,

BOX 12.3

Examples of Institutional Recreation Programs

- **Individual Activities**

Passive	Television, radio, movies, books, computing
Active	Weightlifting, other exercise, playing musical instruments

- **Organized Group Activities**

Indoor	Board and card games, choirs, bands, aerobics
Outdoor	Basketball, softball, flag football, soccer

- **Hobbies/Arts and Crafts**   Ceramics, woodworking, painting, sketching, leather-working

- **Creative Writing, Poetry, Theater**

- **Talent Shows**

- **Community Volunteers**   Music festivals, comedy shows, plays, inspirational speakers

- **Service Clubs**   Jaycees, Key Club, lifer groups

stress, tension, and a lack of productive outlets for inmates can increase the volatility and instability of the environment in some prisons.

The President's Commission on Law Enforcement noted that "recreation would ease institutional tensions."[19] Prison recreation programs may help reduce the probability of institutional violence. Inmates, regardless of educational level or age, can be involved in positive activities. Recreational programs also can be easily modified to serve inmates with mental or physical disabilities. Effective recreational programs can help teach and develop social skills useful in life outside the prison. To be successful in a recreation program, the inmate must learn the value of cooperation, fairness, teamwork, anger management, and socially acceptable methods for resolving conflict.

Another important benefit of recreational programs is the opportunity for inmates to forge links with the community. Interaction with community volunteers and outside recreation events provide important contacts for the inmate upon release and give the inmate a model for appropriate behavior.

The National Correctional Recreation Association (NCRA) is the primary professional organization for prison recreation and leisure program specialists. This organization is responsible for setting professional standards for recreational workers and recreational facilities.

Facility accommodations can be grouped into three broad categories: sports and leisure areas, creative arts areas, and administrative areas. Sports and leisure areas include softball fields; basketball, racquetball, and tennis courts; weightlifting rooms; gyms with locker rooms; multipurpose areas (open field space encircled by a running track); and shaded leisure areas. Creative arts areas include theaters (auditoriums), band and chorus rooms, and crafts rooms. Administrative areas include recreation staff offices, equipment storage rooms with checkout areas, and meeting rooms. These areas can be used for a variety of recreational activities.

Recreational staffing needs vary from one institution to the next due to a variety of factors, including the physical facilities, age and custody level of the inmate population, time and money available for programs, and types and number of recreational activities to be offered. The NCRA recommends that two recreational staff members are needed to plan and implement a recreation program in a small (less than 100 inmates) institution. These staff members should hold at least a bachelor's degree in recreation/leisure services or a related field and have experience in correctional recreation. Inmate and civilian volunteers become invaluable in the effective performance of a recreation program. Part-time staff members and interns are also useful.

• Mental Health •

In 2000, one of every eight state prisoners was receiving some mental health therapy or counseling. About 10 percent were receiving psychotropic medicines such as anti-psychotic drugs. Fewer than two out of every 100 state prisoners were actually housed in a 24-hour mental health unit.[20] However, there are wide disparities in the reported numbers of mentally ill inmates, which may be due to the different ways that mental and emotional illness is defined (see Chapter 10 for additional information).

By midyear 2005, the Bureau of Justice Statistics reported that more than half of all prison and jail inmates had a mental health problem (i.e., having a recent history or symptoms of a mental health problem). Of state prisoners in 2005, 43 percent met criteria for mania, 23 percent had symptoms of major depression, and 15 percent met criteria for a psychotic disorder. The rate of serious mental illness is nearly five times that of the general U.S. population.[21] Many inmates suffer from both a mental disorder and substance abuse problems. Treatment programs are needed that are designed to address mental illness and alcohol and other drug abuse simultaneously.

There is growing concern that mentally ill offenders are more likely than other inmates to be violent recidivists. According to a 2006 Bureau of Justice Statistics report of repeat offenders, 47 percent of mentally ill state inmates had a current or past sentence for a violent offense, compared to 39 percent of other inmates. These figures are similar for jail detainees as well as federal inmates.[22]

In most correctional facilities, treatment for mental and emotional disorders takes the form of individual or group therapy in conjunction with the use of psychotropic medications. Antipsychotic drugs and anti-depressants are used to stabilize the disturbed inmate's behavior so that more traditional forms of counseling and psychotherapy can be utilized. Box 12.4 provides a brief description of some of the more traditional counseling and correctional treatment strategies.

Antipsychotic medications have been successful in general. Psychiatrists often prescribe other medications in conjunction with antipsychotic drugs in an attempt to lessen their adverse side effects. Despite

BOX 12.4

Correctional Counseling and Psychotherapy Approaches

1. **Behavioral and Social Learning Strategies:** Together with cognitive strategies, social learning and behavioral interventions show promise in the successful treatment of offenders. Behavioral and social learning approaches focus on making the offender deal with events in the present. Behavioral strategies, in particular, emphasize identifying and decreasing problem behaviors. Such decreases often come as a result of a system of rewards and punishments. Behavioral therapists may also seek to replace problem behaviors with desirable alternative behaviors. Social learning strategies emphasize the importance of observational learning through which offenders observe and imitate desirable behaviors. Social learning programs tend to be efficient and cost-effective because much of the observational learning can take place in group settings.

2. **Cognitive Treatment:** Cognitive treatments are concerned with examining the ways that people think. Offenders are taught in group and individual sessions how to recognize irrational thought patterns. Once such thought patterns are identified, offenders can begin to replace irrational thoughts with more rational thoughts. An honest counselor can be the catalyst for such a replacement to be made. Cognitive skill training sessions focusing on empathy for self and others, self-control, problem-solving, coping, and planning ahead may be useful to offenders.

BOX 12.4 *(continued)*

3. **Group Work:** Group approaches are popular in correctional treatment because they cost far less in time and resources than individual treatment. Ideally, a counselor meets with a group of five to 10 offenders twice a week. Sessions may last from 60 to 90 minutes. The counselor may use a wide range of approaches, including behavioral and cognitive strategies. Group therapy may have several advantages that individual therapy lacks, including an exchange of information among the group members and counselor, a support network for group members that helps provide hope, and a chance to develop interpersonal skills.

4. **Family Therapy:** Family therapy seeks to address an important factor in whether an offender is able to adjust to life outside of prison: his or her family environment. However, this type of therapy is not readily available to offenders. Practitioners of family therapy use different treatment approaches, including social learning, communications, structural, and psychoanalytic. In all of these approaches, the offender's family is seen as a system rather than just a collection of individuals. The counselor or other treatment professional addresses the problem as that of the entire family rather than just the offender.

Source: Adapted from Antonowicz, P.H., and R.R. Ross (1994). "Essential Components of Successful Rehabilitation Programs for Offenders." *Journal of Offender Therapy and Comparative Criminology* 38:97-104.

side effects, there has been a great deal of success associated with the use of psychotropic drugs. Antipsychotic medications have reduced violent episodes in psychotics, reoriented schizophrenics to reality, and reduced hallucinations in paranoid individuals.

• Developmentally Disabled Offenders •

According to the American Association on Mental Retardation, an individual is considered mentally retarded if he or she has an "intellectual functioning (IQ) below 70-75, significant limitations exist in two or more adaptive skill areas, and the condition is present from childhood (defined as age 18 or less)."[23] It is important to note the distinction between mentally retarded/developmentally disabled individuals and individuals with mental illnesses. Mental retardation and developmental-disabilities manifest as permanent and untreatable diminished mental capacities. Mental illnesses, on the other hand, may affect highly intelligent individuals and may be treatable in some cases. As noted in Chapter 10, the Mental Health Act of 1974 prompted the release of thousands of developmentally disabled individuals from mental institutions into the community. The intent of this legislation was to improve the quality of life for the developmentally disabled. However, in many cases, it resulted in "deinstitutionalized" individuals being placed in jails and prisons. Although some developmentally disabled individuals committed crimes, for many, ending up in correctional institutions resulted from an inability to care for themselves in the community.

Developmentally disabled offenders, by definition, have impaired adaptive functioning. Adaptive functioning refers to the skills an individual needs to cope with daily life. Impairment of these coping skills can make living in a correctional environment difficult for the developmentally disabled offender. He or she may be slower to adjust to prison rules and routines, less likely to take part in rehabilitation programs in order to mask their disability, and likely to become the victim of jokes, exploitation, and sexual harassment.[24] Developmentally disabled offenders are also more likely to spend more time in prison than other prisoners for the same offense and more likely to be denied parole.[25]

• The Antisocial Offender •

Offenders diagnosed with antisocial personality disorder exhibit a pervasive pattern of disregard for societal norms and social relationships.[26] These individuals have a lack of empathy for others and are unable to consider the perspective of another. Antisocial persons often participate in behaviors that are self-destructive (e.g., substance abuse). Typically, antisocial individuals act irresponsibly, and are manipulative, impulsive, and given to mood swings. Their interpersonal relationships are intense, unstable, and frequently violent.

It is important to keep in mind that an inmate with a personality disorder is not always easy to handle. However, correctional personnel should be trained to recognize these behaviors. A referral to the appropriate mental health staff should be made in order to assess the needs of the inmate. Many offenders who display characteristics of antisocial personality respond better to more structured counseling and treatment programs.

• Substance Abuse •

The abuse of alcohol and other drugs and the criminal activity related to it are major problems in today's society. Society can draw direct benefits from effective correctional drug treatment programs—for instance, declines in criminal activity and reductions in the cost of dealing with drug use problems. Offender-addicts who are successfully treated and adjust to the community can become taxpayers rather than tax burdens.

Alcohol and other drug abuse is predominant in inmate populations. According to the National Institute of Justice, in more than half of the 38 sites of male adult arrestees evaluated in 2000, more than 65 percent of the arrestees had recently used one or more of the five standard drugs named by the National Institute on Drug Abuse (the NIDA-5: cocaine, marijuana, methamphetamines, opiates, PCP).[27] The same study's clinically based alcohol dependency screen, which calculates the risk for drug dependence, showed large proportions of arrestees at risk for alcohol dependence and therefore needing treatment. In half of the sites, 34 percent or more of those who said they used alcohol were at risk, with a range of 22 percent (San Antonio) to 47 percent (Albuquerque).[28] As a result, most correctional facilities in the United States offer some type of alcohol and other drug treatment programming. The goal of these treatment programs is to prepare the inmate for eventual release back into the community.

Some people view correctional substance abuse treatment programs with skepticism and cynicism. Such programs often meet with resistance from correctional staff who may view treatment as unnecessary or ineffective. Constraints on resources may result in replacing treatment-effective programs with cost-efficient programs. The latter programs may include a greater number of inmates participating in interventions but may be less likely to supply participants with the coping skills they will need to avoid relapse and a return to prison.

Treatment programs vary in philosophy, approach to recovery, length of time spent in recovery, and intensity of services. Programs may include self-help groups, group therapy, relaxation techniques, educational videos, or medicines to help combat addiction, and any combination of these treatment strategies may be used together. Counselors and other treatment professionals make decisions concerning which type of treatment programs will work best for particular offenders. Treatment programs are developed based on theories that have basic underlying assumptions about offenders and addiction. Box 12.5 provides a description of some of the more common treatment theories.

In prison, one of the most common substance abuse treatment formats is the self-help model. Alcoholics Anonymous (AA) and Narcotics Anonymous (NA), which are based on this model, are the two most prevalent examples of such treatment programs in correctional facilities today. According to AA and NA, the only requirement for membership is a desire to stop drinking or using other drugs. AA and NA members believe that one of the keys to success is the therapeutic value of addicts working with addicts. AA and NA encourage their members to observe complete abstinence from alcohol and/or other drugs. They utilize a series of personal activities known as the "12 steps" to achieve abstinence. The steps include an individualistic interpretation of a higher power that helps the abuser to confront his or her problem by changing the behavior. Ultimately, a spiritual awakening and continuing personal reflection help keep the abuser sober.

BOX 12.5

Substance Abuse Treatment Theories

1. **Disease:** These theories are based on the medical model that views addiction as a sickness that needs to be cured. In order for the offender-client to become "well" again, he or she must gain control over the illness. Proponents of this model believe that the focus should be withdrawal of the alcohol or drug from the body.

2. **Progression:** These theories focus on the process of becoming an addict. These theorists believe that recreational use of less serious drugs can be a gateway to use of more serious drugs. Users may experience a high that they seek to increase, which eventually leads to addiction.

3. **Sociological:** These theories examine the structure of society and the social environment of the substance abuser. Such factors as age, race, education, neighborhood, poverty, and opportunity all play a role in substance abuse. Treatment may focus on changing the socio-economic opportunities available to the offender, changing the environment, and changing the peer group with which the offender interacts.

4. **Psychological:** These theories examine the needs and emotional traits of the client. Issues such as self-esteem and adjustment problems from childhood are studied within the context of personality analysis. However, some psychological theorists also examine drug addiction from a behavioral orientation. They view the addict as receiving a psychological reward from drugs.

5. **Learning:** These theories examine the social environment and the personality of the individual, which are both thought to contribute to addiction. From this perspective, the methods of taking drugs and drinking alcohol are learned behaviors, and the influence of the peer group is paramount to substance abuse. The counselor focuses on changing the peer associations as well as the behaviors of the client.

The primary benefit of AA and NA programs is that abusers can meet in a group setting to discuss their addictions and experiences with other abusers. Because the members share similar experiences, it is less likely they will be able to deceive each other regarding their recovery. However, because AA and NA participation may be mandatory for parole consideration, some groups may be filled with offenders who are not serious about recovery and may simply attend the meetings to improve their chances for parole.

Substance abuse programs are not limited to AA and NA. Many other programs have been established in prisons to treat substance abusers. Some of the newer programs are based on "reality therapy," by which the counselor refuses to accept the offender's excuses for inappropriate behavior. Reality therapy is most commonly utilized in a group therapy setting in which the abuser interacts with other abusers. Reality therapy is designed to help the abuser (1) face his or her antisocial behavior, (2) examine why he or she behaves in certain ways, and (3) ultimately, stop the behavior.[29]

Aversive therapy has also been used as a treatment option. In aversive therapy, the abuser may be mandated, as a condition of release, to ingest antabuse (which causes an adverse physical reaction if mixed with alcohol). However, some offenders may fail to ingest the drug as instructed, and in other cases, abusers may even continue to drink without any adverse effects.

OFFENDERS WITH SPECIAL TREATMENT NEEDS

As discussed in Chapter 10, in correctional populations, there often exists a subset of prisoners for whom some physical, emotional, environmental, and/or psychological characteristic differentiates them from the general prison population. Such offenders can be classified as "special needs" offenders because they may require accommodations by the correctional institution that the average offender does not receive. Such accommodations range from providing telecommunication devices for the deaf (DDS) to arranging for separate housing units for certain types of offenders. Although special needs may include a wide variety of conditions and problems, some of the most common categories of offenders needing special treatment strategies are sex offenders, HIV/AIDS-infected offenders, elderly offenders, and terminally ill offenders.

Counseling and treatment professionals may have to resolve several issues in the treatment of special needs offenders. A fundamental issue is whether the offender needs to be segregated from the general population. Factors that may be considered include whether the offenders are at risk of harm by other offenders and whether the offender may harm himself or herself or others.

• Sex Offenders •

A sex offender is an individual who is convicted of committing a sexual act that is prohibited by law (see Chapter 10 for additional discussion). In 2000, state prisons held an estimated 30,400 males for rape and 82,200 males for other sexual assaults. They also held 300 females for rape and 900 females for other sexual assaults.[30] Greenfeld notes that "about 234,000 offenders convicted of rape or sexual assault are under the care, custody, or control of corrections agencies. About 60% of these sex offenders are under conditional supervision in the community."[31] It is important to note that the majority of sex offenders will eventually be released back into the community, often under the supervision of parole officers.[32] Box 12.6 lists the five categories of sex offenses that account for the majority of treatment program participants.

Sexual aggression can be a form of addictive behavior that requires an individualized treatment plan. A thorough assessment is the first step in developing such a plan. This assessment should include questions about the client's offending as well as those probing for other problems that may contribute to the offending (e.g., alcohol abuse). The emotional readiness and suitability of the client to engage in treatment should also be examined. A special area of consideration for sex offenders is a sexual development history that includes past sexual experiences, a history of sexual victimization, and attitudes toward sex. For male sex offenders, penile plethysmography may be useful at the assessment stage to help determine arousal patterns. During treatment, follow-up assessments should be made to evaluate the effectiveness of

BOX 12.6

Types of Sex Offenses

1. **Rape** and attempted rape is sexual intercourse/sexual penetration or attempted sexual intercourse/sexual penetration of an individual by force or coercion.

2. **Child molestation** or pedophilia refers to sexual contact or sexual intercourse with a person less than 18 years of age.

3. **Incest** is sexual intercourse with persons who are closely related. Many state statutes extended the definition of incest to include individuals who are not biologically related.

4. **Exhibitionism** is the act of exposing one's genitalia in order to achieve sexual arousal or gratification (e.g., sex between a stepfather and stepchild).

5. **Voyeurism** refers to obtaining sexual arousal or gratification through visual stimulation (e.g., viewing sexual acts).

6. **Miscellaneous offenses** (breaking and entering, arson, etc.) are included when there is a sexual motivation.

the treatment. There are three main categories of treatment strategies for approaching sex offending: behavioral strategies, cognitive strategies, and organic strategies.

Behavioral strategies focus on decreasing deviant sexual arousal as a way to decrease sexual offending. This treatment approach may encourage the offender to develop a nondeviant sexual fantasy. A goal of treatment is that the deviant fantasy is replaced by the nondeviant fantasy through behavioral conditioning. Aversive imagery involves pairing inappropriate sexual stimuli and feelings with some unpleasant consequence. Aversion therapy is the most commonly used treatment for sex offenders. Aversion therapy is similar to aversive imagery in that something unpleasant is paired with the inappropriate stimuli, for example, mild electric shocks or unpleasant odors.

Cognitive strategies include social skills training, empathy training, and role-playing. The goal of these strategies is to confront irrational ideas and beliefs that allow the offender to commit a deviant act. Social skills training addresses these beliefs by helping the offender develop appropriate social skills and ways of communicating with their peers. It is hoped that the offender can then engage in healthy adult relationships. Empathy training is designed to expose offenders to victims in a discussion group setting. The offender will then be expected to discuss the effects of victimization. Role-playing is a way for the offender to confront distorted thinking patterns.

Organic strategies involve physical interventions designed to reduce deviant drives. Examples of techniques in this category are surgical or chemical castration and antiandrogen drug therapy. Because these techniques address symptoms of sexual offending rather than causes, they are rarely used.

The treatment plan should provide for an eventual return to the community. Some areas that might be covered include helping the offender find support networks outside the correctional institution and developing appropriate recreational activities. Because sex offenders may be more likely to face hostility from communities, counselors and treatment professionals should prepare the offender for such reactions. For example, legal developments such as "Megan's Law" are designed

> To search the national sex offender registry, go to www.nsopr.gov.

to provide the public with information about convicted sex offenders, who may be potential re-offenders living in the community. Megan's Law was enacted as a result of the rape and murder of Megan Kanka by a neighbor, a man who had twice before been convicted of sexually assaulting children. This highly publicized case prompted New Jersey to enact sex offender registration and notification laws, which sparked a trend across the country.[33]

• Offenders with HIV/AIDS •

HIV/AIDS is another major counseling and treatment issue in correctional institutions. The prevalence of inmates admitting intravenous drug use and the sharing of needles was reflected in the National Prison Project, where inmates admitting intravenous drug use represented the majority of inmates with AIDS[34] (see also Chapter 10). As a result, most prisons within the United States have adopted some form of HIV/AIDS screening test. Because inmates have demonstrated a high rate of HIV infection, many lawmakers and correctional administrators have called for mandatory HIV screening of inmates. In 2004, the Bureau of Justice Statistics indicated that 20 state correctional systems had implemented policies requiring all inmates to be screened for HIV.[35]

The following elements are considered to be crucial to screening inmate-patients for HIV: (1) pretest counseling focusing on the significance of the test; (2) HIV/AIDS education stressing risk-reducing behaviors; (3) referrals for any medical needs; (4) confidentiality measures, especially regarding test results; (5) support for HIV seropositive inmates, to include medical, mental, and social services; and (6) HIV counseling and education following testing for all inmates, to encourage behavioral changes.[36] These recommended procedures help safeguard staff and inmate health and inmate dignity.

Once an inmate has been identified as HIV-infected, the correctional facility has a duty to protect the inmate and provide adequate medical care.[37] Health care should begin immediately after the notification of a positive test result. The HIV counselor has the obligation to inform the inmate of the significance of a positive test result and refer the inmate to medical, psychological, and social services. The staff should administer the appropriate treatment given the stage of the disease and work toward preventing further transmission. One of the ethical considerations when treating an HIV-infected offender is confidentiality. Inmates must feel they can trust counselors and medical staff with personal and private disclosures. Without an atmosphere of trust, inmates are less likely to confide in the medical staff.

• Elderly Offenders •

As noted in Chapter 10, in prison an individual is considered "elderly" at the chronological age of 50.[38] The reason for using this early age is because many offenders may have had inadequate access to health care, including preventive medicine, and been involved in risky lifestyles (e.g., substance abuse). Elderly offenders represent a growing segment of the inmate population; in fact, the number of elderly inmates in state and federal institutions is expected to double approximately every four years.[39] Cromwell notes that "longer prison sentences and a reduction in the use of parole have resulted in the rapidly expanding numbers of elderly inmates in the correctional population."[40]

Elderly inmates may need treatment for chronic disorders associated with aging, such as cancer, diabetes, heart disease, kidney failure, and Alzheimer's disease. Such treatment is often costly. Because elderly offenders may be at risk of harm from younger offenders, they may also require segregated housing or additional protection. Elderly offenders may also need special diets, hearing aids, visual aids, wheelchairs, dentures, and other accommodations.

A hospice worker at Iowa State Penitentiary in Fort Madison, Iowa, tends to a patient in the Assisted Daily Living ward. The Penitentiary's hospice facility is one of four in the state's prison system.

There is currently a continuing debate about releasing elderly offenders. At the heart of this debate is whether the offender would pose a threat to community safety. The stereotype of the elderly offender is of a long-term inmate who committed a crime many years ago. However, approximately half of older offenders who are admitted to prison are classified as new offenders.[41] Of prisoners age 55 or older, 67 percent are in prison for some type of violent crime.[42] Some people feel that violent offenders, elderly or not, are not suitable candidates for release from correctional institutions.

Counseling and treatment professionals should make special efforts to prepare elderly offenders for transition into the community, especially if the offender has been in prison for an extended period of time. In some cases, the offender may have outlived his or her peers and family members. Technologically and culturally, the community may bear little resemblance to when the offender was first imprisoned. Care should be taken to provide job skills, locate living arrangements, and establish support networks for the elderly offender if he or she is expected to make a successful transition upon release.

• Terminally Ill Offenders •

As mentioned in Chapter 10, approximately 3,200 inmates die in U.S. prisons annually.[43] Correctional healthcare professionals must keep up with the challenges presented by these special needs inmates. Many correctional facilities have scarce resources, which hinders efforts to provide adequate medical care to terminally ill inmates.

One way correctional facilities are attempting to address the medical needs of terminally ill prisoners is through the use of hospice programs. The nationwide hospice movement addresses the special needs of dying patients. Hospice care does not seek to cure illnesses; instead, it focuses on pain management and is designed to make the patient as comfortable as possible. According to the National Prison Hospice Association, hospice "is an interdisciplinary comfort-oriented program of care that allows seriously ill and dying patients to live and die with dignity and humanity with as little pain as possible."[44] Hospice programs offer a variety of services, including pain management, spiritual support, psychological counseling, and grief counseling for the bereaved families.

In 2001, the Louisiana State Penitentiary, nicknamed "Angola," was given the American Hospital Association's Circle of Life Award,[45] which recognizes innovations in end-of-life care. Labeled one of America's most inhumane prisons three decades ago, the prison now serves as a model for caring for terminally ill patients. Warden Burl Cain, who came to Angola in 1995, said he began to think about prison deaths when he presided over his first execution. He said it bothered him that he did not talk to the condemned man about the man's soul. In 1997, after coming across a newspaper article about hospices, which have a strong spiritual component, he decided Angola needed one.[46]

Angola's hospice program involves medical personnel, security officers, and spiritual advisors, but at its heart are prisoner volunteers who visit and befriend terminal patients. They serve as "arms" and "legs" for the patients—fetching things, writing letters, or wheeling them to whatever activity they want to attend. These volunteers receive 30 hours of training in comforting and caring for the dying. They are trained to recognize the physical stages, the emotional process, and the spiritual dynamics of death and dying. Volunteers learn how to bring companionship and a sense of peace to those who may not know how to ask for them. They also learn when to begin the around-the-clock vigil that ensures that the hospice patient does not die alone. Because hospice focuses on quality of death, rather than on extending the life of a terminally ill patient, it is not universally embraced by the medical community. However, among the nation's prisoners, hospice care is a welcome alternative to dying alone in prison. Many feel that hospice care brings compassion and humanity to those who have been all but forgotten by the criminal justice system. Cheryl Price, Hospice Coordinator for the Dixon Correctional Center in Dixon, Illinois, claims that hospice has the potential not only to impact the lives of dying inmates but also the inmate-volunteers.[47] Many of the inmate-volunteers may feel that they are making a significant contribution for the first time in their lives. Price observes:

> I close my eyes and listen: the words of encouragement and understanding and the search for self-knowledge that I hear from the inmate-volunteers are the same words I heard on the outside . . . [but when] I open my eyes, I am surrounded by

eight murderers, two armed robbers, one sex offender, and two men who solicited for murder. The chance to volunteer, the chance to succeed, the chance to atone, the chance to be "good" is so much more important in the prison setting.[48]

Inmates, like patients in the community, may shy away from a program that confronts them with the fact that they are dying. To confront dying is a major life step, regardless of where one is living. Inmates may be hesitant to come into the hospice program for several reasons:

- If an inmate accepts that his or her condition is terminal, he or she doesn't want to die in prison. Nothing signifies defeat as much as dying in prison. Inmates want to prolong curative treatment even if it only gives them a couple of months, because they prefer to be with family and friends at the end of life.

- Inmates may not trust correctional medical care in general, and the hospice falls under that umbrella. They may perceive it as the State's attempt to deny life-saving or other more expensive treatment options.

- Hospice acknowledges the patient's vulnerability, but inmates cannot afford to appear weak and needy. They may be fearful of being exploited or of losing their dignity.[49]

Another concern for correctional staff dealing with terminally ill prisoners is the anxiety, depression, hopelessness, and confusion that patients commonly experience at the end of life. The prevalence of depressive disorders among the terminally ill has been reported to be as high as 77 percent, while delirium or confusion affects an estimated 85 percent of persons near life's end.[50] Despite their prevalence, such psychiatric and psychosocial disorders remain underrecognized and undertreated. Inattention to these disorders by healthcare providers may be due to the belief among healthcare professionals that feelings of depression or hopelessness are part of the experience of dying.[51]

In traditional healthcare settings, patients often voice concerns about feelings of hopelessness, loss of dignity, and the sense of being a burden to one's family as the primary sources of suffering. However, the additional burden of being incarcerated may increase feelings of hopelessness for terminally ill offenders. In addition, inmates may have fewer options available to them to make important end-of-life decisions.

Price states that the most important thing to keep in mind when treating and caring for terminally ill prisoners is that:

It doesn't matter what the inmate did to bring him to prison. It doesn't even matter what kind of person he is now. The prison hospice makes the leap of faith: it doesn't matter! This suspension of judgment means providing good care regardless of background. You don't have to like each inmate, but you are obligated to provide good care.[52]

OTHER SPECIAL CONCERNS

Correctional treatment professionals face many special challenges that are unique to the correctional environment.

• Prison Overcrowding •

The recent "get tough on crime" movement has resulted in an increase of offenders in correctional programs and facilities. In fact, from 1980 to 2006, prison populations have increased by 367 percent.[53] Because overcrowded prisons generally are more dangerous for inmates and staff, offenders in overcrowded institutions may be less receptive to traditional rehabilitation and treatment programs and more concerned with personal safety issues. As a result, counselors and other treatment professionals may have to spend an inordinate amount of time engaged in various forms of "crisis intervention."

• Large Caseloads •

Even without the additional strain of overcrowded institutions, counselors are often expected to deal with large numbers of offenders. In some large institutions, counselors may have caseloads of more than 100 inmates. Rapid turnover of inmate populations adds to the problem. With large caseloads and a rapid turnover, the counselor may be limited to seeing each individual offender for only a few minutes every month.

Under conditions in which counselors have a large number of clients with a variety of needs and problems, he or she must be careful not to indulge in what is called the "YAVIS syndrome,"[54] which takes place when the counselor feels inclined to focus on only the Young, Attractive, Verbal, Intelligent, and Successful clients. These clients are the most satisfying to work with and may provide the most enjoyable interactions. However, the counselor should keep in mind the responsibilities of his or her job—namely, to help all clients in need.

• Lack of Institutional Support •

The support received by a counselor may vary substantially from institution to institution. Three types of administrative organizations have been identified: the coactive administration, the diffuse administration, and the discriminative administration.[55] The coactive administration places safety and security as the primary goals. While the counselor is seen as being useful in reducing inmate frustration (and subsequently helping to create a safer environment), treatment itself is not given much support by the administration. In the diffuse administration, a treatment orientation may be seen at the surface. However, upon closer examination, the collection of treatment programs fails to take into account actual inmate needs, and a serious commitment to treatment by the administration is lacking. The discriminative administration offers the most serious commitment to treatment. In this administrative organization, a real effort is made to match inmate needs with treatment pro-

BOX 12.7

Dealing with Anger

You have been a counselor for 10 years, but this is one part of your job that has never gotten any easier.

Doug, an inmate at the institution where you work, has just been turned down for parole for the second time in six years. The two of you are sitting at the hearing room table silently staring out the barred window. You can see the tears silently streaming down Doug's face. You can sense the anger and humiliation he is feeling and the explosion within himself that he is fighting to contain.

Doug has a good prison record with respect to both his conduct and his commitment to rehabilitation programs. The problem is apparently a political one. The local judge simply does not want Doug released in his county. As the institutional counselor, you know of several other inmates who have been granted parole to that particular county. They were paroled despite their having committed more serious offenses than Doug and having been much less receptive to the various institutional rehabilitation programs. Doug also knows of these paroles. To make matters worse, the parole board did not even give him a reason for rejecting his application, nor did they tell him what he could do to increase his chances for parole.

Doug spent weeks in preparation for his parole hearing. The letters of recommendation, the acquisition of his high school diploma, and other related material had in the end meant nothing. The board had convened less than 10 minutes to make a parole decision based on six years of Doug's life. The chairperson simply told you that Doug's parole had been denied and for you to pass the decision along to Doug. You had reluctantly done so, knowing that Doug could see the decision in your eyes before you even spoke. So here the two of you sit, bitter and disillusioned.

Will Doug give up? Will his anger get him into trouble with the administration or other inmates in the cellhouse? How will this affect your relationship with him, as you were the one who encouraged him to apply? You are not sure what to do or say, but somehow you have to try to help Doug pick up the pieces.

Source: Braswell, M., T. Fletcher, and L. Miller (1998). *Human Relations and Corrections*, 4th ed. Prospect Heights, IL: Waveland.

grams. The discriminative administration provides the most productive workplace for the correctional counselor. In this type of administrative organization, the custody and administrative staffs are in agreement concerning the importance of counseling and treatment.

• Racial and Ethnic Groups •

Minority groups are overrepresented in correctional facilities. Among the more than 2.3 million offenders incarcerated in 2006, approximately 534,200 (close to 22%) were black males.[56] This may lead to a special concern for counselors—the tendency to resort to racial bias or prejudice when dealing with people different from oneself. The danger is the tendency to view one's own race or group as superior to another race or group. Stereotyping—judging people on the basis of assumed group characteristics rather than as unique individuals—is a concept that is closely related to discrimination. Within a correctional setting, both prejudice and stereotyping are attitudes that are detrimental to the effectiveness of the counselor.

Multicultural, or "cross-cultural," counseling is one approach that may be helpful in working with a racially or ethnically skewed population.[57] A racially and ethnically sensitive approach can aid the counselor in avoiding problems of racial discrimination and stereotyping by allowing him or her to better understand the cultural traditions of different racial and ethnic inmate groups.

• Confidentiality •

While counselors are expected to maintain professional standards of ethics, some situations pose special problems. In corrections, confidentiality is one of the most difficult ethical issues that a counselor faces. In the outside world, the counselor and client often act in two different social spheres. That is, the client and counselor often do not share the same friends or interact beyond the confines of the counselor's office. However, in a correctional setting, the counselor and client, by necessity, must interact in the same social environment. For example, counselors may have to contact cellmates, other inmates, or staff members to obtain information about a particular client. Persons who participate in or overhear them may not keep such conversations confidential.

When working in a correctional institution, the counselor must be willing for his or her individual position concerning confidentiality to be appropriately and clearly stated. Professional standards may offer guidelines. Most professional standards state that the counselor keep information confidential unless the information poses a risk to the client or to others.

The counselor should expect some initial reserve from the client if he or she finds it necessary to state his or her views on confidentiality. If handled properly, this should not necessarily be a problem after several sessions. Trust and respect gained by the counselor from being truthful and "up front" can outweigh the short-term benefits of any deception. Any dishonesty that is discovered by an inmate-client can adversely affect the particular relationship as well as ruin the counselor's reputation with other inmates. It should be noted that issues surrounding confidentiality are not always black and white. There is a substantial gray area when dealing with problems such as drug use when a counselor wants to maintain an offender's trust yet adhere to correctional rules and security needs of the facility.

• Stress and Burnout •

Correctional counseling can be a stressful career due to its many special problems and challenges. Large caseloads, prison overcrowding, mixed institutional support, and the special needs of different types of offenders are just several of the challenges that correctional counselors may have to face. Stress is not always harmful; in fact, stress in small amounts may actually be helpful in motivating a person to work harder or do a better job. However, in large amounts, stress can be destructive. Excessive amounts of stress can lead to career burnout. Burnout is the end product of long-standing stress. It may be viewed as stress in its most serious form.

The symptoms of stress are easy to identify. Some of the symptoms include an inability to concentrate, feelings of hopelessness, swift mood swings, impatience, and a lack of motivation and energy. Counselors should be aware of the signs of stress and work to alleviate stress-producing conditions before the problem becomes one of burnout. Although there are many ways to deal with stress, one of the easiest is to find an activity that is enjoyable and use that activity to reduce job-related tension. For example, engaging in satisfying recreational activities can help reduce stress and improve one's general health. Another effective way of dealing with stress is to form a network of support. Such a group of caring friends and/or colleagues in whom the counselor may confide helps relieve his or her stress and work through job-related difficulties.

HOW EFFECTIVE ARE CORRECTIONAL COUNSELING AND TREATMENT PROGRAMS?

To be able to determine the effectiveness of correctional counseling or treatment programs, one must first be able to determine what is meant by the word "effective." One perspective is that "effective" means whatever allows the prison schedule to run smoothly, with little thought to preparing the offender for readjustment to the outside community. Another perspective is that "effective" refers to the programs that are the cheapest to implement and maintain. Still another perspective is that the effective program is one that improves the consistency and accuracy of correctional counseling and treatment program evaluations while at the same time maintaining institutional efficiency and economy. Regardless of the perspective one takes, the debate concerning the role, function, and success of a particular offender treatment program has included various criteria, ranging from a concentrated emphasis on community reintegration and/or rehabilitation to little or no reliance on correctional counseling and treatment programs.[58]

Although a number of approaches have been employed in attempts to measure offender treatment program effectiveness, the most prevalent approach is what can be called the "before and after" or "rate of recidivism after release" approach. In this approach, the offender commits a crime, is incarcerated, receives some counseling and other related treatment programs, and is released. After release, a record is kept of whether the offender resumes criminal activities. If the offender fails to resume criminal activity, the counseling and treatment program is generally considered to have been effective. On the other hand, if the offender resumes his or her criminal activity, then the counseling and treatment is considered ineffective.

Other approaches have been used to evaluate counseling and treatment programs. For example, Gendreau reviewed offender treatment literature and conducted a meta-analysis in order to identify some characteristics that effective intervention programs had in common. First, he noted that services provided to clients need to be intensive and should utilize behavioral strategies.[59] Specifically, most behavioral programs are based on the precept of operant conditioning. Central to operant conditioning is the concept of reinforcement, which refers to developing and strengthening an appropriate behavior in the hope that the behavior will be repeated in the future. One of the most effective ways to achieve this goal is to use positive reinforcers (something that the offender-client finds enjoyable or desirable), such as special privileges. These reinforcers should be contingent on the offender demonstrating the desired behavior. Conversely, inappropriate behavior should be met with negative reinforcement, that is, the withholding or removal of positive reinforcements such as visitation time. The goal of negative reinforcement is to suppress the undesirable behavior. However, it is recommended that positive reinforcers substantially outweigh negative ones. The bottom line for program contingencies and behavioral strategies is that they should be enforced in a firm but fair manner.

According to Gendreau, behavioral programs should address the "criminogenic needs of high-risk offenders."[60] Treatment is most effective when it is matched with the needs of the offender-client. The needs of high-risk offenders can be identified through the use of a risk assessment evaluation, which helps to identify high-risk behaviors such as substance abuse, antisocial attitudes, self-control issues, and inappropriate peer associations.

Other methods of program evaluation include long-term studies, follow-up measures, case studies, experimental designs, and psychological tests. Each of these methods has advantages and disadvantages. Box 12.8 outlines seven elements that can contribute to a more effective correctional treatment program.

BOX 12.8

Principles of Effective Correctional Treatment

1. **"A cooperative treatment community"** in which healthcare, educational, vocational, recreational, mental health, and substance abuse professionals work together in a comprehensive, integrated approach in intervening with offenders and promoting prosocial, productive behavior.

2. **"Administrative and institutional support"** in providing adequate resources and opportunities to develop and implement meaningful treatment and related programs.

3. **"A variety of practical life skills and treatment experiences"** that reinforce personal accountability and relevance both within the institution and in the community. Programs should address a variety of offender educational levels, abilities, and psychological needs. Programs should encourage service to others and positive participation in one's community.

4. **"A method for matching characteristics of the offender, therapist, and program,"** referred to as the principle of responsivity. Simply put, responsivity is the ability of a treatment program to facilitate the offender in learning new prosocial skills.

5. **"Program evaluation"** is essential in understanding which programs work and which ones do not. In addition, such evaluations can monitor strengths and weaknesses of effective programs, which can lead to opportunities for improvement.

6. **"A willingness to change"** challenges the status quo and tries creative treatment alternatives.

7. **"Providing relapse prevention strategies"** offers the offender assistance in the community upon completion of the formal phase of a treatment program in prison or a community residential center.

Another research study examined 32 meta-analyses and determined that there is some consensus among researchers about the effectiveness of certain types of treatment programs.[61] According to the findings, group therapy approaches received mixed evaluations. Some researchers have found group therapy to be completely unsucessful,[62] while many others have concluded that it is successful under certain conditions. Still other researchers have found its potential usefulness to be unclear.[63]

The debate concerning correctional treatment effectiveness is not new. A primary source of this debate is a paper by Robert Martinson in which he initially made the claim that "nothing works."[64] Martinson arrived at this conclusion after he and several colleagues reviewed and evaluated the success claims of numerous correctional treatment programs. Other researchers have reviewed the same programs Martinson did with differing conclusions, and even Martinson himself later tempered his claims. The current consensus among many researchers could be summed up as follows: Correctional treatment programs work with some inmates under certain conditions.

CONCLUSION

Correctional counseling and related treatment programs have evolved through the years from having a primarily religious orientation to a focus on the medical model to an emphasis on behavioral science principles. Currently, the trend seems to be pulling between a more punitive, restrictive mindset and more open, creative efforts that are represented by peacemaking, restorative justice, and community justice programs.

There are different types of correctional treatment and related programs in both institutional and community-based settings. In the community, probation, parole, mental health, drug treatment, halfway houses, and educational and vocational training are some of the services and programs that are offered. Many of these same programs are also offered in prisons along with crisis intervention and prerelease counseling.

Just as in the general population, offenders and inmates come in a variety of shapes, sizes, and colors, and have different needs. Some are developmentally disabled, others have infectious diseases such as AIDS, and still others are terminally ill. Designing effective counseling and treatment programs for such special-needs groups is essential.

Other challenges and concerns that can make the delivery of effective correctional counseling and treatment services difficult include prison overcrowding, large caseloads, lack of institutional support, and the diverse needs and demands of different racial and ethnic groups. With security and custody being a priority, particularly in prison, counselor/offender–client confidentiality may also be tested. As in any active, professional, helping environment, stress and burnout among treatment professionals are also significant issues.

Finally, researchers continue to examine questions addressing how effective or ineffective correctional treatment and related programs are in changing offender behavior into more positive, law-abiding lifestyles. Evaluation research has improved the ability to answer such questions and expand innovative correctional treatment efforts.

▶ Ethics Focus: Trust or Security?

You have been working as a counselor at the community correctional center for three years. You feel good about your job and the results you have achieved. No inmate has ever questioned your ethics or integrity.

You are presently working on an interesting case. A young 22-year-old, second-time offender named Ted has really been opening up to you and seems to be turning around in terms of his personal values and motivation. The trust between the two of you is apparent. In fact, just several days ago, the superintendent commented on how much better your client seemed to be since you had taken him on your caseload. However, during the last counseling session your client disclosed something that could severely disrupt your relationship with him, and you are not sure what to do about it.

Halfway through your last session, in a moment of frustration, Ted blurted the whole thing out. Apparently, he and two other inmates had been planning an escape for some time. After Ted became your client and began making progress, he began to have second thoughts about being involved in an escape. The other two inmates, however, threatened to implicate him if anything went wrong with their attempt. The escape attempt is planned for the following night. Ted is distraught as to what he should do, and because you are his counselor, you are also quite concerned.

As a correctional counselor you are not only responsible for inmates, but you have implicit security responsibilities as well. If the escape attempt is allowed to continue as planned, correctional officers, inmates, or both might be seriously injured or killed. If the plan is quashed, you will have failed to honor the confidentiality of your client, and Ted will probably suffer repercussions. Needless to say, your counseling relationship with him will be severely damaged.

It seems you have to either sacrifice Ted, your counseling relationship with him, or the security of the correctional center. Confidentiality or security? Can there be another way?

Source: Adapted from Braswell, M., T. Fletcher, and L. Miller (1990). *Human Relations and Corrections*, 3rd ed. Prospect Heights, IL: Waveland.

▶ At the Movies . . . .

Dead Man Walking, 1996.

Sister Helen Prejean works with a death row inmate as he struggles with his life, the crimes he has committed, and coming to terms with his inevitable execution. She is torn between his needs and the feelings of the victims' family members.

The Spitfire Grill, 1996.

A young woman with a hard past is paroled to a small town in Maine where she is employed at a local café. The challenges of a parolee in a new community after being incarcerated is portrayed as well as the therapeutic potential of supportive community members.

DISCUSSION QUESTIONS

1. How has correctional counseling changed from its beginnings in the 1800s?

2. How can a correctional counselor deal more effectively with the unique challenges and situations he or she faces (for example, large caseloads, stress/burnout, and lack of institutional support)?

3. What changes occurred in the medical services provided to inmates as a result of *Estelle v. Gamble*? How do you feel the law should impact on correctional counseling and treatment?

4. What are some of the most common healthcare problems facing correctional medical and treatment staff today?

5. How can educational and vocational programs help lower recidivism rates?

6. What types of religious services are provided/allowed in prison? What do you think the role of religion should be in corrections?

FURTHER READING

Andrews, D., and J. Bonta (2006). *The Psychology of Criminal Conduct,* 4th ed. Newark, NJ: LexisNexis Matthew Bender.

Braswell, M., J. Fuller, and B. Lozoff (2001). *Corrections, Peacemaking and Restorative Justice.* Cincinnati: Anderson.

Braswell, M., L. Miller, and D. Cabana (2006). *Human Relations and Corrections*, 5th ed. Prospect Heights, IL: Waveland.

Burkhead, M. (2005). *The Search for the Causes of Crime*. Jefferson, NC: McFarland and Company.

Masters, J. (1997). *Finding Freedom*. Junction City, CA: Padma.

Van Voorhis, P., M. Braswell, and D. Lester (2007). *Correctional Counseling and Rehabilitation*, 6th ed. Newark, NJ: LexisNexis Matthew Bender.

NOTES

1. Braswell, Fletcher, and Miller, 1990.

2. *Estelle v. Gamble*, 1976.

3. Anno, 1996.

4. *Bell v. Wolfish*, 1979.

5. Anno, 1996.

6. Anno, 1996.

7. Anno, 1996.

8. Anno, 1996.

9. See National Center for Educational Statistics at http://www.npha.org

10. Violent Crime Control and Law Enforcement Act, 1994.

11. Ryan and Mauldin, 1994.

12. Harer, 1995.

13. Matthews, 1998, 101.

14. Garland, 1990.

15. Clear et al., 2000.

16. Dammer, 1992.

17. "Weight Lifting in Prisons and Correctional Recreation," 2003.

18. H.R. 663, 1995.

19. President's Commission on Law Enforcement and the Administration of Justice, 1967.

20. Beck and Maruschak, 2001.

21. James and Glaze, 2006.

22. James and Glaze, 2006.

23. American Association on Mental Retardation, 1992.

24. Santamour and West, 1985.

25. Santamour and West, 1985.

26. Yalow, 1970.

27. Taylor et al., 2001, 3.

28. Taylor et al., 2001, 16-17.

29. Glasser, 1965.

30. Harrison and Beck, 2002.

31. Greenfeld, 1997, 5-6.

32. Perkins, 1994.

33. Jacob Wetterling Crimes Against Children and Sexually Violent Offenders Registration Act, 1996.

34. Harlow, 1993.

35. Marushack, 2004.

36. Freudenberg, 1989.

37. *Estelle v. Gamble*, 1976.

38. Cromwell, 1994.

39. Cromwell, 1994.

40. Cromwell, 1994, 3.

41. Aday, 2002.

42. Butterfield, 1997.

43. Bureau of Justice Statistics, 2000.

44. National Prison Hospice Association, 2003.

45. Stolberg, 2001.

46. Stolberg, 2001.

47. Price, 1998.

48. Price, 1998, 5.

49. Breitbart et al., 1999.

50. Breitbart et al., 1999.

51. Price, 1998.

52. Price, 1998.

53. Available at Bureau of Justice Statistics web site at http://www.ojp.usdoj.gov/bjs

54. Schofield, 1964.

55. Johnson, 1974.

56. Sabol, Couture, and Harrison, 2006.

57. Dillard, 1987.

58. Palmer, 1992; Whitehead and Lab, 1989.

59. Gendreau, 1996.

60. Gendreau, 1996, 122.

61. Palmer, 1992.

62. Romig, 1978.

63. Van Voorhis, Braswell, and Lester, 2007; Garrett, 1985; Wright and Dixon, 1977.

64. Martinson, 1974.

REFERENCES

Aday, R.H. (2002). *Aging Prisoners: Crisis in American Corrections*. Westport, CT: Praeger.

American Association on Mental Retardation (1992). *Mental Retardation: Definition, Classification, and Systems of Supports*, 9th ed. Washington, DC: author.

American Correctional Health Services Association (1996). In M.D. McShane and F.P. Williams III (eds.), *Encyclopedia of American Prisons*. New York: Garland.

Anno, B.J. (1996). "Health Care." In McShane, M.D. and F.P. Williams III (eds.), *Encyclopedia of American Prisons*. New York: Garland.

Bartollas, C. (1988). *Introduction to Corrections*. Englewood Cliffs, NJ: Prentice Hall.

Beck, A., D. Gilliard, L. Greenfeld, C. Harlow, T. Hester, L. Jankowski, T. Snell, and J. Stephan (1993). "Survey of State Prison Inmates, 1991." *Bureau of Justice Statistics Bulletin*. Washington, DC: U.S. Government Printing Office.

Beck, A.J., and L.M. Maruschak (2001). "Mental Health Treatment in State Prisons, 2000." *Bureau of Justice Statistics Special Report*. Washington, DC: U.S. Government Printing Office.

Braswell, M., T. Fletcher, and L. Miller (1990). *Human Relations and Corrections*, 3rd ed. Prospect Heights, IL: Waveland.

Breitbart, W., H. Chochinov, L. Cohen, L. Ganzini, and J. Shuster (1999). "Shedding Light on Psychiatric Disorders Among the Dying." *PDIA Newsletter*.

Bureau of Justice Statistics (2002). *Death Among Sentenced Prisoners Under State or Federal Jurisdiction*. Washington, DC: U.S. Government Printing Office.

Butterfield, F. (1997). "America's Aging Violent Prisoners." *The New York Times*, July 6, 1997, E3(N), E3(L).

Clear, T.R., P.L. Hardyman, B. Stout, K. Lucken, and H.R. Dammer (2000). "The Value of Religion in Prison:An Inmate Perspective." *Journal of Contemporary Criminal Justice* 16(1):53-74.

Cromwell, P. (1994). "The Graying of America's Prisons." *Overcrowded Times* 6:3.

Cullen, F., J. Wright, and B. Applegate (1995). "Control in the Community: The Limits of Reform?" In A. Harland (ed.), *Choosing Correctional Interventions That Work: Defining the Demand and Evaluating the Supply*. Newbury Park, CA: Sage.

Dammer, H.R. (1992). *Piety in Prison*. Ann Arbor, MI: University Microfilms.

Dillard, J.M. (1987). "Multicultural Counseling." *Journal of American Psychiatric Counseling* 5:3.

Freudenberg, N. (1989). *Prisoners, in Preventing AIDS: A Guide to Effective Education for the Prevention of HIV Infection*. Washington, DC: American Public Health Association.

Garland, D. (1990). *Punishment and Modern Society*. Oxford, MA: Clarendon.

Garrett, C. (1985). "Effects of Residential Treatment on Adjudicated Delinquents: A Meta-analysis." *Journal of Research in Crime and Delinquency* 22:287-308.

Gendreau, P. (1996). "The Principles of Effective Intervention with Offenders." In A.T. Harland (ed.), *Correctional Options That Work: Defining the Demand and Evaluating the Supply*. Thousand Oaks, CA: Sage.

Gilliard, D.K., and A.J. Beck (1998). "Prisoners in 1997." *Bureau of Justice Statistics Bulletin*. Washington, DC: U.S. Government Printing Office.

Glasser, W. (1965). *Reality Therapy: A New Approach to Psychiatry*. New York: Harper and Row.

Greenfeld, L. (1997). "Sex Offenses and Offenders: Executive Summary." *Bureau of Justice Statistics Bulletin*. Washington, DC: U.S. Government Printing Office.

Hammet, T., L. Harrold, M. Gross, and J. Epstein (1993). "1992 Update: AIDS in Correctional Facilities." *Bureau of Justice Statistics Bulletin*. Washington, DC: U.S. Government Printing Office.

Harer, M. (1995). "Recidivism among Federal Prisoners Released in 1987." *Journal of Correctional Education* 46:98-128.

Harlow, C.W. (1993). "HIV in U.S. Prisons and Jails: Bureau of Justice Statistics Special Report." *Bureau of Justice Statistics Bulletin*. Washington, DC: U.S. Government Printing Office.

Harrison, P.M., and A.J. Beck (2002). "Prisoners in 2001." *Bureau of Justice Statistics Bulletin*. Washington, DC: U.S. Government Printing Office.

James, D. J., and L.E. Glaze (2006). "Mental Health Problems of Prison and Jail Inmates." *Bureau of Justice Statistics Special Report*. Washington, DC: U.S. Government Printing Office.

Johnson, E. (1974). *Crime, Corrections, and Society*. Homewood, IL: Dorsey.

Latessa, E.J., and P. Smith (2007). *Corrections in the Community*, 4th ed. Newark, NJ: LexisNexis Matthew Bender.

Martinson, R. (1974). "What Works? Questions and Answers about Prison Reform." *The Public Interest* 35:22-54.

Maruschak, L. (2004). "HIV in Prisons and Jails 2002." *Bureau of Justice Statistics Bulletin*. Washington, DC: U.S. Government Printing Office.

Marvell, T.B. (1995). "Sentencing Guidelines and Prison Population Growth." *The Journal of Criminal Law and Criminology* 85:696-709.

Matthews, S. (1998). "Each Day Is a Lifetime: A Journal by a Prison School Teacher." *Corrections Today* 60:98-101.

McShane, M.D., and F.P. Williams III (1996). *Encyclopedia of American Prisons*. New York: Garland.

National Center for Educational Statistics (1997). *The Digest of Educational Statistics*. Available at http://nces.ed.gov

National Institute of Justice (1996). "1995 Drug Use Forecasting Annual Report on Adult and Juvenile Arrestees." *Bureau of Justice Statistics Bulletin*. Washington, DC: U.S. Government Printing Office.

National Institute of Justice (1990). "Drug Use Forecasting Annual Report." *Bureau of Justice Statistics Bulletin*. Washington, DC: U.S. Government Printing Office.

National Prison Hospice Association (2003). *Mission Statement*. Available at http://www.npha.org

Palmer, T. (1992). *The Re-emergence of Correctional Intervention*. Newbury Park, CA: Sage.

Perkins, C. (1994). *National Corrections Reporting Program, 1992*. Washington, DC: U.S. Government Printing Office.

President's Commission on Law Enforcement and the Administration of Justice (1967). *The Challenge of Crime in a Free Society*. Washington, DC: U.S. Government Printing Office.

Price, C. (1998). *To Adopt or Adapt? Principles of Hospice Care in the Correctional Setting*. American Correctional Association's 128th Congress of Correction, Detroit.

Robins, L.N., and D.A. Reiger (eds.) (1991). *Psychiatric Disorders in America: The Epidemiological Catchment Area Study*. New York: Free Press.

Romig, D. (1978). *Justice for Our Children*. Lexington, MA: Lexington Books.

Ryan, T., and B. Mauldin (1994). *Correctional Education and Recidivism: An Historical Analysis*. Columbia, SC: University of South Carolina.

Sabol, W.J., H. Couture, and P.M. Harrison (2006). "Prisoners in 2006." *Bureau of Justice Statistics Bulletin*. Washington, DC: U.S. Government Printing Office.

Santamour, M., and B. West (1985). "Sourcebook on the Mentally Disorder Prisoner." *Bureau of Justice Statistics Bulletin*. Washington, DC: U.S. Government Printing Office.

Schofield, W. (1964). Psychotherapy, *The Purchase of Friendship*. Englewood Cliffs, NJ: Prentice Hall.

Stolberg, S.G. (2001). "Behind Bars: New Effort to Care for the Dying." *The New York Times,* April 1, 2001, A1, 4.

Taylor, B.G., N. Fitzgerald, D. Hunt, J.A. Reardon, and H.H. Brownstein (2001). "ADAM Preliminary Findings on Drug Use and Drug Markets: Adult Male Arrestees." *Bureau of Justice Statistics Bulletin*. Washington, DC: U.S. Government Printing Office.

Van Voorhis, P., M. Braswell, and D. Lester (2007). *Correctional Counseling and Rehabilitation*, 6th ed. Newark, NJ: LexisNexis Matthew Bender.

"Weightlifting in Prison and Correctional Recreation." Available at: http://www.strengthtech.com

Whitehead, J., and S. Lab (1989). "A Response to 'Does Correctional Treatment Work?'" Unpublished paper.

Wright, W., and M. Dixon (1977). "Juvenile Delinquency Prevention." *Journal of Research in Crime and Delinquency* 14:35-67.

Yalow, I.D. (1970). *The Theory and Practice of Group Psychotherapy*. New York: Basic Books.

COURT CASES

Bell v. Wolfish, 441 U.S. 520 (1979).

Estelle v. Gamble, 429 U.S. 97 (1976).

Issues in Correctional Administration and Management

CHAPTER 13

What You Need to Know

▶ Corrections generally uses one of three basic models of administration and management: an authoritarian model, a bureaucratic model, or a participative model. In practice, a correctional agency often uses a mixed model.

▶ Administration focuses on leadership, providing direction and guidance toward an established institutional mission. Management is supervision of the daily operations of the agency.

▶ Correctional philosophies such as retribution and rehabilitation have influenced correctional administration and management.

▶ Other factors affecting administration and management include both politics and the law.

▶ Correctional administrators and managers need to be aware of threats to institutional safety including drugs, sexual coercion, violence, and gangs—and how to deal with them.

▶ Correctional agencies provide programs and services relating to the physical and mental health of offenders as well as educational and vocational programs.

▶ Correctional administrators and managers must deal with the needs of correctional personnel in addition to those of offenders.

▶ An important concern is infectious diseases such as tuberculosis, hepatitis, and HIV/AIDS. Additional concerns are employee stress and employee unionization.

▶ The growth of prisons and the prisoner population and the costs associated with this growth are critical issues facing today's administrators and managers. Several states are taking steps to deal with these issues, such as using alternatives to sanction technical parole violators.

▶ Another issue is to implement correctional programs that the research evidence indicates are effective and to avoid programs that are clearly ineffective. It is important to try to implement evidence-based suggestions.

INTRODUCTION

There are currently more than 7.2 million people in the United States who are under some form of correctional supervision.[1] That amounts to about one of every 31 adults in the United States.[2] More than 5 million people are on probation or parole, more than 750,000 are in local jail facilities, and just under 1.5 million are incarcerated in state or federal prisons.[3] In simple terms, corrections has been a growth industry, and the job of managing that industry has been getting increasingly difficult. This chapter tries to understand the dimensions of that difficult task.

Corrections encompasses agencies involved with probation, parole, jails, and prisons. Probation and parole are mainly noncustodial entities. They are often considered to be community supervision because the offender is not confined within a correctional facility. Jails and prisons are custodial agencies in which offenders must stay for a given period of time. The administrative structures and management issues pertaining to noncustodial corrections (i.e., probation and parole) are significantly different from those of custodial corrections.

Visit the web site of the Bureau of Justice Statistics at www.ojp.usdoj.gov/bjs. The Bureau issues numerous statistical updates on correctional populations, including those of prisons, jails, probation, and parole. It also issues topical reports.

Jail and prison administration and management also differ significantly. Jails are short-term facilities in which the population is primarily unconvicted; the majority (58.5%) of local jail inmates are just awaiting court action on their current charges.[4] Jails also hold a variety of persons for different reasons at various stages in the judicial process. For example, a jail may hold persons awaiting arraignment, trial, conviction, or sentencing. A jail inmate may be a mentally ill person waiting to be transferred to a mental health facility, or a person under protective custody.[5] It is an environment characterized by constant change.

Prisons, on the other hand, have fairly stable criminal populations. Prisons usually house only offenders who have been convicted and sentenced to serve time for a felony. Increasingly, however, the population of our state prisons is comprised of parole violators, individuals who were released from a sentence on parole but violated that parole in some way. In 2005 new court commitments accounted for 62 percent of state prison admissions, and parole violators accounted for 34 percent of new admissions. Admissions of parole violators in 2005 were 14 percent higher than the number of admissions of parole violators in 2000.[6]

Prison populations grow because of new commitments, parole revocations, increases in the amount of time served, and decreases in the number of inmate releases.[7] These factors lead to increased overcrowding and strain on correctional resources. As a result, competent administration and management is crucial. Because prisons consume the bulk of correctional expenditures, house our most violent and persistent offenders, and are the focus of much public and media scrutiny, this chapter mainly focuses on correctional administration and management as it pertains to this type of correctional facility. However, we do mention some issues in community corrections, including the impact of parole revocations on prison populations.

• Organizational Theory •

Before discussing the concepts of administration and management, and some of the major issues involved within the correctional environment, it is necessary to describe the structure of the environment through which corrections takes place. We use organizational theory to conceptualize "how authority is distributed within an organization and how it is used to accomplish the agency's mission and goals."[8]

Authority is a tool used to get tasks completed toward fulfillment of the organization's mission. Persons with authority make decisions pertaining to institutional functions. Levels of authority, as well as the flow of that authority throughout an organization, can be different from one facility to another. In fact, each institution is a "complex mixture of people, personalities, programs, rules, and behaviors" and is "composed of people who act individually and collectively and create a culture."[9]

While different organizations have variations and adaptations of organizational principles, corrections generally involves one of three basic models: an authoritarian model, a bureaucratic model, or a participative model.[10] The authoritarian model is characterized by a forceful leader who establishes and maintains firm control over the institutional environment. Staff or inmates who behave contrary to this leader's dictates may be subject to harsh discipline. This type of organizational style is highly centralized and regimented with strict adherence to rules and regulations. All decisions are made through the central leader, even if other personnel could make better decisions. In this model, lower-level staff are denied decision-making responsibilities and flexibility. This model can be dangerous for an institution because placing authority within one individual may result in abuse of that power—and corruption may be inevitable.

The bureaucratic model also is hierarchical, but involves more individuals with authority. Control is distributed throughout the hierarchy via a chain of command and formal communication processes. In this model, the institutional functions are not dependent upon only one person and do not reflect only one personality. The disadvantage to this structure is that bureaucracies may also be characterized by inflexibility, inability to change quickly, and few rewards for staff creativity and innovation.

The participative model is significantly different from the other two models. Administrative personnel are more willing to allow democratic and open consideration of suggestions, ideas, and problems. In fact, staff participation is encouraged as critical to the institution's functions. Sometimes, inmates are allowed to offer input into the process as well. In this model, "agency and correctional goals are more efficiently accomplished when all staff have participated in reaching a consensus on how to proceed."[11] In this manner, staff members feel "an increased sense of ownership in planning and operations, often resulting in better attitudes toward and support of routine events and new initiatives."[12] The drawback to participatory models is that they require greater commitments in terms of time and energy on everyone's part.

American correctional institutions rarely employ the participatory model of management. Administrators frequently question the perceived lack of structure and are reluctant to delegate decision-making authority among all the personnel. More frequently, agencies attempt to employ a mixed model, involving the bureaucratic style but adapted to include some participatory elements. In this type of agency, daily decisionmaking is decentralized, and staff involvement is encouraged in many areas. This hybrid is "considered quite effective" for organizational administration.[13]

• Defining Administration and Management •

Although the terms "administration" and "management" often are used interchangeably, they do not actually reflect the same concepts. Administration is a broad term that encompasses the ideas of leadership and management. An administrator leads by providing direction and guidance toward an established institutional mission or vision. Management is more supervisory and more concerned with the daily operations of the facility. A manager uses institutional policies and procedures as a tool for institutional maintenance. Administration is the tool through which leaders and managers accomplish their tasks, which in the case of correctional administration is the insurance that criminal offenders are effectively and efficiently maintained while under the care of the correctional agency.

Correctional administrators often have conflicting roles. They are responsible for making sure that the facility can operate, which includes budgeting, personnel, and facility maintenance. In addition, they must make sure that the facility is safe both for inmates and staff, that offenders are offered effective programs to fulfill the goals of the facility, and that operational procedures are followed. To accomplish these tasks, management personnel must plan, organize, staff, direct, and control.[14]

Correctional planning usually pertains to short-term issues, such as staffing, expansion because of increasing populations, or budgeting. Correctional planning is often necessary for ensuring that the facility can handle both expected and unexpected incidents that might impact it. Forecasting prison populations is one type of planning that helps administrators anticipate significant changes in the numbers of inmates expected to become incarcerated. This forecasting is also used in decisions to expand existing correctional facilities or build new facilities to handle increasing populations.

The danger with this method is that forecasted changes may never occur. Forecasting is based on past trends, and trends sometimes change. When the "war against drugs" was implemented in the 1980s, for example, forecasters had not anticipated the resulting dramatic increases in prison populations. Correctional officials were left to scramble for space in which to house all the new inmates.

The drug war policy, in combination with "truth in sentencing" laws, has contributed to significant overcrowding in our nations correctional facilities. This is a problematic issue for the administration and management of corrections. At yearend 2006, for example, 23 states and the federal prison system were operating at more than 100 percent of their highest capacity.[15]

Organizing within corrections involves both the structure and function of organizational roles. The structure defines the relationships among roles, often arrayed in some sort of hierarchy and chain of command, with the administration at the top level and the front-line workers/correctional officers at the bottom. Within this structure, each level has clearly defined duties (functions) that contribute to the overall mission of the agency. Often, written policies created by upper-level administrators define expectations, while procedures developed by mid-level managers detail how those policies are to be accomplished. These procedures result in specific sets of instructions for employees at the lower levels to guide them in the completion of their duties.

The correctional administrator also is responsible for managing the staffing of the organization. Although most facilities have human resource departments to recruit staff, ensure adherence to mandated hiring practices, and monitor performance appraisals, management ultimately is responsible for the quality of the personnel. Maintaining this quality is also management's responsibility. This includes monitoring staff performance, providing opportunities for additional training and staff development, and mentoring employees.

Managers also must provide direction. This often entails instructing staff with "how to" information. As the "drill sergeants" of the organization, they give orders from a detailed policy and procedure manual, telling the "grunts" (line staff) what to do (policy) and how to do it (procedure). Most management styles involve a clear chain of command, from the top of the hierarchy to the bottom.

In addition to directing the activities of the organization, managers must also make sure that these directions are followed and make a positive contribution toward the organization's mission. It is the manager's job to control operations through a monitoring of policy, procedure, and program effectiveness. Line staff are supervised to make sure they are following policy and procedure. Feedback from staff and inmates also can provide insight into effectiveness. Occasionally, more formal "process" or "impact" evaluations of policy, procedures, and programs can assist managers in controlling operations by revealing weaknesses that need modification.

Although the titles change and the duties vary slightly, correctional administration and management appear fairly similar among levels and jurisdictions. The primary work of corrections is to enforce sentences imposed on offenders by the courts (with the exception of jails, which often house suspects who are awaiting trial). Correctional administrators are entrusted with the task of overseeing the management of the correctional facilities in which inmates complete their sentences.

To help maintain administrative consistency throughout various correctional systems, the American Correctional Association (ACA) has developed a set of standards that agencies can strive to meet for accreditation. According to the ACA, 80 percent of all state department of corrections and youth services are active participants in accreditation, as well as the Federal Bureau of Prisons and some private prisons.[16] The ACA standards pertain to services, programs, and operations essential to good correctional management, and include "administrative and fiscal controls, staff training and development, food service, and rules and discipline."[17] In addition to institutional guidelines and accreditation standards, administrators often are guided by overriding correctional, governmental, political, and legal philosophies.

ADMINISTRATION IN CONTEXT

• Correctional Philosophies •

Throughout this text we have pointed out that many correctional philosophies are rooted in religious principles. Both retribution and rehabilitation are based upon such principles. Retribution involves punishment-oriented penalties and makes offenders "pay" for their offenses (either financially, psychologically, or physically). Rehabilitation, on the other hand, does not view the offender as someone who needs punishing but as someone in need of assistance or treatment. As noted in Chapter 1, this view evolved as society developed the belief that individuals who behaved in nonconforming ways either were lacking something, such as job skills or education, or were "ill" and needed treatment. Being ill could mean an addiction to alcohol or other drugs, or being psychologically or spiritually troubled. This view enjoyed immense popularity in the 1970s as correctional systems developed and implemented many rehabilitative programs. Prisoners who were lacking education or job skills could be educated and trained behind bars. Prisoners who were "ill" could receive treatment.

Historically, various correctional philosophies have influenced the administration and management of correctional environments. The prevailing philosophy at any given time is often determined by several factors. These factors include the current political environment, the current social environment, crime rates, patterns and trends, and the state of social, medical, and psychological research. One of the most influential sets of administrative determinants is related to government, politics, and the law.

• Correctional Administration and Government •

Local, state, and federal governmental systems affect nearly every aspect of correctional administration, from the location of the facility, to the garments the inmates wear, to the daily operations of the facility. The form and function of the U.S. governmental system is central to the idea of an American democracy. People first wanted to come to America to escape governments that were too powerful and too restrictive. This nation's founders wanted to make sure that the citizens would have roles in their own governance and that the power of government would be distributed among three different branches: legislative, judicial, and executive.

The legislative branch is concerned with making laws. Local, state, and federal governments can make laws that affect their own jurisdictions. Local ordinances are created by local governments (county or city) and apply only within their boundaries. One example of a local ordinance would be a noise ordinance that would prohibit people from playing their stereos at a high volume in certain areas at certain times. State laws are passed by state legislatures and affect an entire state. Most familiar laws are state laws such as those against robbery, theft, driving while intoxicated, and homicide. Federal laws are enacted by the federal government (U.S. Congress) and apply to the entire nation. Federal legislation often appears in the form of an Act, such as the Civil Rights Act of 1967, which provides protection against discrimination based on race, sex, religion, and national origin.

State and federal legislatures create and apply laws that impact correctional administration in many ways. Aside from the creation of laws that criminalize certain behaviors or omissions, they create legislative mandates to regulate the functions of the various components of the criminal justice system. For example, a state government may mandate that all law enforcement officers receive a certain number of hours of firearms training every year. Likewise, states and the federal government pass legislation that significantly impact the operations of corrections.

The Prison Litigation Reform Act (PLRA)[18] is one such piece of federal legislation that targets the litigation behaviors of inmates and increases the administrative responsibilities of the correctional institution.

Corrections and law enforcement are parts of the executive branch of government. The executive branch is comprised of managers and administrators. Mayors, governors, and the President of the United States are all government administrators. What many people do not realize is that law enforcement and correctional officials are also government administrators. They are responsible for seeing that the day-to-day functions of law enforcement and corrections are fulfilled. Law enforcement officials are responsible for enforcing laws created by legislatures. Correctional officials primarily are responsible for enforcing sanctions (sentences) passed by the courts.

This system of checks and balances is beneficial in that it spreads the power of government over multiple agencies, and provides citizens with various levels of support. However, having power and discretion spread over multiple agencies also serves to hamper the ability of these agencies to make coordinated decisions. This has been referred to as "jurisdictional separation and functional fragmentation," which is characterized by "lack of cooperation, insufficient coordination, and territorial rivalries."[19] Police officers who arrest suspects, sometimes after long, intensive investigations, are often disappointed and frustrated when the suspects are released on bail, or when prosecutors decide not to pursue a case and suspects are released. Likewise, prosecutors must rely on law enforcement to conduct legal and thorough investigations, or they have no choice but to dismiss cases. Correctional officials may also experience disillusionment and disappointment when they see offenders more in need of education, drug treatment, or psychiatric or medical care than harsh punishment. Everyone connected with the system is disheartened to see high rates of recidivism and the failure of "justice."

• Correctional Administration and Politics •

The job of the correctional administrator also is affected by politics. The two dominant political parties in the United States embrace different political philosophies. Republicans are inclined to advocate more powerful state governments and a weaker federal system, characterized by fewer social welfare programs, a market-driven economy, and tax breaks for corporations and businesses. Democrats, on the other hand, tend to favor a stronger federal government geared toward supporting citizens, characterized by more social welfare programs and more social services but also higher taxes. Democrats also are more likely to favor a tax system that asks for bigger contributions from those with higher incomes and more assets.

These overriding philosophies are reflected in each party's platform presented to the American public. Each year, politicians make issues related to crime and justice central to their campaigns because "corrections and correctional policies are equally attractive political platforms that can be simplified and symbolized to capitalize on public sentiments."[20]

Crime-related issues, including correctional philosophies, starkly emphasize party differences, and as governments undergo changes of political leadership, correctional priorities are apt to change. The Republican platform on crime, for example, includes emphasis on the following: (1) more state and local controls of law enforcement efforts; (2) "no-frills prisons, with productive work requirements;"[21] (3) more resources dedicated to the fight against drugs, including increased penalties; (4) rehabilitation, where appropriate; (5) community-based diversion programs for first-time, nonviolent offenders; and (6) reform of the "exclusionary rule." In contrast, the Democratic platform emphasizes the following: (1) victims' rights; (2) effective drug treatment for prisoners; (3) strictly supervised parole with employment assistance; (4) stricter punishment for drug-related crimes; (5) stronger gun laws; (6) harsher punishments for hate crimes; (7) protection for the "most vulnerable citizens,"[22] such as children and the elderly; (8) focus on domestic violence; and (9) dedication to prevention.

The tendency to position corrections within political symbolism has significant implications for correctional decisionmakers. Correctional policies and procedures "are likely to be monitored more closely,"[23] criminal justice reform proposals may not be well received, and administrators may be more likely to resort to "short-term, reactive solutions. . . that will require more control and will result in increased numbers of offenders under correctional supervision and in institutional confinement."[24]

• Correctional Administration and the Law •

The U.S. Constitution protects citizens from abuse by the state. The first 10 amendments to the Constitution, known as the Bill of Rights, outline the rights of citizens and delineate limits on state power. Because corrections falls under the domain of the government, correctional officials must conduct their business with careful consideration of these constitutional protections. The constitutionality of correctional treatment is often questioned.

When inmates believe that their constitutional rights have been violated, they generally file lawsuits against prisons through the federal courts. This requires filing suit based on 42 USCA §1983 (1988),[25] which provides that a suit may be initiated against a person who has acted as a representative of the state according to state law (e.g., a correctional officer or administrator) to deprive a person of guaranteed constitutional or federal rights. These types of suits often involve conditions of confinement, such as inadequate medical care, abuse by officers, religious discrimination, and inadequate living conditions.[26] In fact, during 1995, 23 percent of state facilities were under court order for these types of specific conditions.[27]

In 2005 almost 10 percent of all civil cases filed in federal courts were prisoner complaints about conditions or civil rights violations.[28] Approximately 98 percent of these cases eventually are dismissed by the courts; of the 2 percent that go to trial, less than one-half are resolved in the inmate's favor.[29] Some examples of unsuccessful suits have involved "melted ice cream, bad haircuts, and a broken cookie."[30]

Other cases, however, do involve clear violations of inmate rights and result in policy and procedure changes within an institution. The state of Michigan, for example, failed to provide inmates with winter coats, hats, and gloves. The federal court ruled in *Knop v. Johnson*[31] that this subjected the prisoners to cruel and unusual punishment. As a result, Michigan institutions had to begin providing the inmates with proper winter clothing.

In 1996, President Clinton signed into law the Prison Litigation Reform Act (PLRA),[32] the purpose of which was to curtail "frivolous" prison litigation brought under Section 1983. The PLRA mandates early dismissal of frivolous suits, more thorough screening of cases, and "exhaustion" of administrative remedies. This last mandate requires that an inmate "first avail himself [sic] of whatever prison internal grievance process is in place at his [sic] correctional institution before filing suit in federal court."[33]

Requiring inmates to first participate in internal grievance programs may have multiple benefits.[34] For example, the burden on federal courts will be reduced and will decrease the amount of judicial oversight of correctional operations. Steinman claims that many correctional administrators believe that "federal courts are not equipped to properly engage in microscopic oversight or management of prisons or jails," and that correctional administration is best left to correctional administrators.[35]

More reliance on the internal process may also allow administrators to have a better sense of their correctional environment. Clear and Cole believe that management can be improved because "by attentive monitoring of the complaint process, a warden or commissioner is able to discern patterns of inmate discontent that may warrant actions to prevent the development of more serious problems."[36]

This process also may benefit the inmates who are dissatisfied. Steinman argues that in this situation "a resolution that is generally satisfactory to both sides is more likely to occur during the prison internal process than during litigation."[37] Administrators must ensure, however, that policies and procedures are in place to protect complaining inmates from reprisals by correctional officials, and to ensure that inmates understand

BOX 13.1

Human Rights Watch Proposals to Revise the Prison Litigation Reform Act

Critics of prison inmate lawsuits like to cite so-called frivolous cases such as suits about being forced to eat three cheese sandwiches a day for one week in disciplinary confinement or being served reconstituted milk instead of fresh milk. The Prison Litigation Reform Act was supposed to reduce such suits.

Critics of the Act, however, claim that the law has created problems by requiring inmates to follow all prison complaint procedures before they can file a lawsuit and punishing criminals for missing technical requirements such as failing to submit a grievance within 48 hours. Human Rights Watch alleges that the stringent requirements of the law have made it difficult for fifteen female prisoners in New York State to get redress for alleged staff sexual abuse. The women alleged sexual assault, harassment, rape, oral sexual acts, voyeurism, demeaning sexual comments, and other abuses. In 2005 the state moved to dismiss the suit on the grounds that the prisoners did not exhaust administrative remedies. The judge was taking considerable time to rule on the state's motion.

Additionally, the act prevents prisoners from recovering damages for sexual humiliation if there is no more than minor physical injury. Due to this requirement, courts have dismissed complaints about a female correctional officer who had grabbed a male prisoner's penis and about two women prisoners who claimed they were strip-searched by male officers.

Source: Human Rights Watch Testimony Regarding Proposed Revision to the Prison Litigation Reform Act. Available at http://www.hrw.org

their right to follow through with a federal complaint if the internal process is not resolved satisfactorily. Alarcon suggests that one way to help administrators and prisoners resolve their disputes—and prevent many lawsuits—is to use an independent corrections ombudsman. An ombudsman is a neutral party, much like a referee or umpire. Iowa and Hawaii have already adopted this measure.[38]

THE INSTITUTIONAL ENVIRONMENT

While correctional administrators always must function within philosophical, political, and legal environments, they also must consider the institutional environment within which they operate. The primary consideration of the institutional environment is that of safety, both for the staff and for the inmates. Additionally, administrators are obligated to provide basic programs and services for inmates under their care. Those programs and services often are limited by safety considerations. Thus, possible threats to institutional safety must be carefully evaluated by the administration. The likelihood of these threats often will guide administrators to the development and implementation of new policies or to the revision of old ones. Some of these threats include substance abuse (alcohol and other drugs), sexual coercion, gangs, and violence.

• Drugs •

High levels of alcohol and other drug use are found among significant proportions of criminal offenders. According to a recent analysis, about 80 percent of state and federal inmates either committed drug-related offenses, were under the influence of alcohol or other drugs at the time of their crimes, committed their crimes to support drug habits, or had histories of serious substance abuse.[39] In fact, drug levels among tested arrestees across the nation indicate that a median rate of 64 percent of the men and 67 percent of the women tested positive for at least one drug.[40]

At the local level (i.e., jails), in 1998, about 70 percent of all inmates either had committed a drug offense or used drugs regularly.[41] In a comprehensive survey of inmates, 32 percent of state prisoners and 26 percent of federal prisoners said they had committed their current offense while under the influence of drugs. Most inmates (83% of the state prisoners and 79% of the federal prisoners) also reported prior drug use.[42]

Offenders do not necessarily stop using drugs when they are incarcerated. This threatens the rehabilitative goals of the facility, inmate and staff safety, public confidence, and perhaps even the safety of the community when the drug-using offenders are released. Despite confinement and close supervision, illegal drugs are often easily obtained. Drugs can be imported by visitors, through the mail, and even by staff.

Correctional administrators have adopted a variety of methods to prevent drugs from entering the correctional environment. These include verbal questioning, patdowns, clothing exchanges, and body cavity searches.[43] Inmates are most often subject to clothing exchanges and body cavity searches, while staff and visitors receive verbal questioning and patdowns. Random drug testing of inmates, or testing on suspicion of use, is frequently also used as an interdiction method. Some states, however, have developed innovative solutions to their drug problems.

During the mid-1990s in Pennsylvania, for example, the problem of drug use in prisons was perceived to be growing and was becoming a significant management issue. Pennsylvania's governor charged the Secretary of Corrections, Tom Horne, with eliminating drugs in the system.

As a result, Secretary Horne established the Drug Interdiction Program (DIP), a "broad-based strategy combining interdiction methods, drug testing, and drug treatment."[44]

Feucht and Keyser described and evaluated Pennsylvania's DIP. The program consists of a zero-tolerance drug policy, with those caught with drugs to be criminally prosecuted and those testing positive for drugs to serve disciplinary time. This policy requires close surveillance both of inmates and visitors, frequent random urinalysis, increased cell searches, and the use of drug-sniffing dogs.

Technology also played a role in the beefed-up surveillance. Ion mobility spectrometers scan people and packages, detecting drugs that individuals, including correctional staff, may try to convey to prisoners. In addition, a new phone system was installed to allow random monitoring of inmate calls. These changes were implemented between 1995 and 1998.

In addition to the DIP, all Pennsylvania inmates undergo an evaluation to determine their need for substance abuse treatment (approximately 92% require it). Each of the state's prisons offer drug treatment, and seven of the facilities maintain therapeutic communities in which severe substance abusers are separately housed to undergo intensive, long-term treatment. In 1997, Pennsylvania opened a substance abuse treatment prison especially for inmates who require specialized drug treatment and ongoing care.

The DIP's effectiveness in reducing drug use in Pennsylvania's prisons was measured by combining hair analysis with the urinalysis already in place. Hair and urine samples were collected from nearly 1,000 randomly selected male and female inmates at five prisons. Inmates who had been incarcerated for less than three months were excluded because hair analysis can detect drug use within the past 90 days, and researchers did not want to detect drug use prior to incarceration. Measures were taken in 1996 before the DIP was initiated, and then again in 1998, after two years of operation. Results indicated a "dramatic decrease in the use of drugs in the prisons."[45] While nearly 8 percent of all tested inmates had at least one drug in their systems in 1996 (before the DIP), only 1.4 percent did so in 1998.

This decline in drug use in Pennsylvania's prisons has been linked with fewer drug finds (a 41% decrease), fewer assaults on staff (a 57% decrease), fewer inmate-on-inmate assaults (a 70% decrease), and fewer weapons found during searches (a 35% decrease). While the reduction and possible elimination of drugs in prisons improves the institutional environment and reinforces institutional authority and control, it also helps the inmates to refrain from drug use during their sentences, which would seem to be an obvious first step to long-term rehabilitation.[46]

Correctional administration can take steps to address the threat of drugs within correctional environments. Zero-tolerance policies coupled with stringent enforcement efforts can have positive effects on the institutional environment. Pennsylvania's experience indicates that a reduction in drug use within the facility also may reduce associated problems with violence, helping create a safer environment for everyone. Because each facility is different, each correctional environment may require different tactics. Clearly, however, administrators must carefully evaluate and define the drug-related problems within their own facility and implement policies, such as Pennsylvania's DIP, to deal with them effectively.

• Sexual Coercion •

Although it has been noted that "sexuality will be expressed within institutions,"[47] it is associated with a plethora of management problems.

AP Photo/Dave Martin

Alabama State Representative Barbara Boyd talks with reporters outside the Statehouse in Montgomery. In 2004, the Alabama Senate gave final approval of a bill making it a felony for a corrections officer or other prison official to have sexual relations with an inmate. Boyd pushed for passage of the bill.

Sexual contact can be of two types within two domains. Types of sexual contact can roughly be divided into contact that is consensual (e.g., self-manipulation, or both parties agree without force or coercion) and contact that is unwanted (forced or coerced). The two domains are staff-inmate and inmate-inmate. Staff-inmate contact is never considered to be consensual, given the power-relationship that exists and the vulnerability of the inmate in the correctional environment.

Staff-inmate contacts are particularly troubling. While the actual frequency of this behavior is unknown, some studies estimate that from 19 to 45 percent of all incidents of sexual contact in the correctional environment may involve staff members to some degree.[48] The majority of incidents involve male officers and female inmates. In fact, the Human Rights Watch reports that in some cases, "male officers are sexually abusing female prisoners while the state and federal government look the other way."[49]

Stewart examined the issue of managerial response to sexual misconduct between staff and inmates by reviewing the practices of a Federal Correctional Institution (FCI) for female felons in Danbury, Connecticut.[50] He found that there are several costs of sexual misconduct, not only for the inmate, but also for the staff member, the correctional facility, and the community. They are as follows:

- *Financial.* The staff member faces the potential loss of employment and income. The institution also faces the cost of investigating the allegations, the cost of training a new employee, and perhaps the cost of litigation if a terminated employee or inmate victim decides to file suit.

- *Social and emotional.* The staff member may suffer the loss of reputation and career. His or her family may also suffer humiliation from the termination and media exposure. There is a great likelihood of separation or divorce.

- *Employee morale.* This is "the most serious consequence" for an administrator. Sexual misconduct cases often divide staff, disrupt operations, and generally depress the whole institution. Many coworkers of the officer who committed the offense suffer stigmatization and a loss of self-respect, respect for their roles, and respect for their occupation (p. 82).

- *Public confidence.* Extremely damaging is the effect of the misconduct on the public perception of the correctional facility. If misconduct repeatedly occurs, public confidence and respect begins to erode. Citizens question the integrity and ethics of the system, and wonder whether management can properly handle staff selection and training.

Stewart emphasizes the importance of maintaining organizational integrity. He claims that a clear understanding of the organization's mission, principles, and core values is essential to that end. Each member of the organization must feel tied to these ideals, so that they share the responsibility for helping the organization do what it must to succeed. Supervisors and managers must make these core values part of their daily operations and teach staff how to use those values in daily decisionmaking.

The Federal Bureau of Prisons (BOP) has attempted to address sexual misconduct by focusing on supervisors and managers. The BOP training for probationary employees during institutional familiarization, academy training, and annual refresher training incorporates the subjects of ethics and integrity. In addition, each male employee that is working with female inmates for the first time must complete a self-study program that reviews issues related to the management of female offenders. Both supervisory and management staff must complete the training.

According to Stewart, "supervisors play a critical role in preventing inappropriate behaviors, especially sexual misconduct, by ensuring high standards of professional behavior."[51] This includes effectively communicating standards of conduct, implementing reasonable procedures to ensure that staff meet those standards, taking all allegations seriously, reporting all staff who may be involved, and using discipline appropriately.

Training supervisors also can prevent cases of sexual misconduct by making them more aware of commonalities or patterns of behavior among staff considered to be at risk for engaging in sexual activities with inmates. Common themes and personal or situational factors that precede misconduct can indicate to attuned supervisors the need for preventive measures, such as counseling.

Some warning signs that supervisors should look for include a severely stressed officer or one who has recently experienced significant personal loss, special treatment of a particular inmate, and misconceptions about female inmates, such as believing that females should be treated differently or are in need of protection. While female inmates do have significantly different needs than male prisoners, response to these needs should be based on management principles, not on a "special treatment" basis.

Stewart suggests several strategies to prevent staff sexual misconduct. These include:

- Awareness: of staff problems and activities; of inmate/staff interactions

- Early intervention: correction of staff showing warning signs; rotation of inmate assignments; identification of manipulative inmates

- Prevention: installing windows in office and closet doors; regular but random visits by supervisors

- Prosecution: treating sexual misconduct as a serious felony[52]

While information on sexual activity between staff and inmates usually becomes known only after media attention or inmate litigation, sexual activity among inmates is often even more hidden. Research in this area is sparse and often focuses on ancillary issues, such as the spread of sexually transmitted diseases (STDs).[53]

Studies that attempt to document the incidence of sexual contact among inmates are rare, and primarily center on sexual assault. It is this unfortunate connection with violence that makes inmate sexual activity an important one for correctional administrators. In fact, one study concluded that "the threat of sexual violence actually dominates the prison environment and structures much of the everyday interaction that goes on among inmates," and that "the threat of sexual victimization becomes the dominant metaphor in terms of which almost every other aspect of 'prison reality' is interpreted."[54] The argument here is that it matters very little whether the actual incidence of sexual assault is high or low; the perception is that the "threat of victimization" is very real.[55] Although correctional administrators should be aware of the actual incidence of sexual activity within their facilities, they should also be concerned with the perceived threat because people typically construct their realities from their perceptions and behave accordingly.

As noted in Chapter 7, one recent research study reported that about 20 percent of both male and female prisoners reported sexual victimization.[56] A national study prompted by the Prison Rape Elimination Act found overall prevalence of sexual victimization to be approximately 4.5 percent, with some prisons having rates as high as 13 to 15 percent.[57]

As difficult as it is to obtain accurate information about prisoner victimization of other prisoners and guard victimization of inmates, especially in women's prisons, it is imperative for administrators to be aware of such victimization and to take appropriate steps to prevent it. Recommendations for dealing with sexual coercion within the prison environment often are targeted at correctional administrators. Enhanced inmate classification systems, for example, would be beneficial in determining which inmates are at risk, either of becoming a victim or a perpetrator.[58] Staff training programs could help officers understand the factors that contribute to sexual coercion, increasing their awareness of situations, places, and persons most likely to become involved. Finally, administrators should convey their willingness to hear reports of sexual coercion, to institute preventive measures, and to respond swiftly and justly to founded reports.

• Violence •

The possibility of violence within the walls of correctional facilities is a given. Inmates often are viewed as societal outcasts, convicted of violating the norms and laws that guide conventional behavior and contribute to civilization. The criminal case processing system is often long, tedious, and frustrating. A variety of problems also make the U.S. criminal justice system patently unfair, such as sentencing disparities and the prevalence of plea bargaining. As a result, prisons often house individuals who are angry and frustrated, and who feel that they were not dealt with justly and fairly by our system. Many of these prisoners have substantially good arguments to support their beliefs. Additionally, prisoners have a diverse mix of temperaments and personalities, and are from a variety of racial, ethnic, social, educational, and cultural backgrounds. Their criminal histories and crimes of choice are widely varied. It seems only logical that violence will exist.

Violence does exist. The latest available statistics show that within state and federal facilities in fiscal year 1999-2000 there were 34,355 inmate assaults on other inmates and 17,952 inmate assaults on staff.[59] This represents a rate of 28 assaults on inmates per 1,000 inmates and 14.6 assaults on staff per every 1,000 inmates.[60]

Although the public often perceives all prison inmates to be violent, many inmates are not serving sentences in our correctional facilities for violent offenses; the most recent available statistics show that about

52 percent of state prisoners and 20 percent of federal prisoners were sentenced to prison for a violent crime.[61] The correctional environment still is volatile, and prison violence has emerged as a significant management problem at various points throughout the history of corrections. Infamous prison riots, such as those in Ohio, New York, and New Mexico, have been valuable learning experiences for those involved in correctional administration.

Numerous studies of prison violence have indicated possible connections between violent acts and overcrowding,[62] gang-related tensions,[63] the inmate subculture as powerless, bored, and sexually frustrated,[64] and the importation of street cultures characterized by violent behaviors.[65] More recently, studies indicate that prison violence may stem from multiple factors with a triggering event.[66]

Irwin and Austin discuss four factors that significantly contribute to prison violence.[67] Restricted freedom refers to the constraints placed on inmate actions while in the facility, including physical mobility, correspondence and visitation, and sexual activity. Resources and contacts, such as educational, vocational, and recreational programs, have been reduced because of a decreased emphasis on rehabilitation as well as declining budgets. Inmates also tend to view the disciplinary procedures as arbitrary punishment, the goal of which is to maintain order within the facility rather than to render fair and impartial decisions. So-called "chickenshit rules" that further restrict the behaviors and individuality of the inmates are those that may ban decorations in cells or the possession of clothing, furniture, "knick-knacks," or pets. Each of these seems to be related to the distribution of power within the institution. Prisoners lose autonomy and feel they are completely under the control of the institution.

A distinction also can be made between violent acts based on the origin and scope of the conflict.[68] Interpersonal violence originates from a personal conflict between individuals, and usually involves a few inmates. Collective violence originates from conflicts between groups of individuals. Prison riots and disturbances are examples of collective violence that involve prisoners acting against the staff and administration. Gang-related conflicts also may be categorized as collective violence.

• Gangs •

Scholars debate whether new inmates enter the prison and begin to conform to the prison culture, or whether those incoming inmates import a particular culture from the outside.[69] Whichever it is, part of the cultural environment centers on gang activity, which poses a significant threat to the safety of both inmates and correctional staff. A 1999 survey of 133 adult state correctional facilities indicated that approximately 16 percent of inmates in minimum-security facilities, 24 percent of those in medium-security facilities, and 33 percent of those in maximum-security facilities were affiliated with a gang. In one-sixth of the facilities, correctional staff members surveyed had been assaulted by gang members; they had been threatened by gang members in nearly one-half. This level of involvement persists despite the fact that 66 percent of the facilities have disciplinary rules prohibiting gang recruitment.[70]

Traditionally, prison gangs were an extension of street gangs because many of the gang members ended up serving time together. To provide group cohesion, gangs such as the Crips and Bloods continued their street gang activities within the prison, such as establishing and protecting turf, recruitment, violence, and drug dealing. Some gangs, such as the Mexican Mafia and the Black Guerilla Family, originated within the prison environment, when prisoners from the same racial and/or ethnic background joined together for support.

Gang members provide support and protection for each other. In

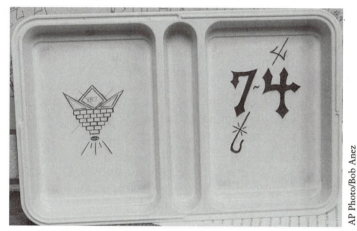

A food tray from the Montana State Prison in Deer Lodge, Montana, bears gang-related graffiti. Gang activity is part of the cultural environment of prison life and poses a significant threat to the safety of inmates and staff.

AP Photo/Bob Anez

addition, they form a powerful negotiating team to make demands on the administration. Because these groups are organized along racial and ethnic lines, the integrated prison environment is particularly subject to gang tension and conflict. Many inmates request protective custody to avoid becoming caught in the middle of a gang war.

Aside from placing large segments of the inmate population in protective custody, how can administrators address their gang problems? Several strategies involve the early detection of potential gang members, possibly through the classification process. Members often try to hide their affiliation from staff, but want to ensure that other inmates recognize them as gang members. Gang affiliation is marked through special clothing, haircuts, body piercings, hand signals, graffiti, tattoos, colors, and turf. Correctional staff can be trained to recognize these signs to identify potential gang members. In fact, gang training was provided to correctional officers in about two-thirds of institutions surveyed in 1999.[71] Other methods of early detection include self-admission, identification through a presentence investigation report, staff information, disciplinary records, records from prior incarcerations, confiscated documents or paraphernalia, and known associates.[72]

Once individuals are identified, they must be carefully observed. Close surveillance is necessary so patterns of gang behaviors can be determined. This will allow staff to possibly anticipate gang movements and behaviors, as well as to regulate the gang balance within the institution.

Gang activity is controlled within the institution in a variety of ways. Gang-involved inmates may be subject to the following restrictions:

- more frequent cell searches and/or strip searches
- an increase in their custody level designation
- limitations on their work and/or program participation
- more intensive monitoring of mail and phone contacts
- placement in administrative segregation
- transfers[73]

In addition, some states transfer gang members and leaders to higher-security facilities, then place them in a type of segregation. Other states, such as Illinois, are attempting to create correctional environments free from gang influence.

In 1996, the state of Illinois converted Taylorsville Correctional Center (TCC) into a "gang-free" facility, housing only inmates who were identified as nongang members. The idea was that if inmates were in an environment free from gang-related tensions and issues, they might be more willing to take advantage of offered programs and services. An evaluation of the program's implementation indicated mixed success. Disciplinary reports decreased, and both inmates and staff perceived the environment as safer. However, staff at other Illinois facilities have claimed that, within their facilities, disciplinary reports have increased, concentrations of more "dangerous" inmates have increased, and they feel more at risk than before the Taylorsville program.[74]

Institutional concerns are at the forefront of administrative agendas primarily because they are at the heart of institutional control and safety. Consequently, the control and safety of the institution significantly affect personnel and public safety. Threats to safety within the institutional environment, such as drugs, sex, violence, and gangs, probably will never be eliminated. These can be controlled, however, through the effective planning and implementation of policies and programs. While prevention is the ultimate goal, control is a significant step in that direction.

PROVISION OF SERVICES AND PROGRAMS

The role of the administrator is complicated. He or she must effectively control the operations of a correctional institution within philosophical, political, and legal boundaries in an environment rife with threats to personal and institutional security. In addition, he or she also must guide the organization toward the attainment of certain goals. Although scholars debate whether prisons should maintain a rehabilitative purpose, most agree that the goal of corrections is to "improve offenders both as an end in itself and as a means of reducing recidivism and of protecting society."[75] "Improving" offenders may refer to their physical and psychological health, as well as to their social, educational, and vocational needs and aptitudes. Toward this holistic improvement, correctional facilities may offer services that provide basic medical, dental, and psychological care, as well as programs geared either toward educational and vocational skills or toward treatment.

The administrator's role is to develop and implement policies related to the provision of these programs and services. He or she must ensure that the classification procedures are current, and screen inmates according to their rehabilitative needs. This entails being informed about current treatment options, any theoretical developments related to inmate rehabilitation, recent legislative initiatives or mandates, and trends or patterns in inmate intakes. When changes are necessary, the administration must alter policies and procedures accordingly and successfully communicate these changes throughout the institution. Additionally, the administration is responsible for overseeing the evaluation of existing policies and procedures related to inmate programs and services. Correctional facilities may conduct internal evaluations, or correctional systems may require periodic evaluation of programs and services offered within their jurisdictions. Alternately, facilities and systems may receive evaluation from an outside entity, such as a private research foundation or local university.

• Physical Health •

Inmate health care has become a critical issue in the administration and management of facilities. Dramatically increasing prison populations, an increasing proportion of older inmates, longer sentences, and fewer releases all mean that more offenders are going to be spending more time under the care of correctional facilities. As a result, prisons are becoming responsible for the health care of more inmates for longer periods of time. (See Chapter 10 for more on healthcare issues within prisons.)

This growing burden drastically affects a facility's budget. In recent years prison healthcare costs have been growing about 10 percent annually. A 2004 study found that prison medical costs totaled $3.7 billion a year and made up about 10 percent of correctional spending. Just one state, California, spent more than $1 billion on healthcare in fiscal year 2004-2005.[76]

A variety of factors influence the cost of inmate medical care. A significant proportion of the inmate population may not have received adequate health care for chronic disorders before they were incarcerated, so prison systems may be forced to make up for this deficiency. Other factors may be related to the state in which the system is located. Some states may be characterized by above-average medical costs, high rates of risky behaviors that cause disease, or a large number of high-cost medical cases, such as AIDS or kidney failures.[77]

Inmates also are more likely than others to have serious, undetected health problems requiring specialized care,[78] resulting from neglected health care in the past and the predominance of alcohol and other drug abuse. Such abuse is associated with medical problems such as gastrointestinal disorders, liver disease, and heart disease. Other conditions, such as venereal disease, HIV/AIDS, tuberculosis, and hepatitis, appear frequently in the correctional setting, requiring expensive long-term care.

Health services provided to inmates vary widely among facilities. The Federal Bureau of Prisons (BOP), for example, operates Federal Medical Facilities to provide special care for medically needy inmates. Most frequently, however, prison systems contract with local health professionals who provide on-site medical services. Additionally, the facility may have a contract with a local hospital, public health agency, or other healthcare agency for circumstances requiring more specialized or long-term treatment.

Contractual arrangements are used to some extent in nearly every correctional facility. How much they are used often depends on the ability of the facility to provide its own services. Moore lists six factors that hamper the provision of health services to inmates:

- health care is not a priority of the institution
- the institution has limited financial resources
- difficulties in staff recruitment
- the absence of a current manual of healthcare policies and procedures
- the isolation of the institution from community health care
- lack of a constituency for inmate health services[79]

Moore argues that an increasing reliance on contractual health services can address many of these difficulties. Prison administrators who institute policies involving contracted services will not have to worry about the recruitment of staff, the formulation of a medical program, or the creation and maintenance of appropriate conditions for the delivery of medical care.

Moore warns, however, that "too often the existence of appropriate policies on paper may not translate into quality health care" and that "the only criteria for filling positions may be that the candidate is licensed and breathing."[80] Administrators ultimately are responsible for making cost-effective and efficient contractual arrangements that deliver quality healthcare services to those incarcerated within their facilities. To accomplish this, the administration must create a well-planned contract that clearly defines all expectations related to service delivery, includes payment provisions that reward efficiency, and institutes monitoring procedures that quickly detect and resolve problems.

• Mental Health •

Mental health services encompass counseling (group and individual) and medication for inmates diagnosed as suffering from mental health problems such as depression, anxiety, and stress, or more serious ailments such as obsessive-compulsive disorders and schizophrenia. Prison staff psychologists usually handle the more common ailments, while the prison contracts with outside psychiatrists for the more serious problems.[81]

Part of the classification process used when new inmates are admitted to correctional facilities involves extensive psychological testing to determine whether and to what extent they need services. Psychological plans can be developed to address each inmate's particular needs, such as individual therapy, group counseling, or prescribed medication. More serious problems may require that the inmate be transferred to a facility that specializes in the care, treatment, and custody of mentally ill offenders. As noted in Chapter 7, it is estimated that more than half of all prison and jail inmates have a mental health problem.[82]

Mental illness is usually associated with a host of other problems. Mentally ill offenders, for example, may be more likely than other offenders to have been homeless prior to their arrest, to have been sexually or physically abused in their lives, or to have ever received public assistance. Mentally ill women are more likely to be victims of sexual or physical abuse than are mentally ill men. The mentally ill also were more likely to be violent repeat offenders; about 53 percent of mentally ill inmates had committed a violent offense, compared to 46 percent of other inmates, and more than 75 percent of the mentally ill had prior sentences to incarceration or probation.[83] Interestingly, only 61 percent of mentally ill inmates in state prisons and 41 percent in local jails reported that they had received treatment for their illnesses, primarily consisting of medication (34% of those receiving treatment).[84]

• Inmate Programs •

The second biggest inmate-related expense generally is for the provision and operation of inmate programs. These programs involve "academic and vocational training, substance abuse awareness and treatment programs, religious activities, parenting, job search preparation, life skills training, recreation and exercise, and related activities."[85] It is difficult to provide estimates on how much states spend per inmate per day because many states cannot separate inmate program spending from general operating costs. One reason is that other agencies often pick up some of the costs. State health departments may provide substance abuse treatment, or state departments of education may help pay for the costs of academic or vocational training. However, Stephan estimates that, on average, states spent $3.28 per day per inmate on programming.[86] Regionally, these expenses ranged from a low of $1.74 in the South to a high of $5.32 in the Northeast.

• Substance Abuse Treatment •

Substance abuse treatment is actually a hybrid creation that is part medical service, part psychological service, and part educational program. Again, inmates are targeted for treatment after the classification procedure. Offenders with self-admitted drug problems or those with drug-related offenses are good candidates. Most prisons with substance abuse programming usually must maintain waiting lists of offenders because these types of programs are in such great demand. Recent reports indicate that more than half of state prisoners and 45 percent of federal prisoners show either drug dependence or drug abuse.[87]

These programs attempt to address the complex relationship between drugs (including alcohol) and behavior. While the correlation between drug use and criminal behavior is very strong, research that indicates causation is lacking. Correctional systems, however, continue to focus on alcohol and other drugs as correlates of crime because public belief in this connection is pervasive. To illustrate, 40 percent of state prisoners and about half of federal prisoners had participated in drug treatment or programs after admission to prison.[88]

These programs can be effective at reducing reoffending. Treatment while in prison and while under post-incarceration supervision (e.g., parole) can reduce recidivism by about 50 percent.[89] With the Violent Crime Control Act of 1994, the federal government provided for funds to be made available to states for the implementation of Residential Substance Abuse Treatment (RSAT) programs. All states may participate in the program, but sites will only be funded if the following guidelines are met:

- The offender is involved in the program for six to 12 months;

- The residential treatment is in a separate facility from the general correctional population;

- There is a focus on the inmate's substance abuse problems;

- The program aims to develop the inmate's behavioral, social, cognitive, vocational, and related skills to address the substance abuse problems;

- The program uses urinalysis and/or other acceptable forms of alcohol an other drug monitoring of qualified inmate participants.[90]

Preliminary evaluations of state participation in this program indicate that states have increased their substance abuse treatment capacity within correctional facilities. Participating states also have developed screening and assessment tools that identify inmates amenable to treatment, which has resulted in better use of correctional resources. Evaluations of RSAT programs' impact on recidivism are still ongoing, but results from Delaware indicate significant success, especially when inmates are provided with continued aftercare upon release from custodial facilities.[91]

Some scholars argue, however, that the excitement over the preliminary success stories may overshadow practical limitations on nationwide implementation. Barriers to developing treatment programs in correctional settings, such as a limited availability and emphasis on aftercare, or the possibility of a coercive environment, may limit their effectiveness.[92] These researchers worry that, although model programs such as therapeutic communities have shown encouraging results, these model programs may not be adequately replicated. The authors claim that "the rapid and poorly planned implementation of correctional treatment programs places these [non–model programs] at risk of being less effective than the programs after which they were modeled."[93]

In addition to institutionally based programs, many correctional facilities offer inmates the opportunity to participate in self-help programs, such as Alcoholics Anonymous (AA) and Narcotics Anonymous (NA), which are coordinated and implemented by the inmates themselves. The leaders of these types of groups are usually inmates who previously have struggled with substance abuse problems but who are reformed or recovering.

• Educational and Vocational Programs •

Programs and services are implemented within the correctional environment because, at some point and at some level, research has indicated a link between the program or service and the goals of the institution (e.g., rehabilitation). Nowhere is this more readily apparent than with inmate educational and vocational programs.

Research has shown a considerable relationship between education and behavior. Moreover, education is related to employment. Correctional populations tend to be less fortunate in both education and employment in comparison to the general, nonincarcerated population. In 1997, 41 percent of state prison inmates had not finished high school. About 45 percent of prisoners were either unemployed or working part-time during the month before their arrest. A full 70 percent of the inmates reported incomes of less than $15,000 per year.[94]

Educational and vocational programs are a significant part of correctional systems. In 2000, 91 percent of state prisons and all federal prisons had educational programs for inmates, with the possibility of obtaining a high school diploma or GED; 27 percent of state prisons and 81 percent of federal prisons offered college courses.[95] More than half (56%) of state prisons and more than 90 percent of federal prisons had vocational training programs (welding, carpentry, electronics), and most facilities offered inmates the opportunity to participate in some type of work program. The most common work was related to facility support services, such as the prison laundry, kitchen, or facility maintenance.

Vocational training is especially useful. One study found that inmates who completed a vocational training program in a federal prison were 33 percent less likely to recidivate than inmates who did not.[96] The authors argue that a greater likelihood of employment was the reason for the reduced recidivism.

The philosophy underlying the provision of these programs is that inmates will be released with the educational aptitudes or vocational skills required to secure and to maintain basic employment. Often, a portion of an inmate's educational experience within the facility is devoted to job readiness, that is, teaching inmates how to complete applications, how to interview, and how to follow directions and work with other people.

Administratively, the challenge in providing inmate services and programs is to balance budgetary constraints with the need for quality and effectiveness. Eventually, this becomes a question of "pay now or pay later." If a correctional administrator hopes to save money by restricting services and providing programs of questionable quality, he or she may eventually pay more when an inmate fails to receive what he or she needs to avoid reincarceration, and the facility ends up housing that same offender over and over again. Administrators who realize the link between effective programs, quality services, and reduced recidivism rates may indeed save money by not succumbing to the "revolving door" pattern.

MANAGING CORRECTIONAL PERSONNEL

While the most obvious and most publicly scrutinized tasks of the correctional administrator are related to the development of policies and procedures to manage inmate behaviors and the provision of programs and services, a significant portion of administrative responsibility is devoted to the management of correctional personnel. Correctional facilities are not ideal workplaces, and the role of the correctional employee is complex and sometimes dangerous. In addition, this field is characterized by rapid growth, given significant expansions in inmate populations. Role complexity and the institutional environment, combined with the relationship of the correctional process to that of institutional and public safety, contribute to a lack of qualified applicants for correctional positions.

Another consideration is that correctional administration must be conducted within the government rubric, which is characterized by political bureaucracies and associated "red tape." With the growing popularity of the private prison industry, government-supported facilities are discovering that they must compete for personnel, public support, and money. Private facilities have many attractions for potential employees, not the least of which is the absence of government bureaucracy.

One reason that talented correctional employees may choose to work in the private rather than the public sector is that the rigid, hierarchical structure of government entities reduces administrative flexibility, restricts imaginative solutions, and impedes innovation. DiIulio suggests, however, that despite the governmental umbrella, correctional managers can successfully lead and innovate if they follow three basic principles.[97] First, administrators should "stick to the basics of inmate care and custody" and follow the MBWA principle—"management by walking around." Second, these administrators should be "open to both human resource and technical innovations" to aid them in basic management. Third, administrators must be realistic enough to understand their roles as public servants who operate under intense public scrutiny. They must be "pragmatic professionals and political realists" who are "responsive to reasonable external demands."[98]

Despite the challenges in attracting and retaining qualified personnel, administrators recognize that qualified staff members are crucial to the attainment of institutional goals. In fact, Freeman calls correctional employees "valuable investments that provide long-term returns to the organization if they are effectively developed and utilized."[99] Responsibility for the effective development and utilization of personnel belongs to the correctional administrator. It entails several concerns. First and foremost, qualified and dedicated applicants must be recruited. Once hired, they must be trained. As they progress, their skills must be developed through continuing education programs, and they may be groomed for promotion to higher ranks. Retention of these qualified and trained employees becomes a major concern because of high turnover rates that often characterize correctional institutions.

Intimately related to the recruitment, development, and retention of officers are issues related to the care and maintenance of their personal and professional needs as correctional employees. Correctional facilities inherently involve unique concerns for those who work within the walls. Health-related concerns, including stress, exposure to communicable diseases, and psychological well-being, affect the work of correctional employees and should be priorities for the administration.

• Health Concerns •

As indicated earlier, health concerns become magnified within the prison environment. This is true both for inmates and for correctional staff. The institutional environment affords the opportunity for the spread of several communicable diseases that are better contained and more easily treatable among the general public. Tuberculosis, hepatitis, and HIV have troubled correctional institutions for years and have become significant management concerns.

Controlling the spread of such illnesses within the close correctional environment is not easy. Staff are sometimes affected. In New York, for example, several inmates and one correctional officer died in 1991 from tuberculosis. This unfortunate incident spurred the New York Department of Correctional Services (DOCS) to significantly redesign the delivery of health care for both inmates and employees.[100] The major change was to create a unit of communicable disease–consultant nurses that provided the staffing necessary to enhance the disease prevention program.

Subsequently, the DOCS established five elements committed to protect the health, well-being, and safety of its employees: (1) education and training, (2) employee assistance programs, (3) monitoring and surveillance, (4) health services, and (5) clear directives, policies, and planning. These elements receive widespread support from the governor, the Corrections Commissioner, and employee unions.

Employees receive wellness training, which begins during an employees' initial training at the academy, and can continue through retirement. They are taught safety education, disease prevention, federal and state standards, the safe handling of chemical agents, and stress training. Ongoing education is part of each employee's 40 annual training hours.

Staff and inmates also are monitored for acute infectious diseases. The DOCS mandates and provides annual tuberculosis testing for everyone in the system. Staff and inmate education is also important in the recognition of symptoms to enhance early detection.

HIV/AIDS prevention is a major focus of the DOCS efforts. The New York system was among the first to recognize the need for intense prevention efforts targeted at this disease because significant portions of this system's inmate population are infected. The DOCS maintains stock kits containing medications that have been suggested as prophylaxis to reduce the risk of acquiring the infection after potential exposure.

Lastly, the DOCS maintains current and clear directives, policies, and planning initiatives as the "backbone of employee health, well-being and safety."[101] A Health and Safety Committee, which includes health services workers, members of employee unions, and facilities-planning personnel, meets regularly to review these written guidelines and to propose revisions, if necessary. Wright notes that each employee is entitled to work in a safe and healthy environment and that "the key to meeting the staff health and wellness needs of each employee is to implement an employee wellness plan that protects against known risks and is adaptable to meet future ones."[102]

• Stress •

The administration's ability to recognize and respond to staff health-care needs is critical to maintaining good personnel relations. However, correctional staff often have additional problems that may be overlooked or minimized. Along with obvious health threats like tuberculosis, hepatitis, and HIV, correctional workers may face a potentially greater threat from stress, the symptoms of which may go unnoticed. In turn, stress may lead to a variety of physical and emotional illnesses, such as high blood pressure, cardiovascular disease, depression, and substance abuse. Stress also affects the organization in both effectiveness and turnover.

Research on stress has shown that a significant source of stress for many correctional employees is the organization. The good news is that supervisors can make a difference. For example, a recent study of occupational stress in Australian correctional officers found that supervisor support was a strong predictor of both job satisfaction and work-related psychological well-being. More importantly, the findings suggested "that adverse psychological outcomes associated with organizational stress can be avoided to some extent, if adequate levels of supervisor support are accessible."[103] In addition, if correctional agencies adopt the principles of effective treatment programs as suggested by the research on correctional interventions, they may improve employee job satisfaction and reduce stress and burnout. As research on job burnout has indicated, part of the problem is a lack of a sense of personal accomplishment.[104] So if correctional organizations can implement effective interventions with offenders, the effectiveness of those interventions should translate into higher feelings of personal accomplishment and less burnout for correctional employees.

• Employee Organizations •

Although correctional administrations generally are responsive to the needs of correctional staff, bureaucratic governmental organizations sometimes need prodding to initiate action. One way in which correctional employees may emphasize their concerns is through the power of employee unions. Correctional administration, especially as it pertains to human resource issues, is often impacted by the presence of labor organizations or unions designed to protect the interests of correctional officers.

The relationship between these organizations and the correctional administration is "an integral part of prison management."[105] Whenever individuals work within a highly structured, hierarchical environment that is characterized by rules, regulations, policies, and procedures that dictate behaviors, they may feel a loss of control and become dissatisfied with certain institutional conditions. Just as inmates seek to redress their grievances through the formation of inmate coalitions and through the filing of lawsuits, so too may correctional officers.

Many government agencies are unionized. Phillips and McConnell imply, however, that correctional environments can remain union-free if management is sensitive to employee needs. In fact, they state that "the formation of a union is (at least in part) evidence of an inability on the part of managers to properly balance the equally legitimate needs of the workplace and the worker."[106]

The authors cite a 1970s study of 379 union elections wherein 74 percent were won by the unions. Three reasons were offered to explain the overwhelming success of the union movement: (1) "apparent management indifference to complaints" about employee wages or other economic issues and "the organization's lack of credibility with employees about issues such as costs and operating circumstances"; (2) "antimanagement sentiment . . . brought about by employee perceptions of poor working conditions"; and (3) "anxiety produced by widespread lack of knowledge about what was truly taking place."[107]

The common thread seems to be communication. As in most hierarchical environments, communication difficulties are the source of most problems. Directives issued by the administration may not reach those at the bottom levels, which may lead to confusion, misperception, mistrust, anxiety, and stress. Unions offer individuals the opportunity to have their concerns addressed by an entity that will listen and has the collective bargaining power to effect real change. Individuals may attempt to convey their needs and concerns to management for years and may never receive any sort of satisfactory conclusion. Unions, on the other hand, are much more effective because they utilize the power of groups of individuals who are reaching for some common goal. This power is enhanced by the National Labor Relations Act (NLRA) and the National Labor Relations Board (NLRB). Under the NLRA, a union can charge an organization with unfair labor practices. If the NLRB rules in the union's favor, the union will obtain the power to operate as a recognized bargaining agent without the requirement of a representation election.

When unions are present in the correctional environment, the administration must function differently. Union contracts will be developed that detail specific rules and regulations within which the daily activities of the facility must operate. Often, managing within a union environment becomes somewhat easier because a great deal of subjective interpretation is replaced by contract specifications. Regular union meetings often provide an opportunity for union officials and the administration to monitor the development of institutional problems and work together on addressing them. However, Phillips and McConnell warn that "individual managers are [not] relieved from their responsibility to communicate with their staff" and that "the presence of a union does not mean [managers] can back off in . . . communications with employees and simply wave the contract at them."[108]

The administrative challenges of managing personnel within a correctional environment require the creation and maintenance of a delicate balance between institutional needs and the needs of the human beings who are involved. Too often, institutional needs and human needs conflict with one another. Individuals, for example, need to feel they have valuable contributions to make in the workplace and that their welfare is of utmost concern to their employers. They need to feel fairly compensated and to have their grievances justly addressed. Frequently, however, institutional requirements dictate that administrators focus on rules, regulations, policies, procedures, budgets, politics, and legal concerns.

For example, an administrator may realize that pay rates are too low. Budgetary constraints, however, may not allow salary adjustments unless the number of personnel is reduced or benefits are cut. Reducing personnel is an institutional concern that affects staff and inmate safety. Reducing benefits when salaries already are too low may seriously damage morale and lead to increased rates of turnover. In either case, institutional safety is again a consideration. An effective administrator, however, understands that without a dedicated, professional staff, there is no institution. This realization should motivate correctional administrators to pay particular attention to personnel concerns and address them without sacrificing safety or other institutional goals.

BOX 13.2

Top Reasons Why Correctional Officers Leave Their Jobs

The Georgia Department of Corrections tries to track the reasons why correctional officers quit their jobs. Turnover in 2004 was more than 20 percent. The top reasons for leaving are the following, with the percentage of officers stating that reason for leaving:

1. Other job opportunities, 42%

2. Infrequent pay increases, 14%

3. One's efforts not well rewarded, 13%

4. Entry salary too low, 12%

5. Leave availability, 11%

6. Health insurance, 10%

Percentages do not add up to 100% due to rounding.

Source: Adapted from Udechukwu, I., W. Harrington, T. Manyak, S. Segal, and S. Graham. "The Georgia Department of Corrections: An Exploratory Reflection on Correctional officer Turnover and Its Correlates." *Public Personnel Management* 36 (3):247-269.

THE FUTURE OF CORRECTIONAL MANAGEMENT AND ADMINISTRATION

In addition to existing challenges outlined in this chapter, the field of corrections faces a future of changes. These changes undoubtedly will bring new challenges to correctional administrators, who must constantly be aware of developments in the field that impact their tasks. While these future considerations are diverse, they all can be related to rapidly growing correctional populations and the financial strains that result from attempts to handle them effectively and efficiently. In fact, the most critical issue facing correctional management is the pressure of growing prisoner populations.

• Addressing the Costly Growth in Prison Populations •

As noted in several chapters, prisons are bursting at the seams. The Bureau of Justice Statistics put the prisoner population at more than 1.5 million at yearend 2006,[109] but even more recently the Pew Center on the States reported that one in every 100 American adults is now incarcerated in a jail or prison.[110] A dramatic example is found in Florida, where the inmate population increased from 53,000 in 1993 to more than 97,000 in 2007. Based on projections, Florida will run out of prison bed space in 2009 and will need to add more than 15,000 beds to have enough space for future prisoners.[111]

The growth in prisons and prisoners is costly. Thirteen states now spend more than $1 billion a year on their correctional systems. California spent almost $9 billion on corrections in 2007, and Texas spent approximately $3.3 billion.[112] Some of this is attributable to overtime pay. In 2006, for example, California spent more than one-half billion dollars in overtime pay, with 15 percent of correctional employees earning at least $25,000 in overtime pay that year. Six correctional employees earned more than the $212,000 salary of Governor Arnold Schwarzenegger.[113]

Go to www.pewcenteronthestates.org to find their recent report *One in 100: Behind Bars in America: 2008*. This report gives recent statistics, including statistics for each state on prison populations and prison costs and suggestions for managing prison growth.

This spending on corrections has been affecting other state spending priorities dramatically. On average, states are spending just under 7 percent, or one of every 15 dollars, in state discretionary spending on corrections. Some states are spending one of every 10 or 11 dollars. Meanwhile, spending on priorities like education is slipping. Between 1987 and 2007, state spending on education, adjusted to 2007 dollars, increased 21 percent while spending on corrections increased 127 percent.[114]

BOX 13.3

Getting a New Prison Not Always a Plus for the Locality

Many counties have tried to have new prisons built within their boundaries on the belief that a new prison brings positive benefits such as new jobs. A study of prison siting in New York State noted some problems in this area. First, only about 33 to 40 percent of the jobs go to local residents. The rest go to residents of other areas. Second, not all the jobs that do go to local residents are full-time jobs. Third, the county loses tax revenue if a private company had owned the site prior to the prison construction. Fourth, a new prison can cause environmental concerns such as water treatment and waste disposal issues. The authors caution that their research is not definitive; more work needs to be done in this area.

Source: Adapted from King, R.S., and M. Mauer (2004). "An Analysis of Prison Siting in Rural Communities." *Criminology and Public Policy* 3:453-480.

A significant part of this spending is for healthcare for inmates. California spent just over $1 billion on health care in one recent fiscal year. For example, it can cost as much as $30,000 to treat one case of Hepatitis C.[115] Moreover, the graying of the prison population is costly. The average cost of housing an older prisoner is $70,000, which is two to three times more costly than a younger prisoner.[116]

Several states have started to tackle the problem of prison growth and costs. On the front end, states are expanding community corrections and diverting offenders away from prison. The use of drug courts is one such expansion of community corrections. Another way to reduce prison admissions is to expand the options for dealing with probationers or parolees who violate the conditions of their supervision: the so-called technical violators. Instead of sending technical violators to prison, states are now using sanctions such as day-reporting centers, electronic monitoring, and community service. For example, Kansas offered grants to community correctional agencies to cut revocations of probation and parole by 20 percent.[117]

Another strategy is to ensure that parole agencies are granting paroles at the desired level. In other words, parole agencies are checking to make sure that they are actually releasing as many prisoners as they targeted to be out on parole. And states are using "earned time" as an incentive to encourage inmates to complete educational or treatment programs in prison and to behave well. Nevada, for example, recently expanded the use of earned time credits, which allow prisoners to get out early.[118]

States such as Kansas, Nevada, and Texas have taken steps to reduce state spending on corrections. This is clearly one of the most important tasks facing correctional managers.

• Adopting Evidence-Based Practices •

A second critical issue facing management is the call to adopt "evidence-based practices." What this means is that managers are encouraged to try to find out what the research evidence indicates is effective and efficient. "Effective" means that a practice achieves the goals and objectives it claims it can achieve. "Efficient" means that a practice achieves what it claims with acceptable use of resources such as financial resources. In other words, being efficient means using practices that do not make excessive use of budgets and staff. If two practices are both effective—they both achieve the desired end results—efficiency dictates that we choose the practice that costs less financially or makes fewer demands on resources such as the number of personnel needed or the time frame necessary to achieve the results.

The ideal of evidence-based practices is research using an experimental or quasi-experimental design including a control group. Such designs provide the best evidence; they are the designs used in pharmaceutical research to test the effectiveness of new medicines.

There are several evidence-based choices for administrators in corrections at this time. The most important evidence-based practice is the need to implement treatment programs that follow the directions that research has shown to be effective. As noted in other chapters, the treatment research has indicated that effective treatment programs address the principles of risk, need, and responsivity. The risk principle means that treatment efforts should be directed to high-risk offenders. The need principle means that treatment efforts should address criminogenic needs, needs that are directly related to criminal behavior. An example of a criminogenic need is addiction; an example of a noncriminogenic need is self-esteem. The responsivity principle notes that treatment personnel should tailor programs to the specific needs and conditions of the particular offender.[119]

Additionally, it has been proven that cognitive-behavioral programs are effective. On the other hand, programs that simply address factors such as self-awareness are not effective.

What this line of research shows correctional managers is the need to implement these principles and programs in prisons, halfway houses, probation and parole agencies, group homes, and community correctional agencies. Research on effective treatment interventions indicates that successful programs can reduce recidivism significantly, for example, from a baseline of 50 percent down to 30 percent.[120]

A clarification is critical: the evidence-based research on correctional treatment does not mean that prisons, parole, and probation are currently using effective programs and that they need to continue to do so. As Lipsey and Cullen point out, many correctional programs involve education and vocational training that do not follow the principles of effective interventions. A dramatic example of this is vocational training that is simply a work assignment.[121] Moreover, some programs just ignore the research. A recent program in Los Angeles targeted at repeat juvenile offenders tried to build self-esteem and used individual and group counseling even though the research has found cognitive-behavioral approaches to be most effective.[122] Related to this, even if a prison implements a program that the research has shown to work, that does not mean that the prison will necessarily implement the program the way it is supposed to be run. Faulty implementation can mean that it will not be effective with prisoners.[123]

So the challenge is for correctional managers to make sure that they are familiar with what the correctional research indicates is effective and then to try to faithfully put such programs into place.

• Additional Evidence-Based Suggestions for Corrections •

While implementing evidence-based treatment programs is critical, research offers additional suggestions for correctional managers. Here we discuss some of the suggestions that recent research offers for improving corrections. Recently there has been a great deal of attention given to reentry, prisoners returning to their communities after release from prison, mainly because so many prisoners are being released each year.

• Reentry and Parole •

Reentry is one problem that correctional managers must address if the American public is going to consider corrections successful. The Urban Institute has been conducting research on reentry in four states. Here we note some of the findings from Cleveland, Ohio, based on interviews with almost 300 men who were interviewed one year after release from prison.

Critical reentry factors are obtaining employment, close contact with supportive family members, stable housing, and abstaining from drug use. One year after release, about half of the men reported that their housing was temporary. A year after release, about half of the former prisoners were employed but less than 40 percent were employed full-time. More than half reported a chronic physical condition. More than one-third of the men reported recent alcohol or other drug use. The men who returned to prison cited drug use as the most frequent reason for their return to prison. Finally, nearly one-third reported committing a crime (typically drug possession and dealing), and 40 percent reported being arrested.[124] In short, the evidence-based research is quite clear that prisoners reentering society have several significant problems that need to be addressed.

Less clear, however, is how to tackle those problems successfully. One suggestion for parole is to use behavioral contracting. Joan Petersilia notes that traditional parole contracts are one-sided agreements telling the parolee all the things he or she cannot do and specifying the negative sanctions if he or she violates the terms. She argues that incentive-based parole contracts would be much more effective in encouraging prosocial behavior. She contends that early release is the incentive that parolees most desire and suggests that the maximum parole term be three years, with the parolee able to reduce that to only six months if he or she remains crime-free, completes victim restitution, and participates in self-improvement programs or remains fully employed. Because the first six months are critical, every parolee would serve at least that amount of time on parole. Because remaining arrest-free for one year reduces the chances of recidivism, offering incentives to get off parole well before the three-year maximum term would encourage offenders to stay crime-free and participate in intervention efforts that would enhance their chances of staying that way.[125]

Contrary to Petersilia's call for behavioral contracting in parole and using incentives to make parole a year or less with incentives is Farabee's call for making parole considerably tougher, having much smaller caseloads, and using GPS tracking. He also wants parole to be three years in length and to be extended with any violation of parole rules. He does not, however, rule out treatment on parole. If a parolee thinks that he or she needs education or job training or substance abuse treatment, Farabee suggests vouchers that the parolee could redeem with community treatment providers. He argues that his suggestions follow the principles of classical criminology by emphasizing deterrence and the free will of the offender,[126] and that they are evidence-based. However, as noted above, most researchers conclude that the research on correctional treatment does show that programs can be effective in reducing recidivism.[127] Therefore, most researchers want to make treatment essential, not just an option like Farabee suggests.

Michael Jacobson, a former Commissioner of Corrections and Probation in New York City, agrees with Petersilia that parole programs need to focus on the time right after release as the critical adjustment period. Jacobson argues that it makes sense to devote the most services to parolees at this important juncture. He disagrees with Farabee's call to use vouchers. Jacobson thinks that government-paid parole officers would resist vouchers because it would threaten their jobs. He also thinks that much of the prison overcrowding crisis is due to states returning too many parole rule violators to prison. He argues that states should use other means to punish parole violators, including weekends in jail and day-reporting centers where parolees can perform community service and also get treatment.[128]

There are some promising signs that reentry programs can be effective. In California, the Preventing Parolee Crime Program (PPCP) was a multi-dimensional, parole-based reintegration program that included substance abuse treatment, employment readiness training, and job placement assistance. Participants had lower recidivism than nonparticipants, and increasing levels of participation (meeting more program goals) were associated with even lower recidivism.[129] In North Dakota, a reentry program included enhanced services (compared to traditional ones), community service by the parolees, parole officer supervision, and supervision by surveillance officers who performed additional home visits and drug testing. Program parolees were less likely to test positive for drugs and had a 60 percent lower likelihood of being arrested after controlling for risk factors.[130] While these programs are far from definitive, they suggest that there are ways to improve the reentry process for at least some offenders.

A change that could open up employment opportunities for returning offenders is to "ban the box." This refers to eliminating the "box" on city employment application forms asking the applicant if he or she has ever been convicted of a past crime. A government agency could do a criminal background check or inquiry only after a tentative offer of employment has been made. At that point in the hiring process, a criminal record would only be relevant if it created an unacceptable risk that the applicant could not fulfill the job's requirements. In Boston, there are no background checks except for positions involving youths, the elderly or the disabled, and the police department. Boston has also applied its "ban the box" policy to private contractors who work with the city. All of these efforts are intended to help offenders find jobs. They are based on research that has found an inverse relationship between having a criminal record and employability.[131]

Bushway and Sweeten offer a more nuanced argument. They argue that, in the short term, many offenders released from prison are at high risk of reoffending. However, after a few years, the risk of reoffending drops to the same level of risk as everyone else in the population. Therefore, they argue that employment bans may be necessary in the short term but should cease after a period of time. They also note that a complete ban on discriminating against ex-offenders could very well lead to employers using race as a proxy for risk and thus discriminating against all blacks, not just black (or white) ex-offenders. They also note that some bans affect loans, grants, and work-study assistance for getting an education.[132]

Another suggestion is to abandon felon disenfranchisement policies. Felon disenfranchisement is the denial of voting privileges to those convicted of a felony. All states except Maine, Massachusetts, Vermont, and Utah have such laws. It has been argued that part of the reason for the spread of such laws in the South was racist efforts to prevent blacks from voting in the post-Reconstruction Era.

Crutchfield argues that felon disenfranchisement increases racial inequalities in crime and criminal justice. He argues, for example, that the war on drugs, particularly at the federal level, has been waged disproportionately on blacks. For example, 28 percent of those charged with a drug offense in U.S. District Courts in 1999 were black. To disenfranchise these voters does not add deterrent value to their sentences but does hinder their reintegration into society "if civic reengagement is important to the prevention of reoffending."[133]

All of these suggestions are intended to address the reentry crisis. With more than 650,000 prisoners returning to communities every year and with all the problems noted, it is clear that correctional managers need to address reentry issues. Otherwise, many of these returning prisoners will simply wind up back in prison, contributing again to the population problem noted earlier.

• Privatization •

As an alternative way to deal with the population growth issue noted above, some jurisdictions have turned to private prisons to handle increasing correctional needs. Private prisons are built and operated by private businesses. They contract with government entities to provide community corrections services or house convicted offenders. Private facilities also may contract to offer intermediate sanctions and services for offenders, such as substance abuse counseling and anger management.

As of yearend 2006, more than 110,000 (113,791) state and federal prisoners were held in privately operated facilities. This was a 5 percent increase over the number held in 2005. The federal system had almost 28,000 prisoners in privately operated facilities.[134] The Corrections Corporation of America (CCA) operates about 72,500 beds and manages approximately 70,000 inmates.[135]

Proponents of privatization argue that this movement "elevates industry performance as a whole in several key respects: taxpayer cost savings, quality assurance, and operational effectiveness."[136] Opponents, however, claim that any potential savings result from cutting corners in staffing, services, and security. An inmate in one private prison alleged, for example, that the prison cut corners by serving ground turkey and processed meats and by providing only limited recreational equipment.[137] Opponents also cite abuses such as escapes and assaults that occurred at a private prison that was opened before guards had sufficient training.[138]

What seems clear is that if a state opts for even partial privatization, monitoring is required to ensure that the private company operates its prison(s) in accordance with its contract with the state. Companies cannot simply be trusted to be benevolent. The history of prisons has clearly shown that both public and private prisons have had problems. Neither government nor private operators can simply be relied on to operate humane and decent prisons without any oversight.

• Riot Prevention •

If management does not do its job, whether in a public or private prison, one possible consequence is a prison riot. Two famous prison riots were in Attica, New York, and near Sante Fe, New Mexico. Thirty-two inmates and 11 guards died at Attica, and 33 inmates died in New Mexico.

Boin and Van Duin argue that poor living conditions and deficient institutional security can set the stage for a riot. Another critical factor is how the administration responds if a disturbance begins. Proper crisis management can defuse a crisis before it becomes a riot, and conversely, poor crisis management can escalate a crisis into a riot. Some critical parts of proper crisis management include planning, assigning roles for crisis situations, flexibility, and resilience.[139]

• Changing Focus •

Society's efforts to develop solutions to problems of correctional administration and management also include reconsidering the focus of corrections. As previously discussed, the focus is driven by the prevailing philosophy that society and society's representative (i.e., government) embraces at any given time. As mentioned throughout this text, while correctional practices over the years have reflected a hodgepodge of philosophies, one usually tends to prevail depending on societal trends. These philosophies influence correctional policies, which in turn influence the work of correctional administrators.

Currently, the dominant correctional philosophy appears to be retributive. All jurisdictions have embraced some form of three-strikes legislation, mandatory minimum sentences, or truth-in-sentencing laws.[140] Many states have abolished or significantly restricted parole releases.[141] These policies have contributed significantly to overcrowding and all the associated ills discussed in previous sections.

However, the fallout from get-tough policies has forced consideration of alternatives. As we have noted, states such as California are facing escalating cost pressures due to prison population increases. As a result, such states are turning to experts for ways to reduce prison populations and costs. Most positively, a few states have already begun to

BOX 13.4

How Not to Prevent a Prison Riot: Lessons from Australia

The Woodford Correctional Centre opened in March, 1997. Three weeks later a major riot erupted. This prison was a public prison but one that tried to use lessons from the private sector. Specifically, the prison promised to deliver "value for money" (Rynne, Harding, and Wortley, 2008:127). Rynne, Harding, and Wortley argue that the following factors contributed to the riot.

1. More than one-half (58%) of the staff had no prior custodial corrections experience.

2. The general manager (warden) had no prior experience as a general manager (warden).

3. The prison adopted new unit and case management approaches (continual presence of officers in the living areas and no physical barriers between staff and inmates) too quickly.

4. Filling the new prison too quickly, with maximum capacity reached in one month.

5. Program staff and guard staff wore very similar uniforms so both prisoners and staff had difficulty knowing which staff were which.

6. A new meal preparation and delivery system failed to deliver hot meals.

7. Despite prisoner protests, the prison planned to ban smoking. Although this ban was not actually carried out, the plan greatly agitated the inmates.

8. The authors think that much of the difficulty stemmed from the desire of the public sector to win a market test against the private sector. In their opinion, this would not have happened if a private company had won the bid to operate this prison because "the commercial realities of profit margin would drive the private sector to require a contract variation to fund more resources" (Rynne, Harding, and Wortley, 2008:137). Given that the Corrections Corporation of America, a private operator, opened a prison too quickly at Youngstown, Ohio, at about the same time and experienced two fatal stabbings, 47 assaults, and several escapes (Mobley and Geis, 2005), it appears that all prison operators, public or private, need to apply sound management principles or suffer the consequences.

Sources: Rynne, J., R.W. Harding, and R. Wortley (2008). "Market Testing and Prison Riots: How Public-Sector Commercialization Contributed to a Prison Riot." *Criminology and Public Policy* 7:117-142. Mobley, A., and G. Geis (2005). "The Corrections Corporation of America: aka The Prison Realty Trust, Inc." In M.C. Braswell, B.R. McCarthy, and B.J. McCarthy, *Justice, Crime and Ethics*, 5th ed. Newark, NJ: LexisNexis Matthew Bender.

implement suggestions such as day-reporting centers for parole violators to try to reduce costs. It is possible that budget pressures, if nothing else, will influence states to turn to practices that are less punitive.

The future holds promise for corrections as we consider restorative and community justice,[142] specialized courts, innovative sentencing structures and options, and technologically advanced alternatives.[143] The task for correctional administrators will be to adapt—to respond effectively to impending changes while simultaneously balancing institutional, personnel, inmate, and public needs.

CONCLUSION

Correctional administration is a complex process, influenced externally by prevailing correctional, governmental, political, and legal philosophies. These philosophies are intimately related. Political party preferences determine the governmental composition, which in turn helps to form legal philosophies. The correctional philosophies supported by citizens are reflected in their political choices. It would be nearly impossible to effect a change in one without impacting any of the others. As a result, the ability of correctional administrators to initiate change or to institute far-reaching reform is somewhat constrained.

Internal influences also help define the role of the correctional administrator. Behaviors and social problems that helped inmates find their way into the correctional environment often follow them into the institution and become magnified. Concentrated groups of persons with various criminal histories and various backgrounds, many with violent tendencies or substance addictions, all share one commonality: they are unwillingly under the control of the state. It often has been said that the inmates run the institutions and that, if they really wanted to, they could take over an institution at any time. Inmates certainly outnumber officers. In a sense, then, the inmates are instrumental in determining the correctional environment and helping to shape the role of the administrator. This relationship, however, is symbiotic. The administrator responds to the inmate culture by developing or changing institutional policy to affect inmate behavior when necessary and working to ensure the safety of the inmates, the staff, and the public.

These external and internal factors dictate, to a great extent, the programs and services that a correctional system offers. Theoretically, inmate need is the primary determinant of both services and programs. Such services and programs however, are created and offered within the boundaries set by the external influences (i.e., the law, governmental policies, etc.). Basic services (e.g., health care) must be provided, but the extent of those services is often very limited (e.g., prison physicians may only be available one day a week) and programs usually are not required.

Correctional administrators must operate within narrowly defined boundaries, but they are not powerless to effect change. Effective administrators can recognize and respond to the need for change within their institutions while still maintaining compliance with legal and ethical codes. Awareness and understanding of inmate and staff cultures, and of the surrounding communities, will assist administrators in anticipating the need for adjustment. With responsive administrators who can anticipate and adapt, institutional corrections will be able to progress successfully.

▶ Ethics Focus: "To Ban or Not to Ban?"

You have been superintendent of the state prison for five years. Having to house, feed, and provide recreation and treatment for 2,000 inmates in a prison built for 1,200 has not made your life easy. With the correctional officer's union threatening to strike, a stack of inmate lawsuits on your desk, and the typical problems of contraband and cellblock assaults, all you need is another problem. Yet here it is—a letter from Reverend Jones, President of the Ministerial Association:

> Dear Superintendent:
>
> As a Christian brother, I entreat you to ban the subversive book circulating among the inmates by the self-proclaimed spiritual teacher who goes by the name of Yogi Bo. His book clearly encourages rebellion against the authority of the State and of God. Our chaplains have a difficult enough time reforming the unfortunate who find themselves in prison with the help of the Good Book. As difficult as it is, they are doing a remarkable job. To allow a book or other writings which challenge the God-given principles our country was founded on to circulate among the inmates will create an overwhelming burden to them and other God-fearing counselors, not to mention the risk of insurrection it poses to prison security. The Ministerial Association is unanimously recommending that you ban this objectionable book. We are praying that you will make the proper decision.

You shake your head, partly in frustration and partly in amusement, and take a deep breath. You were raised as a child in a Protestant church, and you and your wife have raised your children likewise. While you share most of Reverend Jones's beliefs, a great number of inmates don't feel or think the same way. Your prison is made up of Protestant Christians, Catholics, Native Americans, Black Muslims, two Hindus, one Buddhist, and a number of people who, if they believe in anything at all, probably believe in violence.

Ethics Focus - *continued*

On the one hand, you have Reverend Jones and his supporters, who want you to ban Yogi Bo's book. On the other hand, you have a relatively small yet vocal group of inmates who follow the teachings of Yogi Bo. You have read the book and although you personally disagree with some of its ideas, you have found nothing advocating violence or rebellion. In fact, its message is basically a positive one and, to your surprise, you find yourself agreeing with a lot of the points Yogi Bo makes.

The easy thing to do would be to ban the book. Because the prison is located in a small rural area where Reverend Jones has substantial influence, such a decision would be good for you and the prison's image. If you don't ban the book, you will be criticized, letters will be written, and you might not even be re-elected elder in your church. Still, you don't like being pressured from the Ministerial Association, and the book is not the threat that Reverend Jones and others think it is. In fact, you wonder if they have even read it.

Religious beliefs are very personal and powerful. There will be trouble either way you decide. What are some issues at stake here regarding the inmates' wishes and rights and the community's expectations? What role should your conscience play in your decision?

▶ At the Movies . . . .

Brubaker, 1980.

This film, starring Robert Redford and Yaphet Kotto and directed by Stuart Rosenberg, is based on a real warden who faced an uphill battle in reforming the state prison in Arkansas.

The Shawshank Redemption, 1994.

This film, starring Tim Robbins, Morgan Freeman, and William Sadler, can offer administrators and managers an understanding of how it feels to be a prisoner, especially if that prisoner has little or no hope.

DISCUSSION QUESTIONS

1. Discuss the role of the government in correctional administration, including the tasks of each branch. For example, describe how a law is made that impacts correctional administration, and follow this law through each of the branches.

2. What effect does the politicization of correctional issues have on correctional administration?

3. Discuss inmate litigation. How can we balance inmate rights with institutional and public safety needs? Do you feel that inmate suits should be limited? If so, how and to what extent?

4. How can an administrator address the threat of drug use within the institution? What precautions can be taken to prevent the importation of drugs?

5. Given that drug use and sex do occur within prisons, should administrators take precautions to prevent the spread of diseases associated with these activities, such as HIV? For example, should prisons provide clean needles for drug users or condoms for safer sexual activity? What concerns might administrators have about such policies?

6. Discuss the policy of segregation/protective custody within correctional institutions. Would separating dangerous inmates (gang leaders, known sexual predators, etc.) from the general population be a good strategy? Discuss the advantages and disadvantages.

7. Would you agree to fund more or better inmate programming in the areas of treatment, education, and vocational training if research clearly indicated that such programming reduced crime and recidivism? Why or why not?

8. Discuss the unionization of correctional agencies. What benefits do unions provide for correctional personnel? What might be some disadvantages to unionization? What are the challenges for correctional administration?

9. Discuss evidence-based suggestions for correctional managers. Will politicians and the public be open to suggestions that are less punitive? How can correctional managers convince the public that changes are necessary?

FURTHER READING

Ross, J.I., and S.C. Richards (2002). *Behind Bars: Surviving Prison*. Indianapolis: Alpha.

Ross, J.I., and S.C. Richards (2003). *Convict Criminology*. Belmont, CA: Wadsworth/Thomson Learning.

Jacobson, M. (2005). *Downsizing Prisons: How to Reduce Crime and End Mass Incarceration.* New York: New York University Press.

Carceral, K.C. (2006). *Prison, Inc.: A Convict Exposes Life Inside a Private Prison.* New York: New York University Press.

NOTES

1. Glaze and Bonczar, 2007
2. Glaze and Bonczar, 2007
3. Sabol, Couture, and Harrison, 2007.
4. Beck, Karberg, and Harrison, 2002, 10.
5. Beck, Karberg, and Harrison, 2002, 8.
6. Sabol, Couture, and Harrison, 2007.
7. Beck, 2000, 1.
8. Carlson, 1999.
9. Carlson, 1999, 27.
10. Carlson, 1999, 27.
11. Carlson, 1999, 28.
12. Carlson, 1999, 28.
13. Carlson, 1999, 28.
14. Koontz, O'Donnell, and Weihrich, 1986.
15. Sabol, Couture, and Harrison, 2007.
16. American Correctional Association.
17. American Correctional Association.
18. Prison Litigation Reform Act (PLRA), 18 USCA §3636 (1996).
19. Stinchcomb and Fox, 1999.
20. Merlo and Benekos, 1992.
21. Republican National Committee.
22. Democratic National Committee.
23. Byrne, 1989.
24. Merlo and Benekos, 1992, xii.
25. 42 USCA §1983 (1988).
26. Eisenberg, 1993; Maahs and Del Carmen, 1995.
27. Stephan, 1997.
28. *Jones v. Bock,* 549 U.S. 2007 and Administrative Office of the U.S. Courts, Judicial Facts and Figures, available at http://www.uscourts.gov/judicialfactsfigures

29. Hanson and Daly, 1995.

30. Steinman, 1999.

31. *Knop v. Johnson*, 667 F. Supp. 467 (1987).

32. Prison Litigation Reform Act (PLRA), 18 USCA §3636 (1996).

33. Steinman, 1999, 242.

34. Steinman, 1999, 244.

35. Steinman, 1999, 244.

36. Clear and Cole, 1997.

37. Steinman, 1999, 244.

38. Alarcon, 2007.

39. Center on Addiction and Substance Abuse, 1998.

40. National Institute of Justice, 2000.

41. Wilson, 2000.

42. Mumola and Karberg, 2006.

43. Dorsey and Zawitz, 2000.

44. Feucht and Keyser, 1999, 11.

45. Feucht and Keyser, 1999, p. 13.

46. Feucht and Keyser, 1999.

47. Tewksbury and West, 2000.

48. Struckman-Johnson et al., 1996.

49. Thomas et al., 1996.

50. Stewart, 1998.

51. Stewart, 1998, 83.

52. Stewart, 1998, 85.

53. Tewksbury and West, 2000.

54. Smith and Batiuk, 1989, 30.

55. Smith and Batiuk, 37.

56. Struckman-Johnson and Struckman-Johnson, 2000.

57. Beck and Harrison, 2007.

58. Dumond, 1999.

59. Stephan and Karberg, 2003.

60. Stephan and Karberg, 2003.

61. Sabol, Couture, and Harrison, 2007. See also, Brown and Langan, 1999; Harrison and Beck, 2002.

62. Ekland-Olson, 1986; Gaes and McGuire, 1985.

63. Montgomery and Crews, 1998; Irwin, 1980.

64. Jacobs, 1977.

65. Fleisher, 1989.

66. Montgomery and Crews, 1998.

67. Irwin and Austin, 1997.

68. Braswell, Montgomery, and Lombardo, 1994.

69. Irwin and Cressey, 1962.

70. Knox, 2000.

71. Knox, 2000.

72. National Institute of Corrections, 1991.

73. Toller and Tsagaris, 1996.

74. Gransky and Patterson, 1999.

75. Cullen and Applegate, 1998, xiv.

76. Pew Center on the States, 2008.

77. Pew Center on the States, 2008.

78. Pew Center on the States, 2008.

79. Moore, 1998, 47.

80. Moore, 1998, 56.

81. Lamb, Weinberger, and Gross, 1999.

82. James and Glaze, 2006

83. Ditton, 1999.

84. Ditton, 1999.

85. Stephan, 1999, 9.

86. Stephan, 1999.

87. Mumola and Karberg, 2006

88. Mumola and Karberg, 2006

89. The National Drug Control Strategy, 1998.

90. "Reducing Offender Drug Use Through Prison-Based Treatment," 2000.

91. Martin et al., 1999.

92. Farabee et al., 1999.

93. Farabee et al., 1999, 160.

94. Harlow, 2003, 1; Beck et al., 1993, 7.

95. Stephan, 1997.

96. Saylor and Gaes, 1997, 42.

97. DiIulio, 1999.

98. DiIulio, 1999, 33.

99. Freeman, 1999, 363.

100. Wright, 1998.

101. Wright, 1998, 4.

102. Wright, 1998, 4.

103. Brough and Williams, 2007, 565.

104. Whitehead, 1989.

105. Phillips and McConnell, 1996.

106. Phillips and McConnell, 1996, 410.

107. Phillips and McConnell, 1996, 407.

108. Phillips and McConnell, 1996, 419.

109. Sabol, Couture and Harrison, 2007.

110. Pew Center on the States, 2008.

111. Pew Center on the States, 2008.

112. Pew Center on the States, 2008.

113. Pew Center on the States, 2008.

114. Pew Center on the States, 2008.

115. Pew Center on the States, 2008.

116. Pew Center on the States, 2008.

117. Pew Center on the States, 2008.

118. For a discussion of downsizing prisons, see Jacobson, 2005.

119. For excellent summaries of the research on effective treatment interventions, see Lipsey and Cullen, 2007, and MacKenzie, 2005.

120. Lipsey and Cullen, 2007.

121. Lipsey and Cullen, 2007.

122. MacKenzie, 2005.

123. Correctional researchers have developed a measure of program integrity, the Correctional Program Assessment Inventory (CPAI), that allows managers to see how well their programs are actually following the principles of effective interventions. See Gendreau and Andrews, 1996.

124. Visher and Courtney, 2007.

125. Petersilia, 2007.

126. Farabee, 2005.

127. Lipsey and Cullen, 2007.

128. Jacobson, 2005.

129. Zhang, Roberts, and Callanan, 2006.

130. Boufard and Bergeron, 2006.

131. Henry and Jacobs, 2007.

132. Bushway and Sweeten, 2007

133. Crutchfield, 2007, 711.

134. Sabol, Couture, and Harrison, 2007.

135. See http://www.correctionscorp.com

136. Massengale, 1998, 60.

137. Carceral, 2006

138. Mobley and Geis, 2005.

139. Boin and Van Duin, 1995.

140. Tonry, 1999b.

141. Tonry, 1999b.

142. Kurki, 1999.

143. Fabelo, 2000.

REFERENCES

Administrative Office of the U.S. Courts, Judicial Facts and Figures. Available at http://www.uscourts.gov/judicialfactsfirgures

American Correctional Association. Available at http://www.aca.org/standards

Beck, A.J. (2000). "Prisoners in 1999." *Bureau of Justice Statistics Bulletin*. Washington, DC: U.S. Department of Justice.

Beck, A.J., J.C. Karberg, and P.M. Harrison (2002). "Prison and Jail Inmates at Midyear 2001." *Bureau of Justice Statistics Bulletin*. Washington, DC: U.S. Government Printing Office.

Beck, A., D. Gilliard, L. Greenfeld, C. Harlow, T. Hester, L. Jankowski, T. Snell, J. Stephan, and D. Morton (1993). "Survey of State Prison Inmates, 1991." *Bureau of Justice Statistics Bulletin*. Washington, DC: U.S. Government Printing Office.

Beck, A.J., and P.M. Harrison (2007). "Sexual Violence Reported by Correctional Authorities, 2006." *Bureau of Justice Statistics Special Report*. Washington, DC: U.S. Government Printing Office.

Boin, R.A., and M.J. Van Duin (1995). "Prison Riots as Organizational Failures: A Managerial Perspective." *The Prison Journal* 75:357-379.

Boufard, J.A., and L. E. Bergeron (2006). "Reentry Works: The Implementation and Effectiveness of a Serious and Violent Offender Reentry Initiative." *Journal of Offender Rehabilitation* 44(2/3):1-29.

Braswell, M.C., R.H. Montgomery, and L.X. Lombardo (1994). *Prison Violence in America*, 2nd ed. Cincinnati: Anderson.

Brough, P., and J. Williams (2007). "Managing Occupational Stress in a High-Risk Industry: Measuring the Job Demands of Correctional Officers." *Criminal Justice and Behavior* 34:555-567.

Brown, J.M., and P.A. Langan (1999). "Felony Sentences in the United States, 1996." *Bureau of Justice Statistics Bulletin*. Washington, DC: U.S. Government Printing Office.

Bushway, S.D., and G. Sweeten (2007). "Abolish Lifetime Bans for Ex-Felons." *Criminology and Public Policy* 6:697-706.

Byrne, J. (1989). "Reintegrating the Concept of Community into Community-Based Corrections." *Crime & Delinquency* 35(3):471-499.

Carceral, K.C. (T.J. Bernard, ed.) (2006). *Prison, Inc.: A Convict Exposes Life Inside a Private Prison*. New York: New York University Press.

Carlson, P.M. (1999). "The Organization of the Institution." In P.M. Carlson and J. Simon Garrett (eds.), *Prison and Jail Administration: Practice and Theory*, 25-31. Gaithersburg, MD: Aspen.

Carlson, P.M., and J. Simon Garrett (eds.) (1999). *Prison and Jail Administration: Practice and Theory*. Gaithersburg, MD: Aspen.

Center on Addiction and Substance Abuse (1998). *Behind Bars: Substance Abuse and America's Prison Population*. New York: Columbia University Press.

Clear, T.R., and G.F. Cole (1997). *American Corrections*, 4th ed. Belmont, CA: Wadsworth.

Crutchfield, R.D. (2007). "Abandon Felon Disenfranchisement Policies." *Criminology and Public Policy* 6:707-716.

Cullen, F.T., and B.K. Applegate (eds.) (1998). *Offender Rehabilitation: Effective Correctional Intervention*. Dartmouth, UK: Ashgate.

Democratic National Committee. Available at http://www.democrats.org

DiIulio, J.J. (1999). "Leadership and Innovation in Correctional Institutions: New Challenges for Barbed-Wire Bureaucrats and Entrepreneurs." In P.M. Carlson and J. Simon Garrett (eds.), *Prison and Jail Administration: Practice and Theory*, 32-40. Gaithersburg, MD: Aspen.

Ditton, P.M. (1999). "Mental Health and Treatment of Inmates and Probationers." *Bureau of Justice Statistics Bulletin*. Washington, DC: U.S. Government Printing Office.

Dorsey, T.L., and M.W. Zawitz (2000). "Drugs and Crime Facts." *Bureau of Justice Statistics Bulletin*. Washington, DC: U.S. Government Printing Office.

Dumond, R.W. (1999). "Inmate Sexual Assault—The Enigma which Endures." Public Service Psychology—[APA] *Division 18 Newsletter*, 24(3):8-9, 18.

Eisenberg, H.B. (1993). "Rethinking Prisoner Civil Rights Cases and the Provision of Counsel." *Southern Illinois University Law Journal* 17:417-490.

Ekland-Olson, S. (1986). "Crowding, Social Control, and Prison Violence: Evidence from the Post-Ruiz Years in Texas." *Law and Society Review* 20(3):289-421.

Fabelo, T. (2000). "Technocorrections": The Promises, the Uncertain Threats. Papers from the executive sessions on sentencing and corrections, No. 5. Washington, DC: National Institute of Justice.

Farabee, D., M. Prendergast, J. Cartier, H. Wexler, K. Knight, and M.D. Anglin (1999). "Barriers to Implementing Effective Correctional Drug Treatment Programs." *The Prison Journal* 79(2):150-162.

Feucht, T.E., and A. Keyser (1999). "Reducing Drug Use in Prisons: Pennsylvania's Approach." *National Institute of Justice Journal* (October):11-15.

Fleisher, M.S. (1989). *Warehousing Violence*. Newbury Park, CA: Sage.

Freeman, R.M. (1999). *Correctional Organization and Management: Public Policy Challenges, Behavior, and Structure*. Boston: Butterworth-Heinemann.

Gaes, G.G., and W.J. McGuire (1985). "Prison Violence: The Contribution of Crowding Versus Other Determinants of Prison Assault Rates." *Journal of Research in Crime and Delinquency* 22(1):41-65.

Gendreau, P., and D.A. Andrews (1996). *Correctional Program Assessment Inventory*, 6th ed. Saint John, New Brunswick: University of New Brunswick.

Glaze, L.E., and T.P. Bonczar (2007). "Probation and Parole in the United States, 2006." *Bureau of Justice Statistics Bulletin*. Washington, DC: U.S. Government Printing Office.

Gransky, L.A., and M.E. Patterson (1999). "A Discussion of Illinois' 'Gang-Free' Prison: Evaluation Results." *Corrections Management Quarterly* 3(4):30-42.

Hanson, R.A., and H.W. Daly (1995). "Challenging the Conditions of Prisons and Jails: A Report on Section 1983 Litigations." *Bureau of Justice Statistics Bulletin*. Washington, DC: U.S. Government Printing Office.

Harlow, C. (2003). "Education and Correctional Populations." *Bureau of Justice Statistics Special Report*. Washington, DC: U.S. Government Printing Office.

Harrison, P.M., and A.J. Beck (2002). "Prisoners in 2001." *Bureau of Justice Statistics Bulletin*. Washington, DC: U.S. Government Printing Office.

Henry, J.S., and J.B. Jacobs (2007). "Ban the Box to Promote Ex-Offender Employment." *Criminology and Public Policy* 6:755-762.

Irwin, J. (1980). *Prisons in Turmoil*. Boston: Little, Brown.

Irwin, J., and J. Austin (1997). *It's About Time: America's Imprisonment Binge*, 2nd ed. Belmont, CA: Wadsworth.

Irwin, J., and D. Cressey (1962). "Thieves, Convicts, and the Inmate Culture." *Social Problems* 10:142-155.

Jacobs, J.B. (1977). *Stateville: A Penitentiary in Mass Society*. Chicago: University of Chicago Press.

Jacobson, M. (2005). *Downsizing Prisons: How to Reduce Crime and End Mass Incarceration*. New York: New York University Press.

James, D.J., and L.E. Glaze (2006). "Mental Health Problems of Prison and Jail Inmates." *Bureau of Justice Statistics Special Report*. Washington, DC: U.S. Government Printing Office.

Knox, G.W. (2000). "A National Assessment of Gangs and Security Threat Groups (STGs) in Adult Correctional Institutions: Results of the 1999 Adult Corrections Survey." *Journal of Gang Research* 7(3):1-45.

Koontz, H., C. O'Donnell, and H. Weihrich (1986). *Essentials of Management*, 4th ed. New York: McGraw-Hill.

Kurki, L. (1999). *Incorporating Restorative and Community Justice into American Sentencing and Corrections*. Papers from the executive sessions on sentencing and corrections, No. 3. Washington, DC: National Institute of Justice.

Lamb, H.R., L.E. Weinberger, and B.H. Gross (1999). "Community Treatment of Severely Mentally Ill Offenders under the Jurisdiction of the Criminal Justice System: A Review." *Psychiatric Services* 50:907-913.

Lipsey, M.W., and Cullen, F.T. (2007). "The Effectiveness of Correctional Rehabilitation: A Review of Systematic Reviews." *Annual Review of Law and Social Science* 3:297-320.

Maahs, J.R., and R.V. del Carmen (1995). "Curtailing Frivolous §1983 Inmate Litigation: Laws, Practices, and Proposals." *Federal Probation* 59:53-61.

MacKenzie, D.L. (2005). "The Importance of Using Scientific Evidence to Make Decisions about Correctional Programming." *Criminology and Public Policy* 4:249-258.

Martin, S.S., C.A. Butzin, C.A. Saum, and J.A. Inciardi (1999). "Three-Year Outcomes of Therapeutic Community Treatment for Drug-Involved Offenders in Delaware: From Prison to Work Release to Aftercare." *The Prison Journal* 79(3):294-320.

Massengale, D.K. (1998). "Reinventing an Industry: Free Enterprise in Corrections." *Corrections Management Quarterly* 2(2):58-65.

Merlo, A.V., and P.J. Benekos (eds.) (1992). "Introduction: The Politics of Corrections." In P.J. Benekos and A.V. Merlo (eds.), *Corrections: Dilemmas and Directions*, ix-xvii. Cincinnati: Anderson.

Mobley, A., and G. Geis (2005). "The Corrections Corporation of America: aka The Prison Realty Trust, Inc." In M.C. Braswell, B.R. McCarthy, and B.J. McCarthy, *Justice, Crime and Ethics*, 5th ed. (pp. 349-370). Cincinnati: Anderson.

Montgomery, R.H., and G.A. Crews (1998). *A History of Correctional Violence: An Examination of Reported Causes of Riots and Disturbances*. Lanham, MD: American Correctional Association.

Mooney, J., and A. Reiley (1939). *The Principles of Organization*. New York: Harper and Row.

Moore, J.M. (1998). "Privatization of Inmate Health Care: A New Approach to an Old Problem." *Corrections Management Quarterly* 2(2):46-57.

Mumola, C.J., and J.C. Karberg (2006). "Drug Use and Dependence, State and Federal Prisoners, 2004." *Bureau of Justice Statistics Special Report*. Washington, DC: U.S. Department of Justice.

National Drug Control Strategy. Available at http://www.whitehousedrugpolicy.gov

National Institute of Corrections (1991). "Management Strategies in Disturbances and with Gangs/Disruptive Groups." *Bureau of Justice Statistics Bulletin*. Washington, DC: U.S. Government Printing Office.

National Institute of Justice. (2000). "Arrestee Drug Abuse Monitoring (ADAM) Program: 1999 Report on Drug Use Among Adult and Juvenile Arrestees." *Bureau of Justice Statistics Bulletin*. Washington, DC: U.S. Government Printing Office.

Pew Center on the States (2008). *One in 100: Behind Bars in America 2008*. Washington, DC: Pew Center on the States.

Petersilia, J. (2007). "Employ Behavioral Contracting for 'Earned Discharge' Parole." *Criminology and Public Policy* 6:807-84.

Phillips, R.L., and C.R. McConnell (1996). *The Effective Corrections Manager: Maximizing Staff Performance in Demanding Times.* Gaithersburg, MD: Aspen.

"Reducing Offender Drug Use Through Prison-Based Treatment" (2000). *National Institute of Justice Journal.* Washington, DC: U.S. Department of Justice.

Republican National Committee. Available at http://www.rnc.org

Sabol, W.J., H. Couture, and P.M. Harrison (2007). "Prisoners in 2006." *Bureau of Justice Statistics Bulletin.* Washington, DC: U.S. Government Printing Office.

Saylor, W.G., and G.G. Gaes (1997). "Training Inmates Through Industrial Work Participation and Vocational and Apprenticeship Instruction." *Corrections Management Quarterly* 1(2):32-43.

Steinman, R.M. (1999). "Are Inmate Lawsuits Out of Control: Yes." In C.B. Fields (ed.), *Controversial Issues in Corrections,* 239-247. Boston: Allyn & Bacon.

Stephan, J. (1999). "State Prison Expenditures, 1996." *Bureau of Justice Statistics Bulletin.* Washington, DC: U.S. Government Printing Office.

Stephan, J. (1997). "Census of State and Federal Correctional Facilities, 1995." *Bureau of Justice Statistics Bulletin.* Washington, DC: U.S. Government Printing Office.

Stephan, J.J., and J.C. Karberg (2003). *Census of State and Federal Correctional Facilities, 2000.* Washington, DC: U.S. Department of Justice.

Stewart, C.H. (1998). "Management Response to Sexual Misconduct Between Staff and Inmates." *Corrections Management Quarterly* 2(2):81-88.

Stinchcomb, J., and V. Fox (1999). *Introduction to Corrections,* 5th ed. Upper Saddle River, NJ: Prentice Hall.

Struckman-Johnson, C., and D. Struckman-Johnson (2000). *Sexual Coercion Rates in Ten Prison Facilities in the Midwest.* Paper presented at the annual meeting of the Academy of Criminal Justice Sciences, New Orleans, LA.

Struckman-Johnson, C., D. Struckman-Johnson, L. Rucker, K. Bumby, and S. Donaldson (1996). "Sexual Coercion Reported by Men and Women in Prison." *Journal of Sex Research* 33:67-76.

Tewksbury, R., and A. West (2000). "Research on Sex in Prison During the Late 1980s and Early 1990s." *The Prison Journal* 80(4):368-378.

Thomas, D.Q., S. Lai, J. Weschler, J. Mariner, and R. Ralph (eds.) (1996). *All Too Familiar: Sexual Abuse of Women in U.S. Prisons.* New York: Human Rights Watch Report.

Toller, W., and B. Tsagaris (1996). "Managing Institutional Gangs: A Practical Approach Combining Security and Human Services." *Corrections Today* 58(6):110-111, 115.

Tonry, M. (1999). *Reconsidering Indeterminate and Structured Sentencing.* Papers from the executive sessions on sentencing and corrections, No. 2. Washington, DC: National Institute of Justice.

Visher, C.A., and S.M.E. Courtney (2007). *Returning Home Policy Brief: One Year Out: Experiences of Prisoners Returning to Cleveland.* Washington, DC: Urban Institute. Available at http://justice.urban.org

Whitehead, J.T. (1989). *Burnout in Probation and Parole.* New York: Praeger.

Wilson, D.J. (2000). "Drug Use, Testing, and Treatment in Jails." *Bureau of Justice Statistics Bulletin*. Washington, DC: U.S. Government Printing Office.

Wright, L.N. (1998). "Protecting the Health of Correctional Employees Is Long-Term Endeavor." Corrections Today, 1-5. Available at http://www.corrections.com/aca/cortoday/april98/wright.html

Zhang, S.X., R.E.L. Roberts, and V.J. Callanan (2006). "Preventing Parolees from Returning to Prison through Community-Based Reintegration." *Crime & Delinquency* 52:551-571.

COURT CASES

Jones v. Bock, 549 U.S. ____ , 127 S.Ct. 910 (2007).

Knop v. Johnson, 667 F.Supp. 467 (W.D. Mich. 1987).

The Death Penalty in America

CHAPTER

14

What You Need to Know

▶ More than two-thirds of the countries worldwide have abolished the death penalty. The United States joins such countries as China, Iran, and Iraq as countries that retain the death penalty. Mexico is one country that has recently abolished the death penalty.

▶ The United States has executed more than 800 prisoners since 1976. Most were executed by means of lethal injection.

▶ Problems with the death penalty include the execution of innocent persons, racial inequities, and problems with obtaining adequate defense counsel for accused murderers.

▶ The death penalty is actually quite expensive, at times costing more than $2 million dollars per execution.

▶ There is considerable debate about the deterrent effects of capital punishment. Most scholars conclude that there is no deterrent effect.

▶ The death penalty does achieve incapacitation: execution guarantees that a murderer cannot murder again. However, life without parole could also offer a high degree of incapacitation.

▶ Some of the moral arguments over the death penalty are based on religion, the thought of philosophers such as Immanuel Kant, and public opinion.

INTRODUCTION

Capital punishment is a complex issue that can be studied and debated from various perspectives.[1] The death penalty is a policy of the criminal justice system, and can be evaluated as other policies are—for effectiveness, cost, and unintended consequences. It is a legal issue, and its use in the United States can be critiqued in terms of the standards set by the Constitution and by Supreme Court decisions. Capital punishment is also a human rights issue; international law is increasingly concerned with its use.

The death penalty is a moral issue as well, one that arouses strong convictions and passionate arguments between its proponents and those who oppose it. Many religious denominations have taken a formal stand on the issue, and discussions about the death penalty often draw on religious ideas and writings. For the families of victims and offenders, certainly, capital punishment is an intensely personal issue.

Finally, the death penalty is a political issue of enormous symbolic importance. In many jurisdictions, capital punishment has assumed the status of a litmus test for elected officials who wish to present themselves as being tough on crime. This is unfortunate because the tone of modern American politics is not conducive to the deliberate consideration of the empirical, legal, and moral issues raised by capital punishment. The complexity of the concerns raised by the issue requires calm and reasoned consideration, not slogans and sound bites. It is the purpose of this chapter to provide an overview of the information necessary to form a reasoned opinion on the death penalty, and to refer interested readers to the best recent literature on the topic.

THE DEATH PENALTY WORLDWIDE

More than two-thirds of the countries in the world have abolished the death penalty in law or in practice (see Table 14.1).[2] Countries that no longer use the death penalty share certain characteristics. They tend to be stable democracies with advanced industrial and technological economies, or emerging democracies that have rejected the death penalty as part of a new commitment to human rights. The glaring exception to this pattern is the United States.[3]

Some of the major countries that have abolished the death penalty for all crimes since 2002 are Yugoslavia, Armenia, Greece, Turkey, Mexico, and the Philippines. Besides the United States, major countries that still retain the death penalty are China, Cuba, Egypt, Iran, Iraq, Pakistan, and Vietnam.[4]

International law is moving toward the abolition of the death penalty.[5] A number of treaties restrict the use of capital punishment, and the United Nations Human Rights Commission recently voted in favor of a universal moratorium on executions.[6] The international tribunals established to try crimes of war and genocide in Rwanda and the former Yugo-

TABLE 14.1
The Death Penalty Around the World

Abolished completely:	91
Abolished except for war and extraordinary crimes	11
Abolished in practice:	33
Total abolitionist countries:	135
Total retentionist countries:	62

Source: Amnesty International (2007). "Facts and Figures on the Death Penalty." Available at http://www.amnesty.org

slavia do not impose capital punishment.[7] The European Union requires the abolition of the death penalty as a condition of membership.[8]

Mark Costanzo notes that by retaining capital punishment, the United States puts itself "in the company of some of the cruelest and most repressive governments in the world. . . ."[9] What accounts for America's continued commitment to lethal punishment even after so many other nations around the world have repudiated the death penalty? Why is the United States, which prides itself on being a leader in human rights, so out of step with international law and the policies of other Western democracies? To understand America's commitment to the death penalty at the beginning of the twenty-first century, it is necessary to examine the history of capital punishment in America, and to explore the ways in which that history has influenced the politics of modern crime policy.[10]

THE HISTORY OF THE DEATH PENALTY IN THE UNITED STATES

The English brought the death penalty to the American colonies, just as they brought other aspects of their law and culture. American colonial law specified a number of capital crimes, including religious offenses such as idolatry, blasphemy, and witchcraft. After the American Revolution, the states restricted the number of capital crimes and began to divide murder cases into degrees of severity, thus greatly reducing the number of cases in which the death penalty could be used.[11] More than 19,000 people have been executed since George Kendall was hanged in the Jamestown Colony in 1608.[12]

The history of the death penalty in the American South is closely connected with the region's racial history. Slave codes and black codes in Southern states specified punishment by racial combination of defendant and victim, reserving the harshest punishment for blacks convicted of crimes against whites. Later capital statutes were not discriminatory on their face but continued to be so in their enforcement. This was especially true of executions for rape, which were overwhelmingly used against

TABLE 14.2
Executions Between 1930 and 1967, By Race of Defendant

Years	For all crimes			For rape		
	Total	Number black	Percent black	Total	Number black	Percent black
1930-34	776	395	50.9%	52	49	94.2%
1935-39	891	421	47.3%	73	66	90.4%
1940-44	645	362	56.1%	97	83	85.6%
1945-49	639	419	65.6%	103	96	93.2%
1950-54	413	209	50.6%	58	49	84.5%
1955-59	304	167	54.9%	44	40	90.9%
1960-64	181	91	50.3%	28	22	78.6%
1965-69	10	2	20.0%	–	–	–
Total	**3,859**	**2,066**	**53.5%**	**455**	**405**	**89.0%**

Source: Figures computed from Bureau of Justice Statistics (1986). *Capital Punishment 1984*, Table One. Washington, DC: U.S. Department of Justice.

black men accused of assaulting white women (see Table 14.2). Executions often were carried out months, weeks, or days after brief trials that did not observe even minimal due process; many people were executed with no appeal of their cases. Trials and legal executions sometimes bore a striking resemblance to lynchings, especially when a threatened mob attack had been averted. The frequent presence of mobs around or even within the court during trials, as well as the collusion and sometimes active involvement of law enforcement officers in lynchings, served to blur the distinctions between judicial and extrajudicial executions.[13]

After the 1930s, there was a marked decline around the country in the use of the death penalty. Executions fell from a high of 199 in 1935 to only two in 1967. Although death penalty statutes remained on the books and juries continued to sentence defendants to death, an unofficial moratorium on executions began after 1967. Public support for the death penalty declined during this time; for a brief period in the 1960s, polls indicated that a slight majority of Americans opposed capital punishment.[14]

In the late 1960s, lawyers for the first time broadly challenged the death penalty, arguing that it violated the Eighth and Fourteenth Amendments. In the 1972 case *Furman v. Georgia*, the U.S. Supreme Court ruled five-to-four that the death penalty as administered was unconstitutional. The Court's per curiam ruling read:

> The Court holds that the imposition and carrying out of the death penalty in these cases constitute cruel and unusual punishment in violation of the Eighth and Fourteenth Amendments. The judgment in each case is therefore reversed insofar as it leaves undisturbed the death sentence imposed, and the cases are remanded for further proceedings.[15]

Each Justice wrote a lengthy concurring or dissenting opinion. The message of *Furman* was somewhat unclear, beyond its emptying the country's death rows. From the five concurring opinions, two significant themes did emerge: the death penalty as administered was fatally flawed by racial disparities, and it was imposed in an arbitrary and capricious manner.

Almost immediately after the Court's ruling in *Furman*, state legislatures began rewriting their death penalty statutes in an attempt to remedy the faults the Court had identified. Four years later, in 1976, the Supreme Court considered several cases testing the constitutionality of the new laws. The Court ruled that mandatory statutes, which required imposition of the death penalty upon conviction of certain crimes, were unconstitutional,[16] but it approved statutes that provided juries with aggravating and mitigating circumstances to guide their sentencing discretion.[17] With some modifications, these statutes are still in force, and have served as models for death penalty laws around the nation.

BOX 14.1

Furman v. Georgia (1972)

In the 1972 landmark case of *Furman v. Georgia*, the Supreme Court issued a one-page *per curiam* opinion holding that the imposition and carrying out of the death penalty constituted cruel and unusual punishment in violation of the Eighth and Fourteenth Amendments, but the justices articulated their views on the controversial subject in more than 200 pages of concurrence and dissent. Only Justices Brennan and Marshall believed the death penalty to be unconstitutional in all instances.

The *Furman* Court consisted of Chief Justice Warren E. Burger, and Associate Justices Harry Blackmun, William J. Brennan Jr., William O. Douglas, Thurgood Marshall, Lewis F. Powell Jr., Potter Stewart, William Rehnquist, and Byron White. Justices Brennan, Douglas, Marshall, Stewart, and White offered concurrences; Justices Burger, Blackmun, Powell, and Rehnquist offered dissents.

The guided discretion statutes attempted to avoid arbitrary and capricious sentencing by creating several safeguards. First, capital trials were redesigned to consist of two separate phases. In the first phase, the jury decides whether the defendant is guilty, and if so, of what crime. If the defendant is convicted of first-degree murder, the jury then hears evidence about whether the defendant should be sentenced to death or to some alternative sentence. The jurors consider aggravating and mitigating circumstances to guide their sentencing decision. The death penalty statute lists aggravating circumstances, which typically include factors such as the offender having previous convictions for violent crimes or whether the

homicide was committed in the course of a felony or was especially heinous, atrocious, or cruel. Juries are able to consider any relevant aspect of
the defendant's life or crime in mitigation of the sentence.[18] In addition, the
new statutes provide for state-level appellate review of all death sentences.
Despite much evidence (reviewed below) that the new laws operate in
much the same way and with the same results as the pre-*Furman* laws, the
Supreme Court has rejected broad challenges to their constitutionality.

In the late 1970s and 1980s, the death penalty became a political
issue of great importance in the United States, at the local, state, and
even national level. Rising rates of violent crime and the resulting fear
and concern of the public, combined with a general hardening of attitudes on issues of crime and justice, led to increased public support for
harsh punishments; support for the death penalty increased to a high of
80 percent in 1994.[19] Politicians were quick to exploit public attitudes,
and being "tough on crime" became almost a prerequisite for holding
elective office, including local judgeships. This politicization of a particular criminal justice policy is a largely American phenomenon, and has
contributed to the continuing use of capital punishment in the United
States after it has ceased to be used by most other democracies.

CURRENT USE OF THE DEATH PENALTY IN THE UNITED STATES

The 10-year moratorium on executions came to an end on January
17, 1977, when Utah executed Gary Gilmore. Gilmore had dropped his
appeals and made strenuous efforts to be executed. A little more than
two years later, John Spenkelink in Florida became the first inmate to
be executed after losing his appeals. In the 26 years since executions
resumed, 812 prisoners have been put to death by 32 states and the federal government (see Table 14.3).[20]

As of December 31, 2006, there were 3,228 condemned inmates
in the United States.[21] Despite the growing number of executions, the
population of death row remains stable or increases, because equal or greater numbers of prisoners are being sentenced to death than are being executed or leaving death row by other means (sentence reduction,

Go to www.oojp.usdoj.gov/bjs for official
statistics on the death penalty, especially an
annual report on capital punishment. For
additional information on the death penalty
go to www.deathpenaltyinfo.org, the web
site of the Death Penalty Information Center.

new trial, commutation, suicide, and natural death). Even if an execution occurred every day, it would take more than 10 years to execute
those already on death row, and at the end of that time, at current sentencing rates, we could have a new death row population of more than
2,000 prisoners.

TABLE 14.3
American Jurisdictions and the Death Penalty, 2008

Number of executions, as of December 7, 2007		Death penalty law but no executions	No death penalty
Federal	2	Military	District of Columbia
Alabama	24	Connecticut	Alaska
Arizona	22	Kansas	Hawaii
Arkansas	24	New Hampshire	Iowa
California	10	New Jersey	Maine
Colorado	1	New York	Massachusetts
Delaware	13	South Dakota	Michigan
Florida	53		Minnesota
Georgia	31		North Dakota
Idaho	1		Rhode Island
Illinois	12		Vermont
Indiana	9		West Virginia
Kentucky	2		Wisconsin
Louisiana	27		
Maryland	3		
Mississippi	5		
Missouri	59		
Montana	2		
Nebraska	3		
Nevada	9		
New Mexico	1		
N. Carolina	22		
Ohio	5		
Oklahoma	52		
Oregon	2		
Pennsylvania	3		
S. Carolina	28		
Tennessee	1		
Texas	288		
Utah	6		
Virginia	87		
Washington	4		
Wyoming	1		
Total	**812**		

Source: Death Penalty Information Center (2008). "Facts About the Death Penalty." Available at http://www.deathpenaltyinfo.org

The current death penalty differs greatly from the pre-*Furman* system of capital punishment, both in the number of people on death row and in the length of time between sentencing and final disposition of cases.[22] According to the Bureau of Justice Statistics, the average length of time between imposition of the death sentence and execution is more than 11 years,[23] but this figure obscures the fact that many inmates have been on death row much longer. A stay of 15 years is not unusual, and several inmates are close to or beyond their twenty-fifth year on death row. These inmates are in fact serving life sentences while they are under sentence of death.

Another new development under current laws is the popularity of lethal injection as a method of execution. Since 1977, people have been executed by electrocution, gassing, hanging, and firing squads, but the great majority have been put to death by lethal injection. On the one hand, lethal injection may make executions appear like routine medical procedures, thus perhaps desensitizing officials and the public to the severity of executions. On the other hand, at least two dozen executions by lethal injection have been botched—generally when technicians could not find a vein or when the injection equipment malfunctioned. Moreover, several apparently have caused considerable physical pain to the offender.[24]

In 2008, the Supreme Court has ruled that lethal injection is not cruel and unusual punishment. See Box 14.2 for a list of United States Supreme Court cases dealing with the death penalty.

In many other ways, however, the modern death penalty is very similar to the system it replaced. There continues to be a strong "Southern emphasis" to executions.[25] Hugo Bedau has noted that the death penalty is distributed along three geographic tiers. The first is northern, running from Maine to Alaska: "here the death penalty either is abolished or plays a very minor role." The second tier runs from Pennsylvania to California; in this region "executions since 1977 have been few and slow in coming despite large numbers on death row."[26] The third tier begins

TABLE 14.4
Executions by Method Since 1976

Lethal Injection	929	(84.5%)
Electrocution	154	(14%)
Gas Chamber	11	(1%)
Hanging	3	(.3%)
Firing Squad	2	(.2%)
Total	**1099**	

Source: Death Penalty Information Center (2008). "Facts About the Death Penalty." Available at http://www.deathpenaltyinfo.org.

BOX 14.2

United States Supreme Court Cases on the Death Penalty

Issue raised	Case	Holding
Death qualification of jurors	*Lockhart v. McCree*, 476 U.S. 162 (1986)	The Constitution does not prohibit the removal of jurors for opposition to the death penalty.
Execution of insane	*Ford v. Wainwright*, 477 U.S. 399 (1986)	Execution of the insane is unconstitutional.
Execution of juveniles	*Roper v. Simmons*, 543 U.S. 551 (2005)	Execution of a person whose crime was committed under age 18 is unconstitutional.
Execution of mentally retarded	*Atkins v. Virginia*, 536 U.S. 304 (2002)	Execution of the mentally retarded is unconstitutional.
Factual innocence	*Herrera v. Collins*, 506 U.S. 390 (1993)	Set standard for reviewing claims of factual innocence made after "error-free trial"; made review very difficult.
Factual innocence	*Schlup v. Delo*, 513 U.S. 298 (1995)	Set somewhat more lenient standard for reviewing claim of factual innocence made with claim of constitutional error at trial.
Ineffective assistance of counsel	*Strickland v. Washington*, 466 U.S. 688 (1984)	Set standards for reviewing claims of ineffective assistance of counsel.
Lethal injection	*Baze et al. v. Rees*, 553 U.S. __ (2008)	Kentucky's lethal injection protocol satisfies the Eighth Amendment.
Mitigating evidence	*Lockett v. Ohio*, 438 U.S. 586 (1978)	Defendant must be allowed to present mitigating circumstances beyond those in statute.
Proportionality review	*Pulley v. Harris*, 465 U.S. 37 (1984)	Proportionality review of death sentence is not required.
Racial disparities in death sentences	*McCleskey v. Kemp*, 481 U.S. 279 (1987)	Showing of intentional discrimination is necessary for relief.
Restriction on successor habeas petition	*Felker v. Turpin*, 518 U.S. 1051 (1996)	Provisions of Antiterrorism and Effective Death Penalty Act are not unconstitutional.
Victim impact statements	*Payne v. Tennessee*, 501 U.S. 808 (1991)	Statements of the impact of victim's murder on family and friends are not unconstitutional.

Source: Much of the information in this table is drawn from Bedau, H.A. (ed.) (1997). *The Death Penalty in America: Current Controversies*, 238-241. New York and Oxford: Oxford University Press.

with the southeastern states and runs through Arizona; here there are "many executions amidst clamor for more, hundreds on death row and more on the way."[27] Texas stands out even among the states of the third tier; it has executed 36 percent of all the inmates put to death under current laws.[28]

Executions of women in America have always been rare, and continue to be exceptional under current statutes. Victor Streib notes that "women are unlikely to be arrested for murder, extremely unlikely to be sentenced to death, and almost never executed."[29] Of the 1,099 people executed between 1977 and late 2007, only 11 were women, and only 55 (1.7%) of inmates currently on death row are women.[30] Women commit many fewer homicides than men, and very rarely commit felony homicides against strangers; thus, it is to be expected that there would be fewer women than men on death row. Whether a tendency toward leniency in sentencing women convicted of murder also contributes to the rarity of death sentences for women is not entirely clear.[31]

Go to www.supremecourtus.gov for the complete text of important Supreme Court cases on the death penalty. For example, in *Atkins v. Virginia*, the Court ruled that the death penalty is unconstitutional for the mentally retarded. In *Roper v. Simmons*, it ruled that the death penalty cannot be used with juveniles. In *Baze et al. v. Rees*, the Court ruled that lethal injection is not cruel and unusual punishment.

Thirty-five percent of the inmates executed under current statutes were African-American.[32] Approximately half of the victims of homicide in America each year are white, but 81 percent of the victims of those executed between 1976 and September 2002 were white.[33] The racial breakdown of those currently on death row is: white, 45 percent; African-American, 42 percent; Hispanic, 11 percent; Other, 2 percent.[34] The overwhelming majority of condemned prisoners are poor. Mental illness is common among death row inmates, and a significant number are mentally retarded.[35] Most condemned prisoners have a horrific history of childhood neglect and abuse, often including severe head trauma.[36] Many of the people on death row were victims of violent crime as children, suffering repeated assault, rape, and even attempted murder. The personal histories of death row inmates frequently include extreme victimization within the family, resulting in removal to some sort of foster or institutional care, where further abuse and neglect occurs, contributing to worsening emotional and behavioral problems.[37] These problems often include impulsiveness, substance abuse, inability to control anger, and difficulties with personal relationships. In general, the people who wind up on death row in America have faced "the multiple risk factors of poverty, chronic neglect, emotional and physical abuse, and extreme familial instability with little to buffer them from the predictable harm."[38] These factors have affected their ability to function in society.

Although the numbers of persons executed and on death row may seem high, especially when the United States is compared to other countries, it is important to understand that executions occur in only a tiny fraction of homicide cases. Death has always been a rare punishment. Hugo Bedau computed the following estimates for the mid-1990s:

- One person is executed each year for every 1,000 criminal homicides.

- One person is executed each year for every 700 arrested for criminal homicide.

- One person is executed each year for every 450 convicted of criminal homicide.

- One person is executed each year for every 100 on death row.

- One person exits death row each year by execution for every 10 who are admitted to death row.[39]

As Bedau notes, these numbers can support differing interpretations. Some would argue that they show the death penalty is not working—so many homicides, so few executions, and the continuing large death row populations indicate a failing system. Others might argue that the death penalty should be a rare punishment, imposed only upon the most culpable of offenders in the most egregious cases, and that its rarity indicates that it is working as it should. This conclusion assumes that those few who receive the death penalty are indeed the worst of the worst, an assumption examined in the next section of the chapter.

HOW THE MODERN DEATH PENALTY FUNCTIONS

Post-*Furman* death penalty laws were intended to provide a rational system for distinguishing among offenders, reserving the death sentence for the very worst among them. These laws have been in effect since the early 1970s, and much research has been done to examine how they function. This body of research has identified three major ways in which the new laws have failed to live up to their promise. First, mistaken convictions of the innocent continue to occur. Second, the extralegal factor of race exerts a systematic influence on sentencing outcome. And third, the imposition of the death penalty is often influenced by sheer chance and caprice.

These failings would not be so serious if they were reliably corrected by the appellate process. Death sentences are subjected to several levels of appellate review, a process that often takes many years to complete. James Liebman's study of capital appeals documents an astonishingly high reversal rate: 68 percent of the death sentences imposed are overturned by the courts. As Liebman and colleagues note, such a high level of error would not be tolerated in "any other private- or public-sector activity. . . . Any system with this much error and expense would be halted immediately, examined, and either reformed or scrapped."[40] The high reversal rate should not be interpreted to mean that the cases that are upheld on appeal are free from serious error. A study of executions in Missouri revealed that those cases upheld by the appellate courts and denied clemency by the governor had the same sorts of serious errors as the cases that were granted relief.[41]

• The Condemnation and Execution of Innocent People •

If there is one point of agreement between abolitionists and retentionists, it is that no one wants to execute an innocent person. This is the worst outcome possible from everyone's point of view. There are three main questions raised by the issue of innocence and the death penalty: Are innocent people really sentenced to death and executed? How can the risk of this happening be minimized? What level of risk is acceptable? The first question is empirical, the second practical, and the third moral.

There is no definite agreement on how many innocent people have been executed. The most frequently cited number, 23 between 1900 and 1985, is almost certainly low.[42] There are great difficulties in establishing innocence after execution, particularly in older cases. While the exact number of innocent persons executed has not been established, and probably never will be known, Radelet and Bedau note a growing agreement among supporters and opponents of capital punishment regarding the inevitability of some wrongful executions.[43]

More information is available on innocent persons condemned to death and exonerated before execution than on those who were actually executed. Since 1973, 126 people condemned to death have been exonerated and released.[44] While this fact is not in dispute, abolitionists and retentionists differ in their interpretation of what it means. Abolitionists point to these cases as evidence of the system's failure. Proponents of the death penalty argue that these are cases of innocent people not being executed, and thus demonstrate that the system is working, because the mistakes were corrected. Abolitionists counter that such cases prove the system does make mistakes, and we have no way of knowing how many other mistakes have not been caught and rectified. They point to the high level of chance that has contributed to the discovery of many such cases, and note that only the prolonged appellate process has allowed them to come to light. A report on innocent persons released from death row found that the average length of time they spent under sentence of death before being cleared was seven years.[45] Several innocent persons have been exonerated after spending as much as 20 years on death row.

This leads to the second point, which is how the risk of wrongful conviction can be lessened. DNA testing stands out as a new and important development, though it should be noted that there are many capital cases in which convictions are not supported by evidence that could be confirmed or disconfirmed with DNA testing. The risk of wrongful convictions could be lowered by better pretrial investigations and forensic work, support for high ethical and professional standards among police and prosecutors, more funds for defense teams and expert witnesses, scrupulous observance of due process requirements, extreme caution with the testimony of witnesses who stand to benefit from a conviction (e.g., jail cellmates to whom defendants "confess" as well as codefendants with plea bargains), and a meticulous appellate process that allows defendants to raise issues of factual error.[46] All these cost time and money, however, in a system that is already much criticized for being too slow and too expensive.

What level of risk is acceptable? The only way to run absolutely no risk of executing the innocent is to have no executions. Retentionists sometimes point out that many endeavors run the risk of death for innocent people; we try to minimize the risk, but accept that some fatal errors will be made.[47] For instance, we do not abolish cars because innocent people die in traffic accidents. Retentionists argue that the benefits of capital punishment, especially its purported deterrent effect, outweigh the risk of executing the innocent. Abolitionists counter that the death penalty has no demonstrated benefits, and that the decision to take a particular person's life when alternatives such as life imprisonment are available is qualitatively different from accepting a broadly spread risk to many people from activities that have clear social benefits.

• Race and Capital Punishment •

The post-*Furman* statutes attempted to overcome the history of racial discrimination in the use of capital punishment with equitably imposed, racially neutral statutes. A large and sophisticated body of research indicates, however, that racial inequities still influence the use of capital punishment, and not only in Southern states. Racial disparities in the post-*Furman* era tend to be found more in the race of victims than of defendants. That is, people who are convicted of killing whites are more likely to receive the death sentence than those convicted of killing blacks. As society's ultimate punishment, the death sentence tends to be reserved for the killers of the most highly valued victims, who are usually white. A synthesis of studies done by the General Accounting Office of the federal government in 1990 concluded:

> Our synthesis of the 28 studies shows a pattern of evidence indicating racial disparities in the charging, sentencing, and imposition of the death penalty after the *Furman* decision. In 82 percent of the studies race of victim was found to influence the likelihood of being charged with capital murder or receiving the death penalty. . . . This finding was remarkably consistent across data sets, states, data collection methods, and analytic techniques. . . .

BOX 14.3

A Case of Innocence in Illinois

Anthony Porter Case

Date	Event
1982	Marilyn Green and Jerry Hillard were killed in Chicago. Anthony Porter was convicted and sentenced to death for their murders.
September 1998	Porter came within 48 hours of being executed. Execution was stayed to determine his mental competence, not his innocence. Porter has an IQ of 51.
Fall 1998	Case was investigated by journalism students from Northwestern University as a class assignment. Alstory Simon is implicated by his estranged wife, and confesses on videotape to the murders.
February 5, 1999	Porter was released from death row.
February 7, 1999	Alstory Simon was arrested for murders of Green and Hillard.
September 7, 1999	Alstory Simon was sentenced to 37 years for murders of Green and Hillard.
January 2000	Governor Ryan declared a moratorium on executions in Illinois, partly because of his concern over the Porter case.

Quotes on Porter Case	
George Ryan, Governor of Illinois	"I think everybody understands what's at stake here. An innocent man was about to die, and thank God he didn't. And now we want to make sure that scenario doesn't . . . come back and haunt us again."
Dave Urbanek, Spokesman for Governor	". . . [T]he system worked. The process did work. Sure it took 17 years, but it also took 17 years for the journalism professor to sic his kids on that case."
The Chicago Tribune	"Something has gone terribly, chillingly wrong here, and innocent people have almost paid with their lives. . . . How could this case come so horrifyingly close to the point that an innocent man would be put to death? Does Illinois want to answer these questions before an innocent person dies, or after that happens?"
Anthony Porter	"I don't know how I'm going to get those years back. I'm just thankful to be alive."

Sources: Jeter, J. (1999). "A New Ending to an Old Story." *The Washington Post*, February 17, 1999, C:01; Belluck, P. (1999). "Convict Freed after 16 Years on Death Row." *The New York Times*, February 6, 1999, A:7; Pallasch, A.M. (1999). "Man Makes Plea Deal in Case That Freed Death Row Inmate." *Chicago Sun-Times*, September 8, 1999, 12; Berlow, A. (1999). "The Wrong Man." *The Atlantic Monthly*, November 1999, 66-91.

To summarize, this synthesis supports a strong influence of the race of the victim.[48]

Perhaps the most important post-*Furman* study of race and capital sentencing was done in Georgia under the lead authorship of David Baldus.[49] This study, using a sophisticated research design and method of statistical analysis, found evidence that the race of victims exerted a substantial effect on death sentencing in Georgia. The authors found that the odds of receiving death were 4.3 times greater when victims were white, even after they took into account a large number of other variables. The U.S. Supreme Court considered Baldus's study in *McCleskey v. Kemp*, which dealt with the case of Warren McCleskey,[50] a black defendant condemned to death for the murder of a white police officer. The Court found itself in an awkward position, given that it had rejected the pre-*Furman* death penalty largely on the basis of much weaker evidence of discrimination. The Court accepted Baldus's statistics as valid, but ruled by a five-to-four margin that the inequities documented by Baldus did not rise to the level of a constitutional violation. The majority held that McCleskey's evidence of discrimination was not enough to invalidate his death sentence. The Court held that to make a showing of racial discrimination sufficient to overturn a death sentence, a defendant would have to demonstrate that some decisionmaker—judge, prosecutor, or jury—acted with "discriminatory purpose" against him.[51] Such evidence, however, is exceptionally difficult to document. In effect, the Supreme Court held that a system that produces racial inequities does not violate the constitutional rights of those who lose their lives because of those inequities, although similar evidence is substantial enough to prevail in employment discrimination suits. In a scathing dissent, Justice Brennan wrote:

> It is tempting to pretend that minorities on death row share a fate in no way connected to our own, that our treatment of them sounds no echoes beyond the chambers in which they die. Such an illusion is ultimately corrosive, for the reverberations of injustice are not so easily confined. . . . and the way in which we choose those who will die reveals the depth of moral commitment among the living.[52]

The *McCleskey* decision brought an end to broad-based challenges against the death penalty as it is currently applied. Research conducted since *McCleskey* continues to find disturbing evidence of racial disparities in death sentencing.[53] Recent research also found that in death penalty states, 97.5 percent of the district attorneys (who make the decision to seek the death penalty) are white.[54] Despite the unwillingness of the Supreme Court to grant relief on the basis of racial discrimination, the evidence is overwhelming that the death penalty as it is used in America today continues to be influenced by race.[55]

• Capricious Imposition of the Death Penalty •

In addition to the problem of discriminatory imposition of capital punishment, there is substantial evidence that the penalty is also applied in a capricious manner; that is, without logical distinctions between those who receive a sentence of death and those who receive a lesser sentence. The current statutes are designed to guide jury decisionmaking so that only the very worst offenders, convicted of the very worst crimes, will be sentenced to death. In practice, however, people often are sentenced to death based on factors that do not relate to their culpability.

A host of extraneous factors can enter into the way in which potential capital cases are handled, including geography, politics, and jurors' decisions. This chapter has already noted that the likelihood of being sentenced to death varies greatly by geographic region of the United States. There are substantial variations in the likelihood of receiving death within regions and within states as well.[56] Among the factors that may increase likelihood of a death sentence are committing the crime in a rural area and being a stranger to that area.

The death penalty system is not immune to political pressures. The Death Penalty Information Center has documented cases in which elected judges have "abandoned the independence of their office by such actions as throwing a noose over a tree outside the courthouse, coming into court displaying brass knuckles and a gun, revealing their death verdicts before the defendant even comes to trial, boasting about being a 'hanging judge,' and issuing press releases prejudicing a capital defendant during trial. . . ."[57] Political pressures extend to state appellate judges as well, with several having been removed from the bench for making unpopular decisions in death penalty cases.[58]

Another source of caprice lies with the jurors who must make the decision of life or death. The Capital Jury Project,[59] directed by William J. Bowers at Northeastern University, has carried out more than 1,200 interviews with jurors in capital cases in 14 different states. These interviews indicate that jurors have great difficulty understanding the legal standards that are to guide their decisions. Jurors often reach decisions based on mistaken interpretations of the law or accidental or irrelevant factors, and occasionally decide cases based on impermissible factors such as their eagerness to be finished and to go home.

• Quality of Counsel •

A disturbing aspect of capital sentencing is the role that money and luck play in the quality of the defense that capital defendants receive. Defendants who are unable to obtain the assistance of first-rate lawyers are more vulnerable to conviction and condemnation than are defendants who have more resources to hire lawyers, or who simply have better luck in the process of being appointed an attorney. Highly skilled and dedicated lawyers with substantial resources to hire investigators and expert witnesses are much better able to assist their clients at every stage of criminal proceedings.

The U.S. Supreme Court set standards for what constitutes effective assistance of counsel in the case of *Strickland v. Washington*.[60] In general, appellate courts have been reluctant to find lawyers ineffective. Appellate courts have refused to grant relief to capital defendants whose attorneys engaged in the following behavior: sleeping during the trial, being arrested on the way to trial for drunk driving, using illegal drugs during trial, making racial slurs against their own clients in front of the jury, being absent from the courtroom during crucial stages of the trial, not having read the state's death penalty statute, and filing an appellate brief consisting of 33 words.[61] One "effective" attorney's entire penalty phase presentation to the jury consisted of the following:

> Defense Counsel: Ladies and Gentlemen, I appreciate the time you took deliberating and the thought you put into this. I'm going to be extremely brief. I have a reputation for not being brief. Jesse, stand up. Jesse?
>
> The Defendant: Sir?
>
> Defense Counsel: Stand up. You are an extremely intelligent jury. You've got that man's life in your hands. You can take it or not. That's all I have to say.[62]

Not surprisingly, the jury returned a death sentence. The defendant was executed.

This does not mean that every capital defendant is poorly represented. Several jurisdictions have provided substantial funding for the services of lawyers, expert witnesses, and jury consultants. New York pays lead attorneys $125 an hour in capital cases.[63] In a number of other states, however, fees are severely limited:

> Alabama limits compensation for out-of court preparation to $20 per hour, up to a limit of $1,000. . . . [In a case in which lawyers devoted substantial time to preparation] they were still paid $1,000 each, or $4.05 and $5.32 per hour.
>
> In some rural areas in Texas, lawyers receive no more than $800 to handle a capital case. . . . A study in Virginia found that, after taking into account an attorney's overhead expenses, the effective hourly rate paid to counsel representing an indigent accused in a capital case was $13. In Kentucky, the limit for a capital case is $2,500.[64]

The Fifth Circuit Court of Appeals wrote of one Texas case, "The state paid defense counsel $11.84 an hour. Unfortunately, the justice system got only what it paid for."[65] Some indigent defendants are lucky enough to be represented by excellent lawyers, who may be well paid, poorly paid, or not paid at all, but who provide high-quality representation at trial and/or on appeal. While this is fortunate for those individuals, the role of luck once again points out the highly capricious nature of the U.S. capital sentencing system.

If the death penalty is being imposed in a discriminatory and capricious manner, why don't we do whatever is necessary to correct the problem and ensure that it is imposed fairly? The difficulty, of course, is that the problems are not easily fixed. Every current death penalty statute is an effort to correct the problems of arbitrary and capricious imposition identified in *Furman*, yet those problems persist. On the practical side, the death penalty is already prohibitively expensive, and improving our current system would be likely to make it even more costly.

THE COST OF CAPITAL PUNISHMENT

In recent years, there has been much discussion of the economic costs of capital punishment. Robert Bohm summarized what is known: "The evidence clearly shows that capital punishment systems in the United States are always more expensive than punishment systems without capital punishment because 'super due process' is required in the former but not in the latter."[66] There are three points about cost that will be addressed below: What does the death penalty cost compared to long-term imprisonment, why is the death penalty so costly, and should the cost of the penalty influence whether we use it?

Every study of the cost of capital punishment has concluded that it is more expensive to execute prisoners under our current system than it is to keep them incarcerated for many years. The most thorough study done to date compared capital and noncapital cases in North Carolina, and concluded that it costs at least $2.16 million dollars more per execution than it would have cost to try defendants without the possibility of a death sentence and to keep them in prison for life.[67]

When people think about the cost of the death penalty, they often ask what it costs the state to execute a single inmate versus what it would cost to keep that inmate in prison for many years. Framing the question in this way is somewhat misleading, however, and will result in underestimating death penalty expenses, because we must support an entire system of capital punishment before any executions result. In other words, taxpayers cannot buy a single execution; they must buy the whole system that ultimately may produce that execution. This is important because the system has such a high attrition rate. Recall the figures given earlier in this chapter indicating that only one or two inmates are executed each year for every 100 on death row. All the expenses of pretrial investigation, trial, appeals, and maintenance on death row, however, must be paid for all of these cases.

It is important to realize that many of the costs of capital punishment are borne on the county level. Counties with a low tax base can be hard-pressed to pay the costs of capital trials, but even large urban counties can feel the strain. Mark Costanzo reports that commissioners in Harris County (Houston) Texas sought a tax increase to pay for capital trials; when voters refused the increased tax, fire and ambulance services were cut.[68] See Box 14.4 for descriptions of how some counties are struggling to pay the costs of capital punishment locally.

Supporters of a quicker, more efficient, and less costly death penalty system point out that cutting back on appeals and perhaps even on due process at trials could greatly streamline the process and lower expenses. This is no doubt true, but true at a cost. As the above sections demonstrate, our current system is not operating particularly well even with all its safeguards. We could cut back on those safeguards to obtain a quicker and more efficient system, but is it possible to do this without risking increasing the number of errors and miscarriages of justice?

What influence should cost have on policy in this instance? In a moral sense, the whole issue of cost may be irrelevant to whether we should use capital punishment. If the death penalty has demonstrable benefits that outweigh the benefits of alternate punishments, we should use it even if it is more costly than the alternatives. After all, we could save the billions of dollars we spend on police, courts, and corrections by simply abolishing the entire criminal justice system, but no one proposes this as a cost-cutting measure. If, on the other hand, the death penalty does not benefit society more than alternative sentences, and it is substantially more expensive than those alternatives, then cost considerations may well influence us to use the more cost-effective sentences. If the death penalty actually inflicts social harm, then its greater cost is simply another reason to abolish it.

THE EFFECTS OF EXECUTIONS

Despite the problems with the way the death penalty is currently imposed, it is possible that capital punishment delivers certain benefits to society that are unavailable from any other penalty. If this is so, those benefits might outweigh the problems of racial disparities, wrongful convictions, and capricious imposition. Proponents of the death penalty frequently assert that the penalty provides two such benefits, each of which is discussed below. They assert that the death penalty saves the lives of innocent people, by preventing murder either through deterrence or incapacitation, and that the death penalty benefits victims' families by giving them the closure and peace of mind that only the death of the offender can provide.

BOX 14.4

Counties and the Cost of the Death Penalty

The Death Penalty Information Center cites the following examples of counties struggling with expenses in recent death penalty cases:.

- "Officials in Washington state are concerned that costs for a single death penalty trial will approach $1 million. To pay for the trial, the county has had to let one government position go unfilled, postponed employee pay hikes, drained its $300,000 contingency fund and eliminated all capital improvements. The Sheriff's request to replace a van which broke down last year for transporting prisoners has been shelved."

- "Thurston County in Washington state has budgeted $346,000 in 1999 alone, to seek Mitchell Rupe's 3rd death sentence. Rupe is also dying of liver disease. Washington has made extreme efforts to save Rupe from a natural death just so it can execute him. Since 1997, Thurston County budgeted nearly $700,000 for the most recent sentencing hearing alone—expenses above the daily costs absorbed by the county prosecutor's office."

- "In Imperial County, California, the county supervisors refused to pay the bill for the defense of a man facing the death penalty because the case would bankrupt the county. The county budget officer spent three days in jail for refusing to pay the bill. [The case] ended up costing the County half a million dollars. In the criminal trial, the defendant was acquitted."

- "[In] Lincoln County, Georgia [. . .] the county commissioners also refused to pay the defense costs when the attorney won a new trial for a death row inmate Johnny Lee Jones. As in California, the commissioners were sent to jail. . . . The first trial alone cost the county $125,000. . . . [In] the second trial . . . the defendant received a life sentence."

- "In Mississippi, Kemper and Lauderdale Counties recently conducted a border survey battle to avoid responsibility for a capital murder trial. Faced with a case that could cost the county $100,000, Kemper County wanted to show that the scene of the murder was outside their border and conducted two surveys of the site. . . . Kemper County is considering how much it will have to raise taxes just to pay the initial costs of the prosecution."

Sources: Examples drawn from Dieter, C. (1994). *Millions Misspent: What Politicians Don't Say about the High Costs of the Death Penalty*. Washington, DC: Death Penalty Information Center; Death Penalty Information Center (1999). Available at http://www.deathpenaltyinfo.org/dpic.r08.html

• Deterrence •

The deterrent effect of the death penalty has been more extensively researched than any other aspect of capital punishment. Scores of studies testing for a deterrent effect have been published since the mid-1800s when researchers first used statistics to address the issue. These studies have ranged from the very simple to those using highly complex statistical techniques and research designs. Despite the large number of studies, their results are not difficult to summarize. The overwhelming majority have found no evidence of a deterrent effect beyond that exerted by a long term of imprisonment. Increasingly sophisticated studies have confirmed the findings of the simpler earlier studies. The few studies concluding that the death penalty deterred more homicides than long imprisonment were severely flawed in their methods.

Before looking at the research evidence, it is important to be clear about just what researchers are trying to learn when they test for a deterrent effect of the death penalty. First, deterrence must be distinguished from incapacitation, which is punishment that renders the offender incapable of committing another crime. A potential offender is deterred when he or she weighs the benefits of crime against the costs and decides that the price is too high. For most punishments, this decision can be made with reference to the offender's own previous experience with the punishment (specific deterrence) or with reference to his or her knowledge of the experience of others with the punishment (general deterrence). Therefore, any deterrent effect the death penalty has can only be general. A final point of clarification concerns what is sometimes called marginal deterrence. In public discussions of deterrence, the issue is often framed as though we are testing whether the death penalty has any deterrent effect at all. However, no one is proposing that we abolish all punishment for murder. What we need to know is whether the death penalty deters more so than the available alternative punishments. Any deterrent effect of capital punishment above and beyond that of the alternative punishment is referred to as the marginal or superior deterrent effect of the death penalty.

A review of the vast research literature on deterrence and capital punishment is beyond the scope of this chapter. Following Bailey and Peterson's review of this research,[69] it is possible to mention at least the major types of deterrence studies. Early studies often used what Bailey and Peterson call the "comparative method"; researchers compared homicide rates in similar jurisdictions that do or do not use capital punishment, or in the same jurisdiction before and after a change in law. These studies consistently failed to show a superior deterrent effect of the death penalty over alternate punishments.

In the 1970s, researchers began to take a more sophisticated approach, using multivariate statistics and control variables. The best known of these studies, by Isaac Ehrlich, is one of the few to indicate that the death penalty has a marginal deterrent effect.[70] Ehrlich's work has been thoroughly critiqued and his conclusions strongly disputed (and some would say discredited) by other researchers.[71] This literature does not yield itself to a simple summary; the issues are complex and technical. However, the consensus of the majority of scholars and the results of the majority of these studies indicate no superior deterrent effect of the death penalty over the deterrent effect of other punishments. An important contribution to the literature on deterrence is a study testing the deterrent effect of the death penalty in Texas between 1984 and 1997. The authors concluded, "The number of executions did not appear to influence either the rate of murder in general or the rate of felony murder in particular."[72]

Another approach to testing deterrence focuses on the publicity generated by executions. Researchers have reasoned that the more publicity executions receive, the greater the deterrent effect should be, and therefore the greater the decrease in the homicide rate. Researchers have examined the number of homicides in the weeks or months before and after highly publicized executions. The vast majority of these studies give no indication that homicides decrease as deterrence theory predicts; indeed, a number of these studies show an increase in homicides after highly publicized executions. Studies examining the effects of the first executions in many years in Oklahoma, Arizona, and California found a significant increase in certain types of homicide.[73] A final type of research is that which tests whether the death penalty offers any special protection to police or correctional officers. Few studies have addressed this question; those that have fail to show that the death penalty deters more homicides than other punishments.[74]

Why doesn't the death penalty work as an effective deterrent? Why don't people always wear seat belts, obey the speed limit, and stop for red lights? Rationality has a rather limited role in shaping human behavior, especially when we act under the pressure of overwhelming emotion, as is often the case in homicides. Recall our discussion of the background of many capital defendants. Their histories of neurological and cognitive impairment, horrific childhood abuse and neglect, multiple substance abuse, and poor judgment and social adaptation do not argue for the likelihood that they rationally and realistically weigh the results of their actions. It is true, of course, that some killings are calmly deliberated, and one might expect these to be deterrable. Recent research on criminal decisionmaking, however, indicates that when offenders pause to ponder the consequences of their actions, they simply convince themselves that they won't get caught at all and therefore need not be concerned with any legal penalties.[75] Any rational offender who calculates the odds of being executed for any particular murder will quickly learn that the chances of such a result are extremely slight.

As mentioned above, some research has found evidence that executions may increase rather than decrease homicides. This is referred to as the brutalization effect, meaning that the use of lethal punishment by the government may increase lethal behavior by citizens. The intended deterrent effect of an execution may be reversed if potential murderers identify not with the criminal being punished but with those doing the punishing. In this case, the message received may be that killing is acceptable if the person killed is perceived as deserving death.[76] At this time, the brutalization hypothesis has not been tested thoroughly enough to support definite conclusions, though some studies of single jurisdictions are strongly suggestive of such an effect. The overall state of knowledge about deterrence has been summarized by Bohm: "...capital punishment has virtually no effect on crime, capital or otherwise...."[77]

• Incapacitation •

The death penalty permanently incapacitates offenders; that is, it renders them incapable of committing further crimes. There is no disputing this point, and retentionists often refer to it as one of the strongest arguments in support of capital punishment. While it is clear that an executed inmate cannot kill any more victims (at least outside of prison), what is not clear is how many more victims he or she would have killed had he or she not been executed.

James Marquart and Jonathan Sorensen[78] have done the most complete study of this question. They obtained data on 558 of the 613 inmates whose death sentences had been overturned by *Furman v. Georgia*, and tracked their behavior over a period of 15 years. In prison, the 558 inmates were responsible for four killings of prisoners and two killings of correctional officers after their death sentences were reduced. A total of 239 of the previously condemned inmates were released from prison. At the time of the study, the subjects had spent an average of five years in society. One of them committed a second homicide after release. Thus, Marquart and Sorensen found a total of seven homicides that would have been prevented by the execution of these 558 inmates.

As is so often the case, abolitionists and retentionists interpret the same data to support different conclusions. Many retentionists argue that the lives of the seven innocent victims who could have been saved were well worth the guilty lives the executions would have taken. However, abolitionists would be quick to counter that at least six of the 558 inmates were innocent and have since been cleared of the crimes for which they were condemned.[79] Thus the executions of 553 guilty inmates, and five wrongful executions of the innocent, would have saved seven victims' lives. The proper balance of the value of lives of innocent and guilty persons is a moral question, and thus cannot be answered by empirical research, but Marquart and Sorensen's research does indicate that a large number of executions would be required to prevent a small number of subsequent homicides.

• Families of Victims and Defendants •

> There is little enough we can do to ease the pain of grieving survivors, but hanging murderers would help. Many families can find no peace as long as the slayer of their loved one lives. They are filled with rage and despair, they want the killer dead. By seeking the death penalty for willful murderers, society can offer these families a measure of comfort, and assure them that their loss is taken seriously.[80]

Many people would agree with the above statement, including many murder victims' family members. The long-term effects of executions on homicide victims' families, however, simply are not known. Despite the great importance of this issue, systematic research has not been done to learn whether executions do have positive effects for the victims' families. It is hoped that research will be done soon to provide this important information. If the death penalty does benefit victims' families more than a sentence of imprisonment, in many people's minds, that single benefit will outweigh all of the negative aspects of capital punishment.

It should not be forgotten, however, that a substantial number of victims' families do not want the death penalty. There are various reasons for their opposition. Some victims' families oppose capital punishment for moral or religious reasons; others feel that the memory of their relative would be diminished by an act of violence. Some families may wish to resolve the whole matter as quickly and finally as possible, thereby avoiding the prolonged contact with the criminal justice system that the current system of death penalty appeals involves. A few families may hope for eventual mediation or reconciliation with the offender; this is perhaps most likely when victim and offender are members of the same family.[81] In her book, *Dead Man Walking*, Sister Helen Prejean noted that the father of a murder victim told her that he would have been satisfied with imprisonment for his son's murderer; what he really wanted—and got—was an apology.[82]

The defendant's family is often overlooked in discussions of the effect of the death penalty. Albert Camus' description of their experience continues to ring true, although the "long months of waiting" are now long years, or even decades, of waiting:

> The relatives of the condemned man then discover an excess of suffering that punishes them beyond all justice. A mother's or a father's long months of waiting, the visiting-room, the artificial conversations filling up the brief moments spent with the

condemned man, the visions of the execution are all tortures.
. . . [The death penalty] punishes, in iniquity, their innocence
and their misfortune.[83]

Families of condemned prisoners grieve for their relatives' deaths
for years in advance of the event. They must cope with their personal
loss knowing that many people actively desire their relative's death, and
they feel the public shame and disgrace of the death sentence.[84] Any
benefit that executions may have for the families of the victims should
be weighed against the anguish that the death penalty causes the families
of the condemned.

• Moral Arguments •

It is possible to recognize the flaws in the way the death penalty is
administered and still to support it as a morally justified and necessary
punishment. Doing so shifts the ground of the debate from empirical
evidence to moral argument. This chapter cannot begin to give adequate
coverage to the moral arguments for and against the death penalty, and
so only outlines their main points.[85]

Moral arguments fall into three major categories: those that rely on
religion, those that rely on moral reasoning, and those that rely on public opinion. Religiously based arguments are absolute, grounded in faith,
and not susceptible to falsification. If people believe that God has either
ordained or forbidden the death penalty, it is unlikely that discussion of
the issue will change their views. The same religious texts can be perceived as commanding and forbidding capital punishment, and members
of the same religions often disagree. It is noteworthy, however, that in
the United States, "Religious organizations are nearly unanimous in their
condemnation of capital punishment. More than 40 such organizations
(including American Baptists, Catholics, Episcopalians, Jews, Lutherans,
Mennonites, Methodists, Presbyterians, Quakers, and Unitarians) have
issued statements calling for the abolition of capital punishment."[86]

A second type of argument proceeds from moral principles. Primary among these is the retributivist argument for the death penalty.[87]
Grounded in the philosophy of Immanuel Kant, retributivism holds
that executions are necessary to restore the moral order that has been
disrupted by the offender's acts. Not only does the criminal deserve
his or her punishment, but society fails in its duty if it does not punish him or her to the full extent deserved. Kant believed that a rational
actor who chooses to behave in a certain way toward another person
"implicitly authorizes similar action by his fellows toward him."[88] Thus,
the defendant's act of murder justifies the state in taking his or her life.
Any other potential benefits of capital punishment, such as deterrence
or incapacitation, are secondary to the moral requirement to punish

A German postage stamp bearing the likeness of Immanuel Kant. Kant's concept of retributivism is often cited by capital punishment proponents as a morale rationale for the death penalty.

as deserved. Ernest van den Haag, who has written extensively in support of the death penalty on retributivist grounds, states: "Retribution, as deserved by the crime, is the paramount moral purpose of punishment. It is an end in itself, a categorical imperative."[89]

Retributive justice requires the careful calibration of the severity of punishment to the severity of crime.[90] As the most severe punishment, the death penalty is well-suited to punish murder. To quote van den Haag once more: "Is the death penalty too severe? It stands in a class by itself. But so does murder. Execution is irreparable. So is murder. . . . The death penalty thus is congruous with the moral and material gravity of the crime it punishes."[91]

Retributivism is probably the strongest philosophical argument for the death penalty, although it works better as a theoretical justification for capital punishment than as a justification for the death penalty system as it actually functions. It may be problematic to support a punishment by an abstract appeal to justice when so much evidence indicates that the punishment is imposed unfairly in practice.[92] Another challenge to retributivist support for the death penalty argues that proportionality requires only that the harshest punishment be reserved for the worst crime, but does not specify what that punishment must be. A society that used life without parole as its most severe punishment and imposed it on its worst criminals would thus meet the requirements of retributivism.

A third type of moral argument asserts that the death penalty should continue to be used in the United States because the public supports its use.[93] It is true that a majority of Americans continue to express support for the death penalty when pollsters ask the simple question of whether people support or oppose capital punishment. A growing body of research on public opinion indicates that death penalty support may not be as strong as it first seems, however. When people are asked to choose between the death penalty and a sentence of life without parole for convicted murderers, the majority chooses life without parole, especially if it is combined with some form of restitution to the victim's family.[94] These results have been found in many states and nationally, indicating that although only a minority of Americans absolutely opposes the death penalty, a majority prefers a sentence that keeps the defendant in prison for his or her entire natural life. Many states now offer a sentencing option of life without parole for persons convicted of first-degree murder,[95] although the public, jurors, and even legislators are often unaware of the alternate sentence, or do not believe that it is enforced.

CONCLUSION

The evidence of public willingness to accept an alternative to the death penalty brings us back to the question posed at the beginning of this chapter. How long will the United States continue its use of the death penalty, given that a majority of the public appears ready to accept real life sentences as an alternative? Predicting the future is not easy. It seems safe to say, however, that the United States is unlikely to wholly abandon capital punishment any time soon.

On the other hand, it is conceivable that the death penalty in America is approaching its end. Several recent developments could contribute to this outcome. The steep decline in homicide and other violent crimes that has occurred in the last decade may lessen public and political enthusiasm for capital punishment. Indeed, public support for capital punishment fell sharply in the late 1990s, and has not risen significantly in response to the terrorist attacks or other high-profile crimes. The great expense and delay of the current system and increasing international pressure to abandon the death penalty may eventually make the enforcement of the penalty more trouble than it is worth to its supporters. In this regard, it may be significant that the pace of executions and of death sentencing have slowed in the past few years.

A surprisingly strong movement for a moratorium on executions has sprung up recently, partly motivated by the exoneration of a number of condemned prisoners. This movement does not necessarily call for the abolition of the death penalty but only for a temporary pause in executions while the system is studied and reformed. The moratorium movement draws support from people who favor the death penalty but who are troubled by the persistent problems in its current use. The effort to achieve a moratorium began in 1997 with the American Bar Association's call to suspend executions until the legal system adequately addresses problems of racial discrimination, capricious imposition of death sentences, and wrongful convictions. Moratorium legislation has been introduced in a number of states, and was passed by the legislatures in both Nebraska and New Hampshire, although vetoed by the governors. As discussed earlier, in 2000, Governor George Ryan of Illinois declared a moratorium on executions in that state due to his concerns about the number of innocent people on death row. Governor Parris Glendening of Maryland followed suit in May of 2002, declaring a moratorium until the completion of a study of racial disparities in the state's death sentencing.

A final possibility is that the U.S. Supreme Court may at some point revisit the issue and rule that the death penalty is unconstitutional.

Although the Court has abolished the death penalty for the mentally ill and for juveniles, this possibility seems remote. In 2008, by a seven-to-two vote, the Court upheld the constitutionality of lethal injection. On the other hand, although Justice John Paul Stevens concurred with the judgment about lethal injection, he wrote a lengthy opinion arguing that the death penalty is not necessary for incapacitation, deterrence, or even retribution. He ended by saying that he had reached the conclusion that the death penalty is no longer constitutional:

> In sum,...I have relied on my own experience in reaching the conclusion that the imposition of the death penalty represents "the pointless and needless extinction of life with only marginal contributions to any discernible social or public purposes. A penalty with such negligible returns to the State [is] violative of the Eighth Amendment.[96]

DISCUSSION QUESTIONS

1. Can the administration of the death penalty be improved by changing the laws? Draft a model death penalty statute that you think would adequately guide juror discretion.

2. What are some ways society could help murder victims' family members beyond convicting and sentencing the offender?

3. A Supreme Court ruling now prevents juveniles from being sentenced to death. Do you support or oppose this ruling, and why?

4. Should the policies of the United States' criminal justice system be influenced by practices in other countries? Why or why not?

5. A number of recent executions have been "botched"—that is, the prisoners' deaths were prolonged and possibly quite painful. Does the state have an obligation to provide a quick and painless means of death?

6. Some people support a moratorium on executions until the system can be studied and any flaws that are found can be corrected. Others argue that the moratorium effort is really an attempt to abolish the death penalty permanently. Discuss the pros and cons of a moratorium.

7. How large a part should the wishes of the victim's family play in determining a sentence? If family wishes should be given great weight, what should be done when members of the same family disagree as to the proper punishment?

8. How much, if any, consideration should be given to the effect of a death sentence on the prisoner's family? Is this a sufficient reason to spare people from execution?

▶ Ethics Focus: Life Without Parole

After the Supreme Court ruled that the death penalty is unconstitutional for juveniles (*Roper v. Simmons*, 543 U.S. 551, 2005), many people thought that this solved the problem of inappropriate sentences for juvenile murderers. What has happened, however, is that now many juvenile murderers are receiving Life-without-Parole sentences (LWOP). The latest available information shows that some 2,225 juveniles are serving LWOP sentences (Feld, 2008).

Critics argue that LWOP sentences are also inappropriate for juveniles. The same rationale that influenced the Supreme Court to rule capital punishment unconstitutional for juveniles—that juveniles are developmentally immature and therefore not fully accountable for their actions—applies to LWOP sentences. In other words, many argue that the psychological immaturity and impulsivity of juveniles should also rule out a sentence of life without parole. Feld, for example, argues that juveniles' lack of complete development should dictate a sentence of no longer than 20 to 30 years for even the most serious crimes.

In the *Roper* decision, Justice Antonin Scalia argued that he would leave the decision of the penalty for a murder by a juvenile in the hands of the jury in that case. He argued that the jury should take into account the possible immaturity of the juvenile and decide whether to impose the death penalty. So, arguably, he would argue for such jury decisionmaking concerning life without parole. Recall also, however, that youth (immaturity) is supposed to be a mitigator that juries consider to reduce sentences down from the death penalty. In practice, though, juries often use youth (young age) as an aggravator; juries often think that if an offender is young he represents a greater danger and therefore should receive a harsher or longer sentence.

What do you think?

Source: Feld, B.C. (2008). "A Slower Form of Death: Implications of *Roper v. Simmons* for Juveniles Sentenced to Life Without Parole." *Notre Dame Journal of Law, Ethics, and Public Policy* 22:9-65.

▶ At the Movies . . . .

Dead Man Walking, 1996.

Starring Sean Penn and Susan Sarandon, this movie gives the account of Sister Helen Prejean's work as a spiritual advisor for a prisoner in Louisiana.

The Life of David Gale, 2003.

This movie, starring Kevin Spacey and Kate Winslet, is about a college professor who wants to demonstrate in real life some of the problems with the death penalty.

FURTHER READING

Grisham, J. (2006). *The Innocent Man: Murder and Injustice in a Small Town*. New York: Doubleday.

Masters, J. (1997). *Finding Freedom: Writings from Death Row*. Junction City, CA: Padma.

Prejean, H. (2005). *The Death of Innocents: An Eyewitness Account of Wrongful Executions*. New York: Random House.

NOTES

1. For a thorough review, see Bohm, 2007.

2. Amnesty International, 2007.

3. Amnesty International, 2007.

4. Amnesty International, 2007.

5. Schabas, 1997.

6. *The New York Times*, 1999, A:4. The countries opposing the moratorium were the United States, China, Bangladesh, Botswana, Indonesia, Japan, Pakistan, Rwanda, South Korea, Sudan, and Qatar.

7. Sharf, 1997, 58.

8. Morris and Patterson, 1999.

9. Costanzo, 1997, 153.

10. Prinzo, 1999.

11. Paternoster, 1991, 6.

12. Espy, 1997.

13. Wright, 1990; Marquart, Ekland-Olson, and Sorensen, 1994; Tolnay and Beck, 1995.

14. Bohm, 2007

15. *Furman v. Georgia*, 408 U.S. 238, 1972, 239-240.

16. *Woodson v. North Carolina*, 428 U.S. 280, 1976; *Roberts v. Louisiana*, 428 U.S. 325, 1976.

17. *Gregg v. Georgia*, 428 U.S. 153, 1967; *Proffitt v. Florida*, 428 U.S. 242, 1976; *Jurek v. Texas*, 428 U.S. 262, 1976.

18. *Lockett v. Ohio*, 43 8 U.S. 586, 1978.

19. Bohm, 1998a, 28.

20. Death Penalty Information Center, 2008.

21. Bureau of Justice Statistics, *Capital Punishment, 2006—Statistical Tables*; available at http://www.ojp.usdoj.gov

22. Crocker, 1998.

23. Bureau of Justice Statistics, *Capital Punishment, 2006—Statistical Tables*; available at http://www.ojp.usdoj.gov

24. Denno, 1998, 574-576.

25. Harries and Cheatwood, 1997, 30. For an excellent overview of this issue, see Lofquist, 2002.

26. Bedau, 1997, 21. It should be noted, however, that New York reinstated capital punishment in 1995, and that there have been repeated attempts to pass a capital statute in Massachusetts.

27. Bedau, 1997, 21.

28. Death Penalty Information Center, 2008.

29. Streib, 1998, 203.

30. Death Penalty Information Center, 2008.

31. See Rapaport (1990) for a history of the execution of women in America and a discussion of the issues of leniency and severity in sentencing women to death.

32. NAACP Legal Defense and Educational Fund, Inc., 2002, 5.

33. NAACP Legal Defense and Educational Fund, Inc., 2002, 5.

34. Death Penalty Information Center, 2008.

35. The United States Supreme Court has ruled that the execution of mentally retarded individuals is a violation of the Eighth Amendment protection against cruel and unusual punishment, *Atkins v. Virginia*, 122 S. Ct. 2242, 2002.

36. Lewis et al., 1988, 1986.

37. Haney, 1995. No one claims that the experience of abuse and poverty is a necessary and sufficient cause of later violence. At most, the claim is that people who have had these experiences are more likely than others to be violent. This is a probability statement, and thus allows for exceptions.

38. Haney, 1998, 364.

39. Bedau, 1997, 32. Note that these figures may have changed somewhat since Bedau's figures were gathered. The overall point of the rarity of executions as a response to homicide remains valid.

40. Liebman et al., 2000, 1865.

41. Burnett, 2002.

42. Radelet, Bedau, and Putnam, 1992; Bedau and Radelet, 1987.

43. Radelet and Bedau, 1998, 239.

44. Death Penalty Information Center, 2008.

45. Dieter, 1997a.

46. For discussion of these and other safeguards, see Berlow, 1999, 88, 91.

47. van den Haag, 1998, 148.

48. U.S. General Accounting Office, 1997, 271, 272.

49. Baldus, Pulaski, and Woodworth, 1990.

50. *McCleskey v. Kemp*, 481 U.S. 279, 1987.

51. *McCleskey* at 297.

52. *McCleskey* at 344.

53. Among other studies see, Baldus et al., 1998; Sorensen and Wallace, 1999; Thomson, 1997a; Dieter, 1998.

54. Pokarak, 1998, 1817.

55. Amnesty International, 1999.

56. See Harries and Cheatwood, 1997, 34-37, for examples.

57. Dieter, 1996, iii. See also Bright and Keenan, 1995.

58. See Bright, 1998, 123-124, and Dieter, 1996, 2-5, for examples.

59. For an overview of the Capital Jury Project, see the symposium issue of the *Indiana Law Journal*, 1995. More recent publications from the Capital Jury Project include Bowers, Sandys, and Steiner, 1998; Bowers and Steiner, 1999; Bentele and Bowers, 2001.

60. *Strickland v. Washington*, 466 U.S. 668, 1984.

61. Bright, 1997; see also Coyle, Strasser, and Lavelle, 1990.

62. *Romero v. Lynaugh*, 884 F.2d 871, 1989, 875.

63. Finder, 1998. The rate was $175 an hour until late 1998, when it was cut.

64. Bright, 1997, 285.

65. *Martinez-Macias v. Collins*, 979 F.2d 1067 (5th Circuit 1992), quoted by Bright, 1997, 285.

66. Bohm, 1998b, 456; See Bohm, 2007.

67. Cook and Slawson, 1993.

68. Costanzo, 1997, 61.

69. Bailey and Peterson, 1997.

70. Ehrlich, 1975.

71. Among the many critiques of Ehrlich's work, see especially Baldus and Cole, 1975; Bowers and Pierce, 1975; Klein, Forst, and Filatov, 1978.

72. Sorensen et al., 1999.

73. Cochran, Chamblin, and Seth, 1994; Thomson, 1997b; Thomson, 1999.

74. Bailey and Peterson, 1994; Wolfson, 1982.

75. Tunnell, 1992; Wright, 1997.

76. Bowers and Pierce, 1980.

77. Bohm, 2007, 193.

78. Marquart and Sorensen, 1989.

79. In their paper, Marquart and Sorensen note that four of the inmates had been exonerated. Since their paper was published, at least two other inmates on death row at the time of the *Furman* decision have been cleared of the crimes for which they were condemned. See Death Penalty Information Center, 2000b. It is quite possible that others will be exonerated in the future.

80. Jacoby, 1996.

81. Vandiver, 1998.

82. Prejean, 1993, 244.

83. Camus, 1961, 205.

84. For a personal account, see Gilmore, 1994.

85. Readers seeking thorough and balanced treatment of these issues are referred to Steffen, 1998, and Pojman and Reiman, 1998.

86. Costanzo, 1997, 132-133.

87. For an excellent statement of this position, see Berns, 1979.

88. Pojman and Reiman, 1998, 90-91.

89. van den Haag, 1998, 139-140.

90. This calibration of severity does not require any crude physical correspondence between crime and punishment, however. Thus, it is not necessary to reproduce the damage done the victim upon the property or body of the offender. It is merely necessary to ensure that punishment is proportional to offense.

91. van den Haag, 1997, 453.

92. It is worth reflecting on whether Americans would tolerate a death penalty statute that was written to reflect the reality of our system honestly. Would we accept a law stating that executions, with some few exceptions, are reserved for indigent male defendants with poor legal representation, who killed white victims? If not, we should consider why we are willing to accept such a system in practice.

93. It is questionable, of course, whether public support can lend legitimacy to a policy if that policy is morally flawed. Large segments of the American public have supported many clearly immoral policies in the past, among them slavery, the expulsion and killing of Native Americans, and legal segregation.

94. Bowers, Vandiver, and Dugan, 1994; Dieter, 1997b.

95. Dieter, 1997b, 119.

96. Stevens, J., concurring opinion, *Baze et al. v. Rees*, 553 U.S. _____ (2008). Quoting Justice White in *Furman*, 408 U.S. 238 at 312).

96. *Callins v. Collins*, 510 U.S. 1141, 1994, 1130.

REFERENCES

Amnesty International (2002a). "Facts and Figures on the Death Penalty." Available at http://www.amnesty.org

Amnesty International (2002b). "Indecent and Internationally Illegal: The Death Penalty Against Child Offenders." Available at http://www.amnesty.org

Amnesty International (2007). "Death Penalty Statistics—2007." Available at http://www.amnestyusa.org

Amnesty International (1999). "Killing with Prejudice: Race and the Death Penalty in the USA." Available from Amnesty International USA, 322 8th Avenue, New York, NY 10001.

Bailey, W.C., and R.D. Peterson (1997). "Murder, Capital Punishment and Deterrence: A Review of the Literature." In H.A. Bedau (ed.), *The Death Penalty in America: Current Controversies*, 135-161. New York and Oxford: Oxford University Press.

Bailey, W.C., and R.D. Peterson (1994). "Murder, Capital Punishment and Deterrence: A Review of the Evidence and an Examination of Police Killings." *Journal of Social Issues* 50:53-74.

Baldus, D., and J. Cole (1975). "A Comparison of the Work of Thorsten Sellin and Isaac Ehrlich on the Deterrent Effect of Capital Punishment." *Yale Law Journal* 18:170-186.

Baldus, D., C. Pulaski Jr., and G.W. Woodworth (1990). *Equal Justice and the Death Penalty: A Legal and Empirical Analysis*. Boston: Northeastern University Press.

Baldus, D.C., G.W. Woodworth, D. Zuckerman, N.A. Weiner, and B.S. Broffitt (1998). "Racial Discrimination and the Death Penalty in the Post-*Furman* Era: An Empirical and Legal Overview, with Recent Findings from Philadelphia." *Cornell Law Review* 83:1638-1770.

Bedau, H.A. (ed.) (1997). *The Death Penalty in America: Current Controversies*. New York and Oxford: Oxford University Press.

Bedau, H.A., and M.L. Radelet (1987). "Miscarriages of Justice in Potentially Capital Cases." *Stanford Law Review* 40:21-179.

Bentele, U., and W.J. Bowers (2001). "How Jurors Decide on Death: Guilt Is Overwhelming; Aggravation Requires Death; and Mitigation Is No Excuse." *Brooklyn Law Review* 66:1011-1080.

Berlow, A. (1999). "The Wrong Man." *The Atlantic Monthly*, November 1999, 66-91.

Berns, W. (1979). *For Capital Punishment: Crime and the Morality of the Death Penalty*. New York: Basic Books.

Bohm, R.M. (2007). *Deathquest III: An Introduction to the Theory and Practice of Capital Punishment in the United States*. Newark, NJ: LexisNexis Matthew Bender.

Bohm, R.M. (1998a). "American Death Penalty Opinion: Past, Present, and Future." In J.R. Acker, R.M. Bohm, and C.S. Lanier (eds.), *America's Experiment with Capital Punishment*, 25-46. Durham, NC: Carolina Academic Press.

Bohm, R.M. (1998b). "The Economic Costs of Capital Punishment: Past, Present, and Future." In J.R. Acker, R.M. Bohm, and C.S. Lanier (eds.), *America's Experiment with Capital Punishment*, 437-458. Durham, NC: Carolina Academic Press.

Bowers, W.J., and G.L. Pierce (1980). "Deterrence or Brutalization: What Is the Effect of Executions?" *Crime & Delinquency* 26:453-484.

Bowers, W.J., and G.L. Pierce (1975). "The Illusion of Deterrence in Isaac Ehrlich's Research on Capital Punishment." *Yale Law Journal* 18:187-208.

Bowers, W.J., M. Sandys, and B.D. Steiner (1998). "Foreclosed Impartiality in Capital Sentencing: Jurors' Predispositions, Guilt-Trial Experience, and Premature Decision Making." *Cornell Law Review* 83:1476-1556.

Bowers, W.J., and B.D. Steiner (1999). "Death by Default: An Empirical Demonstration of False and Forced Choices in Capital Sentencing." *Texas Law Review* 77:605-717.

Bowers, W.J., M. Vandiver, and P.H. Dugan (1994). "A New Look at Public Opinion on Capital Punishment: What Citizens and Legislators Prefer." *American Journal of Criminal Law* 22:77-150.

Bright, S.B. (1998). "The Politics of Capital Punishment: The Sacrifice of Fairness for Executions." In J.R. Acker, R.M. Bohm, and C.S. Lanier (eds.), *America's Experiment with Capital Punishment*, 117-135. Durham, NC: Carolina Academic Press.

Bright, S.B. (1997 [1994]). "Counsel for the Poor: The Death Sentence Not for the Worst Crime But for the Worst Lawyer." In H.A. Bedau (ed.), *The Death Penalty in America: Current Controversies*, 445-456. New York and Oxford: Oxford University Press.

Bright, S.B., and P.J. Keenan (1995). "Judges and the Politics of Death: Deciding Between the Bill of Rights and the Next Election in Capital Cases." *Boston University Law Review* 75:759-835.

Bureau of Justice Statistics. *Capital Punishment, 2006—Statistical Tables*; available at http://www.ojp.usdoj.gov

Burnett, C. (2002). *Justice Denied: Clemency Appeals in Death Penalty Cases*. Boston: Northeastern University Press.

Camus, A. (1961). "Reflections on the Guillotine." In Albert Camus (trans. J. O'Brien), *Resistance, Rebellion, and Death*, 175-234. New York: Knopf.

Cochran, J.K., M.B. Chamblin, and M. Seth (1994). "Deterrence or Brutalization? An Impact Assessment of Oklahoma's Return to Capital Punishment." *Criminology* 32:107-134.

Cook, P.J., and D.B. Slawson (1993). *The Costs of Processing Murder Cases in North Carolina*. Durham, NC: Terry Sanford Institute of Public Policy, Duke University.

Costanzo, M. (1997). *Just Revenge: Costs and Consequences of the Death Penalty*. New York: St. Martin's Press.

Coyle, M., F. Strasser, and M. Lavelle (1990). "Fatal Defense: Trial and Error in the Nation's Death Belt." *National Law Journal* 40: 30-44.

Crocker, D. (1998). "Extended Stays: Does Lengthy Imprisonment on Death Row Undermine the Goals of Capital Punishment?" *The Journal of Gender, Race and Justice* 1:555-574.

Death Penalty Information Center (2002a). "Number of Executions by State Since 1976." Available at http://www.deathpenaltyinfo.org/dpicreg.html

Death Penalty Information Center (2002b). "Innocence and the Death Penalty." Available at http://www.deathpenaltyinfo.org/innoc.html

Death Penalty Information Center (2008). "Facts about the Death Penalty." Available at http://www.deathpenaltyinfo.org .

Denno, D.W. (1998). "Execution and the Forgotten Eighth Amendment." In J.R. Acker, R.M. Bohm, and C.S. Lanier (eds.), *America's Experiment with Capital Punishment*, 547-577. Durham, NC: Carolina Academic Press.

Dieter, R.C. (1998). *The Death Penalty in Black and White: Who Lives, Who Dies, Who Decides: New Studies on Racism in Capital Punishment*. Washington, DC: Death Penalty Information Center. Available from Death Penalty Information Center, 1320 18th St. NW, 5th Floor, Washington, DC 20036.

Dieter, R.C. (1997a). *Innocence and the Death Penalty: The Increasing Danger of Executing the Innocent*. Washington, DC: Death Penalty Information Center. Available from the Death Penalty Information Center, 1320 18th St. NW, 5th Floor, Washington, DC 20036.

Dieter, R.C. (1997b). "Sentencing for Life: Americans Embrace Alternatives to the Death Penalty." In H.A. Bedau (ed.), *The Death Penalty in America: Current Controversies*, 116-126. New York and Oxford: Oxford University Press.

Dieter, R.C. (1996). *Killing for Votes: The Dangers of Politicizing the Death Penalty Process*. Washington, DC: Death Penalty Information Center. Available from the Death Penalty Information Center, 1320 18th St. NW, 5th Floor, Washington, DC 20036.

Ehrlich, I. (1975). "The Deterrent Effect of Capital Punishment: A Question of Life or Death." *American Economic Review* 65:397-417.

Espy, W. (1997). *List of Confirmations, State by State, of Legal Executions as of January 15, 1997*. Available from Capital Punishment Research Project, P.O. Drawer 277, Headland, AL 36345.

Finder, A. (1998). "New York's Highest Court Cuts Fees for Defense Lawyers in Death Penalty Cases." *The New York Times*, December 24, 1998, B:5.

Gilmore, M. (1994). *Shot in the Heart*. New York: Doubleday.

Haney, C. (1998). "Mitigation and the Study of Lives: On the Roots of Violent Criminality and the Nature of Capital Justice." In J.R. Acker, R.M. Bohm, and C.S. Lanier (eds.), *America's Experiment with Capital Punishment*, 351-384. Durham, NC: Carolina Academic Press.

Haney, C. (1995). "The Social Context of Capital Murder: Social Histories and the Logic of Mitigation." *Santa Clara Law Review* 35:547-609.

Harries, K., and D. Cheatwood (1997). *The Geography of Execution: The Capital Punishment Quagmire in America*. Lanham, MD: Rowman and Littlefield.

Indiana Law Journal (1995). Symposium issue on Capital Jury Project, Volume 70.

Jacoby, J. (1996). "Twisted View of Compassion." *The [Memphis] Commercial Appeal*, December 16, 1996, A:9.

Klein, L., B. Forst, and V. Filatov (1978). "The Deterrent Effect of Capital Punishment: An Assessment of the Estimates." In A. Blumstein, J. Cohen, and D. Nagin (eds.), *Deterrence and Incapacitation: Estimating the Effects of Criminal Sanctions on Crime Rates*, 336-360. Washington, DC: National Academy of Sciences.

Lewis, D., J.H. Pincus, B. Bard, E. Richardson, L.S. Prichep, N. Feldman, and C. Yeager (1988). "Neuropsychiatric, Psychoeducational, and Family Characteristics of 14 Juveniles Condemned to Death in the United States." *American Journal of Psychiatry* 145:584-589.

Lewis, D., J.H. Pincus, M. Feldman, L. Jackson, and B. Bard (1986). "Psychiatric, Neurological, and Psychoeducational Characteristics of 15 Death Row Inmates in the United States." *American Journal of Psychiatry* 143:838-845.

Liebman, J.S., J. Fagan, V. West, and J. Lloyd (2000). "Capital Attrition: Error Rates in Capital Cases, 1973-1995." *Texas Law Review* 78:1839-1865.

Lofquist, W.S. (2002). "Putting Them There, Keeping Them There, and Killing Them: An Analysis of State-Level Variations in Death Penalty Intensity." *Iowa Law Review* 87:1505-1557.

Marquart, J.W., S. Ekland-Olson, and J.R. Sorensen (1994). *The Rope, the Chair and the Needle: Capital Punishment in Texas, 1923-1990*. Austin, TX: University of Texas Press.

Marquart, J.W., and J.R. Sorensen (1989). "A National Study of the Furman-Commuted Inmates: Assessing the Threat to Society from Capital Offenders." *Loyola of Los Angeles Law Review* 23:5-28.

Morris, C., and T. Paterson (1999). "EU Warns Turkey to Spare Ocalan; Don't Expect to Join if Kurdish Leader is Executed, Ankara Told." *The Guardian* (London), November 26, 1999, 2.

NAACP Legal Defense and Educational Fund, Inc. (2002). *Death Row U.S.A.*, Fall 2002. Available from NAACP Legal Defense and Educational Fund, 99 Hudson Street Suite 1600, New York, NY 10013-2897.

The New York Times (1999). "U.N. Panel Votes for Ban on Death Penalty." *The New York Times*, April 29, 1999, A:4.

Paternoster, R. (1991). *Capital Punishment in America*. New York: Lexington Books.

Pojman, L.P., and J. Reiman (1998). *The Death Penalty: For and Against*. Lanham, MD: Rowman and Littlefield.

Pokorak, J. (1998). "Probing the Capital Prosecutor's Perspective: Race of the Discretionary Actors." *Cornell Law Review* 83:1311-1820.

Prejean, H. (1993). *Dead Man Walking: An Eyewitness Account of the Death Penalty in the United States*. New York: Vintage Books.

Prinzo, K.T. (1999). "The United States—'Capital' of the World: An Analysis of Why the United States Practices Capital Punishment While the International Trend Is Towards Its Abolition." *Brooklyn Journal of International Law* 24:855-889.

Radelet, M.L., and H.A. Bedau (1998). "The Execution of the Innocent." In J.R. Acker, R.M. Bohm, and C.S. Lanier (eds.), *America's Experiment with Capital Punishment*, 223-242. Durham, NC: Carolina Academic Press.

Radelet, M.L., H.A. Bedau, and C.E. Putnam (1992). *In Spite of Innocence*. Boston: Northeastern University Press.

Rapaport, E. (1990). "Some Questions about Gender and the Death Penalty." *Golden Gate University Law Review* 20:501-565.

Schabas, W. (1997). *The Abolition of the Death Penalty in International Law*, 2nd ed. New York: Cambridge University Press.

Sharf, M.P. (1997). *Balkan Justice: The Story Behind the First International War Crimes Trial Since Nuremberg*. Durham, NC: Carolina Academic Press.

Sorensen, J., and D.H. Wallace (1999). "Prosecutorial Discretion in Seeking Death: An Analysis of Racial Disparity in the Pretrial Stages of Case Processing in a Midwestern County." *Justice Quarterly* 16:559-578.

Sorensen, J., R. Wrinkle, V. Brewer, and J. Marquart (1999). "Capital Punishment and Deterrence: Examining the Effect of Executions on Murder in Texas." *Crime & Delinquency* 45:481-493.

Steffen, L. (1998). *Executing Justice: The Moral Meaning of the Death Penalty*. Cleveland, OH: Pilgrim Press.

Streib, V.L. (1998). "Executing Women, Children, and the Retarded: Second Class Citizens in Capital Punishment." In J.R. Acker, R.M. Bohm, and C.S. Lanier (eds.), *America's Experiment with Capital Punishment*, 201-221. Durham, NC: Carolina Academic Press.

Thomson, E. (1999). "Effects of an Execution on Homicides in California." *Homicide Studies* 3:129-150.

Thomson, E. (1997a). "Discrimination and the Death Penalty in Arizona." *Criminal Justice Review* 22:65-76.

Thomson, E. (1997b). 'Deterrence Versus Brutalization: The Case of Arizona." *Homicide Studies* 1:110-128.

Tolnay, S.E., and E.M. Beck (1995). *A Festival of Violence: An Analysis of Southern Lynchings, 1882-1930*. Urbana and Chicago: University of Illinois Press.

Tunnell, K. (1992). *Choosing Crime: The Criminal Calculus of Property Offenders*. Chicago: Nelson-Hall.

U.S. General Accounting Office (1997 [1990]). "Death Penalty Sentencing: Research Indicates Pattern of Racial Disparities." In H.A. Bedau (ed.), *The Death Penalty in America: Current Controversies*, 268-274. New York and Oxford: Oxford University Press.

van den Haag, E. (1998). "Justice, Deterrence and the Death Penalty." In J.R. Acker, R.M. Bohm, and C.S. Lanier (eds.), *America's Experiment with Capital Punishment*, 139-156. Durham, NC: Carolina Academic Press.

van den Haag, E. (1997). "The Death Penalty Once More." In H.A. Bedau (ed.), *The Death Penalty in America: Current Controversies*, 445-456. New York and Oxford: Oxford University Press.

Vandiver, M. (1998). "The Impact of the Death Penalty on the Families of Homicide Victims and of Condemned Prisoners." In J.R. Acker, R.M. Bohm, and C.S. Lanier (eds.), *America's Experiment with Capital Punishment*, 477-505. Durham, NC: Carolina Academic Press.

Wolfson, W. (1982). "The Deterrent Effect of the Death Penalty upon Prison Murder." In H.A. Bedau (ed.), *The Death Penalty in America*, 3rd ed., 159-173. New York: Oxford University Press.

Wright, G.C. (1990). Racial Violence in Kentucky 1865-1940: *Lynchings, Mob Rule, and "Legal Lynchings."* Baton Rouge: Louisiana State University.

Wright, R. (1997). *Armed Robbers in Action: Stickups and Street Culture*. Boston: Northeastern University Press.

COURT CASES

Atkins v. Virginia, 536 U.S. 304 (2002).

Baze et al. v. Rees, 553 U.S._____ (2008).

Callins v. Collins, 510 U.S. 1141 (1994).

Felker v. Turpin, 518 U.S. 1051 (1996).

Ford v. Wainwright, 477 U.S. 399 (1986).

Furman v. Georgia, 408 U.S. 238 (1972).

Gregg v. Georgia, 428 U.S. 153 (1976).

Herrera v. Collins, 506 U.S. 390 (1993).

Jurek v. Texas, 428 U.S. 262 (1976).

Lockett v. Ohio, 438 U.S. 586 (1978).

Lockhart v. McCree, 476 U.S. 162 (1986).

McCleskey v. Kemp, 481 U.S. 279 (1987).

Martinez-Macias v. Collins, 979 F.2d 1067 (5th Cir. 1992).

Payne v. Tennessee, 501 U.S. 808 (1991).

Pulley v. Harris, 465 U.S. 37 (1984).

Proffitt v. Florida, 428 U.S. 242 (1976).

Romero v. Lynaugh, 884 F.2d 871 (5th Cir. 1989).

Roberts v. Louisiana, 428 U.S. 325 (1976).

Roper v. Simmons, 543 U.S. 551 (2005).

Schlup v. Delo, 513 U.S. 298 (1995).

Strickland v. Washington, 466 U.S. 668 (1984).

Woodson v. North Carolina, 428 U.S. 280 (1976).

The Evolution of Corrections: What Does the Future Hold?

CHAPTER 15

What You Need to Know

▶ One possible future for corrections is that current trends may continue: the get-tough approach, an emphasis on effective interventions, an emphasis on cutting costs, restorative justice, and restorative rehabilitation.

▶ There are also more speculative possibilities, including the end of probation, the remedicalization of corrections, or the increased use of technology in corrections.

▶ As corrections began with the Quakers and others emphasizing religious reformation, one possibility for the future is to focus on the reintroduction of the spiritual dimension in corrections. Efforts such as faith-based prisons are evidence that this is a possibility.

▶ Whatever direction the future of corrections takes, there are several critical issues that must be addressed and resolved.

INTRODUCTION

Because no one has a crystal ball that enables them to predict the future, it is difficult to forecast what corrections will be like 10 or 20 years from now. This chapter can attempt to do two things, however. First, we can suggest what the future will *probably* be like. We can use current trends to predict developments that may take place in corrections in the next decade. This approach is based on the assumption that the future often is an extension of the present. Second, we can explore what the future could *possibly* be like. With this view, we can be more daring and speculate on less likely but more dramatic changes that could take place. We will do both of these in this chapter. We will first list the current trends and then note the more speculative predictions. We will also note some critical issues that corrections will face in the next decade or more. Previous chapters have noted most if not all of these critical issues. However, we think it is important to revisit these issues as we close.

CURRENT TRENDS CONTINUING INTO THE FUTURE

One current trend that is likely to continue is the punitive or get-tough approach to corrections, including the building of more prisons, processing more juveniles as adults in criminal court, the continued use of capital punishment, continued de-emphasis of parole, and turning probation into a type of community policing with increasingly more drug testing and less rehabilitation. For example, there are about 40,000 individuals serving life-without-parole sentences, including more than 2,000 juveniles.[1] One reason that this trend is likely to continue is that it is politically appealing. It makes politicians appear "tough" on crime. Many elected officials think that this is the way to get elected or re-elected. It also satisfies simple beliefs that getting criminals off the streets is a logical way to reduce and prevent crime and that harsh prisons deter crime (see Box 15.1).

A dramatic example of the get-tough approach is an effort to make probation similar to community policing. Referring to this approach as "broken windows" probation, proponents argue that probation officers should be like community police officers and get out in the community, spend more time checking up on probationers, enforce conditions quickly, and participate in community crime prevention efforts. In this model, a probation officer would be like a police officer on the beat.[2]

A second possible path based on current thinking is to attempt to return corrections to a more traditional focus of trying to rehabilitate offenders. An important issue in deciding which direction to take is the effectiveness of corrections.

BOX 15.1

A New Version of Scared Straight

In Salt Lake City, Utah, the local sheriff is running a new version of Scared Straight. Scared Straight was an inmate-run program in the 1970s in which prisoners showed and told delinquents or predelinquents about the horrors of prison life. The prison tours and talks were intended to scare kids "straight"—to frighten them out of a life of crime.

The Salt Lake sheriff allows adults and kids to spend the night in jail to get a taste of incarceration. This is intended to frighten the young people and to give interested adults a firsthand experience of what jail is like. The "prisoners" are photographed and searched like regular prisoners, and then processed and locked into their cells. One guard, dressed as a prisoner, even pretends to go crazy, and a team of guards in riot gear comes in to remove him. This illustrates to the citizen participants one of the many dangers guards face in prison.

What do you think? Can one night in jail or prison give an accurate picture of what incarceration is like? Is it likely that one night in incarceration will deter a delinquent or predelinquent from a life of crime? Are there any dangers in conducting this type of program?

Source: Adapted from "A Bed and Breakfast That's Tough to Leave." *Time*, January 31, 2000.

As seen in previous chapters (see Chapters 9 and 13), there is a converging consensus about the principles of effective correctional interventions. A number of researchers agree that behavioral programs that target criminogenic needs, address responsivity, use primarily positive reinforcers, and use trained therapists are effective in reducing recidivism.[3] Therefore, one possible path for corrections is for such research on effectiveness to continue and to justify greater reliance on rehabilitation efforts in corrections. Such a commitment would require allocating appropriate correctional financial and personnel resources. The possibility of this trend continuing or growing may be even greater since the publication of the first edition of this text because now there is additional evidence about correctional interventions that are effective.

A third possible trend is what we will call economic pragmatism. What we mean by this is that whatever their position on punishment and treatment, a number of experts agree that states should pursue policies that save money. Michael Jacobson's proposal is a good example of this position. Jacobson's main concern is that prison populations have mushroomed and something must be done to stop this or else the financial costs will be astronomical. In fact, he points out, they are already quite threatening. So, as noted in Chapter 13, he proposes graduated sanctions for parole violators so not as many of them will be sent back to prison. He also argues for devoting most parole services and help in the first year after release from prison because that is the critical juncture in the transition out of prison.[4]

Another possible path for the future is to pursue restorative justice. As noted in Chapter 6, in contrast to retributive justice, which focuses on vengeance, deterrence, and punishment, restorative justice "is concerned with repairing the damage or harm done to victims and the community through a process of negotiation, mediation, victim empowerment, and reparation."[5] Continued development of restorative justice would involve increased emphasis on victims, victim-offender mediation programs, restitution programs, and sentencing circles, as well as attention to the development of offender competencies. This trend is likely to continue because concern for victims is popular politically.

Another possible trend would be to combine the principles of restorative justice and those of rehabilitation. Cullen, Sundt, and Wozniak call this "restorative rehabilitation."[6] They argue that the principles of restorative justice call for offenders to accept responsibility for their actions and to restore victims. Both apologizing for their crimes and making restitution are two specific ways to attempt to restore victims to their state prior to their victimization. Rehabilitation is important because it is a "legitimate and important correctional goal"[7] and because of the empirical research that has been demonstrating that certain interventions are indeed effective in reforming offenders.[8]

Another trend that could continue into the future is privatization. As noted in Chapter 13, companies such as Corrections Corporation of America (CCA) are building and operating increasingly more prisons and jails. In 2006, the number of state prisoners in private prisons reached more than 86,000 inmates, and the number of federal prisoners in private prisons reached almost 28,000 prisoners.[9] Privatization is appealing to some politicians because it is seen as a method to expand the number of prisons and prisoners at a reasonable cost. There have been some problems with privatization, however. For example, a prison built in South Carolina by the Corrections Corporation of America (CCA) was rejected by the South Carolina state government due to a lack of need.

The possible scenarios noted above are all conservative predictions. By conservative here we do not mean politically conservative; we mean that because they all are logical extensions of current practice, it is conservative, or cautious, to predict that such trends will continue. There are also a few directions corrections might take that are less likely to happen. Here we are being more speculative; there is less likelihood that these speculative predictions will turn out to be accurate.

SPECULATIVE DIRECTIONS IN CORRECTIONS

One speculative possibility is the demise of certain components of corrections such as probation. A task force in Wisconsin, for example, recommended the elimination of felony probation (probation terms for offenders convicted of felonies) and replacing it with a sort of halfway-house institutional correctional program.[10] Parole, too, is a program that could face elimination. A number of states have eliminated all traditional parole in which a parole board has the discretion to release offenders early. Other states have abolished parole for violent or felony offenders. As a result, more than half of the offenders who entered parole supervision in 2006 did so through a mandatory release from prison (they had served all the time required of them).[11] However, while the abolition of correctional programs such as probation and parole is a distinct possibility, our best guess is that this will not take place. Both probation and parole are traditional components of corrections that serve several functions. Probation is a form of punishment for those offenders not considered serious enough to be sent to prison. Parole can be a safety valve to relieve prison overcrowding. In addition, bureaucratic inertia stands in the way of any attempt to eliminate these programs. Once a government program has been in operation for any length of time, it takes considerable effort to remove it. Finally, the recent emphasis on reentry has generated new suggestions for parole, such as those noted in Chapter 13.

Another remote possibility is what can be called the "remedicalization" of corrections. This means that medicines may eliminate many of the problem behaviors that lead to some crimes. Although the medical model was found wanting in corrections, increasingly more problems—generalized anxiety disorder, obsessive-compulsive disorder, hyperactivity, depression—are being treated with drugs such as venlafaxine (Effexor), paroxetine (Paxil), fluoxetine (Prozac), and methylphenidate (Ritalin). Something similar is medical treatment for nicotine addiction; nicotine patches and gum help tobacco users fight their addiction. If psychiatry, medicine, and biochemistry continue to discover physiological or neurological bases of behavior amenable to pharmacological treatments, the next decades may see more opportunities to medicalize criminal behaviors.

Another scenario may be increased use of technology in prisons and community corrections. Some technologies currently in development are telemedicine, videoconferencing, and tracking devices. Telemedicine would allow inmates to be diagnosed remotely without a physician making face-to-face physical contact. A related development would be psychological evaluations by teledevices. Varying types of videoconferencing would allow inmates to have court hearings without leaving the prison or jail and allow probationers to report via computers instead of directly to a probation officer. Tracking devices under development offer the hope

BOX 15.2

An Example of One Spiritual Journey in Prison

Jarvis Masters became a committed Buddhist while serving his sentence on death row in San Quentin Prison. One day his observation of unusual behavior in the prison yard led him to conclude that a friend of his was about to stab a gay prisoner—a stranger to Masters—in the middle of the prison yard. At risk to his own life, Jarvis intervened and was able to stop his friend from committing the stabbing. In effect, Masters *saved* two lives—his friend's and the other prisoner's.

After the intensity of the moment, Masters reflected on what he had done:

> "He [the stranger] meant nothing to me—except that he was as human as the rest of us. He *never* came back to our yard after that day, but the incident left me with many questions. Am I alone? Am I the only Buddhist out here? Does this mean that I, the Lone Buddhist Ranger, am expected to try to stop this madness by myself?" (Masters, 1997:173)

These are important questions in a prison environment. They are also important questions for all of us outside the prison. Is it our responsibility to "stop the madness" in our world? What is our obligation to change our world?

Source: Adapted from Masters, J. (1997). *Finding Freedom: Writings from Death Row.* Junction City, CA: Padma.

of detecting if an offender enters a tavern via mapping of longitude and latitude coordinates.[12] The development of personal alarms would allow guards to set off alarm signals from anywhere in the prison so that there would be no locations in prisons that are without communication.

Another possible path is the reintroduction of the spiritual dimension into correctional practice. Skepticism implies that this is probably only a remote possibility. Our consumer culture churns on. Some, however, suggest that there is hope that the spiritual dimension can be reintroduced into corrections. There is evidence that although the spiritual perspective is not for everyone, there is a substantial minority of offenders who are receptive. Medical research indicates that religious faith and practice have positive effects on health.[13] Interest in the spiritual dimension seems alive and well. Books such as *Chicken Soup for the Soul*,[14] *Soul Stories*,[15] and *The Purpose Driven Life*[16] have attracted impressive numbers of readers. In an issue of a criminal justice journal that was devoted to the role of spirituality in criminological theory and criminal justice practice, one article addressed the role of religion in prisons.[17] These trends may demonstrate the longing of the human spirit for nourishment and growth. (We will discuss this possibility in more detail later in this chapter.) Finally, as noted in Chapter 7, faith-based programming has received both attention and funding in the last few years, including by the Florida Department of Corrections, which operates two faith-based prisons. Therefore, this possibility may not be as speculative as we thought in the first edition of this text. In the next few pages, we will offer more details on the possible trends we just presented.

• The Punitive Ideal (The "Get Tough" Movement) •

Several factors may stop or slow down the continuation of the punitive or "get tough" approach. One such factor is cost considerations. Recent estimates show that it costs about $24,000 per year to keep one prisoner in prison for one year and that it costs approximately $65,000 to build one prison bed. Simply adding 100 prisoners to a state's prison population adds $2.4 million to the operating budget, and it would cost $6.5 million to build those 100 additional cells.[18] Such cost considerations may influence politicians to refrain from building more prisons or enacting legislation (especially sentencing legislation) that would send more criminals to prison. One prison official said that cost considerations will force society and politicians to imprison only the dangerous in the year 2025: "Our prisons then will be reserved for those 'we are afraid of' rather than those we are simply 'mad at.'"[19]

A second factor that could slow down prison populations is a change in our country's war on drugs. Drug legalization has been mentioned by both politicians and scholars as one tactic to reduce the antidrug frenzy in the United States. Although California and Arizona did legalize marijuana for medical use in 1996, it is questionable whether the movement toward legalization has the popular support necessary for legislative approval. A more likely development that would reduce the criminal justice processing of drug users would be a return to a therapeutic model that looks on addiction as an illness requiring treatment rather than a crime requiring incarceration.[20]

• Privatization •

As noted in Chapter 13, privatization is a current trend in institutional corrections. Although the usual development is private construction or operation of prisons, privatization also applies to community corrections. One type of privatization is for a private agency to contract with a state to operate a probation-like agency for certain offenders. A major argument for such contracting is economic in nature. The private agency argues that it can provide such supervision at less cost than a state probation agency.

A different form of privatization takes place when private agencies contract to provide specific services for offenders on probation or after-care. In Florida, private vendors have been contracting with the Department of Corrections to provide treatment services for probationers. In 1995, Florida spent about $25 million for mental health and substance abuse programs. For example, one agency would provide eight hours of anger management training at $40 per offender. Sex offender treatment cost between $780 and $2,082 for two years of treatment.[21] However, there seems to be little proof of effectiveness other than testimonials from offenders. There is also the issue of accountability, given that private agencies may not be required to adhere to the same standards that state and federal agencies have to follow.

A realistic concern about privatization is the possibility of abuse. A Youngstown, Ohio, private prison apparently opened too soon with too many new prisoners; within 14 months, there were two murders and 47 assaults.[22] To make matters worse, private prison officials waited more than two hours before notifying local authorities of prisoner escapes. In Texas, out-of-state prisoners from Colorado were locked up in an old industrial warehouse with inadequate ventilation, one bathroom for 26 prisoners in a cell area, temperatures reaching almost 105 degrees, and guards refusing to turn off the lights at night. Despite such intolerable conditions, the State of Colorado was paying $20,000 a day for these prisoners.[23]

None of this is to say that there have been no problems with public prisons. Indeed, there have been notorious abuses in public prisons as well. One report showed, for example, that the Louisiana State Penitentiary (Angola) runs an inmate rodeo that is questionable in its respect for inmate safety and dignity.[24] Of particular concern, though, is the profit orientation of private prisons. This profit orientation raises the question of whether the corrections companies will put the public and prisoner welfare first or will emphasize making a profit.

• The Remedicalization of Corrections •

There are problems with any effort to bring back the medical model and treat conditions with drugs. In many cases, harmful side effects of the drugs do not come to light until years after initial claims of effectiveness. A temptation with the use of these drugs is to prescribe a medication instead of trying to address underlying or surrounding problems. In normal medical practice, for example, it appears that health maintenance organizations (HMOs) encourage the use of medications to the neglect of talk therapies because counseling is more expensive than simply prescribing a medication.[25] Thus, while the most desirable treatment might be long-term psychotherapy because it actually helps the offender deal with his or her problems, the fact that it is time-consuming and expensive may lead prisons to prescribe offenders medications that mask their problems.

• Technological Advances •

Current electronic monitoring devices allow intensive supervision programs to determine if an offender is home when a computer-generated phone call rings in the offender's home or when a probation officer drives by. Technology could be developed so that correctional workers could track the precise whereabouts of offenders and not just confirm that they are at their residence. Such tracking and recording might be a powerful incapacitation and deterrence tool. Offenders could be forewarned that agencies would have accurate records of their comings and goings. Such records would be strong evidence if the offender was recorded as being at the scene of a crime.

One concern about the proliferation of technology in prisons and probation is that many of the technologies under development seem to reduce human contact. One might reflect upon how it feels when one calls a business with a concern and has difficulty actually reaching a person. Kiosk reporting, for example, means that a probationer would enter a kiosk at the probation office and answer computer-generated questions (e.g., Are you still residing at your same address? Are you still employed at Acme Manufacturing? Any changes since your last report?) As efficient as such technologies might be, they reduce or eliminate the human contact between an offender and a correctional worker that could be the basis for change in that offender's life. A computer cannot form an affective relationship with an offender that will influence him or her to think about his or her life and life choices. Putting increasingly more computers into schools and prisons might save dollars in the short run but cost more in the long run.

• Restorative Justice •

The restorative justice model is attractive because it offers a plausible alternative to the get-tough rhetoric that is currently popular. It focuses on the victim as well as the offender and the community. It seeks to make the offender more competent and productive in an effort to bond the offender more closely to the community.

Several jurisdictions have implemented the restorative justice model. For example, Allegheny County, Pennsylvania, has received federal government training and assistance to start such a program emphasizing offender accountability, community protection, and competency development. Part of the program involves youths growing a garden in their neighborhood and using the crops to cook and deliver meals to homeless people. This is an example of meaningful community service. Some of the youths have learned gardening skills that have enabled them to obtain jobs.[26] Restorative justice has a track record of success (see Chapter 6 and Kurki[27] for discussions of restorative justice programs that have been successful).

Possible problems with restorative justice include that offenders do not always complete their restitution payments, the model would require drastic changes in prison and probation agency practice, and there may be racial or class biases linked to the ability to pay restitution. Perhaps the potentially most damaging criticism is that restorative justice does not tell us how to deal with serious and repetitive criminal activity and thus does not contribute to crime control.[28]

Still another problem with restorative justice is that it assumes that communities care about their members. Some question this assumption. Robert Putnam,[29] for example, argues that social capital is decreasing. What this means is that community life is decreasing. People do not join voluntary civic organizations (Kiwanis, Rotary, Lions Club, for example) as much as they did in the past. Generational change, employment changes, and the prevalence of television watching are just some of the developments that account for less community involvement and more individual activity. To use Putnam's graphic phrasing, people are now "bowling alone" rather than in leagues with friends and co-workers. The problem for restorative justice is that mediation programs, sentencing circles, and the like all assume that private citizens are willing and able to participate. If people would rather "bowl alone," then there will not be enough people to staff the necessary elements of the restorative justice movement. Nevertheless, this would not preclude the worthiness of working with restorative justice efforts in doing "what we can, where we can."

• Restorative Rehabilitation •

As part of what they label restorative rehabilitation, Cullen and his colleagues[30] suggest that we should eliminate inmate idleness, imbue inmate activities with a restorative purpose, encourage contact with virtuous people, get inmates to participate in rehabilitation programs that have been demonstrated to be effective, maintain an inmate standard of living that is as high as possible, encourage guards to work as "correctional" officers, and be aware that the "virtuous prison" would not be for all inmates. This idea of the virtuous prison would be quite different from today's prisons, in which many prisoners are idle much of the time or are engaged in activities simply meant to pass time with little or no thought given to the possibility of making a contribution to society. For example, Cullen and his colleagues would like to see inmates engaged in making toys for the needy or building homes for Habitat for Humanity.[31]

This proposal is admittedly idealistic. It sets high standards that would take considerable change and effort to reach. Critics might say that this proposal is simply too costly and unrealistic. Proponents might say that we have not been aiming high enough and that this proposal corrects that mistake.

• Reintroducing the Spiritual Dimension •

Similarly idealistic is the proposal to reintroduce the spiritual dimension into corrections. This would entail efforts of corrections workers, whether prison counselors, chaplains, or probation officers, to help offenders find greater meaning in their lives. Lozoff and Braswell contend that all the major religions teach four classic virtues (honesty, courage, kindness, and a sense of humor). According to this perspective, reductions in recidivism and programs such as counseling or vocational training are still important but they are considered external. The deeper goal is internal personal change: "The primary goal is to help build a happier, peaceful person right there in the prison, a person whose new-found self-honesty and courage can steer him or her to adjust to the biases and shortcomings of a society which does not feel comfortable with ex-offenders."[32] Personal transformation comes first. Peaceful, ethical persons create peaceful communities. From personal transformation come positive institutional changes.[33]

Both prisons and probation can try to address the spiritual needs of prisoners. Prisons and jails have always had chaplains and religious services as part of their programming. Prisons and probation/parole could also take additional steps to incorporate the spiritual dimension into correctional practice.[34]

First, correctional workers—correctional counselors, probation officers, parole officers, and correctional officers—can all attempt to help offenders focus on the question of meaning in their lives. In group sessions and individual reporting, these workers can encourage offenders to think about the meaning of their lives. Reality therapy founder William Glasser recounts one young adult client reporting that Glasser was the first person who had asked him what he intended to do with his life.[35]

Second, correctional workers have the simple but potentially profound example of their own lives. They can come to work every day showing a sense of purpose and meaning in their lives and in their interactions with prisoners. This may influence any or all who come in contact with them. Almost everyone can attest to the existence of persons who show by their lives that there is something that energizes them and inspires them despite the difficulties they face. This is in stark contrast to those workers who exert a negative influence in the prison or in the parole office. For example, in one women's prison, some guards came in and plopped down in front of the television to watch hours of sports.[36] In some Canadian correctional facilities, guard supervisors created an environment rife with sexual harassment.[37] In one Massachusetts prison for women, guard sexual abuse of prisoners was commonplace.[38] At the very least, workers need to refrain from abuse, harassment, and anything else that detracts from prison as a place where offenders can think about the meaning of their lives.

BOX 15.3

Using Stories to Help Offenders Change

Kurtz and Ketcham argue that just as personal connections and sharing stories have been a staple of the Alcoholics Anonymous movement, such connections and stories can help offenders and any of us who feel the need for change in our lives.

They offer the example of the story of a recovering alcoholic who upon waking prayed to God for another day of sobriety. Then at night he thanked the divinity for another day of sobriety. A friend asked him how he could be sure it was God who answered his prayers. The man answered that it had to be God because God was the only one he had asked.

These are important questions in a prison environment. They are also important questions for all of us outside the prison. Is it our responsibility to "stop the madness" in our world? What is our obligation to change our world?

Source: Kurtz, E., and K. Ketcham (2002). *The Spirituality of Imperfection: Storytelling and the Search for Meaning*, p. 209. New York: Bantam Books.

Attempts to inject the spiritual dimension into correctional practice face the difficulty that this goes against much of the American consumer culture. Part of the correctional mission has been to make offenders "successful" jobholders who then become avid consumers. The underlying assumption in corrections has been that if we can offer offenders education and job training, then they will obtain jobs that allow them to buy into the "American dream" of a car (or two), a house, two kids, and ever-increasing purchasing power.

In contrast to this, prison ministry worker Bo Lozoff argues that the world's great religions all teach that we are serving time in our life's journey rather than here simply to accumulate wealth and to spend as much as possible.[39] In the field of social work, Canda and Furman note that in their national survey of social workers, surprisingly high percentages of the workers polled indicated that they think it is appropriate to raise spiritual issues when a client is experiencing life events such as terminal illness, loss of a loved one, or a criminal justice event like arrest or sentencing. Specifically, 73 percent considered it appropriate with clients experiencing terminal illness, and 40 percent considered this appropriate in criminal justice–related problems.[40]

One task of corrections may be to help that segment of offenders who are open to asking and seeking answers to the perennial questions about life: Why am I here? What is the meaning of life? What is happiness? Should I just seek more money and prestige, or are their other more important goals in life? Do I just consider myself, or should I think about others? Am I making moral or immoral choices? As one thinker puts it, am I seeking "significance through engagement in the processes of reflection, creativity, compassion, and the gift of self to others?"[41] None of this should lead to proselytizing or to erasing the separation of church and state. No correctional worker should impose his or her religious beliefs on inmates or probationers.

Some may protest that attempting to inject the spiritual into correctional practice is too ambitious a project. If corrections cannot accomplish the basic objective of keeping offenders crime-free, then how can it be expected to help offenders become better persons spiritually? This objection may have it backwards. Perhaps one reason that corrections has had such an uninspiring record with recidivism is that it makes no effort to help offenders in a search for meaning and purpose in their lives. If the implicit objective of corrections is that offenders need only buy into the American dream, and if that dream is questionable and uninspiring and one that ignores the deeper potential of human living, then it may be no surprise that probation does little to improve recidivism.

• Two Additional Issues: Race and Prevention •

Before we close, two additional issues need some consideration.

One critical need that corrections must address in the future is the issue of race. Progress has been made in the last 50 years in combating discrimination in policing, prosecution, and sentencing. That progress is far from perfect, however. As Tonry notes, on the positive side, the percentages of people arrested for crimes such as robbery and homicide who are black were much lower in 2005 than in 1987. On the negative side, black imprisonment rates continue to be much higher than white imprisonment rates. For example, the Bureau of Justice Statistics calculated that about one-third of black males born in 2001 will spend some time in prison.[42] Two things need to be done to address the issue of race in criminal justice and corrections. First, criminal justice and corrections officials need to do all that they can to eliminate race as a factor in policing, prosecution of crimes, sentencing, and correctional decisions such as parole release. Second, and more important, the United States must deal with societal, political, economic, and cultural factors that encourage or permit racism.

This second line of attack on racism is beyond the scope of this chapter and this textbook, but it needs to be noted that what sociologists call macro or social structural factors are associated with black crime rates and black imprisonment rates. Tonry argues that such factors as income inequality, de facto housing segregation, religious beliefs, and political paranoia are behind criminal justice practices such as capital punishment, life without parole, and three-strikes laws—practices that Tonry claims "are unimaginable in most other Western countries."[43]

One thing that can be done is to be aware of malign neglect in criminal justice policies. The concept of malign neglect means that often lawmakers do not consider the effects of new laws and policies on minority groups such as blacks. When legislators pass laws to start policies and practices such as sentencing guidelines or life-without-parole sentences, they rarely consider how such laws will affect minority groups. If such implications were considered prior to passing the legislation, there might be greater care in the legislation so as to minimize or eliminate unequal racial impacts.[44]

Again, we do not have the space to address this matter fully, but it is important to realize that corrections does not exist in a vacuum. Economic, political, social, and cultural factors all affect corrections. Just as colonial life influenced the corrections of that era, and Quaker beliefs affected the rise of penitentiaries in the early 1800s, so too today are politics, economics, and religion affecting our correctional policies and programs. We need to be aware of the larger forces at work in American society and how those forces are currently shaping corrections. A simple but dramatic example is the fact that the richest school districts in the country spend more than $25,000 more per elementary school pupil than the poorest school districts.[45] Practices such as this have dramatic impact on crime and criminal justice. To think that states can offer a simple program in prison to counteract forces such as spending on education is unrealistic.

Progress has been made in addressing discrimination, and that progress needs to continue. Hopefully, at some point in the future we will not have to talk about race in criminal justice because it will be an issue of the past, but that day is not here yet.

The point regarding elementary school spending leads naturally to a second point: the importance of prevention. A number of criminologists have been researching what causes delinquency and what prevents it. They have identified risk factors that lead to delinquency and protective factors, such as effective parenting, that help to prevent delinquency. Critically, they have also found interventions that can prevent delinquency.

The research on pathways to delinquency and crime has come to a number of conclusions about what can be done at an early age, between birth and early adolescence. For example, research has shown that school programs, such as discipline management and classroom management, can reduce delinquency, and delinquency can be prevented by parent education, parent management training, and daycare services.[46] This is only a bare outline of a delinquency prevention plan. The important conclusion is that "[i]n medicine and public health, it is widely accepted that prevention is better than cure. The same is true of offending."[47]

CONCLUSION

A pessimistic view is that the most likely future of corrections is more of the same. States will keep building prisons and executing murderers. Probation will stumble on with high caseloads, technological innovations, varying levels of recidivism, and technical violations for drug use and other problems. Band-aid solutions will persist. Imprisonment, capital punishment, decreased use of parole, and intensive supervision all offer the illusion that we are doing something about crime. Even so-called positive interventions may not be the complete answer.

Traditional programming offers the hope that offenders can become more like those in the outside society. They will be able to work at jobs so that they can increase their spending power and then consume more goods, services, and entertainment. For many offenders, as for many law-abiding citizens, this is enough. Some, however, search for something deeper.

One possibility is that prison crowding and costs will pressure policy-makers to do something to save money if nothing else. This may not be the noblest reason for acting, but cost pressures are very powerful motivators to change.

Some warnings are in order concerning privatization. First, privatization can make the bottom-line profit the main objective. If cost considerations become the only consideration, then abuses can more easily proliferate. Second, the welfare of workers may also be at stake. In a labor-intensive industry such as the prison system, there are only a few ways to reduce costs. If private prison companies reduce costs by reducing salaries or benefits for workers, there may not be much left to retain their services.

There are more hopeful alternatives. One is to emphasize rehabilitation. Another is to emphasize restorative justice. A third is to combine the two, as Cullen and his colleagues call for with restorative rehabilitation.[48] A fourth alternative is to emphasize a reintroduction of the spiritual dimension in corrections.

Any one of these courses of action bears considerable promise for the future of corrections. All assume that offenders share in common human dignity and destiny and deserve fair treatment. The latter three alternatives also bode well for crime victims because they suggest, either implicitly or explicitly, that offenders need to make amends to their victims.

Restorative justice sets noble goals: helping the victim back to where he or she was before the crime and helping the offender be a responsible and accountable member of the community. Another positive aspect of restorative justice is that it attempts to involve the community in the criminal justice process, something that has been lost in the last 50 years.

Restorative rehabilitation is a bold plan for prisons. The concept of the virtuous prison is a noble ideal that would set high goals for wardens, correctional officers, prison counselors, and inmates. All would be involved in a common pursuit of restoring victims and changing offenders. Both are needed tasks that could make staff, prisoners, the public, and politicians feel that corrections is centered on meaningful objectives.

The path of reintroducing the spiritual dimension into corrections is also salutary. In our view, the Quakers did have it right: the spiritual dimension is critical. For 100 years, however, the United States has been running correctional institutions and programs as if the spiritual dimension of life is nonexistent or unimportant. The results have been far from ideal. Perhaps if we go back to our correctional roots and reintroduce the spiritual dimension back into corrections—with appropriate safeguards against proselytizing and violating individual freedom of religious choice—the future of corrections will be more promising. (For still another set of suggestions for the future of corrections, see Box 15.4.)

BOX 15.4

Austin and Irwin's Suggestions for the Future of Corrections: Humanizing Prisons

After detailing the folly of continued prison building, Austin and Irwin offer still another prescription for the future of corrections. They argue that the necessary course of action is to pursue a goal of humanizing our nation's prisons. Such humanizing would involve several tasks. First, it is imperative to ensure that there is no cruel and unusual punishment going on in our nation's prisons. Second, our prisons must be safe places—not places where attacks, rapes, and murders are the order of the day. Third, prisoners should have adequate health care. Fourth, prisoners should have access to rehabilitation—education, vocational training, and treatment programs. Fifth, there should be re-entry assistance, possibly provided by community-based programs run by nonprofit organizations. If we fail to achieve these objectives, we "will continue to deliver excessive and irrational punishment to our prisoners and dump them back out into the 'streets,' damaged and handicapped, ready to descend into the growing urban pit called the 'underclass' or to be recycled again through prison" (Austin and Irwin, 2001:249).

Source: Austin, J., and J. Irwin (2001). *It's About Time: America's Imprisonment Binge*, 3rd ed. Belmont, CA: Wadsworth.

A final comment stems from Oscar Wilde's observation that "a cynic is a man who knows the price of everything and the value of nothing." As we approach the challenges and difficulties of the future of corrections, it is important that we keep an open and skeptical attitude, one that does not accept solutions at face value because they "feel good" or are politically popular and expedient. At the same time, it is also important that we do not resort to the cynicism Wilde alludes to wherein we choose short-term, more economical responses to correctional problems with little or no regard for more effective long-term corrections policies and practices.

Perhaps a fitting conclusion to this chapter and to this textbook is a reminder that an obsession with crime and corrections is not the answer to the major problems facing the United States. Our society must ask itself what kind of society it wants and what are the steps necessary to get there. Once we decide those basic questions, then we should take steps to achieve such a society. Those steps can have positive consequences. Focusing on crime prevention alone, however, often leads to problems:

> ...the stigma associated with crime prevention undermines the capacity of developmental programs to provide nurture. Efficient crime control singles out children at risk, whereas efficient education and youth development welcome all youths. The problem with calling a program crime prevention is that it *becomes* a program of crime prevention, operating without the optimism and trust that make education work. The negative labels and social stigma of social services motivated by crime worries cannot be neutralized by good intentions or brave words.[49] [emphasis in original]

Concern about crime is important. More important, however, are efforts to enhance opportunities for all citizens. If we keep crime and corrections in perspective, we will achieve better results than if we become obsessive and paranoid about crime, criminals, and delinquents.

▶ Ethics Focus: "Where Do We Go From Here?"

The possible futures addressed in this chapter include a continued emphasis on punishment, devoting more resources to correctional treatment, pursuing restorative justice, and greater attention to spiritual values.

Which of these alternatives are more economically efficient in the short run? In the long run? Which are more morally responsible?

▶ At the Movies . . . .

Mother Teresa, 1986.

This film, narrated by Richard Attenborough, is a powerful documentary about a simple but profound woman who made a dramatic impact with her life. In the documentary, Mother Teresa tells one interested party who wants to know more about her work, "Come and see." This is a message for all of us.

Crash, 2004.

This movie, directed by Paul Haggis and starring Sandra Bullock, Don Cheadle, and Matt Dillon, is a film that shows how we are connected to one another, even to people that we fear or abhor. In fact, our life might depend on someone we both fear and hate.

DISCUSSION QUESTIONS

1. Discuss the possible future scenarios for corrections noted in this chapter. Note the advantages and disadvantages of each scenario.

2. Of all the possible paths that corrections may pursue noted in this chapter, which two are your choices for the best options? Discuss why you chose the two options you selected.

3. One possible direction for corrections is to reintroduce the spiritual dimension into corrections. This is very possible because it has already begun; Florida, for example, has two faith-based prisons. What do you think about trying to reintroduce a spiritual dimension in corrections? Is this a positive direction for prisons, probation, and parole? Or should we focus on such traditional efforts as education, job training, and substance abuse treatment?

4. Can you think of any other directions that corrections can or should take in the next few years? Explain.

FURTHER READING

Kurtz, E., and K. Ketcham (2002). *The Spirituality of Imperfection: Storytelling and the Search for Meaning*. New York: Bantam Books.

Lozoff, B. (1999). *Deep and Simple: A Spiritual Path for Modern Times*. Durham, NC: Human Kindness Foundation.

Lozoff, B. (2004). *We're All Doing Time: A Guide for Getting Free*. Durham, NC: Human Kindness Foundation.

NOTES

1. Tonry, 2008
2. Corbett et al., 1999.
3. MacKenzie, 2006; Lipsey and Cullen, 2007.
4. Jacobson, 2005.
5. Bazemore and Maloney, 1994, 28.
6. Cullen, Sundt, and Wozniak, 2001.
7. Cullen, Sundt, and Wozniak, 2001, 279.
8. Cullen, Sundt, and Wozniak, 2001.
9. Sabol, Couture, and Harrison, 2007.
10. Mobley and Geis, 2005.
11. Glaze and Bonczar, 2007.
12. Fabelo, 2000.
13. Koening, 1999.
14. Canfield and Hanson, 1993.
15. Zukav, 2000.
16. Warren, 2002 . Some prisons are using Rick Warren's book in their prisons.
17. Clear et al., 2000.
18. Pew Center on the States, 2008.
19. Austin and Irwin, 2001.
20. Riveland, 1999, 193.
21. Lucken, 1997.
22. Mobley and Geis, 2005.
23. Dyer, 2000.
24. Bergner, 1999.
25. Groopman, 2000.
26. Hsia, 1997.
27. Kurki, 2000.
28. Levrant et al., 1999.
29. Putnam, 2000.
30. Cullen, Sundt, and Wozniak, 2001.
31. Cullen, Sundt, and Wozniak, 2001.
32. Lozoff and Braswell, 1989, 2.

33. Braswell, Fuller, and Lozoff, 2001.

34. For a more complete discussion, see Whitehead and Braswell, 2000.

35. Glasser, 1965.

36. Girschick, 1999.

37. McMahon, 1999.

38. Rathbone, 2006.

39. Lozoff, 2000.

40. Canda and Furman, 1999.

41. Staples, 2000, 22.

42. Tonry, 2008.

43. Tonry, 2008, 3.

44. Tonry, 1995.

45. Kozol, 2005.

46. Farrington and Welsh, 2007. In their book, Farrington and Welsh give a state-of-the-art summary of effective prevention interventions.

47. Farrington and Welsh, 2007, 3. Farrington and Welsh probably share the comment of Zimring (see quote in the Conclusion, at Note 49) that it is not necessarily best to call a program a "delinquency" prevention program.

48. Cullen, Sundt, and Wozniak, 2001.

49. Zimring, 1998, 193.

REFERENCES

Austin, J., and J. Irwin (2001). *It's About Time: America's Imprisonment Binge*, 3rd ed. Belmont, CA: Wadsworth.

Bazemore, G., and D. Maloney (1994). "Rehabilitating Community Service: Toward Restorative Service Sanctions in a Balanced Justice System." *Federal Probation* 58 (1):24-35.

Bergner, D. (1999). *God of the Rodeo: The Quest for Redemption in Louisiana's Angola Prison*. New York: Ballantine.

Braswell, M.C., J. Fuller, and B. Lozoff (2001). *Corrections, Peacemaking, and Restorative Justice*. Cincinnati: Anderson.

Canda, E.R., and L.D. Furman (1999). *Spiritual Diversity in Social Work Practice*. New York: The Free Press.

Canfield, J., and M.V. Hanson (eds.) (1993). *Chicken Soup for the Soul: 101 Stories to Open the Heart and Rekindle the Spirit*. Deerfield Beach, FL: Health Communications.

Clear, T.R., P.L. Hardyman, B. Stout, K. Lucken, and H.R. Dammer (2000). "The Value of Religion in Prison: An Inmate Perspective." *Journal of Contemporary Criminal Justice* 16:53-74.

Corbett, R.P. et al. (1999). *"Broken Windows" Probation: The Next Step in Fighting Crime*. New York: Manhattan Institute.

Cullen, F.T., J.L. Sundt, and J.F. Wozniak (2001). "The Virtuous Prison: Toward a Restorative Rehabilitation." In H.N. Pontell and D. Shichor (eds.), *Contemporary Issues in Crime and Criminal Justice: Essays in Honor of Gilbert Geis*, 265-286. Upper Saddle River, NJ: Prentice Hall.

Dyer, J. (2000). *The Perpetual Prisoner Machine: How America Profits from Crime*. Boulder, CO: Westview Press.

Fabelo, T. (2000). "'Technocorrections': The Promises, the Uncertain Threats." *Bureau of Statistics Bulletin*. Washington, DC: U.S. Department of Justice.

Farrington, D.P., and B.C. Welsh (2007). *Saving Children from a Life of Crime: Early Risk Factors and Effective Interventions*. New York: Oxford University Press.

Girschick, L.B. (1999). *No Safe Haven: Stories of Women in Prison*. Boston: Northeastern University Press.

Glasser, W. (1965). *Reality Therapy*. New York: Harper & Row.

Glaze, L.E., and T.P. Bonczar (2007). "Probation and Parole in the United States, 2006." *Bureau of Justice Statistics Bulletin*. Washington, DC: U.S. Department of Justice.

Groopman, J. (2000). "The Doubting Disease." *The New Yorker*, April 10, 2000, 52-57.

Hsai, H.M. (1997). "Allegheny County, PA: Mobilizing to Reduce Juvenile Crime." *Bureau of Justice Statistics Bulletin*. Washington, DC: U.S. Department of Justice.

Jacobson, M. (2005). *Downsizing Prisons: How to Reduce Crime and End Mass Incarceration*. New York: New York University Press.

Koening, H.G. (1999). *The Healing Power of Faith: Science Explores Medicine's Last Great Frontier*. New York: Simon and Schuster.

Kozol, J. (2005). *The Shame of the Nation: The Restoration of Apartheid Schooling in America*. New York: Crown.

Kurki, L. (2000). "Restorative and Community Justice in the United States." In M. Tonry (ed.), *Crime and Justice: A Review of Research* (Vol. 27), 235-303.

Levrant, S., F.T. Cullen, B. Fulton, and J.F. Wozniak (1999). "Reconsidering Restorative Justice: The Corruption of Benevolence Revisited?" *Crime & Delinquency* 45:3-27.

Lipsey, M.W., and Cullen, F.T. (2007). "The Effectiveness of Correctional Rehabilitation: A Review of Systematic Reviews." *Annual Review of Law and Social Science* 3:297-320.

Lozoff, B. (2000). *It's a Meaningful Life: It Just Takes Practice*. New York: Viking.

Lozoff, B., and M. Braswell (1989). *Inner Corrections: Finding Peace and Peace Making*. Cincinnati: Anderson.

Lucken, K. (1997). "Privatizing Discretion: 'Rehabilitating' Treatment in Community Corrections." *Crime & Delinquency* 43:243-259.

MacKenzie, D.L. (2006). *What Works in Corrections: Reducing the Criminal Activities of Offenders and Delinquents*. New York: Cambridge University Press.

Masters, J.J. (1997). *Finding Freedom: Writings from Death Row*. Junction City, CA: Padma.

McMahon, M. (1999). *Women on Guard: Discrimination and Harassment in Corrections*. Toronto: University of Toronto Press.

Mobley, A., and G. Geis (2005). "The Corrections Corporation of America: aka The Prison Realty Trust, Inc." In M.C. Braswell, B.R. McCarthy, and B.J. McCarthy, *Justice, Crime and Ethics*, 5th ed., 349-370. Cincinnati: Anderson.

Pew Center on the States (2008). *One in 100: Behind Bars in America 2008*. Washington, DC: Pew Center on the States.

Putnam, R.D. (2000). *Bowling Alone: The Collapse and Revival of American Community*. New York: Knopf.

Rathbone, C. (2006). *A World Apart: Women, Prison, and Life Behind Bars*. New York: Random House Trade Paperbacks.

Riveland, C. (1999). "Prison Management Trends, 1975-2025." In M. Tonry and J. Petersilia (eds.), *Prisons: Crime and Justice: A Review of Research* 26:163-203. Chicago: University of Chicago Press.

Sabol, W.J., H. Couture, and P.M. Harrison (2007). "Prisoners in 2006." *Bureau of Justice Statistics Bulletin*. Washington, DC: U.S. Government Printing Office.

Shichor, D., and M. Gilbert (2001). *Privatization in Criminal Justice*. Cincinnati: Anderson.

Smith, M.E., and W.J. Dickey (1999). "Reforming Sentencing and Corrections for Just Punishment and Public Safety." *Bureau of Justice Statistics Bulletin*. Washington, DC: U.S. Government Printing Office.

Staples, J.S. (2000). "Violence in Our Schools: Rage Against a Broken World." *Annals of the American Academy of Political and Social Science* 567:30-41.

Tonry, M. (2008). "Crime and Human Rights—How Political Paranoia, Protestant Fundamentalism and Constitutional Obsolescence Combined to Devastate Black America: The American Society of Criminology 2007 Presidential Address." *Criminology* 46:1-33.

Tonry, M. (1995). *Malign Neglect: Race, Crime, and Punishment in America*. New York: Oxford University Press.

Warren, R. (2002). *The Purpose Driven Life: What on Earth Am I Here For?* Grand Rapids, MI: Zondervan.

Whitehead, J.T., and M.C. Braswell (2000). "The Future of Probation: Reintroducing the Spiritual Dimension into Correctional Practice." *Criminal Justice Review* 25(2):207-233.

Zimring, F.E. (1998). *American Youth Violence*. New York: Oxford University Press.

Zukav, G. (2000). *Soul Stories: Practical Guides to the Soul*. New York: Simon & Schuster.

Index